中国产业研究报告·物流与采购

·中国物流与采购联合会系列报告·

中国物流发展报告

中国物流与采购联合会
China Federation of Logistics & Purchasing
中国物流学会
China Society of Logistics

China Logistics Development Report (2014–2015)

中国财富出版社
China Fortune Press

图书在版编目（CIP）数据

中国物流发展报告．2014－2015／中国物流与采购联合会，中国物流学会编．—北京：中国财富出版社，2015.5

ISBN 978－7－5047－5683－1

Ⅰ．①中…　Ⅱ．①中…②中…　Ⅲ．①物流—经济发展—研究报告—中国—2014～2015　Ⅳ．①F259.22

中国版本图书馆 CIP 数据核字（2015）第 082875 号

策划编辑　葛晓雯　　**责任印制**　何崇杭
责任编辑　葛晓雯　　**责任校对**　梁　凡

出版发行　中国财富出版社
社　　址　北京市丰台区南四环西路 188 号 5 区 20 楼　　**邮政编码**　100070
电　　话　010－52227568（发行部）　　010－52227588 转 307（总编室）
010－68589540（读者服务部）　　010－52227588 转 305（质检部）
网　　址　http://www.cfpress.com.cn
经　　销　新华书店
印　　刷　中国农业出版社印刷厂
书　　号　ISBN 978－7－5047－5683－1/F·2368
开　　本　787mm×1092mm　1/16　　**版　　次**　2015 年 5 月第 1 版
印　　张　29　　**印　　次**　2015 年 5 月第 1 次印刷
字　　数　584 千字　　**定　　价**　120.00 元

《中国物流发展报告》（2014—2015）

编　委　会

《中国物流发展报告》(2014—2015)

特约撰稿人

(按姓氏笔画排序)

马增荣　中国物流与采购联合会汽车物流分会主任
万　莹　中国物流与采购联合会电商物流与快递分会秘书长
王　坚　新杰物流集团股份有限公司总经理、中物联公路货运分会当值会长
王继祥　《物流技术与应用》杂志常务副主编
王国清　兰格钢铁信息研究中心主任
王玉鹏　新松机器人自动化股份有限公司智能移动事业部副总经理
田　征　大连海事大学交通运输管理学院副教授
冯耕中　西安交通大学管理学院副院长、教授
刘伟华　天津大学管理与经济学部副教授
江　宏　《物流技术与应用》杂志执行主编
李红梅　中国物流与采购联合会标准化工作部主任
李倩雯　上海海事大学　上海国际航运研究中心国内航运研究室
吴志华　南京财经大学营销与物流管理学院副院长、教授、博士生导师
张晓东　北京交通大学交通运输学院副院长
张　洁　中国工程机械工业协会工业车辆分会秘书长
张永锋　上海海事大学　上海国际航运研究中心国际航运研究室副主任
张　滨　吉林大学珠海学院教授
洪　涛　北京工商大学商业经济研究所所长、中国食品(农产品)电子商务研究院院长
赵　楠　上海海事大学　上海国际航运研究中心港口发展研究室副主任
姜超峰　中国物资储运协会名誉会长
姜荣奇　昆明昆船物流信息产业有限公司副总经理
恽　绵　德利得物流总公司运营总监
秦玉鸣　中国物流与采购联合会冷链物流专业委员会秘书长
晏庆华　中国物流与采购联合会网络事业部主任

徐　勇　快递物流咨询网首席顾问
郭肇明　中国物流与采购联合会教育培训部主任
梅赞宾　中国外运长航集团有限公司研究室高级研究员
曹允春　中国民航大学经济与管理学院副院长、教授
崔　雄　上海精星仓储设备工程有限公司总经理
韩永生　天津科技大学物流工程系教授
覃　拥　国药集团医药物流有限公司副总监
靳　伟　中国物流与采购联合会托盘专业委员会常务副主任
潘增友　中国汽车技术研究中心

《中国物流发展报告》（2014—2015）

编 辑 人 员

主　　编：贺登才
副 主 编：周志成

联系方式：

中国物流与采购联合会研究室：010－58566588 转 135
网　　址：中国物流与采购网（www.chinawuliu.com.cn）
电子信箱：yanjiushibj@vip.163.com

2014 年我国物流业发展回顾与 2015 年展望

（代前言）

一、2014 年我国物流业发展回顾

2014 年，我国物流业面对复杂多变的市场形势，积极调整应对，加快转型升级，主动适应经济发展“新常态”，较好地发挥了基础性、战略性作用。

（一）《物流业发展中长期规划（2014—2020 年）》发布，产业地位显著提升

2014 年 6 月 11 日，李克强总理主持召开国务院常务会议，讨论通过《物流业发展中长期规划（2014—2020 年）》（以下简称《中长期规划》），9 月 12 日以国发〔2014〕42 号文正式发布。这是继 2009 年国务院《物流业调整和振兴规划》出台以来，又一个指导物流业发展的纲领性文件。党的十八大以来，习近平总书记、李克强总理等多次考察物流企业，对物流业发展做出重要讲话和批示。此次出台的《中长期规划》，把物流业定位于支撑国民经济发展的基础性、战略性产业，是物流业产业地位进一步提升的重要标志。规划要求，到 2020 年，基本建立布局合理、技术先进、便捷高效、绿色环保、安全有序的现代物流服务体系，明确了中长期发展的战略目标。规划提出三大发展重点、七项主要任务、十二项重点工程和九项保障措施，抓住了制约物流业发展的关键问题，明确了发展方向，是指导我国物流业“新常态”下健康发展的顶层设计蓝图。

（二）增长速度高位趋稳，需求结构稳步调整

总体运行温和增长、质量提升。2014 年全国社会物流总额

213.5 万亿元，同比增长 7.9%，与上年相比小幅放缓，但仍高于同期 GDP 增速，处于中高速增长区间。2014 年社会物流总费用 10.6 万亿元，同比增长 6.9%，增速延续小幅回落态势。2014 年社会物流总费用与 GDP 的比率为 16.6%，物流业发展的质量和效率有所提升。中国物流景气指数全年于 55% 上下区间波动，物流运行总体趋稳。

需求结构深度调整。钢铁、煤炭、水泥、有色等生产资料物流需求增速进一步放缓，进出口贸易依然疲软。全国铁路完成货物周转量 2.75 万亿吨公里，同比下降 5.6%，规模以上港口货物吞吐量和外贸货物吞吐量增速同比分别回落 4.1 个和 3.8 个百分点。最终消费对经济增长的贡献率持续走高，电商物流、冷链物流等消费品物流需求保持快速增长。全年单位与居民物品物流总额增速超过 30%。冷链物流需求规模预计 1.05 亿吨左右，增速在 18% 上下。以服务电商为主的快递业保持快速增长，全年业务件量达 140 亿件，同比增长 52%，我国首次超过美国成为世界快递业第一大国。

（三）资本和技术双轮驱动，市场主体趋于集中

资本介入力度加大。电商物流、快递快运、物流地产、冷链物流等细分市场成为投资热点。京东商城、阿里巴巴上市带动物流概念升温。宅急送等快递企业获得资本投资，启动差异化战略。普洛斯获得中资财团投资，继续巩固领先地位。平安不动产、中信产业基金、复星集团等产业资本加大物流地产投入，万科等房地产企业进入物流市场。《铁路运输企业准入许可办法》发布，鼓励社会资本投资铁路建设和经营。

技术推动行业变革。物流企业纷纷“触网”。中外运推出“海运订舱网”，进军物流电商领域。好运宝、好多车、车旺等一批车货匹配 APP 系统受到资本热捧，集中上线不下 50 家。大数据平台发力。菜鸟网络精准预测“双十一”快递业务情况，缓解高峰期爆仓压力。“以机器替代人”的趋势日益明显。自动化立体仓库、自动分拣设备、智能物流设备等机械化、自动化、智能化装备进入快速发展期。京东商城“亚洲一号”正式启用，分拣处理能力 16000

万件/小时，达到国际一流水平。

市场集中度稳步提升。截至 2014 年年底，我国 A 级物流企业超过 3000 家，其中，5A 级企业近 200 家。《2014 年度中国物流企业 50 强排名》中，第 50 名物流业务收入为 22.4 亿元，入围门槛比上年提高 2.1 亿元。快递、电商、零担、医药、物流地产等细分物流市场品牌集中、企业集聚、市场集约的趋势进一步显现。在公路零担市场，卡行天下、安能物流等加盟型网络依托资本和技术优势，集聚了一批小微物流企业。卡行天下加盟网点增加至 1300 家，安能物流网点增加至 2000 家，货运市场集约化步伐加快。

（四）平台整合、产业融合，经营模式变革创新

平台思维改变传统模式。园区基地平台、公路货运平台、电商物流平台、物流金融平台等风起云涌。传化公路港、林安物流、宝湾物流等园区经营企业加紧连锁复制，编织园区资源、信息和服务平台。“三通一达”联合组建峰网投资平台，抱团深耕产业链。“中国物流金融服务平台”上线运行，金融物流风险管控引起关注。国家物流公共平台受到重视。全国道路货运车辆公共监管与服务平台正式上线，国家交通运输物流公共信息平台推动信息互联对接。

产业联动融合走向深入。物流业与制造业、商贸业、金融业等“多业联动”，产业合作层次从运输、仓储、配送业务向集中采购、订单管理、流通加工、物流金融、售后维修、仓配一体化等高附加值增值业务，个性化创新服务拓展延伸。企业凭借自身优势跨界经营。零担快运企业凭借网络优势推出快递业务。快递企业凭借客户优势进入电商、冷链和 O2O 市场。合同物流企业凭借资源优势承接客户外包服务，从单一的物流服务商向综合服务商转型。

各种组织模式、管理模式和商业模式创新成为热点。在公路货运领域，车货匹配平台整合货源和车源，引入货运“淘宝”和“滴滴打车”模式。易流科技推出“云平台”模式，整合社会车辆超过 30 万辆。在快递电商领域，“网订店取”“智能快递箱”等配送模式得到推广，快递业务趋向“定制、精准和安全”的体验式服务。在仓储园区领域，中储股份与普洛斯建立合资公司，探索混合

所有制模式。外高桥物流中心推广监管新模式。专业性的快递、电商、冷链物流园尝试建立产业生态体系。在合同物流领域，宝供物流发布“四轮驱动、两翼齐飞”发展战略，打造互联网时代新模式。在铁路货运领域，随着铁路货运改革，全国铁路4000多个营业站敞开受理零散货物，日发送货物超过7万吨。电商班列、高铁行包等新兴业务受到市场欢迎。

（五）渠道下沉、海外布局，服务网络纵深发展

网络渠道加紧深耕细作。德邦物流在全国开设直营网点5200余家，全年网点增长近千家，继续向中西部和三四线城市延伸。日日顺物流在全国2800多个县建立了物流配送站和17000多家服务商网点，逐步形成大件商品送装一体化的服务网络。顺丰速运启动快递下乡计划，业务覆盖的县级市或县区已超过2300个。阿里巴巴启动“千县万村”计划，拟投资建立1000个县级运营中心和10万个村级服务站。京东推出“先锋站”计划和“村民代理”模式。据统计，2014年农村新增快递网点近5万个，农村包裹超过20亿件。社区物流服务深入推进，解决“最后一公里”问题。

国际物流市场面临新机遇。跨境电商迎来爆发期，海外物流布局成为重点战略。阿里巴巴、顺丰、圆通等电商、快递企业与境外快递邮政企业合作，开辟全球物流市场，试水跨境电商和物流业务。中邮速递推出“中邮海外购”，打造跨境电商转运平台。中远集团为天猫国际跨境电商业务提供全程物流服务。各类企业看好跨境电商业务，“海外仓”建设吸引大批资金。与此同时，中远物流、中外运股份等大型物流企业继续保持工程物流领域的优势地位，跟随国内工程建设企业“走出去”，在港口、园区等物流战略资源方面取得积极进展。

（六）互联互通、一体化发展，区域物流进一步优化

基础设施加强互联互通。全年完成铁路公路水路固定资产投资2.5万亿元，其中，公路完成投资15256亿元，铁路完成投资8088亿元。物流园区、物流中心等基础设施仍是地方政府支持重点。传

化公路港推出“智能公路港”模式，在青岛、天津等地兴建公路智能网络平台体系。“一带一路”战略受到全球瞩目，基础设施互联互通取得成效。国际货运班列加快整合，西、中、东三条中欧铁路通道加紧建设，预计全年将开行 300 列。国家物流大通道建设开始起步，优化区域物流通道网络布局。安吉物流、长久物流、中铁特货等企业积极推进汽车铁路物流和滚装物流发展。鲁辽陆海货滚甩挂运输大通道航线实现首航。甩挂运输、海铁联运等多式联运有新的进展。“无水港”“无轨货场”“虚拟空港”“卡车航班”等新的物流组织方式促进多种运输方式互联互通。

区域物流一体化加速。按照区域发展战略要求，京津冀、长江经济带、广东地区三大区域通关一体化改革全面实施。京津冀三地签署多项物流合作协议，推进物流业协同发展。长江经济带启动综合立体交通走廊建设，完善区域综合交通运输体系。广东、天津、福建再设三个自由贸易园区，推动更高水平对外开放。郑州、武汉多地启动区域物流中心建设，完善物流基础条件和政策环境。

（七）政府重视行业发展，治理环境持续向好

基础性工作稳步推进。《物流标准化中长期发展规划》编制工作启动，截至 2014 年年底，我国已发布的各类物流标准超过 800 项。物流教育培训成效显著，全国已有 470 多所本科院校、1000 多所高职高专院校开设了物流专业，已有 30 多万人取得相关物流资格证书。物流业信用体系建设获得多部门支持，政府和协会积极探索专业物流领域信用建设。物流安全引发社会关注，公路安全生命防护工程启动，危化品货物运输加强管理，强化重大风险源报备制度。国家提出节能减排阶段性目标，物流业减排压力加大。多地出台新能源汽车补贴政策，物流和快递用车成为支持重点。

物流政策环境持续改善。有关部门发布一系列支持物流业发展的政策文件。国家发改委支持冷链物流、粮食物流、公共信息平台和物流诚信建设，国家级示范物流园区工程已完成前期设计；交通运输部重视物流通道建设，继续开展甩挂运输试点和城市配送便利通行工作，积极推进车型标准化；商务部继续开展城市共同配送示

范试点，商贸物流标准化、电子商务与快递协同发展试点工作启动；工信部加强物流信息化引导，开展物流供应链推进工作；邮政局全面开放国内包裹快递市场，简化快递资质审批。全国现代物流工作部际联席会议加强政策协调，部门间统筹协调机制有望加强。《中长期规划》发布后，有关部门积极推进政策落实，《促进物流业发展三年行动计划》（以下简称三年行动计划）正式出台，明确了五个方面、62 项重点工作任务的牵头部门以及具体目标和完成时限。

总体来看，2014 年我国物流业顺应经济发展“新常态”，总体运行保持了较强的发展韧性。但是我们也要看到，物流整体市场环境较为严峻，企业经营仍然困难，产业间合作还有很大空间。中物联监测的重点物流企业收入利润率持续走低，地方保护、不正当竞争、诚信体系缺失等问题依然存在，资金短缺、人才短缺问题难以缓解，创新驱动的内生机制还没有建立，企业经营压力持续加大。与此同时，国家支持物流业发展的政策有待落实，物流企业审批多、收费高、行路难和税负重等问题还没有实质性改善。这些都对物流业在“新常态”下转型升级、健康发展提出了严峻挑战。

二、2015 年我国物流业发展展望

当前，世界经济仍处在国际金融危机后的深度调整期，我国经济发展步入“新常态”。就物流业面临的形势来看，正处于产业地位的提升期、现代物流服务体系的形成期和物流强国的建设期。

《中长期规划》明确了物流业在国民经济发展中的基础性、战略性地位，极大地提升了产业地位，也对物流业发展提出了新的更高要求。物流业只有适应经济发展的“新常态”，通过调整市场结构、转换经营模式，加快产业升级和创新驱动，才能取得应有的产业地位。

到 2020 年，基本建立布局合理、技术先进、便捷高效、绿色环保、安全有序的现代物流服务体系，是《中长期规划》提出的战略目标。现代物流服务体系，需要物流需求的专业化、社会化，物

流企业的规模化、集约化，也需要物流基础设施的一体化、网络化以及法制化的营商环境。

同时，我们也要清楚地看到，我国是物流大国但不是物流强国，成本高、效率低、集约化水平不高、产业支撑度不足，诚信、标准、人才、安全、环保等“软实力”不强，尚不能满足现代物流国际竞争的需要。

我们要充分认识物流业发展“三期叠加”的阶段性特征，准确把握新的趋势。

从物流需求看，随着消费对经济贡献增大，消费需求将成为主要推动力。以终端消费者为对象，个性化、多样化的物流体验成为电子商务条件下消费者的核心诉求。企业物流需求加快向供应链延伸，专业化、一体化的物流服务成为增长点。城镇化的加速推进，农村物流和社区物流潜力巨大。

从发展方式看，随着增长速度放缓，质量与效率的提升成为市场衡量标准。物流企业更加注重服务体验和解决方案，稳步提高服务能力和运行效率。企业联盟合作成为常态，产业融合加快发展。资源共享、合作共赢、可持续发展的产业生态圈正在形成。

从内生动力看，随着市场竞争层次的提升，整合与创新助推转型升级。企业流程再造、兼并重组、联盟合作更加普遍，功能整合、组织整合、信息整合和平台整合充分发挥资源利用效率。技术创新、组织创新、模式创新、管理创新成为发展新引擎，打造差异化竞争优势，培育核心竞争力，才能引领企业抢占竞争制高点。

从外部拉力看，随着市场开放和互联网经济的发展，资本和技术驱动力度加强。更多的外部企业将携资本优势跨界进入物流市场，依托互联网经济的新模式改变原有的游戏规则，物流市场格局将加快调整，加速洗牌。

从资源要素看，随着各类资源要素全面紧缺，物流业已经进入高成本时代。物流用地落实难，仓库租金仍将延续持续上涨态势。人口老龄化日趋发展，企业“员工荒”现象加剧，劳动力成本逐年上涨。企业加大设施设备和信息系统投入，资金压力加大。对存量资源的调整和增量资源的优化大有文章可做。

从基础设施看，随着国家基础设施投资进入新阶段，物流基础设施网络初步成型。铁路运能进入集中释放期，原有运输格局加快调整。“五纵七横”公路网和“八纵八横”铁路网已经形成，物流园区、物流中心等物流节点初具规模，物流基础设施互联互通，网络后发优势明显，对行业发展的“硬约束”逐步消退。

从环境约束看，随着国家和社会对生态环境的重视，绿色低碳物流成为趋势。环境承载能力达到或接近上限，国家应对气候变化力度加强，还将出台更加严格的节能环保政策，环境对行业发展的约束力加大，倒逼绿色低碳循环物流体系建设。

从政策调控看，随着《中长期规划》和三年行动计划的落实，现代物流工作部际联席机制逐步完善，物流业政策环境将趋于宽松，统一开放、竞争有序、监管有力的现代物流管理体制逐步完善。

这些趋势表明，我国物流业适应经济发展“新常态”，将进入以转型升级为主线的发展新阶段，物流业将逐步从追求规模速度的粗放式增长转变为质量效率集约式增长，从增量扩能为主转变为调整存量、做优增量并存的深度调整，从要素驱动、投资驱动转变为整合发展、创新驱动，逐步释放发展潜力。

2015 年是全面完成“十二五”规划的收官之年，也是《中长期规划》和三年行动计划的启动之年，物流业发展面临新的机遇和挑战，企业要有新思路、新模式、新对策。我们应该更加关注客户需求的新变化，不断开发个性化、体验式服务，着力提升服务质量；更加关注物流服务的新市场，向农村、社区延伸服务链条，同时利用好国际市场，着力拓展物流服务网络；更加关注组织经营的新模式，特别注意资本和技术驱动对传统经营模式的颠覆性创新，着力形成市场竞争新优势；更加关注物流新技术特别是信息技术的推广应用，通过大数据、云计算、物联网、移动互联网等新兴技术，改造业务流程、组织架构和业务模式，着力提升运行效率；更加关注物流人才培养，加强教育培训，持续投资于人，着力提高绩效水平；更加关注承担社会责任，坚持守法经营、诚信经营，大力发展绿色物流，积极服务社会、回报社会、造福社会，着力塑造物流新形象；更加关注行业协会的建设与发展，着力发挥协会桥梁和纽带作用。同时，我们也要注意防控和化解市场风险、技术风险、重组风险、资金风险、法律风险、信用风险，处理好增长与稳定的关系，通过改革创新推动整合优化、增进效率，有序推进全行业转型升级。

随着《中长期规划》和三年行动计划开始实施，我们也希望政府有关部门进一步加大改革开放和法治建设力度，加强部门间的统筹协调，形成促进物流业健康发展的合力。业界迫切希望困扰物流企业发展的税收、交通、用地、审批、融资等方面的政策得到落实，一些长期制约行业发展的问题取得突破。中国物流与采购联合会作为行业社团组织，将继续加强调查研究、积极反映企业诉求、协助政府推进政策落地，为物流业发展适应“新常态”做出新的贡献。

何黎明

（作者：何黎明，现任中国物流与采购联合会会长、中国物流学会会长）

Review of China's Logistics Industry Development in 2014 and Prospect in 2015

(Foreword)

1. Review of China's Logistics Industry in 2014

In 2014, facing complex and volatile market situation, China's logistics industry has actively adjusted the response and speeded up transformation and upgrading. Logistics industry actively adapted to the 'new normal' of economic development, playing a better role in the infrastructure and strategic level.

(1) Publishing the Long – term Planning and Dramatic increase in status of the logistics industry

The Long – term Development Planning of China's Logistics Industry (2014 – 2020) (Named Long – term Planning for short in the following) has been discussed and adopted in executive meetings of the State council which preside by LI Keqiang prime minister in June 11, 2014, published by the State Council issued[2014]No. 42 document in September 12. This was another programmatic document to guide the development of the logistics industry, after the China's Logistics Industry Restructuring and Revitalization Plan issued by the state council in 2009. After the 18th CPC National Congress, General Secretary XI Jinping and LI Keqiang prime minister and some other government leaders has made several visits to the logistics enterprises, making the important speech and instructions to the development of logistics industry. Locating the logistics industry in infrastructure and strategic industry to support national economic development in the introduction of Long – term Strategy, which is an important indicator of the industry to further enhance the status of the logistics industry. The strategy claimed that, by 2020, basically establishing a modern logistics service system with reasonable layout, advanced technology, convenience and efficiency, green and environmental protection, safety and order, clear the long – term development strategic goals. The strategy shows that there are three major focus of development, seven main tasks, twelve key projects and nine safeguard measures, seizing the key problem restricting the development of the logistics industry, clarifying direction of development, which is the top – level design blueprint guiding China's logistics industry under the ‘new normal’ to healthy development.

(2) Stable high growth rate and the structure of demand adjusting steadily

The overall operation get modest growth, and the quality achieve growth. The annual total sum of logistics was expected to exceed 210 trillion yuan, an 8% increase over the same period last year. The added value of logistics business was expected to exceed 3.4 trillion yuan, a 9% increase over the same period last year. The two indices were showing the signs of slower growth than last year, but they were still higher than the GDP growth rate, in the speed region of medium and high. The total social logistics costs was expected to exceed 9.7 trillion yuan, an 8% increase over the same period last year, the growth continuing to trend down slightly. The ratio of total logistics costs to GDP is about 17%, the quality and efficiency of the logistics development has improved. The LPI are in the 55% upper and lower range, logistics industry operation get overall stabilization.

The structure of demand has been deeply adjusted. The logistics demand of means of production such as steel, coal, cement and non – ferrous metal are developing slowly. Import and export trade was still weak. The railway freight turnover was expected to decline by about 6%, the growth rate of above scale port cargo throughput and the foreign trade cargo throughput year – on – year fell 4.1% and 3.8%. The contribution rate of eventual consumption to economic growth continued to rise, then the demand of consumer logistics such as e – business logistics and cold chain logistics were maintaining a rapid growth. The growth rate of the annual sum of item logistics is over 30%. Cold chain logistics demand was expected to 105 million tons, whose growth rate is around 18%. The Express industry which is given priority to servicing e-business maintains rapid growth, and the annual business volume reached 1.4 billion, increasing of 52%. For the first time, China surpass American to become the first world in superpower express industry.

(3) With the ‘two – wheeled’drive of capital and technology, the market tends to focus on one subject

The intensity of capital coming into this field was increasing. Market segments such as e – commerce logistics, express delivery, logistics real estate, cold chain logistics and etc, have become hotspots of investment. The concept of logistics has been heated up by Jingdong Mall and Alibaba’s appearing on the market. Express enterprises as ZJS Express gain access to capital investment and start the differentiation strategy. With the investment from Chinese consortium, Global Logistics Properties continue to consolidate its leading position. Ping' an property, CITIC Industrial Fund, Fosun Group and other industrial capital increase their investment in logistic real estate, while Wanke and other real estate enterprises set foot in the logistics market. According to The Regulation of admittance license of the Railway Transport Enterprise, it's encouraged social capital to invest in railway construction and operation.

Technology pushes the revolution of the whole industry. Logistics enterprises get into the Internet industry one after another. Sinotrans has launched the website for booking shipping online, marching towards the field of electronic businesses. Applications that match goods and vehicles such as Haoyunbao, Haoduoche and Chewang are sought after by capital and there are more than fifty of them have been put on – line simultaneously. The Big Data Platform send its force. Rookie network making the accurate prediction of express delivery business situation on Nov. 11 to relieve the pressure of warehouse explosion in the peak period. The trend to replace humans by robots has been getting increasingly obvious. Automated stereoscopic warehouse, automatic sorting equipment, intelligent logistics equipment and other mechanized, automated and intelligent equipment has been entered a rapid development period. The warehouse named 'Asia's No. 1' of Jingdong Mall was officially used with the sorting ability of 160 million pieces per hour, reaching to world – class level.

The market's concentration ratio improves steadily. Up to the end of 2014, the number of A – level logistics companies in China has been more than 3000, and of which the number of 5A – level logistics companies has been closed to 200. In the 2014 Annual Ranking of the Top 50 Chinese Logistics Enterprises, the business income of the 50th logistics enterprise was 2. 24 billion RMB and the threshold has increased 0. 21 billion RMB compared to the last year. The logistics market segments, for instance, express delivery, e – commerce logistics, less – than – carload freight, medical logistics and logistic real estate, have a revealing trend of brand concentration, enterprise cluster and market intensivism. In the highway LTL market, KXTX, ANE and other join – type network relying on the advantages of capital and technology have gathered a number of small logistics enterprises. The franchise outlets of KXTX Company increased to 1300 and that reached to 2000 of ANE, thus proving the pace acceleration of the intensivism in freight market.

(4) Platform integration, Industrial convergence and reform and innovation in Business mode

Platform thinking transformed traditional operation mode. Logistics park base platform, road freight transport platform, online retailer logistics platform and logistics financial platform are raging like a storm. The Enterprises managing Logistics Park such as Transfar road bay, Linan Logistics Company, Baowan Logistics have been making chain replication, establishing park resources information and service platform. YTO Express, STO Express, ZTO Express and Yunda Express created Feng net investment platform together to focus on industry chain. 'China Logistics Finance Service Platform' beta, financial logistics risks management raise concerns. National public logistics platform received attention. National road freight vehicles public supervision and service platform has been running on the line officially, national transport logistics public information platform promoting information docking.

Linkage and fusion between industry have gone further. Logistics industry has been linking with Manufacturing industry, trade industry, financial industry etc. Industry cooperation level has been developing from transport, storage, distribution to high value – added business and personalized innovation service such as centralized purchasing, order management, distribution processing, logistics finance, after – sale repairing, storage integration etc. Companies run crossover rely on their advantages. LTL express enterprises promote express service based on their network advantages. Express companies enter the fields of e – business, cold train and O2O. Contract logistics enterprises change their role from single logistics service to comprehensive service by undertaking outsourcing services of clients.

Now, various innovation of management modes, organization modes and commercial modes become hotspots. In highway transport filed, car – freight matching platform integrates freight resources and car resources. Introduces 'Taobao mode' and 'Didi Taxi' mode in freight filed. Yiliu Technology promotes 'Cloud Platform' mode, integrate cars of society which are more than 300 thousand. In express electronic commerce filed, some delivery ways such as Net book store 'intelligent delivery box' has been promoted, express service runs to customized, accurate, safe experience service. In storage park filed, China Material Storage and Transportation Company and Global Logistics Properties established a joint venture company, exploring the mixed ownership model. WGQ Logistics Center promoted new mode for supervision. Professional express, electronic commerce, cold chain park has been trying to set up manufactory ecological system. In contract logistics filed, P. G. Logistics published a developing strategy four – wheel drive, Wings fly together' to create new mode in internet age. In railway freight transport filed, with the reformation of railway transport, more than 4000 operating station national wide have opened to accept scattered cargo, and daily cargo delivery has been more than 70 thousand tons. Some emerging services such as online retailer's train, high - speed rail luggage and parcel etc. achieved popularity of the market.

(5) Channel sink, Overseas layout and Further development of the service network

Network channels developed in the direction of deep and thin. There are more than 5200 Deppon Logistics retail outlets in China, continuing to extend to the Midwest and the four - tier cities, and the number kept growing by approximately 1000 every year. RRS logistics has established over 2800 logistics distribution stations and service provider network in more than 17000 counties, and will eventually form a large commodity mounted integrated service delivery network. The plan about express delivery in the countryside of SF Express program started, covering more than 2300 county - level cities and counties. Alibaba started 'Thousands of Villages County' program, with 1000 county operation centers and 100 thousand village service stations to be funded. Jingdong launched the 'Pioneer Station' program and the 'villagers' proxy mode. Statistics showed that, in 2014, the number of newly - set - up Express outlets reached 50 thousand, and rural parcels was over 2 billion. Logistics service in communities has been further promoted to solve the 'last mile' problem.

International logistics market was facing a new opportunity. The cross - border online retailers embraced the outbreak period, and overseas logistics distribution was becoming the key strategic role. Online retailers and postal enterprises like Alibaba, SF Express and YTO Express have cooperated with foreign postal enterprises, opening up the global logistics market, testing the water of cross - border Online retail and logistics business. CNPEX launched the 'CNPEX overseas purchase' service, creating cross - border retailer transfer platform. COSCO Group provided logistics services for Tmall international cross - border retail business. Various types of enterprises look a further increase of cross - border retail business, the establishment of 'overseas warehouse' attracted huge amount of capital investment. At the same time, COSCO, Sinotrans and other large - scale logistics enterprises which continued to maintain a dominant position in the field of project logistics, following the domestic construction enterprises to 'go out', have made positive progress in port strategy, park strategy, and other resource logistics strategy.

(6) Interconnection, Integrated development and Further optimization of regional logistics

Infrastructure interconnection was strengthening. The highway and waterway investment grew at the rate of 9. 2% , of which the highway investment was expected to grow by 11. 4% , the annual railway investment was expected to reach 800 billion yuan. Local government continued to invest mainly on logistics park, logistics center and other infrastructure. Transfar road bay launched the 'Smart way port mode', to build the system of the highway intelligent network platform in Qingdao, Tianjin and other places. 'One Belt and One Road' strategic has attracted global attention and infrastructure interoperability has succeeded. To speed up the integration of international freight trains, West, East and Central Railway has sped up the pace of construction and been expected to open 300 lines. The construction of the national logistics channel has started, which optimized the regional logistics network layout. Enterprises like AnJi logistics, Changjiu logistics and CRSCS actively stimulated the development of automobile and ro – ro logistics. Achieve first flight in the routes of land and sea cargo transportation avenue roll rejection linked between Shandong and Liaoning provinces. Transport, rail transport and multimodal transport have made new progress. New ways of logistics such as 'dry port', 'no rail freight yard', 'virtual airport' and 'truck airline' have promoted the interoperability of a variety of modes of transport.

Regional logistics integration accelerated. In accordance with the requirements of the strategy of regional development, three regional integration clearance reform, which is the Beijing Tianjin Hebei region, the Yangtze River economic belt, and Guangdong area, has been comprehensively implemented. Signed a number of logistics cooperation agreement, Beijing, Tianjin and Hebei promoted the coordinated development of the logistics industry. Construction of a comprehensive three – dimensional transport corridor has been started along The Yangtze River economic belt, improving the regional comprehensive transportation system. Guangdong, Tianjin, Fujian set up three free trade zone, to promote a higher level of opening to the outside world. Zhengzhou, Wuhan started the construction of regional logistics center, improving the logistics infrastructure and policy environment.

(7) Government attached importance to the development of the industry and Governance environment continued to improve

Fundamental work moved forward steadily. The preparation work of Long – term

Development Planning of China ' s Logistics Industry has started, at of the end of 2014, more than 800 pieces of all kinds of logistics standardization have been released in China. Logistics education and training have been paying off. There are more than 470 colleges, 1000 vocational colleges setting up a logistics professional and more than 300000 people with relevant qualification certificate in logistics. The construction of the logistics industry credit system has gained multi – sectoral support. Government and social communications actively explored the credit construction in professional logistics field. Logistics security has arisen social concern. Highway safety protection project has started, transport of dangerous chemical materials was under strengthening management. The filing system of sources of significant risk was improving. The country has put forward the milestone of energy saving and emission reduction, the logistics industry was under pressure of reducing emission. Subsidy policy has been introduced towards new energy vehicles in many regions of which logistics and express delivery vehicles took a large proportion.

Logistics policy environment continued to improve. The relevant departments issued a series of supporting document of the development of the logistics industry policy. The national development and Reform Commission has been in support of construction of the cold chain logistics, food logistics, public information platform and integrity of logistics, the preliminary design of a national demonstration logistics park project has completed; Ministry of transportation underlined the importance of logistics channel construction, continuing the drop and pull transport pilot and urban distribution convenient traffic, and actively promoted the standardization of vehicle models; the Ministry of Commerce continued to carry out urban common distribution demonstration pilot project, commercial logistics standardization demonstration model the pilot project, and synergetic development of e – commerce and express demonstration pilot project has started; Ministry of Industry and Information strengthened to guide logistics to informationize, promoting the function of logistics supply chain ; post offices opened up the domestic parcel delivery market comprehensively, and simplify the examination and approval of the qualification in express. The modern logistics work of the ministerial joint meeting strengthened the policy coordination and inter sectoral co-ordination mechanism was expected to strengthen. After the release of Long-term Strategy, the relevant departments have actively promoted the implementation, The Three Years Action Plan to Promote the Development of Logistics Industry (here in after referred to as The Three Years Action Plan) was promulgated, noticing the five aspects, the lead department of the 62 key tasks as well as specific targets and time frame for completion.

Overall, China's logistics industry kept pace with 'new normal' of the economic development, the overall operation has kept developing with toughness in 2014. But we also have to see that the overall logistics market environment was still serious, and the companies had difficulties to operation. There is great space for inter – industry cooperation. Key logistics enterprises under China Federation of Logistics & Purchasing monitoring continued to develop with a declining profit rate , issues like local protection, unfair competition, lack of integrity of the system still existed, funds and professionals was still of shortage, and innovation – driven endogenous mechanism has not been established, and the pressure of companies continued to increase. At the same time, national policies need further implementation to support the development of the logistics industry, complex examination and approval, high fees, difficulties in functioning and heavy tax burden for logistics enterprise still need substantial improvement. All above have put forward severe challenges to the upgrade in the 'new normal' and healthy development of logistics industry.

2. Prospects of China's Logistics Industry in 2015

Currently, the world economy is still in the situation of deep transforming after the global financial crisis. China's economy goes into the 'new normal'. In the sense of the situation that the logistics industry is facing, the industry is going through the period of the upgrading of the standing of the industry, the forming of modern logistics service systems and the building of a country with strong logistics industry.

Long – term Planning has clarified that logistics plays a fundamental and strategic role in economy development, which significantly upgraded the industry status and suggested higher command for further industry development. Only by adapting to 'new normal' economy, adjusting market structure, switching operation mode , accelerating the industry upgrading and stimulating innovation, can the deserved industry status be acquired.

The strategic goal of Long – term Planning is that to build a modern logistics service system, which is properly situated, high – technological, convenient, efficient, eco – friendly and safe. To build this system, professionalizing and socializing of logistics demand, centralizing of logistics companies, integration and networking of logistics infrastructure and legalized business environment, are all needed.

At the same time, we also need to be aware that China's logistics industry is large in scale but not strong in efficiency. High cost, low efficiency, low level of integration, lack of industrial support, lack of soft power such as honesty, standardization, talents, safety and environment protection, are all deficiencies of the industry that cannot fulfill the need of facing international logistics competition.

We must be fully aware of the 'three - term - integrated' periodic characteristic of logistics industry and understand the new development trends.

From the perspective of logistics demand, with the consumption contributing more to the economy, the consumption demand may become a main stimulating power. Focusing on the final consumers, personalized and diversified logistics experience will become the core demand of consumers in the e - commerce environment. Logistics demand of companies will speed up extending to supply chain management. Professionalized and integrated logistics service will become the new growth point. With the acceleration of urbanization, rural logistics and community logistics have huge development potential.

From the perspective of development path, with the slowing of growth rate, the improvement of quality and efficiency becomes the new criteria for market measurement. Logistics companies will pay more attention to service experience and solution plan, enhancing service and operation efficiency steadily. Alliance and cooperation among companies will become normality. The integration of industries accelerates. The resource - sharing win - win - oriented sustainable industry eco - system is forming.

From the perspective of internal growth force, with the improvement of market competition level, integration and innovation stimulates the transforming and upgrading of the logistics industry. Reforming of operation process, merger and acquisition, alliance and cooperation become more common among the whole industry. Integration of function, organization, information and platform improves the utilization of resources fully. The innovation of technology, organization, mode and management becomes the new engine for development. Only by focusing on developing differentiation competitive advantages and nurturing the core competencies, can the companies acquired dominant places in competition.

From the perspective of external growth force, with the opening market and the development of internet economy, the driven force of capital and technology will be strengthened. More external companies will bring the advantages of capital then cross - border into the logistics market, relying on the new internet economy mode to change the original rules of the game. The logistics market structure will speed up the adjustment and accelerating the shuffle.

From the resource elements, with the overall shortage of elements in a variety of resources, logistics industry has entered the era of high cost. Logistics land is difficult to be implemented, and warehouse rents will continue rising. Aging population development is increasing, corporate ‘employee shortage’ phenomenon being intensified, labor costs being rising year after year. Enterprises increase investment in facilities, equipment and information systems, increasing the pressures of financial. In Adjusting and increment of optimize resource stocks has a lot of essay to do.

From the infrastructure, as the country enters a new stage of investment in infrastructure, logistics and infrastructure network have shaped initial. Railway transport enter the period of concentrated release of transportation capability, the intrinsical transportation pattern expedites the adjustment. ‘Five vertical and seven horizontal’ highway network and ‘eight vertical and eight horizontal’ railway network have been formed. Logistics parks, logistics centers and other logistics node have taken shape and the interconnection and interworking between logistics infrastructure has come into being. The late – starting advantage of networks obvious, the development of the industry's ‘hard constraints’ gradually subsided.

From environmental constraints, with the emphasis on the ecological environment in state and society, green low – carbon logistics becomes a trend. With the carrying capacity of environment having reached or get close to upper limit, the state will strengthen efforts of the response to climatic change and it will also introduce more stringent energy saving policies. The constraining force of environment for development of the industry will be increased, forcing green carbon cycle logistics system to be built.

From a policy regulation, with the implementation of the Long – term Planning and three – year action plan, modern logistics inter – ministerial joint mechanism will be gradually improved. The logistics industry policy environment will become more relaxed, a unified, open, competitive and orderly, modern and effective supervision logistics management system will be gradually perfected.

These trends show that China's logistics industry adapts to the ‘new normal’ economic development features and it will enter a new stage of development being the main line of transition upgrade. The logistics industry will gradually shift from pursuing for scale extensive growth rate to the intensive growth of quality and efficiency. The logistics industry will gradually realize the profound adjustment from increments and expanding capacity to both adjusting stock and doing better in increment, from factor driven, investment – driven to integration the development and innovation – driven, realising development potential.

The year of 2015 is the final year of China's 12th Five – Years Planning, and it is also the start of China Long – Term Planning and Three – Year – Execution Plan. Faced with new opportunities and challenges, it is necessary for logistic companies to come up with new ideas, new modes and new strategies. In order to improve the quality of service, we should pay more attention on the change of new demands of consumers and develop personalized and experienced services constantly. We should expand logistics service to villages and communities, and take good advantages of international market to develop a network of logistic service as well. We should, to take a place of the market competition, focus on the development of the new organization mode, particularly on the capital and technology driving which overturn traditional operation pattern. We should reform business process, operation framework and business pattern to improve working efficiency by using new international technology such as Big Data, Cloud Computing, Internet of Things and the Mobile Internet. Education is also important for us which we should enhance the training of talents and invest on human, to improve the level of performance Undertaking for social responsibilities show also be put into attention, abiding by the law and integrity, and green logistic should also be focused on, serving and bringing back a report for the society, to the new image of logistics. We should set up a bridge and link among the members of the industrial association. Moreover, we should also deal with the relationship of development and steadiness by preventing and defusing risks on marketing, technology, fund, law, credit and so on. Through reform and innovation to promote the integration optimization and improve efficiency, in order to promote the transformation and upgrading of the entire industry.

Accompany by the execution of Long – Term Planning and Three – Year – Execution Plan, we hope the relevant government departments further intensify the reform and opening and the legal system construction, and strengthen co – ordination between departments, to form a joint force to promote the healthy development of the logistics industry. Things matters to logistic companies like revenue, transportation, land use, examination and financing are expected to be solved, and long-term problems which restricted the development of the industry are hoped to have a breakthrough. As an industrial association, China Federation of Logistics & Purchasing will devote ourselves to the development of the logistic industry on the adjustment of ‘new normal’ by enhancing investing, reporting demands of companies and helping the government to carry forward policies.

(Author: He Liming, Chairman of the China Federation of Logistics and Pur-Chasing, China Society of Logistics)

目 录

第一篇 综合报告

第二篇 专题研究

第三篇　资料汇编

CONTENTS

Part 1 General Reports

Part 2 Special Topics

Part 3 Information Collection

第一篇

综 合 报 告

第一章

2014 年中国物流业发展的环境

2014 年，我国经济社会持续平稳发展，结构调整出现积极变化，发展质量不断提高，民生事业持续改善，经济发展进入“新常态”，物流业面临新的社会经济环境、市场环境和政策环境。

一、国民经济实现中高速增长

2014 年，全年国内生产总值 63.65 万亿元，按可比价格计算，比上年增长 7.4%。

分季度看，一季度同比增长 7.4%，二季度增长 7.5%，三季度增长 7.3%，四季度增长 7.3%。

分产业看，第一产业增加值 5.83 万亿元，比上年增长 4.1%；第二产业增加值 27.14 万亿元，增长 7.3%；第三产业增加值 30.67 万亿元，增长 8.1%。

第一产业增加值占国内生产总值的比重为 9.2%，第二产业增加值比重为 42.6%，第三产业增加值比重为 48.2%。第三产业增加值占比连续两年超过第二产业，如图 1 所示。

（一）工业生产平稳增长

2014 年，全年全部工业增加值 22.8 万亿元，比上年增长 7.0%。规模以上工业增加值增长 8.3%。

在规模以上工业中，分经济类型看，国有及国有控股企业增长 4.9%；集体企业增长 1.7%，股份制企业增长 9.7%，外商及港澳台商投资企业增长 6.3%；私营企业增长 10.2%。

分门类看，采矿业增长 4.5%，制造业增长 9.4%，电力、热力、燃气及

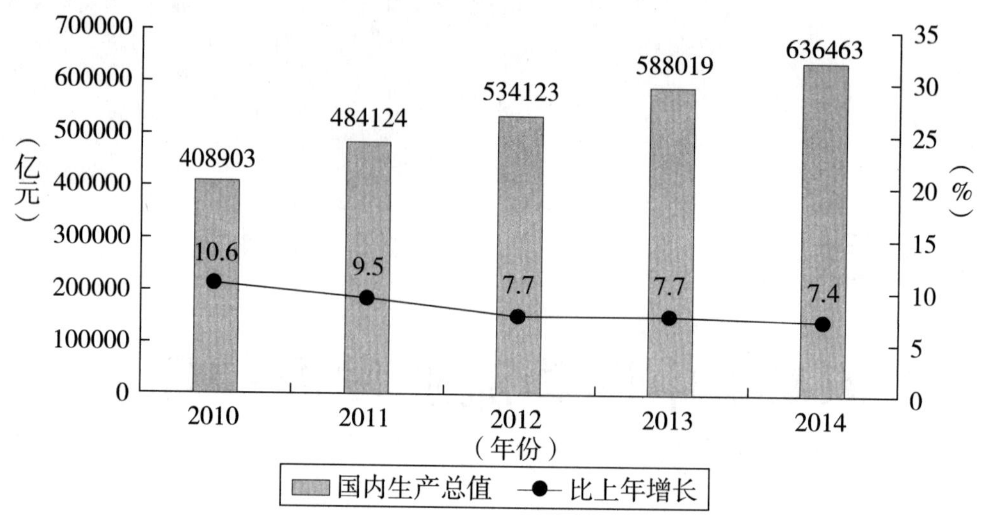

图 1　2010—2014 年国内生产总值及其增长速度

水生产和供应业增长 3. 2%。

分地区看，东部地区增加值比上年增长 7. 6%，中部地区增长 8. 4%，西部地区增长 10. 6%。

分产品看，464 种产品中有 329 种产品产量比上年增长。

全年规模以上工业企业实现利润 6. 47 万亿元，比上年增长 3. 3%，其中国有及国有控股企业 1. 4 万亿元，下降 5. 7%；集体企业 538 亿元，增长 0. 4%，股份制企业 4 . 3 万亿元，增长 1. 6%，外商及港澳台商投资企业 1. 6 亿元，增长 9. 5%；私营企业 2. 23 万亿元，增长 4. 9%，如图 2 所示。

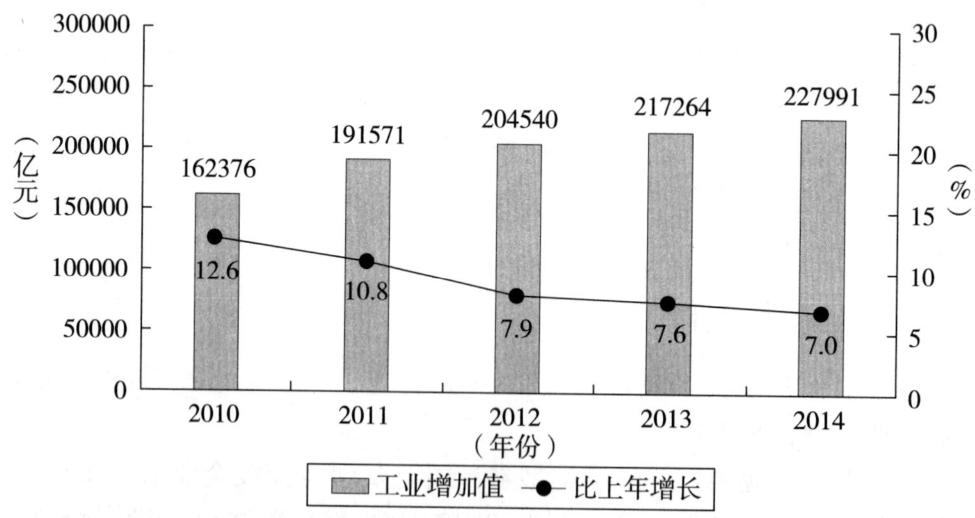

图 2　2010—2014 年全部工业增加值及其增长速度

（二）国内贸易较快增长

2014 年，全年社会消费品零售总额 26.24 万亿元，比上年增长 12.0%，扣除价格因素，实际增长 10.9%，如图 3 所示。

按经营地统计，城镇消费品零售额 22.64 万亿元，增长 11.8%；乡村消费品零售额 3.6 万亿元，增长 12.9%。

按消费类型统计，商品零售额 23.45 万亿元，增长 12.2%；餐饮收入额 2.79 万亿元，增长 9.7%。商品零售额中，限额以上单位商品零售额 12.5 万亿元，增长 9.8%。

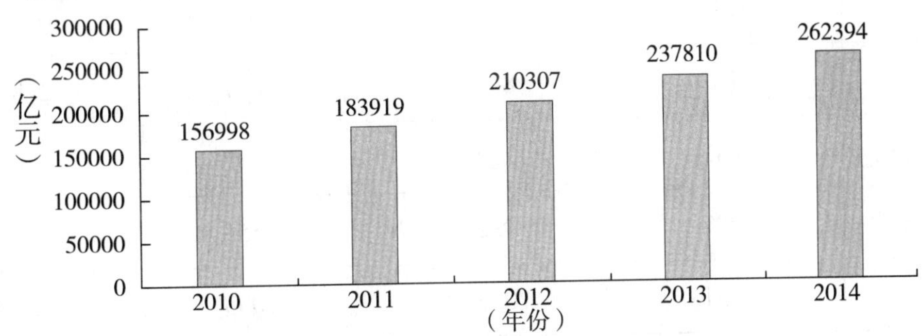

图 3　2010—2014 年社会消费品零售总额

全年网上零售额 2.79 万亿元，比上年增长 49.7%，其中，限额以上单位网上零售额 4400 亿元，增长 56.2%。

（三）进出口贸易增速回落

2014 年，全年货物进出口总额 26.43 万亿元，比上年增长 2.3%。其中，出口 14.39 万亿元，增长 4.9%；进口 12.04 万亿元，下降 0.6%。进出口差额（出口减进口）2.35 万亿元，比上年增加 7395 亿元，如图 4 所示。

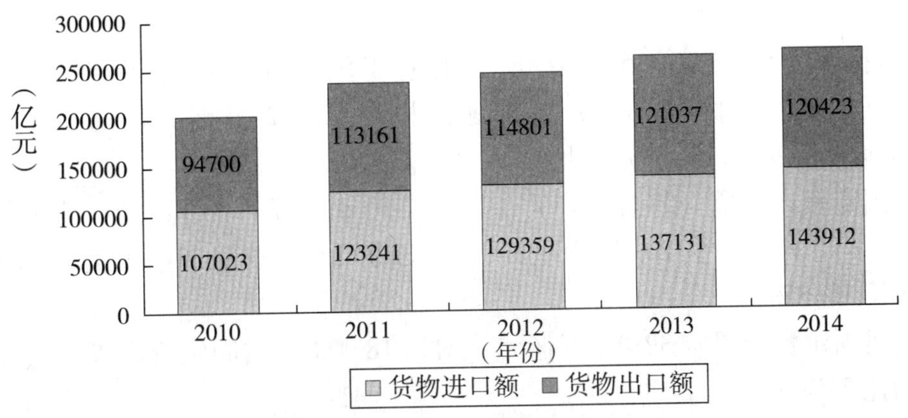

图 4　2010—2014 年货物进出口总额

表 1　2014 年对主要国家和地区货物进出口额及其增长速度

国家和地区	出口额（亿元）	比上年增长（%）	进口额（亿元）	比上年增长（%）
欧盟	22787	8.3	15031	9.7
美国	24328	6.4	9764	3.1
东盟	16712	10.3	12794	3.3
中国香港	22307	-6.6	792	-21.5
日本	9187	-1.4	10027	-0.5
韩国	6162	8.9	11677	2.8
中国台湾	2843	12.7	9337	-3.9
俄罗斯	3297	7.2	2555	3.7
印度	3331	10.7	1005	-4.6

全年服务进出口总额 6043 亿美元，比上年增长 12.6%。其中，服务出口 2222 亿美元，增长 7.6%；服务进口 3821 亿美元，增长 15.8%。服务进出口逆差 1599 亿美元。

（四）固定资产投资增速放缓

2014 年，全年全社会固定资产投资 51.28 万亿元，比上年增长 15.3%，扣除价格因素，实际增长 14.7%。其中，固定资产投资（不含农户）50.2 万亿元，增长 15.7%；农户投资 1.0 8 万亿元，增长 2.0%，如图 5 所示。

东部地区投资 20.65 万亿元，比上年增长 15.4%；中部地区投资 12.41 万亿元，增长 17.6%；西部地区投资 12.92 万亿元，增长 17.2%；东北地区投资 4.61 万亿元，增长 2.7%。

在固定资产投资（不含农户）中，第一产业投资 1.2 万亿元，比上年增长 33.9%；第二产业投资 20.81 万亿元，增长 13.2%；第三产业投资 28.19 万亿元，增长 16.8%。

民间固定资产投资 32.16 万亿元，增长 18.1%，占固定资产投资（不含农户）的比重为 64.1%。

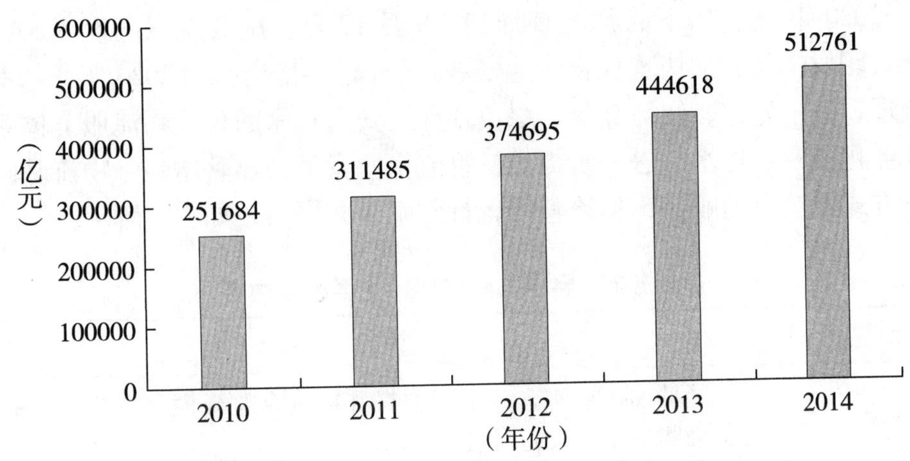

图 5　2010—2014 年全社会固定资产投资

表 2　　2014 年固定资产投资新增主要生产与运营能力

指　标	单　位	绝对数
新增 220 千伏及以上变电设备	万千伏安	22394
新建铁路投产里程	千米	8427
其中：高速铁路	千米	5491
增、新建铁路复线投产里程	千米	7892
电气化铁路投产里程	千米	8653
新建公路里程	千米	65260
其中：高速公路	千米	7394
港口万吨级码头泊位新增吞吐能力	万吨	43553
新增民用运输机场	个	9
新增光缆线路长度	万千米	301

二、政策环境持续向好

（一）国家规划和意见陆续出台

1. 国务院发布《物流业发展中长期规划》

2014 年 6 月 11 日，国务院常务会议讨论通过了《物流业发展中长期规划

（2014—2020年）》（以下简称《规划》）。9月12日，国务院以国发〔2014〕42号文正式印发，部署加快现代物流业发展。《规划》指出，到2020年，基本建立布局合理、技术先进、便捷高效、绿色环保、安全有序的现代物流服务体系。物流的社会化、专业化水平进一步提升，物流企业竞争力显著增强，物流基础设施及运作方式衔接更加顺畅，物流整体运行效率显著提高，如表3所示。

表3　　《物流业发展中长期规划》主要框架内容

项目	内容
发展重点	一是着力降低物流成本，二是着力提升物流企业规模化集约化水平，三是着力加强物流基础设施网络建设
发展任务	一是大力提升物流社会化、专业化水平，二是进一步加强物流信息化建设，三是推进物流技术装备现代化，四是加强物流标准化建设，五是推进区域物流协调发展，六是积极推动国际物流发展，七是大力发展绿色物流
重点工程	一是多式联运工程、二是物流园区工程、三是农产品物流工程、四是制造业物流与供应链管理工程、五是资源型产品物流工程、六是城乡物流配送工程、七是电子商务物流工程、八是物流标准化工程、九是物流信息平台工程、十是物流新技术开发应用工程、十一是再生资源回收物流工程、十二是应急物流工程
保障措施	深化改革开放、完善法规制度、规范市场秩序、加强安全监管、完善扶持政策、拓宽投资融资渠道、加强统计工作、强化理论研究和人才培养、发挥行业协会作用

2. 国家发改委等部门印发《促进物流业发展三年行动计划》

12月12日，为落实《物流业发展中长期规划（2014—2020年）》，国家发展改革委会同有关部门印发《促进物流业发展三年行动计划（2014—2016年）》（以下简称《行动计划》）（发改经贸〔2014〕2827号）。《行动计划》共分五个方面62项重点工作任务，如表4所示。

表4　　《促进物流业发展三年行动计划》主要框架内容

主要方面	重点工作任务
着力降低物流成本	简政放权、深化物流行政审批制度改革；切实加大对公路“乱收费”、“乱罚款”的清理整顿力度；打造物流大通道；完善城市配送车辆运行管理；落实税收支持政策
着力提升物流企业规模化、集约化水平	鼓励物流企业开展跨区域网络化经营；积极培育规模化物流企业；落实和完善支持物流企业发展的用地政策；拓宽物流企业投资融资渠道；鼓励物流业对外开放和“走出去”

续 表

主要方面	重点工作任务
着力加强物流基础设施网络建设	加快多式联运设施建设；发挥物流园区的示范带动作用
加快推进物流业重点工程建设	推进粮食仓储物流设施建设；推进棉花现代物流设施建设；加强农产品冷链物流设施建设；加强资源型产品物流设施建设；加快完善城乡配送网络体系；发展电子商务物流；加快推进物流标准化；加快物流公共信息平台建设；推进绿色物流发展；完善应急物流体系
抓好行业基础性工作	进一步明确物流业的产业地位；完善法律法规；规范市场秩序；加强安全监管；加强统计工作；强化人才培养

3. 国务院发文加快发展生产性服务业

2014 年 8 月 6 日，国务院发布《关于加快发展生产性服务业促进产业结构调整升级的指导意见》（国发〔2014〕26 号）。提出以产业转型升级需求为导向，进一步加快生产性服务业发展，引导企业进一步打破“大而全”、“小而全”的格局，分离和外包非核心业务，向价值链高端延伸，促进我国产业逐步由生产制造型向生产服务型转变。重点发展研发设计、第三方物流、融资租赁、信息技术服务、节能环保服务、检验检测认证、电子商务、商务咨询、服务外包、售后服务、人力资源服务和品牌建设等生产性服务业。

（二）管理体制改革有新进展

1. 部际联席会议加大政策协调力度

2014 年 7 月 14 日，全国现代物流工作部际联席会议在北京召开。会议由国家发改委副主任连维良主持，部际联席会议成员单位及部分与物流工作相关的部门和协会参加了会议。

会议研究了物流信用体系、物流通道建设、降低物流成本等重点工作，听取了关于规范道路货运市场管理和治理超限超载等有关工作情况的介绍，会商了快递企业设立分支机构批准时限、在用车辆加装尾板等企业反映的有关具体问题。会议要求，凡是在部际联席会议机制范围内能够解决的问题，都要协调解决，创造良好的政策环境，促进行业持续健康发展。

2014 年年底，部际联席会议办公室制定了议事暂行规则，议定每两月召开一次会议，由国家发改委、商务部、交通运输部、工业和信息化部和中国物流与采购联合会等成员单位轮流主持召开，协调解决物流业发展中的重大问题。

2. 国家铁路局正式成立

2014 年 1 月 6 日，国家铁路局正式揭牌成立。国家铁路局是 2013 年铁路政企分开改革后新组建的国务院铁路行业监管部门。新组建的国家铁路局由交通运输部管理，负责监管全国 18 个铁路局的安全生产、铁路运输市场、服务质量等。国家铁路局下辖 7 个监管局。

3. 全面深化交通运输改革

2014 年 12 月 30 日，交通运输部发布了《关于全面深化交通运输改革的意见》（以下简称《改革意见》）（交政研发〔2014〕242 号）。《改革意见》提出全面深化交通运输改革，总目标是推进交通运输治理体系和治理能力现代化。

《改革意见》共 11 个部分、42 条改革任务，可分解为 150 多项改革举措。十一个部分：一是全面深化交通运输改革的指导思想、总目标和基本原则；二是完善综合交通运输体制机制；三是加快完善交通运输现代市场体系；四是加快转变政府职能；五是加快推进交通运输法治建设；六是深化交通运输投融资体制改革；七是深化公路管理体制改革；八是深化水路管理体制改革；九是完善现代运输服务体系；十是完善交通运输转型升级体制机制；十一是加强全面深化交通运输改革的组织领导。在第九部分中，《改革意见》提出，完善交通运输促进物流业发展体制机制。

4. 加快推进价格改革

2014 年 11 月 15 日，国务院总理李克强主持召开国务院常务会议，部署加快推进价格改革，更大程度让市场定价。11 月下旬以来，国家发展改革委会同有关部门先后印发了 8 个文件，放开 24 项商品和服务价格，下放 1 项定价权限。涉及物流业的是放开民航货运、铁路运输价格及港口竞争性服务收费，如表 5 所示。

表 5　　涉及物流业的价格改革情况

发文单位	商品和服务	项目
国家发改委	铁路运输价格	铁路散货快运、铁路包裹运输价格，社会资本投资控股新建铁路的货物运价、客运专线旅客票价
民用航空局、国家发改委	国内民航货运价格	全面放开民航国内航线货物运输价格
交通运输部、国家发改委	港口竞争性服务收费	集装箱装卸、国际客运码头作业等劳务性收费，以及船舶垃圾处理、供水等服务收费价格，由现行按作业环节单独设项收费改为包干收费、综合计收，不得另行对货主和旅客收取费用

2014 年 4 月 1 日，国家发改委下发通知，明确新建的淮池铁路开通运营后，货

物运价实行市场调节，由铁路运输企业与用户、投资方协商确定具体运价水平。

5. 行政管理体制改革逐步深化

（1）工商登记制度改革取得进展

2014 年 2 月，国务院印发《注册资本登记制度改革方案》（国发〔2014〕7 号），从 3 月 1 日起在全国实施，实行注册资本认缴登记制，简化注册登记手续。全国 17 个省区市先行启动了“先照后证”改革，一些地方积极试点工商营业执照、组织机构代码证和税务登记证“三证合一”，实行一窗口受理、并联审批等创新举措，提高审批效率。

（2）取消和调整行政审批项目

2014 年，国务院三次下发《关于取消和调整一批行政审批项目等事项的决定》，全年取消和下放 246 项行政审批事项，取消评比达标表彰项目 29 项、职业资格许可和认定事项 149 项，一批物流业行政审批项目等事项得到取消和调整，如表 6、表 7、表 8 所示。

表 6　　国务院决定取消和下放管理层级的行政审批项目目录摘录

序号	项目名称	审批部门	设定依据	处理决定	备注
1	省际普通货物水路运输许可	交通运输部	《国内水路运输管理条例》（国务院令第 625 号）	下放至省级人民政府交通运输主管部门	此为“国内水路运输、水路运输业务经营审批”项目的子项
2	有关作业单位防治船舶及其有关作业活动污染海洋环境应急预案审批	交通运输部	《防治船舶污染海洋环境管理条例》（国务院令第 561 号）	取消	此为“船舶所有人、经营人或者管理人以及有关作业单位防治船舶及其有关作业活动污染海洋环境应急预案审批”项目的子项
3	国家公路运输枢纽总体规划审批	交通运输部	《公路运输枢纽总体规划编制办法》（交规划发〔2007〕365 号）	取消	只取消交通运输部审批，地方人民政府交通运输行政主管部门的审批仍然保留

续　表

序号	项目名称	审批部门	设定依据	处理决定	备注
4	引航员任职资格审批	交通运输部	《中华人民共和国船员条例》（国务院令第494号）《中华人民共和国引航员管理办法》（交通运输部令2013年第20号）	下放至直属海事系统分支机构	
5	从事海员外派业务审批	交通运输部	《对外劳务合作管理条例》（国务院令第620号）《中华人民共和国海员外派管理规定》（交通运输部令2011年第3号）	下放至直属海事管理机构	
6	报关单修改、撤销审批	海关总署	《中华人民共和国海关法》	取消	
7	报关员资格核准	海关总署	《中华人民共和国海关法》	取消	
8	铁路企业国有资产产权变动审批	国家铁路局	《国务院办公厅关于保留部分非行政许可审批项目的通知》（国办发〔2004〕62号）	取消	
9	铁路企业公司改制事项审批	国家铁路局	《国务院办公厅关于保留部分非行政许可审批项目的通知》（国办发〔2004〕62号）	取消	

续　表

序号	项目名称	审批部门	设定依据	处理决定	备注
10	铁路运价里程和货运计费办法审批	国家铁路局	《国务院办公厅关于保留部分非行政许可审批项目的通知》（国办发〔2004〕62号）	取消	
11	经营港口理货业务许可	交通运输部	《中华人民共和国港口法》《港口经营管理规定》（交通运输部令2009年第13号）	下放至省级人民政府交通运输行政主管部门	
12	内河运输危险化学品船舶污染损害责任保险证书或者财务担保证明核发	交通运输部	《危险化学品安全管理条例》（国务院令第591号）	取消	
13	船员适任证书核发	交通运输部	《中华人民共和国船员条例》（国务院令第494号）	下放至省级及以下海事管理机构	

表7　　国务院决定改为后置审批的工商登记前置审批事项目录摘录

序号	项目名称	实施机关	设定依据	处理决定
1	国际海上运输业务及海运辅助业务经营审批	交通运输部	《中华人民共和国国际海运条例》（国务院令第335号）	改为后置审批
2	国际船舶管理业务经营审批	省级人民政府交通运输行政主管部门	《中华人民共和国国际海运条例》（国务院令第335号）	改为后置审批

续　表

序号	项目名称	实施机关	设定依据	处理决定
3	国内水路运输、水路运输业务经营审批	交通运输部及流域管理机构和设区的市级以上地方人民政府负责水路运输管理的部门	《国内水路运输管理条例》（国务院令第625号）《国务院关于第六批取消和调整行政审批项目的决定》（国发〔2012〕52号）《国务院关于取消和下放一批行政审批项目的决定》（国发〔2014〕5号）	改为后置审批
4	港口经营许可	港口行政管理部门	《中华人民共和国港口法》	改为后置审批
5	经营港口理货业务许可	省级人民政府交通运输行政主管部门	《中华人民共和国港口法》《港口经营管理规定》（交通运输部令2009年第13号）	改为后置审批
6	从事国际道路运输审批	省级人民政府道路运输管理机构	《中华人民共和国道路运输条例》（国务院令第406号）	改为后置审批
7	道路运输站（场）经营业务许可证核发	县级人民政府道路运输管理机构	《中华人民共和国道路运输条例》（国务院令第406号）	改为后置审批
8	机动车维修经营业务许可证核发	县级人民政府道路运输管理机构	《中华人民共和国道路运输条例》（国务院令第406号）	改为后置审批
9	机动车驾驶员培训业务许可证核发	县级人民政府道路运输管理机构	《中华人民共和国道路运输条例》（国务院令第406号）	改为后置审批
10	食品流通许可	县级以上地方人民政府食品药品监管部门	《中华人民共和国食品安全法》《中华人民共和国食品安全法实施条例》（国务院令第557号）《国务院办公厅关于印发国家食品药品监督管理总局主要职责内设机构和人员编制规定的通知》（国办发〔2013〕24号）	改为后置审批

续　表

序号	项目名称	实施机关	设定依据	处理决定
11	铁路运输企业准入许可	国家铁路局	《国务院对确需保留的行政审批项目设定行政许可的决定》（国务院令第412号）	改为后置审批
12	从事内地与台湾、港澳间海上运输业务许可	交通运输部	《国务院对确需保留的行政审批项目设定行政许可的决定》（国务院令第412号）	明确为后置审批
13	设立引航及验船机构审批	交通运输部或交通运输部海事局	《国务院对确需保留的行政审批项目设定行政许可的决定》（国务院令第412号）	明确为后置审批
14	从事海洋船舶船员服务业务审批	交通运输部海事局	《中华人民共和国船员条例》（国务院令第494号）《国务院关于取消和下放一批行政审批项目等事项的决定》（国发〔2013〕19号）	明确为后置审批

表8　　国务院决定取消的职业资格许可和认定事项目录摘录

序号	项目名称	实施部门（单位）	资格类别	设定依据	处理决定	备注
1	机动车驾驶员培训机构教学负责人、机动车驾驶员培训结业考核人员从业资格	交通运输部	准入类	《道路运输从业人员管理规定》（交通部令2006年第9号）	取消	
2	公路水运工程试验检测人员资格	交通运输部	准入类	《公路水运工程试验检测管理办法》（交通部令2005年第12号）	取消	
3	理货人员从业资格	交通运输部	准入类	《关于印发〈理货人员从业资格管理办法〉等三个办法的通知》（交水发〔2007〕575号）	取消	

2014 年 9 月 3 日，交通运输部发布《关于加快转变政府职能　深化行政审批制度改革的意见》。提出六项主要任务，一是加大行政审批事项取消和下放力度；二是健全行政审批管理制度；三是规范行政审批运行机制；四是加强事中事后监管；五是优化职能配置；六是促进法治政府部门建设。

2014 年 1 月 8 日，邮政局印发《〈快递业务经营许可证〉变更审核流程优化方案》（国邮发〔2014〕3 号），该方案于 2014 年 3 月 1 日起正式施行。采取形式审查与实地审查相结合，对许可变更事项实行分项管理的方式提出了优化方案。对法定代表人等七项变更事项采取形式审查，不再进行实地审查，对企业名称等四项变更事项采取形式审查与实地审查相结合的审核方式。对于同时拥有省内许可和国际许可的“双证”企业，其变更审核流程进一步简化。7 月 21 日，国家邮政局发布《关于贯彻落实〈《快递业务经营许可证》变更审核流程优化方案〉的通知》（以下简称《方案》），要求各级邮政管理部门进一步贯彻落实《方案》精神，减轻快递企业负担。

（3）整顿和规范涉企收费

2014 年 6 月，国务院办公厅印发《关于进一步加强涉企收费管理减轻企业负担的通知》（国办发〔2014〕30 号）。通知要求，建立和实施涉企收费目录清单制度，对涉企行政事业性收费、政府性基金和实施政府定价或指导价的经营服务性收费实行目录清单管理并对外公开，接受社会监督。

2014 年 7 月 30 日，发改委等多个部门发出《关于整顿规范进出口环节经营性服务和收费的通知》（发改电〔2014〕198 号）。整顿规范工作范围是，海关、出入境检验检疫、港口码头、口岸等部门单位，以及相关经营企业、商（协）会等直接涉及进出口环节的经营性服务和收费。重点领域是，港口码头服务、口岸检验和查验、进出口管理平台服务三个环节。

2014 年 12 月，财政部、国家发改委发出《关于取消、停征和免征一批行政事业性收费的通知》（财税〔2014〕101 号），决定自 2015 年 1 月 1 日起，取消或暂停征收 12 项中央级设立的行政事业性收费。对小微企业（含个体工商户，下同）免征 42 项中央级设立的行政事业性收费。其中，对 100 总吨以下内河船和 500 总吨以下海船予以免收船舶港务费、船舶登记费沿海港口和长江干线船舶引航收费、沿海港口和长江干线船舶引航收费。

（4）简化分支机构备案管理

2014 年 6 月，国家邮政局印发了《经营快递业务的企业分支机构备案管理规定》，决定将经营快递业务的企业分支机构备案职能下放到省级以下邮政管理机构，并简化了备案流程。该规定于 6 月 1 日起正式实施，主要内容包括立法目的和依据，适用范围和管理部门，备案内容和流程，备案监督检查等共计

14 条。

6. 财税体制改革的新举措

（1）国际货代服务实现免征增值税

2013 年 1 月，财政部对《财政部　国家税务总局关于将铁路运输和邮政业纳入营业税改征增值税试点的通知》（财税〔2013〕106 号）中国际货代业免税政策进行了解读。2014 年 7 月 4 日，国家税务总局发布《关于国际货物运输代理服务有关增值税问题的公告》（2014 年第 42 号）。规定试点纳税人通过其他代理人，间接为委托人办理货物的国际运输、从事国际运输的运输工具进出港口、联系安排引航、靠泊、装卸等货物和船舶代理相关业务手续，可免征增值税。自 2014 年 9 月 1 日起施行。

（2）“营改增”后运输业务税负增加引起重视

2012 年营业税改征增值税试点以来，物流企业运输服务税负大幅增加问题逐步受到重视。据中国物流与采购联合会调查显示，2014 年，百家规模以上物流企业增值税税负与营业税体制下相比增长 51%，其中，运输型企业平均增长 123.3%。在行业协会和社会各界的积极努力下，物流企业“营改增”后税负增加的问题已经引起高层领导重视。

（3）土地使用税减半征收政策到期

2012 年起，国家实施物流企业大宗商品土地使用税减半征收政策。3 年来，这项政策取得积极成效，受到行业普遍欢迎。据中国物流与采购联合会调查显示，2014 年，百家规模以上物流企业中，享受土地使用税减半政策的企业平均减少土地使用税 34.2%。为做好政策延续工作，《促进物流业发展三年行动计划》提出，由财政部和税务总局牵头，研究下一步物流企业土地使用税政策的延续问题。

（4）小微企业税收优惠获得支持

2014 年 9 月 25 日，财政部、国家税务总局发布《关于进一步支持小微企业增值税和营业税政策的通知》（财税〔2014〕71 号）。通知指出，自 2014 年 10 月 1 日起至 2015 年 12 月 31 日，对月销售额 2 万元（含本数，下同）至 3 万元的增值税小规模纳税人，免征增值税；对月营业额 2 万元至 3 万元的营业税纳税人，免征营业税。

2014 年 4 月，财政部、国家税务总局发布《关于小型微利企业所得税优惠政策有关问题的通知》（财税〔2014〕34 号），规定自 2014 年 1 月 1 日至 2016 年 12 月 31 日，对年应纳税所得额低于 10 万元（含 10 万元）的小型微利企业，其所得减按 50% 计入应纳税所得额，按 20% 的税率缴纳企业所得税。

（三）重点领域行业监管逐步加强

1. 危险品运输加强安全监管

近年来，危险品运输安全生产重特大事故时有发生。2013 年年底，交通运输部以交通运输部令 2013 年第 2 号发布了《危险货物运输管理规定》，涉及条款多，调整幅度大。2014 年，国家继续加大危险货物运输的整理和监管力度。10 月 14 日，交通运输部印发《关于加强危险品运输安全监督管理的若干意见》（交安监发〔2014〕211 号），涉及危险品运输安全监督管理六大方面，重点包括市场准入、监督管理、风险管控、调查处理等各个环节，为今后道路运输管理机构更好地开展市场整治提供了政策手段，危险品运输管理逐步标准化、规范化、科学化，如表 9 所示。

表 9　　2014 年危险品运输主要涉及文件

时间	发文单位	题目	主要内容
7 月 31 日	国务院安委会	关于集中开展“六打六治”打非治违专项行动的通知	重点突出煤矿、交通运输、建筑施工、消防等重点行业领域，集中开展“六打六治”。其中要求，打击危化品非法运输行为，整治无证经营、充装、运输，非法改装、认证，违法挂靠、外包，违规装载等问题
8 月 12 日	交通运输部	交通运输部关于加强“平安交通”建设集中整治安全生产若干问题的意见	重点整治、打击非法违法生产经营建设行为、公路隧道安全隐患、道路危险货物运输、中韩客货班轮老旧船、港口危化品罐区和油气输送管线安全和水上危险货物运输等十方面 35 类违法违规行为
8 月 26 日	交通运输部办公厅	关于全国道路客运、危货运输安全生产整治实施工作的通知	从 9 月开始到年底分三个阶段开展全国道路客运、危货运输安全生产整治工作。重点任务：一是深入整治道路客运安全问题；二是深入整治道路危险货物运输问题；三是严格整治重点营运车辆动态监控存在的问题

续　表

时间	发文单位	题目	主要内容
9月9日	交通运输部办公厅	关于开展港口危险化学品安全专项整治的通知	整治设施安全，检查新建、改建、扩建港口危险化学品建设项目；整治档案建设，检查港口危险化学品企业对储罐及管线的信息档案建设情况；整治重大危险源管理，检查辖区内港口危险化学品企业登记备案、安全管理等工作；整治应急管理，检查企业应急预案、应急器材、应急救援演练等情况；整治标准化建设，检查企业推进港口危险化学品企业安全生产标准化建设、建立完善企业标准情况
10月14日	交通运输部	交通运输部关于加强危险品运输安全监督管理的若干意见	涉及严格危险品运输市场准入、强化危险品运输安全监督管理、推进危险品运输安全生产风险管控、加强从业人员培训和监管队伍建设、严肃危险品运输安全生产事故调查处理以及建立危险品运输安全生产长效机制六大方面
11月28日	国务院办公厅	关于实施公路安全生命防护工程的意见	提出要加大对超限超载违法运输车辆驾驶人、车辆所有人、运营管理者及货物托运人的处罚，研究推动将车辆超限超载违法运输行为列入以危险方法危害公共安全行为，追究有关人员刑事责任
2015年1月4日	交通运输部	关于开展危险货物道路运输电子运单管理制度试点工作的通知	决定在北京、江苏、浙江、四川、重庆、陕西六省（市）开展危险货物道路运输电子运单管理制度试点工作

2. 交通运输部要求规范公路路政执法

2014年6月5日，交通运输部发布《关于加强公路路政执法规范化建设的若干意见》（以下简称《意见》）（交公路发〔2014〕106号）。《意见》对公路路政执法队伍规范化建设、违法行为查处、路政执法责任、加强路政交警、路政运政协作等方面作出明确规定。《意见》指出，到2017年年底，基本建立较为完善的公路路政执法运行机制和工作格局，实现执法制度健全、执法行为规范、执法监督严密、经费保障有力、公路安全保护达到较高水平。

3. 加强土地节约集约利用

2014 年 5 月 22 日，国土资源部以国土资源部第 61 号令发布《节约集约利用土地规定》，此规定是我国首部专门就土地节约集约利用进行规定的部门规章，2014 年 9 月 1 日起正式施行。其中对低价出售工业用地、以土地换项目、囤积和改变土地用途等作了明令禁止。

2014 年 9 月 12 日，国土资源部下发《关于推进土地节约集约利用的指导意见》（国土资发〔2014〕119 号），明确了未来一段时间目标，一是建设用地总量得到严格控制，二是土地利用结构和布局不断优化，三是土地存量挖潜和综合整治取得进展，四是土地节约集约利用制度更加完善。

4. 食品的贮存运输的规范要求

2014 年 12 月 22 日，食品安全法的修订草案再次提交审议，进一步强化对食品的贮存运输的规范管理。本次修改中关于仓储物流企业对食品的贮存运输规定增加了如下内容：非食品生产经营者从事食品贮存、运输和装卸的，贮存、运输和装卸食品的容器、工具和设备应当安全、无害，保持清洁，防止食品污染，并符合保证食品安全所需的温度等特殊要求，不得将食品与有毒、有害物品一同运输。

（四）有关部门支持物流行业发展

1. 积极部署商贸物流工作

2014 年 10 月 24 日，国务院办公厅印发《关于促进内贸流通健康发展的若干意见》（以下简称《意见》）（国办发〔2014〕51 号），部署加快发展内贸流通，引导生产、扩大消费、吸纳就业、改善民生，进一步拉动经济增长。《意见》分推进现代流通方式发展、加强流通基础设施建设、深化流通领域改革创新、着力改善营商环境、加强组织领导五部分。

2014 年 9 月 22 日，商务部印发《关于促进商贸物流发展的实施意见》（以下简称《意见》）（商流通函〔2014〕790 号），围绕提高物流社会化、专业化、标准化、信息化、组织化和国际化水平，部署促进商贸物流发展，降低物流成本。《意见》提出了商贸物流发展的工作任务：一是提高社会化水平，二是提高专业化水平，三是提高标准化水平，四是提高信息化水平，五是提高组织化水平，六是提高国际化水平。

2. 城市配送管理引起重视

2014 年 1 月 20 日，交通运输部、公安部、商务部联合发布《关于加强城市配送运输与车辆通行管理工作的通知》（交运发〔2014〕35 号），提出了强化城市配送运力需求管理、加强城市配送车辆技术管理、规范发展城市货运出租汽车、优化城市配送车辆通行管理措施、完善城市配送车辆停靠管理措施、提升城市配送运输服务水平、强化城市配送运输市场监督管理、健全城市配送运输与车辆通行管理工作机制八项具体措施。

2014 年，商务部继续推动城市共同配送试点工作。试点工作开展以来，共有 22 个城市纳入试点范围。商务部还对 2014 年度城市共同配送试点工作进行了综合评审。

3. 甩挂运输试点继续推进

2014 年 6 月 23 日，交通运输部下发《关于开展公路甩挂运输第四批试点前期工作的通知》。第四批公路甩挂运输试点支持主题性试点项目。主题性试点项目是指围绕某个特定主题，以甩挂运输业务为纽带，集约整合 2 ~ 3 个甩挂运输项目，实现站场、车辆、信息资源的共享和优化配置。

4. 引导道路运输行业集约发展

2014 年 3 月 13 日，交通运输部公布《关于促进道路运输行业集约发展的指导意见》（交运发〔2014〕61 号）。指导意见提出，把发展龙头骨干企业作为促进道路运输行业集约发展的重要抓手，目标是通过 5 年左右的努力，在发展龙头骨干企业、促进道路运输行业集约发展方面取得重要进展，形成一批实力雄厚的龙头骨干企业。

5. 积极推动港口转型升级

2014 年 6 月 10 日，交通运输部发布《关于推进港口转型升级的指导意见》（交水发〔2014〕112 号）。指出，到 2020 年，基本形成质量效益高、枢纽作用强、绿色安全、集约发展、高效便捷的现代港口服务体系。提出拓展服务功能，发展现代港口业；完善港口运输系统，推进综合交通枢纽建设；科学配置港口资源，引导港口集约发展等六大主要任务。

6. 促进现代航运服务业发展

2014 年 10 月 31 日，交通运输部公布了《贯彻落实〈国务院关于促进海运业健康发展的若干意见〉的实施方案》。从加快海运结构调整、加快航运服务业转型升级、积极推进港口升级和现代物流发展等 9 个方面提出了 60 项任务措施。1 月 5 日，交通运输部正式发布《关于加快现代航运服务业发展的意见》（交水发〔2014〕262 号），根据《意见》，到 2020 年，基本形成功能齐备、服务优质、高效便捷、竞争有序的现代航运服务业体系。《意见》提出促进传统航运服务转型升级；提升航运交易服务能力；创新航运金融保险服务等十一大主要任务。

7. 应急物流受到重视

2014 年 12 月 24 日，国务院办公厅印发《关于加快应急产业发展的意见》

（国办发〔2014〕63号），明确了应急产业发展的总体要求、主要任务和政策措施，提出到2020年，应急产业规模显著扩大，应急产业体系基本形成，为防范和处置突发事件提供有力支撑，成为推动经济社会发展的重要动力。在重点方向和重点工作中，要求围绕提高突发事件防范处置的社会化服务水平，创新应急服务业态，加强应急仓储、中转、配送设施建设，提高应急产品物流效率。

（五）地方政府加强政策配套和创新

1. 各地落实物流业相关国家规划

2014年，为落实《物流业发展中长期规划》和《促进物流业发展三年行动计划》，各省市陆续出台了一批服务业、物流业、物流园区、冷链、快递等领域的地方规划，如表10所示。

表10　2014年部分省市出台的主要物流相关规划

时间	发文单位	题目	主要内容
7月15日	河南省	河南省物流业发展三年行动计划	强调要以郑州航空港、郑州国际陆港和国际物流园区为核心，打造中西部地区国际物流高地。《计划》提出，要强化国际联运口岸功能，提升国际联运服务效率，打造全国重要的陆路集装箱集疏中心
12月10日	湖南省	湖南省现代物流业发展三年行动计划（2015—2017年）	布局一批重要节点城市，发展一批重点园区，建设一批重点项目，扶持一批重点企业，从政策支持、融资渠道等方面加大扶持力度，加快湖南现代物流业发展
8月	温州市	现代物流业发展规划（2014—2020年），温州市现代物流业发展三年行动计划（2014—2016年）	在全市布局规划4大物流园区，到2016年年底基本建成3个物流园区（一期），启动1个物流园区建设，同时建设16个物流中心、N个配送节点。根据规划，今后3年，将初步建成“4+16+N”三级节点网络平台，力争3A级以上物流企业超过30家，5A级物流企业超过1家

续　表

时间	发文单位	题目	主要内容
8月28日	吉林省政府办公厅	吉林省服务业发展三年行动计划	确定了十余个重点项目。将推广应用电子商务纳入重点工程，要求积极推进长—吉国家电子商务示范城市创建工作；鼓励传统批发、零售企业转变发展方式；加快建设现代仓储物流体系；推动长春市加快建设综合保税区，推进重点电商项目实施等
11月19日	江苏省发改委	江苏省农产品冷链物流发展规划（2014—2020年）	提出了到2020年七项主要任务，包括优化冷链物流业空间布局、构建重点产业冷链物流体系、完善冷链基础设施、壮大冷链物流企业、发展冷链共同配送、提升冷链物流标准化信息化水平、推进冷链物流模式创新等。同时，着力实施产地冷库建设工程、冷链物流示范工程、农产品配送直销平台工程、冷链物流信息平台工程、冷链物流安全工程等五大重点工程
11月4日	四川省	四川省物流园区发展规划	到2017年，初步形成一批布局合理、运营规范、具有一定经济社会效益的示范物流园区，建设国家级和省级示范物流园区10个以上；到2020年，基本形成布局合理、规模适度、功能齐全、绿色高效的全省物流园区网络体系，对推动经济结构调整和转变经济发展方式发挥更加重要的作用，建设国家级和省级示范物流园区20个以上
12月11日	杭州市	快递服务业发展规划	力争到2017年，快递业务收入达到110亿元；快递业务量达15亿件；同城当天达比例达90%以上，与省内90%市县实现快递“当日达”或“次日达”

2. 各地支持物流业健康发展

2014 年，各地为进一步促进物流业健康发展，出台了一系列引导行业发展的指导意见，如表 11 所示。

表 11　2014 年部分省市支持物流业发展的相关文件

时间	发文单位	题目	主要内容
12 月 18 日	河北省	关于促进物流业加快发展的若干意见	五方面支持政策。一是简化审批手续。加强事中事后监管，简化物流企业申请设立审批程序。二是保障物流用地。优先支持省级物流产业聚集区用地。三是加大资金投入。引导银行业金融机构加大对物流企业的信贷支持力度，开展多种形式的银企对接，促进金融业与物流业融合。四是落实税费政策，支持农产品物流发展。五是促进车辆便利通行。对于物流车辆在行驶时间和区域采取限行或禁行措施的城市，制定保障配送车辆通行便利管理办法
10 月 10 日	四川省	现代物流业发展工作推进方案	五项工作重点，一是进一步畅通物流通道。二是着力构建多点多级物流节点体系。三是加快推进物流服务平台建设。四是加快物流一体化进程。五是培育壮大物流市场主体
7 月 4 日	河南省交通运输厅	河南省交通运输推进物流业健康发展实施意见	主要任务包括：加快完善交通基础设施，不断完善综合运输通道和网络，加快推进物流节点设施建设；大力发展先进运输组织方式，推进多式联运发展，加快发展甩挂运输；提升运输装备标准化、专业化、清洁化、轻质化水平；着力优化市场主体结构，培育龙头骨干企业，鼓励中小企业联盟发展；加快推进交通运输物流公共信息平台建设；加快推动农村物流、城市配送、专业物流等重点领域物流发展

续　表

时间	发文单位	题目	主要内容
7月3日	山东省政府办公厅	关于促进快递服务业健康发展的意见	从加强规划编制、加大政策扶持、促进转型升级、推进协同发展、保障便捷通行、完善末端投递、强化人才支撑、严格市场监管、保障行业安全九个方面，明确了加快推进省快递服务业健康发展的政策措施
6月4日	深圳市政府	深圳市发展快递业管理规定	着力解决目前深圳市快递企业遇到的用地用房难、停车通行难、融资发展难、通关查验难、用人用工难、案件立案难“六难”问题；并在保障消费者权益、加强安全监管等方面做出详细规定
10月10日	深圳市	关于促进深圳电子商务物流业发展的若干措施	包括促进创新融合发展、完善基础设施建设、推进行业规范管理、营造发展优质环境、强化发展组织保障五个部分、十七条内容，提出将从当前电商物流行业中存在的共性问题出发，完善电商物流市场监管，规范电商物流城市配送，加快电商物流标准化进程，并将依托协会、商会等，加强行业自律
11月14日	济南市经信委、市发改委、市国土资源局	济南市关于加快制造业与物流业联动发展的实施意见	积极推进实施联动发展示范试点工程。其中，到2020年，主营业务收入过10亿元的工业企业将基本实现主辅剥离，建立或委托第三方物流服务。同时，济南市将推出八项措施鼓励制造业和物流业联动发展。制造与物流联动发展同等条件下优先扶持
8月6日	温州市政府	关于进一步促进现代物流业发展的若干意见	包括支持重大物流项目招商与建设、支持物流企业信息化建设、支持物流设施装备提升、支持物流企业品牌培育、支持物流标准化建设、支持物流企业整合重组、支持航空货运航线发展、支持物流业发展用地保障、支持物流人才培育和引进、强化政府引导管理10个方面内容

续 表

时间	发文单位	题目	主要内容
2015 年 1 月 3 日	福建省商务厅、经信委	关于促进大中型物流企业发展的若干措施	提出福建省将引导大中型工业、商贸企业将物流环节剥离，设立物流企业或外包给第三方物流企业；对剥离物流环节设立物流企业的，按新设立物流企业的注册资本，给予 30 万～50 万元一次性补助

三、资源要素压力持续加大

当前，物流业用地、燃油、劳动力等资源要素依然紧缺，要素成本持续上涨，低成本竞争难以为继。

1. 物流用地更为紧缺

2014 年，全年全国国有建设用地供应总量 61 万公顷，比上年下降 16.5%。其中，工矿仓储用地 15 万公顷，下降 29.9%；房地产用地 15 万公顷，下降 25.5%；基础设施等其他用地 31 万公顷，下降 1.9%。工矿仓储用地下降幅度最大。

据中国物流与采购联合会 2014 年年初对百家物流企业抽样调查显示，2014 年物流用地的平均价格，一线城市为 80 万～100 万元/亩，二线城市为 40～50 万元/亩，三线城市为 10 万～15 万元/亩。其中，一线城市用地价格为二线城市的 2 倍，是三线城市的 7.2 倍。调查显示，一线城市物流用地价格上涨幅度明显大于二三线城市，二线城市涨幅大于三线城市，如表 12 所示。

表 12　2014 年全国主要城市物流用地价格抽样调查结果（万元/亩）

城市	北京	上海	广州	深圳	天津	昆明
地价	150～200	100～200	80～150	100～200	40～55	43～45
城市	沈阳	西安	长沙	南昌	贵阳	
地价	45 左右	24.5～50	32.5 左右	16 左右	26 左右	

地方政府降低土地使用年限。2 月 22 日和 3 月 28 日，上海市政府先后印发和转发了《关于进一步提高本市土地节约集约利用水平的若干意见》《（沪府发〔2014〕14 号文）和《关于加强本市工业用地出让管理的若干规定（试行）》（沪府办〔2014〕25 号文）。文件规定：实行新增工业用地出让弹性年期制，一般工业项目用地出让年期为 20 年，出让年限届满后，对项目综合效

益和合同履约等情况进行评估，采取有偿协议方式，续期或收回土地使用权。

2014 年 6 月 3 日，北京经济开发区也发布文件，规定建设用地出让年限一般不高于 20 年。南京市政府宁政发〔2014〕150 号文规定，工业建设用地出让年限不超过 30 年，土地出让价格提高 50% ~150%。还有一些地市开展工业用地弹性年期出让及低效、存量工业用地退出机制改革试点。在法定的工业用地使用权最高出让年限内，分别设定 10 年、20 年、30 年、40 年、50 年出让年限。

2. 燃油价格持续走低

2014 年 WTI 原油价格从 98.5 美元/桶跌到 52.7 美元/桶，全年下跌 46.5%；布伦特原油价格也从 110.55 美元/桶跌到 56.5 美元/桶，全年下跌 48.88%。

2014 年 7 月后，受国际油价下降的影响，国内柴油价格一路下滑。到 12 月底，北京地区 0#柴油价格从 7.94 元/升的高位下滑至 5.90 元/升，下降 24.5%。这还是在 2014 年度两次提高燃油消费税的情况下实现的。12 月，国家分两次将柴油燃油消费税从 0.8 元/升调至 1.1 元/升，2015 年 1 月，柴油燃油消费税再次上调 0.1 元/升，如图 6 所示。

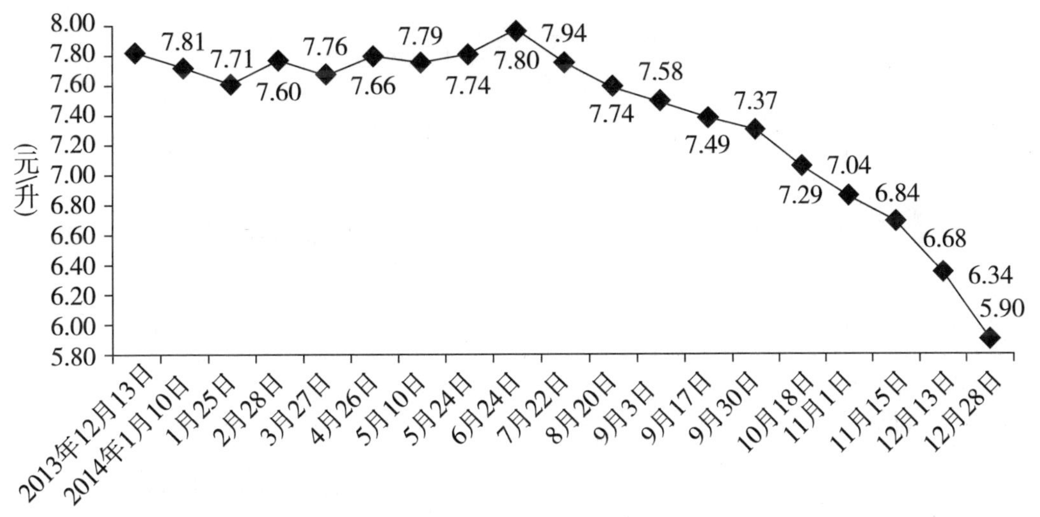

图 6　0 号柴油在 2014 年的价格趋势

注：价格来源于德利得物流成品油监控体系中的中石化零售数据。

3. 劳动力资源依然不足

2014 年年末全国就业人员 7.73 亿人，其中城镇就业人员 3.93 亿人。全年城镇新增就业 1322 万人。年末城镇登记失业率为 4.09%。全国农民工总量为 2.74 亿人，比上年增长 1.9%。其中，外出农民工 1.68 亿人，增长 1.3%；本地农民工 1.06 亿人，增长 2.8%，如图 7 所示。

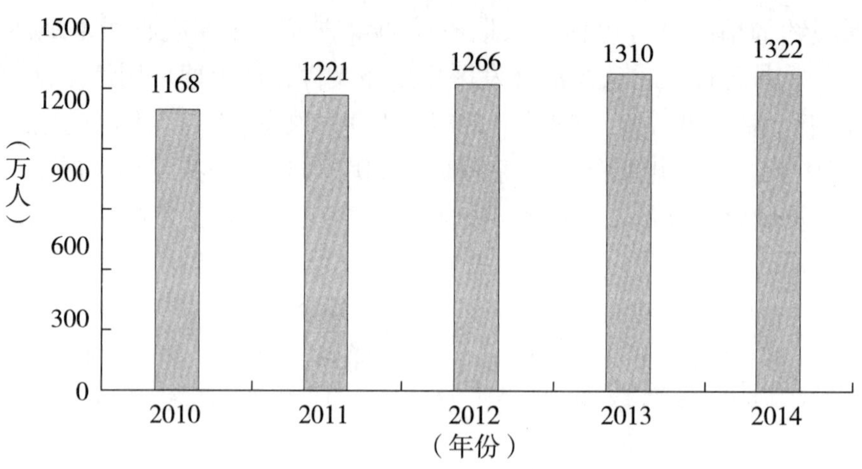

图 7　2010—2014 年城镇新增就业人数

据中国物流与采购联合会 2014 年年初对百家物流企业调查显示，企业人力成本占主营业务成本的 23%。与往年相比，59.5% 的企业反映人力成本上升，其中 17.7% 的认为上升幅度较大，如图 8 所示。

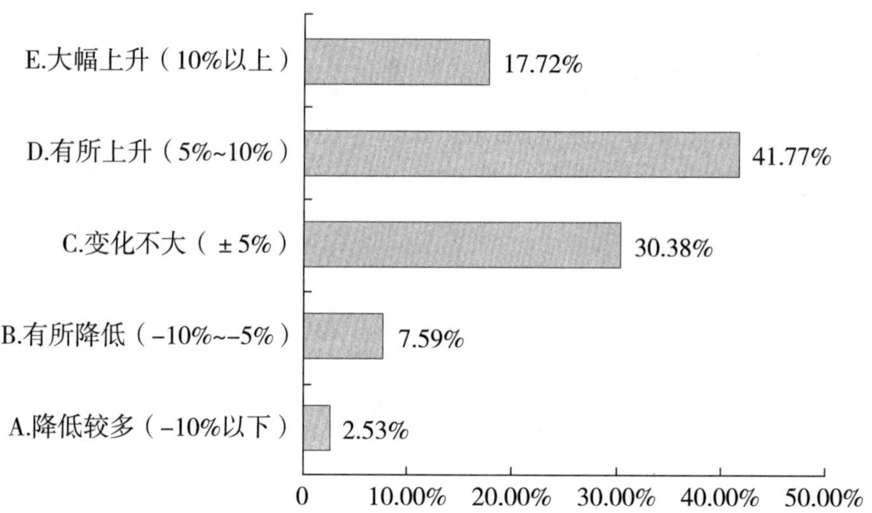

图 8　调查企业 2014 年用工成本与去年同期相比

企业普遍反映，用工成本上升的主要原因是员工工资上调、社保基数上调和福利上调等。

调查显示，企业认为雇用操作型员工有难度的占 44%，认为雇用管理型员工有难度的占 45%。关于员工流失情况，39% 的企业反映操作型员工流失严重。

四、国家强调诚信环境建设

党的十八届三中全会提出建立健全社会征信体系。国家信用系统建设规划纲要出台，部署加快建设信用体系、构筑诚实守信的经济社会环境。物流业信用体系建设指导意见，提出了物流业信用体系建设的纲领和蓝图。

2014 年 6 月 27 日，国务院印发《社会信用体系建设规划纲要（2014—2020 年）》（以下简称《纲要》）（国发〔2014〕21 号），部署加快建设社会信用体系、构筑诚实守信的经济社会环境。这是我国首部国家级社会信用体系建设专项规划。《纲要》指出，到 2020 年，实现信用基础性法律法规和标准体系基本建立，以信用信息资源共享为基础的覆盖全社会的征信系统基本建成，信用监管体制基本健全，信用服务市场体系比较完善，守信激励和失信惩戒机制全面发挥作用。

《纲要》提出要推进重点领域诚信建设，在金融领域信用建设方面，加大对金融欺诈、恶意逃废银行债务、内幕交易、制售假保单、骗保骗赔、披露虚假信息、非法集资、逃套骗汇等金融失信行为的惩戒力度，规范金融市场秩序。交通运输领域信用建设方面，将各类交通运输违法行为列入失信记录。

2014 年 11 月 18 日，国家发改委、交通部、商务部、国家铁路局、中国民航局、国家邮政局及国家标准委联合印发了《关于我国物流业信用体系建设的指导意见》，对物流业信用体系建设工作进行部署。从加强物流信用服务机构培育和监管，推进信用记录建设、共享和应用，构建守信激励和失信惩戒机制，建立完善物流信用法律法规和标准，加强企业诚信建设、推动行业诚信文化形成、大力推进政务诚信建设，充分发挥行业协会作用，开展专业物流领域信用建设试点，加强物流信用体系建设的组织协调等方面提出了具体要求。

五、生态环境建设提出新的要求

国家“十二五”规划纲要明确提出了单位国内生产总值能耗和二氧化碳排放量降低、主要污染物排放总量减少的约束性目标，减排形势十分严峻。国家陆续出台了节能减排的计划和方案，并通过中美联合声明设定了硬性目标，大力推广新能源汽车，争取“十二五”节能减排目标顺利完成。

1. 贯彻落实《节能减排低碳发展行动方案》

2014 年 5 月 15 日，国务院办公厅印发了《2014—2015 年节能减排低碳发展行动方案》（以下简称《行动方案》）。《行动方案》提出了今明两年节能减排降碳的具体目标：2014—2015 年，单位 GDP 能耗、化学需氧量、二氧化硫、氨氮、氮氧化物排放量分别逐年下降 3.9%、2%、2%、2%、5%以上，单位 GDP 二氧化碳排放量两年分别下降 4%、3.5%以上。《行动方案》从 8 个方面明确了推进节能减排降碳的 30 项具体措施。

为加大机动车减排力度，《行动方案》提出，2014 年年底前，在全国供应国四标准车用柴油，淘汰黄标车和老旧车 600 万辆。到 2015 年年底，京津冀、长三角、珠三角等区域内重点城市全面供应国五标准车用汽油和柴油；全国淘汰 2005 年前注册营运的黄标车，基本淘汰京津冀、长三角、珠三角等区域内的 500 万辆黄标车。加强机动车环保管理，强化新生产车辆环保监管。加快柴油车车用尿素供应体系建设。

为强化交通运输节能降碳，《行动方案》提出，加快推进综合交通运输体系建设，开展绿色循环低碳交通运输体系建设试点，深化“车船路港”千家企业低碳交通运输专项行动。实施高速公路不停车自动交费系统全国联网工程。加大新能源汽车推广应用力度。继续推行甩挂运输，开展城市绿色货运配送示范行动。积极发展现代物流业，加快物流公共信息平台建设。大力发展公共交通，推进“公交都市”创建活动。公路、水路运输和港口形成节能能力 1400 万吨标准煤以上，到 2015 年，营运货车单位运输周转量能耗比 2013 年降低 4%以上。

2014 年 11 月 12 日，中美双方在北京发表《中美气候变化联合声明》。中美两国元首宣布了各自 2020 年后应对气候变化的行动目标：美国计划于 2025 年实现在 2005 年基础上减排 26% ~28%的全经济范围减排目标并将努力减排 28%。中方计划 2030 年左右二氧化碳排放达到峰值且将努力早日达峰，并计划到 2030 年非化石能源占一次能源消费比重提高到 20%左右。

2014 年 11 月 19 日，国务院办公厅印发了《能源发展战略行动计划（2014—2020 年）》（以下简称《行动计划》）（国办发〔2014〕31 号），明确了 2020 年我国能源发展的总体目标、战略方针和重点任务，部署推动能源创新发展、安全发展、科学发展。这是今后一段时期我国能源发展的行动纲领。《行动计划》明确了我国能源发展的五项战略任务。一是增强能源自主保障能力、二是推进能源消费革命、三是优化能源结构、四是拓展能源国际合作、五是推进能源科技创新。

2. 推广应用新能源汽车

2014 年 7 月 21 日，国务院办公厅印发了《关于加快新能源汽车推广应用的指导意见》（以下简称《意见》）（国办发〔2014〕35 号）。《意见》明确提出，贯彻落实发展新能源汽车的国家战略，以纯电驱动为新能源汽车发展的主要战略取向，重点发展纯电动汽车、插电式（含增程式）混合动力汽车和燃料电池汽车。《意见》对加快新能源汽车推广应用提出 6 个方面 25 条具体政策措施。

2014 年 7 月 30 日，国家发展改革委下发《关于电动汽车用电价格政策有关问题的通知》，确定对电动汽车充换电设施用电实行扶持性电价政策。《通知》明确，对经营性集中式充换电设施用电实行价格优惠，执行大工业电价，并且 2020 年前免收基本电费。居民家庭住宅、住宅小区等充电设施用电，执行居民电价。电动汽车充换电设施用电执行峰谷分时电价政策，鼓励用户降低充电成本。

2014 年 9 月 16 日，交通部发布《交通运输部关于加快新能源汽车推广应用的实施意见（征求意见稿）》。提出至 2020 年，新能源汽车在交通运输行业的应用初具规模，在城市公交、出租汽车和城市物流配送等领域的总量达到 30 万辆；新能源汽车配套服务设施基本完备，新能源汽车运营效率和安全水平明显提升，新能源汽车对城市交通运输节能减排的贡献率达到 20%。《意见》要求，公交都市创建城市新增或更新城市公交车、出租汽车和城市物流配送车辆中，新能源汽车比例不低于 30%；京津冀地区新增或更新城市公交车、出租汽车和城市物流配送车辆中，新能源汽车比例不低于 35%。到 2020 年，新能源城市公交车达到 20 万辆，新能源出租汽车达到 5 万辆，新能源城市物流配送车辆达到 5 万辆。

随着新能源汽车基础条件的逐步改善，北京、上海、天津、广州、武汉、福建、临沂等各地政府也将物流业纳入新能源汽车重点应用行业，竞相将新能源汽车导入快递物流业。

第二章

2014 年中国物流业发展的特点

2014 年，我国物流业面对复杂多变的市场形势，积极调整应对，加快转型升级，主动适应经济发展新常态，较好地发挥了基础性、战略性作用。

一、总体运行处于中高速区间

（一）物流需求增速回落

2014 年全国社会物流总额 213.5 万亿元，按可比价格计算，同比增长 7.9%，增幅较上年回落 1.6 个百分点，如表 1 所示。

分季度看，一季度 47.8 万亿元，增长 8.6%，增幅较上年回落 0.8 个百分点；上半年 101.5 万亿元，增长 8.7%，回落 0.4 个百分点；前三季度 158.1 万亿元，增长 8.4%，回落 1.1 个百分点，全年呈现“稳中趋缓”的发展态势，仍处于“中高速”增长区间，如图 1 所示。

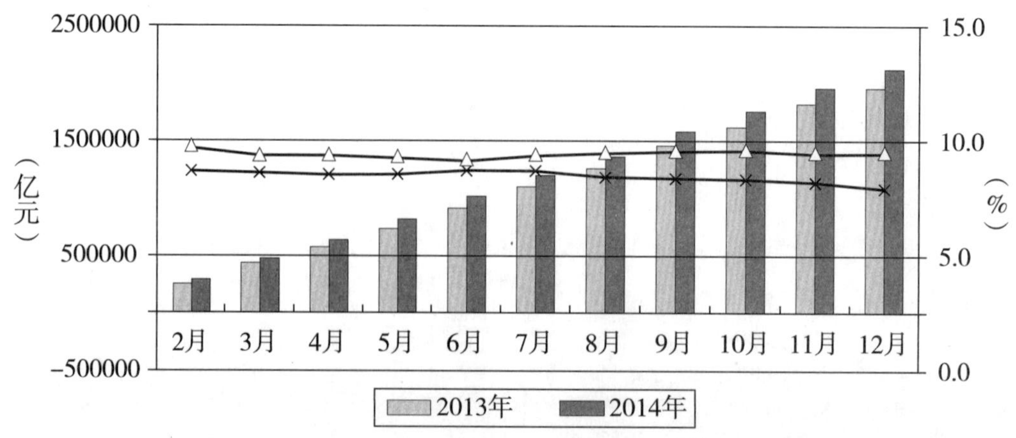

图 1　2013 年以来社会物流总额及增长变化情况

表 1　　2010—2014 年社会物流总额及其增长速度

年份	社会物流总额（万亿元）	同比增长（%）
2010	125.4	29.8
2011	158.4	26.3
2012	177.3	12.0
2013	197.8	11.5
2014	213.5	7.9

（二）物流总费用增速放缓

2014 年社会物流总费用[①] 10.6 万亿元，同比增长 6.9%。

其中，运输费用 5.6 万亿元，同比增长 6.6%，占社会物流总费用的比重为 52.9%；保管费用 3.7 万亿元，同比增长 7.0%，占社会物流总费用的比重为 34.9%；管理费用 1.3 万亿元，同比增长 7.9%，占社会物流总费用的比重为 12.2%，如表 2 所示。

表 2　　2014 年社会物流总费用构成及其增长速度

	绝对值（万亿元）	同比增长（%）	在社会物流总费用中所占比重（%）
运输费用	5.6	6.6	52.9
管理费用	1.3	7.9	12.2
保管费用	3.7	7	34.9

（三）需求结构持续调整

2014 年，钢铁、煤炭、水泥、有色等大宗生产资料物流需求增速进一步放缓。工业品物流总额为 196.9 万亿元，按可比价增长 8.3%，同比回落 1.4 个百分点，增速持续下滑。电商物流、冷链物流等消费品物流需求保持快速增长，促使单位与居民物品物流总额同比增长 32.9%。以服务电商为主的快递业保持快速增长，全年业务件量达 139.6 亿件，同比增长 51.9%，如表 3 所示。

① 由于交通运输部对公路水路运输量统计口径和推算方案的调整，社会物流总费用也进行了相应调整。

表 3　　2014 年社会物流总额构成及其增长速度

	绝对值（万亿元）	同比增长（%）	在物流总额中所占比重（%）
工业品物流总额	196.9	8.3	92.3
进口货物物流总额	12.0	2.1	5.6
农产品物流总额	3.3	4.1	1.5
单位与居民物品物流总额	0.8	32.9	0.4
再生资源物流总额	0.4	14.1	0.2

（四）运行效率有所提升

2014 年，社会物流总费用与 GDP 的比率为 16.6%。按可比口径计算，比上年下降 0.3 个百分点，物流运行效率有所提升。2014 年我国社会物流总费用与 GDP 比率的变化，一方面是受交通运输部对公路水路运输量统计口径和推算方案的调整，以及国家统计局根据第三次经济普查对 2013 年全国 GDP 调整的影响；另一方面也是我国经济结构变化，三产占比高于二产的结果。

2014 年，单位 GDP 的物流需求系数为 3.35，近年来首次出现下降，显示出创造单位 GDP 所需的物流规模有所下降，单位 GDP 的物流需求系数进入回落区间，如图 2 所示。

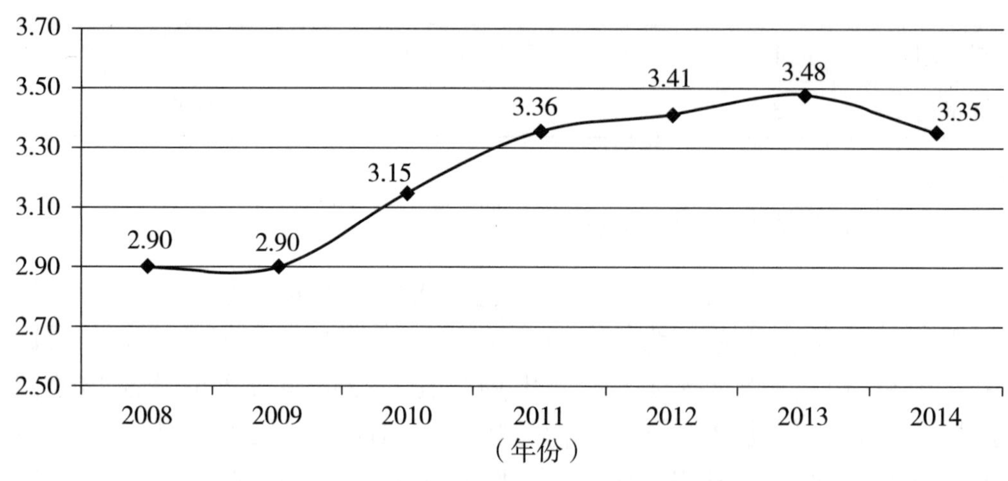

图 2　2008 年以来单位 GDP 的物流需求系数

（五）基础设施投资再创新高

2014 年，交通运输、仓储和邮政业固定资产投资 4.3 万亿元，同比增长

18.6%，增幅较上年提升1.4个百分点，高于全社会固定资产增长水平，如表4所示。

表4　2010—2014年交通运输、仓储和邮政业固定资产投资（不含农户）

年份	2010	2011	2012	2013	2014
交通运输、仓储和邮政业固定资产投资（亿元）	27883.07	27765.89	30881.39	36194.14	42984
同比增长（%）	19.82	-0.42	11.22	17.20	18.6

2014年，全年完成铁路公路水路固定资产投资2.5万亿元。其中，铁路完成投资8088亿元，同比增长24.2%；公路、水运分别完成投资15256亿元和1458亿元，分别增长11.4%和下降4.6%。

铁路投融资改革取得进展。2014年1月26日，国务院发布《关于创新重点领域投融资机制，鼓励社会投资的指导意见》。《意见》要求，改革完善交通投融资机制，加快推进铁路投融资体制改革，按照市场化方向，不断完善铁路运价形成机制。作为铁路投融资改革的平台和基点——铁路发展基金成立，首期募集资金2000亿~3000亿元，吸引社会资本参与。此外，国家出台的铁路土地综合开发政策，全面深化开发铁路区域收益，支持铁路投融资改革进一步深化。

2014年1—11月，仓储业完成固定资产投资4672.5亿元，同比增长24.3%，预计全年投资超过5200亿元，创历年新高。

（六）货物运输量平稳增长

2014年，全年货物运输总量439亿吨，比上年增长7.1%。货物运输周转量18.46万亿吨公里，增长9.9%。全年规模以上港口完成货物吞吐量111.6亿吨，比上年增长4.8%，其中外贸货物吞吐量35.2亿吨，增长5.9%。规模以上港口集装箱吞吐量2亿标准箱，增长6.1%，如表5所示。

表5　2014年各种运输方式完成货物运输量及其增长速度

指　标	单　位	绝对数	比上年增长（%）
货物运输总量	亿吨	439.1	7.1
铁路	亿吨	38.1	-3.9
公路	亿吨	334.3	8.7
水运	亿吨	59.6	6.4
民航	万吨	593.3	5.7

续 表

指 标	单 位	绝对数	比上年增长（%）
管道	亿吨	6.9	5.2
货物运输周转量	亿吨千米	184619.2	9.9
铁路	亿吨千米	27530.2	-5.6
公路	亿吨千米	61139.1	9.7
水运	亿吨千米	91881.1	15.7
民航	亿吨千米	186.1	9.3
管道	亿吨千米	3882.7	10.9

2014 年，全年完成邮电业务总量2.18 万亿元，比上年增长19.0%。其中，邮政业务总量 3696 亿元，增长 35.6%；电信业务总量 1.82 万亿元，增长 16.1%。邮政业全年完成邮政函件业务 56.1 亿件，包裹业务 0.6 亿件，快递业务量 139.6 亿件；快递业务收入 2045 亿元。

（七）物流业处于景气周期

中国物流业景气指数（LPI）中，2014 年 12 月的业务总量指数为 57.5%，全年平均为 56.0%，保持在较高的增长区间，如图 3 所示。

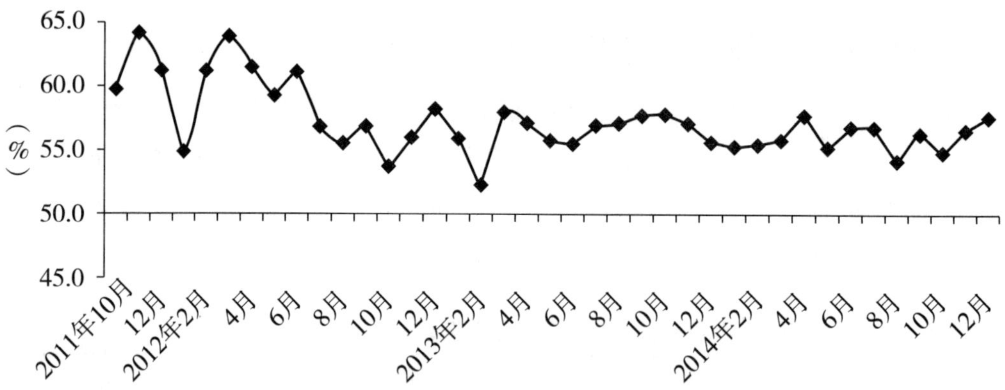

图 3 中国物流业景气指数走势

物流服务价格指数全年在 50% 的临界水平上下波动，平均为 50.4%，显示出物流价格持续低迷的态势。

主营业务利润指数全年平均为 50.7%，保持在较低水平。

固定资产投资完成额指数全年平均为 51.6%，反映出物流运行的基础设施条件呈现改善态势。

二、物流企业寻求转型升级

（一）经营效益有所改善

据中物联重点调查物流企业数据显示，2014 年 1—11 月，重点物流企业主营业务收入增长 8.0%，低于主营业务费用增速 0.1 个百分点；重点物流企业收入利润率为 5.0%，高于去年同期 0.9 个百分点。这些数据表明，我国重点物流企业费用压力依然较大，盈利能力整体较弱，但有所改善，如图 4 所示。

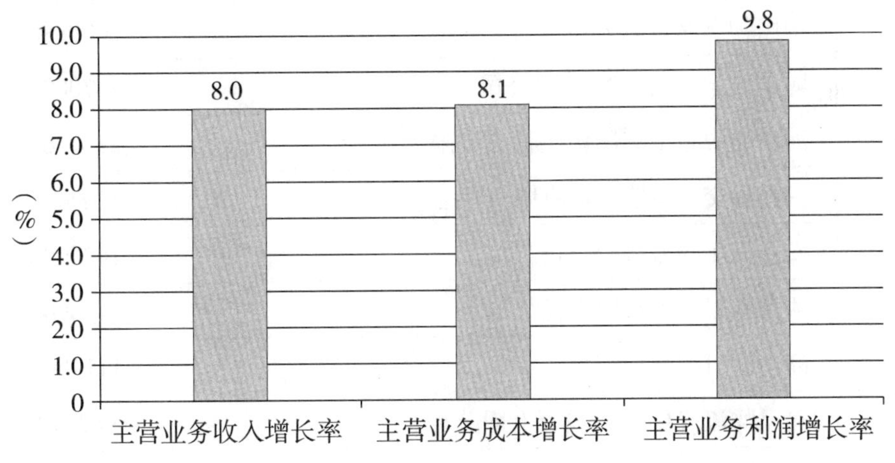

图 4　2014 年 1—11 月重点调查物流企业盈利情况核心指标

（二）市场集中度持续提升

根据中国物流与采购联合会发布的“2014 年度中国物流企业 50 强排名”，2014 年度 50 强物流企业物流业务收入共达 8233 亿元，按可比口径比上年增长 5.5%。50 强物流企业中，排名第 50 位的企业物流业务收入为 22.4 亿元，入围门槛比上年提高 2.1 亿元。

分区域看，东部地区占 80%，同比上升 2%；中部地区占 14%，同比持平；西部地区占 6%，同比下降 2%。分登记注册类型看，国有企业占 34%，同比下降 2%；民营企业占 6%，同比上升 2%；有限责任公司、股份有限公司、股份合作企业分别占 28%，14% 和 2%，港澳台商投资企业、外商投资企业分别占 10% 和 6%，占比与上年同期持平，如表 6 所示。

表 6　　2014 年度中国物流企业 50 强名单

排名	企业名称	物流业务收入（万元）
1	中国远洋运输（集团）总公司	14414820
2	中铁物资集团有限公司	7632421
3	中国海运（集团）总公司	6764517
4	中国外运长航集团有限公司	5828320
5	河北省物流产业集团有限公司	5818003
6	开滦集团国际物流有限责任公司	4423713
7	厦门象屿股份有限公司	3537580
8	中国石油天然气运输公司	3040718
9	中国物资储运总公司	3000880
10	顺丰速运（集团）有限公司	2570000
11	河南能源化工集团国龙物流有限公司	2170563
12	福建省交通运输集团有限责任公司	1767495
13	安吉汽车物流有限公司	1476000
14	朔黄铁路发展有限责任公司	1430905
15	高港港口综合物流园区	1112000
16	嘉里物流（中国）投资有限公司	982218
17	北京康捷空国际货运代理有限公司	959718
18	重庆港务物流集团有限公司	932931
19	中石油北京天然气管道有限公司	926038
20	德邦物流股份有限公司	863333
21	中铁集装箱运输有限责任公司	806659
22	国电物资集团有限公司	781930
23	浙江物产物流投资有限公司	779805
24	中国国际货运航空有限公司	775599
25	中国石油化工股份有限公司管道储运分公司	673795
26	一汽物流有限公司	615565
27	五矿物流集团有限公司	523681

续　表

排名	企业名称	物流业务收入（万元）
28	武汉商贸国有控股集团有限公司	506250
29	中铁现代物流科技股份有限公司	494502
30	重庆长安民生物流股份有限公司	464966
31	中铁快运股份有限公司	441855
32	中外运敦豪国际航空快件有限公司	417295
33	江苏徐州港务集团有限公司	364651
34	中铁特货运输有限责任公司	357913
35	联邦快递（中国）有限公司	356838
36	湖南星沙物流投资有限公司	356764
37	郑州铁路经济开发集团有限公司	352000
38	山西太铁联合物流有限公司	334894
39	广东省航运集团有限公司	334864
40	青岛福兴祥物流股份有限公司	300651
41	中信信通国际物流有限公司	299079
42	中国储备棉管理总公司	296446
43	上海现代物流投资发展有限公司	283987
44	国药控股江苏有限公司	280000
45	北京长久物流股份有限公司	263546
46	天地国际运输代理（中国）有限公司	262885
47	南京空港油料有限公司	260866
48	湖南全洲医药消费品供应链有限公司	244765
49	浙江省八达物流有限公司	225129
50	新时代国际运输服务有限公司	224247

（三）经营模式变革创新

平台思维改变传统模式。2014 年，园区基地平台、公路货运平台、电商物流平台、物流金融平台等风起云涌。物流企业通过平台整合线上线下资源，打通上下游产业链，引导行业集约化、规模化、规范化发展。传化公路港、林安物流、天地汇等园区经营企业加紧连锁复制，编织园区资源、信息和服务平台。卡行天下等公路货运平台依托信息化手段，打造虚实结合的平台，搭建灵活的货运网络。“三通一达”联合组建峰网投资平台，抱团深耕产业链。“中国物流金融服务平台”上线运行，金融物流风险管控引起关注。

产业联动。2014 年，物流业与制造业、商贸业、金融业等“多业联动”，产业合作层次从运输、仓储、配送业务向集中采购、订单管理、流通加工、物流金融、售后维修、仓配一体化等高附加值增值业务，个性化创新服务拓展延伸。

跨界经营。物流企业凭借自身优势，向上下游和中高端市场延伸业务领域。零担快运企业凭借网络优势推出快递业务。快递企业凭借客户优势进入电商、冷链和 O2O 市场。合同物流企业凭借资源优势承接客户外包服务，从单一的物流服务商向综合服务商转型。

模式创新。2014 年，物流领域各种新的组织模式、管理模式和商业模式不断涌现，改变着行业市场格局。在公路货运领域，车货匹配平台整合货源和车源，引入货运“淘宝”和“滴滴打车”模式。在快递电商领域，“网订店取”、“智能快递箱”等配送模式得到推广。在铁路货运领域，随着铁路货运改革，铁路运输企业加快向物流企业转型。在合同物流领域，提升一体化解决方案能力，积极向供应链服务商转型。

（四）资本介入力度加大

基金加大物流业投资力度。各类基金重点关注领域是快递、快运、物流地产、冷链物流等。这些领域的共同特点是行业整体前景看好，普遍处于高速增长阶段，如表 7 所示。

表 7　2014 年物流业部分资本运作事件（基金投资者）

时间	投资方/并购方	目标公司	业务领域	交易模式	投资股权比例（%）	交易规模（百万元人民币）
2014 年 8 月	平安银行	五洲国际	物流地产	股权投资		<1500
2014 年 8 月	复星集团	宅急送	仓储	股权投资		1000
2014 年 7 月	华平资本集团	安能物流		股权投资（C 轮）		5000 万美元
2014 年 7 月	振泰资本许震领投	绿蚂蚁网		股权投资		10

续　表

时间	投资方/并购方	目标公司	业务领域	交易模式	投资股权比例（%）	交易规模（百万元人民币）
2014年7月	弘航集团	田园牧歌		股权收购		
2014年6月	云峰基金	亚峰速递	快递	股权收购		
2014年6月	亿城集团股份有限公司	上海丰树管理有限公司	仓储	股权投资		5000
2014年6月	国药控股与复星集团		医药物流	合资成立	前者40，后者60	5亿～10亿美元
2014年5月	云峰基金	全峰快递	快递	股权投资		
2014年5月	荷兰汇盈资产管理公司	上海益商仓储服务有限公司	仓储	股权投资	20	最多6.5亿美元
2014年4月	香港私募股权公司和狮诚控股国际	上海宇培集团	仓储	股权投资		2.5亿美元
2014年2月	西安世合集团	浙江汇强快递有限公司	快递	股权投资		300
2014年2月	中国财团	普洛斯		股权投资	34	15200
2014年1月	复星国际与美国保险巨头保德信集团		物流地产	股权投资		
2014年1月	华平资本集团	安能物流		股权投资	100	
2014年1月	美国国际数据集团（IDG）	深圳市递四方速递有限公司	电商物流	股权投资		5000万美元

行业兼并重组掀起高潮。2008年金融危机以来，随着国内市场的复苏和物流业的转型升级，行业迎来了新一轮专业化驱动、多元化发展的兼并重组新高潮，如表8所示。

表 8　　2014 年物流业部分资本运作事件（物流从业者）

时间	投资方/并购方	目标公司	业务领域	交易模式	投资股权比例（%）	交易规模（百万元人民币）
2014 年 8 月	普洛斯	中储发展股份有限公司	仓储	股权投资	15.3	2000
2014 年 7 月	天地华宇集团	北京如风达快递有限公司	快递	股权收购	100	
2014 年 7 月	顺丰集团	小红帽落地配		股权收购		
2014 年 7 月	茂业物流	北京创世漫道科技有限公司	移动信息发送	股权收购	100	878
2014 年 5 月	亚马逊公司	上海美味七七网络有限公司	冷链物流	股权投资		2000 万美元
2014 年 1 月	中储股份公司	中储物流地产开发有限公司	物流地产	增资扩股		1000

新市场进入者改变竞争格局。当前，新的市场进入者抓住市场薄弱环节和关键领域，凭借资本、模式、技术优势，正在加快改变行业传统的竞争格局和运作模式。物流业新的市场进入者集中在电商物流领域。万科地产、平安不动产等商业资本和地产投资企业加快进入物流地产市场，如表 9 所示。

表 9　　2014 年物流业部分资本运作事件（市场进入者）

时间	投资方/并购方	目标公司	业务领域	交易模式	投资股权比例（%）	交易规模（百万元人民币）
2014 年 5 月	万科集团	廊坊控股	物流地产	股权投资		
2014 年 5 月	菜鸟	卡行天下		股权投资		250
2014 年 4 月	平安不动产	成都空港物流园仓储物业		股权收购		

续 表

时间	投资方/并购方	目标公司	业务领域	交易模式	投资股权比例（%）	交易规模（百万元人民币）
2014 年 3 月	阿里巴巴	一达通		股权收购		
2014 年 1 月	腾讯集团	华南城控股有限公司	电子商务	股权投资	9.9	15 亿港元

（五）服务网络拓展延伸

网络渠道加紧深耕细作。网络化是物流业的基本特征，也是创造价值的核心竞争力。一些企业已经建立了覆盖全国的物流网络。如，德邦物流在全国开设直营网点 5200 余家，全年网点增长近千家。日日顺物流在全国 2800 多个县建立了物流配送站和 17000 多家服务商网点，逐步形成大件商品送装一体化的服务网络。

国际物流市场面临新机遇。跨境电商迎来爆发期，海外物流网络布局成为重点战略。阿里巴巴、顺丰、圆通等电商、快递企业与境外快递邮政企业合作，开辟全球物流市场。各类企业看好跨境电商业务，“海外仓”建设吸引大批资金。中远物流、中外运股份等大型物流企业继续保持工程物流领域的优势地位，跟随国内工程建设企业“走出去”，在港口、园区等物流战略资源方面取得积极进展。

三、企业物流联动发展

（一）物流成本增速持续回落

2014 年，国家发展改革委、国家统计局和中国物流与采购联合会对 2013 年全国重点工业、批发和零售业企业物流状况和物流企业经营情况进行了统计调查。

调查显示，2013 年工业、批发和零售业企业物流成本比上年增长 10.1%，增幅同比回落 1.9 个百分点，连续 3 年回落。随着经济转型升级和企业管理提升，预计 2014 年企业物流成本仍处于增速回落区间。其中，运输成本受货运量下滑影响持续下降，保管成本受库存增加影响保持高位增长，如图 5 所示。

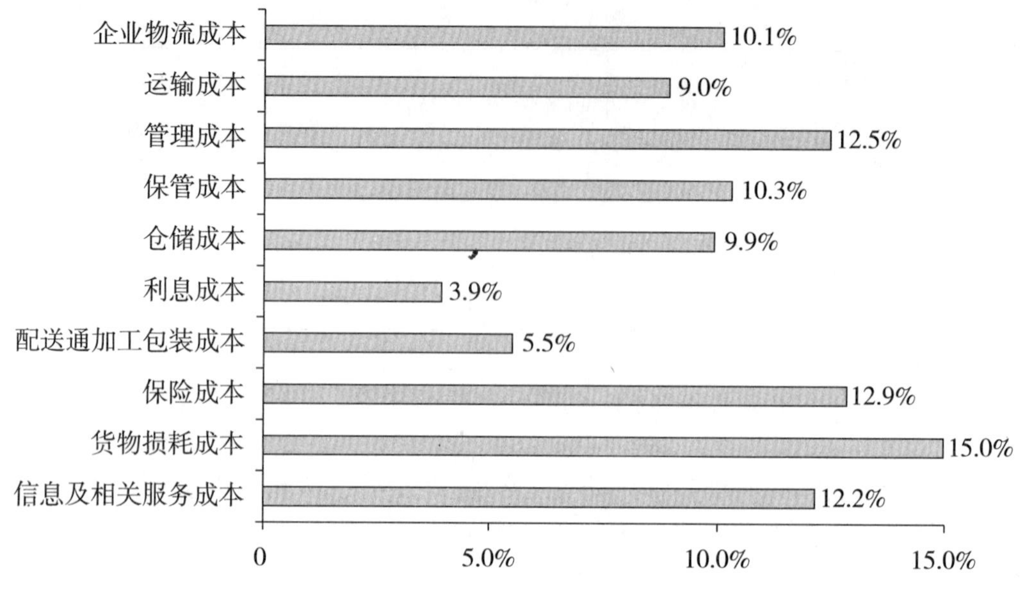

图5　2013年工业、批发和零售业企业物流成本增长情况

（二）物流费用率有所下降

2013年工业、批发和零售业企业物流费用率为8.4%，比上年下降0.2个百分点。其中，工业企业物流费用率为9.1%，下降0.14个百分点；批发和零售业企业物流费用率为7.8%，与上年基本持平。总体上看，近年来我国工业、批发和零售业企业物流费用率呈下降趋势，预计2014年企业物流费用率将维持在8.5%左右。目前，我国工业、批发和零售业企业物流费用率仍高于日本3.6个百分点，如图6所示。

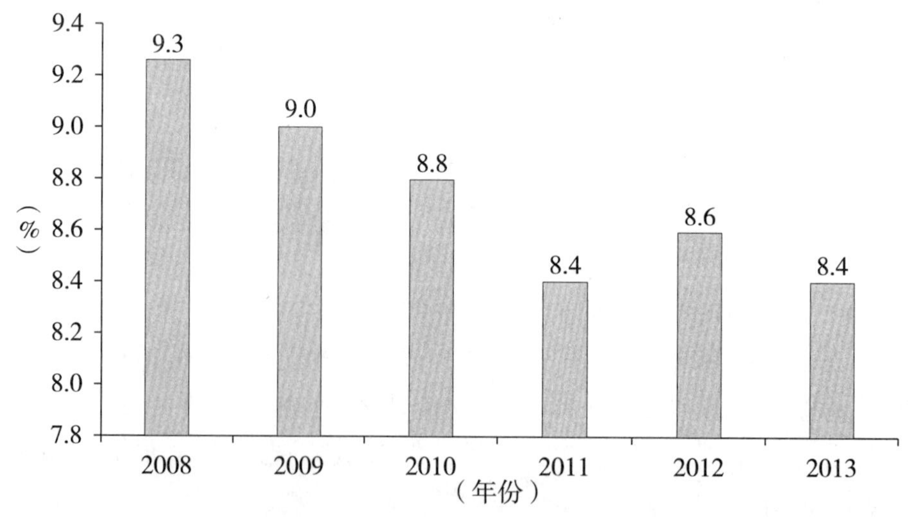

图6　2008—2013年工业、批发和零售业企业物流费用率情况

（三）物流外包比例持续提高

2013 年工业、批发和零售业企业对外支付的物流成本比上年增长 13.5%，占企业物流成本的 62.9%，同比提高 1.9 个百分点。受经济压力增大、企业集中主业影响，预计 2014 年企业对外支付的物流成本占物流成本的 65% 左右，外包比例持续提高，如图 7 所示。

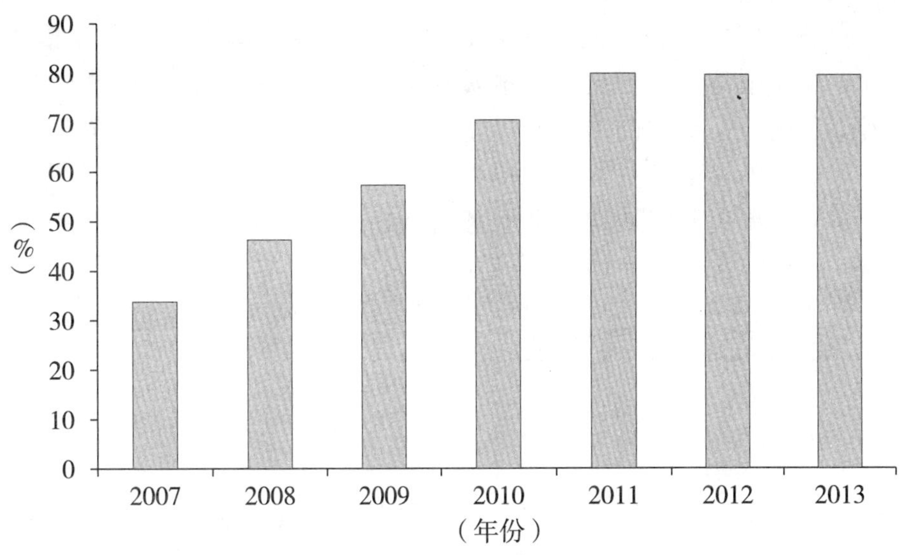

图 7　2007—2013 年工业、批发和零售业企业委托代理货运量占比情况

（四）“两业联动”取得新进展

《物流业发展中长期规划（2014—2020 年）》提出三大发展重点、七项主要任务、十二项重点工程和九项保障措施。其中，制造业物流与供应链管理工程被纳入重点工程中，显示出国家对于推动两业联动发展的高度重视。2014 年 11 月 14 日，济南市发布《关于加快制造业与物流业联动发展的实施意见》，积极推进实施联动发展示范试点工程。其中，到 2020 年，主营业务收入过 10 亿元的工业企业将基本实现主辅剥离，建立或委托第三方物流服务。同时，济南市将推出八项措施鼓励制造业和物流业联动发展。

“两业联动”理念得到普遍认可。在整个经济深度调整的背景下，制造企业也在积极应对变革，谋求联动融合。例如，钢铁生产企业积极向产业链中游流通环节渗透，拓展物流环节，兴办钢铁物流园区，食品饮料行业重点关注冷链及配送环节，服装行业关注通过供应链管理消灭高库存等。产业合作层次从运输、仓储、配送业务向集中采购、订单管理、流通加工、物流金融、售后维修、仓配一体化等高附加值增值业务，个性化创新服务拓展延伸。

（五）供应链管理深入发展

制造业物流的发展趋势是向供应链转型。如，汽车产业链加速拓展，加强零部件入厂、整车物流、售后服务备件物流的管理，向供应链管理领域拓展延伸，取得积极成效。我国供应链发展除了产业链上核心制造企业牵头带动以外，更多地是通过打造供应链一体化服务平台，为供应链上关联企业提供线上线下综合服务，如怡亚通、飞马国际、飞力达、嘉晟物流等，主要集中采购、分销执行、物流服务、平台交易、融资支付等，服务各类企业资源整合和功能提升的需要，这也是我国许多供应链企业的主要发展模式。物流企业贯穿供应链上下游，掌握各类渠道资源，向供应链一体化服务平台转型具有先天优势。未来，一部分物流企业将加快延伸服务链条，承接企业物流业务，提供供应链增值服务，实现向供应链一体化服务商转型。

四、细分市场各具特色

（一）公路货运市场

公路货运市场增速趋缓。2014 年，我国公路完成货运量 334.3 亿吨，同比增长 8.7%，增速比上年同期回落 3.6 个百分点。从各季度看，一季度增长 9%，二三季度增长 9.2%，四季度增长 8.7%。公路累计完成货物周转量 6.11 万亿吨公里，同比增长 9.7%，增速比上年回落 3 个百分点。公路货运量、公路货运周转量分别占货运总量和货运周转量的 76.1% 和 33.1%，分别较上年回落 2.7 个和 2.9 个百分点。考虑到货运量增速回落和持续低迷的运价，公路货运能力过剩局面仍未改变。2014 年，公路货运平均运距 182.9 千米，较上年减少 6.2 千米，如表 10 所示。

表 10　　2010—2014 年公路货运量、周转量及其增长速度

年份	2010	2011	2012	2013	2014
公路货运量（亿吨）	244.8	282.0	318.8	355	334.3
同比增长（%）	15.0	15.2	13.1	11.3	8.7
公路货运周转量（亿吨千米）	43389.67	51374.74	59534.86	67114.50	61139
同比增长（%）	16.7	18.4	15.9	12.7	9.7
公路货物运输平均运距（千米）	177.24	182.17	186.72	189.06	182.9
同比增长（%）	1.4	2.8	2.5	1.3	-3.3

零担货运市场加快集中。零担货运的市场结构主要有两大细分领域：网络型零担主要服务小票零担（30～1000公斤），专线主要服务大票零担（>1000公斤）。

网络型零担中，直营制零担加快分化。德邦物流以全年120亿元的销售额继续领跑，同比增长超过50%，门店超过5200家，增长超过20%。目前，德邦物流的平均货运价格达到2.1元/公斤，远远高于其他零担企业。其他直营制的零担企业，如天地华宇、佳吉快运、新邦物流、盛辉物流等大型零担企业，也都保持了较快增长。此外，区域性零担公司，如长通物流、佳怡物流、卓昊物流、大道物流，深耕区域市场，优化网络布局，逐步走向全国。

网络型零担中，加盟制零担异军突起。加盟制企业凭借较强的运营能力，对加盟网点实行激励的最大化和管理的极简化，保障全网的服务质量。2014年，安能物流、百世快运等加盟制零担实现快速增长。完成C轮投资的安能物流凭借雄厚的资本支持实现了快速扩张，网点数从2013年底的745个增加到现在的2100多个，分拨中心从38个增加至85个。

专线零担中，存在运力过剩局面。行业呈现冰火“两重天”，一些规模化专线线路越开越密，货量越来越大，利润趋好。还有一些专线由于货量下降，生存困难。

专线联盟成为热点。2014年1月18日，大道物流牵头成立了华中大道快运联盟；3月，河南胜邦物流正式成立；8月，蓝盟物流有限公司成立；11月29日，万众（天津）物流集团成立，还有此前成立的好友汇、中中联盟等，中小型企业纷纷抱团发展，结盟发展。

货运平台整合专线资源。卡行天下、商桥物流等平台型企业推动公路货运集约化发展。2014年，卡行天下枢纽中心由2013年的9个增加到23个，网络覆盖全国20个省份，加盟网点由300家增长到1300家，城际间点对点直达货运班车线路从1000条增长到9000条。平台交易运单量和货量激增10多倍。

整车货运市场较为低迷。大宗商品货运量大幅下降，制造业和工业产品增长乏力，整体市场较为低迷。整车货运企业纷纷寻求突破，或往第三方物流、或往平台型企业、或往网络型企业谋求转型。

环保成本逐步显现。2014年4月23日，工业和信息化部发布公告，定于2014年12月31日废止适用于国Ⅲ标准柴油车产品公告，2015年1月1日起国Ⅲ柴油车产品将不得销售。9月15日，环境保护部、发展改革委、公安部、财政部、交通运输部、商务部联合印发《2014年黄标车及老旧车淘汰工作实施方案的通知》。要求确保完成2014年淘汰黄标车及老旧车600万辆任务。加大黄标车及老旧车监管力度，调高黄标车及老旧车使用成本，通过市场手段推进淘汰，通过补贴促进淘汰，车辆更新速度加快。

道路运输车辆动态监管新规启动。2014 年 1 月 28 日，交通运输部、公安部、国家安监总局联合制定颁布了《道路运输车辆动态监督管理办法》（2014 年第 5 号令），并于 2014 年 7 月 1 日起施行。《管理办法》规定，旅游包车、三类以上班线客车、危货运输车辆、重型载货汽车和半挂牵引车在出厂前应当安装符合标准的卫星定位装置。旅客运输企业和危货运输企业监控平台应接入全国重点营运车辆联网联控系统，重型载货汽车和半挂牵引车应接入全国道路货运车辆公共监管与服务平台。

高速公路电子不停车收费推动全国联网。2014 年 3 月 7 日，交通运输部印发了《关于开展全国高速公路电子不停车收费联网工作的通知》（交公路发〔2014〕64 号），决定组织开展全国高速公路电子不停车收费（ETC）联网工作，力争到 2015 年年底基本实现全国 ETC 联网，主线收费站 ETC 覆盖率达到 100%，全国 ETC 用户数量达到 2000 万。截止到 2014 年年底，已经有北京、天津、河北、山西、辽宁、上海、江苏、浙江等 14 个省市实现联网。

（二）铁路货运市场

货运业务量下滑。2014 年，铁路累计完成货运量 38.1 亿吨，同比下降 3.9%，其中，前三个季度分别下降 3.5%、1.5% 和 2.5%，四季度下降 7.8%，降幅有所扩大，上年同期基数较高是重要原因。全国铁路完成货物周转量 2.75 万亿吨千米，同比下降 5.6%。铁路货运量、铁路货运周转量分别占货运总量和货运周转量 8.7% 和 14.9%，较上年分别回落 0.1 和 0.7 的百分点。总体来看，全国铁路货运能力由总体紧张向略有宽松的局面转变。2014 年，铁路货运平均运距 722.6 千米，较上年减少 12.3 千米，如表 11 所示。

表 11　　2010—2014 年铁路货运量、周转量及其增长速度

年份	2010	2011	2012	2013	2014
铁路货物运输量（亿吨）	36.4	39.3	39	39.7	38.1
同比增长（%）	9.28	7.96	-0.72	1.60	-3.9
铁路货物周转量（亿吨千米）	27644.13	29465.79	29187.09	29173.89	27530
同比增长（%）	9.53	6.59	-0.95	-0.05	-5.6

重点物资运输仍然承担骨干角色。2014 年国家铁路完成棉花运量 496 万吨，石油运量完成 1.28 亿吨，煤炭运量完成 16.41 亿吨，粮食运量完成 8260 万吨，分别占全国总产量的 80.52%、60.54%、42.40%、13.61%，在重点物资运输中依然承担骨干角色。2014 年国铁实现货运收入 2854.8 亿元，同比增长 7.3%。

货运产品改革创新。受大宗物资运输需求乏力，消费品运输需求强劲的趋势影响，铁路总公司提出了“稳黑增白”战略，开发出零散货物快运班列、电商快递班列、高铁快递等系列产品。从9月起，铁路开始受理零散货物快运业务。在全路4000余个货运营业站、无轨站敞开受理，形成了覆盖全国的散货办理网络，日发送量在7万吨以上水平。为适应我国电子商务和快递业发展需要，铁路总公司于7月和8月推出了电商快递货运班列。在北京、上海、广州、深圳四地间开行了三对六列电商快递班列。高铁快递服务陆续开通，截止到12月30日，全国高铁快递办理城市已达151个。

物流服务质量全面改善。2014年，铁路总公司以准时制运输、承揽物流外包、拓展增值服务为重点，服务质量得到了全面改善。7月1日调图后，普通货物列车全部实现按时速80公里运行。货车提速加快了货物周转，稳定了运输时刻和货源，保障了货物准时交付。铁路总公司推出了新的货运“一口价”报价收费方式，对所有货物运输探索实行完全市场化的“一口价”。此外，各路局积极拓展仓储、堆存、定制等增值服务，承揽物流外包业务，与企业开展深入合作，加快向物流服务商转型。

货运组织改革不断深入。铁路总公司重新修订了《铁路货运组织改革二十条纪律要求》，针对敞开受理、排队装车、规范收费、门到门运输等方面分别提出了管理要求。一年来，铁路总公司相继发布了近40个文件，加快货运市场的拓展和铁路物流产品的推广。

（三）水路货运市场

水路货运市场平稳增长。2014年，全国水路完成货运量59.6亿吨，同比增长6.4%，增速比上年放缓1.1个百分点，各季度分别增长8%、4.3%、7.7%和5.8%，货运增速在波动中回落。全国水路完成货物周转量9.19万亿吨千米，同比增长9.7%。水路货运量、水路货运周转量分别占货运总量和货运周转量的13.6%和49.8%，分别较上年增长2.7个和3.4个百分点。水路货运平均运距1541.6千米，较上年减少213.4千米，如表12所示。

表12　2010—2014年水运货运量、周转量及其增长速度

年份	2010	2011	2012	2013	2014
水运货物运输量（亿吨）	37.9	42.6	45.9	49.3	59.6
同比增长（%）	18.79	12.41	7.69	7.45	6.4
水运货物周转量（亿吨千米）	68427.53	75423.84	81707.58	86520.56	91881.1
同比增长（%）	18.89	10.22	8.33	5.89	9.7

沿海干散货市场供需矛盾未有明显好转。沿海干散货运输需求整体走弱。2014 年运量前高后低，且季节性特征有所减弱，波动幅度明显减小。沿海干散货运价延续低迷，总体呈现小幅上涨后一路下跌的波动趋势。截止到 2014 年 12 月底，上海航运交易所发布的中国沿海散货综合运价指数（CBFI）全年平均值为 989. 86 点，较 2013 年再次下滑 12. 08%。

国际集装箱货运市场有所回升。2014 年，全球集装箱海运量为 170. 7 百万 TEU，较 2013 年增长 5. 96%。国际集装箱运费持续波动，整体呈现企稳回升态势。截至 12 月 19 日，中国出口集装箱运价综合指数均值为 1087. 31 点，继续维持上年平均水平。从细分航线来看，中国—欧洲、中国—地中海、中国—美东、波斯湾航线等表现较好，其他一些区域内航线运费表现低迷。

运力过剩局面有所缓解。2014 年，中国沿海干散货船舶运力首次出现下滑。截至 6 月 30 日，从事国内沿海运输的万吨以上干散货船共计 1698 艘，5448. 14 万载重吨。其中，2014 年上半年投入营运的新建船舶较上年同期缩减了近一半，而拆解量却增加了近 3 倍。平均船龄继续下降至 7. 56 年，较 2013 年年底下降 0. 44 年。新投入营运的船舶主要集中在 4 万载重吨以上，船舶年轻化、大型化趋势明显。国际集装箱船舶运力规模继续扩大。截至 2014 年年底，全球集装箱船队运力为 1810. 2 万 TEU，同比增长 5. 77%，增幅有所加快。国际集装箱船舶也呈现大型化趋势。

联盟合作抱团取暖。近年来，航运企业通过联盟加强运力控制，提升竞争力。2 月，中远集运、川崎汽船、阳明海运、韩进海运和长荣海运五方组成 CKYHE 联盟，合作范围为亚欧和地中海的航线；5 月，由中远、中海、中外运旗下船队组成“C3 联盟”，在青岛中日航线增投 1500 标箱（TEU）运力；7 月，马士基集团和地中海航运宣布共享 185 艘船舶，总运力 210 万 TEU，组建 2M 联盟，运行跨大西洋航线、跨太平洋航线和亚洲航线。

航运电商化趋势显现。近年来，航运企业纷纷触网，谋求转型发展。中国远洋推出了“中远集运电商”、“泛亚航电商”等平台，中外运开发了“海运订舱网”。2014 年初，中外运推出“易网通”跨境电商平台。7 月，中海宣布与阿里巴巴合作打造跨境电商物流平台，推出“一海通”。11 月，中远集团透露将与阿里巴巴联合打造跨境电商业务。

港口生产增速明显放缓。受国内经济低速增长的影响以及港口吞吐量统计口径的调整，2014 年全国规模以上港口完成货物吞吐量 11. 6 亿吨，较上年增长 4. 8%，增速下滑 4. 9 个百分点。2014 年，我国亿吨以上港口已达到 34 个，其中沿海港口 23 个、内河港口 11 个。吞吐量达到 2 亿吨以上的港口增加 6 个，达到 19 个。外贸港口货物吞吐量好于内贸。2014 年我国规模以上港口累计完成外贸货物吞吐量 35. 2 亿吨，同比增长 5. 9%，内贸货物吞吐量增幅达到

4.92%。沿海港口货物吞吐量好于内河。2014年，沿海规模以上港口完成货物吞吐量76.89亿吨，同比增长5.6%；内河港口完成货物吞吐量35.11亿吨，同比增长3.6%。

集装箱港口吞吐量增速继续下滑。2014年，规模以上港口集装箱吞吐量达到2亿TEU，同比增长6.1%，保持低速增长态势。随着内贸货物通过“散改集”的方式提高运输效率，适箱货范围持续扩大，内贸集装箱将成为港口吞吐量新的增长点。2014年全球集装箱吞吐量排名中，宁波—舟山港超越釜山港，排名全球第五。在全球前五名集装箱港口排名中，除新加坡港外，其余均为中国港口。

（四）航空货运市场

航空货运市场加快回升。2014年，民航累计完成货运量593亿吨，同比增长5.7%，增速比上年提高3.4个百分点；累计完成货物周转量186亿吨千米，同比增长9.3%，增速比上年提高6.4个百分点。航空货运量、航空货运周转量分别占货运总量和货运周转量的0.014%和0.1%，与上年基本持平。航空货运平均运距3136.7千米，如表13所示。

表13　　2010—2014年民航货运量、周转量及其增长速度

年份	2010	2011	2012	2013	2014
民用航空货物运输量（亿吨）	563.04	557.48	545.03	558	593
同比增长（%）	26.38	-0.99	-2.23	2.3	5.7
民用航空货物周转量（亿吨千米）	178.9	173.91	163.89	168.58	186
同比增长（%）	41.73	-2.79	-5.76	2.9	9.3

航空货运积极拓展货源。近年来，跨境电商解决了传统国际贸易分工造成国际航空货源单向性明显的问题。中国国际航空货运比较薄弱，主要是因为运往欧、美、澳的去程货量远大于回程货量，跨境电商货物流向恰恰主要是来自于欧、美、澳和日本四大市场，有效解决了回程货少这一问题。目前，美国到中国的电商包裹运输量日均达750余吨，澳、新地区到中国的电商包裹每年约3万吨。

航空快递业务竞争加剧。继顺丰速运、中国邮政先后组建航空公司后，2014年圆通组建货运航空公司，未来3年内，将实现15架自有飞机、76个机场间互飞、1000余吨日运量的目标。各地机场重点发展航空快件市场。1—10月，石家庄机场货邮吞吐量达到3.7万吨，同比增长12%，其中航空快件增长迅速，增幅超过30%。

航空货运企业延伸服务。航空货运企业在做强主业的基础上，加快向上下游两端延伸，逐步从航空承运商向航空物流商转型。东航物流提出“快递+电商+贸易”的转型目标，2014年“东航产地直达”车厘子包机安排8个全货机航班，累计运载超过400吨车厘子到中国内地市场销售。国内多家航空公司积极开展空铁联运、陆空联运、空空转运等多式联运措施，取得一定成效。

二三线机场加快转型升级。2014年二三线机场货运发展速度较快，郑州、武汉、南京等机场保持高速增长，长沙、宁波、石家庄、沈阳等机场也引来发展契机。2014年郑州机场完成货邮吞吐量37.04万吨，同比增长44.86%；在全国20个大型机场中排名第一。目前，在郑州机场运营的货运航空公司达到17家，货运航线达到32条，国内与国际地区通航点33个，全货机周航班量达到92班。

（五）仓储服务市场

生产资料和大宗商品仓储业务经营趋稳。据中国物资储运协会对60家大型仓储企业的调查显示，2014年样本企业主营业务收入比上年下降28%，但物流收入增长17%；货物吞吐量6137万吨，比上年增长4%；公路运输量增长18%，铁路运输量增长9%；货物年周转次数为10次，比上年增加2.3次；利润总额比上年下降18.6%。库房业务收入增长8.9%，而货场业务下滑2.9%。亏损企业数增加，达到16家，且亏损额大幅增大，如表14所示。

表14　2010—2014年样本企业主营业务增长速度及货物周转次数

年份	2010	2011	2012	2013	2014
主营业务收入增幅（%）	22.1	16	10.5	2.66	-28
货物周转次数（次）	9.6	8.96	7.6	7.66	10

生活消费和网络购物仓储业务持续上涨。受电子商务和第三方物流活跃的仓库租赁需求影响，全国主要城市仓库平均租金同比涨幅5%左右。据中国物流与采购联合会抽样调查显示，2014年仓库租金，一线城市平均为1.2元/（平方米·天），二线城市平均为0.8元/（平方米·天），三线城市平均为0.5元/（平方米·天），继续保持高位增长，如表15所示。

表 15　2014 年主要城市仓库平均租金抽样调查结果　[元/（平方米·天）]

城市	北京	上海	广州	深圳	沈阳
地价	1.45	1.00～1.60	1.00～1.40	1.10～1.60	0.95
城市	大连	西安	长沙	廊坊	
地价	0.9	0.94～1.02	0.74～0.98	0.95～1.00	

新兴仓储物流需求增大。一是电子商务飞速发展，要求仓储业适应小批量、多批次、快交付的要求。电商物流集聚发展。全国规划和建设了一批电商物流中心和基地。在大宗商品电子商务领域，由于生产商要求快速交付，仓库选址分布从产地向消费地转移，消费地仓库需求量增长显著。二是特种仓库需求量增加，如温控仓库、危化品仓库、液体仓库的数量，结构均有较大缺口。三是多式联运型仓库需求大。最突出的是公铁联运、铁水联运。四是农资农产品、快递储物场所需求空间增大。

仓储设施供求紧张局面有所缓解。2014 年 1—11 月，仓储业完成固定资产投资同比增长 24.3%，与往年相比增速有较大下滑。国家统计局第三次经济普查报告显示，截至 2013 年年底，我国仓储业总资产达到 1 .69 万亿元，全国营业性仓储面积拥有量估计在 13 亿平方米以上，其中，一半以上是近五年新建的。仓储设施总体规模与经济需求大体相适应，供需紧张局面有所缓解。但是，一二线城市仓储设施供求紧张的局面还将长期存在。

跨境电商海外仓布局成为热点。电商海外仓能够实现本地发货，加快商品配送速度，提升商品的销售速度，改变了跨境电商零售出口产业的物流生态。国内企业加快海外仓储布点和国际业务的布局。如，出口易、递四方等物流服务商大力建设海外仓储系统，不断上线新产品。

国内外资本市场关注仓储业。由于高端仓储业投资收益较为稳定，仓储业成为投资热点。2014 年，平安不动产 15 亿元注资五洲国际；中资财团 25 亿美元注资普洛斯；嘉民集团和加拿大养老金计划投资委员会（CPPIB）向嘉民中国物流基金注资 5 亿美元，总量达到 15 亿美元；普洛斯入股中储股份，投资 20 亿元，占 15% 的股份，取得第二大股东的位置。

（六）快递服务市场

快递业务保持快速增长。2014 年，全国快递服务企业业务量累计完成 139.6 亿件，同比增长 51.9%，跃居世界第一；业务收入累计完成 2045.4 亿元，同比增长 41.9%。其中，同城业务收入累计完成 265.9 亿元，同比增长 59.8%；异地业务收入累计完成 1130.6 亿元，同比增长 36.4%；国际及港澳台业务收入累计完成 315.9 亿元，同比增长 16.7%，如表 16 所示。

表 16　　2010—2014 年快递业务量、业务收入及其增长速度

年份	2010	2011	2012	2013	2014
快递量（亿件）	23.4	36.7	56.9	91.9	139.6
同比增长（%）	25.8	56.8	55.0	61.5	51.9
快递业务收入（亿元）	574.6	758	1055.3	1441.7	2045.4
同比增长（%）	20.0	31.9	39.2	36.6	41.9

国内包裹快递市场进一步开放。9 月 24 日，国务院总理李克强主持召开国务院常务会议。会议决定，全面开放国内包裹快递市场，对符合许可条件的外资快递企业，按核定业务范围和经营地域发放经营许可。根据国内市场格局，我国全面开放包裹快递市场，短期内不会对国内快递市场造成明显影响。

基础能力建设持续加强。2014 年，我国快递行业共改扩建转运分拨中心 185 万平方米；新增干线车辆 1.2 万台；高铁快件班列覆盖全国 65 个城市、日运输能力达 2000 吨；新增货机专用航线 40 余条、合作航线 200 余条，快递专用货机增至 68 架。据不完全统计，2014 年仅顺丰速运、“三通一达”民营快递总部（包括加盟商）、邮政速递等用于基础设施建设的投资已超过 150 亿元。

市场竞争格局初步显现。目前，外资快递企业在国际快递市场中处于主导地位，顺丰速运占据着国内商务快递和“网购”的高端型市场，中国邮政速递在国家公文、国有企业快递市场中处于核心地位，“三通一达”等民营快递企业占据着国内“网购”经济型快递市场，中国邮政在跨境电商寄递市场中占据主导地位。而大型电商自建快递物流主要为其自身品牌提供服务。

企业低价竞争压力较大。2014 年，我国快递件均收入为 14.65 元，较上年减少 1.04 元，同比下降 6.6%。快递件均收入同比下降，企业盈利能力进一步下滑，“以价换量”模式基本没有改变。多数快递企业呈现“微利化、无利化、亏损化”的趋势，特别是加盟模式民营快递企业的部分加盟商经营较为困难，如表 17 所示。

表 17　　我国快递件均收入

年份	2007	2008	2009	2010	2011	2012	2013	2014
件均收入（元）	28.6	27.0	25.8	24.6	20.7	18.5	15.7	14.65

干线运输条件产生新的变化。2014 年下半年，铁路部门与电商、快递企业合作开行电商班列，一列快递电商班列相当于 45 台 9.6 米的箱式货车，且速度快、时效性强、成本低。铁路与公路和航空运输相比，在 1000～1500 千米干线运输中具有较强的经济优势。随着合作的进一步深入，快递干线运输将逐步形成公路、航空和铁路三种运输方式并重的格局。

“最后一百米”呈现多样化态势。在传统快递“门到门”的基础上，快递“最后一百米”呈现多样化，快递智能快件箱、便利店代理、社区物业代理、校区公共配送平台等新业态加速推广和使用。2014 年，全国有 1.5 万个智能快件箱投入使用，派件量占到总业务量的 1%，业务增速是传统派件业务的 2 倍以上。

民营快递涉足国际快递市场。目前，国际商务快递已经被“国际四大”和邮政速递占据。2014 年，我国多家民营快递进军国际快递市场，业务拓展方式以跨境电商为主。如，申通快递开通了日本专线；顺丰速运开通了俄罗斯小包专线和欧洲小包服务，顺丰速运“优选国际”海购平台正式上线；韵达快递的欧洲快递物流服务中心已在德国运营，美国服务中心网站正式上线；圆通速递推出“俄易邮”专线产品。

快递立法持续完善。2014 年 8 月 4 日，国家邮政局公布《快递条例草案》公开征求意见稿。征求意见稿对快递业务的经营主体、快递服务、用户权益、快递安全等方面做出规定。快递业呼吁多年的加强行业立法，规范和促进行业发展工作取得积极进展。

政策监管更加精细化。2014 年，国家邮政局出台了《邮政业消费者申诉处理办法》、《经营快递业务的企业分支机构备案管理规定》、《快递业务经营许可注销管理规定》、《邮政行业安全信息报告和处理规定》、《寄递服务用户个人信息安全管理规定》、《无法投递又无法退回邮件管理办法》、《无法投递又无法退回快件管理规定》等 7 个规范性文件，以及《快递专用电动三轮车技术要求》、《邮政业标准体系》、《快递营业场所设计指南》等 3 个标准，政策管理要求和规范更加具体明确。

五、行业物流不断创新

（一）电子商务物流

电子商务市场保持快速增长。据艾瑞咨询统计数据显示，2014 年中国电子商务市场交易规模 12.3 万亿元，增长 21.3%，其中网络购物市场交易规模达到 2.8 万亿元，增长 48.7%，仍然维持在较高增长水平。网络购物市场中，B2C 市场增长 68.7%，远高于 C2C 市场 35.2% 的增速，B2C 市场占比达到

45.8%，继续成为网络购物的主要推动力。移动购物市场异军突起，年增长率达239.3%，远高于网络购物整体增长速度，如图8、图9所示。

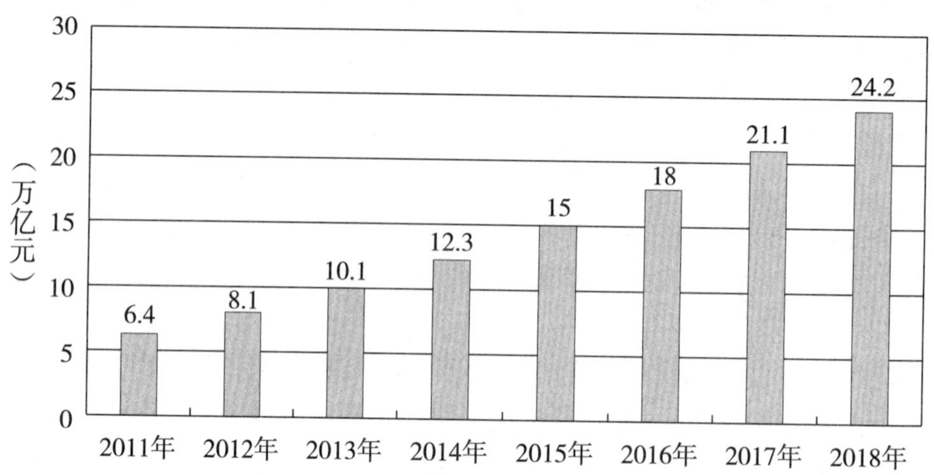

图8　2011—2018年中国电子商务市场交易规模

注：根据艾瑞咨询公开资料整理。

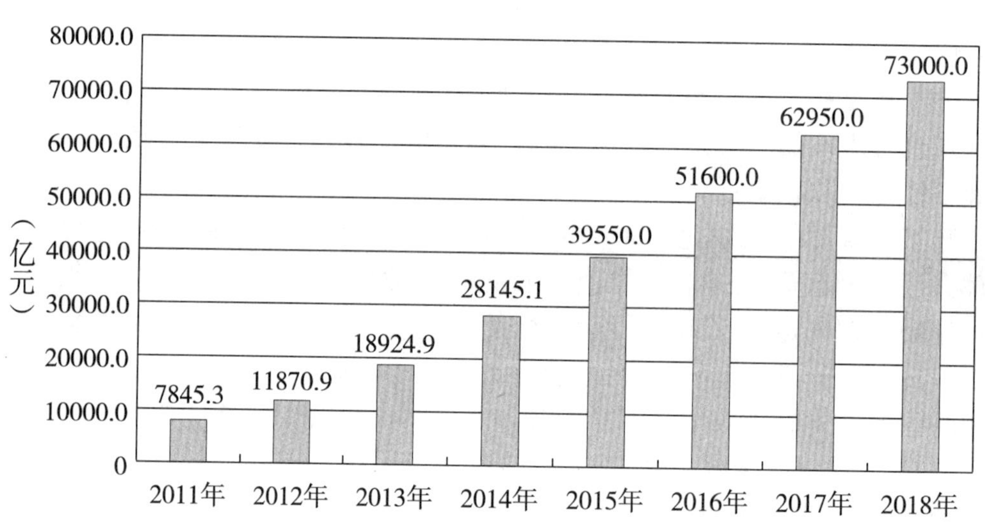

图9　2011—2018年中国网络购物市场交易规模

注：根据艾瑞咨询公开资料整理。

电商加大自建物流投入力度。2014年5月，京东商城成功登陆美国纳斯达克市场，其庞大的自建物流网络成为重要亮点。截至9月30日，京东建立了118个仓库，总面积约为230万平方米。在全国1855个行政区县拥有2045个配送站和1045个自提点、自提柜。菜鸟网络“地网”建设也在紧锣密鼓进行，已在全国14个核心骨干节点城市完成布局，预计于2016年年底交付150万平方米。其他大型电商企业自建物流脚步也进一步加快，积极在全国布局物流基础网络。

差异化服务成为竞争焦点。“送装一体化”服务成服务新标杆。日日顺物流提出为用户提供 24 小时限时达、送装同步等差异化物流服务方案，大大提升了客户的购物体验。物流竞速依然是电商竞争热点。苏宁易购全面实施“半日达”、“急速达”和“一日三送”等物流服务，电商配送时效大幅度刷新。京东陆续推出“夜间配”、“定时达”等新业务，物流时效成为争夺市场和客户的重要手段。此外，退换货的逆向物流服务也越来越成为电商企业关注的焦点。

电商物流效率引领市场发展。京东商城凭借强大的物流基础网络优势支撑“仓配一体化”的电商物流运作模式，根据 IPO 数据显示，2013 年，京东物流费用占营业收入的 5.8%；库存周转天数为 32 天，低于其他电商库存周转70～90 天的水平，远低于其他制造、商贸企业物流水平。2014 年，菜鸟网络以“地网”为载体，以仓聚货、聚人、聚产业，整合了海内外大量物流服务资源，成为电商生态圈的重要组成部分，物流运作效率大大增长，被互联网影响的电商物流行业正在遭遇一场巨大的“变革”。

跨境电商物流多元化发展。目前，由于跨境电商单笔订单的商品数量较少、体积较小，所以在线外贸卖家向海外买家发货一般通过国际快递或国际外贸小包两种方式。随着“备货”模式兴起，通过仓储前置，传统集装箱海运的方式得到青睐。天猫国际和六大跨境电商试点合作，依托港口，批量海运空运到保税区的模式，降低物流成本。同时，传统的快递和物流企业也开始做一些延伸布局，加大对保税仓、第三方转运等业务。跨境物流正在从单一的邮政包裹演变为“邮政包裹为主，其他模式并存”的多元化业态。

电商 O2O 带来物流新挑战。O2O 模式正在成为线下企业电商化的发展趋势。电商企业从线上竞争的“红海”转向线下“蓝海”竞争，线上线下渠道全面打通所形成的物流网络覆盖和服务将成为竞争关键。随着 O2O 的真正发力，电商物流企业为适应客户新的服务要求，其模式将出现创新性变革，具有较大的发展空间。

电子商务物流获得支持。2014 年，按照《促进物流业发展三年行动计划》要求，商务部牵头组织制定《电子商务物流规划》，预计 2015 年出台。2014 年 10 月，财政部、商务部、国家邮政局联合下发《关于开展电子商务与物流快递协同发展试点有关问题的通知》，决定在天津、石家庄、杭州、福州、贵阳 5 个城市开展电子商务与物流快递协同发展试点。

（二）冷链物流

冷链市场规模稳步增长。2014 年冷链需求市场规模进一步增长，达到 1.12 亿吨左右，较上年增长约 22%，地域范围依然集中在中东部经济发达地区，如北京、天津、大连、山东、广东等。全国冷库总量达到 3320 万吨，折合 8300 万立方米，与上年 2411 万吨相比增长 36.9%。

冷链基础设施投入加大。2014 年，冷链物流园区建设成为亮点。据中物联冷链委不完全统计，2014 年全国运作（包含建成、开建、签约不包括建设中的）的重点冷链项目超过 40 个，投资额超过 550 亿元，相较于上年的近 700 亿元降幅较大，但考虑到冷链项目工期一般在 2～3 年，所以冷链基础设施建设依然火热。其中，2014 年完工的冷链项目超过 80 亿元，奠基开工、新签约的冷链项目达到 370 多亿元，涉及冷库 180 多万吨。

冷链物流市场依然分散。冷链物流企业特点依然是规模小、压力大。从中物联冷链委发布的“2013 冷链物流企业百强排名”来看，2013 冷链百强企业总收入为 109.02 亿元，约占全国冷链总收入的 10% 左右。其中，前 50 强占据绝大份额，后 50 强基数较小。在百强排名中，年收入在 5 亿元以上的有 7 家，年收入过亿元的有 25 家，8000 万元以上的有 33 家，6000 万元以上的有 51 家。冷链物流集中度仍较低。

连锁零售发力冷链板块。2014 年，连锁零售企业面对经营压力，纷纷建立生鲜网站、自建和外包生鲜加工配送中心，完善冷链配送系统，为第三方冷链物流企业带来新的机遇。截至 2014 年年底，沃尔玛在中国拥有 11 个生鲜配送中心。

餐饮冷链需求和服务双升级。在食品安全的倒逼下，餐饮企业加大食品安全监管力度，加强食材供应链管理，升级更新食材的温控设施。10 月，商务部、国家发展改革委联合发布《餐饮业经营管理办法（试行）》，餐饮外卖企业须有营业资质和冷链，冷藏保温温控需有保障。政府管理规范餐饮行业发展迈出第一步。

生鲜电商冷链成为发展热点。2014 年，资本和电商纷纷布局生鲜电商领域。由于生鲜电商初期的圈地成本依然很高，冷链设施的购置、全程冷链的设计与配送、消费者理念的培育等，都需要大量的时间和资金成本，大部分生鲜电商企业处于亏损。

冷链物流支持力度加大。2014 年中央一号文件明确提出“完善鲜活农产品冷链物流体系”，继续发力冷链产业。《物流业中长期发展规划》对发展冷链物流提出新的要求。此外，十部委发文促进冷链运输物流企业健康发展，提出九条具体意见，提升冷链运输物流服务水平。

（三）汽车物流

汽车市场整体运行平稳。2014 年，汽车产销分别为 2372. 29 万辆和 2349. 19 万辆，同比增长 7. 26% 和 6. 86%，增幅比上年分别下降 7. 5 个和 7 个百分点，增幅所回落。其中，乘用车产销分别完成 1991. 98 万辆和 1970. 06 万辆，比上年分别增长 10. 2% 和 9. 9%；商用车产销分别完成 380. 31 万辆和 379. 13 万辆，比上年分别下降 5. 7% 和 6. 5%，客车产销比上年分别增长 7. 6% 和 8. 4%，货车产销分别下降 7. 9% 和 8. 9%。2014 年，汽车累计出口 91. 04 万辆，比上年下降 6. 9%。

表 18　　2010—2014 年中国汽车产销量及增长速度

年份	产量（万辆）	增长速度（%）	销量（万辆）	增长速度（%）
2010	1826. 53	32. 44	1806. 19	32. 37
2011	1841. 64	0. 84	1850. 51	2. 45
2012	1927. 62	4. 6	1930. 64	4. 3
2013	2211. 68	14. 76	2198. 41	13. 87
2014	1991. 98	10. 2	1970. 06	9. 9

数据来源：中国汽车工业协会。

汽车物流市场格局加快调整。汽车物流主要包括零部件入厂物流、整车物流、售后服务备件物流三个方面。整车物流市场格局较为稳定，零部件入厂物流对物流和供应链管理要求较高，主要由国际零部件服务企业外包。截至 2014 年年底，全国机动车保有量达 2. 64 亿辆，其中，汽车 1. 54 亿辆，随着汽车保有量的增加，汽车售后备件物流具有广阔的发展潜力。

汽车物流服务日趋完善。汽车物流以零部件入厂物流、整车物流、售后服务备件这三个环节为基础，上游从零部件入厂物流向汽车零部件供应商管理延伸，下游从售后服务备件物流向报废汽车物流以及其他后市场服务延伸，汽车物流产业的纵向延展使汽车物流产业链条更加完整，服务更加完善。

汽车铁路运输快速发展。中铁特货是国家铁路汽车物流核心企业，在铁路商品车物流领域深耕细作，不断创新。为实现“门到门”全程物流，公司实行干线两端由一家配送商负责制，建立规范商品汽车配送队伍 49 支。建设一批大型物流基地，帮助商品汽车生产厂家实现了库存前移。组织汽车整列运输，整列运输比例接近 40%。不断提升运输实效，从柳州开往郑州的“五定”直达班列，从原来的 50 多个小时压缩到 37 个小时。公司在拥有国内先进的运输车（箱）6000 余辆的基础上，不断研制运输多种汽车的新车型。

汽车水路运输有新进展。2014年，沿江沿海整车进口口岸、汽车水运枢纽及配套设施建设又有新进展。各地陆续批复和开建了一批汽车物流中心和汽车滚装码头。6月25日，由南京港集团和安吉物流共同出资合作的南京港江盛汽车码头有限公司正式开业运营，目标三年内达到年中转30万辆规模，建设成为长江最重要的汽车物流枢纽之一。此外，2014年中海集装箱公司等国内领军企业，加大了集装箱在整车物流领域市场开拓的步伐。

企业积极拓展国际市场。汽车物流企业作为汽车工业产业链的一环，为整车基地走出去发展提供保障，也使国内汽车工业更多高利润的业务环节进入海外市场。安吉物流配套上汽泰国工厂运营，从零部件到售后服务，完成了在当地“全产业链”的初步布局。长久物流在德国汉堡注册子公司，并与优特埃（UTi）国际物流建立战略合作关系，将共同开发三大产品，包括欧洲到中国的铁路运输，VMI/生产物流，售后市场零配件配送物流。

车辆标准问题制约行业发展。车辆运输车标准一直以来都是行业关注的焦点问题，被认为是解决公路运输问题的第一步，2014年工信部、交通运输部、公安部、国家标准化委员会会同相关研究机构进行了广泛调研和深入研究，基本形成了一致意见，但终稿仍未出台，解决制约行业发展的老大难问题依旧需要等待。

（四）医药物流

医药流通市场保持较快增长。2014年医药流通行业仍然保持了较快速度增长，但增幅同比略有下降，预计将达到14700亿元左右，增速约在13%左右，比2013年增速下降约3个百分点。由于受经济增速下降和药价调整的影响，医药流通市场增长趋势趋于平稳，医药行业微利化的特征依然存在，如表19所示。

表19　2010—2014年药品流通行业销售总额及其增长速度

年份	销售额（亿元）	增长速度（%）
2010	7084	24.6
2011	9426	23
2012	11122	18
2013	13036	16.5
2014	14700	13

医药物流项目投资依然强劲。随着新版GSP的实施，2014年各医药流通

企业继续加大在物流设施建设上的投入，加快布局现代医药物流中心，提高自身的竞争力。以九州通医药集团投资3.8亿元在武汉东西湖建成全球最大的单体医药物流中心为标志，中国医药物流建设达到了新高潮。

医药电商市场增势迅猛。2014年医药电商市场规模约在70亿元，增势迅猛。截至2014年年底，持有互联网医药交易服务牌照的网站已达到371家，比上年增长169家。2014年，互联网巨头纷纷布局医药电商市场，阿里系的天猫医药馆成为国内规模最大的第三方医药电商平台。5月，国家食品药品监督管理总局公布了《互联网食品药品经营监督管理办法（征求意见稿）》，规定取得相应资格证书的互联网平台不仅可以卖处方药，还可以由第三方物流配送平台进行药品或医疗器械的配送，若这一政策能够落地实施将大大推动医药电商物流的发展。

医药冷链管理水平逐步提高。新版GSP对冷链管理、技术、人才等方面的要求较以前有明显提高，随着新版GSP的实施落地，各医药流通企业加大对冷链管理、技术、人才的投入，取得了一定成果，冷链管理水平有一定程度的提高。

医药物流加快精益化管理。随着医药流通环节毛利逐步降低，行业竞争加剧，传统的低价竞争和粗放式管理已经不能满足客户对物流服务的需求，医药物流精益化管理的时代正在来临。国药物流、华润医药、上海医药均已开展物流精益化管理，并将精益化管理作为战略之一，以期达到降本增效，提高自身竞争力的目的。

医药物流信息化水平提高。新版GSP对医药物流信息提出了更高的要求。医药物流行业加大了对仓库管理WMS，运输管理TMS的投入，越来越多的医药物流企业使用无线射频（RFID）、全球卫星定位（GPS）、无线通信、温度传感等物联网先进技术，提高仓库分拣和冷链物流全程监控，优化业务流程，提高管理水平。

（五）钢铁物流

钢铁市场总体增速放缓。2014年我国钢铁产量继续保持增长，但增速有所放缓。据统计数据显示，2014年我国粗钢产量8.23亿吨，同比增长0.9%。累计生产生铁7.09亿吨，同比增长6.2%；粗钢7.12亿吨，同比增长0.5%；钢材11.26亿吨，同比增长4.5%。我国钢材出口仍然保持了高速增长态势。2014年中国铁矿石进口价格跌幅超40%，在价格剧烈下跌的刺激之下，我国累计进口铁矿砂及其精矿9.3亿吨，同比增长13.85%。我国钢铁市场持续低迷，钢铁行业盈利有所下滑，特别是铁矿石企业下滑明显，如图10所示。

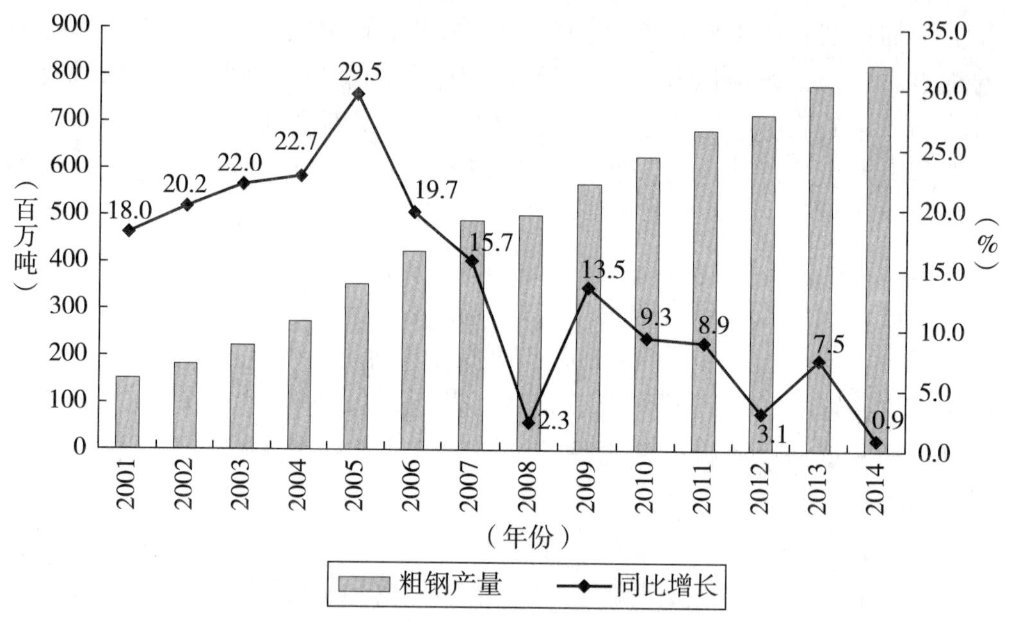

图 10　2001—2014 年钢铁产量及增长情况

数据来源：国家统计局。

钢铁社会库存创下新低。据兰格钢铁信息研究中心市场监测数据显示，2014 年 12 月底，全国 29 个重点城市钢材社会库存量为 871.4 万吨，同比下降 29.7%。目前，钢材社会库存已下降至 2009 年以来最低水平。2012 年以来，全国钢贸商数量从 20 万家迅速缩减至 10 万家左右，市场活跃度进一步降低。许多企业利用自有资金进行货物流转，控制库存成为规避经营风险的重要举措。

钢铁物流园区势头强劲。自 2008 年以来，我国钢铁物流园区建设步伐加快，钢铁企业、钢贸企业以及上下游企业都在尝试钢铁物流发展新路，目前已经建成的大型钢铁物流园区有 300 多家，还有 100 多家钢铁物流园在建和待建，发展势头强劲。但全国各地钢铁物流园区存在盲目快速扩张、一味追求大型化、同质化，无序竞争、效率低下、重复建设等现象。

钢铁电商平台快速发展。由于钢铁行业产能过剩，使得“卖方市场”朝“买方市场”转变，原来的钢铁企业分销体系发生了巨大改变，钢铁电商平台迅速崛起。2014 年，国内钢铁电商发展迅速，钢厂、贸易商、第三方平台等纷纷加大了对钢铁电商平台的投资力度，资本融资也不断创出新高，国内钢铁电商得以蓬勃发展，据不完全统计，目前国内钢铁电商平台有 200 家左右。

（六）危化品物流

危化品市场效益下滑。2014 年，化工行业增加值累计同比增长 10.4%，占全国工业的 6.8%。化工行业主营业务收入 8.8 万亿元，同比增长 8.2%，利润

4312.6 亿元，增长 0.33%，增速分别比去年下降 4.7 个和 11.9 个百分点，利润率 4.9%，比全国工业低 1 个百分点，效益大幅下滑。全年化工行业进口 1864.8 亿美元，同比增长 0.6%；出口 1621 亿美元，增长 11.1%。受下游市场需求不足、产能过剩问题、成本高位运行等因素影响，化工行业下行压力增大，如表 20 所示。

表 20　2010—2014 年化工行业发展情况

年份	增加值同比增长（%）	主营业务收入（万亿元）
2010	34.1	8.88
2011	31.5	11.28
2012	8.29	11.85
2013	8	11.66
2014	10.4	8.8

产品库存高位运行。化工行业物流、能源、财务成本全面上升。全年，化工行业每 100 元主营业务收入成本 87.48 元，同比上升 0.58 元，比全国工业高 1.84 元。由于原油价格大幅下跌带来的降价预期以及下游市场需求低迷，中间商和下游用户的进货意愿不强，使得化工产成品库存同比增长 12.76%，比上年同期提高 4.74 个百分点。此外，电力、天然气价格上升，安全环保、人工成本不断提高。

化工物流园区集聚发展。据不完全统计，我国目前已建成国家级、省级大型化工园区就达 200 多个，各类危险化学品生产、储存、运输、使用、废弃处置企业已达 30 多万家。园区集聚发展有助于提升行业的整体安全水平。目前，危化品仓储设施结构逐步优化，储罐和立体库每年增速在 10% 左右，占仓储设施总量的 70% 以上，平仓只减不增，每年下降幅度在 5% 左右。

危险品运输逐步规范。2001 年以来，国务院在全国范围内开展了道路危险货物运输专项整治活动，危险货物道路运输企业过小、过弱的情况得到了极大改观。危化物流企业平均车辆数由以前的 3 辆增加到 25.9 辆，增加 8.6 倍。目前我国共有道路危险货物企业 8000 多家，经营户 750 多万户，各类运输车辆 30 多万辆，从业人员 120 多万人。道路运输危险化学品货物在 2 亿吨左右，其中易燃易爆油品类达到 1 亿吨。

第三方物流潜力巨大。随着化工产业的规模化、专业化发展，对危化品物流也提出了更高要求。危化品物流企业逐步从生产企业中独立出来，成为企业发展新的增长点。第三方物流企业凭借专业化服务能力，由仓储、运输等传统物流服务向增值服务延伸，并提供供应链一体化服务，提高化工物流和流通效率，提升产业竞争力。

危化品物流环保压力加大。危险品仓储企业是环保监管的重点单位之一，环保部发布的《危险化学品仓储建设项目环境管理要求》、《危险化学品废弃物污染防治办法》、《危险化学品仓储企业环境风险等级划分办法》等一系列法规文件，均对危化品仓储企业的环保工作提出了高标准、严要求，成为危化品仓储企业准入门槛。随着环保要求的提升，危化品仓储企业在防止有害气体挥发，防止毒害品、腐蚀物品、放射性物品泄漏，废旧包装的回收利用，固体废弃物处理，以及洗罐洗桶洗车的污水处理等方面面临更为严峻的考验。

行业监管日益严格规范。2014 年 10 月 14 日，交通运输部印发《关于加强危险品运输安全监督管理的若干意见》，从严格市场准入、强化监督管理、推进风险管控、加强从业人员培训和监管队伍建设、严肃事故调查处理、建立长效机制六个方面入手，坚决遏制危险品运输安全生产事故的发生。不仅如此，国家各相关部门都在各个方面加大了管控力度，出台了严格的管理政策和规范措施。

六、区域物流融合发展

（一）区域物流一体化

长江经济带。2014 年 6 月 11 日，国务院常务会议部署建设综合立体交通走廊，打造长江经济带。会议强调，建设长江经济带，要注重发挥水运运量大、成本低、节能节地的优势，抓好综合立体交通走廊建设。会议要求，改革创新区域协调发展体制机制，打破行政区划“门户”，立足全局、统筹“落子”，通过基础设施共建共享，促进形成统一开放市场体系，让长江这条巨龙带动流域经济和人民生活齐步腾飞。

长江三角洲地区。12 月 11 日，“推进长三角区域市场一体化发展会议暨合作签约仪式”在上海召开。三省一市商务部门签署了“推进长三角区域市场一体化发展合作协议”，建立紧密合作工作机制，围绕六个方面，加强区域合作，建设长三角区域一体化大市场。在流通设施互联方面，要求健全长三角区域基础设施网络，完善长三角综合运输通道和区际交通骨干网络，形成互联式、一体化的交通网络体系。统筹规划，建设和改造一批商业设施、农产品流通设施、物流设施、社区基本生活服务网点等流通基础设施，保障和服务民生。

京津冀地区。2 月 26 日，习近平总书记主持召开专题座谈会，就首都经济圈一体化发展提出七点要求，明确了京津冀协同发展的重大国家战略定位。7 月 31 日，河北省与北京市签署了七份区域协作协议及备忘录，包括《共同推进物流业协同发展合作协议》《交通一体化合作备忘录》等，物流业协同发展成重点。8 月 24 日，天津市与河北省签署了《交通一体化合作备忘录》。提出了包括协同编制交通一体化发展规划、深化港口合作发展、加强铁路项目建设合作、推进公路项目建设合作、促进机场合作发展、深入开展邮政合作六项内容。

珠江三角洲地区。10 月 23 日，广东省政府办公厅印发了《推进珠三角一体化 2014—2015 年工作要点》，明确了推动一体化重点领域的工作内容及相关保障。其中，物流列入十个重点领域。11 月 25 日，广东省政府办公厅印发了《推进珠江三角洲地区物流一体化行动计划（2014—2020 年）》，部署推进珠三角物流一体化发展以及构建珠三角现代物流体系相关工作，提出要推进六个“物流一体化”。

（二）城市物流聚焦配送

1. 各地政府支持共同配送工作

2014 年，为配合国家推进城市共同配送试点，做好城市物流引导工作，一些地方出台了城市配送的政策措施，规划和建设城市配送服务体系，如表 21 所示。

表 21　　2014 年部分地方出台支持城市配送发展的文件

时间	发文单位	题目	主要内容
4 月 16 日	无锡市政府办公室	关于加快城市配送发展的实施意见	提出了完善城市配送基础设施网络；发展先进的城市配送组织模式；加快城市配送信息平台建设，逐步形成全市统一、面向公众的开放型的物流配送公共信息平台；加大市场主体培育和支持力度；优化城市配送车辆通行管控；提升城市配送车辆技术水平；加强城市配送领域市场监管七大工作任务
9 月 9 日	成都市	关于促进城市共同配送发展的实施意见	2014 年年内成都全市将全面启动城市共同配送试点工作，集中配送从超市起步，将来逐步覆盖到电子商务、批发市场等其他业态。根据《意见》的要求，未来成都将引导采取与第三方合作创新的方式，在社区服务机构、大型写字楼、大学校园等有条件的地方设立快件集中投递和收件公共服务网点，利用城市公共建筑配套设施、物业管理用房等设立快递中转站或“快递超市”，未来网购族们收快递肯定将更加方便

续 表

时间	发文单位	题目	主要内容
4月2日	青岛市商务局	关于推进青岛国家城市共同配送试点工作的实施意见	青岛将搭建城市共同配送信息服务平台，布局城区配送节点网络，推进商品配送社会化、信息化、网络化、专业化、标准化发展，不断完善城市配送物流服务体系。根据意见，今年青岛将全面启动各项试点工作，利用3～5年的时间初步建成青岛城市共同配送网络体系基础设施主体框架。试点的核心是要科学决策青岛城市共同配送模式，搭建城市共同配送信息服务平台，加快推进商贸流通领域共同配送，支持大型农水产品、生鲜食品物流配送中心建设，支持城市末端配送，推动先进物流技术应用，完善城市配送物流服务体系
9月29日	江苏省邮政局、商务厅、住建厅、教育厅	关于做好快递末端配送服务工作的实施意见	从加强企业自身能力建设、支持企业开展第三方合作模式、积极探索和推广智能投递等方面，为全省快递末端配送服务提供政策支持并明确操作要求

2. 各地加强车辆通行管理

一些地方通过多种方式保障车辆便利通行；也有一些地方对电动三轮车等采取禁行措施，“最后一公里”物流遇到难题。

银川市印发了《银川市快递车辆通行管理暂行办法》。宁夏5个市邮政管理局与当地交警和道路运输管理部门联合出台了快递车辆便捷通行的管理办法，明确和细化了机动和非机动快递车辆便利通行的优惠政策，实现了快递车辆通行优惠政策在宁夏的全覆盖。

重庆市交管局为快递企业运输车辆核发了绿色通行证，从2014年4月1日起，重庆对在主城区上牌、三轴以下的载货汽车实施不同色度的通行证管理，所有持证车辆必须在限定的范围内错时通行。

2014年，天津三部门联合发布通告，从5月1日起，禁止未悬挂机动车号牌的机动三轮车上道路行驶。10月24日，广州市公布《广州市非机动车和摩托车管理条例（草案征求意见稿）》，提出对电动自行车等非机动车和摩托车进行“全面封杀”。快递“最后一公里”遇到严峻挑战。

（三）农村物流受到重视

1. 粮食物流稳步发展

粮食产量“十一连增”。2014 年，我国粮食总产量达到 12142 亿斤，比上年增加 103.2 亿斤，连续 2 年跨上 1.2 万亿斤台阶；农民增收实现“十一连快”，农民收入增幅连续 5 年超过国内生产总值和城镇居民收入增幅，如图 11 所示。

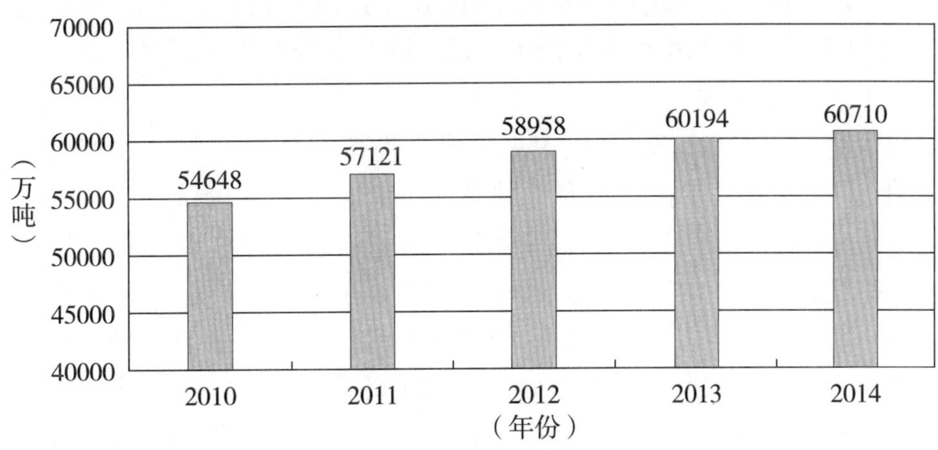

图 11　2010—2014 年粮食产量

粮食储备维持高位。在国际粮食价格总体平稳的背景下，国内粮价受托市收购价格等因素影响长期维持高位，国内外粮价倒挂日益严重，粮食生产与流通成本不断抬高。在双重挤压下，我国粮食收储政策体制和粮食安全面临前所未有的挑战，粮食政策性储备高达 3 亿多吨，保障粮食安全的粮食物流受到政府的高度重视。

国家支持粮食物流建设。2014 年中央安排 10 亿元补助投资，继续支持主要跨省粮食物流通道的节点建设，以提升散粮装卸和中转能力。国家发改委会同国家粮食局下达投资计划，安排中央补助投资 20 亿元，重点在收储矛盾较为突出的东北地区和南方稻谷产区建设仓容 130 亿斤。政府加快推进“危仓老库”维修改造，中央财政补助资金从 2013 年的 10 亿元提高到 20 亿元，其中重点支持省从 2013 年的四个增加到十二个。

2. 农产品市场得到支持

农产品市场受到关注。2014 年中央一号文件提出，着力加强促进农产品公平交易和提高流通效率的制度建设，加快制定全国农产品市场发展规划，落实部门协调机制，加强以大型农产品批发市场为骨干、覆盖全国的市场流通网络建设，开展公益性农产品批发市场试点建设；加快发展主产区大宗农产品现代化仓储物流设施，完善鲜活农产品冷链物流体系；完善农村物流服务体系，推进农产品现代流通综合示范区创建，加快邮政系统服务“三农”综合平台建设。得益于国家政策的扶持，各地积极推进批发市场改造升级，打造功能齐全、服务现代化的农产品物流园区，取得积极成效。

冷链物流获得支持。2015 年将是《农产品冷链物流发展规划》落地实施的最后一年，国家和各地政府继续支持冷链物流发展。2014 年银川市获得中央财政 3200 万元补贴，用于大型农批企业、流通企业的冷链仓储、配送中心建设；吉林农产品冷库获中央财政补助 3638.6 万元；7 月杭州萧山 5 个冷链项目获补助 1250 万元；8 月国家投资 650 万元支持海南冷链物流项目。

3. 农村电商物流成为热点

农村电商高速发展。2014 年中央一号文件首次提出“加强农产品电子商务平台建设”，推进了涉农电子商务的高速发展。据不完全统计，目前全国农产品电商平台已逾 3000 家，农产品网上交易量增长快速，以阿里巴巴平台为例，农产品销售额年均增长超过 200%。包括京东、阿里巴巴和 1 号店在内的主流电商，纷纷布局地方特产项目，开设特色地方馆，用土特产撬动用户对于农产品的需求，拓宽农产品销路，解决县域经济尤其是县域农业的渠道问题。

电商物流网络加快下沉。随着电商市场下沉，物流服务网络向三线、四线城市扩张。顺丰速运启动快递下乡计划，业务覆盖的县级市或县区已超过 2300 个。阿里巴巴启动“千县万村”计划，拟投资建立 1000 个县级运营中心和 10 万个村级服务站。京东推出“先锋站”计划和“村民代理”模式。据统计，2014 年农村新增快递网点近 5 万个，农村包裹超过 20 亿件。随着互联网和移动互联网的发展，三线到六线城市的物流需求激增，这对电商物流服务从深度、广度和速度等方面提出了更高的要求。

七、国际物流持续发力

（一）自由贸易区再扩围

2014 年年底，李克强总理主持召开国务院常务会议，决定在上海自由贸易试验区的基础上，在广东、天津、福建特定区域再设三个自由贸易园区。2015 年 3 月 25 日，中央政治局召开会议，审议通过广东、天津、福建自由贸易试验区总体方案、进一步深化上海自由贸易试验区改革开放方案，自贸区建设进入新的阶段。随着全国自贸区建设的铺开，自贸区各项功能更加完善，自贸区网络逐步形成，自贸区在物流领域的探索和尝试初显成效，我国物流业将迎来重大机遇。

（二）通关环境再提速

国家落实“三互”改革。12月26日，国务院下发了《关于印发落实“三互”推进大通关建设改革方案的通知》（国发〔2014〕68号）。要求强化跨部门、跨区域的内陆沿海沿边通关协作，完善口岸工作机制，实现口岸管理相关部门信息互换、监管互认、执法互助，确保国门安全，力争到2020年，形成既符合中国国情又具有国际竞争力的大通关管理体制机制。通知要求，强化大通关协作机制，完善大通关管理体制，改善大通关整体环境，加强大通关组织领导。

区域通关一体化扩围。5月14日，海关总署公布《京津冀海关区域通关一体化改革方案》，宣布7月1日开始，相关改革率先在北京海关、天津海关启动实施；10月前后，扩大至石家庄海关，实现在京津冀海关全面推开。9月，海关总署为推广区域通关一体化经验，先后发布《关于开展长江经济带海关区域通关一体化改革的公告》和《关于开展广东地区海关区域通关一体化改革的公告》。截至2014年年底，海关通关京津冀、长江经济带、广东地区海关区域通关一体化平台共接受报关单近1800万票。第四季度一体化作业的进、出口平均通关时间比传统口岸清关进、出口平均通关时间分别节省9.18小时和0.31小时。

多式联运监管中心获批。12月11日，青岛多式联运海关监管中心获海关总署正式批复。继西安之后第二家、沿海地区首家多式联运监管中心——青岛多式联运海关监管中心在青岛正式投入使用。

监管创新制度全国推广。上海自贸区成立一年多来，采取了一系列通关便利化措施，如，海关推出“先进区、后报关”、“批次进出、集中申报”等23项监管服务创新举措。检验检疫推出“通关无纸化”、“第三方检验结果采信”等23项改革措施。海事部门推出了船舶安全作业监管、高效率船舶登记流程等15项新制度。据测算，目前在上海自贸区，进口平均通关时间较区外减少41.3%，出口平均通关时间较区外减少36.8%。

（三）“中欧班列”竞相上路

2014年，着眼于服务国家“一带一路”战略，铁路进一步优化中欧班列运输组织，加快构建中欧铁路大通道，打造国际物流知名品牌。按日行1000千米以上，在西、中、东3条通道铺画了中欧班列运行线。全年共开行中欧班列308列，发送集装箱2.6万TEU，较上年同期多开228列，增长285%；组织自欧洲至中国的回程班列28列。12月10日列车运行图调整之后，铁路安排了19条中欧班列运行线，同时安排了15条中亚班列运行线、28条铁水联运集装箱快运列车运行线，积极支持“一带一路”建设，如表22所示。

表22　　2014年中欧班列开行情况统计

序号	班列名称	首趟开行时间	2014年开行列数
1	“渝新欧”班列	2011.03.19	100
2	“蓉新欧”班列	2013.04.26	49
3	“郑新欧”班列	2013.07.18	86
4	“苏满欧”班列	2013.09.30	34
5	“汉新欧”班列	2014.04.23	25
6	“合新欧”班列	2014.06.26	13
7	“义新欧”班列	2014.11.18	1

数据来源：根据网上新闻报道整理。

（四）保税物流平稳运行

保税物流区域稳步增长。2014年，国务院和各部委新批准设立了一批海关监管区域，包括在原有低层次监管区域基础上整合设立的综合保税区。2014年全年及2015年前两个月，综合保税区累计增加9个，较2013年增长近1倍。截止到2015年2月底，我国已设立了44个综合保税区。

保税物流进出口总额有所回落。海关数据显示，2014年全年，我国海关特殊监管区域（包括保税区、出口加工区、保税港区、综合保税区、保税物流园区和珠澳跨境工业区）进出口累计6961.7亿美元，同比下降1.6%；其中，出口3494.5亿美元，同比下降1%；进口3467.2亿美元，同比下降2.2%。相比2013年，我国海关特殊监管区域总进出口额在2014年出现负增长情况，这与国际大环境有一定关系，也与我国政策导向密不可分。

2014年我国各类海关特殊监管区域的进出口数额，保税区以2321亿美元的进出口数额持续领先于其他各类海关特殊监管区域，从同比增量上，呈现出负增长态势。保税港区和珠澳跨境工业区则分别以55.3%和56.8%的增幅位列前茅。但增幅小于2013年67.3%和64.6%的增速。保税物流园区有所好转，2014年我国保税物流园区、出口加工区的进出口增幅情况略有提升，好于2013年的－7.2%及－10.3%的负增长数据。另外，综合保税区以10.3%的增速持续增长，表现较为突出。

（五）跨境电商物流发展快

跨境电商蓬勃发展。据商务部统计数据显示，2013年中国跨境电子商务交易额突破3.1万亿元，预计2014年将超过4万亿元。随着国家对跨境电商政策支持力度的加大，跨境电商成为我国对外贸易的新增长点。

国家支持跨境电商发展。广州、杭州、郑州、深圳、哈尔滨、长春等地先后获批“国家跨境电子商务试点城市”，试点城市将通过“规范贸易制度、制定贸易标准、强化在线支付、完善跨境物流、电商出口退税”五个方面给予政策支持。流程监管创新，通关便利化加速跨境电商的发展。7月29日，海关总署“56号文”、“57号文”相继出台，通过电子商务交易平台实现跨境交易的企业和个人接受海关监管，推广“清单核放、汇总申报”的便利模式，解决了跨境电商货品以个人物品通过行邮的方式出境所存在的难以快速通关、结汇、退税难等问题。

目前，主要有三种类型跨境电子商务B2C模式，即直购进口模式（境外电商与境内消费者之间的B2C模式）、网购保税进口模式（海关特殊监管区域内的电商与境内消费者之间的B2C模式）和一般出口模式（境内电商与境外消费者之间的B2C模式）。

在跨境电子商务经营中，在线批发多采用传统的通关物流方式；在线零售多以商业快件和个人行邮为主要的通关物流方式，并由此衍生出包裹集中后以百家货方式清关到香港转运以及批量货物海外仓转运的模式。

中国跨境电商出口业务70%的包裹都通过邮政系统投递，其中中国邮政占据50%左右的份额，香港邮政、新加坡邮政等也是中国跨境电商卖家常用的物流方式。邮政网络基本覆盖全球，比其他任何物流渠道都要广。但是一般以私人包裹方式出境，不便于海关统计，也无法享受正常的出口退税，且速度较慢。

国际快递对信息的提供、收集与管理有很高的要求，以全球自建网络以及国际化信息系统为支撑。优点是速度快、服务好、丢包率低，尤其是发往欧美发达国家非常方便。

国际电商网络加速向中国渗透。亚马逊2014年与上海自贸区签订战略合作协议，推出六个国家8000万选品直邮中国。从全球范围来说，亚马逊已经在亚洲、北美、欧洲和大洋洲等13个国家建立业务站点。目前有96大运营中心和遍布全球的物流体系提供全球配送，可送至185个国家和地区。

随着我国经济形势的发展，很多企业正在考虑在境外建立海外物流中心，拓展国际物流业务。我国的物流企业在一些发达国家和地区建立配送中心，可以快速反应客户订单；在一些第三世界国家建立海外物流中心，可规避我国境内沿海地区较高的土地成本和劳动力成本，以及一些国内的法律法规。

八、基础设施趋向衔接配套

（一）综合运输体系加紧完善

公路建设增速下滑。2014 年，我国新增公路通车里程 9.38 万千米，其中，高速公路 7450 千米，全年新改建 23 万千米农村公路。至 2014 年年底，公路通车总里程达到 445 万千米，其中高速公路 11.2 万千米。

铁路建设创造新高。根据国务院关于加快铁路建设的部署，铁路采取超常规措施，全面加快推进铁路建设。全年新线投产 8427 千米，创历史最高纪录。至 2014 年年底，我国铁路营业里程达 11.2 万千米，其中高铁线路达到 1.6 万千米，以“四纵四横”为主骨架的快速铁路客运网初具规模，为释放货运潜能创造了有利条件。

水运建设稳步推进。2014 年，新扩建泊位 631 个，其中万吨级泊位 125 个，改善内河航道里程 2068 千米。长江南京以下 12.5 米深水航道建设一期工程、引江济汉通航工程等投入试运行，长江中游荆江河段航道整治工程顺利进行，上海国际航运中心洋山深水港区四期等开工建设。

民航建设加快发展。2014 年，我国境内民用航空（颁证）机场共有 202 个（不含香港、澳门和台湾地区），其中定期航班通航机场 200 个，定期航班通航城市 198 个。

（二）物流园区节点初具规模

园区基础设施初具规模。2014 年 1～11 月，仓储业完成固定资产同比增长 24.3%，与前几年 30% 以上的增幅相比，增速略有下降，物流园区的投资增速有所放缓。目前，全国拥有仓储面积 13 亿平方米左右，其中，一半以上是近五年新建的仓储设施。随着经济增速放缓、货运量下滑、土地指标短缺、资金成本高昂等因素影响，部分地区物流园区出现饱和，投入速度逐步放缓。

物流用地价格难以承受。总体来看，目前，我国土地资源较为紧缺，物流用地难以保障，价格持续上涨，企业难以承受。据中国物流与采购联合会抽样调查显示，一线城市物流用地的平均价格为 80 万～100 万元/亩，二线城市物流用地的平均价格为 40 万～50 万元/亩，三线城市物流用地的平均价格为 10 万～15 万元/亩。一些地方将工业仓储用地土地使用年限缩短到 20 年，大大增加了土地投资成本。

物流园区质量和效益提升。部分物流园区正在走向精益之路。2014 年，中物联物流园区专业委员会对 189 家参评物流园区进行了评价。通过 20 多个指标的测评，50 家园区获批成为优秀物流园区。50 个园区平均物流强度每平方千米吞吐量504万吨，平均就业人数9300人，平均年人均业务收入50万元，均远远高于普通物流园区相关指标数据。

园区开发模式逐步升级。从早期的地产商开发、物流企业租赁运营模式或物流企业独立开发运营模式，到地产商与物流企业合资开发运营，再到第三方整合开发运营模式，还有以政府主导的经济开发区模式，实现了规范化发展。

物流园区积极转型升级。目前，许多物流园区是按照经济高速增长进行规划和建设的，随着当前经济放缓，货运量下滑，导致物流园区必须转型升级，加快向精细化转变。许多园区没有考虑多种运输方式的实现，导致道路车辆运输的货品多，物流成本高，引入新的运输方式成为物流园区转型升级的战略选择。

内陆港建设成为热点。随着"一带一路"战略规划的实施，内陆港建设成为热潮。据不完全统计，2014年约有70个城市的内陆港开始建设或正在规划建设中。一些港口运营商也参加其中，加快从港口运营商向全程物流服务提供商的角色转变。

物流园区向专业化发展。受电子商务旺盛需求影响，电商产业园成为投资热点。此外，农产品冷链物流园、钢铁物流园等各种专业化物流园区不断涌现。

九、物流技术与装备创新驱动

（一）物流技术

1. 物流企业信息化

2014年6月，工业和信息化部信息化推进司发布了《2013年物流信息化监测报告》，从物流信息化基本建设、物流信息技术应用情况和物流信息化应用效果三个方面对物流企业进行了调研。调研显示：

（1）物流信息化投资率有所回落

样本企业在信息化领域的投资率较前两年有所下降，38.14%的企业当年进行了信息化投资。其中，7.69%的企业信息化投资率不足1%，23.08%的企业信息化投资率介于1%～5%，38.46%的企业信息化投资率为5%～10%，7.69%的企业信息化投资率为10%～15%，同时，约有20.08%的样本企业投资率超过15%。

（2）信息平台/门户网站大多用于信息发布

样本企业中，超过85.71%的企业建有自己的门户网站/信息平台；其中，大多数门户网站/信息平台的用途仍是定位在信息发布上，占比达76.67%；只有23.33%的企业将电子交易纳入其中并逐步应用，这一数据较上年略有上升，信息平台的作用由单纯的信息发布逐渐向电子交易等多种形式拓展。

（3）物流信息集成日渐成为建设重点

物流信息集成受到大多数企业的关注，70.97%的样本企业将构建信息平台（内部信息处理、OA、增值业务）作为信息化建设的重点；此外，部分企业将软件开发、RFID/RF/GIS/GPS/条形码等信息技术的应用、数据分析、数据挖掘等作为物流信息化建设的重点。

（4）物流信息技术应用取得成效

条码和电子标签等技术在物流业务中的应用程度继续提升。其中，条码应用率达到58.21%，较2012年增长4.9%；电子标签应用率达到38%，较2012年增长10.44%；而电子单证使用率为48.85%，与2012年相比略有下降。物流信息技术总体发展趋势是毋庸置疑的，这些技术的应用在很大程度上提升了企业的信息化水平，物流信息技术的创新应用是推进物流信息化发展的重要手段。

（5）物流信息化应用效果明显

样本企业调查数据显示，有超过86.67%的物流企业订单（运单）准时率超过70%，其中企业订单（运单）准时率超过90%的企业占比达到70%左右。随着市场竞争日益激烈，企业仍需继续加大信息化建设力度，提升信息技术的应用水平，提高订单（运单）准时率，满足客户需求。

2. 物流信息平台

（1）政府公共信息平台稳步推进

国家交通运输物流公共信息平台：2014年，宁波港集团、萧山机场、传化集团、中兴通讯、华泰财产等单位与国家交通运输物流公共信息平台签订合作协议。平台已经完成东北亚中日韩三国18个港口的信息互联，并按平台统一标准提供信息服务。短短数年间实现从省内、国内到国际的跨越式发展，目前互联中小企业已有30万家，日信息交换量达到200万条。

南方现代物流公共信息平台：2013年12月17日，南方现代物流公共信息平台正式上线。南方平台作为区域级的物流公共信息平台，具有物品及机构统一解析服务，全程实时供应链监控管理服务，电子政务管理服务，物流与信息化行业指数发布服务，物流信息国际互联互通服务5项基础服务功能，以及食品溯源、通关便利化、原产地认证、公用托盘、多式联运、企业诚信等十大增值服务。2014年，广东省经济和信息化委公布了第一批南方现代物流公共信息平台对接项目名单。

长江航运物流公共信息平台：2015年1月，长江航运物流公共信息平台正式启用。是国家交通运输物流公共信息平台在长江水路货运物流信息交换节点，为沿江港航企事业单位免费提供一站式信息化服务。通过这个平台，用户可免费查询船舶、船员、三峡通航、安全、水位气象、水情、水深等管理公共信息；货源、空船期、船舶交易、人才招聘求职等配套服务信息等，港航企业还可通过船货系统、集装箱物流信息系统、危险品物流信息系统，实时了解船货状况，从而为制订生产计划提供切实有用的信息。

中国电子口岸：目前已实现海关与质检、商务、环保等部门之间通关单、自动进口许可证、固体废弃物进口许可证等23种监管证件联网核查，占涉证报关单量的99%以上。在中央层面，电子口岸成员单位已由最初的12家扩展到17家，建设覆盖300多个城市的电子口岸专网，实现与13个部门、20家商业银行，以及欧盟相关部门的联网，开发联网应用项目32个，累计入网企业66万家。在地方层面，各省（区、市）均与海关总署签署《地方电子口岸建设合作备忘录》，并建设36个地方电子口岸平台。电子口岸不仅便利了企业办理进出口手续，还强化了国家宏观调控能力。

（2）第三方物流信息平台热点涌动

2014年，骡迹、货车帮、管车宝、好多车、车旺等一批车货匹配平台集中上线，据不完全统计超过100个。从进入市场的公司类型看，主要有：互联网公司和原为物流企业提供定位服务的软件开发公司、第三方物流、物流园区和其他，全民创业也深入到传统的公路货运行业。资本热捧车货匹配类平台，对传统模式带来重大冲击，加速了行业洗牌，如表23所示。

表23　　部分车货匹配平台情况汇总

名称	成立时间	所属公司	经营特色	融资情况
骡迹物流	2014年6月	北京运科网络科技有限公司	为物流公司、货运公司、配货站、车主、货主提供物流查询、物流专线信息发布等服务，移动信息平台应用包括线上资源整理管理系统、项目管理、O2O信息平台等	2014年7月11日骡迹智慧物流获得真格基金500万元人民币投资；2014年7月13日拿到IDG资本300万美元A轮投资
运满满	2014年11月	上海细微信息咨询有限公司	致力于为公路运输物流行业提供高效的管车配货工具，同时为车找货（配货）、货找车（托运）提供全面的信息及交易服务	物流配货平台运满满获A轮500万美元 欲成物流淘宝平台

续　表

名称	成立时间	所属公司	经营特色	融资情况
运东西	2011年	上海汇通供应链技术与运营有限公司	货主用户可以通过PC、手机微信及手机APP等多种渠道进行比价搜索、在线下单、在线支付、在线买保险、货物在线追踪，同时还可以在地图上追踪到车辆的实时位置，完全实现了物流运作流程的可视化服务。也帮助专线承运商、个体司机等用户增加货源渠道、提高车辆的满载率、顺程填仓、减少空返，提升额外收益	
货拉拉	2013年12月	广州市乔冠网络科技有限公司	主要为有货运需求的货主、面包车配对司机。经营范围包括建材运送、上门搬家、电器家私运输、食品配送、宠物出游、婚纱照包车、展览物资运送等	2015年1月，货拉拉获得由清流资本领投，极客帮、MindWorks Ventures、Sirius Venture Capital、Aria Group及其他个人投资者联合参投的1000万美元
oTMS	2013年1月	北京百川快线网络科技有限公司	提供基于SaaS的社区型运输系统，把货主、第三方物流公司、运输公司、司机、最终收货人等聚合在一起	2013年3月1日oTMS获得紫辉投资数百万元人民币天使投资；2014年11月，oTMS获得由经纬中国、百度投资、紫辉投资的600万美元A轮融资

续 表

名称	成立时间	所属公司	经营特色	融资情况
云鸟配送	2014 年 9 月	北京云中小鸟科技有限公司	通过整合海量社会配送资源，将企业用户与闲散的货车资源进行有效配置，在云鸟极速配送平台进行公开竞价招标的方式，为客户提供高性价比的配送解决方案	2015 年 1 月，云鸟配送获得由经纬中国、金沙江创投、盛大资本联合投资的 1000 万美元 A 轮融资
人人快递	2013 年 1 月	四川创物科技有限公司	通过整合闲散社会资源来解决同城的随程捎带需求，运用移动互联网技术搭建的信息管理平台，采用 P2P 众包模式来运送快递	2014 年 11 月，获得通信产业共赢基金、高榕资本 1500 万美元 A 轮融资
神盾快递	2015 年 1 月	瓦雷拉数据技术（上海）有限公司	同城货运智能调度平台：主要利用移动互联网提供同城货物智能叫车服务	2014 年 11 月获得近千万元人民币的天使投资
1 号货的	2014 年 1 月	广州米豆信息科技有限公司	“1 号货的”利用互联网优势，改变同城货运市场的传统运作模式，整合闲置货车的实时位置信息，发布货主的实际货运需求，让货车跟货主直接对话，减少中间环节，解决找车难、找车贵的问题	上线之前已完成数百万元人民币的天使投资，目前正在进行 preA 及 A 轮融资
蓝犀牛	2013 年 11 月		直接对接司机和用户两端，同时通过加盟的方式，整合社会上的车辆及司机资源来实现同城间的配送	2014 年 12 月，获得了联想旗下君联资本 3300 万元人民币的 A 轮融资
货车帮	2011 年	贵阳货车帮科技有限公司	“货车帮”“物流 QQ”货运信息双平台，为物流行业中的货车司机以及货物主提供需求载体，双方在平台发布各自需求，通过需求匹配，从而形成货物运输交易	

续 表

名称	成立时间	所属公司	经营特色	融资情况
路歌管车宝	2010 年 6 月	合肥维天运通信息科技股份有限公司	路歌管车宝充分利用了互联网技术和基站定位技术，实现了社会车辆的整合优化、定位追踪、证件核查、金融支付、网络车场等功能，有效地提升物流公司整体运营效益	，
车旺	2014 年 9 月	北京中交兴路车联网科技有限公司	车旺“95155 云服务平台”融合了物联网、移动互联、智能交通、云计算、地理信息、位置服务等先进技术，通过对海量行业静态、动态资源和百万有效车源、货源等信息进行智能分析，提供货源车源智能匹配，满足车主找货和货主寻车需求，全面提高物流运输效率	
好多车	2014 年 8 月	深圳市易流车联信息技术有限公司	好多车打造海量、真实的运力资源池，为物流企业免费提供熟车圈管理、找车、竞价调度、运单可视化等服务，为个体司机免费提供车辆状态共享、业务获取、加盟车队、信用积累等服务，让物流企业找车、用车更便捷，让司机接单、运货更容易	
我要物流	2015 年 1 月	广州我要物流网络科技有限公司	是一款快速找车、找货、智能匹配、平台担保、平台公证、信用保险、线上交易一体的物流软件、配货软件	

续　表

名称	成立时间	所属公司	经营特色	融资情况
易货配	2012 年	传化公路港	运力买方（司机）产品是目前司机找货的工具之一，其主要功能就是帮助司机在线上线下找货，通过线上信息及物流基地的显示屏上的信息，实现与货代/货主进行对接洽谈，之后便可通过 APP 或网页端完成整个交易环节	
一站网	2014 年 12 月 13 日	广东一站网络科技有限公司	一站物流交易平台是宝供物流企业集团公司下设的广东一站网络科技有限公司，利用互联网及移动互联网的多项智能化、透明化的技术，在充分的标准化基础设置上面，实现包括物流公司在内的货主与广大货运车辆的智能匹配，对交易完成进行透明化的管理，对装车以后的装车途中全过程的监控，最终实现交易双方的诚信交易。	

3. 新技术应用

物联网：2014 年随着物联网技术的发展，嵌入了物联网技术的物流机械化和自动化智能设备发展很快。如嵌入了智能控制与通信模块的物流机器人、物流自动化设备；嵌入了 RFID 的托盘与周转箱；安装了视频及 RFID 系统的货架系统等都得到了巨大发展。车联网技术飞速发展，物联网对运输系统的覆盖也由过去的车辆追踪与定位开始向车队管理、车辆维修、金融服务、车辆智能调度等领域全方位延伸，极大促进了货运领域的变革。

移动互联：随着信息化时代的快速发展，行业门户应用正在从传统 PC 端互联网向移动互联网延伸，物流业经营平台也开始转向移动互联网。近年来，包括顺丰速运、圆通速递、德邦物流、宝供物流等快递物流企业纷纷推出物流 APP 软件，一批车货匹配平台快速崛起，这标志着物流行业正在加快线下实体产业与移动互联网的融合，一批新的商业模式正在崛起。

大数据：菜鸟网络与国内 13 家物流快递企业签署行业合作框架，合作内容涉及云计算、信息产品、信息安全等多个方面，打造物流大数据平台。通过进一步开放彼此数据，未来大数据平台可实现快递市场分析、质量指数服务、客户挖掘、数据预测等功能。从9月开始，菜鸟网络对各家快递企业“双11”期间包裹总量给出了预估数字，甚至细化到了不同路线、乃至主要营业网点届时可能获得的包裹量，预测数据准确度达到90%左右。

智慧物流：多地积极推进智慧物流建设。甘肃省政府与阿里巴巴共同打造电子商务服务业、现代智能物流、跨境电子商务、云计算和大数据等产业集聚区，推进“智慧甘肃”建设。贵州将推进以智慧物流为重点的信息化网络体系建设，运用信息技术提升物流运行效率。通过智慧物流云、电子商务云的衔接，打造全省统一的物流信息公共服务系统平台。此外，阿里巴巴与中国邮政达成战略合作，双方将在物流、电商、金融、信息安全等领域全面开展深度合作，合力建设中国智能物流骨干网。

（二）物流装备设施

1. 载货车

2014年我国实现载货车生产319.59万辆，销售318.44万辆，销售同比下降8.9%。其中，重型载货车、中型载货车和轻型载货车的生产和销售均比上年下降，微型载货车的产量和销售量同比略有增长。2014年国内进口载货类汽车1.2万辆，较上年同期增长3.4%。其中重型载货车进口3825辆，占进口载货车总量的31.96%，进口重型载货车与国产重型载货车的比值为0.51%，两者比值创近年来新低。

2. 叉车

2014年我国工业车辆的总销量为35.96万台，增幅达9.39%，保持平稳增长，继续位列世界第一大市场。其中，仓储类叉车有20%以上的增长，主要得益于电子商务物流的快速发展，城乡配送需求量明显增加。电动叉车的市场份额明显加大，占27.01%，提高了3个百分点，是近年来增长最快的一年。分行业看，交通运输、仓储物流行业占比达到17.07%，与上年相比上涨了7.86%；电气、机械行业占比达到13.63%，比上年上涨了19.18%。此外，食品饮料、批发零售、石油化工等行业占比也相对较高。

3. 托盘

2014年我国托盘产量约2.5亿片左右，托盘保有量突破11亿片。在托盘标准化方面，根据中国物流与采购联合会托盘专业委员会调查，中国标准规格托盘占托盘总保有量23%左右。根据调查，目前澳大利亚标准规格托盘使用占比最高，托盘保有量中标准规格托盘占95%；欧洲次之，标准规格托盘占总保有量70%；美国第三，标准规格托盘占总保有量55%；亚洲的日本和韩国标准规格托盘占托盘总保有量比例不高，日本为35%，韩国为26.7%。

为推进物流标准化建设，商务部决定与国家标准委在全国范围内开展商贸物流标准化专项行动。该《专项行动》从托盘标准化入手，以降低物流成本，提高物流效率为目标，在快速消费品、农副产品、药品流通领域，率先开展标准化托盘应用推广及循环共用。其主要工作任务包括：提高标准托盘普及率；推进相关领域托盘标准化进程；提升托盘循环共用水平；制定相关服务规范等。

4. 货架

2014 年国内货架行业市场整体保持了较快的增长，增幅超过 20%。总体市场规模在 50 亿~60 亿元。自动化立体仓库货架、以电商需求为代表的组合货架和穿梭小车货架成为市场的三大主力军，占据绝对的市场份额。

货架新技术新产品应用提速，主要集中在两个方面，一是自动化立体仓库货架向更高、更重型方向发展中的应用，二是货架在密集式高效率存储系统发展中的应用。电商行业的货架需求在近两年保持爆发式增长，订单下单量大，工期严苛，加工复杂，对货架公司综合能力考验巨大。

5. 自动化立体库

据不完全统计，2014 年国内建成的自动化立体库接近 300 座，共生产了 2000 多台不同规格型号的有轨巷道堆垛机，自动化立体库的总产值超过 40 亿元人民币。截止到 2014 年年底，全国累计建成的自动化立体库接近 2500 座，在用自动化立体库接近 2000 座。

近几年来，网络技术和电子商务飞速发展，以及各行业规模化企业实力增强，对自动化仓储系统的需求总量越来越大，类型越来越多，推动了自动化立体库的技术发展和创新，自动化立体库呈现出存储单元微型化、SKU 多样化、功能组合增多和作业速度高速化等趋势。

6. 输送分拣设备

根据监测，2014 年输送分拣设备行业市场需求呈现高速增长态势，全年增长预计在 22% 以上，市场规模超过 35 亿元。随着电子商务物流的发展，对物流输送分拣设备的市场需求日益增长。电子商务配送的多品种、小批量、高频次特征，是推动快速分拣市场需求快速增长的基础。输送分拣设备在物流系统中所占比例近年来有较大提升，市场需求增长较快。

传统的输送分拣应用的主要领域还是烟草、医药、流通、邮政、图书等领域，这些领域的输送分拣市场需求量占总需求的大部分比重，也是输送分拣需求增长比较稳定的领域。

十、行业基础工作有序推进

中国物流与采购联合会在政府有关部门和行业企业支持下，致力于推进行业基础工作。2014 年，各项基础工作又取得了新的进展。

A 级物流企业评估发展加速。依据《物流企业分类与评估指标》国家标准，中物联自 2005 年开始组织开展 A 级物流企业综合评估工作。2014 年，完成了第 18 和第 19 批 A 级物流企业评估，评估企业 527 家，复核企业 566 家。自 2005 年以来，共通过了 19 批共 3177 多家 A 级物流企业评估。2014 年，中物联根据行业发展需要，依据商务部发布的质押监管企业评估行业标准，在全国范围内开展了质押监管企业评估，已评出 32 家质押监管企业。

物流企业信用评价加大覆盖。2014 年，中物联完成了第 13 批、14 批物流企业信用评价工作，共评出 A 级信用企业 68 家。自 2007 年以来，共评出 A 级信用企业 376 家。中物联还积极探索与行业龙头企业合作开展物流企业信用评价工作，争取在行业覆盖面上有大的突破。

物流示范基地、试验基地继续推进。“中国物流示范基地”和“中国物流实验基地”自 2001 年设立以来，发挥了行业示范和先行先试的积极作用。2014 年共评出中国物流示范基地、实验基地 11 家。14 年来共评出基地企业 131 家。

统计信息工作发挥重要作用。2014 年，中物联充分发挥 PMI 和物流统计信息的作用，提高信息分析水平，做好宏观经济监测。采购经理指数（PMI）的科学性、权威性进一步提高，影响力进一步扩大，成为国家宏观经济调控决策的重要参考。中国物流业景气指数（LPI）统计、分析、发布体系逐步完善，影响力逐步扩大，已成为观察物流市场走势的风向标。

物流标准化工作加强规划。为落实《物流业发展中长期规划》，受国家标准委委托，中物联正在组织开展《全国物流标准中长期发展规划》的编制工作。2014 年组织编制完成了国家标准 15 项，行业标准 3 项。其中新修订的《物流企业分类与评估指标》和新制定的 7 项物流国家标准正式颁布实施。中物联还开展了“汽车零部件物流标准化倡议活动”、“食品冷链物流、药品冷链物流标准化试点”等标准化宣贯和试点工作，编制了《2014 物流标准目录手册》，物流标准化体系进一步完善。

教育培训工作成效显著。目前，全国已有 443 所本科院校（专业布点数 475 个）、954 多所高职高专院校、中职院校 900 多所开设了物流专业。10 余年间累计为社会各行业培养物流专业本科生 50 多万人，大专生 170 多万人，中专生 30 多万人；自 2003 年开展培训认证项目以来 50 多万学员通过培训中心进行培训，其中 40 多万人分别参加了物流师、采购师认证考试。

学术研究工作全面发展。中国物流学会会员总数达 5500 余名；特约研究员总数达到 326 名；产学研基地总数达到 166 个；第十三次中国物流学术年会参评论文总数达 859 篇，共有 332 篇获得优秀论文奖，113 个课题获优秀课题成果奖，推动了理论与实践的结合和科研成果转化。

第三章

2014 年中国物流业发展的主要问题

为了解 2014 年度物流企业负担及营商环境，发现行业发展的主要问题，中国物流与采购联合会选取 100 家有代表性的物流企业进行了典型抽样调查。被调查的样本企业构成情况如表 1 所示：

表 1　　样本企业构成情况

按所有制性质					
国有及国有控股	私营	股份制	外商及港澳台商投资企业	集体	其他
32.98%	41.49%	10.64%	9.57%	1.06%	4.26%

按业务类型		
运输型	仓储型	综合型
28%	14%	58%

按物流企业综合评估等级			
5A 级	4A 级	3A 级	2A 级
26.92%	33.33%	37.18%	2.56%

按经营规模（年主营业务收入）		
1000 万元以上	1 亿元以上	10 亿元以上
98.9%	67%	30%

调查显示，2014 年我国物流企业各类负担较重，符合行业发展的营商环境还有待完善，影响了企业健康可持续发展，现将有关问题反映如下。

一、业务总量稳中见升，成本增速快于利润

调查显示，主营业务收入较上年增长的样本企业占50.5%，较上年增长或持平的占80.8%；主营业务成本较上年增长的占46.8%，较上年增长或持平的占79.7%；主营利润较上年增长的占47.4%，较上年增长或持平的占67.4%；业务总量较上年增长的占47.1%，较上年增长或持平的占78.8%，如图1所示。

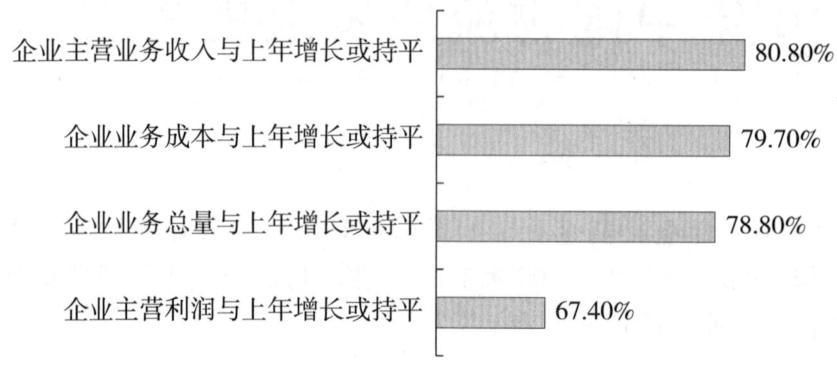

图1　样本企业经营效益情况

总体来看，样本企业经营状况稳中有升，主营业务收入增长的企业超过半数，增长或基本持平的超过八成。但是受主营业务成本增加较快、业务总量增长疲软的影响，主营业务利润增速明显放缓，利润增长的企业占比不到半数，增长或持平的不足七成，显示企业经营效益有所下滑，如表2所示。

表2　　样本企业经营效益情况表

	显著增长（20%）	增长（5%～20%）	基本持平（±5%）	下降（5%～20%）	显著下降（20%）
主营业务收入情况	20.62%	29.90%	27.84%	12.37%	9.28%
主营业务成本情况	18.09%	28.72%	32.98%	12.77%	7.45%
主营业务利润情况	20.00%	27.37%	20.00%	15.79%	16.84%
业务总量情况	18.82%	28.24%	31.76%	17.65%	3.53%

二、税费负担依然较重，运输业务增税幅度较大

调查显示，样本企业中，50%的企业认为企业税费有所加重，其中20%的

企业认为税费大幅加重，企业税费负担总体较重，如图 2 所示。

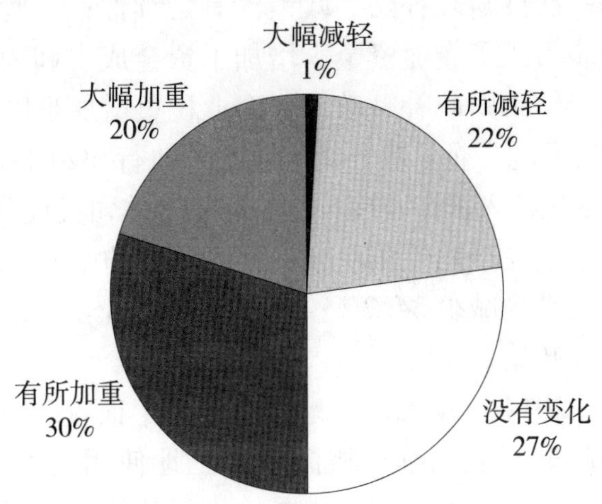

图 2　样本企业税费负担情况

大部分企业（82%）缴纳的法定税费占企业主营业务收入的 15% 以下，12% 的企业占收入的 15% ~25%，还有 6% 的企业占收入的 25% 以上，如图 3 所示。

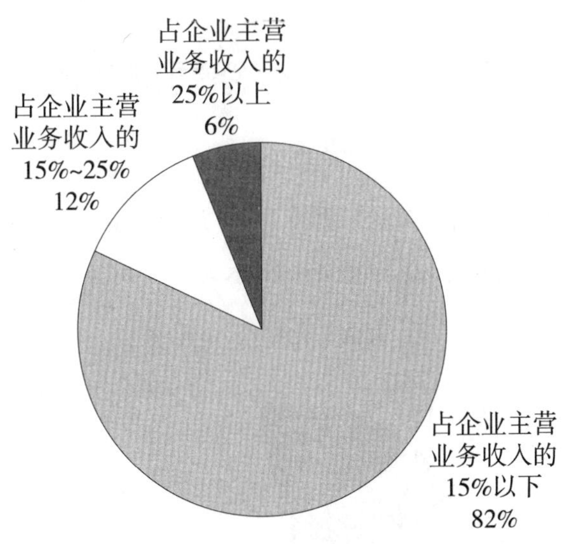

图 3　样本企业法定税费占企业主营业务收入情况

调查显示，样本企业平均缴纳增值税比营业税体制下增长 51%。其中，运输型企业平均增长 123.3%。物流企业普遍呼吁，尽快解决物流企业“营改增”后税负增加问题，完善增值税抵扣链条，减轻物流企业税收负担。

针对各地财政补贴政策，部分企业反映政策不透明、流程烦琐、结算时间长；许多地区 2014 年度财政补贴尚未到位，2015 年度补贴政策尚未明确是否延续；一些地区是一次性财政补贴，政策没有延续性；一些地区将财政补贴改为年度结算，进一步占压了企业资金，增加了资金成本和周转压力；还有一些地区没有出台或已经结束财政补贴政策，企业税负增加难以消化。

为从根本上解决问题，企业呼吁物流业统一执行 6% 的税率，同时将房屋租赁费、过路过桥费尽快纳入抵扣范围，尽快解决个体司机代开增值税发票问题。

调查显示，对于享受土地使用税减半征收政策的企业，2014 年平均缴纳土地使用税与往年相比平均减少 34. 2% 。还有部分企业由于新建设施或企业认定问题没有享受到该项政策。

样本企业反映，2014 年年底，土地使用税减半征收政策正式到期，亟盼延续政策出台。如果政策不能延续，物流企业土地使用税税负将重回高税负水平。更重要的是，由于各地土地使用税单位税额基数普遍提高，税负总水平将远远高于政策实施前的水平。据部分企业反映，三年的减税红利将在政策到期后很短时间内被蚕食。

此外，部分企业反映，对于印花税、防洪保安基金、水利基金等收费存在不合理问题，教育费附加和地方教育费附加存在重复征收，希望予以调整优化，减轻企业负担。

三、通行环境变化不大，公路罚款政出多门、自由裁量权大

调查显示，样本企业中，48% 的企业认为通行环境变化不大，27% 的认为有所好转，20% 认为有所恶化，如图 4 所示。

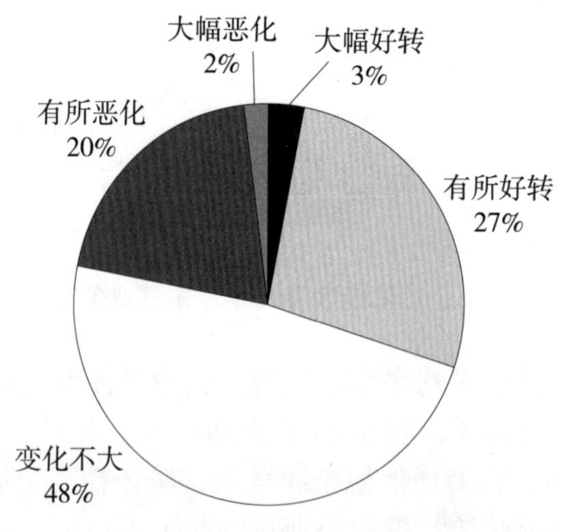

图 4　样本企业车辆通行环境情况

调查显示，样本企业平均燃油费支出占运输成本的30%，与上年相比，43%的企业认为变化不大，40%的企业认为较往年相比下降，17.1%的企业认为较去年增加。

2014年，受国际油价大幅下降影响，我国燃油价格一路下滑。到12月底最低点油价比7月最高点下滑约25%。企业燃油费支出变化除受燃油价格影响外，还与运输业务总量、自有车辆占比有较大关系。此外，与燃油价格下滑幅度相比，燃油费支出下降幅度低，甚至不降反升与营改增后对燃油费发票抵扣需求增加有一定关系，如图5所示。部分企业反映，油价下跌带来的利好与快速上升的人力成本相抵消，企业总成本下降幅度并不高，约在3%左右。

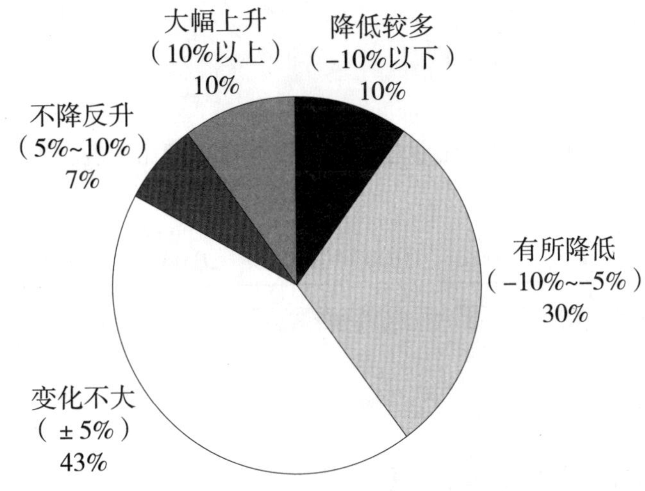

图5　样本企业燃油费支出情况

调查显示，样本企业过路过桥费平均占运输成本的14.9%。其中干线运输物流企业过路过桥费占运输成本的22.7%。与往年相比，55%的企业认为过路过桥费变化不大，26%的企业认为有所下降，19%的企业认为有所上升。

企业路桥费下降的主要原因，一是企业对运输线路进行了优化，采取铁路、水路等多种方式；二是运输业务总量下滑或外包运输业务；三是部分企业将原直接报销路桥费票改为货物运输业增值税专用发票；四是部分地区实行ETC不停车电子收费系统，实现公司统一交费，享受了折扣优惠。

调查显示，30.6%的样本企业反映过路过桥费收费标准偏高，27.50%的反映各地收费标准不统一，18.8%的反映超限收费标准不合理，11.88%的反映计重收费误差较大，11.25%的反映存在超期收费、延期收费问题，如图6、图7所示。

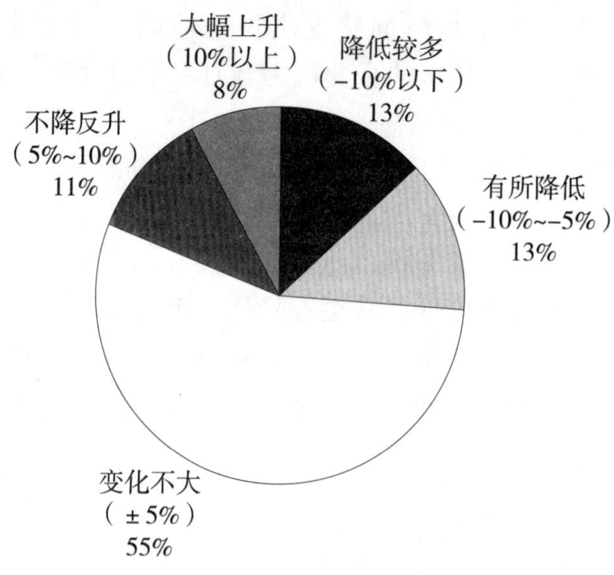

图6　样本企业过路过桥费与往年相比情况

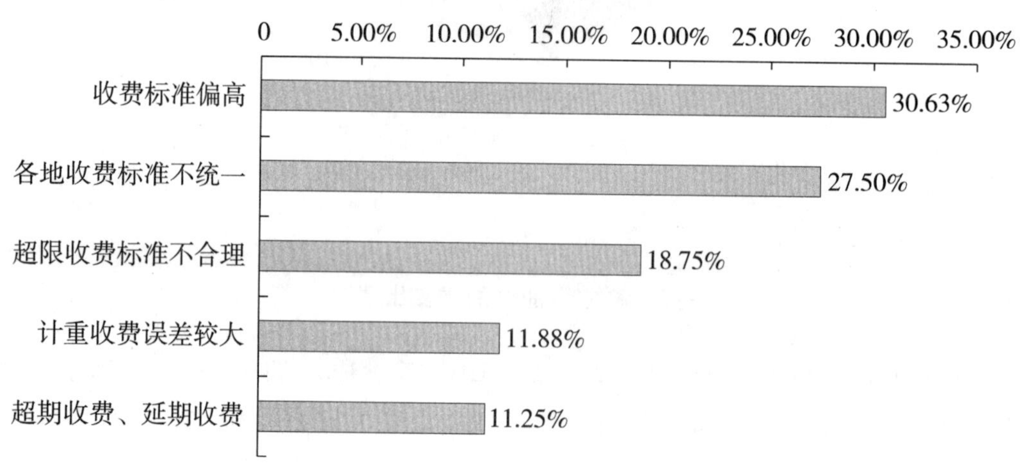

图7　各地过路过桥费存在的主要问题

对于计重收费存在的问题，部分企业反映，计重收费标准较高，特别一些地区的大件运输车辆收费标准过高；往往存在称重不准问题，甚至同一收费站不同收费口称重也不一样；无法使用ETC，导致通行效率低；计重收费后超载现象并没有消除，没有起到限制超载的作用，同时计重收费后不卸载是否可以合法通行存在较大争议。

调查显示，样本企业平均支付公路罚款占运输成本的3.1%。部分大件运输、汽车整车运输、集装箱运输企业公路罚款较多，占运输成本的10%以上。与往年相比，60%的企业认为公路罚款变化不大，19%的企业认为有所降低或降低较多，公路罚款问题有所缓解，如图 8 所示。

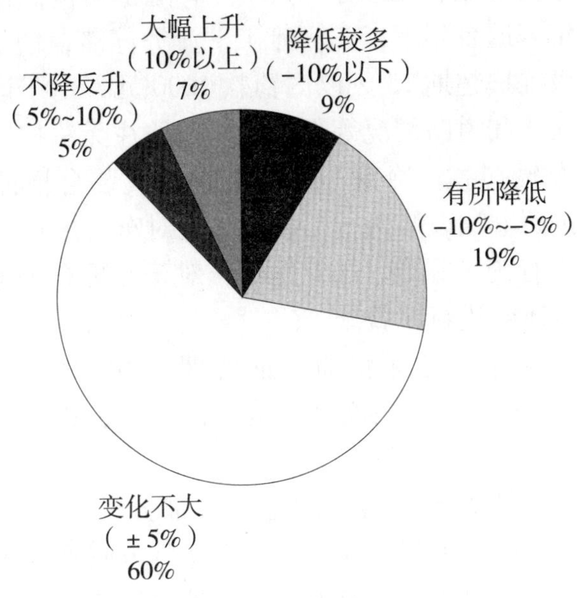

图 8　样本企业支付公路罚款与往年相比情况

物流企业反映，通过加强安全教育和培训，驾驶员交通法规意识增强，公路罚款有所下降。同时，由于各地城市货运车辆禁止通行范围持续扩大，道路限行线路多、时间长、设计不合理造成货车“断头路”，企业被动违法受罚难以避免。部分企业反映，城市货车限行造成客车违法载货配送现象普遍，增加了城市交通压力和空气污染。

调查显示，目前关于公路罚款问题，29. 01% 的企业认为自由裁量权大、随意性强，24. 69% 的企业认为政出多门、标准不统一，24. 69% 的企业认为存在只罚不纠的现象，21. 06% 的企业认为监督管理不严、缺乏举报、问责和处罚机制，如图 9 所示。

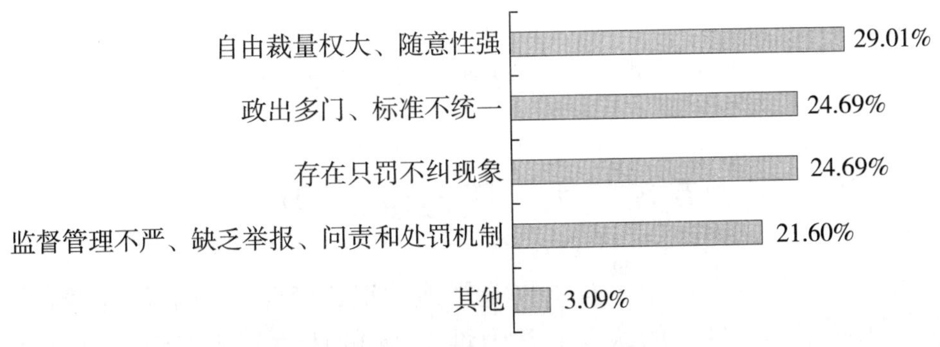

图 9　样本企业公路罚款的主要问题

部分企业反映，司机的道路运输从业资格证每年要进行诚信考核，需到档案所在地签注诚信考核等级，相当于“年审”。由于司机工作地点与户籍地往往不一致，导致每年需返乡年审，车辆停工、业务停滞，增加了企业负担。国家规定营运车辆二级维护超期15天以内罚款1000元，由于运营车辆在全国范围内运行，受运输任务和道路情况等因素影响，往往无法按时回车籍所在地进行二级维护，导致车辆罚款。冷藏车辆改装均有改装合格证，但在实际运行中，一些地区仍会按照非法改装进行罚款。各地对车体广告、车容车貌（例如反光条破旧）罚款没有统一标准，随意性强，对于办理有车体广告备案登记手续的车辆，有些地区还会进行罚款。

调查显示，关于城市配送车辆通行证管理，30%的企业认为申请困难，28%的企业认为区域设限，22%的企业认为标准不一，19%的企业认为通行证数量不足。

企业反映，目前各地办理通行证的地点大部分设置在市内。司机下高速后，需要将货车停在原地，再到市内办理，办完后再回到停车地开车进城。一是极不方便，有时打不到出租车要走很久；二是司机离开车辆造成车辆和货物的不安全；三是有时一下高速就会因没有通行证被处罚。

此外，许多地区采取“一刀切”措施禁止电动三轮车通行，导致“最后一公里”配送压力大大增加，如图10所示。

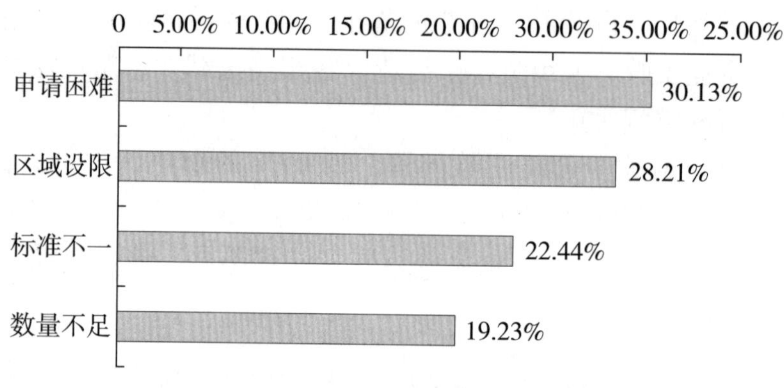

图10　城市配送车辆通行证管理的主要问题

四、用地压力有所加大，用地难、用地贵

调查显示，样本企业中，对于物流用地情况，45%的企业认为变化不大，35%的认为较困难，11%的认为非常困难，8%的认为有所好转。物流企业认为困难的企业占46%，接近半数，显示物流用地压力依然较大，如图11所示。

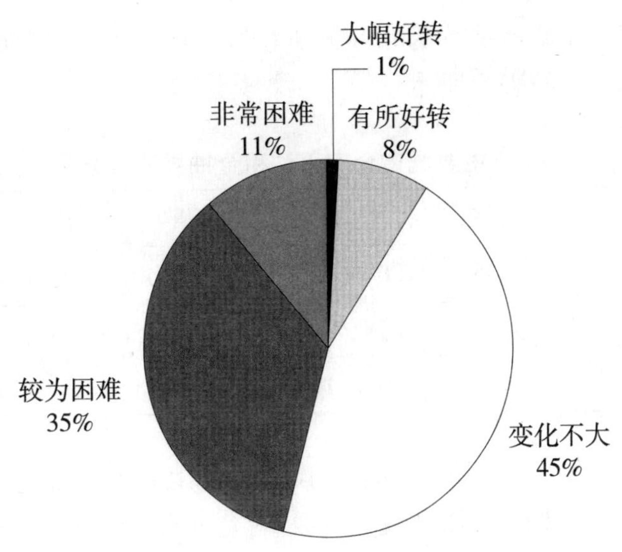

图 11 样本企业物流用地情况

2014 年物流用地的平均价格，一线城市为 80 万 ~100 万元/亩，二线城市为 40 万 ~50 万元/亩，三线城市为 10 万 ~15 万元/亩。其中，一线城市用地价格为二线城市的 2 倍，是三线城市的 7.2 倍，如表 3 所示。

表 3 2014 年全国主要城市物流用地价格抽样调查结果 （万元/亩）

城市	北京	上海	广州	深圳	天津	昆明
地价	150 ~200	100 ~200	80 ~150	100 ~200	40 ~55	43 ~45
城市	沈阳	西安	长沙	南昌	贵阳	
地价	45 左右	24.5 ~50	32.5 左右	16 左右	26 左右	

调查显示，一线城市物流用地价格上涨幅度明显大于二三线城市，二线城市涨幅大于三线城市，如表 4 所示。

表 4 样本企业物流用地平均价格与往年同期相比

城市	降低较多（-10% 以下）	有所降低（-10% ~ -5%）	变化不大（±5%）	不降反升（5% ~10%）	大幅上升（10% 以上）
一线城市	0.00%	2.78%	38.89%	25.00%	33.33%
二线城市	0.00%	6.82%	38.64%	36.36%	18.18%
三线城市	5.13%	2.56%	53.85%	23.08%	15.38%

调查显示，2014 年租用仓库的平均租金，一线城市平均租金为 1.2 元/

（平方米·天），二线城市平均为0.8元/（平方米·天），三线城市平均为0.5元/（平方米·天），如表5所示。

表5　2014年主要城市仓库平均租金抽样调查结果［元/（平方米·天）］

城市	北京	上海	广州	深圳	沈阳
地价	1.45	1.00~1.60	1.00~1.40	1.10~1.60	0.95
城市	大连	西安	长沙	廊坊	
地价	0.9	0.94~1.02	0.74~0.98	0.95~1.00	

调查显示，反映一线城市物流用地投资强度上升的企业较多，占50%；反映二三线城市物流用地投资强度变化不大的企业分别占60%和53%。一线城市物流用地投资强度上涨幅度快于二三线城市。

表6　样本企业物流用地投资强度与去年同期相比

	降低较多（-10%以下）	有所降低（-10%~-5%）	变化不大（±5%）	有所上升（5%~10%）	大幅上升（10%以上）
一线城市	0.00%	10.00%	40.00%	37.50%	12.50%
二线城市	0.00%	6.67%	60.00%	24.44%	8.89%
三线城市	0.00%	15.79%	52.63%	26.32%	5.26%

企业普遍反映，一些地方将工业仓储用地土地使用年限缩短到20年，加速物业折旧，经营成本大增，投资回收压力加大，导致企业投资趋于短缺，影响建筑的可靠性和耐久性，不利于可持续发展。

五、融资渠道不畅，获取资金难度大、成本高

调查显示，对于企业融资环境，39%的样本企业认为变化不大，33%的企业认为较去年紧张，28%的企业认为融资环境较去年有好转，融资环境总体依然较为紧张，如图12所示。

调查显示，未来一年，22%的企业表示资金需求有很大缺口、急需融资，55%的企业表示资金略有缺口、需要融资，23%的企业表示不需要融资，如图13所示。

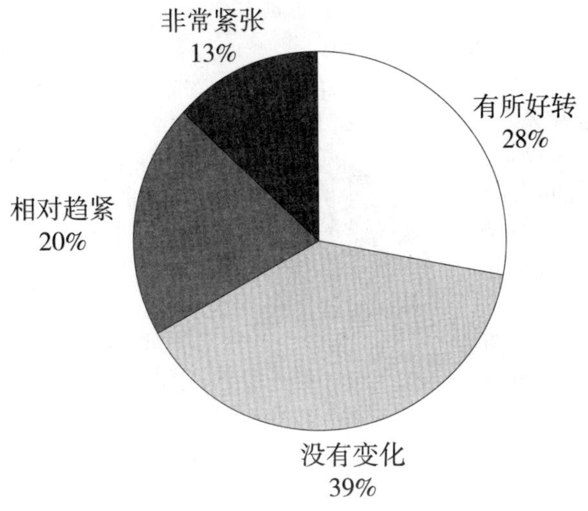

图 12　样本企业融资环境

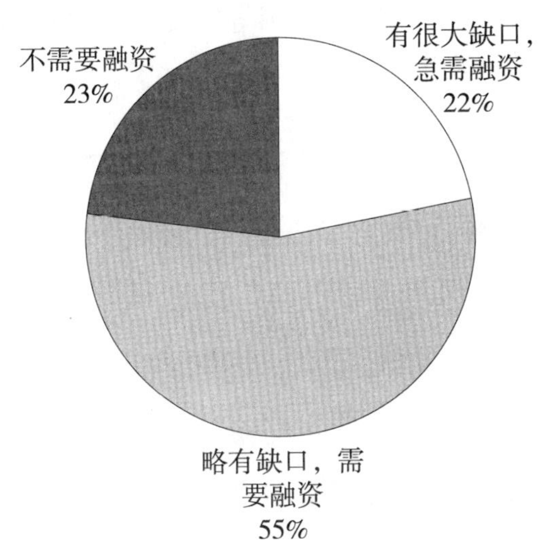

图 13　样本企业未来一年的融资需求情况

调查显示，企业的主要融资渠道，70%的企业通过银行贷款，7%的企业通过民间借贷，6%的企业通过企业债券，3%的企业通过上市融资，3%的企业通过基金和风险投资，银行贷款占七成，仍是企业的主要融资渠道，如图 14 所示。

调查显示，从银行的贷款情况看，18%的企业认为难度较大；64%的企业任务困难，但是可以争取；18%的企业认为较容易获得，不存在困难。

银行贷款融资的主要问题，27.92%的企业反映可抵押物少，折扣率高；16.88%的企业反映贷款额度小；14.94%的企业反映担保体系不完善；9.74%

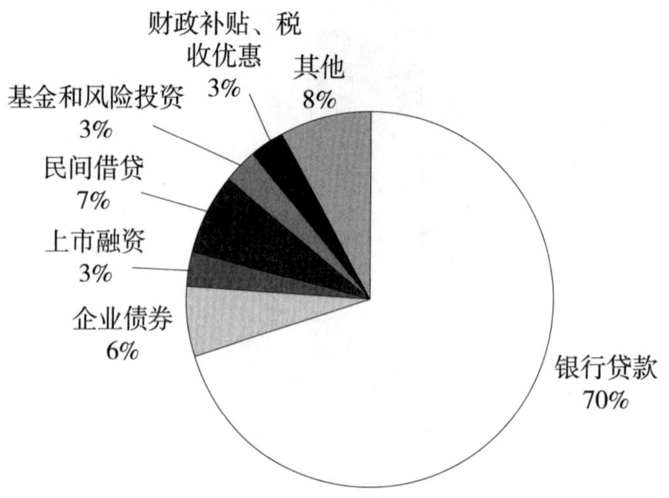

图 14　样本企业的主要融资渠道分布图

的企业反映存贷挂钩，还有企业反映信用等级低、续贷时间间隔长、使用承兑汇票等，分别占 8% 左右，如图 15 所示。

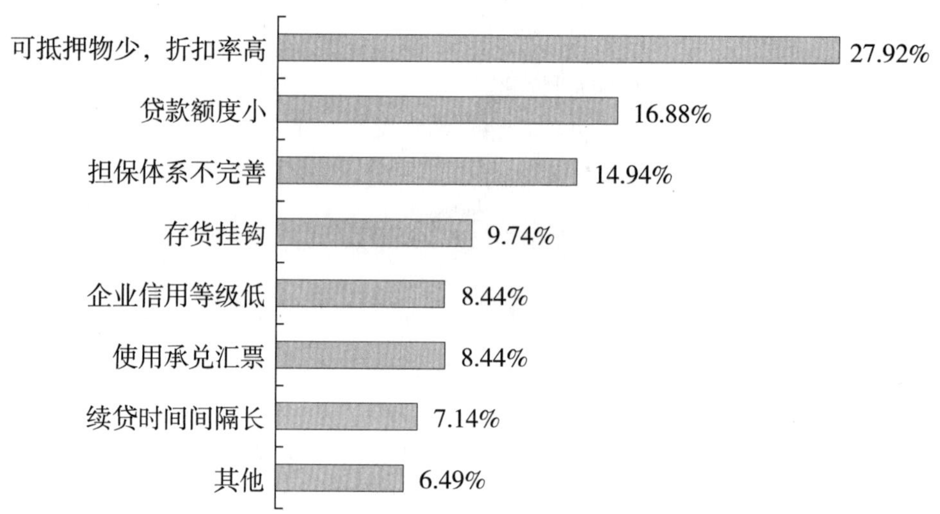

图 15　样本企业从银行融资贷款的主要问题

关于上市融资计划，22% 的企业有计划，正准备上市；32% 的企业希望上市，还没有准备；41% 的企业没有上市计划，5% 的企业已经上市，如图 16 所示。

企业上市融资的主要问题：39% 的企业认为门槛高、31% 的企业认为发行成本高、13% 的企业认为会计制度不完善、9% 的企业认为税收制度不完善等，如图 17 所示。

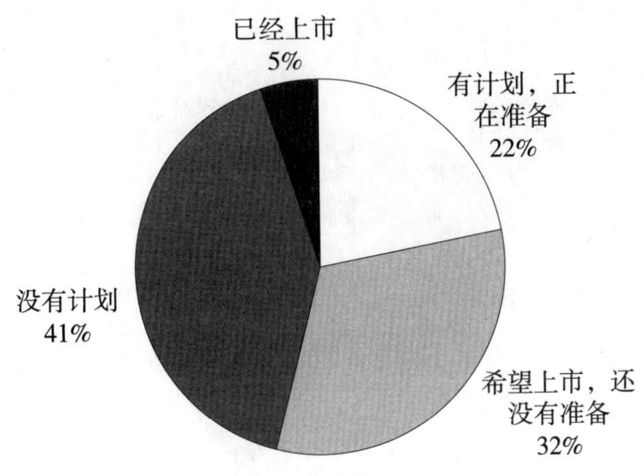

图 16　样本企业上市情况

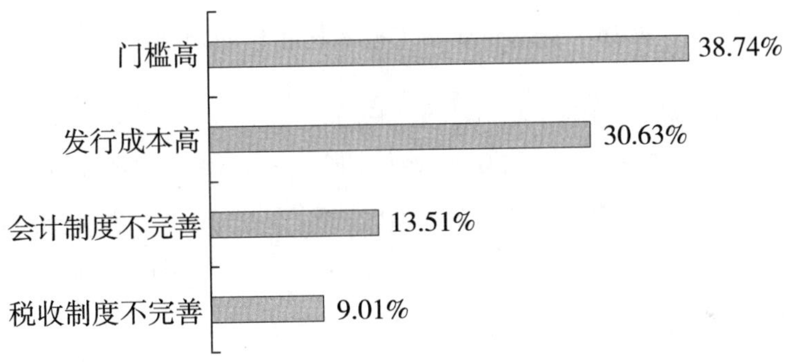

图 17　样本企业上市融资的主要问题

企业普遍反映，由于物流业存在抵押物少、贷款额度低的问题，亟须建立具有公信力且成本低廉的行业贷款担保机制，为企业扩大经营提供融资担保支持。

六、用工成本持续上升，操作型员工流失严重

调查显示，样本企业人力成本占主营业务成本的 23%。企业普遍反映过去一年用工成本上涨在 10% 以上。与往年相比，60% 的企业反映人力成本上升，其中，18% 的认为上升幅度较大，还有 30% 的企业反映变化不大，如图 18 所示。

企业普遍反映，用工成本上升的主要原因是员工工资上调、社保基数上调和福利水平上调等。

调查显示，企业认为雇用操作型员工的有难度的占 42%，认为雇用管理型

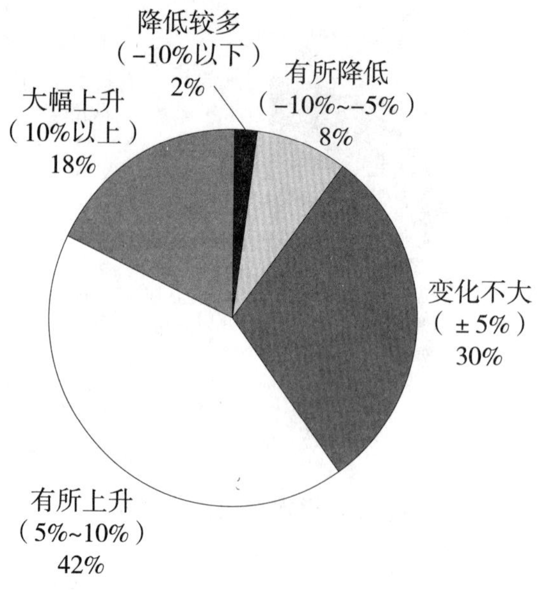

图 18　样本企业用工成本与去年同期相比

员工有难度的占 46%，如图 19、图 20 所示。

部分企业反映，目前货车司机非常紧缺。由于货车司机需要具备 A2 驾照，但是 A2 驾照获得需要 6 年时间，而且扣分超过 12 分将进行降级处理，导致货车司机数量难以满足市场需求。一些企业雇用 B2 驾照的司机代替 A2 驾照司机，存在一定的违规风险。

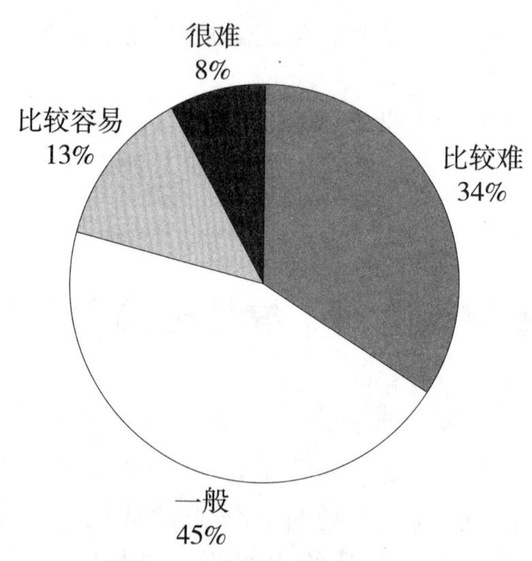

图 19　样本企业雇用操作型员工的难度情况

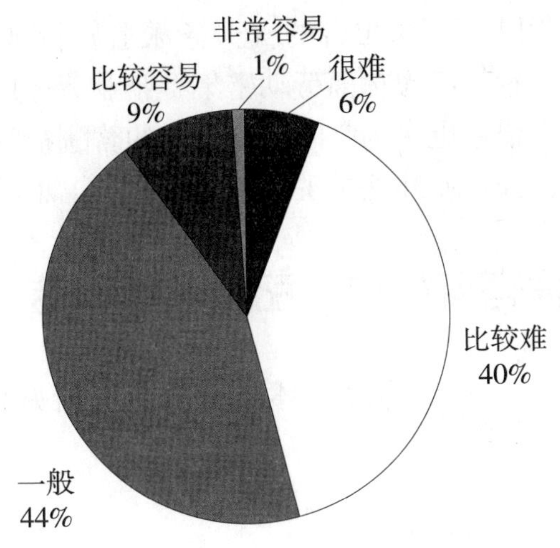

图 20　样本企业雇用管理型员工的难度情况

关于员工流失情况，39% 的企业反映操作型员工流失严重，12% 的企业反映管理型员工流失严重。操作型员工大量流失导致“用工荒”应引起行业重视，如表 7 所示。

表 7　样本企业员工流失情况

	比较严重，对企业影响大	严重，可以接受	一般	无影响
操作型员工	7.14%	31.63%	50.00%	11.22%
管理型员工	1.23%	11.11%	61.73%	25.93%

其中，员工流失的主要影响因素表现为工资待遇 30%、生活成本上涨 24%、职业晋升前景 20%、房价太高 10%、家庭关爱需要 9% 等，如图 21 所示。

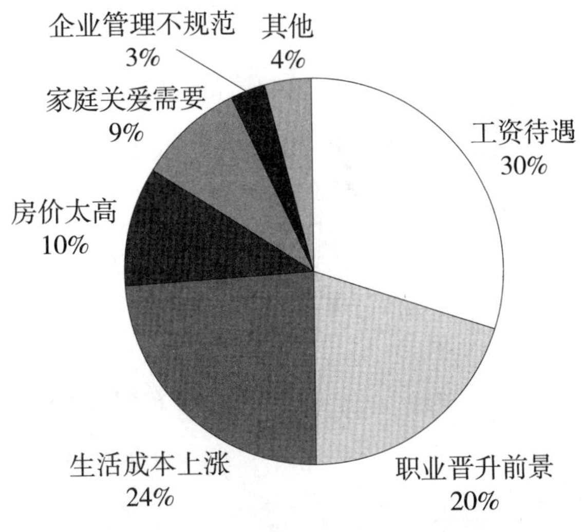

图 21　样本员工流失的主要原因

企业普遍反映，2014 年国家出台的《劳务派遣暂行规定》对企业劳务用工比例进行了明确规定。希望考虑提高劳动密集型企业劳务用工的比例限制，着重研究同工同酬政策，给企业更多的空间改善员工的薪酬福利。此外，社保缴纳比例过高，企业负担重，且企业外地员工比例较高，员工难以享受到社保福利。

七、政务环境有所好转，配套政策有待落实

调查显示，61% 的企业认为政务环境较上年有所好转，政务环境持续向好，如图 22 所示。

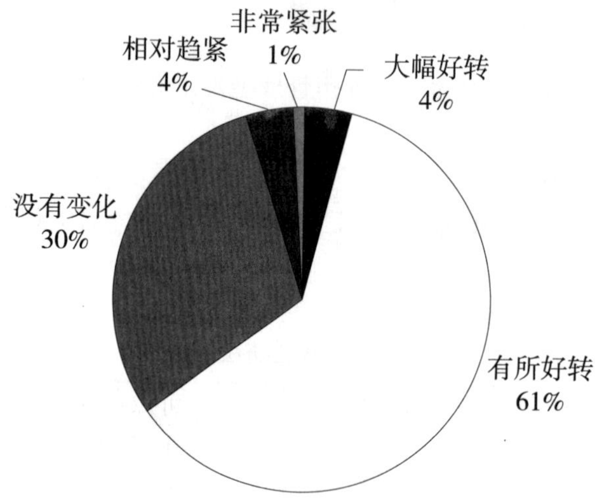

图 22　样本企业政务环境

对于国家推行工商登记制度改革，83% 的企业反映注册审批环节较过去简化，如图 23 所示。

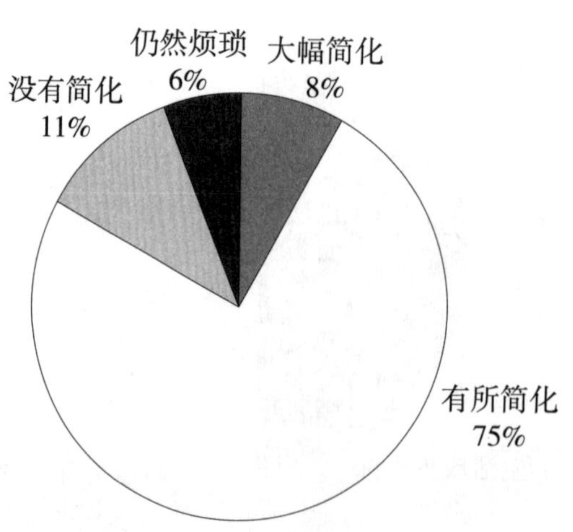

图 23　样本企业手续审批情况

对于相关事项办理手续的看法，较为便捷的有车辆手续、年审手续、工商登记手续、海关进出口手续；较为复杂的有土地手续、营运手续、规划手续、建设手续、消防手续、环保手续、投资手续、外汇管理手续，如表 8 所示。

表 8　样本企业对相关事项办理手续的看法

	很便捷	便捷	一般	复杂	很复杂
车辆手续	6.10%	21.95%	52.44%	14.63%	4.88%
土地手续	0.00%	10.29%	39.71%	26.47%	23.53%
营运手续	2.41%	21.69%	49.40%	20.48%	6.02%
年审手续	10.00%	40.00%	40.00%	8.89%	1.11%
规划手续	0.00%	11.59%	39.13%	27.54%	21.74%
建设手续	1.59%	3.17%	39.68%	26.98%	28.57%
消防手续	4.11%	12.33%	42.47%	24.66%	16.44%
环保手续	0.00%	12.33%	43.84%	26.03%	17.81%
投资手续	1.52%	18.18%	53.03%	18.18%	9.09%
工商登记手续	6.02%	50.60%	32.53%	9.64%	1.20%
海关进出口手续	0.00%	30.91%	43.64%	20.00%	5.45%
检验检疫手续	0.00%	28.30%	41.51%	22.64%	7.55%
外汇管理手续	0.00%	18.37%	51.02%	28.57%	2.04%

近年来，国家和地方出台的一系列支持物流业发展的政策，调查显示，63% 的企业认为对企业的发展有作用，38% 的企业认为政策的落实情况好，7% 的企业认为落实情况不好。

落实情况不好的主要原因：28.33% 的企业反映缺乏配套政策，帮助企业效果不明显；18.33% 的企业反映条件设置门槛高，企业达不到；17.22% 的企业反映办理手续烦琐；17.22% 的企业反映信息渠道不畅通；9.44% 的企业反映政策力度不大，对企业没有吸引力；9.44% 的企业反映难以进入申报体系，如图 24 所示。

样本企业反映，一些地区要求企业在当地设立具有法人资格的子公司，才能开展相应的业务，直接影响了企业扩大经营规模和建立服务网络；企业总部获得的资质分支机构不能享受；一些地方正在推行“先照后证”，希望在物流行业全面推开；同时，随着简政放权进一步深化，希望道路运输许可证、快递经营许可证进行后置审批。

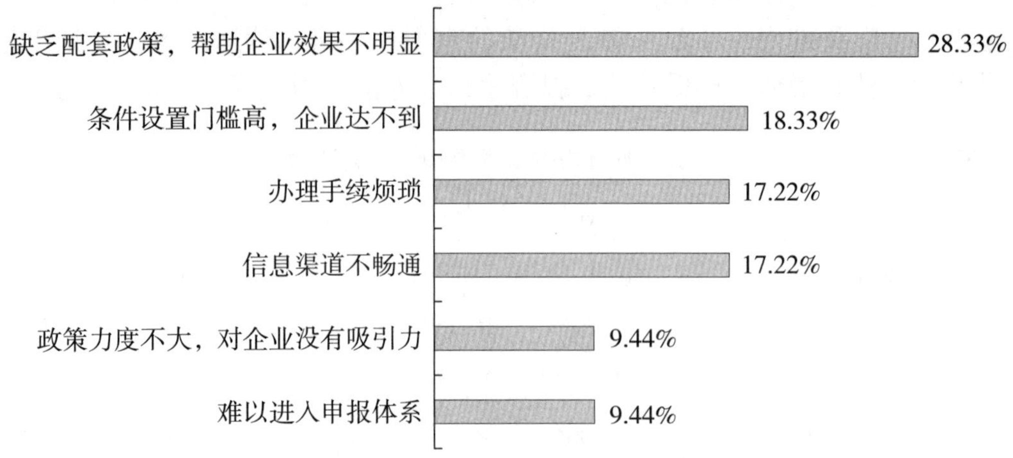

图 24　政策落实情况不好的主要原因

部分企业反映，道路运输许可证年检流程复杂，填写资料太多，一些地方异地办理道路运输许可证需要保证金。

一些资质建议取消，如：法人负责人安全员资格证、航空运输销售代理资格证、快递员职业资格证、国际货运代理备案表、对外贸易经营者备案表等。

八、法律环境变化不大，物流综合立法缺失

调查显示，61%的企业认为所在领域法律环境变化不大，28%的企业认为较去年有所改善，如图 25 所示。

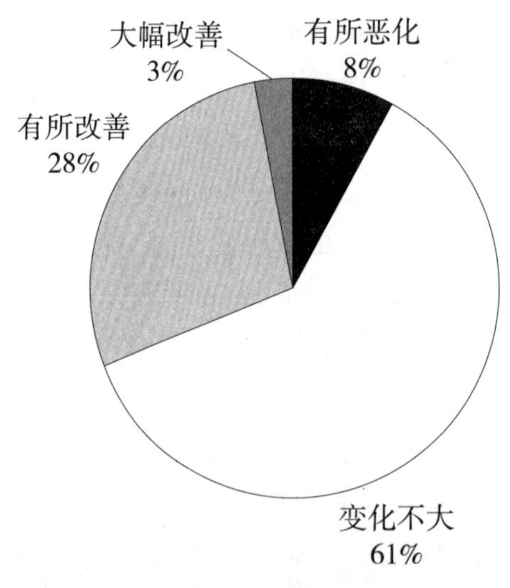

图 25　样本企业所在领域的法律环境情况

关于企业自身的法律情况，50%的企业表示企业有专门的法律部门；47%的企业表示企业无法律部门，但有相关部门代管法律事项。调查显示，60%的企业反映最近三年有法律纠纷，法律纠纷主要涉及合同纠纷51.65%、劳资纠纷17.58%、企业间纠纷16.48%等，如图26所示。

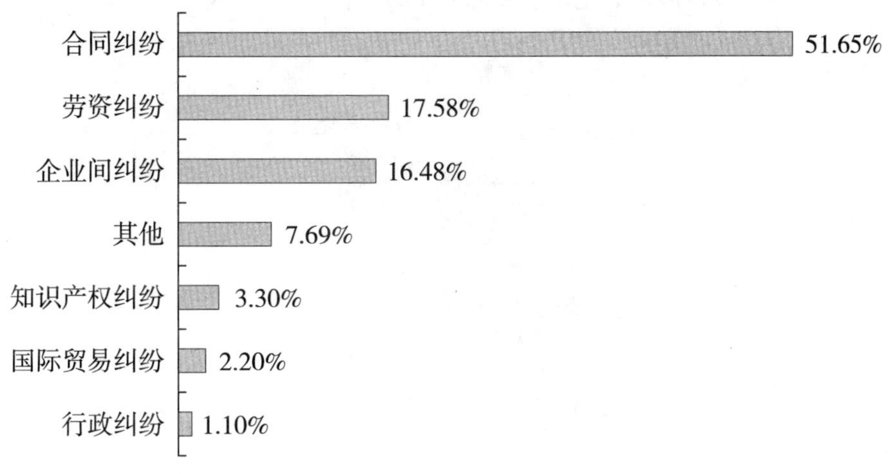

图26　样本企业法律纠纷的主要涉及方面

企业发生法律纠纷，主要解决途径为诉讼解决50%、法律部门跟对方沟通协商32%、非诉讼途径自行解决17%等，如图27所示。

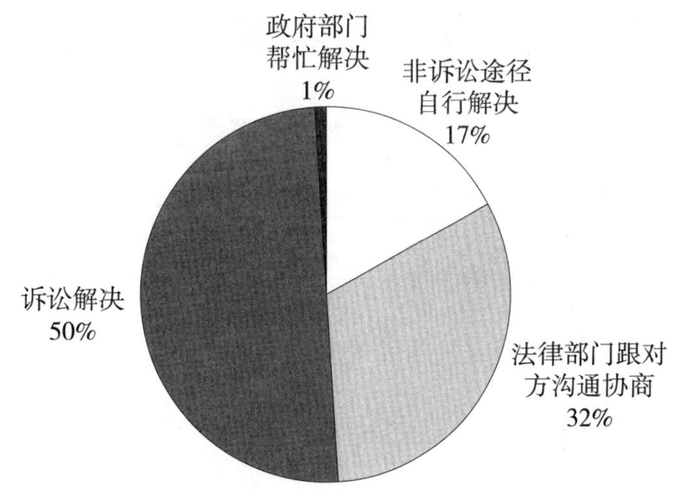

图27　样本企业解决法律纠纷的主要途径

企业普遍反映，我国目前尚无专门的物流立法，物流各领域相关部门规章制度较多，标准不统一，合规成本较高，企业难以适从。

九、诚信问题依然突出，诚信建设亟待加强

调查显示，36%的企业认为2014年企业所在领域的行业诚信环境有所改善，53%的企业认为环境变化不大，如图28所示。

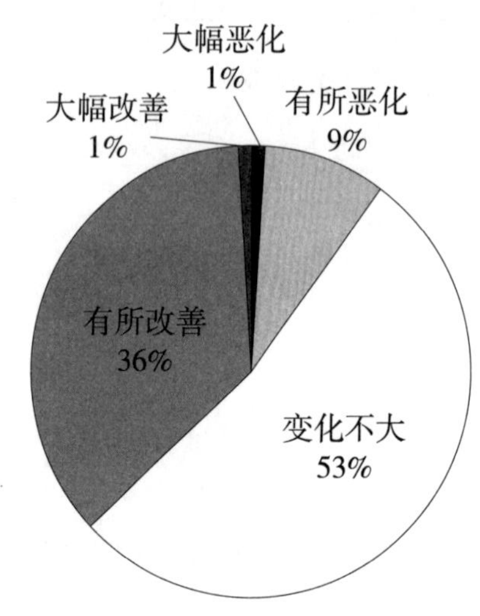

图28 样本企业所在领域的行业诚信环境

调查显示，行业失信现象主要表现为拖欠货款49.29%、合同违约35.51%、虚假信息10.14%等方面，如图29所示。

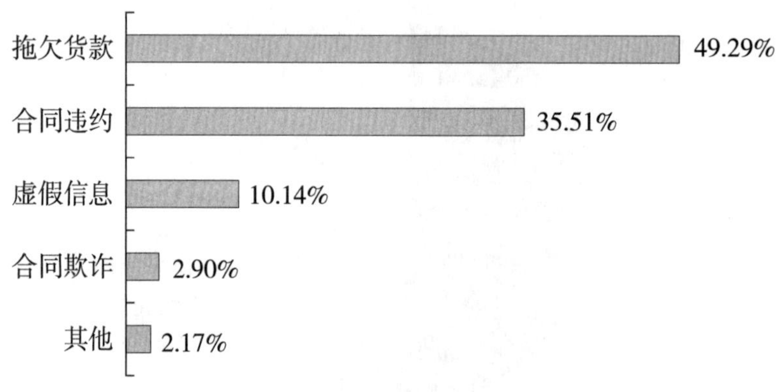

图29 行业主要失信现象

调查显示，90%的企业建立了诚信制度和风险防范体系情况。企业获得诚信信息的渠道主要为行业协会26.59%、同行口碑25.40%、银行或金融机构18.65%、政府部门17.06%等，如图30所示。

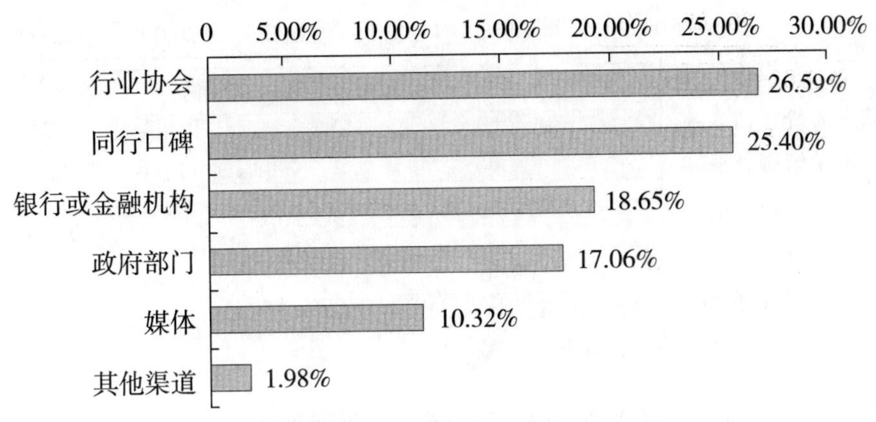

图 30 样本企业获得诚信信息的主要渠道

企业反映，行业信用体系需要完善，对不同信用等级物流企业的差别化管理尚未形成，奖优罚劣机制尚未建立，不守诚信成本总体较低。

十、通关环境持续向好，海外拓展障碍较多

近年来，有关部门大力推进通关环境改革已见成效。调查显示，59% 的企业认为通关环境较去年有所改善，36% 的企业认为变化不大，如图 31 所示。

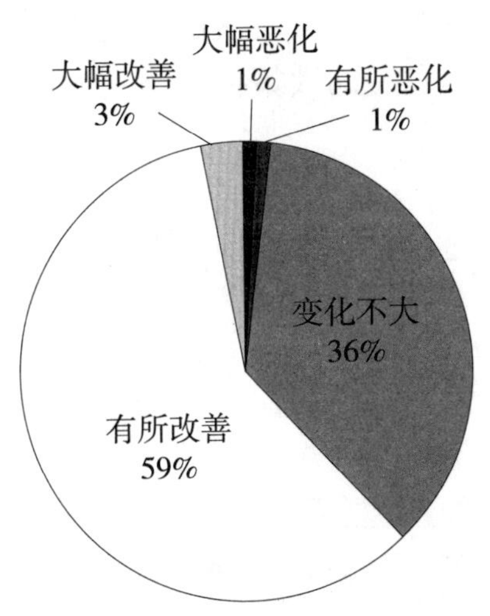

图 31 样本企业反映通关环境情况

企业进行海外市场拓展仍有很多问题，主要表现为缺少海外经营人才 22.83%、不了解投资环境 22.83%、不了解国外法律 17.93% 等，如图 32 所示。

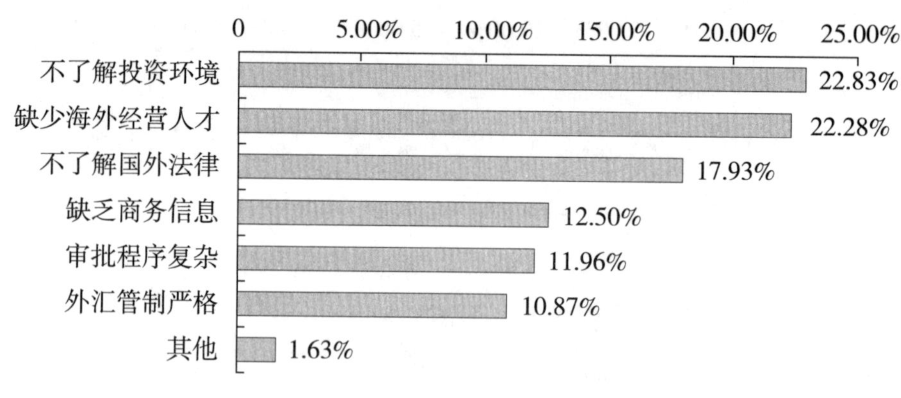

图 32　样本企业进行海外市场拓展遇到的主要困难

十一、未来发展面临挑战，营商环境仍需改善

对于未来三年阻碍企业发展的挑战，调查显示，第一位挑战是经济增长放缓，其次是劳动力成本上涨，第三是税收问题，第四是车辆通行问题，第五是用地问题。此外还有吸引和留住人才、融资问题、法律法规不完善、缺乏合格的人才等，如图 33 所示。

这些问题的解决，一方面需要企业从战略上引起重视，加快模式创新，促进转型升级，适应新常态下经济社会发展的新趋势；另一方面需要政府有关部门，制定和落实促进物流业发展的政策措施，切实减轻企业负担，为行业发展创造良好的营商环境。

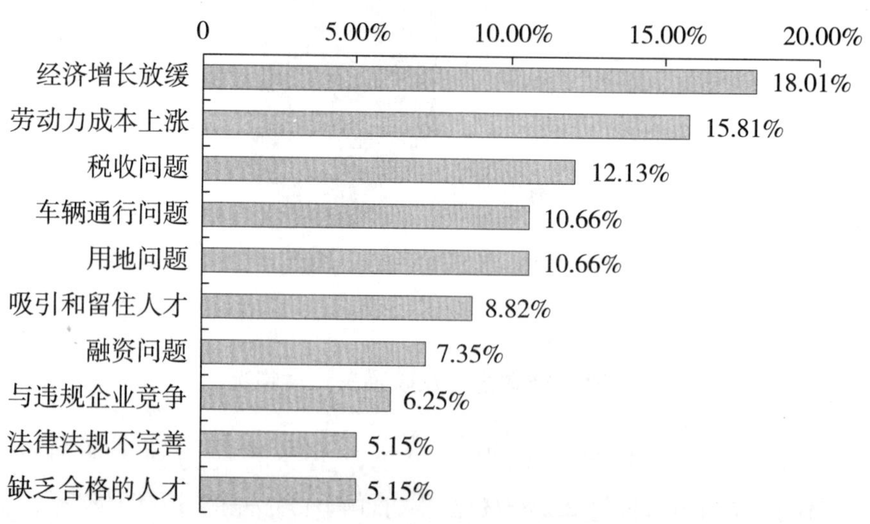

图 33　目前和近三年阻碍公司发展的最大挑战

第四章

2015年中国物流业发展展望

当前，世界经济仍处在国际金融危机后的深度调整期，我国社会经济发展步入“新常态”。就物流业面临的形势来看，正处于产业地位的提升期、现代物流服务体系的形成期和物流强国的建设期，物流业发展面临新的机遇和挑战。

一、总体运行以稳为主

2015年，物流业整体上将保持平稳运行，呈现“增速减缓、结构调整”的趋势。全社会物流总额，按可比价格计算，预计增长7%左右。

从物流需求看，随着消费对经济贡献增大，消费需求将成为主要推动力。电子商务对物流服务的需求成为产业升级的助推器，以终端消费者为对象，个性化、多样化的物流体验成为核心诉求。企业物流需求加快向供应链延伸，专业化、一体化的物流服务成为增长点。城镇化的加速推进，农村物流和社区物流潜力巨大。

从发展方式看，随着增长速度放缓，质量与效率取代规模和速度成为衡量标准。物流企业更加注重服务体验和解决方案，服务能力稳步提升，运行效率不断改进。企业联盟合作成为常态，产业融合加快实现。资源共享、合作共赢、可持续发展的产业生态圈正在形成。

从内生动力看，随着市场竞争层次的提升，整合与创新助推转型升级。企业流程再造、兼并重组、联盟合作更加普遍，功能整合、组织整合、信息整合和平台整合充分发挥资源利用效率。技术创新、组织创新、模式创新、管理创新成为发展新引擎，打造差异化竞争优势，培育核心竞争力，引领企业抢占竞争制高点。

从外部拉力看，随着市场开放和互联网经济的发展，资本和技术驱动集约发展。更多的外部企业将携资本优势跨界进入物流市场，依托互联网经济的新模式改变原有的游戏规则，长期处于静态的市场格局将加快动态调整，实现均衡发展。

从资源要素看，随着各类资源要素的紧缺，物流业已经进入高成本时代。物流用地长期紧缺，仓库租金仍将延续持续上涨态势。人口老龄化日趋发展，企业“员工荒”现象加剧，劳动力成本逐年上涨。企业加大设施设备和信息系统投入，资金压力加大。对存量资源的调整和增量资源的优化成为发展共识。

从基础设施看，随着国家基础设施投资进入新阶段，物流基础设施网络初步成型。铁路运能进入集中释放期，原有运输格局加快调整。“五纵七横”公路网和“八纵八横”铁路网已经形成，物流园区、物流中心等物流节点初具规模，物流基础设施互联互通，网络后发优势明显，对行业发展的“硬约束”逐步消退。

从环境约束看，随着国家和社会对生态环境的重视，绿色低碳循环物流成为趋势。环境承载能力达到或接近上限，国家应对气候变化力度加强，还将出台更加严格的节能环保政策，环境对行业发展的约束加大，倒逼绿色低碳循环物流起步发展。

从政策调控看，随着《物流业发展中长期规划》和三年行动计划加快落实，现代物流工作部际联席机制逐步完善，物流业政策环境将趋于宽松。

二、细分市场加快调整

（一）公路货运市场

2015 年，公路货运量受需求影响将维持稳中有降，运能过剩局面依然没有改变。油价持续低迷与人力成本上涨相互抵消，成本仍然维持高位。加盟制和平台化将是行业整合的重要手段，推动行业集约化发展。部分企业经营不善加快退出市场，市场集中度稳步提高。随着货运联盟从起步走向深入，联盟内部的合作模式和运行机制成为发展关键，新的联盟模式不断涌现。随着政府修订相关政策法规，行业发展将趋于规范，营改增政策将出现利好，特别是无车承运人等新规则的确立，将给行业发展带来新的机遇。最值得关注的是“互联网 +”的商业模式创新，新的进入者不断涌现，不能够实现盈利预期的企业将被迫退出。新的商业模式抓住行业“痛点”，将逐步改变传统行业的运行规则。

（二）铁路货运市场

2015年，铁路货运量继续维持下滑态势，货源结构和运输需求逐步调整。煤炭、石油、棉花等大宗物资运输需求总量将持续下滑，“白货”市场将逐步发展成铁路货运市场的新增长点，对运输组织方式提出新的要求。随着铁路线路建设的不断完善和货运能力的不断释放，铁路快运班列运行向网络化发展将成为必然趋势，充分发挥在综合交通运输体系中的骨干作用。铁路货运将依托“站到站”运输的核心竞争力，拓展两端物流功能，加快铁路货运业务向全程物流的深度拓展。铁路货场加快向铁路物流中心转型，拓展节点服务功能，提升服务水平。随着铁路向市场化改革的深入推进，企业机制创新、管理创新、技术创新不断深化，铁路货运将全面向现代物流转型升级。

（三）水路货运市场

2015年，受需求端持续低迷影响，预计沿海干散货运输需求增速较2014年稳中有降。受前期延迟交付以及近两年新增船舶订单量较大的影响，沿海干散货船运力增速有可能再次反弹，运力过剩局面的缓解程度极其有限。由于货主企业、贸易集团船舶订单的加入，非航运企业订单数量依然高涨，成为近年来沿海散货运输市场运力过剩的主要原因。预计，2015年全球经济增速小幅提升，在发达经济体内生需求不断增强的带动下，全球集装箱海运量将持续回升，同比增长预计将达到6%以上。全球集装箱船舶拆解量会进一步下滑，同时将迎来运力交付高峰期，对国内市场冲击较大。各地将积极落实促进海运业健康发展的若干意见，加强海运企业与货主的紧密合作、优势互补，推动签订长期合同，有序发展以资本为纽带的合资经营。整合各种专项资金，推动运力结构调整、节能减排和运输效能提升。

我国港口货物吞吐量将保持“新常态”的稳定增长，增速预计将达到5%左右。随着欧美经济的逐步复苏，以及我国内贸集装箱业务的快速发展，预计我国港口集装箱吞吐量仍将保持6%左右的稳定增长。其中，受国内产业转移及内贸箱集装箱化率进一步提升影响，内贸箱量增速仍将好于外贸，预计可达到7.5%左右。我国各地港口将深化落实港口转型升级的指导意见。大量中小型内河港口将通过老码头改造，推动港口代际等级的提升，实现专业化、现代化、规模化发展。而沿海港口则将通过发展现代航运服务业、延伸港口服务功能来实现港口转型升级。部分地区港口金融等业务将得到有效发展。随着自贸区建设的推进以及扩围，港口深化改革将得到推进。允许外商独资经营码头的制度改革有望在自贸区试点地区推广，理货市场准入有望得到放开，沿海港口引航机构设置审批管理权限有望下放。

（四）航空货运市场

2015 年，预计航空物流持续稳定增长，货邮运输量增长 6% 左右。受跨境贸易增加带动，全球空运需求将增长 4.5% 左右。航空货运企业完善地面服务网络，加快向物流服务商转型。跨境电商成为国内各大航空货运公司改善货源结构、解决市场单向性问题的重要渠道。生鲜网购市场规模增速将有所放缓，新的竞争者不断涌入，生鲜产品产地直达依旧是航空物流的一个推进点。面对高铁的竞争，航空货运将逐步改变当前多段经营与运输的局面，将散落的环节连接起来，并加强与公路等运输方式的有机衔接，提高运输的整体效率。航空货运将加快取得海关、质检等方面的支持，尽可能缩短流程和时间，以赢得航空物流的市场空间。

（五）仓储服务市场

2015 年，预计仓储服务和仓储投资的增长速度将会有所下降。在一线城市，仓库租金还将有一定幅度的增长，但增速会有所放缓。仓储业投资将有重点选择，对仓储“洼地”进行填平补齐。国家战略涉及区域和产业转入地还会迎来一轮仓储设施建设的热潮。仓储业务结构适应产业结构调整和生活服务需要，原材料等大宗商品仓储企业将积极应对货量不足和场地外迁的变化，生活类仓储企业应对多批次、少批量、快分拣的要求。所有仓储企业都将加快技术改造和转型升级，主动融入供应链，提升自身的综合竞争力。

（六）快递服务市场

2015 年，预计快递业务量将完成 196 亿件，同比增长约 40%；业务收入将完成 2650 亿元，同比增长可达 30% 左右。在快递业务结构中，“网购”快递所占比重进一步提升，将达到 75% 以上，而商务快递的占比会进一步下降。快递专业化成为新的竞争焦点，将按照商品的属性和特性、个性化需求不断细分。中型快递企业专业化转型，小型快递企业个性化转型成为趋势。随着市场逐步饱和，大型快递企业将向综合型物流企业转型，积极向上下游市场延伸拓展。政府部门对快递企业监管将日益完善，简政放权和法治建设加快推进。电商企业“向下走”的农村战略给三四线城市、农村消费带来巨大变化，物流覆盖半径和纵深继续扩大。

三、行业物流深度变革

（一）电子商务物流

2015 年，我国电子商务市场仍将保持较高的增长速度。电子自建物流与第三方物流加快互相渗透、融合发展。电商物流市场旺盛的需求将吸引新进入者，电商物流专业化、个性化、差异化竞争日益增强，定时服务、自提服务、退换货服务、售后服务等增值服务成为行业热点。电子商务缩小了城乡差距，使得生产、消费、物流的改变将带来商业流通体系的重大变革。大数据应用使电商企业与物流行业之间形成联动机制，互联网使物流更“聪明”，电商物流机械化、自动化、智能化水平不断提升，物流效率大幅提高。电子商务借助互联网+优势加快拓展，推动天网、地网的优化重组，新的电子商务生态系统逐步建立。

（二）冷链物流

2015 年，我国冷链物流行业将持续向好。新一届政府对食品安全的重视进一步升级，中等收入人口数量不断增加，对冷链产品的需求越来越大，政府和消费者对冷链物流理念的认识越来越深，冷链投资力度持续加大，冷链市场规模继续扩大。第三方冷链物流企业依然规模较小，资金、网络、模式、人才压力进一步显现。冷链零担和宅配服务市场规模会进一步扩大，“最先一公里”和“最后一公里”配送的综合性差异化服务体验将是竞争核心。传统物流企业和其他领域竞争者进入冷链领域，一方面会为冷链行业注入新的血液和基因，另一方面对于传统冷链格局将带来巨大的冲击和挑战。

（三）汽车物流

2015 年，汽车市场规模增速将有放缓趋势，汽车企业间的竞争将会加剧，物流企业将面临服务收入、质量和渠道下沉等多方压力，行业将面临多重挑战。汽车零部件企业和售后服务备件领域物流市场将会是增速较高的市场，汽车物流领域将会有更多外部竞争者进入。车辆运输车新标准即将出台，整车物流公路运输格局加快调整，公铁水综合运输体系的完善和发展将对目前物流格局产生重大影响。移动互联网时代的汽车流通模式对汽车物流提出挑战。行业领军企业凭市场、技术、资金、人才优势加快国际化发展。“一带一路”的国家战略，为汽车物流企业“走出去”提供了重要保障。

（四）医药物流

2015 年，我国医药物流虽然增速将有所下降，但医药流通行业销售总额将会再创新高。医药电商特别是网络处方药、移动医疗和医疗器械将是主要亮点。由于新版 GSP 的实施，医药流通企业在软硬件投入和升级改造方面仍将会有较大提升空间，全国性的医药物流网络将进一步完善。《互联网食品药品经营监督管理办法》出台在即，第三方物流企业可以介入医药电商，传统医药物流和医药电商物流将加快整合。同时，随着医药电商的快速发展，医药物流“最后一公里”的建设成为一个新的瓶颈。伴随着移动互联网时代的来临，以用户为中心，去中心化、扁平化、平台化，建立新的医药物流生态圈已成必然，医药物流信息化建设将取得积极进展。

（五）钢铁物流

2015 年，我国钢铁业产能过剩问题依然严重，价格总体将处于低位运行。钢铁物流和流通市场需求持续萎缩，大批钢铁流通企业退出市场，企业盈利难度加大。随着高风险融资业务的清退，钢铁流通业正在回归交易的本质。未来一段时期，随着一批国家战略的实施，基础设施投资仍将保持稳步增长，钢铁需求基本稳定，奠定了钢铁行业物流发展的基础。同时，钢铁流通电商化趋势日益明显，通过互联互通、资源共享，新的业务模式不断出现，推动了行业的转型变革。钢铁行业物流业和流通业与上下游产业间的联动融合走向深入，产业链条逐步缩短，流通效率进一步提升。

（六）危化品物流

2015 年，化工行业主营业务收入约 9.5 万亿元，同比增长 8%，利润 4700 亿元，增长 7% 左右，危化品物流预计将保持快速增长。化工企业不仅对仓储设施提出更高要求，对于危化品物流也有更专业的需求，使用第三方物流比例呈扩大趋势。以集约化、规模化、现代化为特征的化工园区为载体，危化品仓储设施不断升级，储罐和立体库占比持续增加。随着传统石化产业向中西部迁移，拉动中西部危化品仓储设施建设，危化品仓储能力将有明显提升。由于危化品物流较高的安全要求，新技术在危化物流上的应用层出不穷。行业安全监管将进一步增强，企业持续加强风险管理。节能环保和低碳循环对危化品物流企业提出新的要求。

四、城乡、区域和国际物流加强协同

（一）国际物流

2015 年，随着自贸区扩围，我国自贸区建设将加快推进，自贸区通关便利化改善发展环境，对区域经济的“溢出效应”和“辐射效应”显著，将逐步形成区域物流节点和重要枢纽，助推区域经济一体化。随着“一带一路”国家战略愿景和行动的发布，区域的互联互通成为主要着力点，交通基础设施建设和物流网络布局成为重要组成部分，以中欧铁路、中亚铁路为核心的物流大通道将加快建设，多式联运积极推进。我国加快实施“走出去”战略，物流业作为重要的配套产业，跟随制造和商贸企业一同走出去，逐步建立覆盖全球的物流服务网络，大大提高产业转移和输出的成功率。随着跨境电商的持续快速发展，新的物流模式和监管政策不断出现，提升跨境电商物流时效，将成为跨境电商的重要保障和核心竞争力。

（二）区域物流

2015 年，随着京津冀协同发展、长江经济带建设，交通一体化成为重要支点，为区域物流一体化创造了良好的条件。京津冀物流协同速度加快，交通一体化将先行先试，物流布局和调整将逐步落地。长三角区域市场一体化加快落实，长三角综合运输通道和区际交通骨干网络将逐步完善，形成互联式、一体化的交通网络体系。珠江三角洲地区物流一体化有序推进，加快建设与港澳地区错位发展的国际物流中心，构建珠三角现代物流体系。

（三）城市物流

2015 年，城市物流仍将重点关注物流配送和快递等重点工作，积极推进共同配送试点，促进电子商务与物流快递协同发展。一批城市制定的共同配送实施方案陆续实施，有序规划和推进物流配送中心建设，加大市场主体培育和支持力度，提高配送车辆技术水平，完善物流配送服务网络，重点支持末端配送节点，解决“最后一公里”问题。城市货运车辆管理日趋严格，城市“禁货”和车辆禁行仍将深刻影响物流配送效率。通过环保手段和车型标准化，城市货运车辆将逐步规范，配送车辆“通行难”可能会有所缓解。

（四）农村物流

2015 年，中央一号文件继续关注“三农”问题，我国将加快农产品市场体系转型升级，加强农产品市场设施建设和配套服务，健全交易制度。政府将持续完善全国农产品流通骨干网络，加大重要农产品仓储物流设施建设力度，提高粮食收储保障能力。各级政府将继续开展公益性农产品批发市场建设试点，强调农业生产全程社会化服务机制创新试点。随着交通运输部等四部门印发《关于协同推进农村物流健康发展、加快服务农业现代化的若干意见》，将探索建立交通运输、农业、供销、邮政管理多部门共同推进农村物流发展的新机制，依托各部门和行业在农村物流发展中的已有基础和优势，加强资源整合共享与合作开发，构建“场站共享、服务同网、货源集中、信息互通”的农村物流发展新格局。

五、基础设施建设重点突破

（一）综合运输体系

2015 年，综合运输体系建设仍将积极推进，重点包括中西部铁路、城际铁路、国家高速公路“断头路”和普通国道“瓶颈路段”、内河高等级航道、新建干线机场等新开工重大项目相关工作。同时深化投融资体制改革，创新投融资模式，进一步鼓励社会资本进入交通基础设施领域，积极吸引社会资本。用好铁路发展基金平台，扩大铁路建设资本金来源。2015 年，铁路投资仍将保持高速增长，预计拟安排投资 8000 亿元以上，投产新线 8000 千米以上，基本完成“十二五”时期交通基础设施发展目标见下表。

“十二五”时期交通基础设施发展目标表

指标	单位	2010 年	2014 年实现值	2015 年
综合交通网总里程	万千米	432	481	490
铁路营业里程	万千米	9.1	11.2	12
公路通车里程	万千米	400.8	445	450
国家高速公路	万千米	5.8	11.2	8.3
内河高等级航道里程	万千米	1.02	1.27	1.3
管道输油（气）里程	万千米	7.85	11	15
民用运输机场数	个	175	202	230

（二）物流园区

2015 年，大规模的物流园区投资将会有所降温。随着土地节约集约利用方针的制定，总量控制力度加大，物流用地将持续紧缺。城镇化、“一带一路”、京津冀、长江经济带等国家战略的实施，物流园区在重点地区和产业仍有较大空间。我国物流园区布局将日益完善，协作共赢的园区网络加快形成。物流园区建设运营向专业化、规范化、标准化发展，物流园区与产业融合逐步深入，配套能力不断加强，园区发展逐步从追求规模扩张向服务提升转变。园区技术装备改造升级，以适应电子商务等快速响应的要求。铁路货运改革对物流园区开展多式联运提供重要机遇。供应链金融借助物流园区的载体，提升物流增值服务水平。

六、政策环境持续向好

2015 年，随着《物流业发展中长期规划》和三年行动计划开始实施，全国现代物流工作部际联席会议加强统筹协调，部门间合力逐步加强。一批物流管理政策措施将陆续出台，一批试点示范项目将逐步开展。政府继续推进简政放权，一批行政审批事项有望进一步放开。商事制度改革继续推进，注册登记制度有望进一步优化，逐步实现“三证合一”。市场准入负面清单加快研究制定，政府权力清单、责任清单加快出台，切实做到法无授权不可为、法定职责必须为。行业法治建设积极推进，危化品运输、黄标车等涉及安全和环保的监管工作日益严格。行业信用体系建设逐步推进，标准化建设进入新阶段，业界重点关注的税收、交通、用地、审批、融资、通关等方面的政策，在一些地方、一定程度上将有望取得突破。

（撰稿：周志成　审稿：贺登才）

参考文献

[1] 何黎明 .2014 年我国物流业发展回顾与 2015 年展望 .
[2] 恽绵 .2014 年第三方物流发展回顾与 2015 年展望 .
[3] 姜超峰 .2014 年仓储业发展回顾与 2015 年展望 .
[4] 王坚 .2014 年公路货运市场发展回顾与 2015 年展望 .
[5] 张晓东 .2014 年铁路物流发展回顾与 2015 年展望 .
[6] 赵楠 .2014 年港口物流发展回顾与 2015 年展望 .
[7] 张永锋 .2014 年国际集装箱运输市场发展回顾与 2015 年展望 .
[8] 李倩雯 .2014 年沿海干散货市场回顾与 2015 年展望 .
[9] 曹允春 .2014 年航空货运市场发展回顾与 2015 年展望 .
[10] 徐勇 .2014 年快递业发展回顾与 2015 年展望 .
[11] 冯耕中 .2014 年物流地产业发展回顾与 2015 年展望 .
[12] 田征 .2014 年保税物流发展回顾与 2015 年展望 .
[13] 刘伟华 .2014 年制造业物流发展回顾与 2015 年展望 .
[14] 洪涛 .2014 年商贸物流发展回顾与 2015 年展望 .
[15] 王国清 .2014 年钢铁行业物流发展回顾与 2015 年展望 .
[16] 马增荣 .2014 年汽车物流行业发展回顾与 2015 年展望 .
[17] 覃拥 .2014 年医药物流业发展回顾和 2015 年展望 .
[18] 秦玉鸣 .2014 年冷链物流发展回顾与 2015 年展望 .

[19] 万莹.2014 年电子商务物流发展回顾与 2015 年展望.
[20] 张滨.2014 年跨境电子商务物流发展回顾与 2015 年展望.
[21] 吴志华.2014 年粮食物流发展回顾与 2015 年展望.
[22] 王继祥.2014 年物流装备业发展回顾与 2015 年展望.
[23] 李红梅.2014 年物流标准化工作回顾与 2015 年展望.
[24] 晏庆华.2014 年物流信息化发展回顾与 2015 年展望.
[25] 郭肇明.2014 年物流教育培训发展回顾与 2015 年展望.

第二篇

专 题 研 究

第一章

物流服务业

2014 年第三方物流发展回顾与 2015 年展望

2014 年，世界经济变幻莫测，中国经济发展进入新常态，互联网经济进入了快速发展期，从资源、制造、分销、零售、消费、服务等各个层面、各个角度快速调整与变化，第三方物流服务也在发生着深刻的变化。

一、2014 年第三方物流发展回顾

（一）经济新常态下第三方物流市场需求发生了重大变化

2014 年是互联网经济的丰收年，阿里、京东相继在美国上市，互联网已经远远不只是一项技术，在电商改变人们的生活习惯从而改变世界的同时，传统制造业、分销业的供应链也应声而动，开始发生重大变化。有研究表明，世界供应链每隔 20 年就有一次重大的重组过程，2014 年正是新轮回的第二年，这一规律得到了验证。经济新常态的到来、科技的进步、社会的变化促使制造业与分销业不断的变革与创新，以适应竞争的需要。由此推动的需求变化是第三方物流发展最大的推手，将促使第三方物流企业逐步从恶性价格竞争的泥潭中拔出，转向物流解决方案与物流优化；并且形成新的规模不断扩大的专业供应链物流服务市场需求，进一步促进我国供应链物流的进步。主要体现在：

1. 客户供应链物流招标的决定因素开始从价格为主转向综合服务能力为主

过去第三方物流客户招标的主要目的是降低直接物流成本，因此价格权重曾高达 70% ~80%。但随着供应链的优化，供应链的效率更加直接地表现在客户的竞争力中，因此客户开始重视物流服务商的供应链服务能力与规划能力。

2014 年价格权重降低的客户越来越多，有的甚至降低到 40%，由过去简单追求降低基础物流服务价格向追求整体供应链的高效率转型。

2. 供应链物流外包逐渐增加

在过去大型制造业与分销业的物流招标中，最重要的是运输、仓储等基础物流服务的招标。而 2014 年招标业务中供应链综合服务、线边物流、生产物流等更高层次的综合性物流服务招标业务有了明显的增长，客户原来以自营物流为主的供应链物流核心操作部分也已经出现外包的趋势。

3. 大型企业集团的供应链业务开始整合

随着经济全球化和中国市场的开放，世界级企业在中国的布局已经进入多元化时代，过去以不同产品制造为核心的独立供应链体系开始打破，一些企业集团开始了跨供应链的一体化物流管理，因此对物流服务提出了在标准化服务基础上的柔性化服务能力要求，原来专业化物流服务开始向多品种、多品系、一体化方向发展，第三方物流服务不仅仅专于某种产品，而且要能够适应从大件、工业到消费品等多品类供应链物流的不同需求，具备全产业链的供应链服务能力。

4. 电商爆发性增长形成了特有的供应链形式

中国电子商务的快速发展，在改变商业模式的同时，也在改变着人们的生活习惯，进而改变了零售模式。京东商城、一号店、亚马逊为首的垂直电商和淘宝、天猫为主的平面电商形成了各具特色的电商供应链生态。垂直电商以自营物流为主建立了高效完整的物流体系，并逐步走向开放的社会第三方物流服务商。阿里的菜鸟则立足于建立适应平面电商的全国性电商节点网络体系，整合社会快递快运形成第三方供应链物流标准化服务体系。电商供应链物流体系的建立为第三方物流开拓了新的市场，同时也引来了新的竞争强者。

5. 制造与分销创新带来了柔性供应链的新需求

随着经济新常态的到来，制造业也在设计、制造、分销、服务上不断创新，带来了供应链的深刻变革，海尔的柔性供应链提出了更好、更快、更高的供应链需求。

第三方物流企业都深深地体会到客户在供应链上的变化，特别是世界五百强的跨国企业，供应链的调整带来了供应链服务需求较大幅度的调整。第三方物流企业将逐步从恶性价格竞争转向物流解决方案与物流优化，从而形成新的规模不断扩大的专业供应链物流服务市场需求，进一步促进我国供应链物流的进步。

（二）第三方物流服务经营环境不断变化

2014 年，供应链物流服务大环境发生了深刻的变化。

1. 互联网思维深入影响整个经济生活

从互联网的“免费”服务开始，传统的一分钱一分货的价值观被打破，物流企业从货代开始抢先踏入免费的行列，深圳的“阿里一达通”，打出了免费服务的大旗，不仅货代免费，对出口企业还实行补贴，颠覆了货代行业服务收费的商业模式。有的物流园区已经在试探仓储免费的思路，而在增值服务、特别是金融服务上寻找新的商业机会。传统企业以产品为核心，以客户为导向，现在互联网思维下开始更加关注的是供应链上的最终用户，以用户的价值为导向成为第三方物流企业和客户一起进行供应链物流优化的关键。

2. 基础性物流服务创新不断，平台与联盟势头正旺

2014 年已经成为物流的平台年和联盟年。这一年中，在安能物流和卡行天下的成功示范作用下，全国各地整合各种运力资源的物流平台和跨区域的物流联盟不断涌现，一部分专线公司通过平台与联盟的建立，利用网络化优势，实现标准化管理，作为第三方物流企业的外包供应商，有利于第三方物流提升物流服务水平。同时，有的专线公司开始计划向专业第三方物流市场发展，抢占第三方物流的低端市场份额。

3. 下半年起燃油价格持续下降抵消部分人力资源成本上涨压力

从 2014 年下半年起，国际燃油价格持续大幅度下滑。截至 2014 年 12 月 28 日，国内物流业使用最广泛的 0 号柴油价格下降了 24.46%，燃油成本占公路运输成本由 36.04% 下降到 28.84%。而人力资源成本却继续大幅度上涨，最低工资标准上涨了 14.1%，人力资源成本由占公路运输成本 22% 增加到 27%，两者相抵，公路运输成本下降 3.02%，有利于降低物流总成本。

4. 政府密集出台政策支持物流业发展

2014 年是政府对物流业支持空前的一年，最重要的是 9 月 12 日国务院印发的《物流业发展中长期规划（2014—2020 年）》，围绕中国物流业发展的多个核心问题，全面表明了政府对物流产业的引导与支持政策。明确了物流业是复合型服务业，具有基础性、战略性的地位。提出了“标准化、信息化、智能化、集约化”的“四化”要求。确定了农产品物流、制造业物流与供应链管理、再生资源回收物流等 12 项重点工程。聚焦了物流业的突出问题。政府着力在物流业发展的关键制约因素，降低物流成本，推动物流企业集约化规模化，改善物流基础设施，简政放权。第三方物流的经营环境获得持续改善。

5. 第三方物流企业逐步从单点创新向系统创新发展

创新已经成为引领第三方物流企业发展的新动力之一，由过去通过物流装备的创新、流程的创新、路径的创新逐步向跨体系，跨客户、跨产业的系统性创新发展，重点体现在供应链一体化服务的创新。

6. 规模物流企业税负较重的局面没有根本改变

根据中国物流与采购联合会的统计，在 2008—2012 年，物流企业税负支出增长幅度比营业收入和营业利润增幅分别高出 5.25 个和 6.52 个百分点；物

流企业税负高于全国同期宏观税负水平1.93个百分点；集团型企业跨区域纳税仍然无法实现，自2013年物流业营改增在全国施行后，规模物流企业特别是运输服务的税负明显增加，持续影响了第三方物流企业的积累和可持续健康发展。

（三）面对新常态，第三方物流服务创新发展

1. 我国物流企业加快国际化步伐

在经济全球化的大潮中，随着中国国力及创新带来的影响力不断提升、物流企业经营能力、服务能力不断增强，我国物流企业走向世界的步伐正在加快，建立强强联合的战略合作关系是基础模式。如长久物流与优特埃国际物流建立了战略合作伙伴关系，长久物流发挥20多年中国企业物流的运营经验，建立起国外汽车企业进口到中国、国内厂商出口（整车/零部件）到海外高效的供应链物流服务桥梁，通过优质的服务，释放更高的价值。中外运、中远等国有物流企业在新常态下重点建设外向型核心竞争力。中外运合同物流事业部与澳大利亚著名家居连锁企业SPOTLIGHT集团签署了综合物流战略协议，为澳方提供集运与物流增值服务。福建象屿集团控股的速传物流在新西兰建立了合资公司后进一步合资成立了联合森林集团，整合新西兰中小林场资源，为产业链上的林场主、砍伐商、物流服务商、终端需求客户构建高效、便捷的供应链渠道。走向世界的不再仅仅是价廉物美的中国制造，中国服务已经迈出了走向世界的大步。

2. 创新驱动应对新常态挑战

2014年对第三方物流来说是关键的模式创新年。过去第三方物流企业由于物流服务与客户的供应链紧密衔接，因此主要创新方向是与客户供应链物流相关的物流优化和物流技术。随着市场竞争的日趋激烈，第三方物流企业也在探索经营模式创新之路。宝供物流在构建以仓储为核心的物流服务王国基础上，提出了“四轮驱动，两翼齐飞”的全新发展战略，依托全国物流节点，推出了整合社会公路运输资源的“宝供快运”和基于移动互联的车货交易平台“一站网”，走向了第三方物流与社会公共物流服务的融合之路。九州通物流在开创“低成本、高效率”的九州通模式的基础上，发力B2B、B2C、O2O医药电商领域，好药师、去买药APP正式上线，打通医药电商最后一公里，开启大健康时代。

3. 产业融合，第三方物流深层次进入供应链物流服务

自2007年国家发改委召开制造业与物流业两业联动大会起，促进了制造业物流外包与第三方物流行业的崛起。到7年后的今天，两业联动已经进入两业融合的新阶段。日日顺物流紧随海尔的制造业变革，提出了“实网＋虚网”

的海尔逻辑，向下延伸打通最后一公里，在阿里资金的支持下快速布局全国城乡，实网上提出“按约送达、送装同步、超时免单”的差异化服务，建立了遍及城乡的专卖店、网店、联络点，融入海尔的柔性化供应链制造体系与O2O分销体系，构建起“用户为王”的海尔价值新体系。这一体系未来将进一步开放成为大家电的价值链开放平台。德利得物流在14年深耕第三方物流服务的经验积累上，2014年进一步发掘客户的深层次需求，提出了针对大型精密医疗设备的全程供应链一体化服务，把原来分散在供应链上，从进口到物流、从专业运输到临时存储的专业化加电通水、加液氦、终端用户的复杂专业化就位等各个环节的专业化、个性化物流需求，整合到一个供应链物流服务平台进行服务，实现效率优化，成本降低，服务标准，信息通畅，与客户的制造、服务紧密融合，成功为跨国医疗设备企业集团实施的一体化供应链全流程服务，供应链物流服务进入新的发展空间。

4. 横向拓展建立战略协同关系

在经济全球化与互联网经济的影响下，第三方物流企业不仅仅围绕客户的供应链深入拓展市场，同时主动出击横向拓展业务疆土，2014年中远物流与宁波市江北区人民政府、中国国际电子商务中心（CIECC）共同发起与建设中远物流电子商务平台项目，以中远物流全面电子化、信息化的操作模式为基础，为客户提供一站式全程供应链服务，打造一流的全球化公共物流平台。中信信通国际物流有限公司与中美天元投资集团签署全面业务合作战略协议，参与中美天元旗下医药产业全面供应链的优化、进口汽车销售及服务、化工产业物流服务以及物流地产的合作。首先，通过与海生药业开展资本层面的合作，全面优化广西海生药业的物流网络、销售通道和产业结构，在物流、仓储、运输、连锁终端等环节导入智慧物流系统，促进企业价值的全面提升，力求强强联合。以供应链、资本、价值链为纽带的新的战略联盟关系正在形成。

5. 紧跟需求与政策导向，拓展新业务领域

互联网时代下企业与社会的多种需求爆发，政府的管理策略也在调整，第三方物流企业紧跟形势创新解决物流中的痛点。招商物流为了解决流动资金链的问题，与招商银行合作，为承运商推出了“运费贷”的服务，切实解决了中小外协承运商“融资难、融资贵”的难题。国药物流紧跟医疗改革深化及新版GSP的机遇，全国整合资源，建立高效率的医药专业供应链体系。北京快行线物流有限公司破冰冷链宅配服务，与美国大使馆共同合作的美国大樱桃宅配，生鲜冷链宅配已经伴随电商的发展深入到百姓生活中，生鲜冷链宅配成为增长最快的专业物流市场之一。快递业龙头老大顺丰速运在优质快递基础上加大了拓展供应链物流服务的力度，成立顺丰冷运开拓冷链运输业务，同时从电商服务一体化物流服务入手进入供应链物流服务领域。

二、2015 年第三方物流业发展展望

2015 年，经济新常态下中国经济发展结构调整将逐步深化，电商化逐步渗透到经济发展的各个层次，互联网技术和其催生的新物流需求将深刻地影响着供应链的变化与调整，与供应链如影随形的第三方物流服务进入快速调整与变革的新时期。

1. 第三方物流的生态环境变化促使第三方物流服务变革

电子商务在终端销售领域爆发性增长的大趋势下，2015 年将逐步延伸影响到第三方物流服务领域，需求的改变，快递快运、专线联盟也开始抢占第三方物流市场，第三方物流服务企业上受到客户需求变化的压力，下受到供应商抢占市场的挤压，第三方物流与传统快递、快运的界限将模糊。快运、快递等社会物流服务企业通过大客户策略凭借基础物流服务优势开始进入第三方物流市场，第三方物流服务企业也将通过自有大客户货源为基础向社会物流平台化发展，新的物流服务格局将逐步产生。同时企业通过资本的介入，兼并重组，集中度将有所上升，第三方物流服务将向平台化和专业化两个方向发展。

2. 大型制造企业集团跨供应链一体化运营将成为常态

市场竞争的加剧与商业模式的变革，促使多元化的大型集团企业越来越重视供应链一体化运营，通过对集团内多个产业板块的供应链协同，从优化采购计划、集中采购、仓储协同、供应商管理库存（VMI）、集中运输、循环配送、线边协同等方式或运作模式，扁平供应链，减少环节，协同供应链运行，减少供应链渠道库存，加快库存周转，实现跨供应链的优化。由于客户跨供应链整合需求出现，物流企业的供应链优化将从第一阶段的成本优化，第二阶段独立的供应链优化，向第三阶段跨供应链优化方向发展。第三方物流企业也必须适应跨供应链协同的需求，提升信息化、标准化、柔性化、个性化的服务能力及供应链物流解决方案服务能力，满足客户跨供应链服务的需求。

3. 供应链物流服务外包需求从简单物流向高层次快速发展

随着竞争从独立的企业竞争走向供应链竞争发展，供应链协同越来越被供应链上的相关企业所共同关注，经营独立的第三方物流服务企业在供应链协同中扮演更重要的角色，解决跨企业的物流优化问题，制造与分销企业则更加关注优化与控制物流成本，通过标准化、精益化、信息化运营等手段降低成本、提高效率。供应链物流服务的外包将从简单的运输、仓储等单一服务向融合线边物流、库存管理、干线运输、分拨配送、产品包装、分拣包装、VMI/JIT、进口/出口等多种供应链物流服务的供应链一体化服务。具备供应链多种服务能力与经验的第三方物流服务企业将有更多的市场机会。

4. 标准化将成为提高供应链物流效率的关键之一

在供应链优化已经进入深层次的时候，无论是制造分销业还是物流业，都越来越意识到标准化是降低行业物流成本，特别是降低各个物流环节衔接成本的重要手段。供应链物流标准化工作重点将从原则与框架性的国家标准向更偏重于实际与应用的行业标准与企业标准发展。参与各种层次标准的制定并在企业的供应链物流服务中真正实施落实，将成为第三方物流企业的重要战略行动之一。

5. 国家强化对物流行业的规范化管理

十八大之后，国家政府部门调整了新常态下物流行业管理的基本思路，近期各部委在同城配送、电子商务、跨境电商等各个领域连续出台了多个行业指导意见，同时在社会诚信建设等方面不断加大力度，伴随新版 GSP 的实施，对医药物流、生鲜冷链等与药品食品安全紧密相关的行业加强监管。今后政府将进一步简政放权，加强行业的监管和行业发展的指导与支持。给第三方物流企业创造了良好的经营环境，第三方物流企业需要抓住机会，适应形势，规范发展。

6. 先进物流技术与装备将快速发展

随着中国经济结构调整的深入，人力资源等成本将持续上升，物流企业减员增效，提高劳动生产率的意愿日益增强，先进物流技术装备需求将出现大幅度增长。物流运营将向智能化方向发展，包括储位优化、配送线路优化、装载优化、库存分布决策、分布式订单优化、柔性供应链服务体系等。京东商城的“亚洲一号”成为大订单量、爆发性波动、单品拣选、快速响应、高效高速的电商仓储分拣系统标杆；九州通的自动化药品分拣仓储系统为医药专业物流的自动化运营创造了样板；各种高效率的自动、半自动分拣设施在物流行业快速应用，并从自动化向智能化快速发展，物联网技术渗入到物流操作的各个环节，实现供应链全程的可视化、可控化，大幅提高供应链物流的效率。中国物流先进装备制造业将伴随物流业的发展共同成长。

7. “互联网＋”趋势下，物流信息化、自动化程度将进一步提升

在移动互联网大潮的冲击下，供应链结构开始调整，以用户为中心、扁平化趋势开始显现，信息化和自动化成为供应链优化的两个重要抓手，目的是实现全链条的可视化、可追溯。大数据、云计算、智能化、模块化、集成化、平台化技术与模式的应用将打造一个新的供应链物流生态体系，为供应链上下游企业、政府监管部门、企业经营管理提供高效、便捷、齐全的云服务；中小型企业更多地选择 SaaS 模式的云服务系统，在提升信息化能力的同时，为平台汇总了大数据，提升了价值。在制造业供应链物流服务的过程中，外资企业也开始改变不与中国物流企业信息对接的固有观念，开始制订包含严格的网络安

全准入制度的供应链信息化 EDI 对接计划。“互联网 +”的趋势将越来越明显。

新常态奠定了中国经济发展的基本格局，“互联网 +”成为供应链物流进步的利器，人才需求、技术需求、装备需求、管理需求将伴随中国经济发展结构的变化而快速增加，中国第三方物流企业发展变革的新机遇来了。

（德利得物流总公司　恽绵）

2014 年公路货运发展回顾与 2015 年展望

一、2014 年公路货运行业发展回顾

2014 年中国公路货运政策环境利好不断、公路货运量出现滑坡、行业变革暗潮涌动，呈现出巨变前各种模式争艳的特征，未来谁将引领潮流，将会在 2~3 年内露出端倪。

（一）行业政策利好不断

1. 国家物流规划发布公路货运受到重视

2014 年物流行业最引人关注的是国务院于 9 月 12 日发布了《物流业发展中长期规划（2014—2020 年）》（以下简称《规划》），作为物流业中最基础运输方式的公路货运，规划中有多项内容涉及。2014 年 12 月 12 日，国家发改委以发改经贸〔2014〕2827 号文下发了《国家发展改革委关于印发〈促进物流业发展三年行动计划（2014—2016 年）〉的通知》，明确了 62 项主要工作和牵头单位，既对公路运输主管部门提出了规范行政、治理三乱的要求，也对公路货运企业提出了规范经营、不得超载超限的要求。同时，对公路枢纽的规划提出了要求。在全国高速公路基本建成后，国家又适时提出公路枢纽的规划，必将对今后货物转运节点和模式产生重要影响。

值得注意的是，在这次规划和行动计划中，国家将物流行业的标准和集装单元化提到了前所未有的高度。随着这些标准的落实，公路货运行业首先是会增加投资，更新采购必要的设备；其次是运输效率的大幅提升，公路货运企业将会从中受益；最后是装载率的下降，整车装载重量下降。

为落实规划和行动计划，全国现代物流工作部际联席会议决定每两个月召开一次会议，协调各部委的物流政策，解决涉及多部门的问题，一些困扰行业多年的老大难问题有望得到解决。

2. 国家领导人多次考察公路货运企业

习近平主席继 2013 年 11 月考察山东临沂物流基地后，又先后于 2014 年 5 月和 12 月考察了河南综合保税物流园区和江苏镇江的惠龙易通物流公司。李克强总理于 2014 年元月春节前在陕西考察了顺丰快递公司，之后于同年 8 月考察了上海外高桥物流中心，又在 11 月考察了义乌的快递网点。这届中央领

导高密度考察物流行业，是新中国成立后从未有过的现象，突显了国家领导人对物流行业的高度重视。

3. 交通运输部全面深化改革

2014 年 12 月 31 日，《交通运输部关于全面深化交通运输改革的意见》发布，这是继铁路运输行政管理划归交通运输部后首次明确了综合运输体系的建立方向，同时也为 2015 年及未来几年进一步深化改革指明了方向。

应国家对简政放权的要求，交通运输部将外商投资道路货运企业的审批权下放至各省市，取消了国家公路运输枢纽总体规划的审批，但保留地方审批权力。明确将道路货物运输、国际道路运输、道路运输站（场）经营业务许可证核发放入后置审批环节，缓解了企业办证的难度。但对于企业比较关心的道路运输许可证、车辆营运证、人员上岗证、车辆二级维护保养等与企业日常经营息息相关的行政许可项目基本未变，因此对企业而言，经营环境变化不大。

4. 车辆动态监督新规出台

2014 年一度引起争议的是 1 月 28 日公布的交通部 5 号令《道路运输车辆动态监督管理办法》。由于各省市要求各监控平台企业必须在各省市备案，并设置了各自不同的条件；实行初期北斗终端设备价格较贵，企业反响较大。后经交通运输主管部门协调后，基本得到解决。

5. 中物联公路货运分会成立

与国家政策环境改善的要求相适应，中物联抓住机遇，于 2014 年 11 月成立了中物联公路货运分会，公路货运企业将依托这个平台向政府反映诉求，推动行业升级转型。

总体而言，公路运输行业的经营环境日益公平和宽松，但真正达到理想状态还需要相当长的时间，不可没有信心，也不能期望过高。

（二）外部环境变化不断

1. 营改增对行业影响较大

2013 年 8 月，全国交通运输行业实现营改增。2013 年年底，道路运输业代开票基本被禁止。承担着 80% 公路货运业务总量的个体司机无法提供合适的发票，为客户提供运输服务的第三方物流企业由于车辆吨位不足甚至没有车辆，无法或无法足额开具 11% 的增值税发票，只能开具 6% 的货运代理业发票，反而是提供挂靠服务的所谓运输公司可以开 11% 的运输业专用发票。营改增后，公路货运企业因其业态不同，税负均有不同程度的增加，以靠人工提供增值服务较多的企业税负增加幅度尤为大。虽然部分地方政府出台了过渡性的财政补助政策，但受国务院 62 号文件《关于清理规范税收等优惠政策的通知》

的影响，各地补助处于观望阶段，让公路货运企业苦不堪言。企业纷纷自寻出路，给个体司机油卡以替代部分运费的情况成为普遍现象，整个行业税务风险极高。部分企业为规避风险，将有车辆的运输部分与实际提供运输服务的部分分拆成两个公司，实际提供运输的公司严格按税法提供6%的增值税发票，降低了企业的竞争力，行业的公平性受到破坏。

2. 移动互联网对行业影响加深

随着3G资费下调，4G网络逐步推开，智能手机广泛使用，80%以上的司机用上了智能手机，微信、移动支付也开始逐步为司机所使用，客观上为司机的移动互联网化做好了外部准备。滴滴、快的打车软件的崛起，让市场认识到司机的智能化手机应用是完全可行的，公路货运行业可能出现滴滴、快的的商业模式。

3. 铁路货运改革快速推进

2013年3月铁路总公司正式成立，2014年铁路总公司动作频频，各路局内的铁路循环货运班车的开立、铁路局间客车化的定班专列开行、规范化收费等。目前，虽未对公路运输形成重大冲击，但是如果解决了装卸、破损等问题，铁路将会对中国长途干线货物运输形成巨大挑战。铁路重回被放弃的零担货运市场，将会如何影响公路货运格局？长途专线会消失吗？公路与铁路如何良性合作？这些问题需要在实践中得到解答。

4. ETC全国联网启动

2014年年底，全国14个省市实现了ETC联网，按照规划，2015年9月底，全国所有省市高速公路将实现ETC联网，这意味着高速公路一卡走遍全国成为现实。高速公路ETC卡作为一种储值卡，意味着大额的资金沉淀，因此ETC卡的大户——卡车公司和卡车司机将成为各地高速公路公司争抢的对象，在ETC卡上的金融功能，如后付费融资等衍生业务拥有巨大的想象空间。同时，ETC卡统一付费，取得一张发票，将有效遏制路桥费假发票的泛滥，减少企业粘贴核查发票的人工成本。

5. 油价进入下行通道

2014年7月以后，受国际油价下降的影响，国内柴油价格一路下滑。到12月底，北京地区0号柴油价格从7.94元/升下滑至5.90元/升，下降约25%。这还是在2014年度两次提高燃油消费税的情况下实现的。12月，国家分两次将柴油燃油消费税从0.8元/升调至1.1元/升（2015年1月，柴油燃油消费税再次上调0.1元/升）。单纯公路货运企业，油价的下跌会带来8~9个点的成本下降，但是考虑到人工成本的快速上升，实际长途干线车辆运输成本下降约3~4个百分点如下图所示。

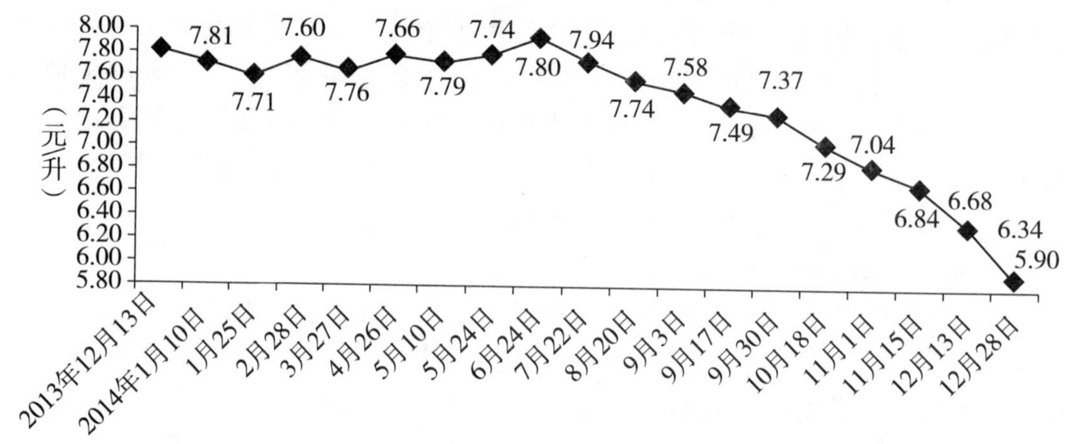

0 号柴油在 2014 年的价格趋势

注：价格来源于德利得物流成品油监控体系中的中石化零售数据。

6. 国四排放车辆靴子落地

国四排放标准原定 2011 年 1 月 1 日执行。2010 年 12 月 21 日，环保部表示，将 3.5 吨以上柴油车国四标准执行时间推迟一年，即 2012 年 1 月 1 日正式实施。此后，又陆续推迟到 2013 年 7 月 1 日，2014 年 1 月 1 日和 2015 年 1 月 1 日。采用国四排放后，由于大部分车辆采用 SCR 技术，需要使用尿素，每千米增加尿素成本约为 0.08 ~ 0.10 元，但由于油耗会下降，总体每千米的运输成本没有变化。在此期间，北京、上海等大城市都已率先推出了地方国四的强制要求。与此同时，国家加大对黄标车的淘汰力度，对黄标车采取扩大限行范围、多次年检等限制手段，并对提前淘汰给予一定的财政补助等政策，鼓励黄标车提前淘汰。这些年来，国家不断提高排放标准，加快了车辆淘汰更新的速度，公路货运企业和个体司机配合国家政策，默默地为环保买单，做出了巨大贡献。

7. 多项法规酝酿修改

涉及公路货运的多项法规、标准由于不能适应当前新的形势，交通运输部正在牵头组织修改。

《道路车辆外廓尺寸、轴荷及质量限值国家标准（GB 1589—2004）》的修改尤为引人关注。目前，长途干线主力车型——17.5 米大型车并不在标准范围内，是否放宽标准至 58 英尺，还是引进汽车列车，成为业界关注的焦点。侧帘车等一些新的车型能否列入国家标准也值得关注。

《道路运输条例》的修改同样值得关注，一般道路运输的经营许可是会放宽乃至取消还是为安全需要给予限制，无车承运人的界定与管理成为公路货运行业关心的问题。

《收费公路管理条例》的修改也值得关心。随着国家高速公路收费期陆续到期，是否继续收费，如何收费是关系到货运企业和个体司机乃至整个行业成本的话题。2014 年年初，山东省政府对山东境内已到期的高速公路延长收费一年的文件在全国引起很大反响，中央政府应给予明确的规定。

《汽车货物运输规则》的修改同样值得期待。1999 年公布的《汽车货物运输规则》，因目前货运形势发生了诸多变化，如到门、上楼、签收等，现有货规明显不符合市场需要，修改势在必行。

8. 在用尾板终于取得合法身份

目前市场上的尾板基本都是车辆获得行驶证后加装的，在部分地方运管部门看来，这属于“非法改装”，要处以巨额罚款。公路货运企业多次呼吁，收效甚微。在交通运输部和中物联的多次协调下，终于以出台新的国家标准的方式，使后装尾板的合法性得到认可。这对行业提高装卸效率，应对劳动力成本的上升，降低人员工伤和货物破损大有裨益。

（三）行业的救赎启动

1. 整体货量下降倒逼行业升级

2014 年中国公路货运行业与其他行业一样面临着产能过剩、供大于求的局面。货量下降会引起一系列的反应：企业效益下降、运输效率下降、新购车辆数下降、员工数量下降。更为重要的是，中国企业经历了几十年的高速增长，对下滑的市场毫无应对经验。但从另一个角度看，货量的下降，要求企业开始追求内部的精益管理，优化作业流程，会对行业的进步产生一定影响。这个过程对每个企业来讲都是痛苦的，但却是必需的。

2. 市场集中度逐步提高

零担物流方面，德邦一骑绝尘，以傲人的 120 亿元销售额继续保持高速增长。佳吉快运推出免费提送货后，抢了专线部分小货。华宇在中信入主后，市场动静不大。区域性零担公司纷纷酝酿突破之道，这类公司如果有资本的引导，组成全国性的零担网络，也许可以异军突起，在零担市场上独树一帜。合同物流受累于经济新常态，增长乏力，人工成本高企使经营步履维艰，但各公司纷纷寻求突破，或往 4PL、或往平台型企业、或往网络型公司谋求转型。专线作为最具操作性的公路货运业态，呈现出冰火二重天的情况。一些专线公司线路越开越密，货量越来越大，利润趋好。部分专线由于货量下降，生存困难。公路货运行业市场集中度的提高由此开启。

3. 货运 APP 各种模式、各路英雄粉墨登场

车货匹配平台纷纷露出水面，滴滴和快的打车软件大战使人们认识到，互联网是可以通过烧钱来培养习惯的，是可以迅速改变一个行业的，也是可以通过 APP 平台将司机和客户连接起来的。虽然货运不像出租车那样有政府监管要

求，但是诚信问题、结算问题、标准化问题同样存在。如何解决这些问题、从哪个角度切入、如何获得车源、如何获得货源，这些虽同为车货匹配公司，实则运营重点及战略部署都有各自不同的地方。具体是做长途整车、长途零担还是市内整车、市内零担哪个细分市场，每个公司又各有不同的侧重。从杀入这场混战的公司来看，主要有这样几类：互联网公司和原为物流企业提供定位服务的软件开发公司、三方物流、物流园区和其他，全民互联网创业也深入到传统的公路货运行业。移动互联网一定可以改变这个行业，但是究竟谁能成功尚不能预测。这个领域中最值得关注的是货车帮和路歌管车宝。

4. 平台类企业发展壮大

前几年崛起的安能物流、卡行天下等平台类企业由于受到资本的青睐，体量迅速扩大。安能物流加盟网点已经达到2100多家、分拨中心已达80家。卡行天下的分拨中心2014年年底达到23家。在这些企业的推动下，传统零担类企业也纷纷转型，佳吉推出免费提送货物服务，将很多专线公司的小货收入囊中。恒路也开展加盟服务，加盟网点也达到800多家。安能、卡行能否成功与资本密切相关，融资成为这些企业能否走下去的核心要素之一。能否获得融资成为部分物流企业的核心能力。

5. 专线联盟快速兴起

2014年另一个值得关注的现象是专线联盟的兴起。由于货量下降，部分专线公司经营不如以前、部分同行公司加入卡行天下等平台引起他们的强烈关注。他们既害怕加入平台后失去独立性，又担心以后会被行业所淘汰，因此联盟也就成为选择之一。所谓联盟就是多条专线公司统一服务标准、统一服务品牌、相互间调剂货物的一种企业联合体，结合得更为紧密的是多条专线公司成立一个合资公司。但目前联盟还刚刚起步，大多数联盟做的事情并不多，多年前老的联盟很多不能维持下去，这波联盟潮是否能持续也是值得关注的。

6. 融资租赁公司尝试大车队模式

以狮桥为代表的融资租赁公司，不但提供交通工具的融资租赁，而且提供合同运力的服务，通过自主招聘、培训驾驶员，提供车辆维修等服务，为货运企业提供全方位的合同运力服务。这种模式是否能成功同样吸引眼球。

7. 资本加快进入行业

2014年行业初创型公司从未像如今这般受到资本的高度关注。车货匹配平台、整合社会资源的公司等在天使轮资本动辄1000万元人民币，A轮拿到1000万美元的公司也为数不少。据公开披露，物流软件服务提供商OTMS获得A轮融资600万美元；长途车货匹配公司运满满A轮融资500万美元；物流招车平台货拉拉融资1000万美元；市内整车货运平台云鸟获得1000万美元的A轮融资；同城整车平台蓝犀牛获得3300万元人民币的A轮融资；物流小秘、神盾快运等都获得融资。再加上大量没有被披露的投资和自己找三五好友做天使的项目，资本的进入使这个行业引进了很多高级人才，将对行业形成重大的冲击，加速行业洗牌。

8. 跨界人士进入行业

跨界人士尤其是从事互联网行业的高级人才杀入这个行业。互联网思维在2014年受到高度重视。传统货运人考虑问题的出发点是从现实出发，我们有哪些制约因素，应该如何达到目标。但新的互联网人士考虑问题的出发点是，这个行业应该是怎样的。他们将打破很多传统观念，挑战传统物流人，未来他们是否能主宰这个行业值得关注。

9. 人工越来越贵，驾驶员越来越难找

2014年的人工维持着过去几年的涨势，大约上涨15%左右。B照及以上驾驶员越来越难招，根据现行规定，要获得可以驾驶牵引车的A2类驾驶执照，必须经过8年时间，大约花费2万多元。而且违章扣分达到12分，驾驶员将会受到降级处理。

各类驾照获取成本和时间表如下表所示：

各类驾照获取成本和时间

驾照类型	价格（元）	可增驾年限（年）	增驾学习时间（天）
C1	4500		
C1 增驾 B2	7000	3年	70 ~ 90
B2 增驾 A2	10000	5	70 ~ 90
B2 增驾 A1	7500	5	70 ~ 90

10. 行业媒体加快变化

由于微信等自媒体的快速发展，个人办自媒体受到了广泛关注，物流名人黄刚创办的物流指闻粉丝就达到10万人以上，每天发表行业新闻和对行业的看法。运联传媒每年举办的活动不少于6场，对行业热点问题给予深入讨论，引起业内人士的高度关注。

总之，无论什么业态，市场的淘汰已经开始，市场集中度在提高，组织化程度在提升，这是一个漫长的过程，如果能借助催化剂——资本的力量，将大大加速行业的整合。

二、2015年公路货运行业发展展望

2015年注定是个精彩纷呈的年代，我们可以展望以下几点：

1. 传统货运面临着外部环境可预期的变化

（1）货量稳中有降；

（2）油价低位徘徊；

（3）装卸工工资维持基本不变，但B照以上驾驶员工资会继续上涨15%左右。

上述条件考验着公路货运企业，随着部分企业退出市场，可以预期的是市场集中度会提高。

值得注意的是，由于驾驶员难招，目前大部分双司机运作模式的车辆可能会逐步改为单司机运作模式，对司机的服务区提出了客观要求。

2. 随着新规则的确立，会给行业带来新的运营模式

无车承运人法律地位的确立，市场会出现一股无车承运人热，一些原挂靠车辆以获得经营资质的企业会将挂靠车辆清出公司。

GB 1589的修订稿将车辆载重限制在49吨，如果严格执法的话，6×4和6×2的牵引车会逐步退出市场，企业会逐步购买4×2的牵引车。

3. 联盟潮起潮落

除了现在不同专线的联盟外，可能出现同一条线路的联盟，可能会对此线路造成垄断。联盟内的企业联合采购也是值得关注的现象之一。

4. 最值得关注的是互联网化

获得投资的公司疯狂跑马圈地，B轮融资会展开，企业估值会有超过1亿美元的公司出现。没有融资或者B轮融资不成功的，又不能实现盈利的公司将退出游戏。现在的车货匹配公司会死掉一批，投资泡沫会破裂。但是用户的使用习惯会被培养起来。这个市场还会不断有新的进入者，行业显现前赴后继的局面。在这个过程中，不断有新的商业模式试错。这不会是个漫长的过程，也许在1~2年中就会尘埃落定。

5. 收费公路政策调整值得关注

《收费公路管理条例》修订稿中，如何规定到期后还贷性和经营性收费同样值得关注，如果高速公路收费下降，必将导致整个公路运输成本的下降和效率的提高。

6. 营改增的进一步深入也值得期待

如果房屋租赁业和高速公路公司列入营改增，公路货运企业的房租和路桥费能够进入抵扣项，必将大大降低公路货运企业的税收负担。

让我们大家都期待着精彩的2015年，并为之添彩！

（新杰物流集团股份有限公司　中物联公路货运分会　王坚）

2014年铁路物流发展回顾与2015年展望

2014年是我国铁路货运组织改革全面推进的一年，是铁路体制机制改革、向现代物流转型升级的关键年。面对我国经济全面进入“新常态”带来的货源结构变化和市场需求新形势，铁路系统积极应对挑战，奋力攻坚克难，推动了铁路货运组织改革全面深化发展。

一、2014年铁路物流发展回顾

（一）铁路建设全面推进

根据国务院关于加快铁路建设的部署，铁路采取超常规措施，加大了在建项目组织实施力度，全面加快推进铁路建设。2014年全路完成固定资产投资8088亿元，同比增加24.2%。建成投产了兰新高铁、贵广高铁、南广高铁、沪昆高铁长怀段等一批重大工程项目，全年新线投产8427千米，创历史最高纪录。至2014年年底，我国铁路营业里程已达11.2万千米，其中高铁线路达到1.6万千米，以“四纵四横”为主骨架的快速铁路客运网初具规模，为释放货运潜能创造了有利条件。

（二）货运生产经营下行压力加大

受相关产业增长放缓，大宗物资货源不足等因素影响，2014年全国铁路完成货物发送量38.1亿吨，同比下降3.9%，其中，四个季度分别下降3.5%、1.5%、2.5%和7.8%。货物运输总周转量27530亿吨千米，同比下降5.6%，分别占全社会货运总量及总周转量的8.68%和14.91%，分别下降0.13%，0.73%。虽然总量下降，但铁路在重点物资运输保障方面依然承担骨干角色，2014年国家铁路棉花运量完成496万吨，石油运量完成1.28亿吨，煤炭运量完成16.41亿吨，粮食运量完成8260万吨，分别占全国总产量的80.52%、60.54%、42.40%、13.61%。一年来，铁路积极适应运输市场变化，加强货运营销和运输组织，大力拓展物流市场，深入实施多元化经营，推进土地综合开发，提升了运输效益。2014年国铁实现货运收入2854.8亿元，同比增长7.3%。

（三）铁路物流产品不断丰富

面对大宗物资运输需求乏力、白货运输物流需求增长强劲的市场新趋势，铁路总公司提出了“稳黑增白”战略，不断创新货运新模式、努力打造国际物流品牌，积极开发了零散货物快运班列、中欧班列、电商快递班列、高铁快递等系列产品。

1. 开展铁路零散货物快运

从2014年9月开始，铁路开始受理零散货物快运业务。铁路敞开车站收货，打破了客运、货运、中间站的分类，凡是具备装卸作业基本条件的车站全部开展散货快运受理和装卸业务；在全路4000余个货运营业站、无轨站敞开受理散货快运，形成了覆盖全国的、最大的散货办理网络，解决了办理点少的问题。

铁路着眼于适应快运市场需求、服务区域经济发展，打造了东北、京津冀、三晋、中原、九州、三秦、长三角、南方、八桂、西部、环疆货物快运等一批区域快运品牌，全国18个铁路局每天面向零散货物开行区域循环货物快运列车70余对，运行线路如下图所示，在京沪、京广、京哈、陇海、襄渝、沪昆等主要干线开行8对跨区域的货物快运列车，切实解决了零散货物无法受理、难以快速集结装运等问题。由此，铁路运量得到了显著提升，其中，2014年9月推行全路零散货物快运后，日发送量由最初的几百吨增加并稳定在200万件、7万吨以上水平，累计发送货物超过400万吨；2014年11月加强108个小品类运输后，运量由前10个月的日均发送1000车增长到1700车以上。

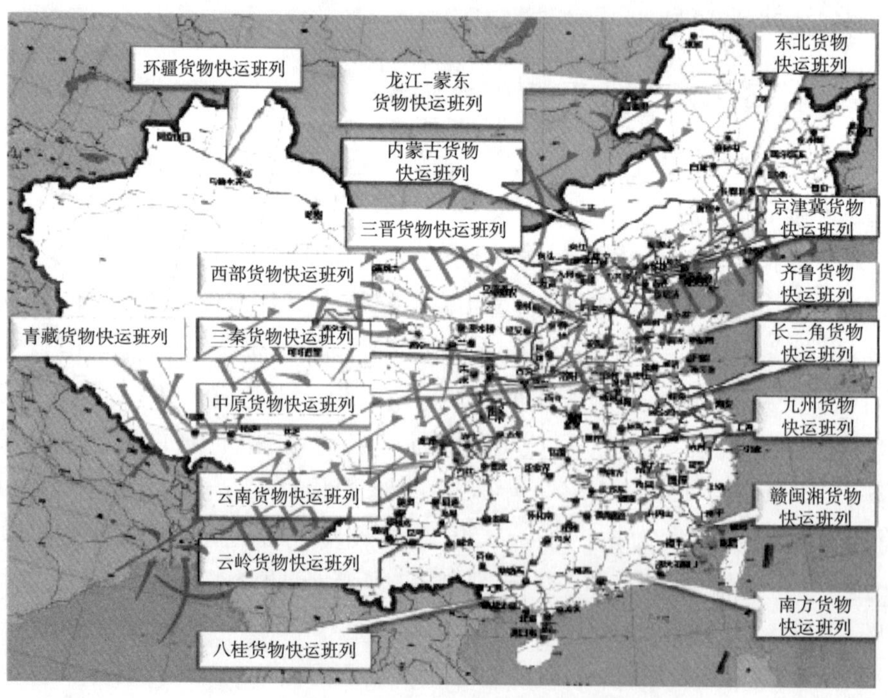

各铁路局零散快运货物班列开行径路示意

更为重要的是，上述零散白货快运班列均采用客车化开行方式，提高了铁路货物列车的准时性，极大改进了传统铁路运输组织方式，对未来进一步开拓物流市场奠定了良好的基础。

2. 优化中欧班列开行

2014 年，着眼于服务国家“一带一路”战略，结合深化货运组织改革，铁路进一步优化中欧班列运输组织，提高铁路国际联运服务质量，加快构建中欧铁路大通道，积极打造国际物流知名品牌。按日行 1000 千米以上，在西、中、东 3 条通道铺画了中欧班列运行线；按照品牌标志、运输组织、全程价格、服务标准、经营团队、协调平台“六统一”的原则，打造中欧班列品牌。全年共开行中欧班列 308 列，发送集装箱 26070TEU，较上年同期多开 228 列，增长 285%；组织自欧洲至中国的回程班列 28 列。表 1 为 2014 年中欧班列开行情况统计。2014 年 12 月 10 日列车运行图调整之后，铁路安排了 19 条中欧班列运行线，同时安排了 15 条中亚班列运行线、28 条铁水联运集装箱快运列车运行线。中欧班列的快速发展，为中欧、中亚沿线各国间经贸发展起到了积极的促进作用，为国家“丝绸之路经济带”建设提供了强有力的运力保障，促进了沿线各国间经贸交流发展。

表 1　2014 年中欧班列开行情况统计

序号	班列名称	首趟开行时间	2014 年开行列数
1	“渝新欧”班列	2011. 03. 19	100
2	“蓉新欧”班列	2013. 04. 26	49
3	“郑新欧”班列	2013. 07. 18	86
4	“苏满欧”班列	2013. 09. 30	34
5	“汉新欧”班列	2014. 04. 23	25
6	“合新欧”班列	2014. 06. 26	13
7	“义新欧”班列	2014. 11. 18	1

资料来源：根据网上新闻报道整理。

3. 开发电商快递班列

为适应我国电子商务和快递业迅速发展的需要，提高铁路服务质量，降低社会物流成本，铁路总公司在广泛市场调查、深入客户对接的基础上，充分考虑客户对速度、时间、价格、仓储与分拣等方面的要求，按照敞开受理的原则，于 2014 年 7 月和 8 月推出了电商快递货运班列新服务。在北京、上海、广州、深圳四地间开行了三对六列电商快递班列，通过优化作业环节，提高安检效率，为我国快递干线运输提供了快速、便捷服务，给电商快递市场降本提效带来了新格局。

4. 扩大高铁快递规模

随着部分高铁线路在2014年的陆续开通，截止到12月30日，全国高铁快递办理城市已达151个，新增了哈密、包头、烟台、威海、湘潭、东莞、汕头等多个高铁快递城市，主要分布在广东、湖南、山东等省高铁沿线，使更多中、小城市的客户能够体验高铁快递安全、准时、快捷的服务。同时为适应高铁快递业务的快速发展，提升服务品质，中铁快运公司在合肥建成全国首家高铁快递呼叫中心并投入运营，为客户详细了解高铁快递开办城市和产品种类提供了实时咨询服务渠道。

除上述货运新产品外，在2014年国庆黄金周和北京APEC会议期间，铁路还成功组织了北京去往浙江、陕西、四川等6个方向的自驾游汽车运输业务试点，取得了良好的市场反应。

（四）铁路物流服务体系逐步完善

以准时制运输、市场化定价、承揽物流外包、拓展增值服务为重点，铁路物流服务质量得到了全面改善，企业发展活力明显增强。

1. 推行准时制运输

2014年7月1日调图之后，和谐型货运机车担当的普通货物列车首次全部实现按时速80千米达速运行。着力于稳定市场、固定发到站、适应高附加值货物运输的运到时限等要求，货车提速加快了大宗和高附加值货物的周转，稳定了运输时刻和货源，保障了货物准时交付，提升了运输效率效益。

2. 探索运价改革

2014年9月全路开办零散货物快运业务之后，铁路建立了与市场对接的货物快运计价体系，在国家政策范围内实行了完全清晰、市场化的一口报价、一次核收。对市场需求大、铁路运量小的白货实行了按实重（体积）计费报价。在此基础上，铁路总公司推出了新的货运“一口价”报价收费方式，对所有货物运输探索实行社会物流业通行的完全市场化的“一口价”。

3. 承揽物流外包项目

面对货源结构的重大调整，为扩大市场份额，适应制造业与物流业融合发展的趋势，铁路放下身段，大力开展市场调查，主动参与生产加工型企业的物流招投标项目，积极承揽物流外包业务。各路局重点展开了对家电、医药等108个小品类货物物流需求特点的分析，掌握了企业物流外包合同履行现状和2015年度物流招投标活动安排，为铁路承揽第一手货源，与企业深入合作，制订个性化投标书和物流解决方案提供了基础。

4. 拓展物流增值服务

以货运场站为突破，在提供货物到发、中转、装卸、搬运服务的基础上，各路局积极拓展仓储、堆存、定制等增值服务，目前各路局均有部分货场可提供上门装卸、仓储、装卸加固材料提供和接取送达服务。此外，部分路局在电子商务、城市配送、金融物流、供应链解决方案等方面也已展开探索。铁路在物流增值服务方面的尝试和完善，有力地增强了铁路在物流市场上的竞争力。

5. 转型发展实现突破

2014 年各铁路局向物流企业转型发展取得了实质进展，当年 3 月，上海铁路局成为首家以铁路局为主体的全国 5A 级物流企业资质单位。“5A 级物流企业”称号的获得对上海铁路局在承揽物流外包项目，拓展服务规模，提升铁路货运服务的品牌效应等方面产生了积极效果。其他路局结合自身实际，积极申报 5A 级物流企业，截至 2015 年 1 月，全路已有 13 个铁路局和 3 个专业运输公司通过审核评估并获得 5A 级物流企业资质，为全面开展承揽物流外包项目创造了有利条件。表 2 是铁路局及专业运输公司获得 5A 级物流企业情况统计表。

表 2　　铁路局及专业运输公司获得 5A 级物流企业情况

<table>
<tr><th>评估通过时间</th><th colspan="2">铁路局及专业运输公司</th></tr>
<tr><td>2005. 7</td><td colspan="2">中铁快运股份有限责任公司</td></tr>
<tr><td>2012. 7</td><td colspan="2">中铁集装箱运输有限责任公司</td></tr>
<tr><td>2014. 2</td><td colspan="2">上海铁路局</td></tr>
<tr><td rowspan="7">2015. 1</td><td>沈阳铁路局</td><td>北京铁路局</td></tr>
<tr><td>太原铁路局</td><td>郑州铁路局</td></tr>
<tr><td>武汉铁路局</td><td>西安铁路局</td></tr>
<tr><td>济南铁路局</td><td>南宁铁路局</td></tr>
<tr><td>成都铁路局</td><td>昆明铁路局</td></tr>
<tr><td>兰州铁路局</td><td>乌鲁木齐铁路局</td></tr>
<tr><td colspan="2">中铁特货运输有限责任公司</td></tr>
</table>

（五）铁路货运改革制度日益规范

随着货运组织改革不断深入，铁路制定并发布了系列改革文件，为铁路发展提供了规范化的制度保障。结合改革实际，铁路总公司重新修订了《铁路货运组织改革二十条纪律要求》，针对敞开受理、排队装车、规范收费、门到门运输等方面分别提出“八不准”、“四必须”、“五严格”、“三禁止”的红线管理要求。为加快货运市场的拓展和铁路物流产品的推广，2014 年铁路总公司相继发布了《关于支持中铁快运发展快递物流业务的意见》、《关于试行批量零散货物快运有关事项的通知》、《关于做好电商快递班列开行工作有关事项的通知》、《关于加强 108 个小品类运输组织的通知》等近 40 份文件，重点明确了在作业标准、考核机制、计费事项、跨局协调、服务质量等方面的要求。此外，铁路加强了关于运价与清算机制、招投标、申办 5A 级物流企业等工作的部署，为进一步推动铁路物流转型升级提供了坚实的保障。

二、新常态下铁路物流面临的机遇和挑战

我国铁路发展正处于经济发展步入新常态的重要战略机遇期，如何适应新常态、把握新常态，推动铁路物流往更系统、更深层次的方向发展，这对铁路而言既是机遇，也是挑战。

（一）新常态为铁路转型发展注入新的动力

随着我国铁路网规模不断扩大，特别是高铁迅速发展，运输能力显著提升，为适应新常态下经济结构调整和内需扩大奠定了基础。2014 年 6 月公布的《物流业发展中长期规划（2014—2020 年）》中，明确提出提高铁路运输比重，在新常态的发展中为铁路货运转型提供了契机。同时，社会物流总量将保持稳定增长，尤其是高附加值货物存在较大市场，这对于铁路发挥干线运输和路网优势、实现货运结构优化、推进多式联运，进一步提高内涵式发展水平和经营效益，提供了重要机遇。

（二）新常态给铁路货运发展带来新挑战

随着国家宏观经济增速放缓，经济结构调整、产业转型升级、节能减排力度不断加大，煤炭、矿石、钢铁等大宗物资的社会运输需求总量将持续下滑，大宗货源形势十分严峻，相反，“白货”市场在新常态的形成中逐步发展成物流市场的新增长点。在新形势下，社会货源结构和运输需求规模发生了重大变化，新的运输市场格局正在加快形成，各种运输方式的竞争更加激烈，而服务水平已成为核心竞争力的重要内容，这对于铁路在经营下行压力持续加大的态势下，适应现代物流发展的新要求，提出了极大挑战。

三、2015 年铁路物流发展展望

2015 年是铁路改革的深化之年，也是全面完成铁路“十二五”物流发展规划的收官之年。根据铁总年度会议精神，2015 年全路将以市场为导向，以效益为中心，主动适应新常态带来的新变化。铁路物流有望在以下几个方面进一步着力，努力开创铁路物流发展新局面。

（一）全面深化铁路货运组织改革

面对新常态带来的新变化，铁路向市场化改革仍将深入推进，制度建设和机制创新将进一步发展，企业发展活力将进一步增强。铁路将主动适应经济发展新常态，推进内部管理体制创新、运输组织改革创新、安全管理创新、铁路技术创新和经营机制创新，铁路货运将向现代物流企业全面深化转型发展。下一步将聚焦提高货运服务质量，提升铁路物流服务功能，重点解决运到时限管理、运价管理、配套能力建设等诸多方面的问题。

（二）大力推进铁路基础设施建设

铁路“十二五”规划发展目标确定到 2015 年年底实现铁路总营业里程 12 万千米左右，快速铁路网营业里程 4 万千米以上，目前，还存在一定的差距。李克强总理 2015 年政府工作报告明确提出今年国家铁路拟安排投资 8000 亿元以上，投产新线 8000 千米以上，其中，将重点完善中西部铁路建设，带动区域经济发展。同时，铁路将通过自主开发、转让、租赁等多种方式盘活利用现有建设用地，以市场化方式引进社会资本实施土地综合开发，促进铁路基础设施建设良性发展，进一步提高铁路建设项目的资金筹集能力和收益水平。

（三）着力打造铁路快运班列网络化开行

随着铁路线路建设的不断完善和货运能力的不断释放，在充分利用路网资源的基础上，使铁路运力资源的配置更加符合市场需求，寻求与各种运输方式密切配合，以满足客户时效需求，铁路快运班列运行向网络化发展将成为必然趋势。首先，各路局将进一步明确适宜铁路快运发展的重要载体城市，从而构建层次分明的快运班列始发、终到、中转城市的网络结构，实现网络节点的有效支撑。其次，各路局平衡协调各自的市场需求和运输能力，拉通跨局节点城市间的线路，采用干线加支线结合的开行方式。最后，全面实现铁路快运班列的快速中转换挂作业，充分考虑集中到达作业时间的要求和场站快速作业的能力匹配，为铁路快运班列网络化开行提供基础保障，从而发挥铁路在综合交通运输体系中的骨干作用、降低社会物流成本。

（四）全面加快货运场站向铁路物流中心转型发展

在货运组织改革深入推进的过程中，铁路货场向铁路物流中心转型升级的需求尤为突出。铁路将结合既有货运场站存在的问题及国内外物流中心发展情况，撰写并出台铁路物流中心设计规范。各路局将依据发到货源的物流需求，规划货场改扩建和物流中心布局、建设，强化物流设施设备建设，拓展节点服务功能。积极打造铁路物流中心服务品牌，依托品牌产品与品牌营运项目，争取全国优秀物流园区称号，提升铁路物流中心服务水平和经营效益。

（五）大力发展铁路全程物流服务

铁路将依托“站到站”运输的核心竞争力，在“门到门”运输基础上拓展两端物流功能，加快铁路货运业务向全程物流的深度拓展。一是提高接取送达能力。铁路将强化两端与公路的衔接，进一步发挥区域间干线运输的优势，形成铁路区域运输、公路末端配送的模式，采取自建和合作的方式提升接取送达能力。二是大力拓展铁路物流外包业务。按照物流整体外包的市场通行规则，铁路将逐步完善跨局物流协调机制，各铁路局将采取独立投标或跨局协作的方式，承揽物流整体外包业务。三是探索发展供应链管理业务。在全程物流服务的基础上，进一步延伸服务链条，深入了解客户的物流运作流程和管理模式，详细分析客户在采购、生产、销售等环节中的物流需求，开展金融物流、商品展览、市场交易等业务。

（六）提升运输组织信息化水平

一体化信息集成平台是铁路完成信息化集中建设的重要任务，铁路将重点构建先进的信息化架构，实现互联互通、资源整合、信息共享、应用集成，与主营业务深度融合，提高总公司信息化能力、增强企业核心竞争力、提升生产经营管理效率和科学决策水平。同时，总公司将组织研究开发基于 12306 网站的货物电子交易平台，推出更加贴近市场的电商业务，这将是铁路货运融入现代物流的更大幅度的突破，会带给铁路货运更深层次的变革。

2015 年，铁路各领域“十三五”发展规划研究编制工作将全面展开，规划将重点探索在经济新常态、新型城镇化、“一带一路”、两型社会建设等一系列国家重大战略的背景下，铁路系统及铁路物流谋求发展的新方向、新思路和新举措。

（北京交通大学交通运输学院物流工程系　张晓东　吴勇锋）

参考文献

[1] 李克强. 2015 年政府工作报告 [R]. 第十二届全国人民代表大会第三次会议, 2015-03-05.

[2] 盛光祖. 以创新发展为主线　主动适应新常态努力开创铁路改革发展新局面 [R]. 中国铁路总公司工作会议, 2015-01-29.

[3] 郭玉华. 在货运营销研讨会议上的讲话提纲 [R]. 全国铁路货运营销研讨会议, 2014-04-28.

[4] 杨欣. 回眸 2014・中国铁路货运 [N]. 人民铁道报, 2015-01-29 (A3).

[5] 卫晓菁, 张晓东, 韩伯领. 铁路货运组织改革发展对策研究 [J]. 综合运输, 2015 (1): 31.

[6] 中国铁道网. 盘点 2014 年铁路大事记　期盼铁路辉煌 2015 [EB/OL]. http://www.chnrailway.com/html/20150122/726954.shtml, 2015-01-22.

2014年港口物流发展回顾与2015年展望

一、2014年港口物流发展回顾

2014年，我国经济增速在保持相对平稳的基础上略有下滑。受全球经济依旧疲软的影响，我国对外贸易下滑明显，除第三季度进出口总额保持7.7%增速外，其他三个季度对外贸易增长均相对乏力。在此背景下，2014年港口生产总体情况不及2013年，增速明显下滑，如图1所示。

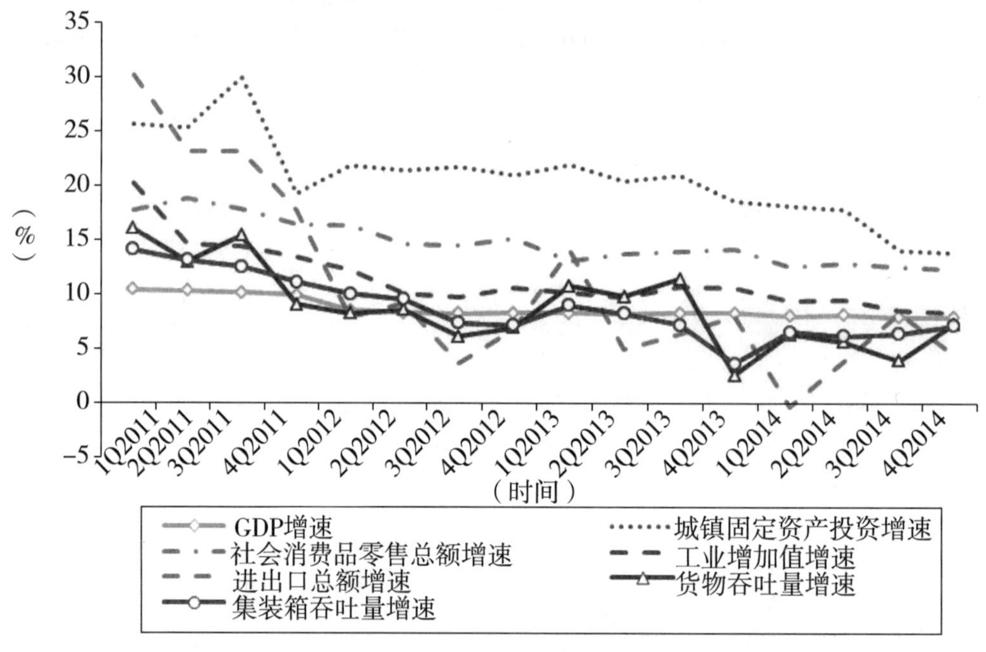

图1　我国主要经济指标与港口吞吐量增长变化趋势

数据来源：国家统计局，中华人民共和国交通运输部。

（一）港口生产增速小幅下滑

受国内经济低速增长的影响以及港口吞吐量统计口径的调整，2014年全国规模以上港口货物吞吐量增速明显放缓，全年共完成货物吞吐量112亿吨，同比增幅仅为5.2%，增速较2013年下滑3.7个百分点。集装箱吞吐量增速虽也有所下滑，但相对保持稳定。2014年，规模以上港口集装箱吞吐量达到2亿

TEU，同比增长5.8%，如表1所示。

表1　2008—2014年我国规模以上港口货物吞吐量及集装箱吞吐量

年份		2008	2009	2010	2011	2012	2013	2014
货物吞吐量	吞吐量（亿吨）	58.7	69.7	80.2	90.7	97.8	106.5	112.0
	同比增长（%）	11.6	18.7	15.1	13.1	7.8	8.9	5.2
外贸货物吞吐量	吞吐量（亿吨）	18.99	21.8	24.73	27.57	30.2	33.1	35.0
	同比增长（%）	6.0	14.8	13.4	11.5	9.5	9.6	5.7
集装箱吞吐量	吞吐量（亿标准箱）	1.29	1.22	1.45	1.64	1.77	1.89	2.00
	同比增长（%）	13.2	-5.4	18.9	13.1	7.9	6.8	5.8

2014年，沿海和内河港口货物吞吐量增速均明显放缓。仅有唐山、湛江、福州、虎门、芜湖、锦州等少数几个港口依然保持两位数增长。其中，唐山港凭借大宗能源运输服务，货物吞吐量保持快速增长。虽然增速较2013年下滑近10个百分点，但仍凭借两位数的增长，在全国排名中由第七位上升为第四位。大部分一线港口货物吞吐量保持低速甚至负增长，例如上海、深圳两港，反映出我国港口发展已进入“新常态”，吞吐量已不能作为考核港口发展的唯一指标。其中，上海港随着黄浦江下游港区和罗泾港区的功能转型，部分散杂货港口装卸业务迁移，对上海港吞吐量增长产生一定影响。

2014年，我国亿吨以上港口已达到34个，其中，沿海港口23个、内河港口11个，芜湖、杭州、锦州三个港口分别以18.1%、6.6%和17.2%的增速进入亿吨大港的行列。除锦州港外，其余两个港口均为内河港口。其中，吞吐量达到2亿吨以上的港口增加6个，达到19个。2012—2014年我国亿吨以上港口货物吞吐量排序情况详见表2。

表2　2012—2014年我国亿吨以上港口货物吞吐量排序

排序	港口名称	2014年		2013年		2012年	
		吞吐量（亿吨）	同比增长（%）	吞吐量（亿吨）	同比增长（%）	吞吐量（亿吨）	同比增长（%）
1（1）	宁波—舟山港	8.73	7.84	8.10	8.87	7.44	9.73
2（2）	上海港*	7.55	-2.71	7.76	5.43	7.36	2.22
3（3）	天津港	5.40	7.78	5.01	5.25	4.76	5.54
4（7）	唐山港	5.01	12.33	4.46	22.19	3.65	16.99

续 表

排序	港口名称	2014 年		2013 年		2012 年	
		吞吐量（亿吨）	同比增长（%）	吞吐量（亿吨）	同比增长（%）	吞吐量（亿吨）	同比增长（%）
5（4）	广州港*	4.80	5.49	4.55	4.84	4.34	1.17
6（5）	苏州（内河）港	4.79	5.51	4.54	6.07	4.28	12.63
7（6）	青岛港*	4.65	3.33	4.50	10.57	4.07	8.53
8（8）	大连港*	4.28	5.16	4.07	9.12	3.73	10.36
9（10）	日照港	3.35	8.41	3.09	9.96	2.81	11.07
10（9）	营口港	3.34	4.38	3.20	6.31	3.01	15.33
11（11）	秦皇岛港	2.74	0.37	2.73	3.80	2.63	3.95
12（13）	烟台港	2.37	6.76	2.22	10.45	2.01	11.67
13（12）	深圳港	2.23	-4.70	2.34	2.63	2.28	2.24
14（14）	南通（内河）港	2.20	7.32	2.05	10.81	1.85	6.94
15（15）	连云港	2.10	3.96	2.02	9.19	1.85	11.45
16（16）	南京（内河）港*	2.09	3.47	2.02	5.21	1.92	10.34
17（17）	厦门港	2.05	7.33	1.91	11.05	1.72	10.26
18（18）	北部湾港*	2.04	9.09	1.87	7.47	1.74	13.73
19（19）	湛江港*	2.03	12.78	1.80	5.26	1.71	8.92
20（20）	黄骅港*	1.78	4.09	1.71	36.80	1.25	12.61
21（22）	泰州（内河）港*	1.56	1.96	1.53	18.60	1.29	29.00
22（24）	重庆（内河）港*	1.48	8.03	1.37	9.60	1.25	10.62
23（25）	福州港	1.44	13.39	1.27	11.40	1.14	11.76
24（23）	镇江（内河）港*	1.39	-1.42	1.41	4.44	1.35	21.62
25（27）	丹东港	1.38	14.65	1.20	25.00	0.96	26.32
26（31）	虎门港*	1.29	17.27	1.10	115.69	0.51	50.00
27（26）	江阴（内河）港*	1.24	-1.90	1.26	-4.55	1.32	3.13
28（30）	岳阳（内河）港	1.20	9.09	1.10	5.77	1.04	15.56
29（29）	泉州港	1.12	1.82	1.10	5.77	1.04	10.64

续　表

排序	港口名称	2014 年		2013 年		2012 年	
		吞吐量（亿吨）	同比增长（%）	吞吐量（亿吨）	同比增长（%）	吞吐量（亿吨）	同比增长（%）
30（-）	芜湖（内河）港*	1.10	18.11	0.93	12.75	0.83	10.53
31（32）	珠海港	1.07	7.00	1.00	29.87	0.77	6.94
32（28）	嘉兴内河	1.01	-7.82	1.10	1.85	1.08	1.89
33（-）	杭州（内河）港*	1.00	6.59	0.94	3.13	0.91	1.85
34（-）	锦州港*	1.00	17.19	0.85	16.02	0.74	-4.63

注：*表示 2014 年吞吐量为预测值；排序中括号内数字为 2013 年排序。

1. 货物吞吐量外贸增速震荡下行，内贸基本保持低速平稳增长

逐月来看，从 2013 年四季度开始，我国港口货物吞吐量增速便一直保持低位震荡。直到 2014 年四季度，受我国内贸吞吐量拉动的影响，我国港口货物吞吐量增速有所回升。总体来看，2014 年上半年我国外贸吞吐量增速好于内贸，但全年外贸货物吞吐量增速整体呈现震荡下行态势。尤其是三季度后，由于 7、8 月步入锅炉等设备检修高峰，钢铁下游市场需求减弱，铁矿石进口量明显减速；再加上国内煤炭企业压低煤价，严重冲击挤压进口煤空间，同时中国煤炭余量增多，电厂负荷未如预期大幅上涨，耗煤量明显减少，煤炭进口量明显缩水。从国际方面看，国家人口红利减弱、物料成本提高、环境压力凸显削弱了国内产品的竞争力，使出口面临周边国家和地区的挑战；而发达国家“再工业化”、货币贬值以及贸易保护策略进一步阻碍了中国外贸进出口的增长。基于上述因素，受我国外贸吞吐量占比较大的大宗能源货物需求减弱，外贸货物吞吐量增速四季度开始逐月走低。相对而言，受圣诞节、春节等节前消费因素影响，内贸吞吐量在四季度表现相对较好。但整体来看，外贸吞吐量的增速仍高于内贸，2014 年我国规模以上港口累计完成外贸货物吞吐量 35.0 亿吨，同比增长 5.7%，内贸货物吞吐量增幅达到 4.92%，如图 2 所示。

就沿海和内河港口来看，从 2013 年开始到 2014 年，沿海港口货物吞吐量增长情况就明显好于内河。2014 年，沿海规模以上港口完成货物吞吐量 76.89 亿吨，同比增长 5.6%；内河港口完成货物吞吐量 35.11 亿吨，同比增长 3.6%。其中，沿海港口的内贸货物吞吐量增长情况好于内河港口内贸吞吐量增速。2014 年，沿海内贸吞吐量达到 44.85 亿吨，同比增长 6.8%；内河港口内贸吞吐量为 31.7 亿吨，同比增长仅为 3.9%，如图 3 所示。

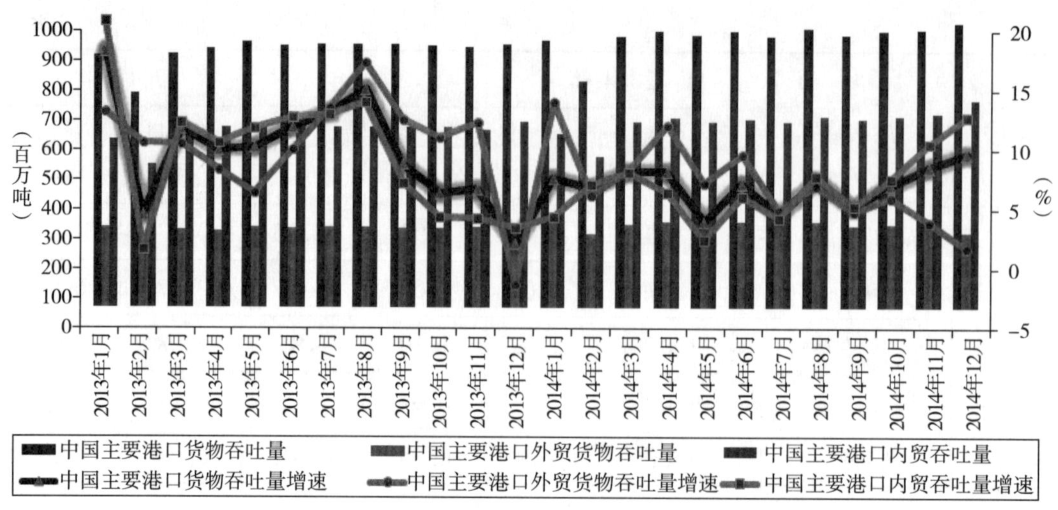

图 2　2013—2014 年规模以上港口内外贸吞吐量

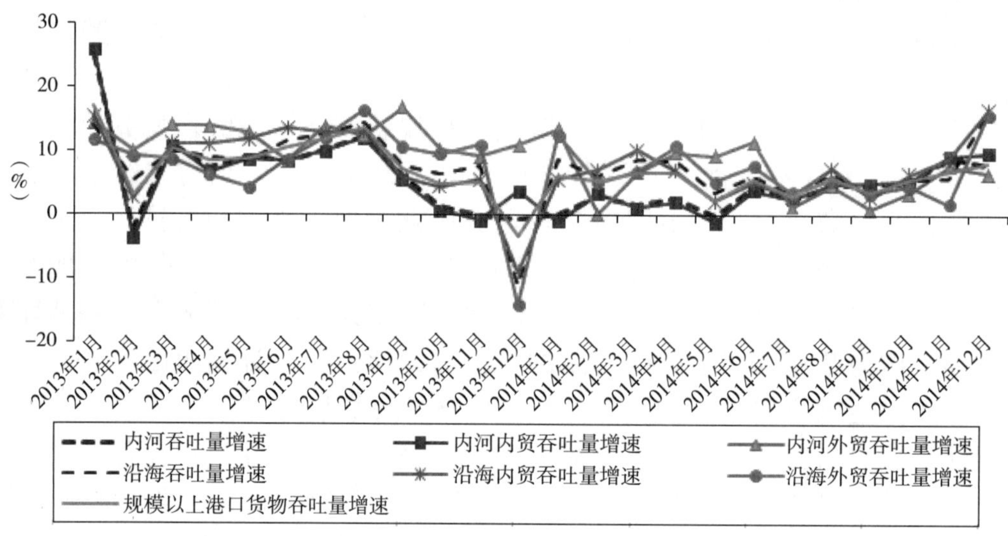

图 3　2013—2014 年规模以上沿海和内河港口内外贸吞吐量增速走势

2. 集装箱吞吐量低速增长成常态，内贸箱增长潜力较大

2014 年，我国集装箱吞吐量增速继续下滑，规模以上港口集装箱吞吐量增幅仅为 5.8%。在我国港口发展新常态的背景下，未来一段时期内，我国集装箱吞吐量可能都将保持低速增长的态势。但随着适箱货范围的扩大，集装箱吞吐量仍将保持增长，如图 4 所示。2014 年，我国集装箱吞吐量排名前二十位的港口保持两位数增长的情况较少，仅有宁波—舟山、虎门、日照、福州、泉州增速超过两位数。其中，宁波—舟山港近两年表现优异，在各港口增速均出现下滑或保持低速增长的情况下，其集装箱吞吐量增长情况连续三年好于其他一

线港口。虎门港继续延续 2013 年的良好涨势，集装箱吞吐量增速超过 50%。2014 年我国港口集装箱吞吐量排名见表 3。

表 3　　2014 年我国港口集装箱吞吐量排名

排名	港口名称	吞吐量（万标准箱）		同比增长
		2014 年	2013 年	（%）
1	上海港	3529	3362	4. 97
2	深圳港	2403	2328	3. 22
3	宁波—舟山港	1945	1735	12. 10
4	青岛港	1658	1552	6. 83
5	广州港	1660	1531	8. 43
6	天津港	1405	1300	8. 08
7	大连港	1013	1002	1. 10
8	厦门港	857	801	6. 99
9	营口港*	562	530	6. 04
10	连云港	501	549	-8. 74
11	苏州（内河）港	445	534	-16. 67
12	佛山（内河）港*	287	271	5. 90
13	虎门港*	284	189	50. 26
14	南京（内河）港*	276	267	3. 37
15	日照港	242	202	19. 80
16	烟台港	236	215	9. 58
17	福州港	224	198	13. 13
18	泉州港	188	168	12. 17
19	丹东港	167	156	7. 05
20	中山港*	136	131	3. 82
21	海口港	135	117	15. 38
22	汕头港*	133	129	3. 10
23	珠海港	117	87	34. 08
24	嘉兴港	116	101	14. 46

续 表

排名	港口名称	吞吐量（万标准箱）		同比增长
		2014 年	2013 年	（%）
25	江门港*	113	92	23.12
26	唐山港	112	73	53.94
27	北部湾港*	110	100	10.00
28	重庆（内河）港	101	91	11.50
29	武汉（内河）港	100	85	17.26

注：＊表示 2014 年数据为预测值。

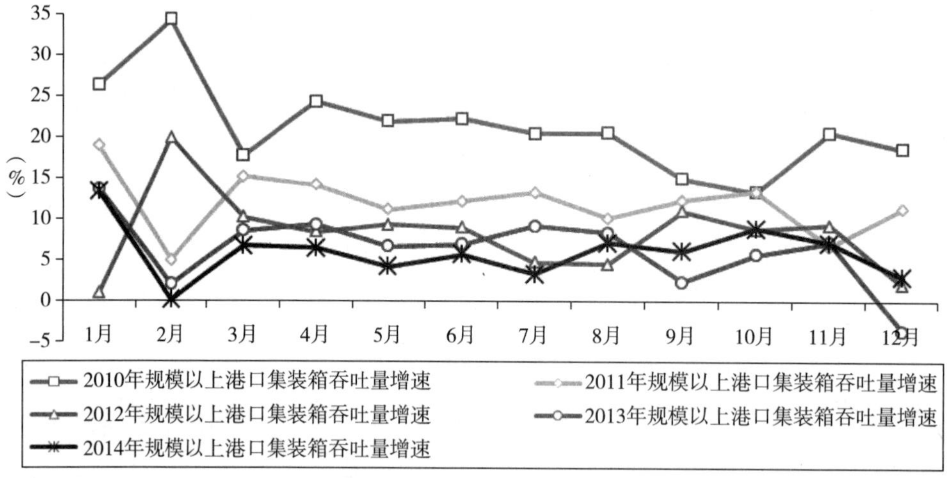

图 4　2010—2014 年我国规模以上港口集装箱吞吐量增幅走势

数据来源：中华人民共和国交通运输部。

从内外贸增长情况来看，2014 年我国内贸集装箱增长仍好于外贸。2014 年前 11 个月，全国规模以上港口完成外贸集装箱 1.16 亿标准箱，同比增长 5.28%；内贸集装箱吞吐量达 6851.4 万标准箱，同比增幅达 7.76%。过去，我国内贸货物大多以大宗散货为主，集装箱化率并不高，在新时期为了加大港口集装箱业务的发展，通过“散改集”的方式推动集装箱量的增长。另外，我国经济方式的转型，各地区经济发展不均衡，中西部地区开发以及产业转移等都为内贸集装箱的增长提供了重要条件。因此，未来一个阶段，内贸集装箱将成为港口集装箱吞吐量新的增长点，如表 4 所示。

从航线来看，2014 年外贸内支线延续 2013 年增速下滑趋势，呈现负增长，成为拖累我国港口集装箱量增长速度的主因。国际航线和内贸线仍保持相对较高的增长水平。国际航线中，受欧洲经济复苏影响，欧线箱量增长明显，同比实现近 8.9

个百分点的增长；美线延续过去两年的良好涨势，今年依旧保持了3.0%的增速。2014年，新加坡航线增速放缓十分明显，由去年的7.8%下降至仅有0.7%的增幅。中国香港、日本、中国台湾等近洋航线都较2013年有明显的提升，如表5所示。

表4　2013—2014年中国港口集装箱内、外贸吞吐量

前11个月累计值	外贸—国际航线		外贸—内支线		内贸	
	总量	出港	总量	出港	总量	出港
2014年/万TEU	9743	5047	1835	875	6851	3422
2013年/万TEU	9207	4731	1790	878	6358	3172
同比增速（%）	5.8	6.7	2.5	-0.3	7.8	7.9

数据来源：中华人民共和国交通运输部。

表5　2013—2014年中国港口部分国际航线集装箱吞吐量

前11个月累计值	中国香港	日本	韩国	新加坡	中国台湾	美国	欧洲
2014年/万TEU	1137	726	617	389	246	1662	1889
2013年/万TEU	1080	712	600	386	216	1613	1735
同比增速（%）	5.3	2.1	2.86	0.7	13.6	3.0	8.9

数据来源：中华人民共和国交通运输部。

由于宁波—舟山港近两年箱量的快速增长，2014年全球集装箱吞吐量排名中，超越釜山港，排名全球第五，在全球前五名集装箱港口排名中，除新加坡港外，其余均为中国港口，如表6所示。

表6　2014年全球前20大港口集装箱吞吐量排名

排名			港口名称	集装箱吞吐量（万标准箱）		
2014年	2013年	走势		2014年	2013年	增长率（%）
1	1	→	上海港	3529	3362	4.95
2	2	→	新加坡港	3387	3258	3.96
3	3	→	深圳港	2404	2328	3.25
4	4	→	香港港	2228	2229	-0.03
5	6	↑	宁波—舟山港	1945	1735	12.10
6	5	↓	釜山港	1865	1768	5.50
7	7	→	青岛港*	1670	1552	7.60

续 表

排名			港口名称	集装箱吞吐量（万标准箱）		
2014 年	2013 年	走势		2014 年	2013 年	增长率（%）
8	8	➡	广州港*	1641	1531	7.18
9	9	➡	迪拜港	1525	1350	12.96
10	10	➡	天津港	1405	1300	8.08
11	11	➡	鹿特丹港	1230	1162	5.83
12	12	➡	巴生港	1095	1035	5.75
13	14	⬆	高雄港	1059	994	6.57
14	13	⬇	大连港	1013	1002	1.07
15	15	➡	汉堡港	970	921	5.32
16	16	➡	安特卫普港	898	858	4.64
17	17	➡	厦门港	857	801	7.02
18	18	➡	洛杉矶港	834	787	5.99
19	19	➡	丹戎帕拉帕斯港*	760	747	1.74
20	20	➡	长滩港	682	673	1.35

注：*表示 2014 年数据为预测值。

3. 煤炭吞吐量增速下滑，铁矿石和原油吞吐量增长相对乐观

2014 年，由于受到南方雨水充沛，水力发电能力增长，火力发电受到影响，煤炭消费需求有所下滑，因此沿海煤炭运输量下滑比较明显，勉强维持正增长。此外，由于国家能源局发文限制低质煤炭进口，外贸进口煤量也有所下滑。2014 年全年，我国规模以上港口共处理煤炭及其制品近 22 亿吨，同比增幅仅为 1.6%。其中，宁波、唐山、黄骅等几个港口表现相对较好，增速均超过 15%。

2014 年，我国铁矿石吞吐量增长相对良好，全年规模以上港口完成铁矿石吞吐量超 16 亿吨，同比增幅达到 11%。其主要原因在于全球铁矿石供过于求，价格大幅下滑，国外铁矿石进口量大幅上涨，带动我国港口铁矿石吞吐量的增长。2014 年，宁波港完成铁矿石吞吐量 10156 万吨，同比增长 15.24%；唐山港处理铁矿石量超 2 亿吨，同比增幅达到近 30%。

2014 年，受美国对伊朗就核问题达成共识，伊朗油类出口明显增长，受美国较高的原油库存及页岩气广泛应用的影响，国际油价不断走低，油类运输市场相对乐观。尤其 2014 年上半年，我国原油进口量保持近 10% 的增速，直至

三季度，由于国内原油消耗量增长并不显著，各地需求维持谨慎、观望态势，港口原油库存持续上扬等因素影响，原油进口量增幅出现下降。但全年来看，我国原油进口依旧保持相对较高的增速，进口原油量达到3.08亿吨，同比增长9.5%。规模以上港口完成石油、天然气及制品7.8亿吨，同比增长4%。主要原油装卸港口，宁波—舟山港和大连港原油处理量分别达到8421万吨和3160万吨，同比增长1.01%和12.77%。

（二）港口建设稳步推进

1. 港口通过能力增长与吞吐量增长基本同步

2014年我国沿海港口产能结构进一步调整，在码头建设稳步推进的同时，码头投资建设增长继续收窄。2014年，我国港口建设投资金额达到890亿元。其中，新建深水泊位80个，较2013年进一步减少。从结构方面来看，新增大型矿石接卸能力得到有效控制，接卸能力适应性由2013年的适度超前转为基本适应。总体来看，我国沿海港口码头实际吞吐能力的增速与吞吐量增速保持一致，沿海港口码头吞吐能力适应性处在适度超前状态。

2. 集装箱枢纽港继续扩能，提升枢纽地位

随着船舶大型化的发展以及航运企业联盟，我国沿海枢纽港之间的竞争愈加激烈，而船舶大型化的发展要求枢纽港具有较高的通过能力和高效的集装箱处理能力。在这一趋势推动下，我国沿海集装箱枢纽港继续扩能，以期提升港口在区域中的枢纽地位。2014年，上海洋山深水港四期工程正式获批建设，该工程预计于2017年完工，工程总投资约139亿元，泊位岸线长近2800米，共建设5个5万吨级和2个7万吨级集装箱泊位，该码头将首次采用最新一代的自动化集装箱装卸设备和自动化生产管理控制系统，真正实现集装箱码头的全自动化运作。洋山四期码头的建成对缓解目前上海港通过能力不足有着重要意义，自动化码头的建设也将对其提升码头作业效率有积极的作用。此外，深圳盐田港也获批将已建成的突堤南端886米岸壁结构调整为1个15万吨级集装箱泊位，兼顾10万吨级、7万吨级集装箱船舶各1艘同时靠泊，新增年通过能力100万标准箱。宁波和舟山两港合作的金塘港区大浦口集装箱码头工程继续推进，广州南沙港区集装箱三期正式投入运营。

3. 内河港口建设再次提速

2014年9月，国务院正式发布《关于依托黄金水道推动长江经济带发展的指导意见》（以下简称《意见》），长江经济带战略上升为国家战略。《意见》提出充分发挥长江黄金水道功能，增强干线航运能力，改善支流通航条件，优化港口功能布局的具体要求。内河港口是长江黄金水道的重要节点通道，《意见》提出要加快上海国际航运中心、武汉长江中游航运中心、重庆长江上游航

运中心和南京区域性航运物流中心建设。提升上海港、宁波—舟山港、江苏沿江港口功能，加快芜湖、马鞍山、安庆、九江、黄石、荆州、宜昌、岳阳、泸州、宜宾等港口建设，完善集装箱、大宗散货、汽车滚装及江海中转运输系统。在长江经济带战略要求下，2014 年内河港口建设继续提速，淮安港、荆州港、安庆港、重庆港口项目得到稳步推进和落实，并在港口转型升级要求下，通过改造老旧码头，实现内河码头的专业化、大型化和现代化。

（三）“21 世纪海上丝绸之路”带动新一轮港口投资与合作

2014 年，“21 世纪海上丝绸之路”上升为国家战略，我国海上丝绸之路沿线港口便陆续结合自身特点重新定位以融入丝路发展的大潮。例如，泉州港积极谋划 21 世纪海上丝绸之路先行区、宁波港提出建设 21 世纪海上丝路重要的支点城市、广州港则要建成海上丝路的交通主枢纽、深圳港着力打造海上丝绸之路的重要枢纽、广西北部湾港定位于 21 世纪海上丝绸之路桥头堡和新枢纽，而斯里兰卡等海外港口也将在 21 世纪海上丝绸之路建设中发挥“至关重要的中心作用”。

在 21 世纪海上丝路战略的大背景下，地区间港口合作正日渐升温。目前，中资码头运营商已投资、运营了斯里兰卡科伦坡港和希腊比雷埃夫斯港。国内深圳港依托新丝路战略与全球 14 个重点港结成友好关系，而北部湾港也开辟了至新加坡、曼谷、海防、胡志明、巴生等港口的多条国际直达航线，并建立了以钦州为基地，覆盖东盟国家 47 个港口城市的中国—东盟港口城市合作网络。

（四）以自贸试验区建设为依托探索港口领域制度改革和政策突破

自 2013 年中国（上海）自由贸易试验区（以下简称“自贸试验区”）获批建设后，以自贸试验区为依托，在港口和航运服务领域等方面进行了有效的探索，对促进我国港口的发展有着积极的意义。2014 年 7 月海关完成国际中转集拼监管方案的制定，之后在外高桥保税物流园区和洋山保税港区各选择一家试点企业，启动国际中转集拼创新业务，业务试点后上海已成功运作两票国际中转集拼业务。中转集拼业务对于提升我国港口国际中转枢纽地位有着重要的意义。

此外，依托自贸试验区，开展沿海运输捎带业务的试点。2014 年 6 月 18 日，海关总署发布《关于调整内外贸集装箱同船运输以及中国籍国际航行船舶承运转关运输货物试点工作的公告》。要求中资航运公司全资或控股拥有的非中国籍国际航行船舶，拟开展承运海关转关运输集装箱货物试点业务的，仅限以上海港为国际中转港、在国内对外开放港口与上海港之间开展。该项政策在 2014 年 12 月 29 日“中远泗水轮”从上海港捎带货物驶往我国天津、青岛两个港口后正式落地。沿海捎带业务有利于防止中转箱量外流，提升我国集装箱中转枢纽港地位。

再者，自贸试验区的试验内容之一在于探索负面清单管理模式。在建立的2014年版的负面清单中，港口服务领域亦实现进一步扩大开放，原国际海运货物装卸、国际海运集装箱站和堆场业务限合资、合作，在2014年版负面清单中被进一步开放，外商可独资投资国际海运货物装卸、国际海运集装箱站和堆场业务。该项政策的突破是我国港口真正建立竞争市场的基础，有利于改善我国港口市场的服务水平。

（五）港口资源整合进一步推进

新时期下，我国港口发展环境正面临一系列变化。一是，随着新港口的开发建设及原港区范围的扩大，港口群内港口密度不断加大，腹地交叉、重叠加剧，港口群内竞争愈加激烈。二是，船舶大型化和航运企业联盟成为航运业发展主流趋势，港口链下游的航运企业联盟挑战了港口的议价能力，同时亦加剧了港口之间的竞争。三是，港口岸线、土地等自然资源具有区域性和稀缺性特点，由于这类资源分散性的特点，在发展阶段这类资源往往被大量开发利用，导致目前我国港口岸线、土地等自然资源利用效率不高。在此背景下，港口群内港口需要通过资源整合来提升资源的利用率，提高港口群整体竞争力，从而应对下游航运业带来的挑战。

从21世纪初，我国便开展了一系列的港口资源整合，2014年，我国港口资源整合得到继续落实和推进。北京、天津和河北三地推动港口资源整合，天津港集团与河北港口集团共同出资20亿元各占50%股权的渤海津冀港口投资发展有限公司，负责京津冀地区港口项目的投资与开发。此外，天津港将在河北唐山、廊坊和天津静海、武清等地新建陆港口岸，使该集团在京津冀地区的陆港口岸增加到10个。京津冀港口的一体化发展有利于高效、统筹利用天津、河北两地的港口资源和航运要素，优化京津冀地区港口的合理分工及产业布局。

此外，在市场主导下太仓港和上海港合作进行资源要素整合，上海港出资参与太仓港集装箱码头的运营，以及将部分原本到外高桥港区转运至洋山的长江中上游地区外贸集装箱业务迁至太仓港。此次合作有利于解决上海港土地、岸线资源不足的问题，对于促进太仓港规模化发展也有积极的意义，有利于两港的互补、错位、双赢发展。

（六）继续推进绿色港口建设

较之国外，中国绿色港口建设起步较晚，但当前对于绿色港口发展的重视再次被提升到新的高度。在2014年《交通运输部关于推进港口转型升级的指导意见》中，明确提出要推动港口绿色发展，而国务院《物流业发展中长期规划（2014—2020年）》也强调大力发展绿色物流，部分沿海港口已率先采取措施，积极营造绿色生态港口体系。目前，我国在推进绿色港口建设过程中不仅聚焦于绿色低碳技术的使用，还包括从管理上推动绿色能源管理体系的建立。例如天津建立码头绿色低碳示范工程、绿色能源管理体系等多项重点工程。从技术的角度来看，岸电技术和对港口配套设施进行“油改气”或“油改电”等措施在越来越多的港口推进，并且港口也积极通过对清洁能源采取补贴的形式进行政策引导，促进了我国绿色港口的建设和发展，如表7所示。

表7　近期中国沿海港口推进绿色港口建设措施

港口名称	措施
宁波	龙门吊“油改电”（2007）、集卡“油改气”（2009）、船舶接岸电、绿色照明、集卡“一拖双挂”（2010）及“双重运输”（2008）等
天津	全自动智能化集装箱码头建设、码头绿色低碳示范工程、绿色能源管理体系等多项重点工程；货物“二维码扫描”技术（2013）等
深圳	每年投入资金2亿元对使用船舶岸电设施和船用低硫油进行补贴（2014）等
青岛	加强绿色低碳技术改造，重点在船舶岸电、绿色照明、清洁能源利用、大型机械运行节能控制、散货作业环保抑尘等领域研究新措施、实施新项目，加快建设无人闸口、无人堆场、无人桥板头、无人理货等智能化港区（2013）等
大连	建设太平湾港城一体化生态示范区；全面推行以节能、低耗和绿色材料等新技术为基础的低碳物流港建设；应用油改电、油改气、太阳能，以及码头岸电等能源替代技术，实现港口清洁化运行；以调整功能布局和运行专业化码头提升对散货粉尘控制等十大生态绿色项目（2013）
上海	轮胎式集装箱龙门起重机采用锂电池供电节能改造（2011）
日照	矿石卸船机综合节能技术（2012）
连云港	新苏港50万吨级矿石码头技能减排综合技术，以岸电技术创新为先导驱动港口绿色发展（2010）

二、2015年港口物流发展展望

（一）港口生产保持稳定增长

2015年，我国经贸环境发展仍然较为复杂，仍将处于经济转型调整期，消化过剩产能、淘汰落后产能仍将是我国经济发展的主旋律。在此背景下，预计

2015 年我国 GDP 将保持 7% 的增速。在此背景下，我国港口货物吞吐量将保持“新常态”的稳定增长，预计增速可达到 5% 左右。

1. 集装箱吞吐量将保持稳定增长

随着欧美经济的逐步复苏，以及我国内贸集装箱业务的快速发展，预计 2015 年我国港口集装箱吞吐量仍将保持 6% 左右的稳定增长。其中，受国内产业转移及内贸箱集装箱化率进一步提升影响，内贸箱量增速仍将好于外贸，预计可达到 7.5% 左右。外贸集装箱国际航线中，欧线和美线仍将保持较好的增长态势，但较 2014 年欧线近 9% 的增幅，欧线增幅将略有下滑，预计在 7% 左右。美线集装箱量仍将保持 3% ~4% 的增幅。

2. 煤炭吞吐量增速将小幅提升，钢铁、石油将保持稳定增长

2015 年，预计北方煤炭下水需求有望得到提升，全年社会用电量将有小幅提升。然而，由于存在较大的不确定性，以及进口煤炭对国内煤炭的冲击，2015 年我国煤炭吞吐量保持高速增长的可能性不大，预计增速将保持在 2.5% 左右。同样，受国家淘汰落后产能等因素影响，钢材需求依然疲弱，2015 年我国钢铁产量仍将维持小幅增长，在此背景下，预计我国铁矿石进口量将保持 5% 左右的增幅。而由于我国居民消费升级，汽车购买量和保有量快速提升，将有力支持我国原油需求，预计 2015 年原油进口量将达到 6% 左右。

（二）港口将全面实现转型升级

2014 年《国务院关于促进海运业健康发展的若干意见》标志着海运业上升为国家战略，明确提出了港口发展适度超前，优化港口布局，积极参与国际海运事务及相关基础设施投资、建设和运营，扩大对外贸易合作。此外，2014 年交通运输部亦发布《关于推进港口转型升级的指导意见》，提出港口转型升级发展目标：到 2020 年，基本形成质量效益高、枢纽作用强、绿色安全、集约发展、高效便捷的现代港口服务体系，适应我国经济社会发展需求。在此背景下，2015 年，我国各地港口将深化落实港口转型升级的指导意见。大量中小型内河港口将通过老码头改造，推动港口代际等级的提升，实现专业化、现代化、规模化发展。而沿海港口则将通过发展现代航运服务业、延伸港口服务功能来实现港口转型升级。部分地区港口金融等业务将得到有效发展。

（三）我国将产生首例港口硫排放限制政策文件

国际海事组织（IMO）组织国际防止船舶污染公约（MARPOL）要求船舶燃料油的含硫量限值为 3.5% m/m。2014 年，香港正式提出靠港船舶使用低硫燃油的要求。中国作为国际海事组织（IMO）组织国际防止船舶污染公约（MARPOL）缔约国之一，该项公约已对中国正式生效。按 2015 年 1 月 1 日生

效的新标准，船舶燃料油的含硫量将集聚缩减至0.1% m/m（2015年前控制区的含硫量上限为1% m/m）。为了推动绿色港口的建设，以及符合公约要求，预计2015年上海港将首先建立关于硫排放控制区的政策文件。

（四）“二十一世纪海上丝绸之路”战略将推动我国港口企业走出去

“二十一世纪海上丝绸之路”战略旨在打通海上丝绸之路通道，通过基础设施投融资合作加强海上丝绸之路的互联互通。在此背景下，我国港口企业将加快走出去进行投资。目前，我国港口企业在探索“走出去”已有成功的经验，包括以船公司为背景的中远码头和中海码头已成功在海外投资运营码头，招商国际也在海外不断拓展码头市场，上港集团已于2010年成功投资欧洲泽布吕赫港。在海上丝绸战略的推动下，2015年我国港口企业将深化走出去战略，在东南亚、南亚等地投资港口基础设施建设，同时继续深化与海上丝绸之路沿线港口的合作发展。

（五）港口改革将得到进一步深化

2015年将是我国深化改革不平凡的一年。一方面，2014年，交通运输部、国家发改委联合发布《关于放开港口竞争性服务收费有关问题的通知》，要求集装箱、外贸散杂货装卸作业，国际客运码头作业等劳务性收费，以及船舶垃圾处理、供水等服务收费，由现行分别实行政府指导价、政府定价统一改为市场调节，由港口经营人、船舶供应服务企业根据市场供求和竞争状况、生产经营成本自主制定收费标准，堆存保管费继续实行市场调节价。这一通知将在2015年1月1日起正式执行，这项改革将对我国港口市场产生一定的影响，有利于改善我国港口市场环境。另一方面，随着自贸区建设的推进以及自贸区在其他地区的扩围，港口领域改革将得到深化和推广。允许外商独资经营码头的制度改革将在自贸区试点地区得到有效推广，理货市场准入有望得到放开，沿海港口引航机构设置审批管理权限将得到下放等。

（上海海事大学　上海国际航运研究中心　赵楠）

2014 年国际集装箱运输市场回顾与 2015 年展望

一、2014 年集装箱市场回顾

1. 世界集装箱贸易量和港口吞吐量稳步增长

2014 年世界集装箱贸易量继续上升，全球集装箱海运量为 170.7 百万 TEU，较 2013 年增长 5.96%。全球集装箱港口吞吐量预计将达 6.51 亿 TEU，较 2013 年增长 4.66%。受全球经贸活力回升影响，港口生产形势有所改善。2014 年亚洲港口集装箱吞吐量为 3.66 亿 TEU，增速回升至 5.72%（2013 年：4.85%），北美港口集装箱吞吐量增速回升至 3.66%（2013 年：2.04%），欧洲地中海港口吞吐量增速回升至 3.67%（2013 年：0.56%），北欧港口集装箱吞吐量增速回升至 3.95%（2013 年：0.92%），如图 1 所示。

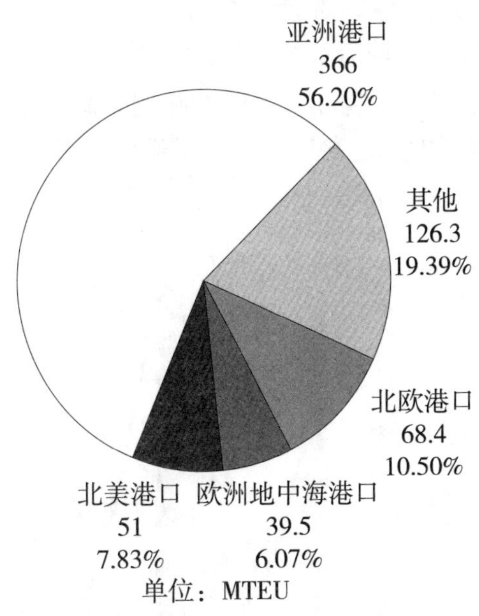

图 1　各区域港口全球份额

数据来源：克拉克森。

2. 大船集中交付，集运市场运力规模继续扩大

截至 2014 年，全球集装箱船队运力为 18102000 TEU，同比 2013 年增长 5.77%，增幅较 2013 年均有所加快。据 Clarkson 统计，截至 2014 年 12 月 8000 以上 TEU 船

型占全球船队总运力 32.71%，其中 12000 + TEU 的万箱船运力占比达 12.02%。

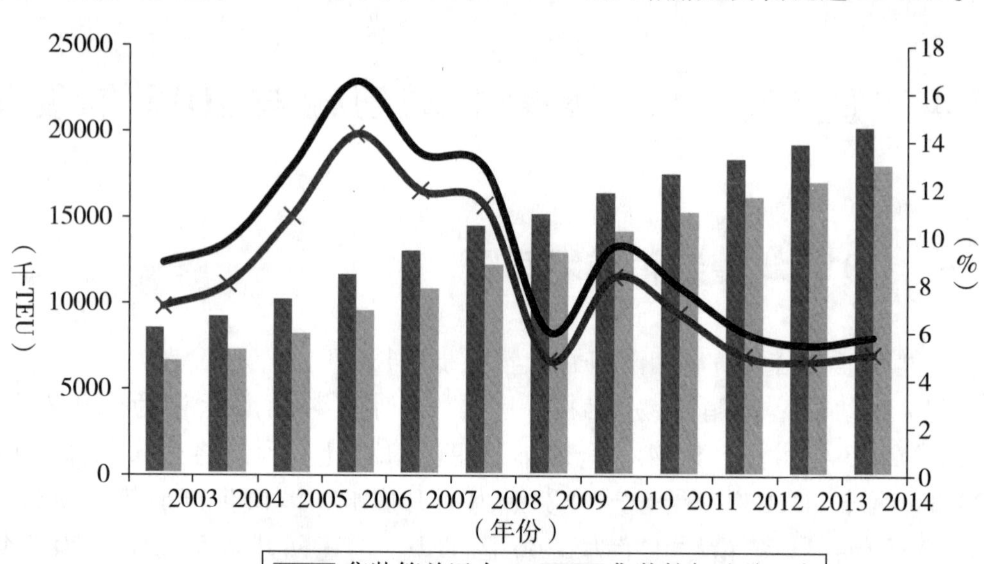

图 2　2003—2014 年全球集装箱市场总运力

数据来源：上海国际航运研究中心整理。

3. 国际集装箱市场运费继续维持低位

金融危机以来，国际集装箱运费持续波动，但是经历了 2013 年的再次下滑后，市场整体呈现企稳回升态势，而复苏步伐依然脆弱。截至 2014 年 12 月 19 日，中国出口集装箱运价综合指数均值为 1087.31 点，继续维持 2013 年水平，如图 3 所示。

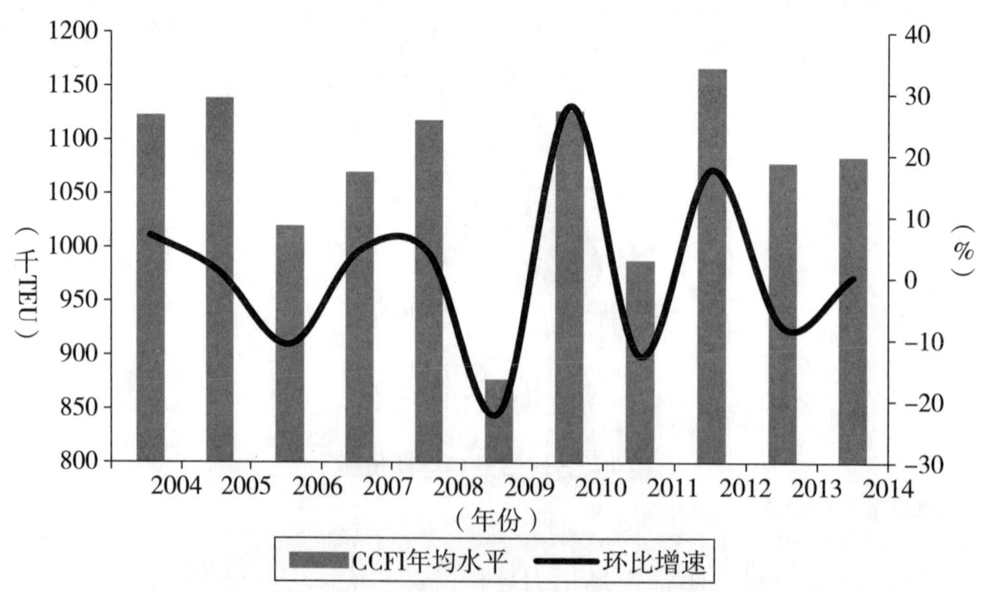

图 3　2004—2014 年集装箱市场运价均值趋势（CCFI）

数据来源：上海航运交易所，上海国际航运研究中心整理。

从细分航线来看，中国—欧洲、中国—地中海、中国—美东、波斯湾航线等表现较好，其他一些区域内航线运费表现低迷，如表1所示。

表1　　分航线即期市场运价（SCFI）

日期	中国—欧洲（基本港）		中国—地中海（基本港）		中国—美西（基本港）		中国—美东（基本港）		台湾（高雄）	
	运价（$/TEU）	同比增幅（%）	运价（$/TEU）	同比增幅（%）	运价（$/TEU）	同比增幅（%）	运价（$/TEU）	同比增幅（%）	运价（$/TEU）	同比增幅（%）
2013	1092.20	-20.89	1160.02	-14.62	2026.89	-11.93	3286.33	-4.39	224.53	-9.51
2014	1173.68	7.45	1379.26	18.90	1970.22	-2.8	3695.42	12.45	220.38	-1.85

日期	中国—东南亚（新加坡）		日本关西（基本港）		日本关东（基本港）		香港（香港）		韩国（釜山）	
	运价（$/TEU）	同比增幅（%）	运价（$/TEU）	同比增幅（%）	运价（$/TEU）	同比增幅（%）	运价（$/TEU）	同比增幅（%）	运价（$/TEU）	同比增幅（%）
2013	232.67	-9.1	337.55	-2.17	346.16	0.37	85.22	-35.04	197.26	8.09
2014	232.60	-0.03	263.30	-22	276.26	-20.19	65.06	-23.65	186.50	-5.46

日期	南美（桑托斯）		澳新（墨尔本）		南非（德班）		西非（拉各斯）		波斯湾（迪拜）	
	运价（$/TEU）	同比增幅（%）	运价（$/TEU）	同比增幅（%）	运价（$/TEU）	同比增幅（%）	运价（$/TEU）	同比增幅（%）	运价（$/TEU）	同比增幅（%）
2013	1374.31	-22.74	811.99	-11.71	803.17	-23.19	1926.78	-7.34	784.59	-21.51
2014	1121.06	-18.43	684.94	-15.65	755.46	-5.94	1844.40	-4.28	819.76	4.48

数据来源：上海航运交易所、CTS，截至2014年12月19日。

4. 单位运力周转次数和闲置运力比例继续低位徘徊

2009年起，集装箱船单位运力周转次数已连续5年在9～10徘徊，表明尽管集运市场供大于求的局面长期存在但未进一步恶化。（单位运力周转次数＝年集装箱海运量/当年全球集装箱船队运力），如图4所示。

班轮公司为了抢夺市场份额，加大闲置运力的释放力度，集装箱闲置运力比重再创近三年新低。截至2014年12月1日，全球集装箱闲置运力230774 TEU，全球总运力占比仅1.2%，如图5所示。

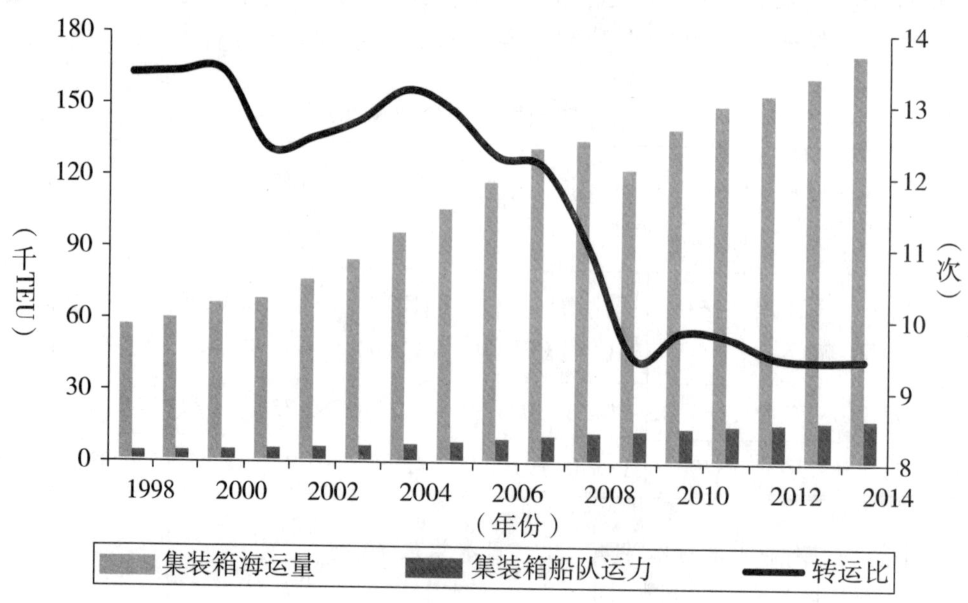

图4　1998—2014年集运市场单位运力周转次数

数据来源：克拉克森。

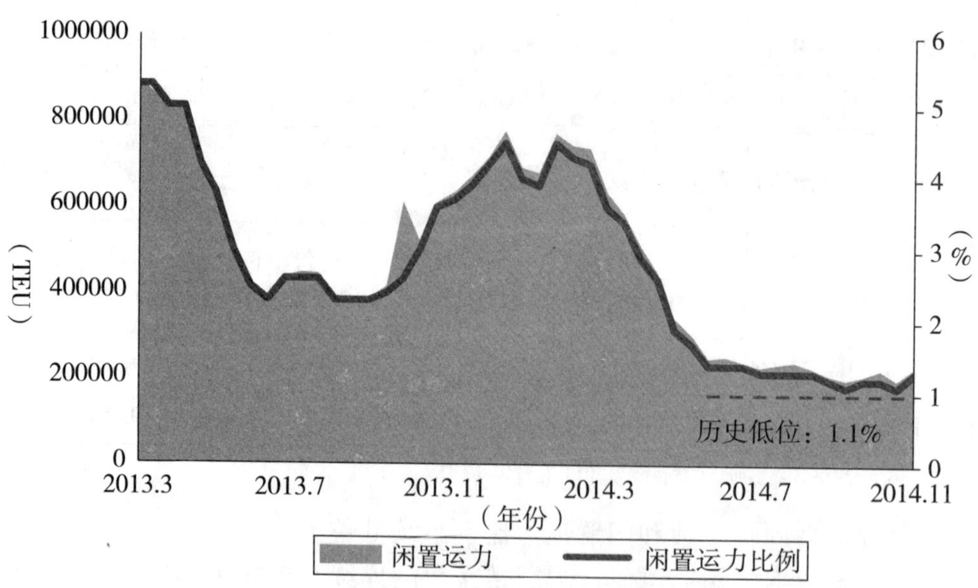

图5　全球集装箱船舶闲置运力比例趋势

数据来源：Alphaliner。

5. 舱位利用率继续低位运行，部分航线略有回升

2014年泛太航线平均周班航次数有所降，较2013年各季度均减少3～5个班次，其船队升级、航线调整频率较高。其东行装载率明显高于西行航线，不

过整体装载率对比 2013 年有所下滑。为了缓解供需压力，提高舱位利用率和盈利水平，班轮公司继续进行航次裁减和合并，2014 年远东/欧洲航线周航次数较 2013 年继续下滑，其东西行航线舱位利用率有所上升，如表 2 所示。

表 2　太平洋航线东/西行舱位利用率

		2013 年	2014 年
东行航线舱位利用率	1 季度	82.61%	81.95%
	2 季度	90.63%	88.11%
	3 季度	96.11%	92.13%
	4 季度	82.92%	81.95%
西行航线舱位利用率	1 季度	53.29%	51.44%
	2 季度	49.68%	48.56%
	3 季度	52.95%	53.79%
	4 季度	50.94%	55.04%

数据来源：德鲁里。

二、2015 年集装箱市场展望

1. 世界经贸继续维持复苏态势，但是复苏脆弱且不平衡

2015 年世界经济增速将略有回升，但仍处于历史较低水平，增速分化态势可能更加明显。IMF 预计，2015 年世界经济将增长 3.8%，较 2014 年增长 0.5 个百分点，如表 3 所示。

表 3　主要机构对 2015 年世界经济的预测　（%）

主要机构	发达经济体	发展中经济体	世界经济
IMF	2.3	5.0	3.8
UN	2.1	4.8	3.1
World Bank	2.4	5.4	3.4

数据来源：IMF、World Bank、UN。

根据 IMF、WTO 等主要机构预测结果显示，2015 年世界贸易状况将持续好转，全球贸易环境整体优于 2014 年。发达经济体正出现稳步复苏的态势，发展势头好于新兴经济体，如表 4 所示。

表 4　　主要机构对世界贸易额增长的预测　　（%）

预测机构	2013	2014（E）	2015（E）
IMF	3.00	3.85	4.98
WTO	2.20	3.10	4.00

数据来源：根据公开资料整理。

2. 预计 2015 年海运量为 182.1 百万 TEU，增幅 6.68%

2015 年全球经济增速小幅提升，全球贸易额增速高于 GDP 的增速，在发达经济体内生需求不断增强的带动下，全球集装箱海运量也将继续增长。

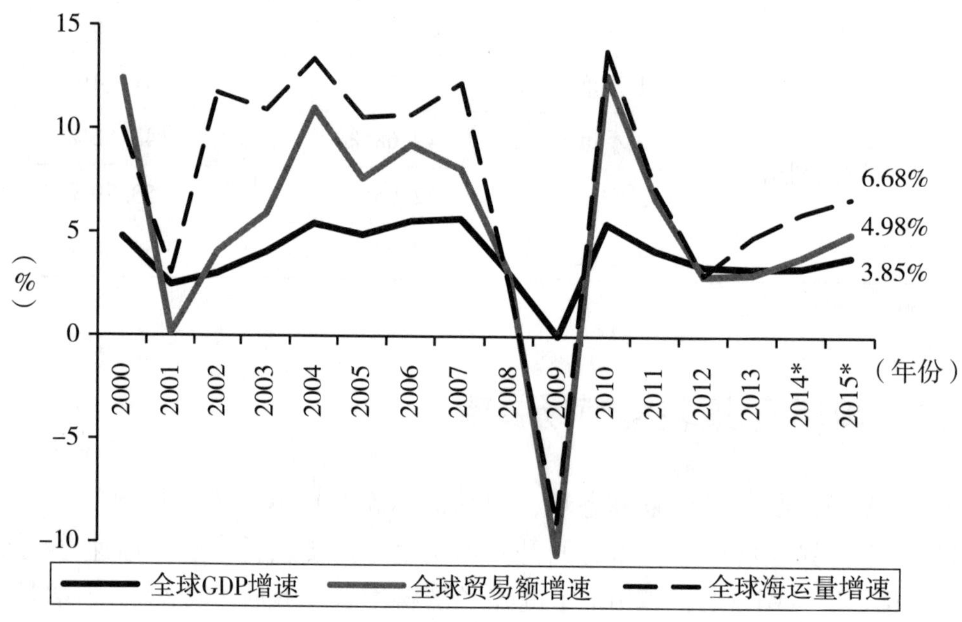

图 6　全球集装箱海运量预测

数据来源：克拉克森，IMF。

综合以上预测，结合实际经济增长，上海国际航运研究中心预计 2015 年全球海运量将达 182.1 百万 TEU，同比增长 6.68%，如图 6 所示。

3. 预计 2015 年迎来运力交付高峰期，市场冲击较大

2014 年全球集装箱船手持订单规模占现有船队的比例为 21.77%，比 2013 年 19.80% 有所回升。随着船队低龄化趋势加速和 2014 年老旧船舶拆解量有所降温，2015 年集装箱船舶拆解量预计会进一步下滑。预测 2015 年集运市场船队总运力规模为 19242 千 TEU，同比增长 6.30%。从 2015 年预计新船运力交付情况看，7500 以上 TEU 船舶依然是交付市场的主力船型，占比将达 82.7%，10000 以上 TEU 船型占比达 49.7%，如图 7 所示。

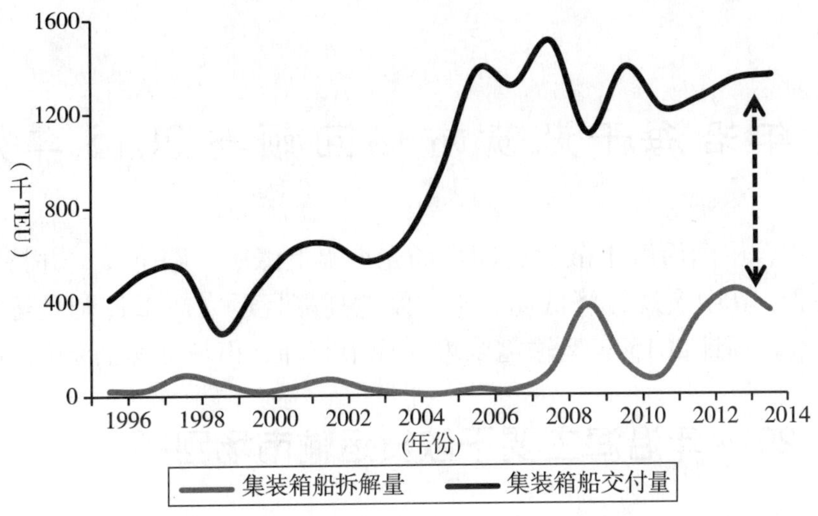

图 7　集运市场船舶交付及船舶拆解趋势

数据来源：Clarkson，上海国际航运研究中心整理。

4. 预计国际集装箱运费整体维持小幅增长态势

展望 2015 年，整体来看，国际集装箱运输市场继续维持缓慢复苏态势，并且在一段时间内缓慢复苏已经成为一种新常态，不过受区域内政策、经济增长、运力供给、市场竞争等因素影响，分航线运价走势会有所分化。个人认为，2015 年国际集装箱运输市场运费平均会好于 2014 年，主干航线表现会继续优于近洋航线，主要考虑是新的班轮联盟格局已经初步形成，班轮公司面临较大的融资压力，对市场运费存在共同预期。各班轮公司涨价会更加谨慎，横向与纵向合作、航线优化、成本控制和稳定大客户仍然是核心内容。而闲置运力比例预计会有所回升。

（上海海事大学　上海国际航运研究中心　张永锋）

2014 年沿海干散货市场回顾与 2015 年展望

2014 年，中国沿海干散货运输市场先小幅上涨后一路下跌，并持续刷新历史最低水平。其中宏观经济低迷、水力发电高涨且运力严重过剩是运价下跌最主要的因素。预计 2015 年运输需求增速稳中有降，市场疲软态势依旧难改。

一、2014 年沿海主要干散货运输市场回顾

1. 沿海干散货运价年均值再次下滑，供需矛盾未有明显好转

受宏观经济增速回调，沿海干散货运价延续低迷，全年较大规模的增长仅出现在第一季度，总体呈现先小幅上涨后一路下跌的波动趋势。其中运力过剩未有明显好转以及旺季需求不高是运价下跌最主要的因素。截止到 2014 年 12 月底，上海航运交易所发布的中国沿海散货综合运价指数（CBFI）全年平均值为 989. 86 点，较 2013 年再次下滑 12. 08%，如图 1 所示。

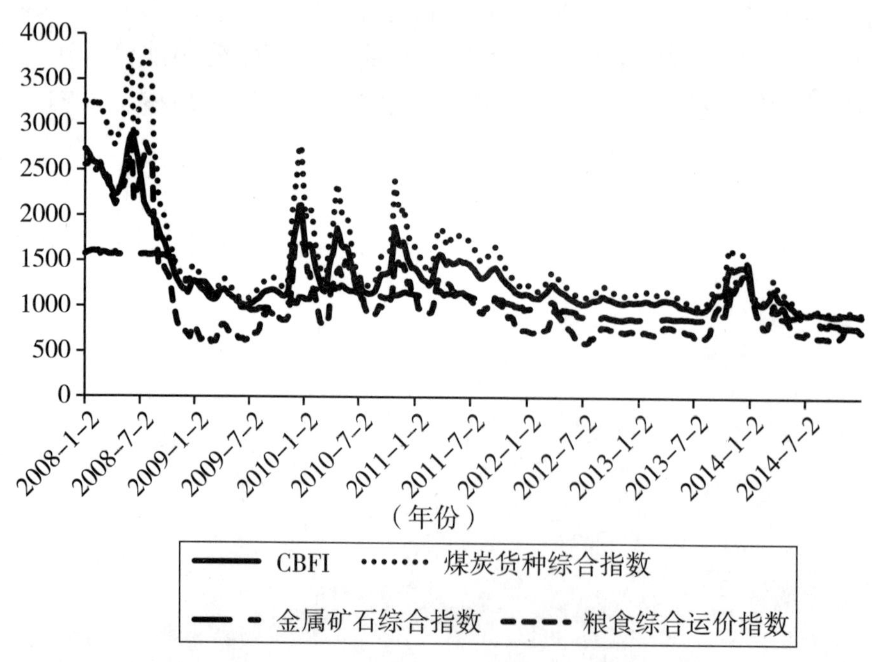

图 1　2008—2014 年沿海散货综合运价指数走势

数据来源：上海航运交易所。

（1）沿海煤炭运价前高后低，季节性特征不再显著。2014 年新版沿海煤炭运价指数均值为 623.02 点，同比下跌 24.14%。2014 年年初沿海煤炭运价跌入谷底，在春季国内煤炭大幅降价与大秦线检修等因素的综合影响下迅速拉涨；夏季受宏观经济低迷、水力发电高涨且高温天气持续时间短暂的影响，沿海煤炭迎峰度夏旺季不旺；随后由于秋季大秦线检修以及国内煤炭价格低廉等因素影响，沿海煤炭运价偶有涨幅。

（2）沿海矿石运价步入下行通道。2014 年沿海矿石运价指数均值为 896.31 点，同比下跌 6.64%。年内，国内外宏观经济增速放缓，房地产、汽车、造船等钢材终端需求表现低迷，加之国家淘汰钢厂等主要高耗能企业，中国沿海铁矿石运价前高后低，第一季度震荡上行，之后持续走低。此外，本年度中期铁矿石进口出现信贷危机，港口积压大量铁矿石也对运价走低造成一定影响。

（3）沿海粮食运价受整体行情拖累止涨下跌。2014 年沿海粮食运价指数均值为 785.76 点，同比下跌 10.10%。2014 年第一季度在国家玉米临储政策下，粮食市场有所回暖，后期步入淡季，加上沿海煤炭运输市场的萧条，沿海粮食市场一路下滑。直到第四季度，受新粮上市及节假日需求的刺激，猪市开始回暖，饲料等下游行业也得以改善，粮食运输需求有所好转。

2. 沿海干散货运量明显下滑，季节性波动有所减弱

2014 年世界经济继续维持“弱增长”格局，中国经济增长出现回落，多个行业出现产能过剩，我国对大宗散货、原材料的需求增速明显回落，沿海干散货运输需求整体走弱。2014 年沿海干散货运量前高后低，1—11 月中国沿海干散货三大货种总运量达 8.75 亿吨，同比上涨 2.2%，较去年的 8.82% 有明显下降，且季节性特征有所减弱，波动幅度明显减小。

（1）沿海煤炭运量增速明显下降，电煤需求降低是主因。2014 年 1—11 月，全国主要沿海港口内贸煤炭发运量累计 6.04 亿吨，同比增长 4.53%，增速降低 10.34 个百分点。同时，全国重点煤矿铁路运量也有所缩水，同比下跌 1.57%。沿海煤炭运量此次下滑的原因首先是南方降水同比增加，火力发电量上行乏力。2014 年 1—11 月，全国发电量总计 49419.1 亿千瓦时，同比上涨 5.05%，涨幅有所收窄；其中火力发电 37868.5 亿千瓦时，同比微幅上涨 0.76%，占总发电量 76.63%，同比降低 3.25 个百分点；全国六大电网耗煤量累计同比下跌 7.27%。其次，内贸煤低价促销跌破 500 元/吨，进口煤冲击减小。2014 年 1—11 月，中国煤炭进口总量为 2.06 亿吨，同比下降 15.74%。其中，动力煤累计进口 10925.89 万吨，同比增加 8.03%，但增速下滑 6.23 个百分点，如图 2、图 3 所示。

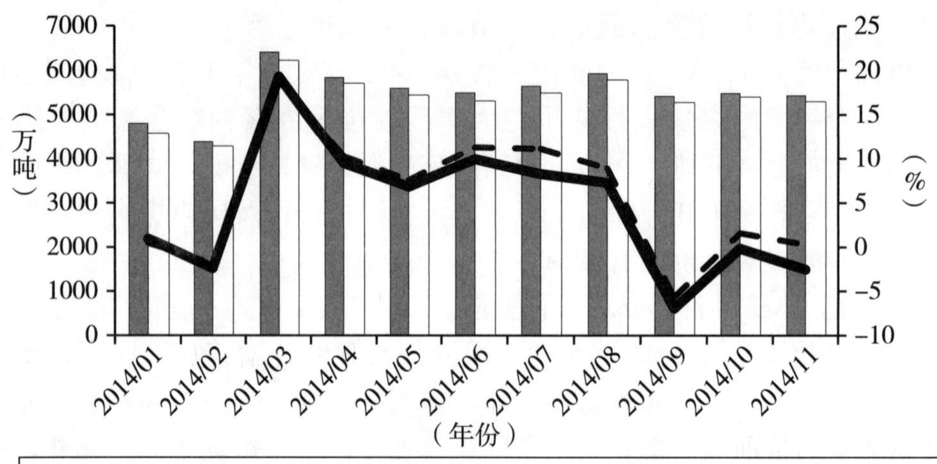

图 2　2014 年全国主要沿海港口内贸煤炭发运情况

数据来源：我的钢铁网。

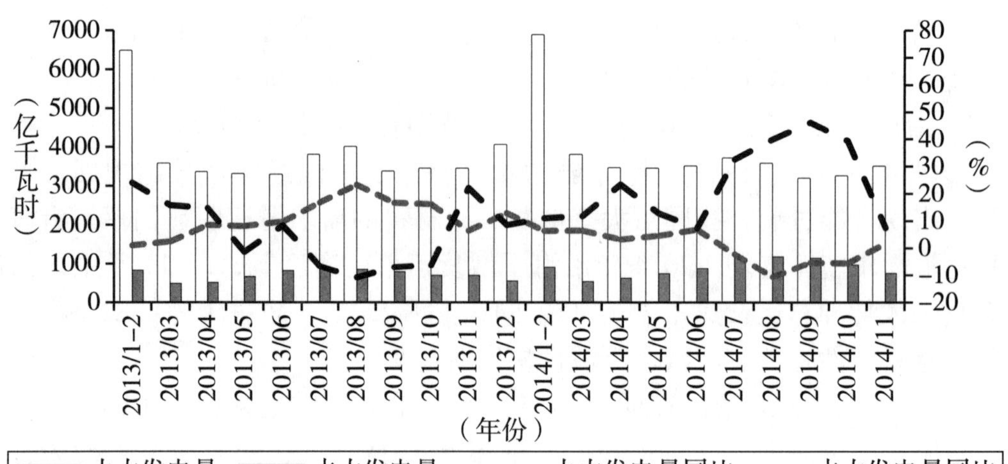

图 3　2013—2014 年全国火力、水力发电量统计

数据来源：国家统计局。

（2）沿海矿石运量增幅萎缩，钢材市场低迷是主要原因。2014 年 1—11 月，全国主要沿海港口内贸铁矿石出港量累计 2.23 亿吨，同比增长 7.23%，增速下降 3.71 个百分点。沿海矿石运量此次增幅萎缩的主要原因包括两方面：首先，钢材产量同比增速明显下滑成为主要原因。2014 年 1—11 月，全国房地产企业新开发房屋面积 164705 万平方米，同比降低 9.0%，增速下降 20.5 个百分点。在此影响下，2014 年钢材生产同比增速明显下滑。2014 年 1—11 月，全国粗钢产量74520.6万吨，同比上涨4.63%，增速下降4.75个百分点。其次，铁矿石供给增速有所放缓，进口量增速高于上年。2014年1—11月，全国铁矿石供应总量达到22.18亿吨，同比增长8.11%，增速小幅放缓0.8个百分点；由于国际矿价明显低于2013年水平，铁矿石进口量增速达到13.30%，增速小幅上涨2.57个百分点，如图4、图5所示。

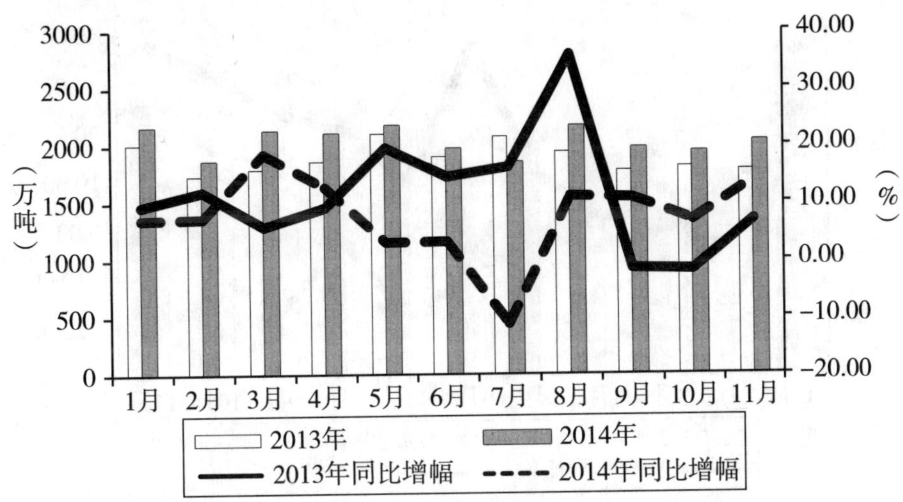

图4 2013—2014年全国主要沿海港口内贸铁矿石出港量统计

数据来源：交通运输部综合规划司。

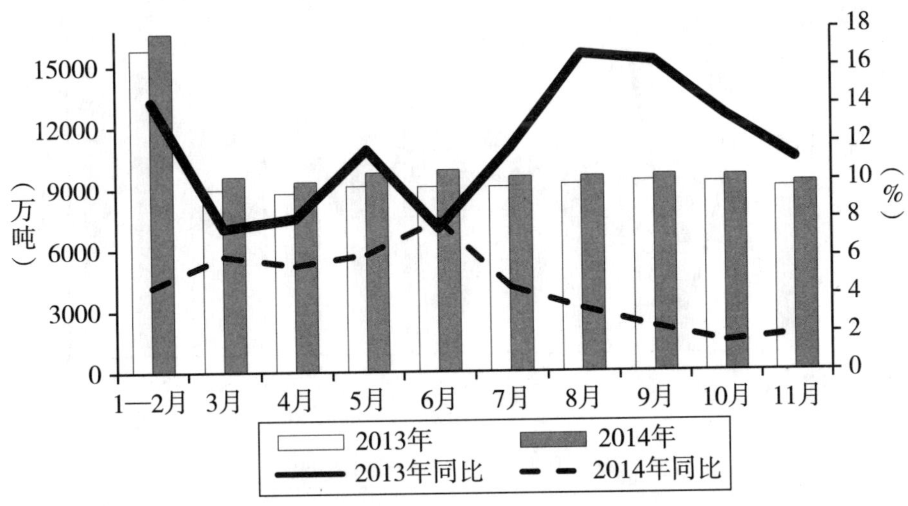

图5 2013—2014年1—11月全国粗钢月度产量

数据来源：我的钢铁网。

（3）沿海粮食运量同比下跌，港口库存波动性减弱。2014年1—11月，全国主要沿海港口内贸粮食出港量累计4774.28万吨，同比下跌1.87%，增速下降 17. 63 个百分点。需求方面，下游行业全年表现低迷，成为拉低沿海粮食运输需求的主要因素；供给方面，虽然北方粮食整体供给充足，但对沿海粮食运输的拉动作用有限。因而全年沿海粮食运量的季节性波动较去年有所增强，年初较高，之后一路震荡下行，后期有所发力，如图 6、图 7 所示。

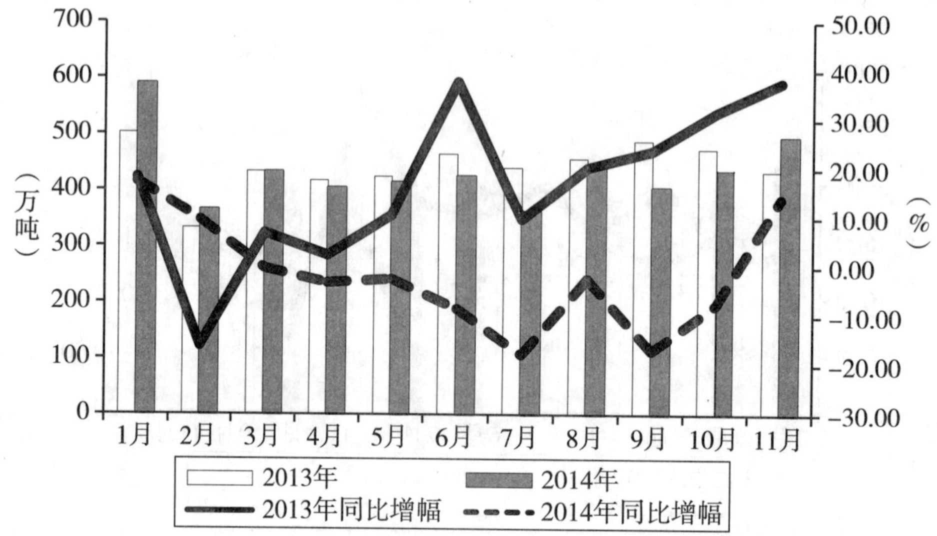

图 6　2013—2014 年 1—11 月全国主要沿海港口内贸粮食出港量统计

数据来源：交通运输部综合规划司。

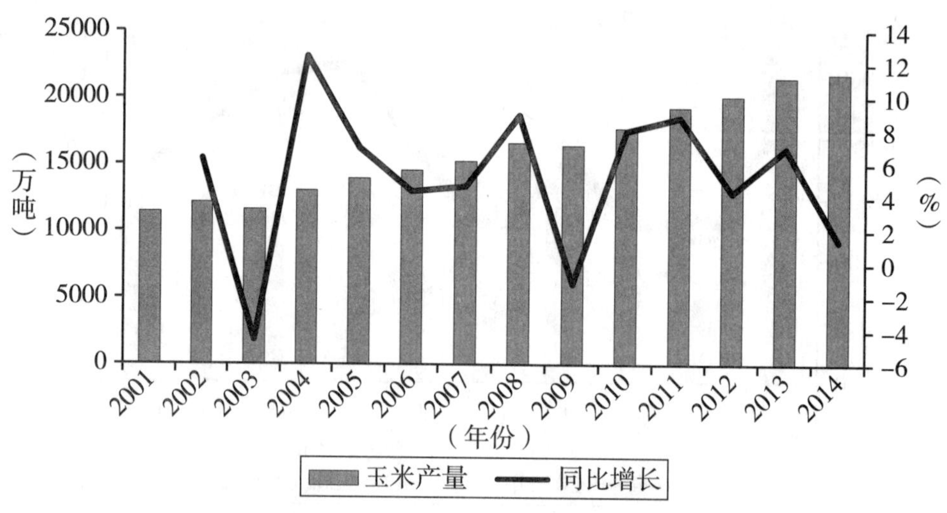

图 7　2001—2014 年全国玉米产量

数据来源：国家统计局，中国粮油中心。

3. 沿海干散货运力首现下滑，新建船舶缩减近一半

2014 年航运企业为控制亏损规模已有意识地控制运力数量，加之国家拆船

补贴政策的影响，大量拆解老旧船舶，2014 年中国沿海干散货船舶运力首次出现下滑。但考虑到部分北方港口上半年进行能力扩张，船舶周转速度加快，目前市场上的运力保有量相对货运量仍然过剩，航运企业、船厂等相关方的盈利情况依然不容乐观。截至 2014 年 6 月 30 日，从事国内沿海运输的万吨以上干散货船（即除去集装箱船，重大件船等特种船之外的普通货船，下同）共计 1698 艘，5448.14 万载重吨，载重吨降幅为 1.27%。其中，2014 年上半年投入营运的新建船舶较去年同期缩减了近一半，而拆解量却增加了近三倍，如图 8 所示。

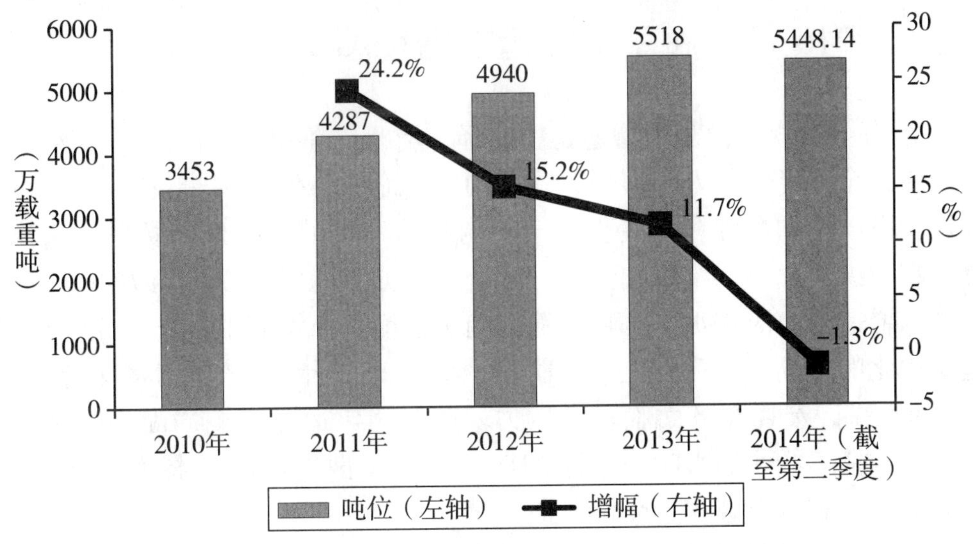

图 8　2010—2014 年第二季度沿海干散货船运力情况

数据来源：交通运输部。

（1）沿海干散货老旧船舶大量拆解，年轻化、大型化趋势明显。受市场低迷、企业主动调整运力结构和国家鼓励老旧运输船舶提前报废更新政策等影响，2014 年上半年，大量老旧运输船舶持续以低于 18 年报废年限提前处置退出市场，导致沿海万吨以上干散货船的平均船龄继续下降至 7.56 年，较 2013 年年底下降 0.44 年。截至 2014 年第二季度，共有 71 艘，267.74 万载重吨的干散货船提前退出市场，较去年全年的拆解总量增加了近一倍。同时，近年来新投入营运的新建船舶主要都集中在 4 万载重吨以上的大吨位船舶，因此 2014 年沿海干散货运输船队的平均吨位也略有增加，但由于今年新投入营运的船舶数量较少，截至 2014 年第二季度，沿海干散货运输船队的平均吨位为 3.21 万载重吨，较 2013 年年底仅小幅增加 0.01 万载重吨。

（2）沿海运输相关企业控制运力增幅，多数公司仅微盈利。截至 2014 年 6 月，中海发展共拥有散货船舶 126 艘，1005.4 万载重吨，同比增长 16.7%，单船平均规模继续上升至 7.98 万载重吨；长航凤凰共有 20 艘船舶资产遭到法院裁定拍卖或市场竞拍出售，公司船舶数量的大幅减少使得公司的经营成本有显著下降；中海海盛拥有散货轮 23 艘，总运力规模 123.13 万载重吨，平均单船规模 5.35 万载重吨，交付量下滑一半以上；宁波海运拥有散货轮 17 艘，总运力规模 80.80 万载重吨，虽然船队运力数量有所减少，但船队结构得到优化。就营业利润来看，选取的部分沿海干散货运输上市企业中，除长航凤凰通过资产处理使利润转正外，仅中海发展和宁波海运两家在 2014 年 1—9 月实现了微弱盈利，其他仍为小幅亏损，可见大部分公司仍在盈亏平衡点附近徘徊。

二、2015 年沿海干散货运输市场展望

1. 沿海干散货运输需求增速稳中有降，增幅仍在 6% 以下

当前，全球经济仍处于缓慢、脆弱的复苏之中，但各国步伐不一。世界经济复苏状态的不均衡性和易变性，短期内将给中国的对外经济贸易带来挑战。此外，在国内资源环境约束加强、国际经济复苏不稳定的双重压力下，我国将进入经济增速趋向潜在水平、物价涨幅趋于适度、新增就业趋于稳定、经济结构趋于优化的“新常态”。在此背景下，预计 2015 年 GDP 增速将保持在略高于 7% 的水平，宏观经济面临较大压力。虽然明年运力过剩局面将略有缓解，但受需求端持续低迷的影响，预计 2015 年沿海干散货运输需求增速较 2014 年稳中有降，仍难以突破 6% 的增长水平。

（1）能源结构调整将影响煤炭运输需求。《大气污染防治行动计划》明确指出，到 2017 年煤炭占能源消费总量比重降到 65% 以下。2014 年 6 月，习总书记提出 5 点要求，推动能源生产和消费革命。随着我国能源结构的不断调整，煤炭消费占比将逐步降低。预计 2015 年的发电结构将有所变化，火电占比继续放缓至 75% 以下。但鉴于国家将继续限制煤炭进口，进口动力煤冲击将减弱，预计 2015 年中国沿海煤炭运输需求增速继续放缓至 6% 以下，全年走势前低后高。

（2）基建需求集中释放将支撑矿石运输需求。2015 年我国基础建设项目需求将集中释放，成为钢材需求增量的主要来源。但在中国环境治理和对钢铁行业加大落后产能淘汰的大背景下，中国铁矿石需求增速还将继续放缓。同时，铁矿石供应过剩问题将进一步加剧，长期来看随采随用模式依旧盛行，因此预计 2015 年中国沿海矿石运输需求增速也将放缓至 5% 附近。

（3）终端刚性需求助涨粮食运输需求。2014 年全国饲料生产专用设备的产量同比微涨，刚性需求仍有一定的发展空间。同时，进口粮食量或将减少，国内供给比例上升拉动沿海粮食运量上行。但由于 2014 年深加工企业亏损严重，加上产能过剩短时间难以化解，沿海粮食运输需求的涨幅有限，因此预计

2015年中国沿海粮食运输需求增速回升至3%左右。

2. 沿海干散货运力增幅可能反弹

鉴于2013年船舶订单数量的大幅回升，2014年下半年的集中交船期仍将存在，但集中交付量较以往要缩减很多。根据上海国际航运研究中心测算，预计2014年年底国内沿海运输万吨以上干散货船将达到5607.12万载重吨左右，全年运力增幅在1.6%左右，将是中国沿海干散货船舶运力数量增速的最低谷。而2015年，受前期延迟交付以及2013年、2014年新增船舶订单量较大的影响，中国沿海干散货船运力增速有可能再次反弹至3.0%附近，这意味着2015年运力过剩局面的缓解程度极其有限，各大船东所谓的理性控制船舶数量较难实现，中国沿海干散货运输市场将继续面临严峻的挑战。

（1）新船订单集中交付。克拉克森的订单统计数据显示，将在2015年交付的船舶中，于2013年和2014年签订造船合同的订单占比为69.5%，前期延迟交付和后期新增订单将集中出现，届时运力增幅有望较2014年小幅反弹。预计2015年中国船东将有110艘，661.47万载重吨的沿海干散货船舶等待交付，较2014年全年上涨54.4%。

（2）非航运企业订单数量依然高涨。根据克拉克森的全部手持订单数量统计，目前来源于中国航运企业（包括拥有海运业务的大型集团公司）的沿海干散货船舶手持订单数量总计为138艘，786.56万载重吨，占总订单数量的58.0%；中国非航运企业的沿海干散货船舶手持订单数量总计为79艘，470.34万载重吨，占比为34.7%；剩余7.4%的为其他未透露公司名称的不知名中国企业。随着近年来船东弃船数量的增加，部分船厂已逐渐成为拥有大量船舶的船东。加之部分金融租赁公司、货主企业、贸易集团的沿海散货船舶订单的加入，非航运企业的订单数量依然高涨，成为近年来沿海散货运输市场运力过剩局面加剧的最大隐患。

（3）运力过剩缓解程度有限。受2013年船舶订单数量大幅反弹的影响，2015年的沿海干散货船舶的交付数量将略有反弹。同时，由于国家拆船补贴政策已施行近一年的时间，可供继续拆解的老旧船舶数量有限，因此预计2015年中国沿海干散货船运力有望达到5776万载重吨左右，较2014年年底的预测值（5607万载重吨）增长3.0%，这意味着2015年运力过剩局面的缓解程度有限，所谓船东理性控制船舶数量较难实现。

3. 沿海干散货运价均值在900至1200点

预计2015年沿海干散货运量增长将略低于GDP增速，为5%～6%。同时，沿海干散货船舶运力增速在3%左右，运力过剩情况将略有缓解。因此，在本报告预测2015年国内气候恢复正常，即夏季高温、降水量缓和的假设下，

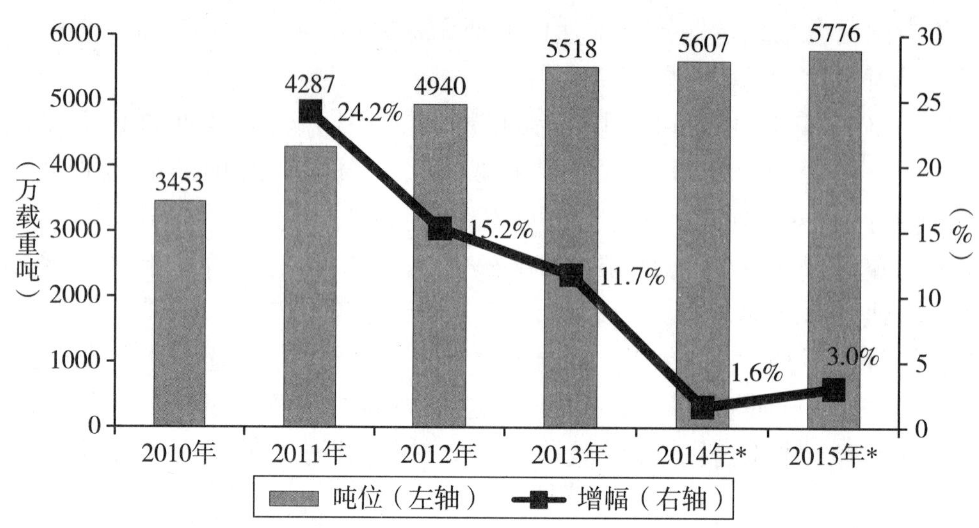

图 9　国内沿海运输的万吨以上干散货船总运力预测

注：*为上海国际航运研究中心预测值。

预计 2015 年沿海干散货运价较今年变化不大，增幅在 4% 以内，沿海干散货运价指数（CBFI）将保持在 900 至 1200 点。全年沿海干散货总体运价前低后高，二季度可能出现较大回落、三季度可能有所走高，如图 9、图 10 所示。

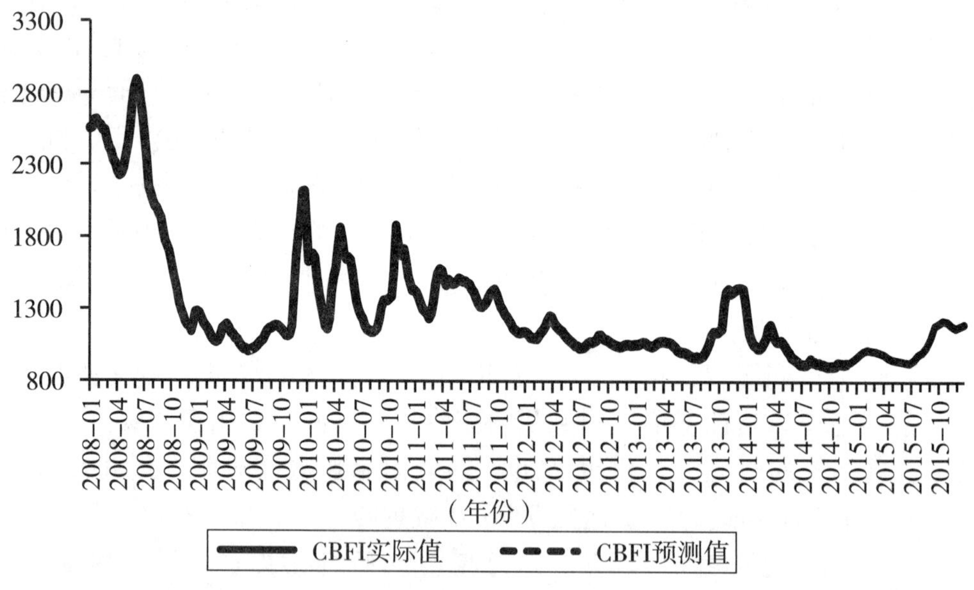

图 10　2015 年沿海散货综合运价指数（CBFI）预测

数据来源：上海国际航运研究中心。

（1）沿海煤炭运价下半年提升幅度有限。2015 年全球经济缓慢复苏，国内经济处于结构调整期，高耗能产业将继续保持低速增长，预计全社会用电量小幅上升，火力发电所占比例将继续下降，国内煤炭需求预期小幅上涨。同时，受国家对进口煤炭征收关税以及下游煤炭需求增长放缓的影响，2015 年全年煤炭进口量增幅将继续放缓，总量占比或将有所下滑。鉴于沿海煤炭运输需求增幅将放缓至 6.0% 以下，同时运力增幅预计在 3% 左右，综合考虑其与粮食市场、矿石市场的联动性及非食品价格涨幅或在 1.3% 左右的预测值，预计 2015 年沿海煤炭运价全年均值止跌上涨 4.5% 左右，波动仍然呈现大 M 型，除极端天气影响外，全年波动将趋于平缓，如图 11 所示。

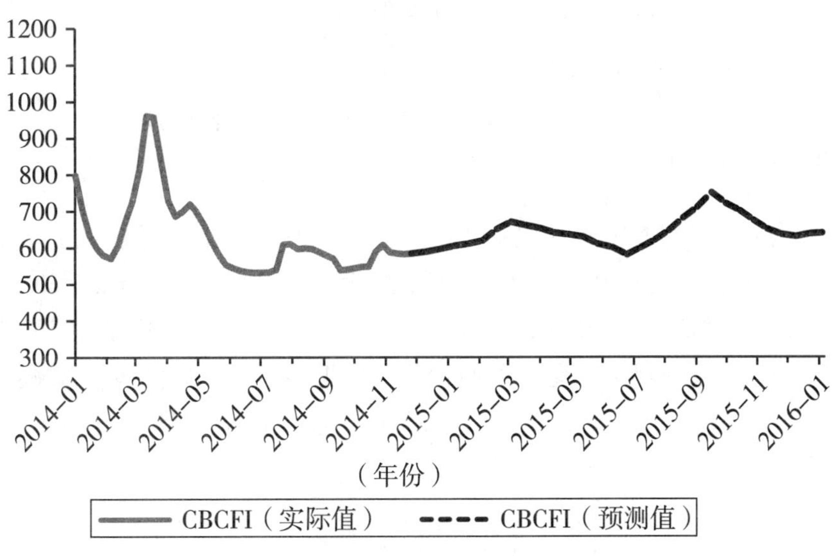

图 11 2015 年新版中国沿海煤炭综合运价预测

数据来源：上海国际航运研究中心。

（2）沿海矿石运价后期在震荡中上行。2015 年全球经济复苏缓慢，钢材需求增长主要依赖国内固定资产投资，因此 2014 年批复的诸多基建项目与城镇化建设的继续推进将成为 2015 年中后期钢材需求的主要增长点。预计 2015 年家电行业、机械行业与汽车产业将保持中低速增长，造船市场或将缓慢复苏，而房地产市场走势不明则成为影响钢材需求的最大不确定性因素。2015 年全国耗钢量将保持低速增长，进口矿石需求将达到 8 亿吨左右，沿海矿石运量呈现低速增长态势，增长幅度为 5% 左右。此外，钢厂矿石“随用随采”的模式也将为沿海铁矿石运价增加一定的不确定性，同时天气因素也会对沿海铁矿石运价产生一定影响。预计 2015 年沿海铁矿石运价将小幅回升，全年均值涨幅在 3% 左右，最高点将出现在第四季度初，如图 12 所示。

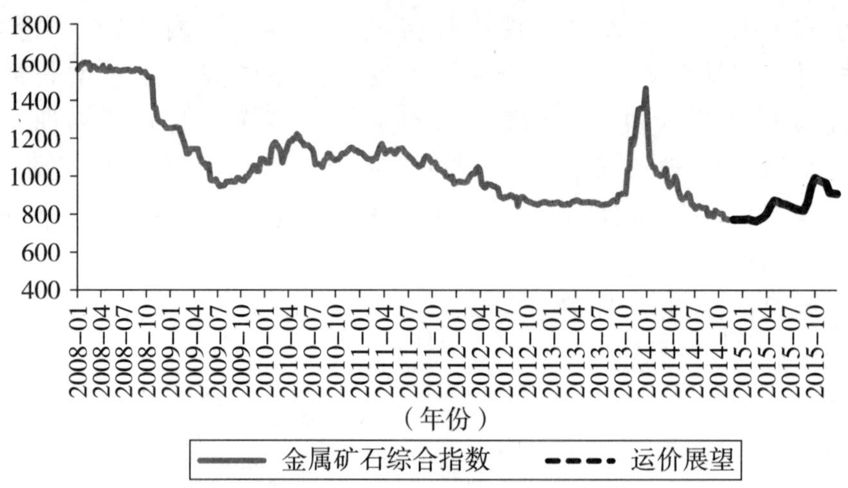

图 12　2015 年沿海金属矿石综合运价指数预测

数据来源：上海国际航运研究中心。

（3）沿海粮食运价季节性特征仍较显著。2015 年国内饲料行业刚性需求将有所增长，深加工行业更是如此，加上粮食进口量继续增长的空间不大，国内粮食供给占比较 2014 年将出现上升，预计沿海粮食运量增幅在 3% 左右。由于沿海粮食运价受沿海煤炭运价影响较大，2015 年沿海粮食运价增幅将与沿海煤炭运价基本保持一致，预计增幅在 4.0% 左右，且沿海粮食运输市场季节波动仍相对平缓，如图 13 所示。

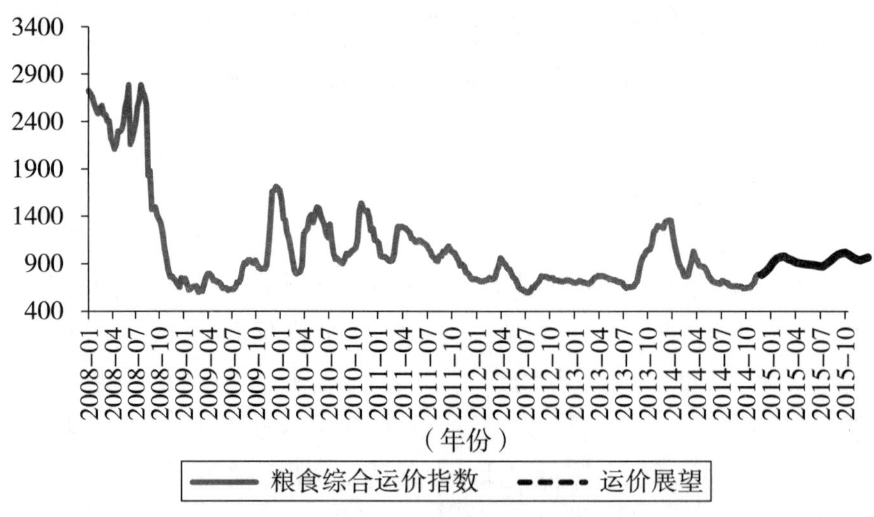

图 13　2015 年沿海粮食综合运价指数预测

数据来源：上海国际航运研究中心。

（上海海事大学上海国际航运研究中心 李倩雯　孟威）

2014 年航空物流发展回顾与 2015 年展望

一、2014 年航空物流发展回顾

过去几年，由于受燃油价格居高不下、航运市场运力过剩等因素的影响，全球航空货运市场前景堪忧。2014 年全球航运量再度达到顶峰水平，使得航空货运市场再次复苏。2014 年度，我国民航累计完成货运量 593 亿吨，同比增长 5.7%，增速比上年提高 3.4 个百分点；累计完成货物周转量 186 亿吨公里，同比增长 9.3%，增速比上年提高 6.4 个百分点。总体来说，作为航空货运转型的关键年，今年我国航空物流发展如火如荼，市场热度居高不下，成果可圈可点。

（一）跨境电商贡献不可小觑

2014 年，伴随着亚马逊中国开通海外站点直邮、阿里巴巴宣布进军全球市场，国内各大电商也相继加入了跨境电商这一持续升温的“狂欢派对”。PayPal 数据显示，预计至 2018 年，中国跨境网购消费者将达 3560 万人，“海淘”规模将达到 1 万亿元。这也预示着，中国正在和美国一起成为全球跨境电子商务的中心。

跨境电商的快速增长，预示着巨大的物流潜力。如果以 2014 年跨境网购规模 1500 亿计算，假设跨境电商物流费用占销售规模的 10%，将带动相关物流支出近 150 亿元。所以跨境电商这块蛋糕，不只吸引着电商大佬们纷纷布局，各大航空货运企业也想从中分一杯羹。各大货航纷纷加大了对跨境电商领域的投入力度，其中最具代表性的要数东航物流旗下的“东航产地直达”。除了收益增加，跨境电商的发展对航空物流的贡献还在于解决了传统国际贸易分工造成货源单向性明显的问题，以往中国通过航空运往欧、美、澳货量远大于欧、美、澳回程中国的货量，而进口到中国的跨境电商包裹货物恰恰主要来自北美（美国为主）、欧盟（英国、德国、荷兰为主）、澳新地区和日本四大市场，跨境电商的出现刚好解决了这一问题。目前，美国至中国的日均电商包裹运输量达 750 余吨，澳新地区至中国的电商包裹运输量每年约 3 万吨。除此之外，跨境电商对口岸城市航空物流的贡献亦不可小觑，中俄间电商交易呈爆发式增长，阿里巴巴俄语版访问量几乎每 2 个月就翻一番，2013 年 11 月起哈尔滨先后开通了12条对俄客运和货运包机航线，一整年间共执飞了100班包机航班，包机总载货量达2000吨，货值突破2亿美元大关，占对俄电商物流包裹总量的40%。

（二）航空快递竞争激烈

每年“双十一”期间，为了能尽量多占有航空舱位，各个快递公司除自家货机外，都要与航空公司签订舱位协议。2014年“双十一”前，各航空公司的货运舱位已基本被物流公司提前抢订；1—10月，石家庄机场货邮吞吐量达到3.7万吨，同比增长12%，航空快件增长迅速。1—10月，石家庄机场货运航空快件所占的比例越来越大，增幅超过30%。以上两个例子仅仅是航空快递受热捧的一个缩影，在航空快递数量快速增长过程中，各物流企业纷纷发力，目的就是谋求更大的市场份额。

继顺丰速运、中国邮政先后组建航空公司后，圆通也开始组建货运航空公司，国内快递业向航空领域的业务竞争即将打响，未来3年内，将实现15架自有飞机、76个机场间互飞、1000余吨日运量的目标。据Flightglobal报道，凭借覆盖整个亚洲的航线网络，亚洲航空日前推出了全新低成本快递服务——Redbox。据悉，Redbox快递计划将在新加坡、印尼、菲律宾、越南、尼泊尔和马来西亚的31个主要城市运营，未来将逐渐延伸至澳大利亚、日本、中国和香港等地。7月，北京锦绣盛世航空投资管理有限公司与陕西天驹投资集团签约《共同开发航空快递项目投资意向书》。根据协议，双方共同投资5亿元，用3年时间在全国建成快递服务网。

（三）关注冷链物流发展

近年来，冷链物流的市场需求旺盛，其原动力一方面来自消费市场对温控商品总需求的日益壮大，另一方面来自消费市场对商品品质要求的提高，一些对品质要求比较高的商品也进入温控产品序列，致使冷链物流市场日渐扩大。

中国社科院《医药蓝皮书：中国药品市场报告》介绍，中国药品市场复合增长率超过20%。2014年，需要航空冷链物流运输的药品市场超过780亿元。除此之外，依托航空冷链物流的发展，国际先进的冷链全程可视、可追溯体系已经在厦门建立，未来厦门市民的餐桌上，不仅食品鲜活，而且具有质量保障。

芝加哥奥黑尔国际机场是一个美国航空枢纽，也是美国最大的药品空运机场。总的药品运输价值量占了奥黑尔机场所有空运货物价值量的11%，药品是奥黑尔机场的第二大出口货物（仅次于飞机零部件）和第三大进口货物（仅次于手机和电脑）。与达到80%～90%的发达国家的食品冷链运输率相比，中国只有10%左右。据中国物流与采购联合会的调查，目前中国冷藏容量仅占货物需求的20%～30%，还有约90%肉类、80%水产品、大量的牛奶和豆制品未实现冷链保障。一个普遍的冷链现象是“两头冷、中间断”，而这段“中间断”的冷链过程也有待规范。中国的冷链产业蕴藏着巨大商机，航空货运业应积极应对，制定出适合的冷链发展战略，创造良好的社会效益和经济效益。

（四）差异化发展战略成焦点

航空物流市场竞争日益激烈，推动错位发展时机成熟，高铁与国外低成本航空公司的不断冲击，迫使机场与物流企业选择差异化发展。

就机场来说，受各方因素影响，武汉机场近两年货运增长缓慢，2012年及2013年增速分别为4%和1%，低于行业水平。2013年湖北机场集团正式提出“门户＋枢纽”发展战略，并以“国际＋中转＋物流”作为差异化竞争策略，首次将航空物流上升到集团战略层面。最终形成统一发展思路：加快货运转型，成立物流板块，搭建货运平台，推动武汉机场航空物流取得新的突破。在实行差异化发展战略后的一年时间里，武汉机场取得的成绩可喜可贺。2014年7月，武汉机场货运吞吐量增幅达到22.8%，创近年来历史单月增幅新高。2014年1～7月，武汉机场货运增速达11%，迎来新的突破。

就物流企业来说，2014年6月19日，乾瀚国际物流旗下新产品——全日达航空特快正式上线。其主要理念是，瞄准生鲜、高值产品，做高端航空特快服务。全日达打破了传统的空运服务标准和流程。与以往航空物流“机场—机场”的服务流程不同的是，全日达提供“门—门”的快递式服务，并自主研发信息系统，为客户提供一站式物流解决方案，针对客户的不同要求提供限时配送的高效服务，以及超时返还运费等承诺保障，保证用户体验。

（五）生鲜产地直达成新宠

从前只能依靠旅游才能享受到的异国或异地美食，如今依靠航空运输最快当日即可搬上餐桌。正是因为航空物流能够将原产地的食品保质保量的运送到全国各地，这是陆路运输所不能的。

正值樱桃丰收的5月。早晨8点，30公斤刚刚从树上采摘下来的新鲜樱桃离开果园，被运往大连机场。10个小时后，樱桃出现在2000公里以外的广州某酒店客房。广州荔枝熟了。上午9点，由批发市场发往大连的500公斤荔枝，当天傍晚就交付到大连多个收件人手中。也就是说，以大连为起点，广州为终点，货品以每秒约76米的速度在流通。

2014年春运十天内，青岛机场共有200吨海鲜“打飞的”去往全国各地。2014年6月11日至8月底，“东航产地直达”车厘子包机安排8个全货机航班，累计运载超过400吨车厘子到中国内地市场销售。2014年8月，喀什机场的水果平均日处理量达20吨。还有部分小机场通过向枢纽机场集中货物，通过枢纽机场发达的航线网络将本地蔬果销向全国，此种做法不仅解决了小机场航线少、本地产品销售困难等问题，更从另一方面增加了枢纽机场航空货运量。

（六）电子货运

电子货运的重要性不仅在于简化了现有的航空物流链上的商务流程，还在于能够提高航空公司对航空货运业务可持续发展的重视。同时，电子货运在提高自身货运处理效率、打造重要货运枢纽等方面也具有重要意义。

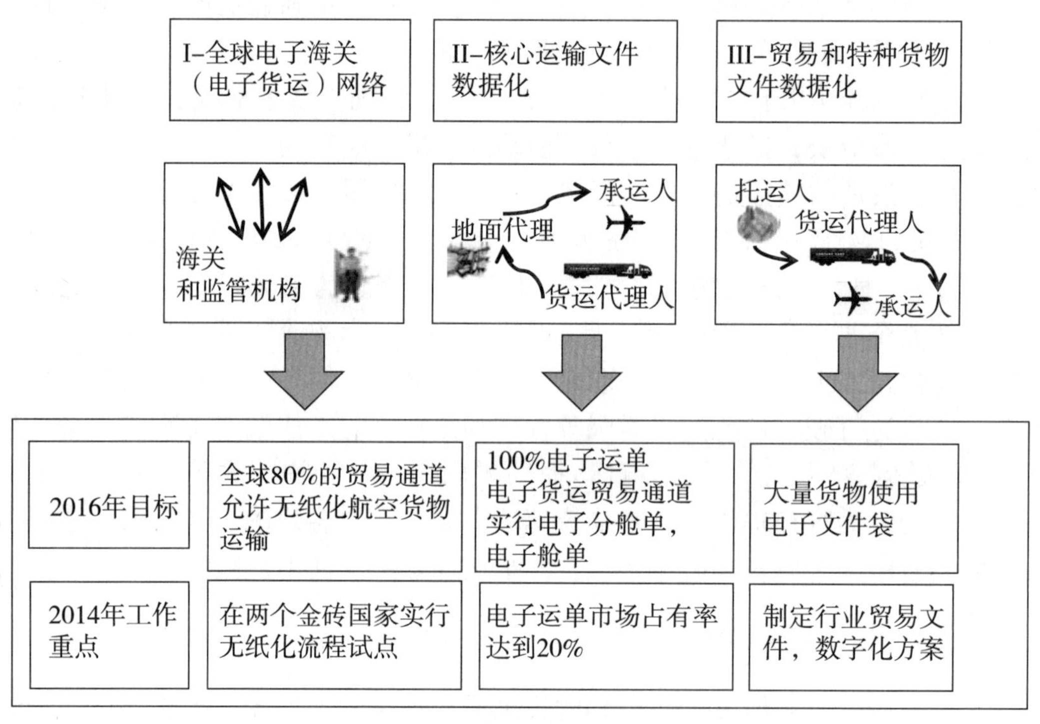

图1　电子货运发展图示

IATA计划的目标是在2015年年底前电子运单达到100%全覆盖。这些目标看起来似乎有些过于自信，但是随着国际航空运输协会的多边电子航空货运单协议的引入，货运行业实际上已经迈出了坚实的一步。业内人士预计，全面实行电子货运计划，全年不仅可为全球货运全价值链带来31亿~49亿美元的净收益，还可同时享受效率提高的好处，如图1所示。

回顾2014年电子货运的发展历程。首先，从总体运量来看，3月国际航空货运电子运单数已达20.6万，达到历史新高。电子运单渗透率（即份额）达到13.4%，环比提高1.2%。其次，从机场排名（按电子货运业务量）来看，香港机场的电子货运业务量全球最多，其占全部业务份额已过半。在电子货运业务中，亚洲机场走在了世界前列。其中，迪拜机场85%的国际货运业务均已实现电子化，占比最高。最后，从航空承运人来看，国泰货运、港龙货运、迪拜货运、阿联酋货运和新加坡货运公司的电子货运业务开展得有声有色，其国际货运业务中电子货运渗透率均已超过3/4。除此之外，国内一些机场也纷纷开展了电子货运业务。

随着2014年11月中旬国家质量监督检验检疫总局发布公告，决定推进无纸化报检工作，电子运单、电子货运的发展也必将实现新突破。

（七）保税物流建设

保税仓库与保税物流中心的建设，其主要作用在于完善机场保税物流功能，健全机场航空口岸设施，有效提升招商引资竞争力。除此之外，可有效带动空港周边物流产业发展，为高新技术产业的高附加值原材料、产成品带来良好的保税物流环境，进一步整合周边物流、仓储、监管、加工、生产型服务、进出口贸易等资源，促进供应链完善，加快产业结构优化。

2014年9月，合肥空港公用型保税仓库获批建设，这预示着合肥及周边地区从事进出口贸易的企业可在该仓库免税存放相关货物，这不仅降低了企业经营成本和产品周转费用，还解决了国际物流仓储和国际联运的难题。同年10月成都空港保税物流中心正式通过国家验收、西咸空港保税物流中心获批。

保税物流一直是空港建设关注的焦点，它直接推动了航空物流的发展，间接提升了空港乃至城市的对外合作高度。所以，每年都会看见各大空港在保税物流上努力建设，也能从中受益匪浅。

（八）高铁冲击

一直以来，航空与快递相结合是不错的运营模式，且因为快递业务对于运输时间要求较高，铁路、公路往往难以和空运形成竞争。但随着火车提速以及铁路网络加密，铁路开始有能力与飞机竞争，这对航企会产生一定影响。7月1日，铁路总局正式开行首批3对6列试点特快电商班列，8月又增开了京广、京沪两列快递专列。

传统意义上，陆路、铁路、航空三种转运方式的竞争距离分别在500千米以内、500~1000千米、1000千米以上，运输时间分别在2小时以内、1~1.5小时、2小时以上。过去以“大宗商品”为主的铁路货运在推进市场化改革方面积极性很高，而且随着高铁速度和密集度的提升，千公里内高铁运输相比航空来说优势更强。所以，高铁进军快递领域对航空货运业带来了不小的打击。公路物流和铁路物流的大势兴起，对航空物流发出了新的挑战，社会生活节奏加快也对航空物流提出了新的要求。

航空运输作为航空物流的重要载体，直接影响和制约着航空物流系统的整体发展。各大型机场均充分整合各种运输方式的经济和技术优势，为开展综合运输创造有利条件。为应对高铁竞争，机场、航空公司单方面的努力是不够的，最好的办法是在竞争中谋求一条合作化道路，也就是齐心协力发展综合运输，致力于解决物流最关心的“最后一公里”。

二、2015 年航空物流发展展望

2015 年，全球货运量有望增长 4.5%，达到 5350 万吨。自 2011 年以来，全球航空货运市场就一直面临着市场疲软和日益激烈的竞争，但 2015 年全球货物运输的成本有望下降 5.8%，货运总收入有望增至 630 亿美元。预计全球 1% 的 GDP 将用于航空运输，总计超过 8200 亿美元，如图 2 所示。

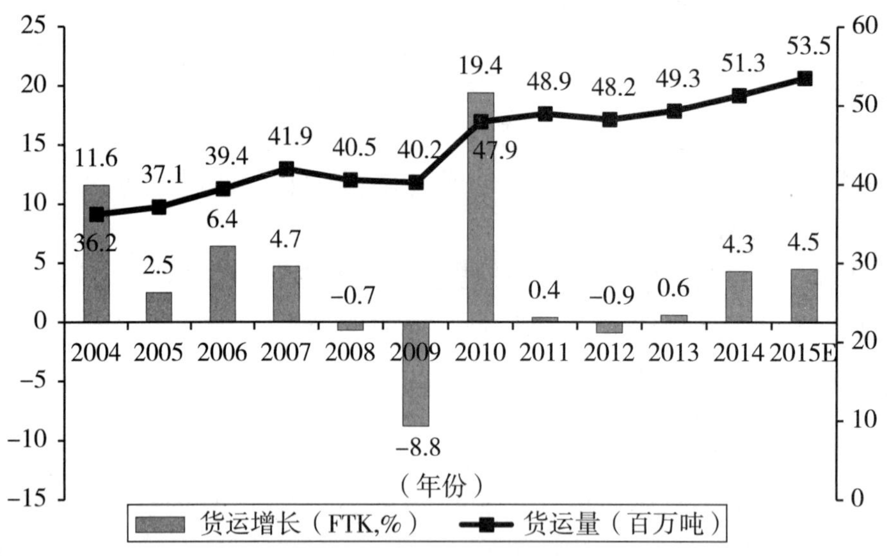

图 2　全球航空货运变化趋势

中国民航业在 2014 年发展势头良好，根据中国民航局统计，2015 年中国民航主要业务指标预期：全行业运输总周转量 817.2 亿吨公里、旅客运输量 4.3 亿人次、货邮运输量 627 万吨，分别比上年增长 10.2%、10.0% 和 6.0%，如图3、图 4 所示。

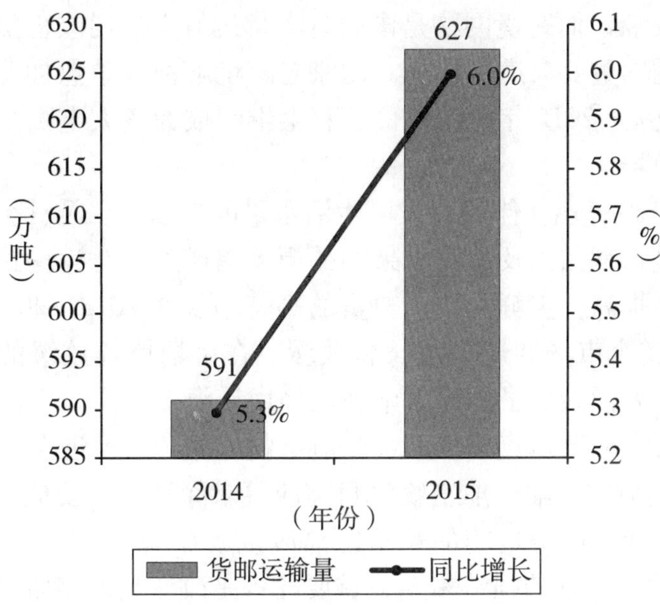

图 3　2015 年预期指标：货邮运输量

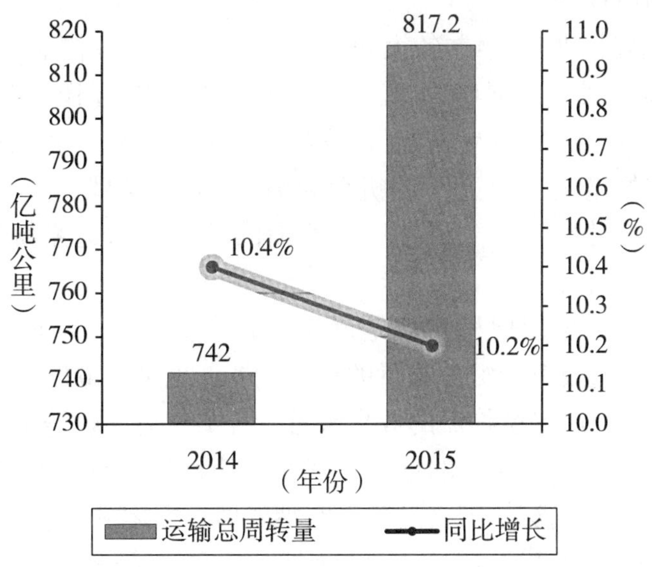

图 4　2015 年预期指标：运输总周转量

2015 年国内航空物流发展方向可以从以下几个方面进行展开：

（1）跨境电商。到 2018 年，中国将占全球跨境电商比例的 50%，PayPal 数据显示，预计至 2018 年中国跨境网购消费者将达 3560 万人，“海淘”规模将达到 1 万亿元。国际航空运输协会（IATA）表示，受跨境贸易增加带动，2015 年全球空运需求将增长 4.5%。跨境电商是中国从“世界工厂”向“世界商场”的转型支点，而跨境网购是国内各大货运航空公司改善货源结构、解决市场单向性问题的重要渠道。伴随着国家对跨境电商政策愈加明朗、行业内部运作形式愈加规范，2015 年跨境电商还将会继续成为各大电商平台与航空货运业逐鹿的重要战场。

（2）生鲜产地直达。伴随着人民生活水平的提高，以及社会生活节奏的加快，国人对于进口食品以及生鲜水果的欲望大幅增加，对运输速度和服务质量的要求也在不断提高。生鲜网购用户量的高速增长在 2013—2014 年基本完成。因此 2015 年，整个市场的规模增长将放缓。在市场增长放缓的前提下，今年又将有新的竞争者涌入。虽然生鲜电商已经由蓝海变红海，但不会影响整体的航空运量，生鲜产品产地直达依旧会是航空物流的一个推进点。

（3）远距离航空运输。航空物流目前应寻求除高效、便捷优势外的竞争优势。对于高铁提速，航空运输的竞争距离应该放在 1500 公里以上远程的货源上。2015 年，面对高铁的强势来袭，首要任务是改变当前多段经营与运输的局面，将散落的环节连接起来，并加强与公路等运输方式的有机衔接。要取得海关、检疫等方面的支持，尽可能缩短流程和时间。总之努力提高运输时效，以赢得航空物流的市场空间。

（4）综合运输。2015 年，各大机场将会继续从机场周边道路建设上下功夫；面对“电商专列”的强势来袭，与“铁老大”的合作也是趋势之一，在运送速度、配送距离、成本支出上将获取“三赢”战绩；除此之外，一些沿海城市机场应利用好坐拥“双港”的机会大力发展“空海联动”。多方努力相结合，多种运输方式并举，才能最终实现所谓的“全球联运系统”，真正达到使航运货物“流”起来的目的。

（5）保税物流。发展保税物流是近几年的热点，各大空港针对保税物流提出的相关政策不仅是吸引投资与项目的重要利器，也是空港航空物流快速发展的保障。通过近几年开展保税物流的成果来看，各个空港都取得了喜人的成绩，保税物流现在可以算是空港建设的标配，一个城市航空物流发展阶段的标识。所以，在 2015 年，保税物流依旧会是各大空港发展航空运输考虑的方向之一。

（6）冷链物流。2014 年冷链物流行业保持 20% 左右的增长，从传统 B2B 的冷链物流服务大规模转向 B2C。数据显示：国内果蔬冷链损耗率高达 25%，而发达国家的果蔬损耗率在 5% 左右，美国部分生鲜电商甚至能将损耗率控制在 1%。冷链物流问题是当前农产品电商的重大瓶颈，冷链物流关键切入点是要“快”，而能切合这个“快”的，就是航空运输。

（中国民航大学　曹允春）

2014年仓储业发展回顾与2015年展望

2014年，我国的仓储业处于艰难的转型期，主要是受经济增速放缓、经济结构调整、土地资源紧缺、东西部发展不平衡等因素的影响。总体看来，仓储业增速放缓，业务结构调整速度加快，仓储技术向机械化、自动化、信息化方向发展。

一、2014年仓储业发展回顾

（一）仓储企业生产经营趋稳，但尚未度过风险期

根据中国物资储运协会对60家大型仓储企业的调查显示，2014年样本企业主营业务收入比上年下降28%，但物流收入增长17%；货物吞吐量6137万吨，比上年增长4%；公路运输量增长18%，铁路运输量增长9%；货物年周转次数为10次，比上年增加2.3次；利润总额比上年下降18.6%。主要特点：一是生活品物流业务增长，生产品物流业务下降。大宗商品物流量和销售价格下跌，造成以大宗商品为主要对象的物资仓库业务下滑，而与百姓生活相关的仓储物流业务增长，抵消了部分下降因素。2014年库房业务收入增长8.9%，而货场业务下滑2.9%。二是租用外仓数量增加。由于本企业仓容不足或客户有特殊要求，样本企业租用外仓达110万平方米，增长30%以上。三是亏损企业数增加，达到16家，且亏损额大幅增大。主要原因在于：高速增长时期过于冒进，对外投资失误；贸易业务上当受骗，做托盘业务不控货；企业被迫搬迁，旧地交出，新地批不下来，客户和业务流失等。

（二）新兴仓储物流需求增大

一是电子商务飞速发展，要求仓储业适应小批量、多批次、快交付的要求。2014年，全国兴起了电商物流热，规划和建设了较多的电商物流中心。在大宗商品领域，电子交易取代了一批中间贸易商，无须见面、直接交易数量增加。同时，由于生产商要求快速交付，仓库的选址分布从产地向消费地转移，消费地仓库需求量增加。二是特种仓库需求量增加，如温控仓库、化危仓库、液体仓库的数量，结构均有较大缺口。由于上述仓库都有一定的危险性，有的城市限制，有的拒绝其入驻。三是多式联运型仓库需求大。最突出的是公铁联运、铁水联运，其制约因素在于缺乏适宜的地块和足够的土地面积，以及土地

价格和设施设备的通用程度。四是农资农产品、快递储物场所需求空间增大。农资下乡、农产品进城、快递送达都需要有相应方便快捷的仓储设施。

（三）仓储业投资加快，仓储设施供求紧张有所缓解

2014 年 1—11 月，仓储业投资额为 4672.5 亿元，同比增长 24.3%，而同期的铁路投资为 5920.6 亿元。另外，国家统计局发布的第三次经济普查报告显示，截止到 2013 年底，我国仓储业总资产达到 16878.6 亿元。比 2003 年增长 14300 亿元，增幅 5.5 倍，比 2008 年增加 11184.6 亿元，增长 196%。此外，2009 年到 2013 年，仓储业投资累计 13027 亿元，年平均增长超过 30%。上述数据表明：一是 10 年来，仓储业投资大幅增长，无论是增长速度还是绝对额，都是前所未有的。二是我国的营业性仓储面积拥有量估计在 13 亿平方米以上。其中一半以上是近五年新建仓储设施。三是仓储设施总体规模大体与经济需求相适应。展望今后几年，仓储业投资仍会增长，主要是因为我国仓储业投资欠账过多，加上城市扩张过快，老仓储设施被驱赶出城，新建仓储设施要逐步到位，但增长速度会适度放缓。其主要制约因素在于：我国经济增速放缓、土地资源紧缺、建设资金供给偏紧、经济结构调整、电子商务的发展等。

（四）物流园区向质量、效益方向发展

无论从需求、供给、市场、资金、土地等各个因素来看，都不支持物流园区无限扩张，部分物流园区正在走精益之路。2014 年，中物联物流园区专业委员会对 189 家参评物流园区进行了评价。通过 20 多个指标的测评，50 家园区获批成为优秀物流园区。50 个园区平均占地面积 4950 亩，平均物流强度每平方公里吞吐量 504 万吨，平均就业人数 9300 人，平均人年业务收入 50 万元。另据观点地产网报道，杭州将加快建设杭州临江传化综合物流产业园、杭州空港物流园区、顺丰（杭州）智能电商物流产业园等一批重点园区。2017 年杭州将初步建成“全国智慧物流中心”运营架构。一般化、低水平的物流园区已经过时，代之而起的是多功能、高质量、智慧型的物流基础设施。

（五）仓储业投资市场活跃

据物流供应链竞争情报报道，2014 年财团加大对仓储业的投资。如平安不动产 15 亿元注资五洲国际；中银集团、厚朴基金、中国人寿等构成的豪华中资财团 25 亿美元注资普洛斯；荷兰汇盈将向易商投资 6.5 亿美元，高盛向易商提供 1.2 亿美元 Pre－IPO 贷款融资；新加坡和中国香港的私募股权公司 RRJ Capital 以及新加坡淡马锡旗下的狮诚控股国际向宇培投资 2.5 亿美元；凯雷集团以及汤森房产集团 2 亿美元投资宇培；嘉民集团和加拿大养老金计划投资委

员会（CPPIB）向嘉民中国物流基金注资5亿美元，总量达到15亿美元。普洛斯入股中储股份，投资20亿元，占15%的股份，并取得第二大股东的位置。据有关报道，普洛斯正在加快转型，由物流地产商向物流运营商转变。这表明，普洛斯已完成了第一阶段的战略布局，正在向纵深扩大战果。

（六）铁路货运改革力度大，货场改造速度加快

2013年铁路总公司启动货运改革之后，推出网上订仓、一口价、零担货运列车、直达货运列车、白货运价下浮等一系列措施。原来的货运场站已不能适应新的需求，铁总启动了货场改造计划，总的方向是增加库房、增加装卸搬运设备等。设施设备的改造使铁路物流的收入结构发生了变化，单一的铁路货运收入逐步向多元经营收入转变。据观察和数据资料分析，铁路物流收入中运输业务收入占75.5%，装卸搬运收入占7%，配送与货代业务收入占5.7%，包装加工收入占2%，仓储收入占1.2%，综合业务收入占6.4%。站到门、门到门业务大幅度提升。

二、仓储业存在的挑战和机遇

（一）仓储设施规划布局不合理

一是随着人口的迅速集聚，城市物流体系不适应性日渐显现。各个城市都在扩建新区，一般情况下，新区面积大过老区。如陕西的西咸新区，面积882平方千米，兰州新区面积1600平方千米，天津滨海新区面积2270平方千米。原有的物流体系被打乱，仓储、货站、道路、铁路、码头、港口的布局需重新规划。二是交通组织管理与需求不相适应。人口和建筑的聚集给城市道路通行带来拥堵、噪声，货车进城受到严格控制。货物供应不足会引起物价上涨，百姓不满。三是土地商品化，有偿使用，把低端商贸和物流驱赶到更远的地方，使用价格更高的土地，使其利润越来越薄，城市内外的货物交换缺少相应的仓储设施。

（二）安全事故后果严重

2015年1月2日13时，哈尔滨市北方南勋陶瓷大市场仓库起火，22时，仓库上部的居民楼坍塌。造成5名消防队员牺牲，14名消防人员受伤。该建筑是20世纪90年代建成，地面三层是库房和商铺，五至八层为居民住宅。仓库和商贸、居住设施混合型建筑，是灾难发生的首要因素。从古至今，仓库都是单独建设的。这是因为，仓库是储存货物的场所，要远离危险源，远离人群。在这样一个地下室做仓库、地面低层做商场、商场以上是居民住宅的多功能叠

加的场所，建筑密度大，交通混乱拥堵，一旦发生事故，无法展开救援。哈尔滨大火不仅伤亡巨大，而且居民积攒多年的财产损毁，后果严重。

（三）仓储用地更为紧缺

据国土资源部统计，2014 年，全国国有建设用地批准面积为近三年同期最低水平，供地结构出现变化。全年供应建设用地共 61 万公顷，同比下降 16.5%。其中，工矿仓储用地 15 万公顷，同比下降 29.9%；房地产用地 15.1 万公顷，同比下降 25.5%；基础设施等其他用地 31.1 万公顷，同比下降 1.9%。

2014 年，有关部门和部分省市纷纷出台了节约集约使用土地的政策。2014 年 2 月 22 日和 3 月 28 日，上海市政府先后印发和转发了《关于进一步提高本市土地节约集约利用水平的若干意见（沪府发〔2014〕14 号文》和《关于加强本市工业用地出让管理的若干规定（试行）（沪府办〔2014〕25 号文)》。文件规定："提高土地市场周转效率。实行新增工业用地出让弹性年期制，一般工业项目用地出让年期为 20 年，出让年限届满后，对项目综合效益和合同履约等情况进行评估，采取有偿协议方式，续期或收回土地使用权。对用地有特殊要求的市重点产业项目，经有关部门批准后，出让年期可为 20 ~ 50 年"。2014 年 6 月 3 日，北京经济开发区也发布文件，规定建设用地出让年限一般不高于 20 年。南京市政府宁政发 2014（150）号文规定，工业建设用地出让年限不超过 30 年，土地出让价格提高 50% ~ 150%。2014 年 7 月 10 日四川日报报道，成都、自贡、遂宁、眉山、南充、简阳、邻水 7 市、县开展工业用地弹性年期出让及低效、存量工业用地退出机制改革试点。在法定的工业用地使用权最高出让年限内，分别设定 10 年、20 年、30 年、40 年、50 年出让年限。

（四）仓储业受资金紧缺的约束较大

中国人民银行发布数据，2014 年，我国广义货币余额 122.8 万亿元，同比增长 12.2%，狭义货币余额 34.84 万亿元，同比增长 3.2%，比上年低 6.1 个百分点。贷款余额 81.68 万亿元，同比增长 13.6%，增速比上年低 0.5 个百分点，非金融企业及其他部门贷款增加 6.48 万亿元。

资金供给相对不足，致使以借贷资金为主建设的仓储设施压力增大，一方面需要建设资金，尽快形成生产能力，另一方面需要增加运营资金，还要支付土地使用成本如土地使用税。一些园区已经开始抛售产权，也有的采取租赁外包方式减轻资金压力。

（五）仓储业的新机遇

一是"一带一路"和依托黄金水道推动长江经济带发展战略的实施，给仓储业的布局提出新要求。同时还要求仓储业走向境外。二是仓储业成为物流中的关键。生产供应功能、城市服务功能、蓄水池功能、货物集散功能、库存管理功能、应急储备功能叠加在一起，需求量增加，给仓储业提出更高的要求。仓储若不能完成这些功能，就会产生物流梗阻。三是仓储业的技术支持更加成熟。无论是库房建造，还是机器装备都有较大的发展。2014 年上海物流装备展上，自动化装卸搬运设备，如机器人、穿梭机、自动分拣机的展位明显增多，表明需求在增大。

三、2015 年仓储业发展展望

2015 年，我国仓储业仍然需要面对严峻的经济环境压力，调结构、降增速、谋布局、重效益成为仓储业发展的主基调。

调结构：是指仓储设施的结构和仓储企业业务结构要适应新的需要。仓储业务的结构要适应产业结构和生活需要，原材料等资源型仓储企业要应对货量不足和场地外迁的变化，生活类仓储企业要应对多批次、少批量、快分拣的要求。所有仓储企业都要主动融入供应链，把眼光放在整体行业的发展和变化上。无数事实证明，不谋全局者不足谋一隅。电商、快运、冷链、化危等产品的仓储设施要专业化，普通仓库设施要柔性化，适应性更强。在过去的一段时期内，快运中转仓库用普通仓库替代，在通道、站台、柱距、纵深等方面造成浪费。冷链仓库不能实现全封闭，节能方面有较大缺陷。

降增速：是指仓储业务和基础投资增长速度会下降。在一线城市，仓租还会有一定程度的增长，但增速会放缓。据中国物资储运协会统计，2014 年样本企业平均每平米仓储面积收入为 321 元，比 2013 年的平均收入 370 元下降了 13%；平均每平米仓储面积创利 34 元，比 2013 年减少了 2 元；市场商铺出租率为 82%，比上年下降了四个百分点。较低的投资利润率会影响到投资者的积极性。2015 年的仓储业投资将有重点选择，对仓储“洼地”进行填平补齐。国家战略涉及区域和产业转入地还会迎来仓储设施建设的热潮。

谋布局：是指仓储业的管理者和经营者都会在全局上考虑仓储业布局。包括城乡仓储设施的位置、数量、规模、业态、服务范围、标准化和网络化等。比如化危仓库的选址、建设标准和安全管理，是推不掉躲不开的事，不如积极应对。城市规划物流先行，物流设施要先于城市建设考虑。应该打造物流网络体系。在物流行业中，最有价值的是网络，建立业务网络、运输配送网络、仓储网络、综合交通物流网络、信息网络。还应该建立完善的国际物流体系。两个丝绸之路经济带建设和长江经济带的发展，是我国新一轮对外开放的重大措施。与国际对接，就要引入国际思维，谋求双赢而不是利益独占；引入国际标准，谋求最优而不是唯我独尊；引进技术装备，谋求集成而不是全面依赖。

重效益：是指应把铺摊子、占土地的路子转移到注重效益的轨道上来。要确立新的评估指标体系，以需求为导向重新评估企业的战略定位，企业的方向应以做强为主而不是做大为主。高主营收入增长率指标要让位于质量、效益和就业指标；以服务为导向调整业务体系。不断从客户的现实需求和潜在需求中找到自己的服务定位，服务标准化、标准透明化，自加压力，提升服务档次。只算计客户不维护客户的合作是不能长久的。比如在质押监管业务中，许多物流企业对提供市场价格信息、回购、确认物权等避之不及，而有的企业则把这样的需求接下来，同时加强风险防控。收入是原来的 4 倍。用供应链管理的理念重新组建业务管理体系，公司业务一盘棋统筹，深圳式的供应链金融业务就包括了供应链融资方案设计、贸易、货代、通关、物流的方案规划、融资、办税、结算、结汇、保险、仓储、运输、配送、加工、包装、市场营销拓展等。一些公司块块式的组织体系显然不合时宜。我们谈了多年的精益化，现在是到了认真落实的时候了。

2015 年，国内外经济处于缓慢复苏调整期，下行压力依然明显，资金供给总体偏紧，引致需求减弱，土地市场上升乏力，地价环比涨幅持续回落。给仓储业带来许多不确定因素，希望行业内企业审时度势，清理半拉子工程，尽快形成生产能力。新项目应谨慎上马，尤其是仓储设施充足的地区。所有仓储企业应尽快融入供应链管理，创造更多的服务产品，服务制造业、服务农业、服务电商、服务人民生活。

（中国物资储运协会　姜超峰）

2014 年国际货代业发展回顾与 2015 年展望

国际货代是为对外经贸提供服务的物流行业。2014 年中国经济的主题词是新常态。受其影响，中国对外贸易和对外承包工程增速放缓，国际货代业也随之进入新常态。本文以新常态为关键词，回顾一年来的行业成就，展望未来的发展趋势。

一、2014 年国际货代业发展回顾

（一）行业全面进入新常态

中国经济进入新常态有三层含义：一是经济发展由高速转入中高速增长，7% 或是一个临界值；二是经济结构不断优化升级，大力提升第三产业的比重；三是经济发展的动力由要素驱动、投资驱动等转向创新驱动。

2014 年 9 月，国务院颁布《物流业发展中长期规划（2014—2020 年》（国发〔2014〕第 42 号），首次将包括货代业在内的物流业明确定位为支撑国民经济发展的基础性、战略性产业，物流业在国民经济中的地位稳步提升。随着中国对外经济贸易进入新常态，国际货代业也将进入新常态，并呈现三大特点：

其一，行业发展整体转向中低速增长阶段。2014 年，我国进出口总值 26. 43 万亿元人民币，以美元计为 4. 30 万亿美元，同比增长 3. 4%，低于年初预期；我国对外承包工程业务完成营业额 8748. 2 亿元人民币，以美元计为 1424. 1 亿美元，同比增长 3. 8%。上游对外贸易和工程承包行业增速下滑，直接导致下游国际物流业增速下滑。2014 年 1—11 月，全国外贸货物吞吐量仅增长 6. 1%，国际货邮吞吐量仅增长 7. 3%。受民生需求的拉动，2014 年，国际及港澳台业务等快递收入完成 315. 9 亿元，同比增长 16. 7%，跨境电商贸易增长 30%。除此之外，绝大多数国际货代和物流业务处于 5% 左右的中低速增长。

其二，行业优化结构和转型升级步伐加快。现阶段，我国国际货代的功能分散，环节单一，订舱、仓储、报关等简单性业务所占比重大。经济全球化必然带来物流服务的专业化和国际化。由于海外网络和行业经验的缺失，国内真正有能力提供高端全程国际物流服务，如工程物流、跨境电商物流、国际采购物流、国际会展、保税物流等和能够提供供应链集成服务的国际货代企业比重还比较低。由于市场环境的变化，近些年来，不少行业企业拓展新业务，加快

向专业化、综合性物流企业迈进。如中国外运股份有限公司工程物流业务持续增长，并在国内合同物流的基础上积极拓展国际化经营，开发了“替代采购+外包仓（VMI）”、“替代采购+国际集拼（Consolidation）”新模式。2014年年底，该公司成功中标世界500强企业澳大利亚Kmart公司超市项目，获得该公司中澳80%的DC管理和运输业务。

其三，创新驱动对国际货代转型升级更具针对性和迫切性。历史的原因造成国际货代是轻资产、重渠道的中间商，2003年取消审批放开市场后，国际货代业快速发展。截止到2014年年底，在商务部备案的国际货代企业总计35000家。10多年来，集成货代功能、延伸业务链条且蓬勃发展的物流业在削弱传统货代的生存空间，并且国际货代业是在电子商务日新月异、上游国际航运市场萎靡不振、行业内部企业资金缺乏且融资成本高、劳动力“红利”日趋丧失等要素供求关系日益偏紧的基础上艰难挺进的。创新驱动是适应我国经济和上下游行业新常态，促进我国国际货代业转型发展的关键一招。

（二）经济新常态带来的机遇和挑战

新常态下，政府以转变职能、简政放权为抓手，为企业松绑，致力于打造一个大众创业、万众创新的营商环境。2014年，伴随着“一带一路”上升为国家战略，中国对外开放迎来了新的发展空间。这对我国国际货代和物流企业创业创新和海外发展带来潜在机遇。

1. 政府简政放权为中小企业生存发展营造良好环境

2014年，中央政府大幅度取消行政审批，力推简政放权，关注中小微企业发展，成为本年度政府行政改革的最大亮点。此举无疑使行业数量占比超80%的中小企业直接受益。

2014年1月1日起，实施多年的报关员统一资格考试制度被取消；7月，政府推出商事登记制度改革，实行“先照后证”；11月，国务院决定取消报检员资格许可，这为中小货代企业延伸业务打开了方便之门。

2014年7月4日，国家税务总局发布国际货物运输代理服务有关增值税问题公告，自2014年9月1日起，将国际货物运输代理服务免税范围由直接与国际运输单位发生业务的代理环节扩大到间接提供国际货物运输代理服务环节。这标志着自2013年以来，行业广泛呼吁的国际货代企业免征增值税的问题得到初步解决，显著减轻了企业的税收负担和经营成本。同时，针对中小微企业融资难、融资贵和税负重的问题，2014年和2015年年初，国务院常务会议多次研究决定降费减税，不断为中小企业创业创新送去“政策大礼包”。

2014年7月，为稳定外贸增长，国家发改委牵头，会同财政部、海关总署、质检总局、商务部和交通运输部集中开展整顿规范进出口环节经营性服务和收费专项工作，取消了一批港口码头、口岸检验和查验等不合理收费，有效维护了企业利益，得到了企业的一致好评。

2014 年，关检部门通力合作，实施了多项贸易便利化通关措施。海关总署在全国 20 个直属海关实施“一次申报、一次查验、一次放行”新模式，提高了口岸通关效率、降低企业经营成本，深受广大货代和货主企业欢迎。同年 9 月和 12 月，海关总署分别在京津冀、长江经济带启动区域通关一体化改革，助力贸易便利化和区域经济发展。

2014 年 12 月 22 日，国务院在总结上海自由贸易试验区设立一年成功经验的基础上，决定在广东、天津、福建特定区域再设 3 个自由贸易园区。自贸区的成立为行业企业创新经营模式、拓展供应链服务创造了难得的条件。

此外，2014 年 6 月，中国国际货运代理协会（CIFA）首次举办 FIATA 亚太区会议，并连续成功举办了十一届中外货代物流企业洽谈会，显著提升了我国国际货代业在亚太及全球的影响力。天津国际货运代理协会等地方行业组织聚焦行业热点问题，搭建信息和会员服务、业务合作交流、政策法律咨询、专业培训等平台，全方位为行业企业服务。

2. “一带一路”战略拓宽国际物流业发展空间

新常态下，我国对外开放高水平“引进来”、大规模“走出去”将会同步发生。现阶段，诸多原因造成国内物流企业“走出去”总体缓慢。我国物流经营的阶段性特点及提升我国物流企业全球竞争力的内涵等要求国内物流企业必须加快“走出去”的步伐。“一带一路”沿线区域、非洲、拉丁美洲等新兴市场将成为我国物流企业“走出去”的重点区域。

新一届中央领导登高望远，统筹国内国外两个大局，适时提出并积极推进以互联互通建设为重点的“一带一路”战略，至少是未来 5 ~ 10 年中国实施全方位对外开放新战略的“先手棋”和突破口。2014 年是“一带一路”国家战略的顶层设计之年。

2014 年 10 月 24 日，由中国发起设立的亚洲基础设施投资银行（AIIB）成立，初始资本 500 亿美元，重点支持“一带一路”基础设施建设。

2014 年 11 月 8 日，在北京 APEC 期间，国家主席习近平宣布中国将出资 400 亿美元成立丝路基金，为“一带一路”互联互通项目提供投融资支持。

2014 年 12 月 4 日，中共中央正式印发“一带一路”发展规划，从战略目标、合作重点、组织领导、优先安排的项目清单等方面明确了时间表和路线图，为该战略的落地实施提供了遵循和保障。该规划明确提出支持国际货代企业参与有关项目建设。

“一带一路”战略建设的重点是加强政策沟通、道路联通、贸易畅通、货币流通、民心相通。这“五通”之间紧密联系、相互促进，关联性强。其中，道路联通、贸易畅通、货币流通同国际货代和物流企业的主业经营密切相关，将为相关企业以海外项目为抓手，绑定国内大型工商企业集群式“走出去”，到沿线区域海外布局、整体输出物流服务和管理等提供了一次重大机遇。

事物都有两面性。客观说，新常态也为行业的发展带来不少挑战。主要表现在：

一是行业增速的下滑不利于企业做大。现阶段，我国的国际货代和物流企业总体规模偏小，保持一个较高的增长速度，对加速行业成长发展、做大企业规模有积极意义。

二是传统货代的生存空间受到吞噬。电商物流和航运电商等跨境电商业务的方兴未艾，正动摇着上游传统外贸的经营模式，客户消费需求和体验的不断升级使得O2O（线上线下）、贸易+金融+物流等新兴模式有望引领行业未来。而目前，很多行业企业仍停留在传统的中间商角色，市场意识、资源条件和技术储备很难有所作为，来适应这一潮流和趋势。

三是行业市场竞争日益加剧。新常态下，我国将按照准入前国民待遇加负面清单的方式，进一步加大国内物流领域向外资的开放。外资跨国物流巨头如UPS、DHL 、FedEx、Schenker 等凭借网络、技术、资产、模式等综合优势将会在国内外快递、工程物流、国际采购物流、高端合同物流、供应链金融和管理、保税物流、国际铁路货运等领域同国内同行展开全方位竞争，这或许会进一步降低国内企业在相关国际业务上的市场占有率。

综上所述，因企业的业务领域、发展阶段、资源条件不同，不同企业对新常态带来机遇和挑战的认识不尽相同。虽如此，求同存异，行业随经济大势进入新常态是客观经济规律，行业增速的放缓恰恰给企业调整结构和创新转型预留了时间和空间。

二、2015 年国际货代业发展展望

（一）新常态下行业发展环境会进一步优化

2015 年是我国全面深化改革的关键之年。各级政府将继续实施简政放权，让利于企业。

从外部看，世界经济复苏的动力仍不足，世界贸易组织预测全球贸易的增长率为3.8%。基于对国内外形势的研判，2015 年我国外贸的年增长率设定为6%。为稳定外贸增长，国家将有望从财税、信贷、通关便利化等方面出台一系列“稳增长，调结构”的组合性政策措施。2 月，国务院发文出台实施有关执法部门信息互通、监管互认、执法互助的“三互”措施，力推大通关建设。

2015 年1 月，国务院颁布《关于加快发展服务贸易的若干意见》，提出积

极发展运输等服务业，大力推动服务业对外投资。

2015 年 3 月，《政府工作报告》首次将“一带一路”、长江经济带和京津冀协同发展战略明确为“三大支撑带”，将着力统筹实施。围绕“一带一路”战略，国家发改委、财政部、商务部、交通运输部等多个政府部门已推出年度重点工作，20 多个省市区地方政府列入政府工作报告，排出具体工作安排，“一带一路”进入全面实质操作阶段。

2015 年也是落实《物流业发展中长期规划》、《促进物流业发展三年行动计划》的启动之年，企业期盼多年的一些政策措施或落地破局。这些政策措施将为国际货代业的发展提供更加有利的营商环境，极大提升行业企业增长的潜力和动力。

（二）新常态下行业发展趋势展望

国际货代是一个重在资源整合、靠管理出效益的行业。新常态下，我国国际货代和物流业的发展将更多转向效益优先、结构调整、创新发展等多策并举的轨道。

1. 优先将效益提升作为考核企业业绩的核心指标

同其他行业一样，主营业务收入和利润是考核物流企业的两个基本指标。总体来看，我国物流企业的经营规模偏小，产业集中度偏低。2014 年，我国前 50 强物流企业的主营收入 8233 亿元，仅占同期我国 500 强企业排名前 50 强企业的 3%，占同期社会物流总费用的 8%。要提升我国物流企业的收入规模，一靠企业自身的内生发展，二靠借用外力并购重组。研究德国邮政（DHL）、美国联合包裹（UPS）、德国辛克（DB Schenker）、荷兰基华（CEVA）、中东致力（Agility）等全球前 10 强物流企业的发展史，大规模的资本并购是他们做大业务规模、拓展新业务、进军新市场的重要手段。结合成长性、经营模式和市场环境看，在目前的国际货代和物流领域，国内企业开展资本并购的机会不大。

在国内外宏观经济增速放缓的新常态下，除跨境电商、国际快递等少数与民生相关的国际物流业务外，国际货代和物流企业要保持前几年主营收入 10% 的年均快速增长，已非常困难。在增量不大的前提下，应把经营重点放在存量的优化和提升上。适应新常态的要求，中小货代企业应主要考核利润增长指标。即便是行业内的一些大型企业，也应把考核增长的重点更多放在主营业务利润率、应收账款周转率等效益指标上。

2. 着力将结构优化作为加快企业转型的重点

传统国际货代业经营的困局主要在于经营模式落后，业务链条短，适应上游外贸、工程承包行业转型升级的需要及物流和供应链发展趋势，行业的优化升级可从以下着眼：

从内容上，对于传统业务，除一些大型企业可继续通过建立订舱平台控制渠道外，中小企业应转变靠以庄家“坐庄”搞订舱代理做大规模的模式，要有效配置有限资源，着力走“专、精、特”专业化经营，以适应上游外贸客户多元化和个性化的需求；对于新兴业务，重点是以全程物流解决方案为引领，向国内外两端尤其是向海外段延伸，通过整合资源、加强海外网络建设和加大属地化设施投资等，大力发展整合的国际货代、工程物流、跨境电商、保税物流、合同物流等专业物流服务，这是推动整个行业结构优化的成败之举。

从地域上看，传统货代业务主要集中欧盟、美加、亚洲（日本、韩国、中国香港等）这三大传统外贸市场，但市场已饱和，货运需求增长缓慢，结构调整的重点是“巩固存量，发展增量”。而“一带一路”沿线国家及非洲、拉美、南太等新兴市场，外贸增长强劲，工程承包规模大，是我们扩大传统货代规模和提升工程物流等专业物流比重需重点锁定的目标市场。为此，应绑定大型工商企业一起“走出去”，以海外网络建设为支撑，采取反向营销、培育人才、实体投资等措施，在管控好风险的同时，搞好属地化经营，以加强在当地的存在，输出自己的行业服务和管理。这或是不少国际货代和物流企业调整业务布局的必由之路。

3. 坚持将创新发展作为引领企业发展的自觉行动

由于国际货运的运输工具主要由承运人掌控，国际货代和物流经营的核心在于国外两端软性资源（网络、渠道、人脉）及必要的支持性硬资源（如堆场、车队）的整合。其中硬件资源少，主要靠软性资源的整合和运作，导致客户黏性较国内物流差、可持续能力不强，这是行业经营的最大软肋。要在新常态下实现行业的可持续发展，增长的动力同样来自创新，也必须来自创新。结合行业特点，主要是管理创新、制度创新和技术创新。

首先，管理创新关乎国际货代和物流企业的成败，是推动行业可持续经营的永恒主题。结合实际，这其中既包括对仓库、车辆、设备、运力等“硬件”的管理优化，又包括对前期投标、客户营销，中期运营流程、风险和分包商，后期财务、资金等及后台支撑系统（商务、人才、文化、团队）等全套“软”系统的创新管理。管理创新的重点在于创新运营机制、构建协同的网络体系、重组优化作业流程、持续培养复合型职业化人才，难点在于营销创新。

其次，大力推动制度创新。重提制度创新对国际货代和物流企业经营有现实意义。在大中型企业内部探索建立骨干员工持股制度，是从制度入手调动人的主观能动性、推动企业可持续发展的破题之举。另外，将民营物流企业的效率、外资物流企业的管理和国有物流企业的资源有机融合，选择工程物流、跨境电商等增长快、市场潜力大的国际物流业务作为突破口，积极探索发展混合所有制经济，应成为新常态下有关各方认真思考的一大问题。

另外，技术创新对行业经营的作用同样不可低估。技术革新使得远洋运输船舶船速大幅提升且运营成本不断下降；优化改进货物包装方式和材料、实施托盘标准化、运用新兴叉车工具等对提升装卸效率和降低企业成本有重大意义。当前，我们已进入互联网时代。行业企业应该学会运用互联网思维改造传统货代业务，努力将信息化打造成为企业的核心竞争力，实现国际物流服务全程的透明和可视化管理，这也是行业转型的重要内容。

4. 发挥政府在推动行业发展中的积极作用

当前，物流企业“走出去”热情高涨，关键是发挥好政府部门在其中的牵引和支持作用。有关部门应从提升国内企业全球供应链管理能力、扩大运输服务贸易出口以及物流是实施“一带一路”重点保障等高度，来深化对加快推动物流企业“走出去”迫切性的认识。商务、财政、发改、交通运输等部门应加强顶层设计，围绕海外网络体系布局、跨境电商海外仓建设、重大海外物流建设项目等焦点，加快研究出台相关的财税扶持政策。

另外，适应国际物流细分市场蓬勃发展的态势，中国物流与采购联合会、中国国际货运代理协会等行业组织可在旗下设立国际物流、工程物流和跨境电商等专业委员会，加强行业自律和专业引领，有关高校要加强对新常态下行业转型发展的前瞻性研究，行业媒体应加大舆论宣传，积累一切有利于行业结构调整、创新发展的“正能量”。

（中国外运长航集团　梅赞宾）

2014 年快递业发展回顾与 2015 年展望

2014 年是我国快递业持续高速发展的第四个年头，是快递业最受国务院、地方政府关注、关心和支持的一年，也是快递业变化最大的一年。

一、2014 年快递业发展回顾

（一）2014 年快递业发展 10 件标志性大事

1. 我国快递业务量超过美国，跃居全球第一大快件国

2014 年，我国快递业务量接近 139.6 亿件，业务收入超过 2045.4 亿元。标志着我国快递业务量超过美国，跃居全球第一大快件国。但是，快递业务收入和件均收入与美国相比还有较大差距。2014 年，我国快递件均收入为 14.65 元，同比差额为 1.04 元，同比下降 6.6%。快递件均收入同比下降标志着我国内资快递企业盈利能力进一步下降，“以价换量”的发展模式基本没有改变。同时，我国内资快递企业在国际快递市场所占份额较低，因此，我国快递业在做大之后的做强之路还很长。

2. 李克强总理先后在西安顺丰速运和义乌中通速递调研

2014 年 1 月 27 日，李克强总理赴西安顺丰速运有限公司调研。11 月 19 日，李克强总理来到浙江义乌青岩刘村的中通快递网点视察。这是我国民营快递业发展二十年以来，第一次迎来总理调研、考察。

目前，我国民营快递企业业务量占全国市场份额 80% 以上，为我国快递业的发展做出了巨大的贡献，也被李克强总理誉为中国经济的一匹“黑马”。这标志着我国民营快递企业已成为社会公认的快递业主力军。

3. 国务院常务会议决定进一步开放国内快递市场

2014 年 9 月 24 日，国务院总理李克强主持召开国务院常务会议，决定进一步开放国内快递市场、推动内外资公平有序竞争。会议指出，扩大全方位主动开放，打造内外资企业一视同仁、公平竞争的营商环境，是我国长期坚持的重大政策取向。这将有利于倒逼国内快递企业改善经营管理、提升服务水平。

因此，外资快递企业进入国内包裹、信件（文件）快递市场将是必然趋势。但是，根据目前国内民营快递占 80% 市场份额的格局分析，我国全面开放国内包裹快递市场，对符合许可条件的外资快递企业，按核定业务范围和经营地域发放经营许可，并不会在短期内对内资快递企业造成明显影响。外资快递

企业短期内很难占有一半以上国内快递包裹的市场份额。我国对外资快递企业开放国内包裹市场的政策利好意义大于实际意义。

4. 快递市场竞争格局进一步显现，市场集中度依然很低

从目前快递市场的竞争格局分析，外资企业在国际快递市场中处于主导地位，顺丰速运占据着国内商务快递和“网购”的高端型市场，中国邮政速递在国家公文、国有企业快递市场中处于核心地位，“三通一达”等民营快递企业占据着国内“网购”经济型市场，中国邮政在跨境电商寄递市场中处于垄断地位。

而大型电商的自建快递物流主要为其自身品牌提供服务，如京东、苏宁、国美、酒仙网、我买网、顺丰优选、日日顺、亚马逊、当当银河一号、1号店、唯品会、聚美优品等都在自建快递板块。

同时，大型快递企业综合化、中型快递企业专业化、小型快递企业个性化的转型趋势已经开始显现。如顺丰速运正在向综合物流企业转型，“落地配”企业的服务更加个性化。由于我国快递企业主要采取以品牌为主导的加盟模式，加盟商拥有自主经营权（包括定价权），因此我国快递业的市场集中度非常低。这也符合产业集中度越低，竞争形式以价格竞争为主；产业集中度越高，则以服务品质竞争为主的规律。

5. 铁路电商班列开通，快递干线运输格局将发生变化

2014年下半年，铁路部门与电商、快递企业合作，最高时速160千米的电商班列开通，这是铁路货运改革的重要标志性成果之一。它将改变快递业目前以公路和航空两种干线运输方式为主的竞争态势，加快形成公路、航空和铁路三种运输方式并重的格局。与公路和航空运输方式相比，铁路电商班列具有速度快（公路汽运平均时速为70千米左右；铁路电商班列平均时速为110千米）、运输规模大（一列快递电商班列相当于9.6米的箱式货车45台）、时效性强、受气候影响极小、运输成本低和节能环保等优势。而且，在1000~1500千米干线运输中，铁路较其他运输方式优势明显。

但是，由于快递企业对运输作业场地具有特殊需求，所以为了适应快递的装卸特点，应采用效率较高的输送设备、装卸模式。这就意味着铁路进入快递业干线运输市场还需要对相关配套设施进行技术改造。

6. 快递电子运单开始推广使用

据抽样调查，2014年电子运单在快递企业的使用率占到8%~20%，预计到2015年年末将达到30%左右。这将会对传统快递运单的应用产生冲击。

对快递企业来说，电子运单的应用不仅可以降低运单成本，还可以降低快递作业的人工成本，提高快递的作业（包括录单、分拣）效率。但是，快递企业或将受制于电商以及为电商提供ERP信息技术的服务商，电商应用ERP的

费用将会转嫁给快递企业，从而增加快递企业的成本。

7. 菜鸟网开始整合快递资源

快递行业的竞争方式，已经开始由快递服务能力的竞争向快递上游发货权的竞争转变。即控制了快递的发货权，就控制了快递的服务资源。

菜鸟网正在准备控制阿里巴巴体系电商“网购”快递物流的发货权。其主要手段是通过免费为电商提供ERP（电子运单）服务，以掌握电商“网购”快件的分配权；制定电商快递的服务标准，从而达到整合快递资源的目的。同时，菜鸟网络联合日日顺物流，全面激活全国2600个区县的物流配送体系，实现了全国93%的区县家电送货入户，降低了对“三通一达”等大型快递企业的依赖度。

8. 快递“最后一百米”呈现多样化的趋势

在传统快递“门到门”的基础上，“最后一百米”呈现多样化，快递智能自助柜、便利店代理、社区物业代理、校区公共配送平台等新业态加速推广和使用。2014年快递智能自助柜“取派件”终端模式的业务量增速在2倍以上。

快递企业纷纷介入“最后一百米”的新业态，如韵达与杭州邮政启动“E邮站”项目战略合作，广州邮政首推“小蜜蜂邮包包”同城配送便民服务，圆通速递北京分公司与小麦公社签署战略合作协议，顺丰速运4000家“嘿店”打通线上线下经营模式，百世汇通在京沪试点运行智能快递柜。

“最后一百米”新型终端模式的飞速发展主要是基于其收寄快件智能化程度高、便利、运营成本低、安全性高等优势。目前，多样化的“最后一百米”新型终端模式已成为了智慧城市、物联网和民生工程的重要组成部分，也成为了社区和校区一道亮丽的风景线。

9. 民营快递企业深入涉足国际快递

目前，国际商务快递已经被“国际四大”和邮政速递所垄断，其中中国邮政占跨境电商快递的80%左右。对于民营快递企业来说，国际快递市场的空间有限，主要切入点应是以跨境电商快递为主的专线快递。对于国际快递业务的拓展方式则应分为三个层级：初级阶段是代理合作；中级阶段以代理为主，自营为辅；高级阶段是以自主快递品牌为主，代理为辅。

2014年我国多家民营快递进军国际快递市场，业务拓展方式以跨境电商为主。例如，申通快递开通了日本专线；顺丰速运开通了俄罗斯小包专线和欧洲小包服务，顺丰速运“优选国际”海购平台正式上线；韵达快递的欧洲快递物流服务中心已在德国运营，美国服务中心网站正式上线；圆通速递推出“俄易邮”专线产品。

10. 蜂网投资有限公司成立

2014年7月，“三通一达”联合组建了投资平台“蜂网投资有限公司”

（简称蜂网）。蜂网的成立标志着“三通一达”之间的市场关系将由竞争向竞合转型。蜂网的投资定位主要是打造快递集约化的投资平台，推动智慧快递、物联网和“云计算”在“三通一达”快递企业的应用，以及推广应用快递智能自助柜，推动“三通一达”在跨境电子商务领域发挥作用等。

与阿里集团所成立的菜鸟网不同，菜鸟网主要是整合快递资源针对普通消费者提供服务；而蜂网则是将快递资源整合，形成规模化效应，针对“三通一达”提供服务。目前，“三通一达”之间的竞争属性一如既往，价格仍是各自定价，不过未来将会以良性的竞争方式来竞争。

（二）政策、法规和标准出台力度最大的一年

2014 年 9 月 24 日，国务院常务会议决定进一步开放国内快递市场。2014 年，国家邮政局出台了《邮政业消费者申诉处理办法》、《经营快递业务的企业分支机构备案管理规定》、《快递业务经营许可注销管理规定》、《邮政行业安全信息报告和处理规定》、《寄递服务用户个人信息安全管理规定》、《无法投递又无法退回邮件管理办法》、《无法投递又无法退回快件管理规定》7 个规范性文件，以及《快递专用电动三轮车技术要求》、《邮政业标准体系》、《快递营业场所设计指南》3 个标准。各地方政府出台了如《青海省邮政条例》、《海南省邮政条例》、《湖北省邮政条例》、《贵州省邮政条例》4 个邮政条例。

各项规范、文件及标准的出台，标志着国家邮政局的监管正向精细化管理转型，对适应快递业发展的新变化、保护消费者合法权益和快递企业的合法权益，起到了积极的促进作用。地方性法规的颁布实施，使得地方邮政管理局实现了依法监管、依法行政。

（三）市场竞争最激烈的一年

2014 年是国内快递企业市场竞争最激烈的一年，也是面临竞争挑战最大的一年。一方面，电商继续利用自身的货源优势打压快递价格，其商业模式由赚取商品差价转变为赚取快递费差价，件均收入的下降幅度为 0.5 ~ 1.5 元；另一方面，快递企业之间的同质化竞争加剧了“价格战”的双重叠加效应，即多数快递企业呈现“微利化、无利化、亏损化”的趋势，特别是加盟模式民营快递企业的部分加盟商经营困难，部分中型快递企业总部亏损现象继续持续。究其原因，与美国相比，我国快递市场品牌集中度不高。同时，新的竞争还在加剧，自建快递物流还在进一步扩张。

经过多年的发展，我国快递业已经进入资本时代。在我国 20 家知名快递品牌或具有一定知名度的快递品牌中，有一半的快递企业总部还没有实现盈利，企业对资本的依赖度很高。因此，不断融资成为民营快递企业成败的关键

要素。同时，资本市场也会利用资本优势重组快递企业，激活快递企业并提升快递产业的品牌集中度。

据统计，2014 年内资快递企业按照快递业务量排名是：申通快递、圆通速递、中通快递、顺丰速运、韵达快递、邮政速递、百世汇通、京东快递、天天快递；按业务收入排名是：顺丰速运、邮政速递、申通快递、圆通速递、中通快递、韵达快递、京东快递、百世汇通、天天快递。2014 年外资快递企业业务量的排名是：中外运敦豪（DHL）、联邦快递（FedEx）、联合包裹（UPS）、天地快递（TNT）、欧西爱斯（OCS）、日本雅玛多（黑猫）、大众佐川急便（中日合资）；业务收入排名是：中外运敦豪（DHL）、联邦快递（FedEx）、联合包裹（UPS）、天地快递（TNT）、欧西爱斯（OCS）、日本雅玛多（黑猫）、大众佐川急便（中日合资）。

（四）基础设施投资力度最大的一年

2014 年，继京东亚洲一号启动后，大型快递企业和大型电商加速基础设施的投资建设。据初步统计，2014 年仅顺丰速运、“三通一达”民营快递总部（包括加盟商）、邮政速递等用于基础设施建设的投资已超过 150 亿元。

例如，2014 年邮政集团公司投资约 1 亿元建立电子支付服务基地；京东商城投资 70 亿元在武汉建设华中物流基地，投资 20 亿元在东莞建设现代服务产业园；苏宁云商借力移动网络计划建设 60 个物流基地；唯品会中部枢纽物流基地正式落户郑州；圆通速递在 12 座城市投资建仓配一体化服务体系。

二、2015 年快递业发展展望

根据 2014 年 9 月 24 日国务院常务会议有关促进快递业发展的政策，和中央经济工作会议对 2015 年重点工作的部署，以及 2015 年初国家邮政局的邮政管理工作会议精神，结合 2014 年我国快递市场的竞争格局。预计，2015 年我国快递业发展环境将进一步改善，鼓励快递业发展的政策还将延续，快递市场还将继续保持高速增长态势。但是，快递企业面临的挑战将进一步加剧，主要表现为以下 5 个方面：

1. 快递业继续保持高速增长态势

预计 2015 年，我国快递业务量的增幅在 40% ~50%，即在超越美国跃居全球第一大快件国的基础上，2015 年快递业务量将在 180 亿 ~210 亿件，与全球第二大快件国——美国之间的差距进一步拉大；快递业务收入增幅将在 35% ~42%；在快递业务结构中，“网购”快递所占比重进一步提升，将达到 75% 以上，而商务快递的占比会进一步下降。

2. 快递企业诚信体系建设开始布局

2014 年，国家邮政局提出建立企业诚信评价体系，开展推动信用等级评定工作。推动企业建立和完善对加盟企业、员工与消费者的诚信记录和评价。目前，占有一半快递业务量一半市场份额的“三通一达”四家快递企业，利用所设立的蜂网公共平台已经完成了《快递员失信管理办法》和《快递客户失信管理办法》，将于 2015 年全面实施。这将对快递业全面推行诚信体系建设起到积极的推动作用。

3. 专业化快递成为新的竞争焦点

快递专业化的特征主要表现为：快递细分市场的专业化。快递业市场细分是快递业发展成熟的重要标志之一。它将按照商品的属性和特性、个性化需求不断细分。例如，跨境电商快递、冷链宅配、酒类宅配、药物宅配、化妆品宅配、即时配送、高铁快递等细分快递市场。在这些细分快递市场中，将会涌现出很多中小型快递企业和专业化的快递企业，这也将成为快递业务新的增长点。

4. 民营快递企业转型趋势开始显现

基于我国快递业的发展历程和发展路径，借鉴“欧美”和日本等发达国家快递业的发展轨迹，我国大型快递企业将向综合型物流企业转型，中型快递企业将向专业化转型，小型快递企业将向个性化转型。

继顺丰速运开始向综合型物流企业转型后，其它民营快递企业将在 2015 年逐步开始转型。随着快递产品单一的同质化“网购”快递市场竞争的加剧，快递企业只有找到自己的转型方向，才能在这场竞争中取得胜利。

5. 制约快递业发展的瓶颈进一步凸显

一是适合我国快递业“最后一公里”配送的交通工具车型标准尚未出台，快递车辆进入市区“行车难”和“停车难”的问题依然存在；二是，目前快递企业所使用车辆的合法性还没有在政府法规的层面上得到突破，各地政府采取的“禁电禁摩”的政策对快递配送的制约越来越大；三是，快递智能自助柜进入社区和校区的地方性政策还存在空白；四是，电商利用货源优势打压快递企业，从中赚取快递费差价的现象日趋普遍。

（快递物流咨询网 徐勇）

2014年物流地产业发展回顾与2015年展望

2014年，全球经济总体增长乏力，复苏进程缓慢，世界贸易投资格局变化不定，我国继续全面深化改革，坚持稳中求进的工作总基调，宏观政策保持了连续性和稳定性，经济发展进入新常态。《国家新型城镇化规划（2014—2020年）》（中发〔2014〕4号）及一系列促进城镇化发展方案的发布和实施为全面优化我国城市群布局提供了依据。同时，新城市群的建立促进了区域产业重心转移，加快了区域产业发展与产业融合，为作为工业地产重要组成部分的物流地产，提供了广阔的发展空间。

2014年9月国务院正式印发了《物流业发展中长期规划（2014—2020年）》（国发〔2014〕42号），提出到2020年基本建立现代物流服务体系，提升物流业标准化、信息化、智能化、集约化水平，在物流基础设施网络建设方面着力加强，标志着我国物流业进入新的发展阶段。另一方面，《物流园区服务规范及评估指标》等物流园区相关国家标准的正式实施，有效促进了我国物流园区的规范化发展。电子商务物流的迅速发展带动了物流地产产业链与价值链的转型升级，有效推动了我国物流地产的快速发展。

一、2014年物流地产业发展回顾

2014年，在我国经济结构进一步优化，经济发展进入"新常态"的背景下，我国物流业各项指标保持良好的发展趋势。物流相关行业固定资产投资保持快速增长，物流基础设施建设稳步推进，物流园区服务能力进一步提升，物流地产进入调整规范阶段。

（一）物流相关行业固定资产投资稳步增长，社会物流总费用占GDP比重有所下降

2014年我国物流基础设施进一步优化，物流相关行业固定资产投资稳步增长。2014年1月以来，我国物流固定资产投资完成额指数均保持在50%以上，反映出物流运行的基础设施条件呈现改善态势。

据2014年国家统计公报显示，2014年我国全社会固定资产投资增速有所放缓，增速由2013年的18.7%下降为2014年的15.3%。相比之下，2014年全国交通运输、仓储和邮政业的固定资产投资继续保持平稳增长，增速为

18.6%，近五年来首次超过全社会固定资产投资增速，如图1所示。

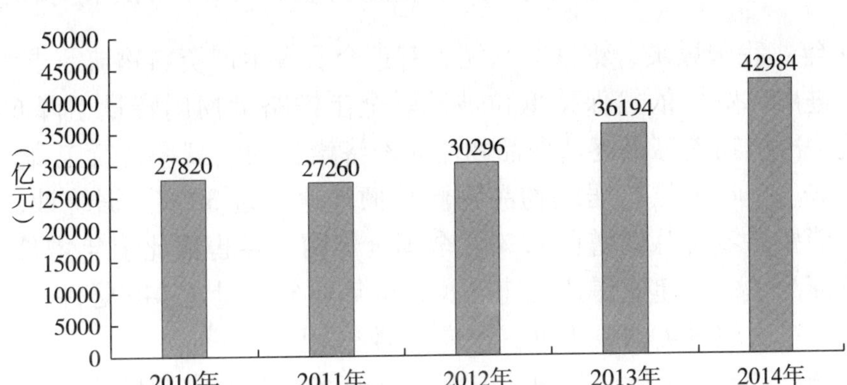

图1　全国交通运输、仓储和邮政业固定资产投资情况

（二）物流服务设施租金继续上涨，市场需求依然看好

2014年，受强劲的消费内需和居民消费习惯改变的支撑，2014年我国“双十一”交易额再创历史新高，从2013年的350亿元增长至2014年的571亿元。电子商务对物流仓储需求的急剧增长，推动物流服务设施租金的不断上涨。

世邦魏理仕（CBRE）亚太区研究部指出，2014年亚太区的仓储物流总供应量同比预计将增长80%，强劲的市场需求将有助于消化新增的物流仓储设施。2014年6月，世邦魏理仕（CBRE）首次发布亚太地区物流市场的趋势报告。报告指出，在全球经济缓慢复苏，亚太地区经济增长相对较快的大背景下，网络购物群体的持续增长、电子商务销量的迅速增多和第三方物流的持续壮大给亚太地区物流市场带来广阔的发展前景，未来仓储物流租金将出现继续上涨的态势。预计2014年亚太区的物流租金将以同比3%~4%的增长速度增长，其中东京、上海和广州的增长速度为4%，香港地区的增长速度为亚太地区最高，将达到7.5%。

2014年我国一线城市的物流仓储用地价格不断上涨。据统计，北京市2014年物流仓储租金平均上升至人民币37.1元/月·平方米，同比上升3.5%。其中北京空港物流园是租金最高的区域，租金为人民币41.8元/月·平方米，同比上涨4.3%。北京通州物流园区租金为人民币39.8元/月·平方米，价格紧随其后。数据显示，2008年至2014年第三季度期间，上海物流仓储用地以年均8%的增长速度增长，其租金水平正在接近行业承受边界。根据戴德梁行的统计，过去五年，上海优质仓储物业平均租金已连续18个季度上涨。我国物流地产仍有较大的发展空间。

（三）物流地产市场需求结构深度调整，电商物流需求快速增长

2014 年，我国煤炭、钢铁、水泥、有色金属等生产资料物流需求增速进一步放缓，进出口贸易依然保持低位波动。全年铁路货物周转量下降 6% 左右。电商物流、冷链物流等最终消费品物流对经济增长的贡献率持续走高，保持快速增长趋势。全年单位与居民物品物流总额增速超过 30%。据统计，2014 年我国社会消费品零售总额增长 12%，全国全年网上零售额比上年增长 49.7%。以服务电商为主的快递业保持快速增长，全年业务件量达 140 亿件，同比增长 52%。我国首次超过美国成为世界快递业第一大国。

据艾瑞统计数据显示，2014 年中国电子商务市场交易规模达 12.3 万亿元，增长 21.3%。其中网络购物增长 48.7%，在社会消费品零售总额中首次突破 10%。戴德梁行中国区工业和物流地产部表示，目前上海仓储用地的需求主要来自制造企业和物流地产投资商两类企业。其中物流地产商对仓储用地的需求非常旺盛。尤其是近两年来快速发展的电子商务，使得电商企业对物流地产的需求更加强劲。数据显示，随着 2014 年网购市场的持续火爆，为能够扩大市场份额，延伸产业链及价值链，各路电商巨头在全国范围内大面积布点，纷纷建立电商物流园区。克而瑞研究总监薛建雄指出："物流地产的兴起，电商自建具有非常大的推助作用。"目前，阿里、京东、大物流（顺丰、德邦、圆通等）都在抢占物流、仓储市场。如京东在物流领域的布局从 2007 年起步，截止到 2014 年 9 月 30 日，其自建物流体系在全国已覆盖 1800 多个区县，总面积约为 230 万平方米，其中大型仓库建成 118 个。

罗兰贝格 2014 年 5 月发布报告预测称，受宏观政策和市场需求推动，中国冷链物流行业未来将保持年均 25% 的高速增长，至 2017 年，市场规模将达到 4700 亿元。继阿里巴巴在北京、上海、广东、深圳、天津、武汉、重庆、成都、宁波等 26 个网购热点城市的生鲜冷链物流配送布局之后，2014 年，拥有物流"终结能力"的顺丰速运推出了定位全球新鲜美食的电商平台"顺丰优选"，随后又完成了一系列在冷链物流方面的战略布局。冷链物流快速抢占物流地产。

（四）物流地产开发运营模式呈现多样化，投资热度不减

2014 年 9 月，国务院发布了《关于依托黄金水道推动长江经济带发展的指导意见》（国发〔2014〕39 号），为我国中部地区尤其是长江经济带沿线城市的经济发展和产业的规模化扩张带来了新的机遇。同时，"新丝绸之路经济带"的提出也极大地促进了我国西部地区经济发展，中西部地区将会迎来新一轮的发展高潮。同时，配套的物流需求将快速增长，物流地产呈现出新的投资

机遇。

物流业的快速发展也促进了物流地产开发建设模式的多样化。物流地产开发建设模式呈现出不断变化的特点。即早期的地产商开发、物流企业租赁运营模式或物流企业独立开发运营模式，到地产商与物流企业合资开发运营，再到第三方整合开发运营模式，发展到现阶段的由政府主导的经济开发区模式，实现了规范化发展，预示着我国物流地产行业正在走向高效化与规范化。

目前我国物流地产还是主要由地产商来进行，但是由于地产商对物流领域不熟悉，很容易造成大量过剩的现象。国内地产商和物流企业已经开始建立重要的战略伙伴关系，合作趋势逐步明显。地产商充分吸收物流企业在选址、规划和运营管理等方面的经验，实现物流地产的良性运转。例如传化物流、林安物流等物流企业开始与各地房地产开发商合作。其中，林安物流致力于在全国连锁建设和运营现代化智慧物流园，实现其以现代智慧物流园区运营和管理，搭建现代物流信息交易服务平台的第四方物流企业的目标定位。

除房地产企业和电商企业纷纷投资物流地产外，保险、银行等企业也开始投资物流地产。2014 年 9 月 15 日，五洲国际控股公告称，将引入平安不动产为战略投资者。据了解，平安不动产计划在 5 年内就五洲国际未来的专业批发市场和物流项目进行不高于人民币 15 亿元的战略投资。除平安不动产外，目前已有多家保险企业的资金进入物流地产领域。2014 年 6 月，中银投资、中国人寿、厚朴基金等知名险资企业先后投入 25 亿美元，宣布和物流地产巨头普洛斯合作，我国物流地产的投资运营模式进一步呈现多样化态势。

（五）物流园区服务能力不断提升，进入规范化发展阶段

按照 2013 年《全国物流园区发展规划》的要求，中国物流与采购联合会物流园区专业委员会（以下简称专委会）在 2013 年工作的基础上，开展了“2014 年度物流园区综合评价”工作。通过对全国 206 家物流园区的基础设施、服务能力、运营效率和社会贡献等几个方面的统计分析和综合评价，评选出全国 50 家优秀物流园区。为我国物流园区的规范化发展指明了方向。

2014 年由国家标准化管理委员会立项、由全国物流标准化技术委员会提出并归口的《物流园区统计指标体系》、《物流园区服务规范及评估指标》和《仓储绩效指标体系》于 7 月 1 日正式开始实施。对我国物流园区经济活动的统计和管理，物流园区服务保障，仓储型物流企业的绩效考核等提出了明确要求，为政府部门、行业组织和物流园区自身提供了科学向导，有力的推进了我国物流园区的规划、建设和规范化运营。2014 年作为国内优秀物流企业之一的传化公路港物流有限公司不仅积极参与了国家标准《物流园区分类与基本要求》、《社会物流统计指标体系及方法》的制订，并率先将标准化、规范化的

原理与方法运用于产业服务链。2015 年 1 月，其浙江分公司承担的升级服务业标准化试点项目——《物流园区管理服务标准化试点》顺利通过现场评估验收。数据显示，杭州公路港通过标准化工作，工商企业物流业务外包率从 36% 上升到 90%，降低物流成本 20% 以上，年节约社会物流成本近 15 亿元。

根据《国务院关于加快发展生产性服务业促进产业结构调整升级的指导意见》（国发〔2014〕26 号）和国家标准委、商务部《关于加快推进商贸物流标准化工作的意见》（国标委服务联〔2014〕33 号）的精神及要求，各省对商贸物流企业纷纷开展了标准实施情况调查，这有助于加强物流园区的规范发展，提高物流园区的运作效率和服务能力。

（六）物流园区纷纷触网融合，转型升级态势明显

为加快我国商贸物流业的快速发展，商务部于 2014 年 9 月印发了《关于促进商贸物流发展的实施意见》（商流通函〔2014〕790 号），提出要大力支持电子商务物流的快速发展，促进商贸物流和电子商务物流的有效协同，加快推进两业的业务流程再造。在物流平台建设方面，物流公共信息平台、物流园区基地平台以及电商和物流金融平台等快速崛起。在经营模式上，园区的组织模式、管理模式和商业模式创新成为热点，如中储股份与普洛斯建立合资公司，探索混合所有制模式等。

随着互联网的快速发展，各地物流园区积极实施改革创新，提高园区总体服务能力和自主创新能力。作为 2014 年度优秀物流园区之一的山东盖世国际物流集团，积极促进物流信息化及物流产业供应链一体化，加快了物流产业的转型升级。深圳市平湖物流园区是深圳市唯一以政府主导投资开发的综合性物流园区，总规划控制范围约 14.75 平方公里，2014 年共投资 100 多亿元，引进 14 个物流项目入驻园区。随着深圳市的产业发展布局不断调整，市政府对物流园区的定位也不断清晰，包括多式联运、国际中转、电商物流、冷链物流等在内的一系列现代化物流功能不断增加，物流园区的服务能力也逐步加强，为深圳市物流业发展提供了重要支撑。

二、2015 年物流地产业发展展望

2015 年是“十二五”规划的收官之年，中国经济发展将继续保持稳中求进，积极推进各项改革工作，物流地产的发展态势亦将继续保持平稳发展，在物流地产的综合效益、规范化、集约化发展方面逐步提升，围绕国际物流、专业领域物流的服务能力力争有所突破。

（一）物流园区布局趋于合理，二三线城市和农村物流中心布局逐步展开

2014年9月25日，国务院发布了《关于依托黄金水道推动长江经济带发展的指导意见》（国发〔2014〕39号），将长江通道建设确定为具有重要战略地位的东西轴线。通过规划与建设，将进一步优化港口功能布局，加快上海国际航运中心、武汉长江中游航运中心、重庆长江上游航运中心和南京区域性航运物流中心建设。同时加强集疏运体系建设，推进港口与沿江开发区、物流园区的物流通道建设，拓展港口运输服务的辐射范围，这为优化长江沿线地区的物流园区布局做出了明确的指引方向。

2014年年底国家发展和改革委员会正式发布《关于印发国家新型城镇化综合试点方案的通知》（发改规划〔2014〕2960号），将江苏、安徽两省和宁波等62个城市（镇）列为国家新型城镇化综合试点地区。试点地区从东、中、西部全国范围和省、市、县、镇不同层次同时展开，其中，在25个县级试点城市中，西北地区占1/5。由于东南沿海地区土地资源日益短缺，物流园区的布局将沿着我国新型城镇化的步伐向中西部地区和二三线城市逐步展开。

从局部地区的物流园区或物流中心布局来看，城镇化的快速发展进一步加剧了产业转移，推动物流设施的迁建与重新布局。从2015年1月开始，北京动物园服装批发市场、大红门服装批发市场的搬迁工作将逐步展开，天津、河北等地纷纷积极行动，争夺已进入白热化。在全国各地类似商贸流通中心的布局调整已纷纷展开。

同样，农村物流基础设施布局也进入快速发展的轨道。《农村电子商务消费报告（2014）》显示，2014年全国农村网购市场总量预计将达1800亿元以上，2016年将突破4600亿元，面对日益凸显的农村电商市场，为了解决配送“最后一公里”问题，各大电商巨头积极布局服务农村的物流中心和配送站。例如，阿里巴巴已在奉化市建立淘宝市级服务中心，占地700平方米。建成后，其将成为300个淘宝服务站的物流和配送中心。类似的，苏宁、京东等电商巨头亦纷纷在县区建立电商服务站或农村电商服务中心，这些服务站将集成物流配送、展示体验、电商培训等功能。更加令人期待的是这些服务站基本同时具备了农产品采购功能，帮助农民推进农产品进城销售问题。在未来几年内，农村物流服务基础设施将逐步丰富和完善，进一步发挥双向流通的重要作用。

（二）满足跨境物流业务需求的物流园区建设将成为新热点

2014年12月12日，国务院召开常务会议，决定在更大范围推广（上海）

自由贸易区建设经验，批准在广东、天津、福建特定区域再设三个自由贸易园区。而进入2015年，包括重庆，湖北武汉，河南郑州，陕西西安，甘肃兰州，山东青岛，辽宁大连，吉林长春、珲春，广西北部湾等9个城市或区域积极申报第三批自由贸易园区，特别是首个内陆自由贸易园区的竞争十分激烈。

2014年12月26日，国务院印发的《落实“三互”推进大通关建设改革方案》中明确提出，进一步推动通关协作，建立完善与推进国际物流大通道建设相适应的通关管理机制，建设多式联运物流监管中心，改进监管方式；加快自由贸易园（港）区和海关特殊监管区域监管制度创新与复制推广，建立“自由贸易园（港）区－海关特殊监管区域－区外”的分级复制推广机制，推动全方位扩大开放。这将是加快我国对外贸易通关便利化的重要举措。

面对我国对外贸易的不断发展，通关模式的逐步优化和完善，跨境电商物流园、保税物流园、保税仓库等物流地产项目的建设将进一步成为落实跨境物流服务的重要支撑。据统计，截至目前我国综合保税区数量逐年递增，现共有39个，如图2所示。

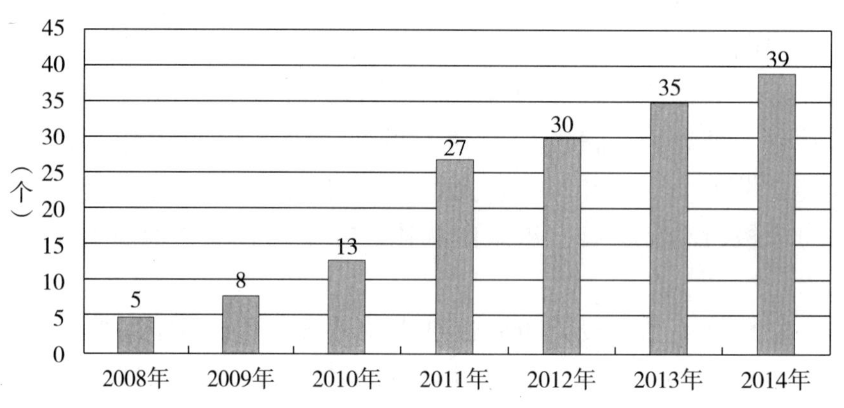

图2　全国综合保税区数量统计

特别是内陆地区，结合跨境电子商务的发展、电子口岸等通关便利条件的逐步完善，保税物流、国际物流将继续蓬勃发展，各种相关的物流基础设施将进一步丰富，逐步满足多样化的跨境物流服务需求。

2015年2月9日，中国（杭州）跨境电子商务产业园（空港园区）正式启动进口业务，杭州跨境电子商务空港园区一期实现规划5平方千米，截至目前已启用了256亩、10万余平方米的保税物流中心场站资源。根据规划，空港园区将在5年内实现航空运输、口岸服务、分拨转运、保税仓储、线上交易、线下展示、支付金融、快递派送等跨境电商的综合服务功能，仅半个小时即可完成通关手续。而在同一天，杭州市萧山区人民政府与京东集团签订战略合作协议，未来双方将在跨境电商、物流技术示范、区域贸易结算等多个领域开展深度合作。这标志着未来一段时期，服务跨境电商的物流园区或中心将继续成为新的开发热点。

（三）物流地产的投资主体多元化趋势将更加凸显

随着信息技术和电子商务的突飞猛进，我国经济发展对现代物流服务设施的需求将进一步增强，服务能力要求将进一步提升，物流地产有较大的发展空间。这进一步促使境外物流地产基金和投资集团、传统房地产商、电子商务企业等抢夺中国物流地产市场。

首先，投资银行、境外投资基金仍然对中国物流地产市场保持高度兴趣。据21世纪经济报道统计，目前，境外资金对国内物流地产商的投资规模已在30亿美元左右，其中，宇培集团4.5亿美元、易商集团超过了8.5亿美元，嘉民集团目前15亿美元，在未来2～3年内将翻一番达到30亿～40亿美元。其在上海、天津、成都、重庆、廊坊、常州、合肥等重点城市的在建项目总面积超过78万平方米。在国内，中国平安银行成立了物流、不动产等部门，已经成功收购Vailog（维龙地产）及民营仓储物流设施，将在物流地产继续开拓业务市场。总体来看，物流地产基金、投资银行对于市场需求大、租金回报率较高的物流地产项目保持着较高积极性，未来将进一步发挥重要作用。

其次，电子商务企业仍将积极布局物流网络，并抢占三四线城市乃至县级农村市场。2014年10月，京东在上海的“亚洲一号”物流中心正式投入运营，在南京雨花台区签下了四个新项目。苏宁也即将在雨花台区建成苏宁雨花二期自动化仓库，项目占地20万平方米，存储能力可达2000万件商品。在管理方面，苏宁已经对集团架构进行了重新调整，成立了苏宁物流集团和苏宁金融集团，将在未来逐步实现物流的社会化运营，并独立运营，向第三方开放。

另外，传统地产商加快了在物流地产领域开拓的步伐。随着中国房地产市场的持续调整，发展增速放缓，房地产供需趋于平衡，原有的传统住宅和商业地产项目利润率已逐步走低。富力、绿地、恒大、合生创展等传统房地产投资商已经投资物流地产，2014年5月，万科集团与廊坊市国土土地开发建设投资有限公司签署了《战略合作框架协议》，标志着万科集团正式进入物流地产领域。据万科透露，进军物流地产将是万科战略转型的重要一步，物流地产围绕大都市周围的高铁、机场布局，空间很大，金融化、专业化是万科做物流地产的方式。8月23日，万科又在贵阳龙里县签下了总投资10.5亿元的综合仓储物流项目，万科表示未来还将覆盖江浙沪地区，并引入黑石、凯雷等战略投资伙伴。万科投资物流地产将是万科城市配套服务商定位中的重要一环，这也将引领中国房地产商进一步争夺物流地产市场。

（四）物流园区将进一步提升规范化、集约化水平

随着《物流业发展中长期规划》（国发〔2014〕42 号）的发布，物流业发展进入了新的历史阶段，物流园区工程作为重点工程之一，规划中强调推进物流园区的基础设施和多式联运设施建设，提升信息化服务能力和综合配套服务能力，特别是加强物流园区的示范带动作用。

2015 年，中国物流与采购联合会将在全国范围内开展第四次物流园区（基地）调研工作，再次对全国物流园区的总数量、分布区域、建设状态、建设情况、运营情况进行系统调查，摸清我国物流园区发展的总体态势。届时共同开展的还有“2015 年全国物流园区综合评价”调查工作，针对物流园区的规范化建设、运营、服务能力等进行全面评估。

在物流园区综合评价调研基础上，即将开展的国家级物流园区示范工程，将进一步引导物流园区在管理体制、服务机制、招商运作方面创新发展，通过示范带动作用，提升我国物流园区的整体发展水平。

随着国家对物流园区规范化发展的要求不断明晰，各地方也通过制定相关政策、开展国家级及省级物流园区规范化发展试点工作等形式对物流园区规范化发展进行快速响应。如贵州省于 2015 年 2 月发布的《省人民政府办公厅关于加快发展现代物流业的若干意见》（黔府办发〔2015〕3 号），提出了全力推动物流企业规模化、集约化发展，积极推广物流标准化，为加快贵州省现代物流业规范化发展指明方向。四川省成都国际集装箱物流园区作为国家级服务业标准化试点，承担的内陆港准口岸国际货代服务标准及准口岸物流服务链协调标准等 80 项标准的起草，为全国物流园区向着规范化、标准化方向发展起到示范性和带动性的作用。

（五）在线供应链金融推动智慧物流园区快速实现

随着电子商务在中国如火如荼的发展，已形成了庞大的产业链条以及周边新生产业。结合云计算、大数据、物联网等新兴产业的发展，智慧物流园区的概念伴随着智慧城市的发展不断清晰。自我国 2012 年发布了 90 个国家智慧城市试点名单以来，据不完全统计，已有近 200 个城市成为了国家智慧城市试点，智慧城市的建设也已从电子化、自动化、智能化逐步向智慧化发展。

在 2014 年 12 月举办的全国智能物流云峰会上，地产投资专家、中房指数研究院院长陈晟先生阐述了物联网发展对物流地产的影响，他指出，随着物联网技术的发展，物流地产将迎来新的发展契机，智慧型物流地产将成为下一个物流地产新的投资热点。

从现实的管理理念和技术手段来看，智慧物流园区的概念也将逐步清晰。

在管理上通过电子商务企业、物流企业、房地产企业的联合运作，实现信息高度互通互联，以数据为基础，进一步加快了信息流、物流的快速传递。在服务模式上，通过电商、物流和银行搭建合作平台，供应链平台化服务格局初显，混合型供应链组织模式正在出现。在线供应链金融的支持推动物流园区的智能化经营和管理。

据报道，杭州市政府正在编制《杭州市建设全国智慧物流中心三年行动计划（2015—2017 年）》，将结合电子商务的发展基础，进一步以传化物流为核心的“智慧物流公路港”和以阿里巴巴电子商务为核心的“智慧物流信息港”为着力点，全力推进智慧物流业发展，计划在 2017 年智慧物流业增加值突破 100 亿元，占物流业总增加值达 20%。江西省由省发改委等 12 个部门联合发布了《江西省物流园区发展规划》，在推进物联网、云计算、3G、4G、移动互联网等高新技术在物流园区的开发应用做出了积极要求，将建成覆盖全省的智慧物流信息平台，全面提升园区在在线调度管理、智能配货、物品可追溯、全自动物流配送等领域的信息化与智能化水平。

随着我国改革的不断深入，现代物流业将进一步发挥其在国民经济中的重要作用，物流基础设施建设将继续稳步推进，物流地产业发展仍处在黄金时期。物流相关领域的制造商、交易商、流通商、服务商等与金融商的合作，在线供应链金融方面的创新思路和应用模式将不断涌现，共同推进智慧物流园区的快速发展，提高我国物流业的整体发展水平。

致谢：本项研究获国家科技支撑计划（2012BAH21F01 和 2012BAH21F03）支持。

（西安市商用信息系统分析及应用工程实验室　刘缨缨　孙雨　陈对对
西安交通大学管理学院　冯耕中　王能民
西安国际陆港投资发展有限公司　刘幼臻）

参考文献

［1］国务院．关于印发物流业发展中长期规划（2014—2020 年）的通知［EB/OL］．中华人民共和国中央人民政府政务网，2014－09－12.

［2］商务部．国家标准委商务部关于加快推进商贸物流标准化工作的意见［EB/OL］．中华人民共和国商务部网，2014－06－12.

［3］商务部．商务部关于促进商贸物流发展的实施意见［EB/OL］．中华人民共和国中央人民政府国务院办公厅政务网，2014－09－22.

［4］国务院．关于依托黄金水道推动长江经济带发展的指导意见［EB/OL］．中华人民共和国中央人民政府国务院办公厅政务网，2014－09－25.

[5] 国家发展改革委．关于印发国家新型城镇化综合试点方案的通知［EB/OL］．国家发展改革委政务网，2014－08－06.
[6] 市场需求空前冷链物流被国外巨头看好［N］．中国食品机械设备网，2015－02－07.
[7] 2014年物流业十大事件盘点［N］．中商情报网，2015－01－26.
[8] 2014年物流地产等产业地产勃发正当时 春潮可期待［N］．中国物流与采购网，2015－01－14.
[9] 2014年社会物流总额过210万亿物流业深度“触网”融合［N］．新华网，2015－01－16.
[10] 2014年中国物流仓储地产开发成亮点［N］．中国行业研究网，2014－03－01.
[11] 中国2015年五大经济主题趋势预测［J/OL］．中商情报网，2014－12－31.
[12] 铁路行业：2015年铁路工作会议重申发展与改革［J/OL］．瑞银证券，2015－01－30.
[13] 石家庄有望成北方新商贸物流中心 重整商贸业［N］．中国经营报，2015－02－07.
[14] 农村电子商务消费报（2014）［R］．阿里巴巴研究院，2014－10－13.
[15] 电商巨头争相“下乡”，农村特产借机进城［N］．浙江省商务厅，2015－02－12.
[16] 基金输血电商物流地产［J/OL］.21世纪经济报道，2014－06－19.
[17] 万科进军物流地产 欲做中国普洛斯［J/OL］.21世纪经济报道，2014－05－22.
[18] 八省份表态今年申报自贸区［N］．南国城报，2015－02－11.
[19] 杭州跨境空港园区开园商品半小时可通关［N］．新民网，2015－02－13.
[20] 萧山区与京东集团签订战略合作协议［N］．萧山日报，2015－02－10.
[21] 杭州拟建14个重点物流园打造智慧物流中心城市［N］．观点地产网，2015－01－20.

2014 年金融物流发展回顾与 2015 年展望

2014 年，金融物流既遇到巨大挫折，又有许多创新，在国有企业全面退出的同时，大量民营企业进入。行业整体处于震荡变动、创新融合的状态和时期。

一、2014 年金融物流发展回顾

2014 年，金融物流延续了上年总体下滑、国退民进、优化整合的态势，且与互联网因素多方结合，又产生了一些新的业务组合。

（一）金融物流业务继续下滑

根据中国物资储运协会的调查，所属会员单位质押融资监管业务大幅下降，融资额同比下降 44%，业务收入下降 46%，利润总额下降 60%，收入利润率下降到 30% 左右。央企四大公司的此类业务也全面萎缩，有的已停止该项业务，有的在清理整顿。与此同时，民营物流企业迅速占领了国企让出的市场，有的地区几乎是全盘接收。

金融物流业务下滑的原因：一是经济形势不乐观，行业资金链条断裂，相互欠债较多，新的多角债务链较为普遍。贸易企业、房地产企业、矿产企业资金占用多、周期长、环节多，最易出现借贷逾期、周转不畅、甚至卷款跑路的情况。二是大宗商品行情不好，钢铁、有色金属、煤炭、铁矿石价格下跌。2014 年 12 月 31 日，螺纹钢平均价格为 2670 元/吨，高速线材 2590 元/吨。钢材的市场价格同比下跌 15% 以上。以价格下行的物资作质押物，银行认为风险较大。三是新的业务事故和诉讼不断出现，尤其是青岛事件，打击了部分银行的信心，使他们感到无可信任的企业，无安全的质押融资业务。四是中央管理的国有企业受管理体制制约较多，只许成功、不许失败的考核机制以及层层审批的制度，对于短期灵活的融资业务不相适应。

（二）质押融资新案频发

相对于 2013 年新增案件极少的情况，2014 年的新案、大案较多。其中案值和影响极大的是青岛案，由于涉案金额巨大，涉案银行众多，案情复杂而备受关注。截至年底，案件还在调查之中，具体情况不明了，但可以大致看到脉络。涉案人陈基鸿，是新加坡籍华人，做有色金属贸易起家。拥有多家企业。作案手法大体三种：一是同一出资人注册多家公司，一家是买方、一家是卖方、一家是担保方、一家是仓储方。买卖双方签购销协议，担保方担保，向银行申请订单融资。银行审贷后、委托仓储方监管质物。银行的过失在于审核贸易的真实性、监管企业的关联性、货物验收的真实性不到位、不严格，给嫌疑人以可乘之机。二是青岛某物流公司有关人员被收买，对应一笔货物出具多张仓单，仓单用于质押。三是存入货物时与仓储企业签署仓储合同，并要求开仓单。作案人用仓单质押融资，用仓储合同提货单提出货物，换库再开仓单质押。这里的问题是没有做到仓单的唯一性，仓单的法律地位不明确，仓储企业没有做到见仓单发货。

青岛骗贷案之所以会发生，与银行的麻痹大意有很大关系。这些骗贷手法并不新奇，重复质押、虚开仓单，在上海钢贸事件中早已臭名昭著，而青岛案中仍有18家银行深陷其中，说明以下问题：虚拟的公司贸易业务是可以瞒过银行的，包括外资银行；银行对出质人、监管人、担保人的形式审查多于实质审查，对做案人的真实状况不清楚；没做到全程控货，别人的教训没能引起自己的警惕，对该业务的流程、风险不清楚便匆匆进入，极其轻率。此外，作案人的外籍身份和从业经历也有很大的欺骗性。

（三）金融物流业务的创新

一是电商、金融、物流三业进一步跨界融合。几乎所有的电子商务公司在提供交易平台的同时也提供融资平台，因此，其网站必然具有两方面的功能，其中一个是融资功能，另外一个是物流功能。为面向买卖双方开展融资，各主要商业银行、股份制银行都推出了专门针对电子商务的融资产品。金融、物流与电商三者紧密联系在一起，就产生了一种新的业务形态，即网上交易、网上融资、网下交付。电子商务环境下，交易不再受时空限制，交易环节缩短，碎片化订单能够更好地反映真实需求。快速交易要求快速交付，能够为小企业提供销售市场，降低融资和交易成本。

二是供应链金融成为年度最受推崇的模式。把供应链管理引入金融物流业务，把业务链条向上向下延伸，为金融物流业务提供了更多的安全保障。2014年，更多的人关注在线供应链金融，利用互联网和大数据，实现供应链融资线上化。在线供应链金融不改变供应链金融实质，包括借贷关系、利益主体、担保关系，但改变业务模式和风险管理技术，如信息对接、放款快速、方便简洁、借还灵活、标准公开透明、额度循环使用、共同监控风险等。

深圳式的供应链金融受到重视。其实质是把商贸、物流、金融融合在一起的业务模式。又分为两类，一类是订货式，即企业通过研究市场需求，发现或设计某种产品，寻找加工企业提供材料委托加工，产品制成后收购或收货，出口国外国内市场销售。贯穿始终的是金融和物流，以融资启动项目，以物流控货保证安全。另一类由外贸代理业务演变而来，贸易代理公司为中小制造企业提供供应链融资方案设计、融资代理、贸易货代通关物流方案规划、海关两检代理、融资、办税、结算、结汇、保险、仓储、运输、配送、加工、包装、市场营销拓展等服务。其收费方式为打包收费，即某些项目免费服务，而在集中物流如租船订舱、大批量运输取得优惠价格和金融服务收入。

三是大数据对金融物流的支撑作用增强。大数据背景下，金融物流业务出现了一系列新的特点：一是速度快，受理、审贷、放款、交付的速度加快。二是流程标准化，进而实现了信息化、平台化。大家之所以相信余额宝，其根本原因就在于它的流程是标准化的，运营规则是透明的，是不会轻易变动的，进而实现了平台化。三是融合化。制造业、商贸业、金融业、物流业与市场之间相互融合。但利用大数据并不容易，因为数据要能够聚焦成指标，指标要与被说明的事物有关联；要寻找准确的参数。包括基础参数、临界参数，是决策的重要依据；要校验数据，验证数据的可靠性。

二、金融物流存在的问题

（一）行业信用风险增大

在 2014 年宏观经济增速放缓的条件下，由于前期扩张过快，核心企业出现负债率过高、或有负债多的问题，此时银行业为自保而抽回贷款，无疑是釜底抽薪。核心企业资金周转困难，便拖欠上游供应商货款，预收下游资金，新的三角债日益严重。核心企业的危机，引发了行业的危机。一些信用一直很好，10 多年没有任何不良记录的企业也突然跑路，这使各种信用评级方法失灵。

（二）在多业融合的同时，业务边界变得模糊

近年来，由于金融物流业务参与者众多，制造企业、商贸企业、物流企业、金融企业、非金融企业、担保企业、基金、供应链管理公司、保理公司、交易所、电商平台公司、中小物流企业从各自的出发点进入金融物流领域。订单融资、保单融资、电商融资、金融物流、贸易融资、应收账款质押融资、预付账款质押融资、进出口项下质押融资、仓单质押、动产质押。担保品管理、保兑仓、保理仓、融资租赁、互联网金融、贸易金融等，其边界不易区分，不易归口管理或制定规则。

（三）法律制度修订速度跟不上金融物流的发展

一是重复抵、质押问题。在法律规定中，允许同一物品重复抵押，但抵押品必须到有关部门登记。不同的抵押物规定了不同的登记部门。未登记的不得对抗善意第三人。质押物没规定登记部门，因此，高法司法解释第三部分第十八条规定，同一财产法定登记的抵押权与质权并存时，抵押权人优于质权人受偿。二是监管与保管的区别。法律上没有对监管的解释，行内约定俗成地认为，监管是监督和管理，并不涉及对担保财产的作业。同时，保管业务不问货物权属、不关心货物的价值、只对存货的数量负责；而监管业务则需关心质物的权属、质物的价格波动；质物的质量是要由质权人来确认的，监管和保管只对担保财产的外观质量负责。三是仓单的法律地位。在合同法中，规定了存货人存入货物，仓储企业应给付仓单。但在实际运作中，几乎所有的仓储企业都不开仓单。这时就出现了问题，是仓储集体违法还是法律条文考虑不周？还有，在供应链金融业务中，仓单是必不可少的工具之一。应该让仓单流动起来，成为可转让仓单。问题是，所有仓储企业是否都有权力开出仓单？这些仓单的金融属性谁来认定？会不会造成仓单这种有价证券泛滥？四是在线供应链金融网站的信用。在很多情况下，从事在线供应链金融业务是由金融机构进行的，它们有较大的注册资本和净资产，有正式的金融机构牌照，接受金融当局的管理，按规定提取存款准备金，一般情况下，可以应对挤提风潮和其他危机事件。但也有一些互联网金融网站，注册资金少，有无资格运作几千亿的资金。

三、2015 年金融物流发展展望

尽管金融物流在 2014 年又遭挫折，但业界对金融物流新模式、新合作、新领域的探索从未停止。据分析，2015 年，全球经济增速有可能加快，中国经济仍将保持中速增长；“一带一路”和自贸区等国家战略实施，铁路货运改革等积极因素，将带来生产和贸易格局的重大变化和新的机遇；利率市场化和竞争的加剧；互联网技术更广泛的应用，会引发金融产品创新热潮。上述因素的变化会对金融物流的发展产生巨大推动力。

一是融资担保方式向信用担保倾斜，但实物担保方式仍是最安全担保方式。信用担保主要靠金融机构对借款人的评估。在大数据条件下，电商企业根据自己掌握的数据，对客户的业务、财务、历史等进行全面分析，在安全范围内提供小量、短期融资，把沉淀在网站平台上的无成本资金盘活。电商规模越大，沉淀资金越多。如果加上吸收存款功能，就变为金融机构；银行业释放出这种灵活性，信用担保就不仅限于大企业，而是可用于中小企业，业务范围将大大扩展。

在信用担保逐步扩大的同时，实物担保必不可少。即使是在诚信体系高度发达的国家，实物担保也是主要担保方式。在当前贸易金融方兴未艾的时期，实物担保有着广泛的应用。贸易金融以真实的贸易为要件，在真实贸易中，仓单、提单、运单都有相应的货品存在。无论是应收账款、预付账款，还是集合贷款、国际贸易等业务模式，都离不开实物。

二是供应链金融业务更加多样化，也更加安全。时刻控货、全程管理，物流企业、保险企业、电商企业、数据企业共同协作，业务安全系数大幅提高。金融物流向实体企业靠拢，甚至向个体农户提供服务。农资、农产品、名贵花木、种畜、奶牛等都在尝试质押融资。招商银行提出打造智慧供应链平台，大力发展行业金融、平台金融、生态金融、产业链金融。平安银行开办了橙 e 网，为建材交易、流通提供平台，同时推出融资、结算、支付、保险、保理等服务。

三是金融物流应在降低借款企业资金成本方面多做努力。近两年来，金融机构和非金融机构的理财、保理、基金、担保、P2P 业务，在满足部分企业资金需求的同时，也提高了借款企业的资金成本。从投资者手上高息揽资，经保险公司、担保公司、小贷公司、P2P 公司，到借款人手里，年化利率已达 20% 左右，如此高的资金成本，是无法促进实体经济发展的。无数“食利者”中，不乏“寄生者”，如何让资金直接进入实体企业，是管理者应认真解决的大问题。

四是新出现的联盟式内部结算模式值得关注。某一个行业的上下游企业组建联盟，成员之间有供应、采购及应收应付的债权债务关系。比如钢厂欠铁矿石贸易商的钱，钢贸商欠钢厂的钱，制造商欠钢贸商的钱，银行资金又难以借到。此时，联盟筹集资金（对投资人承诺较高利息），贷给制造商，制造商归还钢贸商欠款等等，以此类推，直到全链债务解除。发展下去，联盟甚至不需筹集资金，只要在联盟内发行结算单证就可解决多角债务问题。这种方式是否违法还需研究，但要维持运转，联盟内成员之间要高度信任，盟主要公平公正不贪，要有极强的掌控能力。既然有那么多集资跑路的案例，入盟者还是谨慎一些为好。

（中国物资储运协会　姜超峰）

2014 年保税物流发展回顾与 2015 年展望

保税物流是国际物流的一种特殊形式。普通的国际物流，进出口货物跨过边境（关境）时，要办理通过手续，包括上缴进出口关税。而保税物流则是在满足一定条件下提前或者延后办理进出境关税与流通税手续。

中国现阶段有三种形式的保税物流：通过海关特殊监管区域的保税物流、保税手册备案的保税物流以及两国间签署自由贸易协议的进出口物流。2014 年，国务院和各部委又新批准设立了一批海关监管区域，包括在原有低层次监管区域基础上整合设立的综合保税区。同时，广东、天津、福建也被批准为第二批自由贸易试验区，中国的保税物流进入了新阶段。

一、2014 年保税物流发展回顾

（一）海关特殊监管区域建设稳步推进

上海自由贸易试验区成功运作一周年。作为高层次的海关特殊监管区域，自由贸易试验区已经不仅局限于是对外贸易和物流的实验田，而且已经升级为我国政府改革、行政改革的试验田，将在国家新一轮改革开放中起到更为关键的作用。

2014 年年末，上海自贸区实现扩区，将陆家嘴、张江、金桥三个区域纳入，由原来的 28.87 平方千米扩大到 120.72 平方千米。扩区后，将建设几个“区中区”，分别为科技创新区和航运试验区。

2014 年 12 月 28 日，国务院先后批复天津、广东和福建三个自贸区。

中国（天津）自由贸易试验区占地面积 119.9 平方千米，涵盖天津港区域、天津机场区域及滨海新区中心商务区区域。天津自贸区依托天津东疆保税港区离岸金融及融资租赁等业务基础，重点拓展在金融领域的深化改革。天津港作为中国北方第一大港，作为京津冀地区第一开放口岸，将对加快京津冀协同发展增添新动力。

中国（广东）自由贸易试验区占地面积 116.2 平方千米，涵盖深圳前海区域、珠海横琴区域、南沙区三部分。广东自贸区依托深圳港对接香港及澳门，与之前和香港签订的自贸协定（CEPA）相比较，广东自由贸易试验区具有更多的优势。在税收方面，对进入自由贸易区的货物不但可以减免关税还可以免交增值税、消费税等；广东自由贸易区属于境内关外，从地域上分析，对于香港、澳门等土地稀少地区扩展经营地域提供了便利，中国（广东）自由贸易试验区将与 CEPA 相互补充共同发展。

中国（福建）自由贸易试验区占地面积 118.04 平方千米，涵盖平潭区域、厦门区域和福州区域三部分。与广东自贸区类似，福建自由贸易区依托对台区位优势，重点发展对台贸易及交流，同时也是作为《海峡两岸经济合作框架协议》（ECFA）实施的补充。

截至 2014 年 12 月全国自由贸易实验区如表 1 所示。

表 1　　截至 2014 年 12 月全国自由贸易实验区

序号	名称	成立时间	规划面积（平方千米）	备注
1	中国（上海）自由贸易试验区	2013.9.28	120.72	全国第一个自贸区
2	中国（天津）自由贸易试验区	2014.12.28	119.9	天津港 30 平方千米，天津机场 43.1 平方千米，中心商务区 46.8 平方千米
3	中国（广东）自由贸易试验区	2014.12.28	116.2	南沙新区 60 平方千米，深圳前海 28.2 平方千米，珠海横琴 28.2 平方千米
4	中国（福建）自由贸易试验区	2014.12.28	118.04	厦门 43.78 平方千米，平潭 43 平方千米；福州 31.26 平方千米

在此基础上，国家进一步在全国范围内复制推广 28 项改革事项。其中，在投资管理领域包括外商投资广告企业项目备案制、涉税事项网上审批备案等 9 项；贸易便利化领域包括全球维修产业检验检疫监管、中转货物产地来源证管理等 5 项；金融领域包括个人其他经常项下人民币结算业务、外商投资企业外汇资本金意愿结汇等 4 项；服务业开放领域包括允许融资租赁公司兼营与主营业务相关的商业保理业务、允许设立外商投资资信调查公司等 5 项；事中事后监管措施包括社会信用体系、信息共享和综合执法制度等 5 项。此外，在全国其他海关特殊监管区域复制推广的改革事项 6 项，包括期货保税交割海关监管制度、境内外维修海关监管制度、融资租赁海关监管制度 3 项海关监管制度创新，以及进口货物预检验、分线监督管理制度、动植物及其产品检疫审批负

面清单管理3项检验检疫制度创新。

与自由贸易试验区的密集批复和火热申请相比，综合保税区的审批推进显得更加有序。2014年新批复的综合保税区呈现两大特征，一是在原有功能单一的海关特殊监管区基础上通过区域合并、功能整合升级为综合保税区，例如盐田综合保税区；二是继续布局西部地区开发开放，服务丝绸之路经济带。

2014年全年及2015年前两月，综合保税区累计增加9个，较2013年设立数目增长近1倍。截止到2015年2月，我国已设立了44个综合保税区。

新增综合保税区的情况：

（1）深圳盐田综合保税区：2014年1月22日，国务院正式批准设立深圳盐田综合保税区。新获批的盐田综合保税区整合了海关特殊监管区域的所有功能政策，具备保税仓储、国际贸易、国际分拨、国际中转、检测维修、保税展示、研发制造、港口作业等功能。

作为深圳保税区转型升级重点工程，盐田综合保税区在原沙头角、盐田港保税区和盐田港保税物流园区的基础上，实现区域整合、资源整合、功能整合和监管整合。区域整合改变了盐田保税区域数量多、面积小的零散现状，为战略新兴产业、现代商贸服务业、临港服务业等的综合发展提供了空间；资源整合将改变盐田保税区产业联动弱、配套资源不足的现状，为区港全面联动和产业整合优化创造条件；功能整合将改变目前各园区产业功能单一的现状，极大提升片区的产业和土地价值；监管整合改变了狭小区域多重监管的现状，为监管设施的升级和监管机制的优化提升奠定基础。

（2）合肥综合保税区：2014年3月27日，国务院批准设立合肥综合保税区，是安徽省首个综合保税区。获批的合肥综合保税区规划面积2.6平方千米，将在该市新站区建设，东至铜陵北路、南至东方大道、西至新蚌埠路、北至魏武路。合肥综合保税区获批，对进一步承接产业转移，促进地方加快开放型经济发展将产生积极效应。

（3）岳阳城陵矶综合保税区：2014年7月8日，国务院批准设立岳阳城陵矶综合保税区，规划的综合保税区位于岳阳城陵矶临港产业新区核心区内，规划面积2.98平方千米。其中，第一期1.5平方千米，第二期1.48平方千米，分为出口加工区、保税物流区、保税仓储区、综合服务区四个功能区，将建设成为具有示范性的绿色、生态、环保型综合保税区。

（4）兰州新区综合保税区：2014年7月15日，国务院批复设立兰州新区综合保税区，规划面积3.39平方千米，其中围网区域面积约2.86平方千米，配套区域面积约0.53平方千米。总体规划为“一轴两翼多组团”，一轴，即位于综合保税区内的综合服务区、海关查验区和口岸作业区，以及位于综合保税区外的配套办公区和商业区；两翼，即主轴南北两侧的配套区，主要是西南和西北侧的加工物流功能、东南侧的商务功能、东北侧的居住功能；多组团，即综合保税区内的口岸作业、保税加工、仓储物流、综合服务等功能组团。兰州新区综合保税区将着力建设成为政策优惠、功能完善、配套齐全的经济发展高地，打造成为具有强大功能和竞争力的向西开放战略平台，逐步发展成为辐射西北、带动全国的内陆地区自由贸易区，成为推动西北地区经济社会转型跨越发展的重要增长极。

（5）临沂综合保税区：2014 年 8 月 8 日，国务院正式批准设立临沂综合保税区，综合保税区位于国家级临沂经济技术开发区东部，规划面积 3.7 平方千米。具备公路、铁路、航空、海运四位一体的综合交通优势。具有保税加工、保税仓储、保税物流、口岸作业和综合服务等功能，这将为加快临沂商城国际化、推动经济转型升级注入新活力。

（6）新疆喀什综合保税区：2014 年 9 月 2 日，国务院正式批准设立新疆喀什综合保税区，喀什综合保税区规划面积 3.56 平方千米，划定了四至范围。主要规划设置保税仓储、保税物流、保税加工、展览展示、口岸操作、航空货运和综合配套服务七大功能区，具备国际中转、国际配送、国际采购、国际转口贸易和出口加工等功能。

新疆喀什综合保税区是新疆第二个综合保税区，也是南疆首个综合保税区，其设立有助于为喀什发展乃至南疆区域外向型经济增添新动力，搭建新平台。利用综保区贸易、物流、加工等便利条件，发挥喀什国际机场的货运联运优势，打造喀什空港货物中转枢纽，也必将搭建起中国与中亚、南亚乃至欧洲经贸交流的“喀什通道”，其现实意义和战略意义重大。2015 年 1 月 8 日已顺利通过由海关总署、国家发展改革委、财政部、国土资源部等十部委联合验收组的验收。

（7）石家庄综合保税区：2014 年 9 月 15 日，国务院正式批准设立石家庄综合保税区。石家庄综合保税区选址在空港工业园起步区内，位于石家庄正定国际机场东侧，规划面积 2.86 平方千米，围网面积 2.58 平方千米，重点建设海关检查区、口岸物流区、保税物流区、综合服务中心和两个产业单元。功能定位以口岸作业、保税加工、保税物流三大功能为主，积极拓展保税商品展示展销、跨境电子商务、综合保税服务等功能。

（8）南阳卧龙综合保税区：2014 年 12 月 2 日，国务院正式批准设立南阳卧龙综合保税区，成为继郑州新郑综合保税区后，河南省第二个综合保税区。南阳卧龙综合保税区选址在南阳市卧龙区境内的南阳光电产业集聚区北部，面积 3.03 平方千米，一期建设面积 1.05 平方千米；建设周期为 1 年，将于 2015 年年底封关运行。

截至2014年12月全国综合保税区情况如表2所示。

表2　　截至2014年12月全国综合保税区情况

序号	名称	成立时间	规划面积（平方千米）	备注
1	苏州工业园综合保税区	2006/12/17	5.28	国内首个综合保税区
2	天津滨海新区综合保税区	2008/03/10	1.967	
3	北京天竺综合保税区	2008/07/23	5.944	国内第一家直接依托空港口岸设立的综合保税区
4	广西凭祥综合保税区	2008/12/19	8.5	国内第一个在陆地边境线上设立的综合保税区
5	海口综合保税区	2008/12/22	1.93	国内第一个省会城市综合保税区
6	黑龙江绥芬河综合保税区	2009/04/21	1.8	
7	上海浦东机场综合保税区	2009/07/03	3.59	
8	江苏昆山综合保税区	2009/12/20	5.86	
9	重庆西永综合保税区	2010/02/15	10.3	国内面积最大综合保税区
10	广州白云机场综合保税区	2010/07/03	7.385	全国最大的空港综合保税区
11	苏州高新技术产业开发区综合保税区	2010/08/25	3.51	全国首家通过“信息化围网”技术来进行监管的综合保税区
12	成都高新综合保税区	2010/10/18	4.68	
13	郑州新郑综合保税区	2010/10/24	5.073	
14	潍坊综合保税区	2011/01/25	5.17	
15	西安综合保税区	2011/02/14	6.17	西北地区第一个综合保税区
16	阿拉山口综合保税区	2011/05/30	5.6	新疆首个综合保税区
17	武汉东湖综合保税区	2011/08/29	5.41	湖北首个综合保税区
18	沈阳综合保税区	2011/09/07	7.1982	东北地区内陆城市第一个综合保税区
19	长春兴隆综合保税区	2011/12/16	4.89	
20	无锡高新区综合保税区	2012/05/10	3.497	

续 表

序号	名称	成立时间	规划面积（平方千米）	备注
21	济南综合保税区	2012/05/15	5.22	
22	盐城综合保税区	2012/06/18	2.28	苏北第一家综合保税区
23	淮安综合保税区	2012/07/19	4.92	
24	曹妃甸综合保税区	2012/07/30	4.59	
25	太原武宿综合保税区	2012/09/02	2.94	山西省第一家综合保税区
26	银川综合保税区	2012/09/10	4	
27	南京综合保税区	2012/09/17	5.03	
28	西安高新综合保税区	2012/09/22	3.64	
29	舟山港综合保税区	2012/09/29	5.85	
30	衡阳综合保税区	2012/10/25	2.5743	湖南省第一家综合保税区
31	南通综合保税区	2013/01/03	5.29	
32	苏州太仓港综合保税区	2013/05/30	2.07	
33	湘潭综合保税区	2013/09/09	3.12	
34	贵阳综合保税区	2013/09/14	3.01	国内首个山地生态型综合保税区
35	红河综合保税区	2013/12/17	3.29	云南省第一个综合保税区
36	深圳盐田综合保税区	2014/01/22	1.16	
37	合肥综合保税区	2014/03/27	2.6	安徽省首个综合保税区
38	岳阳城陵矶综合保税区	2014/07/08	2.98	
39	兰州新区综合保税区	2014/07/15	3.39	
40	临沂综合保税区	2014/08/08	3.7	
41	新疆喀什综合保税区	2014/09/02	3.56	新疆第二个、南疆首个综合保税区
42	石家庄综合保税区	2014/09/15	2.86	河北省第二个综合保税区
43	南阳卧龙综合保税区	2014/12/02	3.03	河南省第二个综合保税区

（二）海关特殊监管区域全年进出口数据分析

海关数据显示，2014 年全年，我国海关特殊监管区域（包括保税区、出口加工区、保税港区、综合保税区、保税物流园区和珠澳跨境工业区）进出口累计 6961.7 亿美元，同比下降 1.6%；其中出口 3494.5 亿美元，同比下降

1%；进口 3467.2 亿美元，同比下降 2.2%。相比 2013 年，我国海关特殊监管区域总进出口额在 2014 年出现负增长情况，这与国际大环境有一定关系，也与我国政策导向有着密不可分的联系。同时也可以看到，我国海关特殊监管区域在我国外贸进出口事业中仍然有着举足轻重的作用。相关数据如表 3、图 1 所示。

表 3　2014 年 1—12 月全国海关特殊监管区域进出口、出口和进口数值

年/月	进出口（亿美元）	同比（%）	出口（亿美元）	同比（%）	进口（亿美元）	同比（%）
14/01	546.4	-10.3	261.1	-14.2	285.3	-6.3
14/02	402.1	-16.8	187.8	-22.9	214.3	-10.5
14/03	555.1	-39.9	270.2	-40.9	284.8	-38.9
14/04	540.0	-24.2	257.6	-27.5	282.3	-20.9
14/05	543.4	8.9	268.3	8.8	275.1	9.0
14/06	537.4	16.6	273.2	18.7	264.2	14.4
14/07	623.7	14.2	322.5	24.2	301.2	5.0
14/08	611.7	16.4	322.5	25.1	289.2	8.1
14/09	709.2	32.3	344.9	40.0	364.3	25.7
14/10	642.1	18.0	328.0	16.0	314.1	20.1
14/11	617.8	0.2	336.3	1.4	281.5	-1.2
14/12	636.0	2.9	323.2	3.2	312.8	2.7
合计	6961.7	-1.6	3494.5	-1.0	3467.2	-2.2

（三）不同类型海关特殊监管区域发展概况

纵观 2014 年我国各类海关特殊监管区域的进出口数额，可以看出：我国保税区以 2321 亿美元的进出口数额持续领先于其他各类海关特殊监管区域，但从同比增量上，呈现出负增长态势。我国保税港区和珠澳跨境工业区则分别以 55.3% 和 56.8% 的增幅位列前茅。但增幅小于 2013 年 67.3% 和 64.6% 的增长幅度。与珠澳跨境工业区表现截然相反的则是保税物流园区，2014 年我国保税物流园区、出口加工区的进出口增幅情况略有提升，好于 2013 年的 -7.2% 及 -10.3% 的负增长数据。另外，综合保税区以 10.3% 的增速持续增长，表现出不可小觑的实力。如表 4 所示。

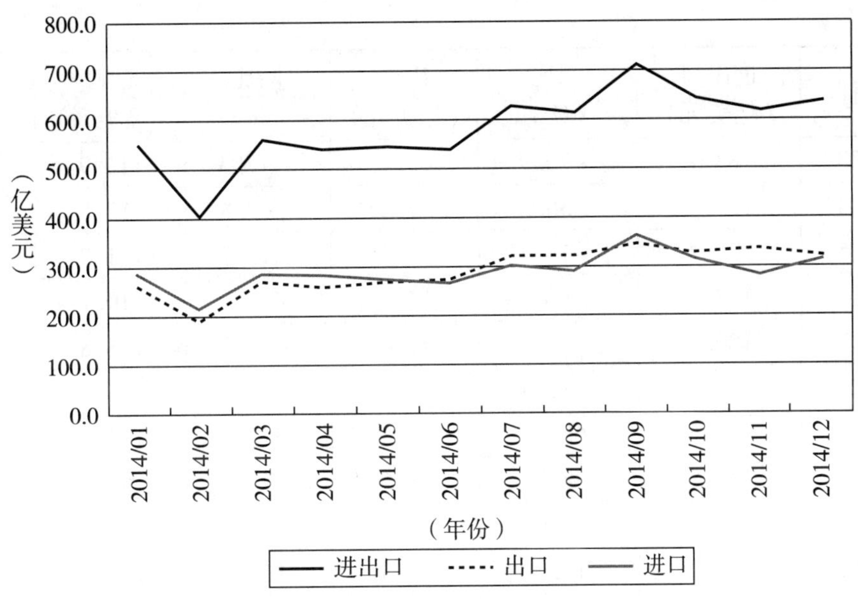

图1 2014年海关特殊监管区域进出口价值

表4 2014年海关特殊监管区域进出口数值汇总

监管区域类型	进出口（亿美元）	同比（%）	进口（亿美元）	同比（%）	出口（亿美元）	同比（%）
保税区	2321.0	-26.8	1484.8	-22.6	836.1	-33.2
出口加工区	1358.3	17.2	521.3	22.4	837.0	14.2
保税港区	911.8	55.3	509.6	51.0	402.2	61.2
综合保税区	2208.2	10.3	884.6	10.6	1323.6	10.0
保税物流园区	159.5	3.9	65.1	3.8	94.3	3.9
珠澳跨境工业区	2.9	56.8	1.6	46.2	1.2	73.1

1. 全国保税区进出口情况

2014年1—12月全国保税区进出口累计2321亿美元，同比增长-26.8%；其中出口836.1美元，同比增长-33.2%；进口1484.8亿美元，同比增长-22.6%。2014年有7个月保税区进出口呈现负增长，直接影响2014年保税区进出口额全年负增长。如表5和图2所示。

表5 2014年1—12月全国保税区进出口、出口和进口数值

年/月	进出口（亿美元）	同比（%）	出口（亿美元）	同比（%）	进口（亿美元）	同比（%）
2014/01	178.8	-43.9	59.5	-54.4	119.2	-36.6
2014/02	127.1	-53.6	41.2	-63.3	86.0	-46.8

续 表

年/月	进出口（亿美元）	同比（%）	出口（亿美元）	同比（%）	进口（亿美元）	同比（%）
2014/03	183.1	-70.9	63.2	-77.3	119.9	-65.7
2014/04	175.1	-56.8	57.2	-67.8	117.8	-48.3
2014/05	173.4	-14.4	62.1	-12.2	111.3	-15.6
2014/06	174.2	0.7	64.1	7.6	110.1	-3.0
2014/07	180.8	-21.4	62.0	-24.3	118.8	-19.7
2014/08	182.5	-12.4	71.0	-9.0	111.5	-14.5
2014/09	290.5	60.3	116.1	97.4	174.4	42.5
2014/10	236.8	38.7	81.5	25.9	155.4	46.4
2014/11	198.4	8.3	78.4	15.4	119.9	4.2
2014/12	221.7	13.7	80.5	13.9	141.3	13.5
合计	2321.0	-26.8	836.1	-33.2	1484.8	-22.6

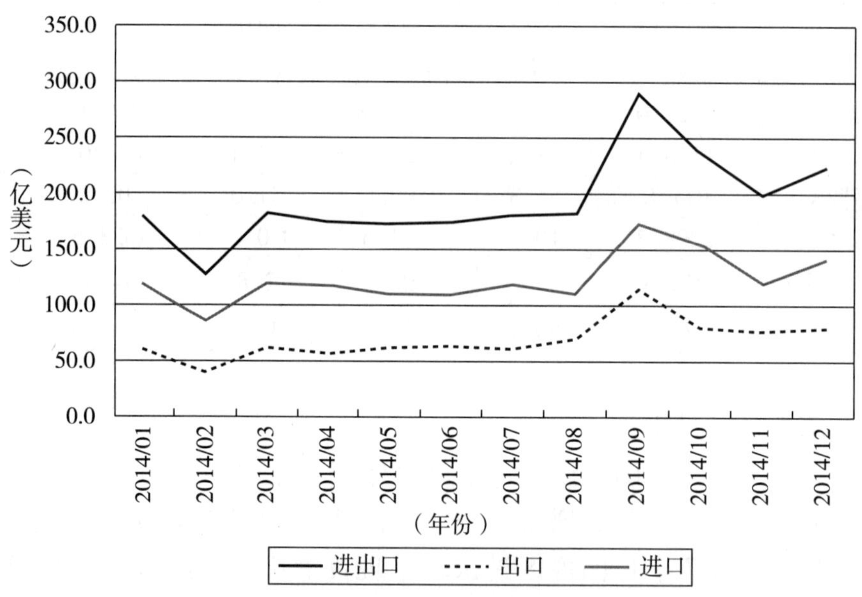

图2　2014年全国保税区进出口价值

2. 全国出口加工区进出口情况

2014年1—12月全国出口加工区进出口累计1358.3亿美元，同比增长17.2%；其中，出口837亿美元，同比增长14.2%；进口521.3亿美元，同比增长22.4%。2014年全国出口加工区进出口情况整体好于2013年。如表6和图3所示。

表 6　　2014 年 1—12 月全国出口加工区进出口、出口和进口数值

年/月	进出口（亿美元）	同比（%）	出口（亿美元）	同比（%）	进口（亿美元）	同比（%）
2014/01	120.9	33.8	67.9	18.0	53.0	61.6
2014/02	83.9	15.5	50.3	-0.7	33.5	53.1
2014/03	107.1	22.6	64.8	14.2	42.3	38.1
2014/04	113.8	25.7	69.9	29.3	43.9	20.3
2014/05	110.7	32.1	69.7	32.1	41.1	32.0
2014/06	98.2	24.9	59.1	17.7	39.1	37.7
2014/07	119.5	27.5	76.5	33.9	43.0	17.5
2014/08	126.1	23.5	77.2	21.8	48.9	26.2
2014/09	121.9	15.2	71.9	13.1	50.0	18.4
2014/10	119.1	9.9	74.1	4.9	45.0	19.5
2014/11	128.4	-1.2	82.8	-2.9	45.6	1.9
2014/12	111.2	-4.9	73.7	2.7	37.4	-17.0
合计	1358.3	17.2	837.0	14.2	521.3	22.4

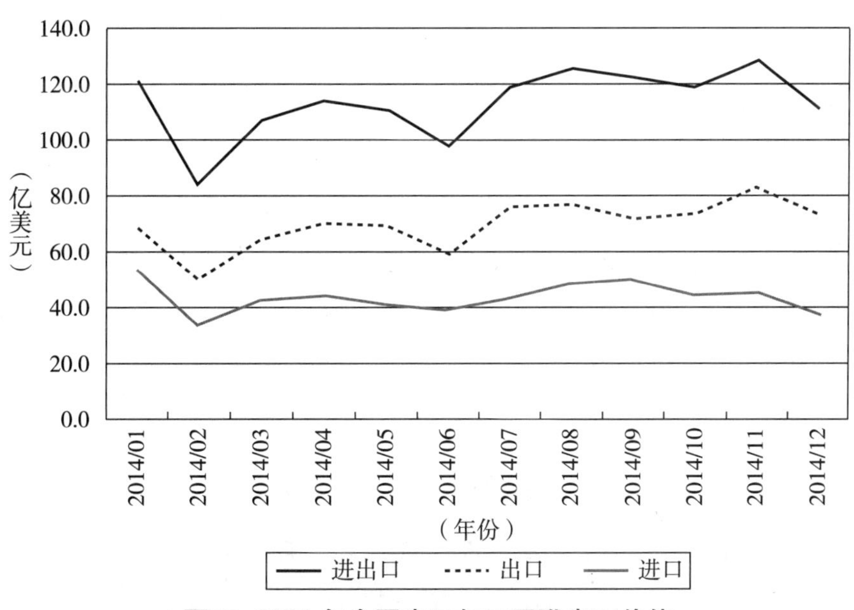

图 3　2014 年全国出口加工区进出口价值

3. 全国保税港区进出口情况

2014 年 1—12 月全国保税港区进出口累计 911.8 亿美元，同比增长

55.3%；其中，出口402.2亿美元，同比增长61.2%；进口509.6亿美元，同比增长51%。如表7和图4所示。

表7　2014年1—12月全国保税港区进出口、出口和进口数值

年/月	进出口（亿美元）	同比（%）	出口（亿美元）	同比（%）	进口（亿美元）	同比（%）
2014/01	84.7	162.5	33.4	163.0	51.4	162.3
2014/02	56.1	92.4	18.0	69.2	38.1	105.8
2014/03	82.0	84.8	33.7	84.9	48.3	84.7
2014/04	75.8	71.6	31.1	57.3	44.6	83.1
2014/05	70.6	63.2	26.1	30.3	44.5	91.6
2014/06	77.1	71.6	36.7	92.0	40.4	56.5
2014/07	117.4	136.7	60.6	198.7	56.9	93.8
2014/08	102.0	109.2	51.7	159.4	50.3	74.5
2014/09	74.6	31.4	31.7	50.2	42.9	20.3
2014/10	66.2	23.6	33.4	32.0	32.8	16.1
2014/11	50.7	-21.6	23.4	-24.0	27.3	-19.6
2014/12	55.0	-27.0	22.8	-27.9	32.2	-26.4
合计	911.8	55.3	402.2	61.2	509.6	51.0

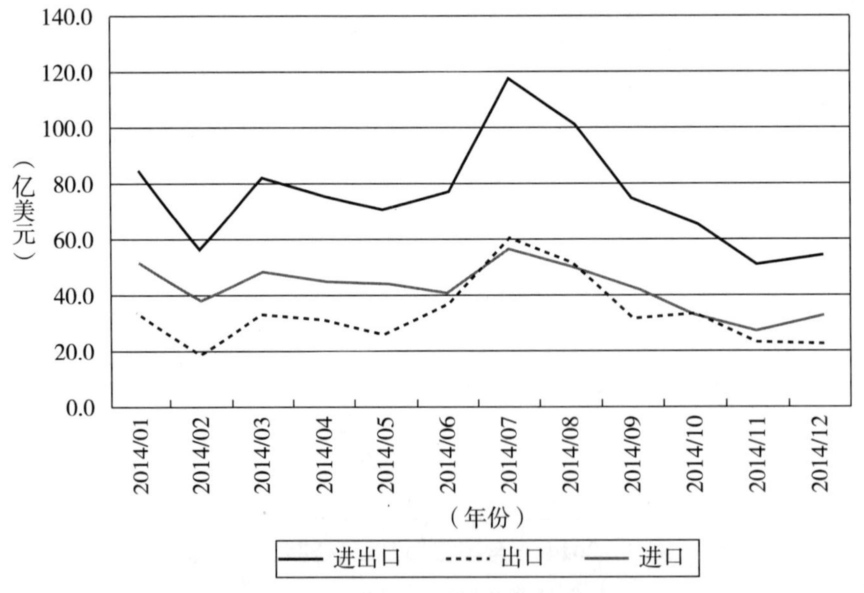

图4　2014年全国保税港区进出口价值

4. 全国综合保税区进出口情况

2014年1—12月全国综合保税区进出口累计2208.2亿美元，同比增长

10.3%；其中，出口 1323.6 亿美元，同比增长 10%；进口 884.6 亿美元，同比增长 10.6%。如表 8 和图 5 所示。

表 8　　2014 年 1—12 月全国综合保税区进出口、出口和进口数值

年/月	进出口（亿美元）	同比（%）	出口（亿美元）	同比（%）	进口（亿美元）	同比（%）
2014/01	147.3	2.1	92.3	1.9	55.0	2.3
2014/02	124.4	27.2	73.2	14.9	51.3	49.9
2014/03	168.8	12.5	101.2	5.5	67.6	24.8
2014/04	161.1	-1.0	91.8	-6.6	69.3	7.6
2014/05	177.2	11.8	103.5	7.3	73.6	18.9
2014/06	174.2	13.2	104.8	11.0	69.5	16.7
2014/07	191.7	19.4	114.4	23.7	77.2	13.4
2014/08	186.3	21.3	112.7	26.9	73.6	13.7
2014/09	207.4	15.6	115.3	20.7	92.1	9.9
2014/10	207.2	4.7	131.4	14.6	75.8	-9.0
2014/11	226.8	1.0	144.1	3.2	82.7	-2.6
2014/12	234.5	7.6	137.9	4.8	96.5	11.8
合计	2208.2	10.3	1323.6	10.0	884.6	10.6

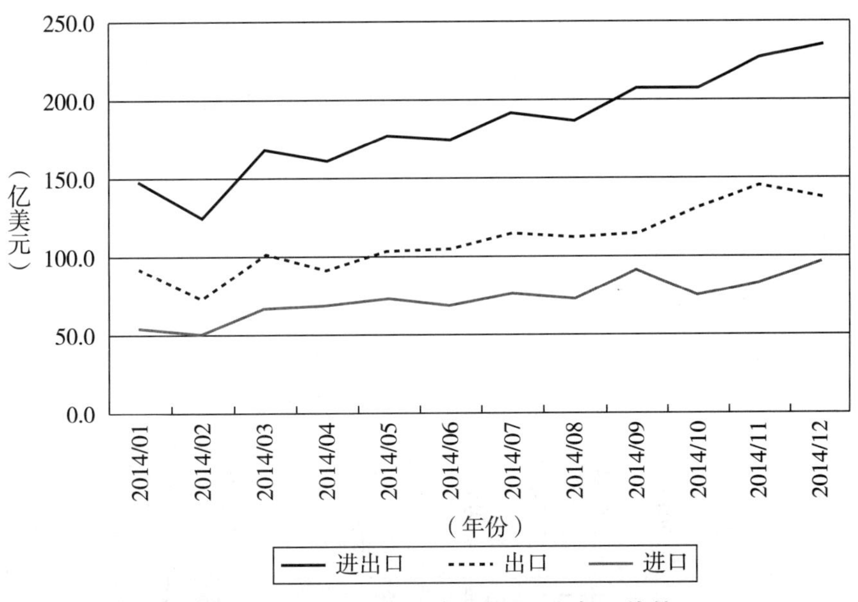

图 5　2014 年全国综合保税区进出口价值

5. 全国保税物流园区进出口情况

2014 年 1—12 月全国保税物流园区进出口累计 159. 5 亿美元，同比增长 3. 9%；其中，出口 94. 3 亿美元，同比增长 3. 9%；进口 65. 1 亿美元，同比增长 3. 8%。如表 9 和图 6 所示。

表 9　2014 年 1—12 月全国保税物流园区进出口、出口和进口数值

年/月	进出口（亿美元）	同比（%）	出口（亿美元）	同比（%）	进口（亿美元）	同比（%）
2014/01	14. 3	-38. 6	7. 8	-40. 5	6. 6	-36. 0
2014/02	10. 4	7. 3	5. 1	-20. 8	5. 3	61. 7
2014/03	13. 9	8. 7	7. 2	-0. 5	6. 7	20. 9
2014/04	14. 0	47. 1	7. 4	32. 9	6. 6	67. 2
2014/05	11. 2	4. 3	6. 8	5. 0	4. 4	3. 4
2014/06	13. 4	29. 6	8. 4	24. 9	5. 0	38. 4
2014/07	14. 1	14. 9	9. 0	15. 9	5. 1	13. 2
2014/08	14. 7	18. 2	9. 8	28. 9	4. 9	1. 2
2014/09	14. 5	14. 7	9. 8	37. 4	4. 7	-14. 6
2014/10	12. 6	-6. 2	7. 5	3. 0	5. 0	-17. 3
2014/11	13. 1	-6. 2	7. 3	-6. 9	5. 8	-5. 4
2014/12	13. 3	7. 2	8. 2	8. 4	5. 1	5. 4
合计	159. 5	3. 9	94. 3	3. 9	65. 1	3. 8

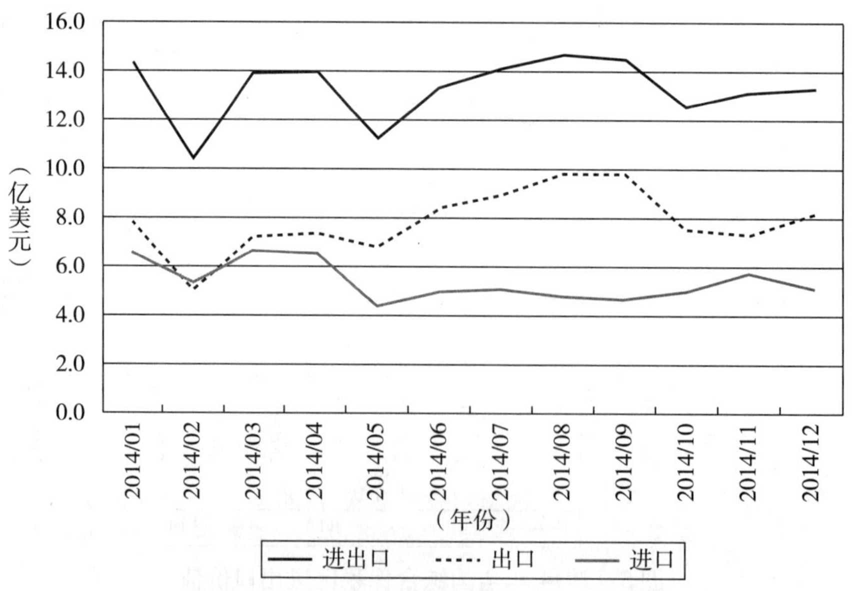

图 6　2014 年全国保税物流园区进出口价值

6. 珠澳跨境工业区进出口情况

2014 年 1—12 月珠澳跨境工业区进出口累计 2.9 亿美元，同比增长 56.8%；其中，出口 1.2 亿美元，同比增长 73.1%；进口 1.6 亿美元，同比增长 46.2%。如表 10 所示。

表 10　2014 年 1—12 月珠澳跨境工业区进出口、出口和进口数值

年/月	进出口（亿美元）	同比（%）	出口（亿美元）	同比（%）	进口（亿美元）	同比（%）
2014/01	0.3	255.6	0.2	334.3	0.2	200.2
2014/02	0.1	209.7	0.1	338.6	0.1	160.4
2014/03	0.2	116.5	0.1	203.2	0.1	80.5
2014/04	0.2	223.9	0.1	402.1	0.1	154.1
2014/05	0.2	86.9	0.1	171.8	0.1	48.9
2014/06	0.2	38.1	0.1	9.4	0.1	58.5
2014/07	0.2	-10.9	0.1	41.4	0.1	-31.3
2014/08	0.2	18.8	0.1	149.7	0.1	-22.4
2014/09	0.3	-1.8	0.1	-37.5	0.2	44.3
2014/10	0.2	23.6	0.1	16.8	0.1	29.5
2014/11	0.4	99.8	0.2	144.1	0.2	71.6
2014/12	0.3	26.8	0.1	19.6	0.2	32.8
合计	2.9	56.8	1.2	73.1	1.6	46.2

（四）跨境电子商务催生新型保税物流

2012 年 8 月，国家批准上海、郑州、重庆、杭州和宁波首批五个跨境电商试点城市。另有 2013 年 9 月批准的广州和 2014 年 9 月批准的深圳。而出口模式对各个城市基本放开，只要提出申请，基本均能批准。北京、安徽、福建、重庆、宁波、金华、苏州、青岛、东莞等省、市也纷纷上马跨境电商园区与平台建设，其中杭州跨境贸易电子商务产业园发展速度较为迅捷，目前已经实现“家门口通关”。

我国跨境电子商务产业的发展远远领先于全球其他国家和地区，跨境电商已成为中国进出口贸易增长最快的领域。电子、时尚、家居园艺、汽配及收藏品成为中国跨境电商零售出口产业销售额最高的前五大品类，而家居园艺、汽配和时尚则成为增速最快的三大品类。

2014 年是中国电商发展关键的一年。2014 年 3 月 5 日，李克强总理的政府工作报告中提到：要稳定和完善出口政策，加快通关便利化改革，扩大跨境电子商务试点；加快电子商务等新议题谈判。2014 年 3 月 4 日海关总署《关于跨境贸易电子商务服务试点网购保税进口模式有关问题的通知》明确了保税进口网购模式。

有三种类型电子商务 B2C 模式，即直购进口模式（境外电商与境内消费者之间的 B2C 模式）、网购保税进口模式（海关特殊监管区域内的电商与境内消费者之间的 B2C 模式）和一般出口模式（境内电商与境外消费者之间的 B2C 模式）。

在跨境电子商务经营中，在线批发多采用传统的通关物流方式；在线零售多以商业快件和个人行邮为主要的通关物流方式，并由此衍生出包裹集中后以百家货方式清关到香港转运以及批量货物海外仓转运的模式。

中国跨境电商出口业务 70% 的包裹都通过邮政系统投递，其中，中国邮政占据 50% 左右的份额，香港邮政、新加坡邮政等也是中国跨境电商卖家常用的物流方式。邮政网络基本覆盖全球，比其他任何物流渠道都要广。邮政为国营，有国家税收补贴，因此价格便宜。但是一般以私人包裹方式出境，不便于海关统计，也无法享受正常的出口退税，且速度较慢。

另外是采用国际快递。国际快递对信息的提供、收集与管理有很高的要求，以全球自建网络以及国际化信息系统为支撑。优点是速度快、服务好、丢包率低，尤其是发往欧美发达国家非常方便。比如，UPS 从中国寄包裹到美国，最快可在 48 小时内到达，TNT 发送欧洲一般 3 个工作日可到达，价格较高。

亚马逊 2014 年与上海自贸区签订战略合作协议，推出六个国家 8000 万选品直邮中国，更让跨境电商业务得到实质性推进。不到一年的时间，亚马逊独步全球全中文“海外购”商店，百分百源自亚马逊美国，并首次将中国市场带入“黑色星期五”狂欢节，几乎掀起了类似国内“双十一”的轰动效应。

从全球范围来说，亚马逊已经在亚洲、北美、欧洲和大洋洲等 13 个国家建立业务站点。目前，有 96 大运营中心和遍布全球的物流体系提供全球配送，可送至 185 个国家和地区。借助全球化的网络，亚马逊在海外购方面的优势明显。

2014 年中国已经成为亚马逊除美国本土之外最大的物流运营网络。目前在中国拥有 13 个运营中心。除了覆盖近 1400 个城市区县的当日达及次日达服务，还以 5000 多个自提点居 B2C 电商的首位。亚马逊也充分利用了大数据分析来提高效率。

国内最大的垂直专业网站开发运营商——生意宝将与谷歌合作，共同帮助中国外贸企业发展跨境电子商务。双方将在关键词广告、外贸出口等方面发挥各自优势资源。

上海市跨境贸易电子商务试点平台于2013年12月28日正式投入运营，并开通直购进口和网购保税进口两种模式，提供外汇、通关、税收、结算等业务的公共服务平台、导购门户网站、跨境电商物流中心等均投入使用。截至目前，共有71家电商企业和14家物流、仓储企业在海关完成备案。通过此平台成交的主要商品类别涉及母婴、箱包、服装配饰、香水、化妆品、进口食品等。

随着我国经济形势的发展，很多企业正在考虑在境外建立保税物流中心，拓展国际物流业务。我国的物流企业在一些发达国家和地区建立配送中心，可以快速反应客户订单；在一些第三世界国家建立保税物流中心，目的是规避我国境内沿海地区较高的土地成本和劳动力成本，以及规避一些国内的法律法规。这将为保税物流增添新的形态，也带来了新的需要研究的问题。预计在2014年境外保税服务行业会有一个井喷式发展。

和沿海城市相比，东北内地过去一直是被我国经济发展大潮遗忘的角落。现在也借电子商务的东风，后起直追，利用地缘优势开展针对俄罗斯的边境贸易。2014年，哈尔滨市共有101架次邮政小包货运包机飞抵俄罗斯莫斯科、叶卡捷琳堡，出境货物1214万件、共计2244.5吨，货值超2亿美元，发货量占全国对俄电商小包总数30%，在国内位居第一。

2014年6月，中国首个对俄电子商务边境仓正式在哈尔滨开仓运营，极大地缩减了电商对俄跨境物流成本。目前，哈尔滨已开通5条对俄客货混载航线，其中，哈尔滨至叶卡捷琳堡航线每月包裹量可达100万件。哈尔滨也成为中国境内对俄跨境电商平台数量最多、对俄出口电商包裹量最多和跨境零售出口额最大的城市。

目前，哈尔滨市启动建设60万平方米的对俄跨境电商基地，拟打造连通俄罗斯、东北亚、北美等地区的国际化跨境电商保税物流园区。同时，将开辟哈尔滨至克拉斯诺亚尔斯克、新西伯利亚等地的货运航线，形成辐射俄罗斯多地的航空网络运输格局。

（五）保税物流通关便利化

1. 推广三项海关监管创新制度

"智能化卡口验放""简化通关作业随附单证""简化统一进出境备案清单"三项上海自贸区海关监管创新制度。

智能化卡口验放是依托电子地磅、条码自动扫描比对等功能，实现智能审核、自动抬杆，省去了原来人工比对、人工抬杆的程序。

简化了通关作业随附单证后，企业申报时可以省去电子随附单证的扫描及上报流程。

简化统一进出境备案清单后将备案清单申报要素由原来的最高 40 项统一简化为 30 项，每票申报工作的工作量仅为原来的一半。

2. 区域通关一体化

为适应国家区域经济发展战略，2014 年 7 月起，海关先后在京津冀、珠三角区域实施了通关一体化改革，建立起区域海关的统一申报、风险防控、专业审单和现场作业四大平台。区域海关间通过改革实现了互联互通，企业可以自主选择申报、纳税、验放地点，使得通关更便利、成本更节约。

9 月 22 日起，在上海、南京、杭州、宁波、合肥海关（以下简称长三角地区海关）启用区域通关一体化通关方式；12 月 1 日在南昌、武汉、长沙、重庆、成都、贵阳、昆明海关启用该通关方式。

长三角地区海关区域通关一体化通关方式适用于上海市、江苏省、浙江省、安徽省（以下简称长三角地区）企业在长三角地区各口岸海关进出口的货物。长三角地区企业可自主选择向经营单位注册地、货物实际进出境地海关或其直属海关集中报关点办理申报、纳税和查验放行手续。

企业可根据实际需要，自主选择口岸清关、转关、“属地申报、口岸验放”、“属地申报、属地放行”、区域通关一体化等任何一种通关方式。

二、2015 年保税物流发展展望

（一）“一带一路”战略构想带来陆路保税物流的发展

2014 年博鳌亚洲论坛年会开幕大会上，李克强总理以“共同开创亚洲发展的新未来”为题发表演讲，阐述了中国的亚洲合作政策，强调要推进“丝绸之路经济带”和“海上丝绸之路”简称“一带一路”的建设。

丝绸之路经济带主要是将我国内陆地区通过铁路和公路运输线将西亚和东欧国家联系起来，开展经济往来。不仅将成为我国内地的经济高速发展的推进器，同时将促进我国对周边国的贸易量迅速增长，对欧洲国家通过铁路进行的国际物流也将出现大幅增长，使得我国对西亚东欧国家的国际贸易和国际物流取得更快进展，铁路保税运输和公路保税运输量将明显上升。

与海运保税物流明显不同，陆运的保税物流形式不仅局限在陆运口岸地区建立海关特殊监管区域，还有可能在经济带沿线各个国家边境到腹地都设立监管区域，以及经济带陆运途中的物品保税。这样，增加了各国海关的监管难度，也提出了保税监管技术、监管政策的新的需求。

（二）航运政策改革突破旧框架

上海自由贸易试验区在2014年年底扩大范围，纳入自贸区版图的洋泾将建设一个区中区：洋泾国际航运试验区，成为航运领域政策突破和制度创新的产业载体。洋泾社区面积7.38平方千米，航运资源要素丰富，已经有1000多家航运企业入驻。

由于上海浦东有两个海港和一个空港，将利用海运航空资源优势和保税政策优势，加快周边地区的综合运输体系建设，在2015年成为浦东海运空运兼营的国际保税物流中心。

（三）区域通关一体化改革继续推进

在京津冀、长江经济带、广东省内海关区域通关一体化基础上，海关2015年计划继续将区域通关一体化改革向全国海关推进，完善海关内部协作、互认共享机制，让跨区域通关更便捷、物流更顺畅。

（四）国民境外购物将成为保税物流的新形式

2014年中国的出境人数已经超过1亿，境外消费已经超过1万亿元人民币，大部分购买的是中国制造的出口商品。原因有几个：一是出口商品退税，是形成价格倒挂的因素之一；二是国内流通成本过高，环节过多；三是国外品牌商对华的定价政策。

随着上海自贸区的设立，居民保税消费的坚冰已经开始融化，中哈霍尔果斯边境自由贸易区允许中国公民购买一定数额下的免税商品，四大自贸试验区均可以试点中国居民进区购物。其他海关特殊监管区域可以尝试复制自贸区入区购物免税政策，跨境电商与监管区域的实体店相配合，形成出口商品转内销的O2O模式。这样，既降低了物流成本，还节约了国民的购物时间。自由贸易试验区将和国际成熟的自由贸易区、自由港差距进一步缩小。最终诞生和中国香港、新加坡几乎一样的真正意义上的自由贸易区，届时中国的世界经济地位将会进一步提升。

（大连海事大学交通运输管理学院　田征
东方海外（天津保税物流园区）有限公司　王涛）

第二章

行业物流

2014 年制造业物流发展回顾与 2015 年展望

一、2014 年我国制造业发展回顾

当前，我国制造业发展趋势与典型工业化国家的一般规律基本吻合，同时也表现出追赶国家的一些特点。一方面，我国工业化率高于典型工业化国家在类似发展阶段的平均水平，呈挤压式增长；另一方面，我国重化工业特点比较明显，制造业的服务投入系数偏低，劳动力、土地等成本上涨压力增大、产能过剩等矛盾也严重制约了制造业的快速发展。面对这些问题，制造业进行转型升级和结构调整已是大势所趋。2014 年制造业发展主要呈现出以下几个突出特点：

（一）PMI 整体呈先升后降趋势

PMI 指数的英文全称为 Purchasing Managers'Index，中文含义为制造业采购经理指数，是国际上通行的宏观经济监测指标体系之一，对国家经济活动的监测和预测具有重要作用。通常以 50% 作为经济强弱的分界点，PMI 高于 50%，反映制造业经济扩张。“十二五”规划时期，是我国实现转型升级，提高产业核心竞争力的关键时期。2011—2014 年，我国官方 PMI 如表 1 所示。

表 1　　规模以上工业增加值同比增长速度①

	2011 年 PMI（%）	2012 年 PMI（%）	2013 年 PMI（%）	2014 年 PMI（%）
1 月	52.9	50.5	50.4	50.5
2 月	52.2	51.0	50.1	50.2
3 月	53.4	53.1	50.9	50.3
4 月	52.9	53.3	50.6	50.4
5 月	52.0	50.4	50.8	50.8
6 月	50.9	50.2	50.1	51.0
7 月	50.7	50.1	50.3	51.7
8 月	50.9	49.2	51.0	51.1
9 月	51.2	49.8	51.1	51.1
10 月	50.4	50.2	51.4	50.8
11 月	49.0	50.6	51.4	50.3
12 月	50.3	50.6	51.0	50.1
全年平均	51.4	50.8	50.8	50.7

从 2014 年全年来看，制造业 PMI 平均水平 50.7%，与前两年平均水平基本相当，并未出现大幅下降，显示经济运行稳定性增强，增速处在适度合理区间。综合来看，经济新常态正在形成。

（二）结构调整与转型升级继续深化

中央经济工作会议明确指出，我国已进入经济发展新常态，认识新常态、适应新常态、引领新常态是当前和今后一个时期我国经济发展的大逻辑。工业是我国经济的根基所在，也是推动经济发展、提质增效升级的主战场。我们必须准确把握经济发展新常态，坚持走新型工业化道路，推进信息化和工业化深度融合，努力发挥工业在经济增长、结构优化和动力转换中的主力军作用。

结构调整和转型升级主要从以下几个方面展开：优化产业结构，发现培育工业领域新增长点，把推动经济结构战略性调整作为转变经济发展方式的主攻方向；实施创新驱动，重塑工业转型发展新引擎，将增强创新能力摆在首要位置，增强中国工业升级的动力；发展智能制造，探索信息化条件下生产新方式，把发展智能制造作为战略重点，抓住新一轮产业变革浪潮和信息化发展趋势，探索智能制造生产方式，建立信息化条件下的工业生态体系。加快绿色发

① 数据来源：国家统计局月度统计数据，http：//www. stats. gov. cn/，作者已经进行整理。

展，推动形成低碳循环发展新模式，坚持生态文明建设与工业文明建设相结合，推动工业走绿色、循环、低碳发展之路。

（三）制造业服务化创新趋势明显

“制造业服务化”是指在经济全球化、客户需求个性化和现代科学技术与信息化快速发展条件下，出现的一种全新的商业模式和生产组织方式，是制造与服务相融合的新的产业形式。这种产业形式使企业实现了从单纯产品或者服务供应商向“综合性解决方案”供应商的转变。

服务化代表着制造业发展的大趋势和升级的大方向。《2014 年中国制造业服务创新调查报告》指出，在信息技术革命的背景下，制造业发展模式正在发生深刻变革。该调查报告指出，中国过去令人瞩目的增长是通过制造业扩张来实现的。中国已经成为制造大国，但要成为制造强国，则必须更加具有服务创新意识。服务创新有助于中国装备制造业摆脱长期以来处于价值链低端而导致的价格竞争，提高自身在国际产业分工中的地位。制造业服务化是制造业的本质回归，服务创新也可弥补技术和产品质量的不足。从国内实践看，我国一些制造企业正在积极探索与服务业有机结合的路子，并已初见成效。比如，中国铁建重工集团近年来积极延长产业链条，针对客户需求提供从产品研发、制造到售后服务的一揽子解决方案，构建了面向产品全生命周期的全新服务模式，极大提升了企业竞争力。

（四）面向信息化与数字化的智能制造开始起步

互联网与生产制造领域渗透融合步伐在 2014 年明显加快，涌现出个性化定制、按需制造、众包众设、异地协同设计等一批“互联网 +”应用新模式。海尔通过众包平台聚集中科院、高通、腾讯等资源研发设计空调产品。北江纺织基于 O2O 开展定制化业务，创维发布了 O2O 移动商业平台“云 GO”。未来，将有一大批制造企业主动拥抱互联网，同时，互联网企业也将加快与制造业深度融合。

大数据技术和应用加速向经济社会各领域快速延伸。大数据正被喻为“未来新石油”，成为构建企业竞争优势的新基础。基于大数据的应用创新将更加活跃，海量多格式和多模式数据将纳入统一管理、实时分析和高效流通，大数据还将与神经计算、深度学习、语义计算以及人工智能等技术结合，促进大数据应用更加智能，可视化手段更加丰富。

2014 年，典型智能工业开始起步。互联网技术、新型感知技术和自动化技术相互融合并快速发展，带动智能制造技术在工业生产、设备管理、环保监测、能源管理、安全生产等领域广泛应用。中石化启动金陵石化智能工厂建设，九江石化即将完成智能工厂的基本框架构建。华纺股份、鲁泰、红豆、上海纺织集团等纺织企业开始部署智能制造。

二、2014 年我国制造业物流发展回顾

2014 年，我国经济发展告别高速增长阶段，物流业也随之驶入“稳中有进”的轨道。产业结构调整，物流需求结构也发生了变化，外贸物流需求增速放缓，与内需有关的物流需求呈现高速发展的态势。制造业生产成本不断攀升、资源环境负责不断加重，整合资源和创新将成为驱动制造业物流业发展的主要动力。

（一）社会物流需求增速平稳

2014 年 1—11 月，全国社会物流总额 196.9 万亿元，按可比价格计算，增长 8.3%，增速与 1—10 月持平，较 1—9 月月回落 0.1 个百分点，较上年同期回落 1.3 个百分点①。

从物流总额构成看，物流市场结构有所优化。工业品物流总额 181.7 万亿元，可比增长 8.3%，增速较 1—10 月回落 0.1 个百分点。进口货物物流总额 11.0 万亿元，可比增长 7.8%。单位与居民物品物流总额继续保持高速增长态势，可比增长 32.5%，较 1—10 月提高 0.6 个百分点，如图 1 所示。

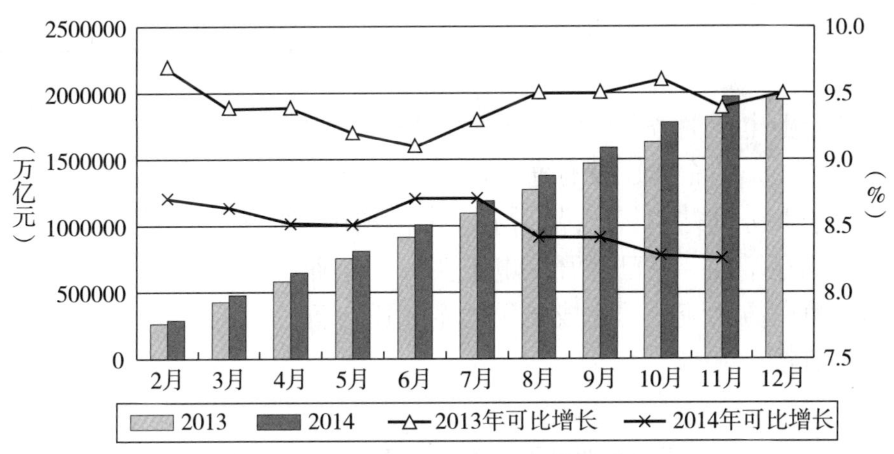

图 1　2013 年和 2014 年各月社会物流总额及增长变化情况

从分项数据来看，各分项物流总额自 9 月以来呈现明显的趋稳回升迹象。工业品物流总额增速也有回升迹象，较上半年回升 0.3 个百分点，但较 2013 年同期回落 0.4 个百分点。在社会物流总额中占绝大部分比重，仍是促进物流规模增大、拉动社会物流总量的决定性力量。

① 数据来源：中国报告大厅，http：//www.chinabgao.com/stat/stats/39746.html，作者已经进行整理。

（二）2014 年制造业物流调查数据与分析①

制造业物流的相关数据显示了制造业物流的运营现状。基于数据调查，可以分析出制造业企业物流的发展趋势。根据国家发改委经济运行调节局和南开大学现代物流中心于 2014 年 1—4 月对我国工商企业物流业务外包总体情况的调查，在工商企业物流总费用占销售收入的比例方面，调查结果显示，22% 的工商企业的物流总费用占销售收入的比例低于 5%，物流总费用占销售收入比例的均值为 9.3%，工商企业物流总费用占销售收入比例的均值相对 2013 年略有下降。如表 2 所示。

表 2　　工商企业物流总费用占销售收入的比例

项目	比例（%）
低于 5%	22
5% ~10%	35
10% ~15%	33
高于 15%	10
合计	100
均值	9.3

在工商企业电子商务运作模式方面，43.4% 的企业开始通过电子商务网站销售产品，56.6% 的企业还没有通过电子商务网站销售产品，23.8% 的企业已准备开拓电子商务网站销售产品。与上一年相比，通过电子商务网站销售产品的企业数量明显增加。在已经开展电子商务的企业中，无论采用何种电子商务平台，利用第三方物流公司完成配送的企业比自营物流配送的企业居多，具体数据如表 3 所示。

表 3　　工商企业电子商务运作模式（有多选）

所采用的模式	比例（%）
自建电子商务平台，自营物流配送	8.2
自建电子商务平台，第三方物流公司完成配送	29.3
借助其他电子商务平台开展业务，自营物流配送	5.9
借助其他电子商务平台开展业务，第三物流配送	63.7

① 本节数据均来源于《中国现代物流发展报告 2014》。

在工商企业物流业务外包的程度方面。调查结果显示，在外包干线运输或配送的工商企业中，37.9%的企业将其70%以上的干线运输或配送业务实施外包，表明干线运输或配送业务外包的程度较高，具体数据如表4所示。

表4　　　　　工商企业物流业务外包程度（有多选）

项目＼程度	10%以下	11%～30%	31%～50%	51%～70%	70%以上
干线运输或配送	17.2	13.7	24.2	7.0	37.9
仓储保管	50.0	15.6	15.2	7.8	11.3
采购管理	66.8	8.2	8.6	0	16.4
包装与流通加工	54.3	0	36.3	9.4	0
产品装配与安装	63.3	18.4	9.0	0	9.4
库存管理	61.7	7.8	7.8	0	22.7
物流信息管理	64.8	5.9	0	5.9	23.4
物流系统设计	40.2	0	19.5	0	40.2

工商企业与物流服务商的合作形式中，90.6%的工商企业通过签订合同与物流服务商合作，17.2%的工商企业与物流服务商结成战略联盟，具体数据如表5所示。

表5　　　　工商企业与物流服务商之间的合作形式（有多选）

项目＼年份	2009	2010	2011	2012	2013
签订合同	93.1	94.6	92.7	92.3	90.6
战略联盟	22.4	25.3	24.0	20.6	17.2
参股物流服务商	4.8	5.9	6.7	1.4	4.3
其他	0.2	0.4	1.1	1.4	2.0

物流信息技术的广泛应用使得工商企业物流的运营效率和效果都得到很大程度的提升。2013年，70.3%的工商企业采用了条码技术，36.3%和22.7%的工商企业采用了全球卫星定位系统和地理信息系统（GPS和GIS）和射频识别（RFID）技术。各种物流信息技术的使用比例略有下降，但是射频识别技术的使用比例却有明显升高，具体如表6所示。

表 6　　　　工商企业采用的物流信息技术种类（有多选）

项目＼年份	2009	2010	2011	2012	2013
条码技术	67.4	72.5	78.7	76.9	70.3
全球卫星定位系统与地理信息系统（GPS 和 GIS）	32.6	38.9	41.3	45.1	36.3
射频识别（RFID）技术	14.3	16.2	15.3	18.2	22.7
电子数据交换系统（EDI）	37.2	37.3	37.0	38.8	19.1
电子订货系统（EOS）	18.6	19.1	25.3	27.6	14.8
自动分拣系统（ASS）	17.2	15.7	14.3	15.4	10.5
其他	14.0	14.1	11.7	7.7	10.5

（三）把握电子商务机遇，制造业物流转型升级继续推进

近年来，随着互联网技术的发展和普及，电子商务迅速崛起，大数据、云计算得到普遍应用，互联网化、拓展供应链布局成为产业发展的一种大趋势。无论是服装、汽车等加工制造业，还是零售等服务性制造业，都在通过互联网手段，不断强化供应链体系建设，进而实现创新发展。

根据《邮政业发展“十二五”规划》和《工业转型升级规划（2011—2015 年）》，在 2015 年，快递将继续在服务制造业发展方面发挥重要作用，也将随我国电子商务的快速发展而获得更大的市场。

另外，近年来我国大宗商品电子商务得到快速发展。2014 年，阿里巴巴上市和世界互联网大会将我国的消费互联网带入巅峰时代，我国电子商务总交易额超过美国。同时，大宗商品电子交易量也随着国际间贸易量的不断增加而急速上升。大宗商品电子商务在其发展过程中，与物流等相关领域的结合越来越紧密。因此我国制造业物流也将随之快速发展，获得更大的市场空间。

（四）制造业物流重点行业物流效率稳步提升

中国物流与采购联合会、中国物流信息中心于 2015 年 2 月发布的重点企业物流统计调查数据显示，2013 年钢铁行业物流效率稳步提升，物流专业化水平持续提高，但总体来看，我国钢铁物流成本依然较高，根据推算规模以上钢铁企业物流总成本达 7900 亿元，降低物流成本潜力较大。

在钢铁行业产能过剩的大背景下，行业物流效率稳步提升，钢铁物流费用率有所下降。重点企业物流统计调查数据显示，2013 年钢铁行业物流成本费用

率为 10.7%，同比下降 0.4 个百分点，较 2009 年下降了 1.3 个百分点，为近年来的最低水平。如图 2 所示。

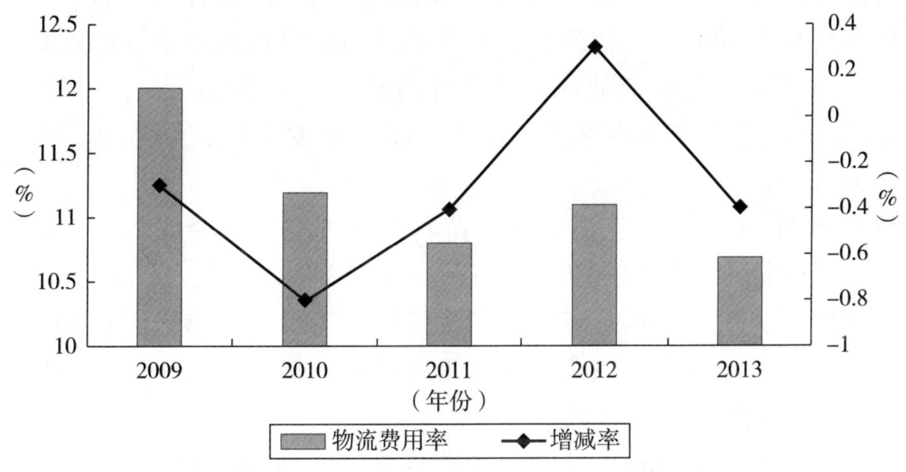

图 2　2009—2013 年钢铁企业物流费用率

近年来在钢铁价格持续低迷、银行限贷等诸多因素影响下，钢铁企业为压缩物流环节费用，积极采取措施，如加大直供比例及电子商务平台的应用，以实现供应链的成本节省和快速响应。2013 年钢铁行业库存率为 11.0%，近年来总体呈下降趋势，较 2009 年下降了 1.6 个百分点。在此背景下，仓储成本和利息成本占比分别下降 0.01 个和 0.2 个百分点，占 4.4% 和 12.2%。如图 3 所示。

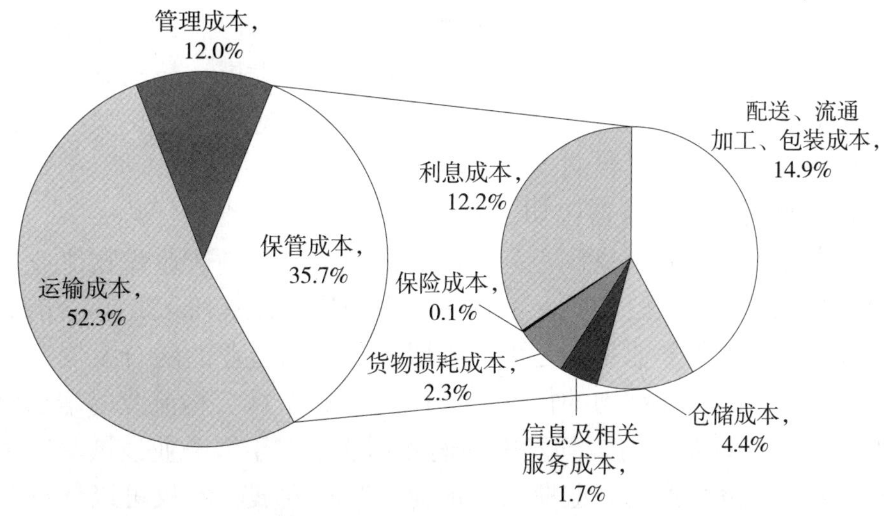

图 3　调查钢铁企业物流成本构成

（五）2014 年制造业与物流业联动发展新进展

随着制造业与物流业的转型升级和现代化产业结构的优化调整，“两业”联动发展变得越来越重要，社会各界对两业联动必要性和紧迫性的认识不断提高。2014 年，制造业与物流业联动发展有以下几方面进展：

1. 制造业物流与供应链管理工程纳入物流业发展中长期规划，两业联动方式转型升级

2014 年 6 月 11 日，李克强总理主持召开国务院常务会议，讨论通过《物流业发展中长期规划（2014—2020 年）》，9 月 12 日以国发〔2014〕42 号文正式发布。规划提出三大发展重点、七项主要任务、十二项重点工程和九项保障措施。其中，制造业物流与供应链管理工程被纳入重点工程中，显示出国家对于推动两业联动发展的高度重视。

在主要任务中，《物流业发展中长期规划（2014—2020 年）》指出，要鼓励制造企业分离外包物流业务，促进企业内部物流需求社会化。优化制造业、商贸业集聚区物流资源配置，构建中小微企业公共物流服务平台，提供社会化物流服务。着力发展第三方物流，引导传统仓储、运输、国际货代、快递等企业采用现代物流管理理念和技术装备，提高服务能力；支持从制造企业内部剥离出来的物流企业发挥专业化、精益化服务优势，积极为社会提供公共物流服务。鼓励物流企业功能整合和业务创新，不断提升专业化服务水平，积极发展定制化物流服务，满足日益增长的个性化物流需求。进一步优化物流组织模式，积极发展共同配送、统一配送，提高多式联运比重。

由国家发改委印发的《促进物流业发展三年行动计划（2014—2016 年）》的通知中，提出要继续深入推动制造业与物流业联动发展，鼓励制造业企业分离外包物流业务，释放物流需求。提高物流企业的供应链一体化服务能力，发挥好物流业对制造业转型升级的支撑带动作用。

2. 制造业物流业关系日益密切，各地两业联动工作继续深化

现代物流是提升制造企业核心竞争力的重要手段，制造业是物流业发展的需求基础。发达国家的经验表明，工业化步入中后期发展阶段，必须借助于服务经济的力量，通过服务业特别是生产性服务业与制造业的融合发展，来推动制造业的转型升级和产业结构的优化。2014 年，整个社会物流业的增加值已占到服务业增加值的 17% 左右，其发展的速度和质量对于服务业发展具有举足轻重的地位。因此，继续推动制造业与物流业的联动发展，不仅可以促进制造业的转型升级，而且可以推动服务业快速发展，对于转方式、调结构，打造中国经济升级版具有十分重要的意义。

2014 年 11 月 14 日，济南市经信委、市发改委、市国土资源局联合发布

《济南市关于加快制造业与物流业联动发展的实施意见》，促进产业升级和经济发展方式转变，积极推进实施联动发展示范试点工程。其中，到2020年，主营业务收入过10亿元的工业企业将基本实现主辅剥离，建立或委托第三方物流服务。同时，济南市将推出八项措施鼓励制造业和物流业联动发展。制造与物流联动发展同等条件下优先扶持。

事实证明，两业联动是促进物流业发展和发挥物流业基础性支撑作用的有效途径，两业联动的理念也已得到了制造企业和物流企业的普遍认可。例如，中化化肥建立了供应商、生产企业到分公司、销售大区、销售网点及核心门店、客户的供应链，中化化肥作为供应链的核心企业，总部设立专职管理机构，在上游生产环节以集中采购和规模化生产使得供应链成本降低，在下游销售环节以市场和客户需求拉动，快速响应市场使公司销售收入提升，通过强化对供应商的考评管理，高度重视客户关系的建设和维护，并以全供应链信息化平台作为管理工具和手段，引导供应商高效运作，为公司应对激烈的市场竞争，完成战略转型提供了有力的支持。

在整个行业深度调整的背景下，行业物流也在积极应对变革，谋求整合提升。例如，钢铁生产企业积极向产业链中游流通环节渗透，拓展物流环节，兴办钢铁物流园区；汽车产业链加速拓展，第三方物流企业在实现汽车零部件入厂、整车物流、售后服务备件物流业务的同时，向供应链管理和物流领域延伸，向汽车后市场领域拓展。将来物流企业要融入客户生产的前期采购、订单环节。物流企业从取货、送货阶段，发展到配合客户进行生产管理，深入到生产过程，甚至直接参与生产线的生产过程。食品饮料行业重点关注冷链及配送环节、服装行业的供应链管理重难点在消灭链条上高库存等等。

3. 物流技术应用步伐加快，供应链模式创新带动产业升级

2014年，是我国新技术革命的重要战略机遇期。随着劳动力的短缺和要素成本上升，以机器替代人力的趋势日益明显。制造业物流将积极通过技术改造和设备升级，提升物流信息化、机械化、自动化水平，提高单位产出效率，创新物流服务模式。大数据，移动互联，智慧物流在制造业物流开始发力，通过整合数据和深入挖掘，为物流经营提供决策支持、为经济运行提供分析预警、为供应链上下游企业提供数据共享和相互协同，用数据创造新的价值，打造智能化竞争新优势。

以上海大众公司为例，上海大众借鉴德国大众新物流概念，建立了基于全流程信息化的拉式零部件供应链体系。以保证零件在正确的时间以正确的数量备货上线，实现零部件供应的同节拍运作，是整车企业物流和供应链管理的新实践。此外，在2014年3月，上海大众官方旗舰店入驻苏宁易购，开启O2O购车新时代：在线或电话咨询预约试驾，线上确认车型并进行支付。通过这种

模式，减少了很多流通环节，有效降低物流成本，在满足客户需求个性化的同时，增加了物流业务的弹性。

物流的核心价值就在于整合，这也是现代物流区别于传统的运输、仓储行业的主要特征。领先企业通过流程再造、兼并重组、联盟合作等多种方式，加快功能整合、组织整合、信息整合和平台整合，挖掘物流整合潜力，发挥资源利用效率，有效提升发展的质量和效益。海尔的日日顺物流推出“送装一体化”服务模式，打造四网融合核心竞争力。

2014 年，制造业物流的一个重要发展趋势是向供应链转型。世界经济发达国家加大了“再工业化”战略的推进力度，依靠的就是对全球供应链的掌控和驾驭能力。以徐州工程机械集团有限公司（以下简称“徐工集团”）为例，充分利用物联网、云计算、数字化、智能化等新技术，着力解决各业务、各产品之间普遍存在的信息孤岛问题，推进徐工集团信息化整体提升，实现企业内外有效协同，提升企业竞争力。2014 年 7 月 1 日，徐工信息技术服务有限公司正式成立运营。信息化作为集团的“智慧大脑”和“价值中心”，开展产品智能化工程，面向装备制造业制造生产、上下游产业链，提供数字化工厂解决方案，优化供应链整体运营。2014 年 11 月，徐工集团阿里巴巴国际站跨境电子商务平台投入运营。平台主营徐工全系列整机与备件产品，依托阿里巴巴国际站面向全球 190 多个国家销售。

总体来看，我国制造业供应链发展除了产业链上核心制造企业牵头带动以外，更多地是通过打造供应链一体化服务平台，为供应链上关联企业提供线上线下综合服务，如集中采购、分销执行、物流服务、平台交易、融资支付等，服务各类企业资源整合和功能提升的需要，这也是我国许多供应链企业的主要发展模式。

4. 制造业物流国际化步伐加速

2014 年，我国制造业发挥在全球产业链中的竞争优势，积极参与价值链体系分配，积极实施走出去战略。制造业企业通过“走出去”转移过剩产能，推动支持境外重大合作项目，引导冶金、化工、建材等重化工业到能源资源富集的国家和地区投资，鼓励轻工、纺织等劳动密集型产业有序“走出去”。以钢铁企业为例，2014 年 9 月初，河北钢铁在南非投资建设的 500 万吨钢铁项目正式启动，这是迄今我国在国外投资建设的最大规模全流程钢铁项目，意味着我国钢铁企业“走出去”有了新开端，将会有企业跟进效仿，积极从外部谋求发展空间。

2014 年，国际物流渠道全面打开，中国物流与全球接轨，积极服务于制造业的全球化发展。亚太经合组织工商领导人峰会之后，谋求亚太经济一体化、共筑亚太梦想成为国际议论的焦点，而实现的关键在于“亚太物流一体化”。

“亚太物流一体化”将积极推进亚太自贸区建设，支持多边贸易体制，促进全球供应链的合作。中海集运与法国达飞海运和阿拉伯联合航运签署合作协议，三家集装箱班轮运营商在亚欧航线、泛太平洋航线和亚洲—地中海航线三条东西向的主干线上展开共同投船、舱位互换和舱位买卖等形式的合作；中国—东盟自贸区建设向纵深推进，物流陆路通道不断扩展，中国与东盟已有近10条重要陆路货物运输通道进行互联互通，有力推动了双方经贸合作。与此同时，各类企业看好跨境电商业务，“海外仓”建设吸引大批资金。中远物流，中外运股份等大型物流企业继续保持工程物流领域的优势地位，跟随国内工程建设企业“走出去”，在港口、园区等物流战略资源方面取得积极进展。

三、2015年制造业物流发展展望

2014年我国经济在宏观调控区间运行，产业结构得到优化，改革取得重大突破；2015年我国经济预计会在政府投资拉动和房地产行业回稳的情况下出现良好发展势头，经济增长目标会在7.1%～7.5%。作为全面实现“十二五”规划的收官之年，2015年经济工作的总基调是稳中求进。2015年制造业物流业将继续维持在“中速增长阶段”，制造业与物流业“两业联动”，逐步走向商贸业、金融业等“多业联动”，合作共赢的“产业生态圈”也将逐渐形成。同时，随着我国从工业大国向服务业强国的产业结构转变新常态的出现，“新常态”将进入制造业物流。在这种形势下，预计2015年制造业物流将呈现出缓步稳定增长的态势。

（一）制造业物流随着电子商务的高速发展继续快速增长

近几年来，我国电子商务出现迅猛发展。根据《电子商务“十二五”发展规划》，到2015年中国电子商务交易额预计可达到18万亿元。在电子商务的带动下，中国的制造业物流也进入了高速增长阶段。2015年将是信息经济全面发展之年。信息经济全面发展，将始于以下新迹象：从产业化向服务化发展，从信息产业向信息经济发展。在互联网带动下，各行各业将联合起来，推动中国经济从工业经济向信息经济发生质变。

以钢铁业为例，通过钢铁电子商务集成性，将分散、碎片化的消费集成起来，使得钢铁行业供需形成对应关系，必然可以在一定程度上抑制产能过剩。钢铁电子商务发展轨迹推动着钢铁流通组织的全过程，而不仅仅停留在交易当中，它能够推动商流、物流统一起来，形成全流程管理以此降低流通成本。通过钢铁电子商务能够把握住在流通领域环节的物控权。

此外，2015年，制造业物流将在如何更好的服务更多顾客的基础上进行发力。互联网将唱响制造业智能化、服务化的主题，从同质化的中国制造，向差异化的高端发展。汽车不再只是钢铁，而是智能移动终端，成为容纳身体的大号手机。房间不再只是水泥，而成为智能家居。中国是制造业大国，如今已进入全球化电商时代，而跨境电商也无疑是电子商务领域的“热词”，更被称为互联网的下一个“风口”，电子商务的一次革命。中国制造要想在全球市场中抢占一席之地，必须借助跨境电商，加快转型升级。

（二）区域物流规划开始发力，跨境制造业物流机遇多

近年来，国家陆续提出跨区域的长江经济带、京津冀协同发展、丝绸之路经济带和海上丝绸之路等一系列区域经济规划。2015 年，物流企业将以区域物流为突破口，推动开发型经济发展。另外，制造业物流也将以平台整合为突破口，逐步完善物流网络。相对于以往分散的公路货运、物流园区、国际货代等领域，平台整合将以多种形式全面铺开，实体基地平台推进全国区域布局的工作也将进行。

以区域物流和物流平台整合为起点，制造业跨境物流将迎来快速发展的机遇。商务部统计数据显示，近年来我国跨境电子商务发展迅速，2011 年，中国跨境电子商务交易额约为 1.6 万亿元，预计到 2016 年中国跨境电商进出口额将增至 6.5 万亿元，年增速超过 30%。跨境电商的快速发展带来对我国跨境电商物流的大量需求，促使我国企业开始逐步建立国际物流网络。因此，2015 年，我国物流将继续向国际延伸，国际物流成为新的增长点。为搭建覆盖全球的国际物流服务网络，我国企业将启动海外战略性物流资源布局，打造区域化、国际化竞争新优势。

随着国内企业“走出去”步伐加快，特别是跨境电商的快速发展，物流网络逐步向国际延伸，国际物流成为新的增长点。境外战略性物流资源布局将开始启动，搭建覆盖全球的国际物流服务网络，以适应制造业、电子商务等其他产业跨境发展需要，打造区域化、国际化竞争新优势。

（三）物流外包加速，供应链管理水平不断提高

受多种因素的组合影响，一些知名外资企业，如松下、日本大金、夏普、TDK 等均计划进一步推进制造基地回迁日本本土。优衣库、耐克、富士康、船井电机、歌乐、三星等世界知名企业则纷纷在东南亚和印度开设新厂，加快了撤离中国的步伐。日本知名钟表企业西铁城在华生产基地——西铁城精密（广州）有限公司宣布清算解散，千余名员工被解除劳动合同，限期离厂。与此同时，微软则计划关停诺基亚东莞工厂和北京工厂，并加速将生产设备运往越南工厂。微软在东莞和北京两地的关厂，将总共裁员 9000 人。2015 年，进入了

制造业发展的真正考验期。2015 年 1 月和 2 月的 PMI 值分别是 49.8% 和 49.9%，低于 50% 的荣枯线，反映出制造经济的低迷态势。尽管这两个月有一定的季节性因素存在，但中国制造业经济陷入低谷是一个不争的事实。在此宏观背景下，制造业物流外包作为降低制造企业成本的有效手段，发展步伐将进一步加速。2014 年以来，制造业物流外包受到国务院的高度重视。国务院先后于 2014 年 8 月 6 日和 2015 年 1 月 16 日发布了《国务院关于加快发展生产性服务业促进产业结构调整升级的指导意见》和《国务院关于促进服务外包产业加快发展的意见》，这两个《意见》明确指出，今后三年将培育一批具有国际先进水平的服务外包知名企业，建设一批主导产业突出、创新能力强、体制机制先行先试的服务外包产业集聚区，因此，2015 年我国物流外包行业将得到快速发展。同时，2015 年我国市场竞争将更加激烈，信息技术也将快速发展。企业为了取得竞争上的优势，减轻自营物流高固定成本造成的制造成本居高不下的压力，将进一步剥离内部物流业务。上述两种因素的综合作用将增加制造业企业物流外包的动力，增加制造业物流业务外包总量，促进外包物流企业不断拓宽业务范围。

根据国家发改委印发的《促进物流业发展三年行动计划（2014—2016 年）》，制造业供应链管理能力将在 2015 年得到进一步提升。一批仓储配送设施和物流信息平台、第三方供应链管理平台等将得到建设和实施，这也将有力地推进供应链管理水平的不断提升。

（四）全球供应链物流转型发展趋势明显

全球供应链是指在全球范围内组合供应链，它要求以全球化的视野，将供应链系统延伸至整个世界范围，根据企业的需要在世界各地选取最有竞争力的合作伙伴。2012 年美国提出的《全球供应链安全国家战略》以及 2014 年亚太经合组织（APEC）贸易部长会议上通过的《建立 APEC 供应链联盟倡议》等文件说明全球供应链发展已经成为世界各国的共识。我国国务院 2014 年印发的《物流业发展中长期规划（2014—2020 年）》中也鼓励物流企业与制造企业深化战略合作，建立与新型工业化发展相适应的制造业物流服务体系，形成一批具有全球采购、全球配送能力的供应链服务商。随着我国制造业“走出去”步伐加快，我国制造类企业将要面对全球化的原料采购、全球化的生产力布局、全球化的产品营销要求。

因此，2015 年，我国制造业物流业企业将加强关键物流节点布局和物流资源掌控，实施供应链一体化管理，进一步加强全球制造业供应链物流的发展战略，建立全球化的供应链体系，提升基于供应链物流的全球资源配置能力，与全球利益各方构建协作共赢的战略合作关系，掌控供应链的主导权。

（五）绿色采购将成为制造企业的新趋势

伴随低碳经济的发展要求，绿色采购成为近年来国家大力倡导的重要采购模式，这一采购模式也将在2015年成为亮点。绿色采购指企业在采购活动中，推广绿色低碳理念，充分考虑环境保护、资源节约、安全健康、循环低碳和回收促进，优先采购和使用节能、节水、节材等有利于环境保护的原材料、产品和服务的行为。环境保护部、商务部、工信部于2014年12月22日联合发布的《企业绿色采购指南（试行）》（以下简称《指南》）鼓励企业要求供应商在产品设计过程中更多采用生态设计技术，以减少环境污染和能源资源消耗，使产品和零部件能够回收循环利用。《指南》还要求企业应不断完善采购标准和制度，综合考虑产品设计、采购、生产、包装、物流、销售、服务、回收和再利用等多个环节的节能环保因素，与上下游企业共同践行环境保护、节能减排等社会责任，打造绿色供应链。《指南》在2015年1月1日开始实施，因此，2015年绿色采购将成为制造业物流的亮点。

（天津大学管理与经济学部　刘伟华　武润泽　朱冬蕾
天津师范大学管理学院　毛乔梅）

2014 年我国商贸物流发展回顾与 2015 年展望

2014 年可以说是商贸物流改革的“设计年”，而 2015 年将是真正的“改革元年”，具体回顾展望如下：

一、2014 年商贸物流发展回顾

2014 年，国务院出台了《关于促进内贸流通健康发展的若干意见》、《物流业发展中长期规划（2014—2020 年）》、《关于依靠黄金水道失去长江经济带发展的指导意见》，商务部出台了《关于促进商贸物流发展的实施意见》、商务部、国家标准委出台《商贸物流标准化专项行动计划》、国家发改委等 7 部委出台《关于我国物流业信用体系建设的指导意见》等相关政策，较系统全面地提出了促进商贸物流业发展的方针政策。

（一）社会消费品零售总额增速趋缓

1. 社会消费品零售总额增幅减缓

2014 年我国社会消费品零售总额增长速度进一步趋缓，2008 年曾经增长 22.7%，2012 年 14.3%，2013 年 13.1%，2014 年为 12%，呈现趋缓趋势，2014 年我国实现社会消费品零售总额 26.2 万亿元，同比增长 12%，扣除价格因素，实际增长 10.9%，比上年同期分别放缓 1.1 个和 0.6 个百分点。

2. 农村消费增幅连续高于城市

2012 年至今 30 多个月，农村消费增速高于城镇，2012 年城乡社会消费品零售总额增幅分别为城市 14.3%，农村 14.5%，2013 年分别为 12.9%、14.6%、2014 年分别为 11.8%、12.9%。三四线城市成为中外零售商竞争的焦点。

我国流通业增幅减缓，但农村消费增幅上涨，这与我国连续 11 年丰收、粮食“十一连增”、农民收入“十一连增”以及我国农村政策的落实具有很大关联性。同时流通业正在由过去追求高速度、大规模的社会消费品流通时期，开始转为追求质量和效率的时期，长期以来低价格竞争的时代已经结束，疲劳促销已经不能够真正满足消费群体消费升级的需要，这表明我国商品流通业进入理性发展的新常态时期。

3. 商品交易市场规模持续加大

2014 年我国亿元以上商品交易市场估计超过 5100 家，交易额超过 10 万亿元。而 2013 年我国亿元以上商品交易市场为 5089 个，交易额达到 99254 亿元。商品交易市场规模越来越大，占地越来越多，2000 亩、3000 亩比比皆是，而且同质化严重，北京、上海、天津、郑州、广州、昆明、杭州、石家庄等城市的商品交易市场陆续外迁，行业加快进入结构调整、交易升级、管理创新的新阶段。

（二）网络零售高速发展

2014 年电子商务继续保持高速增长的态势，进入一个新时期。2014 年我国电商额达到 13 万亿元，增长 25%，增幅较上年减缓，全国网络零售额达到 2.8 万亿元，同比增长 49.7%，增幅较上年有所提高，上半年移动商务交易额达到 2542 亿元，增长 378%，呈现高速增长的态势。从地区来看，浙江省发展较快，2014 年 5641.57 亿元，同比增长约 47.64%。2014 年“双十一”网络零售交易额达到 571 亿元，同比增长 63.14%，全国范围内网络零售额达到 805.11 亿元。

（三）“双十一”网络促销再创新高

从阿里系的“双十一”促销来看，2009—2014 年“双十一”销售额分别为 5200 万元、9.36 亿元、53 亿元、191 亿元、350 亿元、571 亿元，这是阿里从 2009 年到 2014 年“双十一”的支付宝成交额，就在 2014 年“双十一”前几天，阿里股价也达到了 117 美元的新高度，市值 2878 亿美元。数据显示，2014 年 11 月 10 日到 11 月 17 日的 7 天时间，全行业需要处理的快件量近 6 亿件，日最高处理量将接近 1 亿件，是 2014 年以来日常处理量的 3 倍。

（四）跨境电子商务交易额预计超过 6 万亿元

2014 年，我国进出口总值 26.43 万亿元人民币，比 2013 年增长 2.3%。其中，出口 14.39 万亿元，增长 4.9%；进口 12.04 万亿元，下降 0.6%；贸易顺差 2.35 万亿元，扩大 45.9%。按美元计价，2014 年，我国进出口、出口和进口分别增长 3.4%、6.1% 和 0.4%。2014 年跨境电商交易额预计将超过 6 万亿元（上半年为 3.1 万亿元），而 2013 年为 3.1 万亿元。

（五）移动商务市场份额得到提高

移动互联带来了更多碎片化时间，2014 年的“双十一”，阿里无线端销售额占比 45%，而在凌晨最高峰时，甚至达到了 70%。而在 2013 年这一比例仅有 20%。主打本地生活服务的美团网移动端交易额占比达到 90% 以上，移动商务市场快速增长。

（六）农产品目标价格试点开始

根据 2014 年中央一号文件精神，国家进行棉花、大豆目标价格试点，进一步放开棉花、大豆市场，将改变现有的粮食、棉花“政策市”现状。棉花取消收储，定价回归市场，2015 年将根据国内棉花供需形势做好棉花进口的相关工作，除发放按照加入世贸组织承诺的 89.4 万吨关税进口配额、满足纺织配棉等需要外，不再增发进口配额，并引导国内纺织企业多使用国产棉。

收储制度致农产品价格倒挂严重，最低价格收购和临时收储制度始于 2004 年，其目的是由国家指定企业进行低价收购，维护市场价格。但近年来由于该政策使得包括大豆、棉花、白糖在内的不少农产品国内外价差日益增大。以大豆为例，2013 年临时收储价 4600 元/吨，而目前美国大豆进口折算到港成本仅 4200 元/吨不到，南美豆更低只有 4000 元/吨左右，收储价和市场价差高达 400～600 元/吨，而棉花目前国际市场价 1.4 万元/吨左右，国内目标价格为 1.98 万元/吨，差价达到 5800 元/吨。

食糖有望成价改下一站，2014 年一号文件对玉米、油菜籽、食糖保留临时收储，取消了大豆、棉花农产品临时收储政策，并正式启动东北和内蒙古大豆、新疆棉花目标价格补贴试点。未来中国主要农产品价格大幅高于国外会是常态，为此，会继续挑选重要农产品实行农产品目标价格制。目的是尽量拉平国内外市场差价，同时保障农民利益。

从选取的新疆棉花、东北大豆价格试点来看，主要选择的是一些产地比较集中的农产品，且存在的价格倒挂问题比较严重。从这些条件来看，食糖很可能成为下一个试点的农产品，目前我国 70% 以上的食糖集中在广西，而且价格倒挂问题严重。

考虑到小麦、稻米是全国大部分人口的基本口粮，关系到国计民生，而我国的政策是保证“口粮绝对安全”，因此关于稻米、小麦的目标价格制度试点工作会放到最后，在大豆、棉花、玉米价格试点取得一定成效后，才会对其进行目标价格制度改革。

（七）农产品电商融资进入高潮

2014 年农产品电子商务进入第五个发展时期，融资进入高潮：①年初本来生活、美味七七先后得到融资（美味七七获得亚马逊 2000 万美元入股）；②5 月京东上市融资 17.8 亿美元；③我买网融资 1 亿美元；④宅急送获得 10 亿美元投资，探索生鲜农产品电商物配；⑤阿里美国上市融资 218 亿美元，成为最大的融资规模企业；⑥“青年菜君”以半成品生鲜电商特色获千万元 A 轮融资——提出“顾客头天网上下单，次日地铁口自提”模式；⑦进口食品垂直类跨境电商平台“鲜 LIFE（鲜生活）”获千万人民币天使投资。这些融资已经或将大量地投入农产品电子商务。2013 年 12 月底，我国各类淘宝村达到 211 个，淘宝镇达到 19 个，农村电子商务将促进我国“三农”的稳步发展。

（八）农产品网络零售额超千亿

据初步估算，2014 年我国农产品电子商务构成：一是网络期货交易达 32 万亿元；二是大宗商品交易达 25 万亿元；三是商务部等网络交易会交易额超过 100 亿元；四是各类农产品网络零售额超过 1000 亿元。2014 年生鲜农产品电子交易额预计达到 262 亿元，增长 100%。农产品电子商务进入“成长期”和“发展期”，需要培育市场的政策环境等。

（九）零售业进入“关店开店”调整期

自 2012 年以来，我国零售业进入关店时期，但关店与开店并存，关店数大于开店数，据联商网统计，截至 2014 年 12 月 31 日，全国主要零售企业（百货、超市）共计关闭 201 家门店，较 2013 年关闭 35 家，同比增长 474.29%，创历年之最。

百货类门店共计关闭 23 家，其中百盛百货关闭 4 家门店，成为 2014 年关店最多百货企业，华堂商场、中都百货各关闭 3 家，尚泰百货、NOVO 百货、宝莱百货各关闭 2 家，王府井百货、天虹商场、新光百货、摩登百货、春天百货、瑞富奥莱、南宁百货，各关闭 1 家。

超市类门店共计关闭 178 家，其中沃尔玛关闭 16 家门店，成为 2014 年关店最多的超市企业，乐天玛特关闭 6 家，人人乐关闭 5 家，华润万家、家乐福、乐购各关闭 4 家，世纪联华、新华都各关闭 3 家，永辉超市关闭 2 家，麦德龙、北京华联、中百仓储、恒客隆、三江购物、胖东来、佳乐家各关闭 1 家，四川家和超市因资金链断裂关闭 26 家门店，百全超市宣布试水失败，关闭在河南、山东、江西等地 98 家门店。

（十）零售企业网站陆续上线

2014 年有 13 家大中型实体零售企业上线电子商务，如大润发的飞牛网、大商集团的天狗网、步步高的云猴网、万达集团的万达电商、永辉超市的永辉微店 APP 等，使零售企业电子商务网站达到 88 家，在 O2O 模式探索方面有了新的进展。而另一方面，建材家居市场却在不断地开店，市场集中度不断增大，如红星美凯龙、居然之家在 2013 年 130 家、84 家基础上，2014 年继续开店，且销售额也有较大增长。2014 年居然之家开店超过 100 家，达到 107 家，销售额超过 360 亿元。

（十一）商贸物流模式多样化突破

2014 年全国首个“南菜北运”全程冷链果蔬绿色专列——广西百色至北京果蔬绿色专列正式开通运营。2014 年 8 月，首趟电商专列开出，电商专列满载一次，运输量相当于 62 辆 9.6 米长的货车，或者 36 架波音 737 全货机的运力。2014 年 8 月，沈阳局开通“东北货物快运”——鲜活货运快车，采取发电车供电机械式制冷，每组车编挂冻结式保温车、保鲜式保温车和冷藏式保温车 2 ~ 3 辆，适合各种储藏要求的鲜活产品运输，在大连周水子站和哈尔滨香坊站间循环开行，截至 2015 年 1 月 11 日，沈阳局“鲜活”货运快车已运送鲜活物品 18 万件多，1300 余吨。此外阿里菜鸟物流、京东自建物流都有新的进展，许多电商物流也有了新进展，如电子菜箱、智能菜柜、“网购店取”等多种物流业态不断涌现。

（十二）全国市场、园区建设出现盲目发展

全国购物中心、农产品市场、物流园区、电子商务园区出现盲目发展。据统计，全国现有物流园区近 1000 家，电子商务园区达到 500 多家，购物中心（含城市综合体）5000 多家。而且同质化相当严重，许多地方，特别是三四线城市的商业设施供过于求，闲置、空壳、休眠的商业地产大量出现。以体验性业态为主的购物中心，百货店核心店正在由集合店所取代，形成差异化发展趋势。

（十三）商贸物流业诚信体系建设开始试点

2014 年，商贸流通业诚信体系建设已经试点。自国务院出台《社会信用体系建设规划纲要 2014—2020 年》以来，商务部、中宣部、国家工商总局以及中国消费者协会在内的 17 个部委和单位启动了 2014 年“诚信宣传月”，其主题是“合力共筑，诚信强国”，浙江率先在阿里、义乌小商品城进行试点，积累了较好的经验，义乌小商品城成为美国诚信采购点。

二、2015 年商贸物流发展展望

展望 2015 年我国商贸物流的发展，将会更加重视发展的质量和效率，预计将延续 2014 年的发展趋势，在此基础之上会有一个较大的发展，将出现十大趋势：

（一）我国“十二五”规划的收官之年

2011 年《商贸物流发展专项规划》提出 2015 年的目标是：初步建立一套与商贸服务业发展相适应的高效通畅、协调配套、绿色环保的现代商贸物流服务体系，形成城市配送、城际配送、农村配送有效衔接，国内外市场相互贯通的商贸物流网络。各项计划抓紧推进，2015 年将得到进一步落实。

（二）逐步落实国务院等出台的系列文件

2015 年将逐步落实 2014 年国务院等部门出台的关于商贸物流业文件，2014 年国务院先后颁布了一系列促进商贸物流业发展的文件，如《关于促进内贸流通健康发展的若干意见》、《物流业发展中长期规划（2014—2020 年）》、《关于依托黄金水道推动长江经济带发展的指导意见》、《关于促进海运业健康发展的若干意见》、《关于加快发展生产性服务业促进产业结构调整升级的指导意见》、《2014 年食品安全重点工作安排》、商务部颁发《关于促进中小商贸流通企业健康发展的意见》、《商务部关于促进商贸物流发展的实施意见》，李克强主持召开国务院常务会议决定进一步开放国内快递市场，推动内外资公平有序竞争。商务部、财政部《关于开展电子商务进农村综合示范的通知》。商务部等 13 部门颁布《关于进一步加强农产品市场体系建设的指导意见》。

（三）我国社会消费品零售总额将平稳增长

延续 2014 年我国社会消费品零售总额升幅减缓趋势，原计划到 2015 年社会消费品零售总额 32 万亿元左右，年均增长 15% 左右的目标受到影响，2015 年预计以 12% 左右的增长速度发展，全国社会消费品零售总额在 2014 年 26.2 万亿元的基础上，2015 年接近 32 万亿元的规模，2014 年电子商务得到迅速发展，超过 13 万亿元，2015 年将以 26% 左右的增长速度增长；2014 年我国网络零售额预计达到 2.8 万亿元，2015 年以 40% 左右的增长速度增长。

（四）农村消费市场将进一步活跃

2015 年农村社会消费品零售总额将延续 2012 年以来高速发展势头，2014 年我国粮食连续“十一连增”，粮食产量再次超过 6 亿吨，达到 60709.9 万吨（12142 亿斤），比 2013 年增加 516 万吨（103.2 亿斤），增长 0.9%，2015 年农业部提出“稳量增收”的政策，农民收入将得到提高。三四线城市的消费市场将进一步活跃。

（五）生产资料物流市场继续疲软

2015 年我国生产资料销售额将延续 2014 年发展的势头，2014 年我国生产资料销售额为 54 万亿元，但是增长幅度将继续减缓，明显达不到 2015 年规划的 76 万亿元的目标。但是生产资料物流仍然是商贸物流的主要内容。

（六）商贸物流结构应得到调整和优化

2015 年我国商贸物流的规模在结构调整中得到协调发展，如全国物流园区达到 700 多家、电子商务园区超过 510 家（3 月底数据，预计实际超过这一数字）、城市综合体超过 5000 多家、商品交易市场超过 8 万家（其中亿元以上商品交易市场超过 5000 家），2014 年我国“双十一”网络销售额达到 805.11 万亿元，预计在 2015 年在规范发展中增幅减缓。

（七）零售业 O2O 将创新发展

2015 年我国零售业 O2O 将不断创新发展。2014 年我国零售巨头的 O2O 加快转型发展，如苏宁 O2O 全新零售业态（线上线下同价）、国美的 O2M 战略（线下实体店 + 线上电商 + 移动终端）、万达的万百腾共赢的 O2O、银泰与阿里共建大数据 O2O、大润发 O2O（生鲜、门店发货、门店电子屏、千乡万馆 O2O）、步步高本地生活服务平台、大商以 O2O 构建多重零售业态、三胞并购麦考林等推行 O2O 等，被称为是零售业 O2O 转型代表模式。

（八）京津冀物流一体化将加速

2015 年京津冀物流一体化将加快其进程，预计 4 月底《京津冀协同发展规划》下发，铁路、公路、航空、水路、管道等物流一体化将加快进程，市场联动、品牌联动、物流配送快递联动、海关联动、支付联动等将积极行动，北京与白沟、北京与廊坊、北京与石家庄、北京与天津、北京与滨海新区等相互联动，建立物流协同关系。

（九）电商物流得到较快发展

2015 年阿里物流、京东物流将发挥重要作用。2013 年 5 月 28 日，由阿里巴巴集团牵头的物流项目“中国智能骨干网”（简称 CSN、俗称“菜鸟网络”）在深圳正式启动，注册资金 50 亿元。以自营起家的京东则不惜投掷 35 亿元建“亚洲一号”物流工程。同时，淘宝延续网络平台功能，建设了 212 个淘宝村、19 个淘宝镇和 30 多个地方特色馆，京东自建物流也在全国范围内发挥作用。电商专列、冷链动车，以及 140 万快递员队伍，促进电商物流配送快递发展。

（十）“一带一路”进入实质性阶段

“一带一路”是指“丝绸之路经济带”和“21 世纪海上丝绸之路”的简称，2015 年将进入实质性阶段。2014 年义乌打造“一带一路”经贸合作“桥头堡”，西安、新疆、甘肃等省市区，以及浙江、福建泉州等都开始了系列活动，促进“一带一路”进入实质性阶段。同时加快与长江经济带、环渤海经济圈的协同创新。

（北京工商大学商业经济研究所　洪涛）

2014 年钢铁行业物流发展回顾与 2015 年展望

2014 年我国经济形势复杂，处于“经济增长速度换档期、结构调整阵痛期、前期刺激政策消化期”的“三期叠加”时期，经济运行面临下行压力。作为国民经济的支柱产业，钢铁行业在宏观经济新形势下也进入全面调整期，低增长、低效益、低价格、高压力，“三低一高”成为钢铁业新常态。2014 年内，钢铁产量、钢材出口、铁矿石进口量均创新高，钢价跌至近年来新低，社会库存严重收缩，钢铁流通模式正在发生变革。2015 年，新环保法实施，新的铁矿石供应格局有望形成，钢铁电商时代日趋成熟，钢铁行业正式步入加快结构调整、推进转型升级的洗牌期，钢铁行业物流在新形势下也将进入深度调整期，流通方式亟待瞄准平台经济的发展方向进行创新转型。

一、2014 年中国钢铁行业物流发展回顾

1. 2014 年钢铁产量增速放缓，钢材出口量及铁矿石进口量大幅增长

2014 年我国钢铁产量继续保持增长，但增速有所放缓。据国家统计局数据，2014 年我国粗钢产量 82270 万吨，同比增长 0.9%。我国累计生产生铁 70897 万吨，同比增长 6.2%；粗钢 71160 万吨，同比增长 0.5%；钢材 112557 万吨，同比增长 4.5%，如图 1 所示。

2014 年，我国钢材出口仍然保持了高速增长态势。据海关统计，2014 年，我国累计出口钢材 9378 万吨，同比增长 50.5%；累计进口钢材 1443 万吨，同比增长 2.5%。净出口钢材 7935 万吨（2000 年以来我国每年钢材进出口情况详见图 2）。2014 年中国铁矿石进口价格跌幅超 40%，在价格剧烈下跌的刺激之下，我国累计进口铁矿砂及其精矿 93251 万吨，同比增长 13.85%。

2. 2014 年钢铁行业效益同比下滑

2014 年随着中国钢铁产量增速放缓以及三大矿山矿石产量大幅增长，铁矿石供需关系发生变化。兰格钢铁信息研究中心监测数据显示，截至 2014 年 12 月 31 日，进口铁矿石普氏指数由年初的 134.5 美元/吨，下跌至 71.25 美元/吨，跌幅达 47.0%。铁矿石海关进口均价也从 2014 年 1 月的 130.7 美元/吨下跌为 12 月的 75.6 美元/吨，海关进口均价跌幅达 42.2%。铁矿石价格大幅下跌使得钢铁企业成本明显下降，但钢铁市场持续低迷，钢铁行业盈利有所下滑，特别是铁矿石企业下滑明显。国家统计局数据显示，2014 年 1—12 月，黑

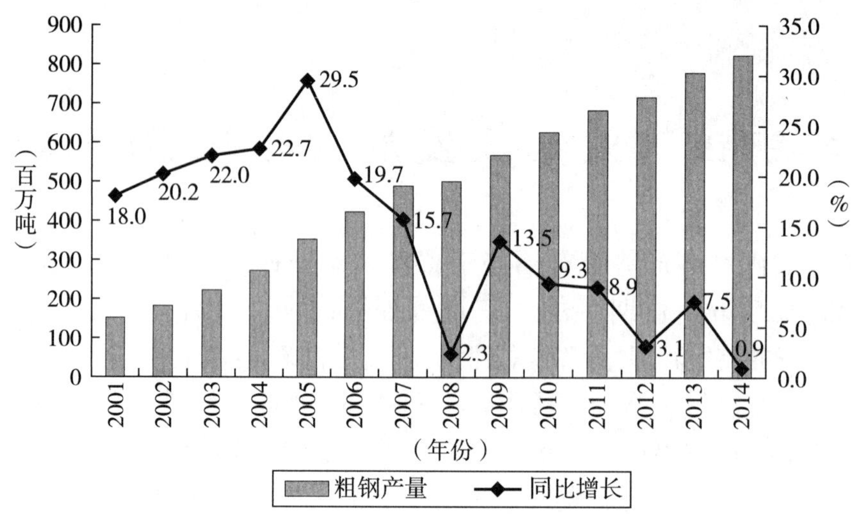

图 1　2001—2014 年粗钢产量及同比增速变化

数据来源：国家统计局。

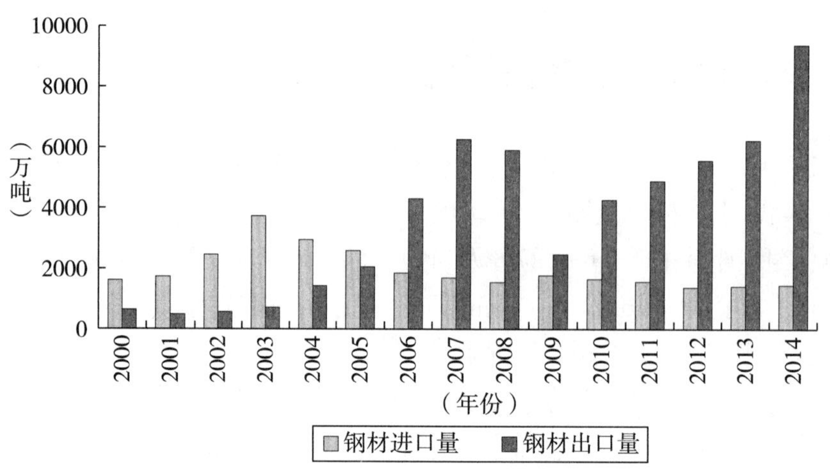

图 2　2000—2014 年我国钢材进出口情况变化

数据来源：中国海关。

色金属矿采选业利润总额 801.2 亿元，同比下降 23.9%；主营活动利润 753.2 亿元，同比下降 29.6%。黑色金属冶炼和压延加工业利润总额 1647.2 亿元，同比下降 2.7%；主营活动利润 1722.5 亿元，同比下降 5.8%。

3. 社会库存创下新低，流通环节规模不断收缩

据兰格钢铁信息研究中心市场监测数据显示，2014 年 12 月底，全国 29 个重点城市钢材社会库存量为 871.4 万吨，同比下降 29.7%。其中建筑钢材社会库存 427.0 万吨，同比下降 29.1%。板材社会库存 444.4 万吨，同比下降 30.3%（详见图 3）。

目前，钢材社会库存已下降至 2009 年以来最低水平。2012 年以来，钢铁

流通企业遭遇大规模洗牌，据不完全统计，上海近70%、全国其他地区近30%的钢贸商退出行业，全国钢贸商数量从20万家迅速缩减至10万家左右，市场活跃度进一步降低，且普遍面临“融资难”的问题。很多企业利用自有资金进行货物流转，因此控制库存成为规避企业经营风险的重要举措。2013年起我国传统的“钢材冬储”操作方式逐渐被淡化，在钢价持续下行、企业资金紧张和避险意识增强等情况下，2014年钢铁流通企业冬储操作仍较为稀少。

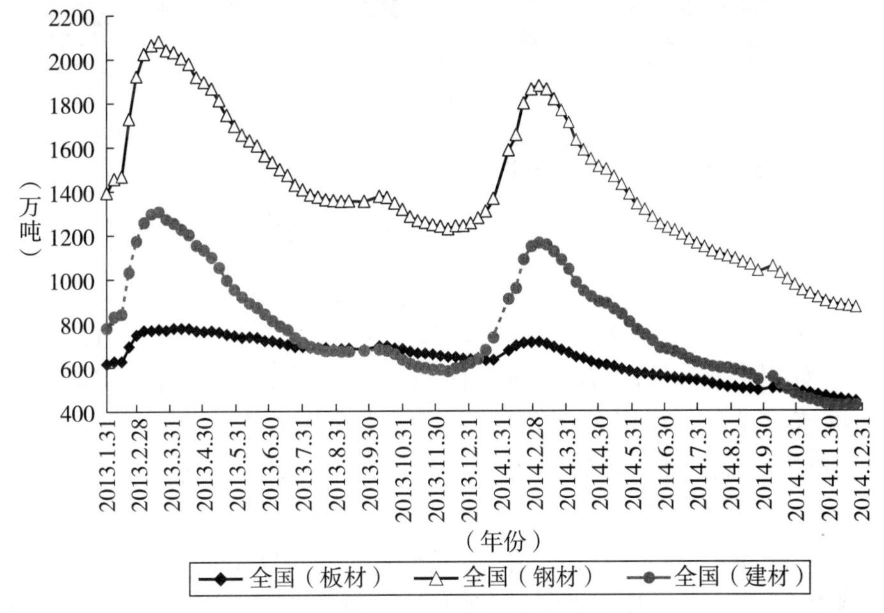

图3　国内每周钢材社会库存走势

数据来源：兰格钢铁信息研究中心。

4. 钢铁行业物流效率稳步提升

中国物流与采购联合会、中国物流信息中心重点企业物流统计调查数据显示，2013年钢铁行业物流效率稳步提升，物流专业化水平持续提高，但总体来看，我国钢铁物流成本依然较高，根据推算，规模以上钢铁企业物流总成本达7900亿元，降低物流成本潜力较大。2013年钢铁行业物流成本费用率为10.7%，同比下降0.4个百分点，较2009年下降了1.3个百分点，（详见图4）。2013年重点调查钢铁企业物流成本较上年同期增长3.9%，近年增幅总体呈下降态势。其中，保管成本同比增幅回落3个百分点。在保管成本中，利息成本和仓储成本增幅分别回落10.4和5.2个百分点。此外，运输成本和管理成本保持平稳增长，比上年同期分别增长5.3%和10.5%。

2013年日本钢铁企业物流费用率为7.7%，尽管其较上年同期上升1.5个百分点；但与日本相比，我国钢铁企业仍高出3个百分点，一方面表明我国钢铁行业物流水平仍存在很大差距，另一方面也显示出我国降低钢铁物流成本的

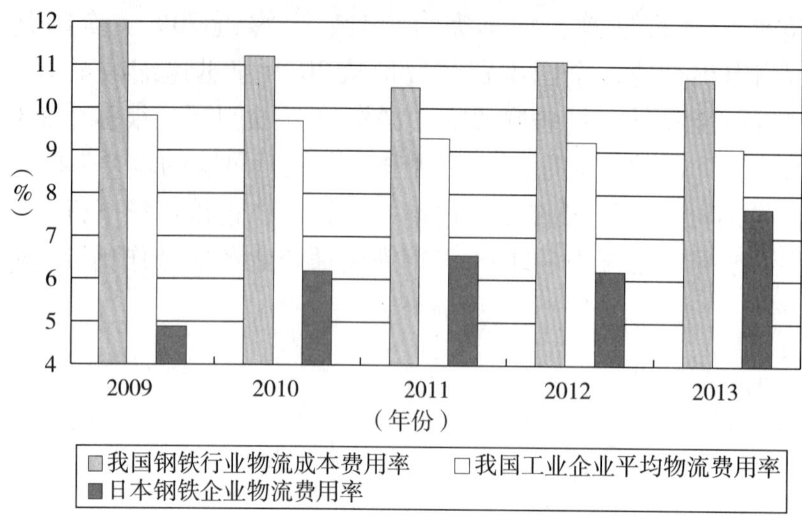

图 4　2009—2013 年钢铁企业物流费用率比较

数据来源：中国物流信息中心。

巨大潜力。数据显示，2013 年我国钢铁行业利润率仅为 2.2%，行业实现利润 2588 亿元。如果我国钢铁物流费用率达到日本水平，意味着可以降低 2000 亿元左右的物流成本，节约的物流成本接近行业全年利润额。

5. 国家积极出台规划政策，引导钢铁行业物流转型发展

2014 年 9 月，国务院正式印发《物流业发展中长期规划》，提出了三大发展重点、十二大重点工程和八项政策措施。其中，与钢铁行业物流相关的有制造业物流与供应链管理工程、资源型产品物流工程和物流园区工程等三项工程。提出要加强与制造业企业紧密配套、有效衔接的仓储配送设施和物流信息平台。要加快资源型产品物流集散中心和物流通道建设。要结合区位特点和物流需求，发展钢铁、煤炭、汽车等专业类物流园区，发挥物流园区的示范带头作用。

为落实《物流业发展中长期规划》，商务部印发了《关于促进商贸物流发展的实施意见》。提出要加快生产资料物流转型升级。鼓励生产资料物流企业充分利用新技术和新的商业模式整合内外资源，延长产业链，跨行业、跨领域融合发展，增强信息、交易、加工、配送、融资、担保等一体化综合服务能力，由单纯的贸易商、物流商，向供应链集成服务商转型。支持生产资料生产、流通企业在中心城市、交通枢纽、经济开发区和工业园区有序建设大宗生产资料物流基地和物流园区，促进产业适度集聚。

这些规划和意见的出台，为下一阶段钢铁流通业发展提供了方向指引和发展机遇。钢铁物流和流通企业要顺应“新常态”发展要求，努力提升自身社会化、专业化、标准化、信息化、组织化水平，建立一体化、个性化、多样化服务体系和经营模式，推动行业规模化和集约化发展。同时，要通过延长产业链，积极向上下游延伸服务，由单纯的贸易商、物流商，逐步向供应链集成服

务商转型，整合分散的企业群体，形成更多的利益共同体，提升市场集中度，建立合作共赢的“产业生态圈”。

6. 国内首批钢铁物流国标在北京通过专家评审

2014年12月24日，由中国物流与采购联合会钢铁物流专委会牵头组织，国家建筑钢材质量监督检验中心、西本新干线、鞍钢、新余钢铁等参与制定的我国首批钢铁物流国家标准，在北京顺利通过专家评审。评审会分别针对《钢铁物流包装标识规范》、《钢铁物流验货操作规范》、《钢铁物流作业规范》三个标准送审稿进行了广泛而深入的论证。与会专家还分别对三项标准对应的起草小组提出修改建议，为标准更具有实用性和可操作性提出积极参考意见。

这预示着市场期盼已久的钢铁物流领域第一批国标即将问世，未来将对提升我国钢铁物流运作效率、社会效益发挥重要作用，对钢铁物流产业的健康、有序发展发挥重要战略意义。

7. 钢铁电商平台发展迅速

自2012年钢贸危机爆发以来，中国钢贸商数量从20万家缩减至10万家左右，钢铁行业产能过剩使得“卖方市场”朝“买方市场”转变，原先的钢铁企业分销体系发生了巨大改变，需要新的营销模式来替代，钢铁电商因而迅速崛起并抢占市场；钢铁电商平台因载体不同，导致平台优劣势各有差异，详见下表。由五矿发展全资子公司五矿电子商务有限公司建设运营的鑫益联于2014年5月正式启动，而五矿发展早在2010年就开始布局电商战略，并于2012年联合国内部分钢材仓储物流、钢贸等企业成立了“钢铁流通e联盟”。2014年，国内钢铁电商发展迅速，钢厂、贸易商、第三方平台等纷纷加大了对于钢铁电商平台的投资力度，资本融资也不断创造奇迹，国内钢铁电商得以蓬勃发展，据相关统计数据显示，目前国内钢铁电商平台有200家左右。

不同类型钢铁电商对比分析

	第三方钢铁电商	贸易商、仓储物流类钢铁电商	钢厂类钢铁电商
代表企业	兰格钢铁网、上海钢联、找钢网	五矿发展、物产中拓、欧浦钢网	宝钢（东方钢铁网、上海钢铁交易中心）、沙钢玖隆电商、华菱荷钢网
主要优势	信息数据服务能力强，平台开放度高，行业整合性强，互联网思维，业务模式灵活	成熟的物流仓储体系，满足客户个性化定制需求，产品多样化	资金实力强，与贸易商、物流仓储企业合作广泛

续 表

	第三方钢铁电商	贸易商、仓储物流类钢铁电商	钢厂类钢铁电商
主要劣势	物流仓储在体外，难以满足客户定制化需求，仓单风险控制难度高，资金实力偏弱	属于重资产行业，异地扩张面临资金、渠道等问题，目前处于线下业务线上化阶段，平台内生性扩张能力不强	平台开发性、多元化性受到竞争对手排斥，产品多样性不足

二、2015 年中国钢铁行业物流发展展望

随着我国经济环境和钢铁产业环境的不断变化，我国钢铁行业物流正在经历着一系列的转变：一是市场由“扩张期”向“后扩张期”转变；二是服务由“单一型”向“复合化”转变；三是企业由“散乱差”向“大强优”转变；四是流通功能由“贸易商”向“供应商”转变；五是经营模式由“虚实分离”向“虚实融合”转变。目前我国钢铁行业物流正在步入新的转型期，如何创新钢铁物流交易模式，加快产业联动成为业界共同关注的问题。

1. 顺应“新常态”创新驱动钢铁行业物流发展

目前我国钢铁业产能过剩问题严重，生产、消费量在峰值区间上下波动，价格总体处于低位运行，企业经营困难长期存在。钢铁行业物流和流通市场需求持续萎缩，大批钢铁流通企业退出市场，企业盈利难度加大。但随着高风险融资业务的清退，钢铁流通业正在回归交易的本质。未来一段时期，随着国家城镇化战略、“一带一路”、长江经济带、京津冀协同发展等国家战略的实施，国家基础设施投资仍将保持稳步增长，钢铁需求基本稳定，奠定了钢铁行业物流发展的基础。同时，借助信息化手段，钢铁流通电商化趋势日益明显，通过互联互通、资源共享，新的业务模式不断创新，加快了行业的转型变革。钢铁行业物流业和流通业与上下游产业间的联动融合走向深入，产业链条逐步缩短，降低物流成本，提升流通效率，通过合作共赢创造新的驱动力，积极融入新常态。

2. 钢铁电商突破发展瓶颈，由“烧钱”向“盈利”跨越

我国钢铁电商近几年发展势头迅猛，特别是风投资本的涌入，钢铁电商“烧钱”规模扩大。钢铁电商平台崛起除了给钢铁在线资源交易带来便利外，电商平台还可利用网络的便捷功能，创造出高效的资源流转体系，从而减少冗杂的流通环节，达到压缩流通成本的目的。因此，通过电商平台降低物流费用

是企业转型发展的创新与突破，它既是销售方式的革命，又是采购方式的革命。

目前，我国钢铁电商遭遇几大发展瓶颈：一是平台模式难定。定位不清晰，没有清晰的盈利模式，最终导致不少电商平台昙花一现。二是物流网络难通。钢铁作为大宗生产资料，受到运输、储存、资金支付等多种因素的影响，线上线下无缝对接的难题成为电商平台发展的掣肘。三是资金线上支付难。钢铁产品所需资金量较大，动辄几百万元、千万元甚至上亿元，电商平台的安全支付渠道如何取信于用户至关重要。四是短时间内难以建立诚信体系。自钢铁行业“爆仓事件”和“钢贸商跑路”事件被曝光后，整个行业都深陷信任危机。作为虚拟平台，钢铁电商同样面临诚信的考验。

未来钢铁电商平台能够盈利至少需要具备：①交易规模巨大，无论卖家还是买家都能够迅速地在平台上找到对方，而且对客户来说具有黏性，交易量是电商平台盈利的前提；②规模化的O2O交易平台以在线交易为核心，还要融合发展仓储管理、物流整合、支付结算、融资服务等生态链服务，并形成信息流、物流、资金流的三流合一，达成交易的完整闭环，全流程闭环钢铁电商的意义一方面在于对交易各环节风险的严格把控，另一方面在于钢铁电商未来的盈利点也立足于平台提供的增值服务，包括供应链金融、仓储、物流等；③对用户交易习惯的培养，从传统的贸易模式转向钢铁电商是巨大的转变，用户习惯的培养一方面包括交易方式的改变，增加用户的黏性，另一方面还要通过为用户提供增值，从而使得用户使用平台供应链金融、仓储、物流等服务。

3. 集中化管理和运营是钢铁物流园区的出路之一

自2008年以来，我国钢铁物流园区建设步伐加快，钢铁企业、钢贸企业以及上下游企业都在尝试探索钢铁物流发展之路，形形色色的钢铁物流园区、钢铁物流中心等在各地拔地而起，目前已经建成的大型钢铁物流园区有300多家，还有100多家钢铁物流园区在建和待建，发展势头十分强劲。但纵观全国各地钢铁物流园区，存在着盲目快速扩张、一味追求大型化、同质化，无序竞争激烈、效率低下、重复建设等现象。因此有必要从大局出发，对钢铁物流园区实行集中化的管理和运营。

钢铁物流园区集中化管理和运营将有利于政府和行业管理部门的管理和监督，有利于国内外钢铁产品信息的及时发布，有利于钢材市场价格的及时调整和管理，有利于发现和杜绝假冒伪劣产品在市场上流通；有利于运用现代物流管理方式和信息技术改造提升钢铁物流业。能够通过整合现有钢铁物流资源和新建钢铁物流设施，建立和完善多种经济形式并存的现代钢铁物流服务网络体系。此外还可以打破行业、地区分割和体制机制的制约，促进国内外资本和企业参与本地区物流企业改制重组、兼并联合，整合改造现有商业、运输、货代、联运、物资、仓储等行业的物流资源。引进、培育和发展一批以仓储分拨、零担快运服务、特定客户服务、综合物流服务和快速运输服务等为主的大型物流龙头企业，推动传统物流向现代物流转变。

随着云计算、大数据、物联网等新兴技术的不断发展和成熟，对传统行业的发展既提出了新的要求，又孕育着新的发展机遇。2015 年是完成“十二五”规划的收官之年，也是钢铁行业物流转型发展的关键之年。钢铁行业物流的发展需要行业内企业凝聚共识、重树信心、加强合作。钢铁物流企业应该顺应行业发展趋势，以创新谋发展，用信心赢未来，加强联动融合，以转型升级应对经济“新常态”，共同推进行业健康发展。

（北京兰格电子商务有限公司　王国清　刘长庆）

2014年汽车物流行业发展回顾与2015年展望

一、2014年汽车物流行业发展回顾

（一）汽车物流市场平稳快速增长

1. 市场规模的横向增大——汽车产销量的中速增长

2014年面对复杂多变的国际环境和艰巨繁重的国内改革发展稳定任务，汽车行业总体实现了良好发展，行业整体运行平稳。据中国汽车工业协会统计数据，2014年，汽车产销分别为2372.29万辆和2349.19万辆，增幅与上年相比有所回落，同比增长7.26%和6.86%，比上年分别下降7.5个和7个百分点，总体呈现平稳增长态势。其中，乘用车产销分别完成1991.98万辆和1970.06万辆，比上年分别增长10.2%和9.9%，增速高于汽车总体产销2.9和3个百分点；商用车产销分别完成380.31万辆和379.13万辆，比上年分别下降5.7%和6.5%，客车产销比上年分别增长7.6%和8.4%，货车产销分别下降7.9%和8.9%。2014年，汽车累计出口91.04万辆，比上年下降6.9%。其中乘用车出口53.30万辆，比上年下降10.6%；商用车出口37.73万辆，比上年下降1%。进口汽车主要车型为越野车、轿车和小型客车；出口主要车型为轿车、载货车和客车。

2. 市场资源的纵向延展——产业链的上下游市场扩张

汽车物流产业链主要包括零部件入厂物流、整车物流、售后服务备件物流三个方面，汽车物流服务以这三个环节为基础，上游从零部件入厂物流向汽车零部件供应商管理延伸，下游从售后服务备件物流向报废汽车物流以及其他后市场服务延伸，汽车物流产业的纵向延展使汽车物流产业链条更加完整，服务更加完善。

（1）汽车零部件企业的发展丰富了物流市场资源

每辆汽车所需零部件种类达7000～10000种，汽车总成本中零部件占到70%～80%，由于汽车产业市场规模巨大，汽车零部件工业也成为宝贵的物流资源。由于国际零部件企业普遍重视物流业务，在物流和供应链管理方面普遍拥有成熟经验，因而是我国汽车零部件企业物流外包的主流企业。

（2）汽车后市场强大需求为汽车物流创造发展潜力

汽车后市场是从汽车销售以后，围绕汽车使用过程中的各种服务。汽车售后备件是后市场服务中的重要环节之一，也是汽车物流服务的重点环节。从全球情况看，汽车制造和维修用零部件所占比例约为80%和20%。截至2014年年底，全国机动车保有量达2.64亿辆，其中汽车1.54亿辆，新注册量和年增量均达历史最高水平。如此庞大的数量，需要的售后备件数量也是巨大的，若每辆汽车一年中替换一个备件，那全年的售后备件量就可达到上亿件，甚至更多，这对汽车售后备件物流的发展既是机遇也是挑战。并且每年汽车销量不断增加，保有量也不断增长，汽车售后备件物流具有广阔的发展潜力。

（3）二手车、报废车市场扩大为汽车物流提供新的关注领域

从中国汽车流通协会了解到，2014年全国共交易二手车605.29万辆，相比上年同期增长16.33%。二手车的运输与报废汽车的回收都是汽车物流发展的新领域。近两年，国家相关部门出台了多项关于开展报废汽车回收、整治的办法和通知，并且加大了老旧汽车报废更新补贴工作力度，这对报废汽车回收工作的开展起到了至关重要的作用。随之而来的是，物流工作如何与汽车报废回收相适应。未来在这些领域，汽车物流的发展空间将会越来越大。

总而言之，2014年汽车物流市场总量随着汽车市场规模的扩大而增长，但业务链条延长，总体增速高于汽车工业增速。

（二）行业政策利好和市场环境日趋规范

1. 相关政策的出台明确了物流发展方向

在宏观政策方面，2014年9月国务院发布《物流业发展中长期规划（2014—2020年）》（以下简称《中长期规划》）。规划要求，到2020年，基本建立布局合理、技术先进、便捷高效、绿色环保、安全有序的现代物流服务体系，明确了中长期发展的战略目标。规划提出三大发展重点、七项主要任务、十二项重点工程和九项保障措施。《中长期规划》发布后，全国现代物流工作部际联席会议加强政策协调，积极推进政策落实，《促进物流业发展三年行动计划》正式出台，明确了五个方面、62项重点工作任务的牵头部门以及具体目标和完成时限。

在涉及物流运输的微观政策方面，交通运输部、公安部、国家安全监管总局公布《道路运输车辆动态监督管理办法》。自2014年7月1日起施行。全面系统地规范了道路运输车辆动态监管工作，为做好道路运输车辆动态监管工作提供了基本制度保障，是指导动态监管工作的纲领性文件。交通运输部、公安部、商务部发布了《关于加强城市配送运输与车辆通行管理工作的通知》，重点解决“最后一千米”的配送运输和车辆通行管理问题。

2. “一带一路”为汽车物流提供了国际合作契机

“一带一路”是“丝绸之路经济带”和“21世纪海上丝绸之路”的简称。习近平主席2013年9月和10月出访中亚四国及印尼、马来西亚期间提出共建“丝绸之路经济带”和“21世纪海上丝绸之路”的宏伟构想。“一带一路”战略的落实为提高各车型出口、加快海外市场拓展步伐提供了内生动力。

3. 车辆运输车标准问题仍旧制约着行业发展

车辆运输车标准一直以来都是行业关注的焦点问题，被认为是解决公路运输问题的第一步，2014年工信部、交通运输部、公安部、国家标准化委员会会同相关研究机构进行了广泛调研和深入研究，基本形成了一致意见，但2014年终稿仍未出台，解决制约行业发展的老大难问题依旧需要等待。

4. “治超”工作开展为汽车物流企业敲响了警钟

2014年，四川省高速交警总队发布了《关于分阶段整治商品车运输专用车相关问题的通知》中提到，2014年7月1日前，允许商品车专用运输车辆通过高速公路，并集中运输积压的商品车。2014年7月1日至12月31日，交管部门将开始集中整治商品运输车的超限问题。需整改的商品运输车的高度不得超过4.2米、宽度不得超过2.55米、整车长度不得超过30米，且专用车尾部伸出货箱部分必须切割。若未达到规定标准的运输车，交警将责令车主、驾驶人按规定整改。这对于汽车整车运输企业来说是一个警示。目前，车辆运输车违规车辆较多，特别是俗称“二怪”的车辆运输车，这些车辆基本不符合要求，四川“治超”严重影响了部分汽车物流企业的运营，需要加快行业标准的出台和规范运输车辆。

（三）相关国家和行业标准继续完善

《物流标准化中长期发展规划》编制工作启动，截至2014年年底，我国已发布的各类物流标准超过800项。汽车行业物流标准工作一直得到国家标准管理机构的高度重视，是标准建设和实施的典型和示范。

1. 出台的新标准

由国家标准化管理委员会批准，汽车物流分会牵头组织的《汽车物流服务评价指标》（GB/T 31149—2014）、《汽车零部件物流塑料周转箱尺寸系列及技术要求》（GB/T 31150—2014）、《汽车整车物流质损风险监控要求》（GB/T 31151—2014）和《汽车物流术语》（GB/T 31152—2014）四项物流国家标准正式发布，已于2014年12月1日开始实施。

2. 即将出台的国家及行业标准

在全国物流标准化技术委员会推动下，分会牵头的《汽车物流统计指标体系》《商用车背车装载技术要求》《汽车零部件物流器具分类及编码》《汽车物流信息系统基础要求》四项国家标准及行业标准通过专家评审，进入报批阶段。《乘用车物流质损判定及处理规范》《乘用车运输服务规范》《乘用车水路运输服务规范》《乘用车仓储服务规范》四项修订的汽车物流行业标准又有新的进展，目前正在完善标准工作组讨论稿，并准备向社会征求意见。《汽车整车出口物流标识规范》（20132702 – T – 469）国家标准已经由国标委批准立项。

3. 标准工作存在的问题

一是汽车物流行业标准体系有待完善，虽然汽车物流标准相继出台，并且针对物流标准体系已经有了一定的研究，但针对行业专业标准并没有完善的体系，标准的完整性还存在一定的问题。另外，由于各个企业借鉴其他国家的标准，有欧美的，有日韩的，标准存在一定的差异性，对于行业资源共享和利用存在一定阻碍。通用性标准和专用性标准要有明确的区分，对于和其他行业相一致的标准，应该由主管部门统一制定，对于有汽车物流行业特点的标准，要根据行业特色进行制修订。二是标准宣传贯彻不尽理想。标准制定后，缺乏系统的宣传，导致企业对于已经出台的行业标准不了解，造成有标准却贯彻不下去的现象。

（四）行业统计和研究工作有新突破

中国汽车物流的发展可以借鉴发达国家汽车物流行业成熟的经验和做法，但是具体到每个细分领域，都需要结合本国国情得出切实可行、符合实际又为未来发展留出空间的方案，因而行业研究工作确属必要。2014 年开始，汽车物流分会每年对汽车物流企业进行年度调研，主要包括整车、零部件、售后服务备件三个方面的调研，调研根据《汽车物流统计指标体系》中指标进行数据采集，共涉及三大类 60 余项指标。调研完成后将对数据进行整理和分析，有利于更好地了解汽车物流行业发展现状，分析行业发展中遇见的问题，进一步优化汽车物流行业发展结构，推动公、铁、水综合运输体系建设，提升零部件、整车至售后服务备件物流的供应链管理水平。

（五）综合运输体系建设更加深化

1. 铁路运输

中铁特货运输公司作为国家铁路汽车物流核心企业，在铁路商品车物流领域深耕细作，不断创新。一是完善全程物流链提效增收。为实现“门到门”全程物流，公司在全国范围内对配送业务进行重新招标；通过优化配送模式，改变以往由于前后端配送商不统一导致质损多、赔付金额大的状况，实行项目两端由一家配送商负责，全程商品汽车质损理赔。经过整合，中铁特货建立规范商品汽车配送队伍 49 支，提高了商品汽车全程物流质量，也大大降低了物流成本。二是建设物流基地筑巢引凤。各汽车生产厂家销售模式开始向规模化的集中区域代理销售方式转变。适应市场需求，依托铁道部政策和地方政府支持，中铁特货积极建设大型物流基地。此举不仅帮助商品汽车生产厂家实现了库存前移，也为公司开展商品汽车全程物流运输工作创造了有利条件。三是量体裁衣做优服务。公司专项投资开发了商品汽车物流管理信息平台。有效提升了铁路汽车物流的全过程管理水平，保证了汽车物流的信息畅通，提高了客户的满意度。公司还通过建立客户维护机制，对客户实行分类分级维护，提高决策效率和市场响应速度，保持公司运量稳定增长。四是积极创新，公司创新制定了《商品汽车铁路装卸作业安全技术管理标准》。在这本 50 页的小册子中，仅汽车启动作业一项就有 20 条要求，细到对简单的开车门的动作都有精确描述。为提高运输时效，公司积极组织整列运输。目前，商品汽车整列运输比例接近 40%。从柳州开往郑州的“五定”直达班列，从原来的 50 多个小时压缩到 37 个小时。同时，公司加强与铁道部、铁路局、站段等的协调，加快重车输送和空车调配，提高车辆周转效率，缩短在途时间。运输装备方面，公司在拥有国内先进的运输车（箱）6000 余辆的基础上，“量体裁衣”，不断研制运输多种汽车的新车型。目前，公司正在研究、设计一种新车型作为铁路汽车物流的专用车型，以“专用 + 通用”为特点，既能运输汽车又能运输常规货物，这种新车型面世后，能够进一步降低汽车企业的物流成本、提升竞争力。同时，中铁特货公司 2014 年还专门就牵引车等商用车运输专用箱进行研究和开发，并基本确定了制造方案。

2. 水运领域

沿江沿海整车进口口岸及汽车水运枢纽及配套设施建设又有新的发展。代表性的区域有：

（1）青岛港：在保税港区内，正在建设 2.79 万平方米的汽车物流展示中心，近百家通过平行贸易方式进口的贸易商在这里聚集，类似于进口汽车的大卖场；青岛保税港区汽车整车进口口岸分两期开发建设，其中，一期工程开通 4 号、5 号汽车专用泊位，建设 8 万平方米汽车堆场、1.1 万平方米检测场站、5600 平方米海关查验场地和 2.7 万平方米青岛国际汽车展厅。二期工程规划建设 3 个汽车专用泊位、码头作业区和 1.01 平方千米国际汽车贸易中心，其中，国际汽车贸易中心包括进出口汽车物流检测区、展示体验区、总部商务区、综合服务商业区、创意研发区五大功能业态。

（2）江苏盐城：大丰港滚装码头工程于 2014 年 10 月 19 日正式开工建设，该项目总投资 1.2 亿元，工期一年，码头等级为 7 万吨级。码头建成后，将形成 40 万台车辆的运送能力，对降低悦达起亚及周边车企运输成本、实现南北对流的内贸输运、促进汽车外贸进出口、发展中韩陆海联运都具有重要意义。

（3）江苏南京：由南京港集团和安吉物流共同出资合作的南京港江盛汽车码头有限公司于2014年6月25日正式开业运营，南京港江盛汽车码头有限公司拟建设3万吨级和1万吨级浮式滚装泊位各1座，目标定位为三年内达到年中转30万辆规模，建设成为长江最重要的汽车物流枢纽之一。

（4）武汉—汉南港项目：2014年5月29日，武汉汉南港正式开港运营。该港已建成投用的是一个3000吨级汽车滚装泊位，年汽车转运能力30万辆，是长江中上游年吞吐量最大的汽车转运港口。汉南港还将配套建设占地700亩的港口物流加工园，形成长江中上游最大的商品车集并、中转、分拨中心。二期项目还将建设3000吨级商品汽车滚装泊位1座、5000吨级通用泊位4座，将具备年运转商品车60万辆、吞吐件杂货640万吨的运作能力。

（5）武汉—江盛项目：2014年7月21日，武汉港务集团（武港集团）与安吉汽车物流有限公司（安吉物流）签订协议，合资组建武汉江盛汽车码头公司。该公司将经营沌口滚装码头和金口滚装码头的汽车滚装及汽车物流业务，为武汉产汽车提供多式联运物流服务，打造中部汽车物流枢纽。

（6）福州银河国际汽车园：该地区已于2014年9月11日开工建设了江阴港银河国际汽车园主体工程，此次动工的银河国际汽车园3号地块占地813亩，总建筑面积78万平方米，预计总投入30亿元人民币。

（7）舟山兴海汽车滚装码头：2014年12月，交通运输部批复了舟山兴海汽车滚装码头项目，该项目位于宁波—舟山港马岙港区小沙作业区，建设1个7万总吨级商品汽车滚装泊位及相关配套设施，使用岸线490米，泊位长度满足2艘2万总吨级商品汽车滚装船舶同时靠泊作业，设计年通过能力为商品汽车60万辆、零部件19万吨。

（8）天津临港经济区安信物流项目：2014年11月6日，安信联合物流有限公司物流总部项目在临港经济区正式开工建设。该项目总投资6.92亿元，占地面积32万平方米。项目位于黄河道以北、渤海二十八路以东，将涵盖整车仓储、整车物流、进口车贸易、物流金融等业务板块。

此外，集装箱运输作为中国水路运输的一种重要形式，多年来发展速度缓慢，2014年中海集装箱公司等国内领军企业，加大了集装箱在整车物流领域市场开拓的步伐，与滚装运输相比，集装箱运输具有网点数量更多、运输自由度大、班期密度更大的特点，适合小批量，多品种，内陆运输和国际联运需求。

（六）领军企业拓展国际市场速度加快

2014年6月4日，MG6轿车在上汽集团泰国春里府工厂驶下生产线，标志着上汽泰国工厂正式投入运作。这是我国自主品牌轿车在海外建成投产的第一座合资整车厂，其生产的MG轿车将以泰国为核心，加入东南亚汽车市场的竞争。安吉物流也在泰国实现了布点，从零部件到售后服务，完成了在当地“全产业链”的初步布局。在泰国等东南亚市场，长期以来日系汽车品牌占据绝对市场份额，中国汽车品牌要进入并非易事。上汽泰国整车工厂建设之初，当地日本品牌零部件供应商采取封锁态度，不跟上汽整车工厂配套；泰国本地汽车零部件基础薄弱，使得项目一度面临巨大挑战。完备的产业链为整车基地后续发展提供保障，也使得国内汽车工业更多高利润的业务环节进入海外市场。

2014 年长久物流在德国汉堡注册了子公司，开始实施国际物流业务，打通了一条横跨欧亚国际铁路的新通道，率先启动了国家倡导的“一带一路”发展战略。长久物流与优特埃（UTi）国际物流于 2015 年年初建立战略合作，能够使长久物流汲取国际领先的物流技术和管理水平；将优特埃全球海运、空运网络与长久物流欧亚铁路网络的资源整合，形成海、铁、空立体的国际化物流网络。此举一方面推进中国“一带一路”步伐，同时加快双方业务发展，为长久物流早日成为国际化物流企业打下坚实基础；另一方面利用长久物流在国内的客户资源，将优特埃的技术和管理理念在中国的汽车厂加以推广和应用，这必将加速中国汽车物流产业的发展。双方在战略合作阶段将共同开发三大产品包括欧洲到中国的铁路运输，VMI/生产物流，售后市场零配件配送物流。尤其是欧洲到中国的铁路运输将为中国的客户提供更可靠、高效、低成本的中欧之间门到门铁路运输及海铁联运等多式联运服务。

（七）行业横向跨界融合创新

（1）物流服务和技术服务的融合创新。以往的物流服务与技术装备供应是汽车物流业务的两个环，近年来呈现一体化融合发展的趋势，部分行业企业取得创新突破。中世国际物流有限公司是由长久物流、奇瑞汽车和大连港组建的合资公司。公司在按照既定目标，打造航运、码头、物流管理为一体的“全供应链一体化服务”的综合性国际物流公司的同时，拓展了汽车企业现场器具和耗材的开发、设计、研制，以及清查、损坏器具维护送修等附加业务，不仅稳定了物流链而且创新了价值链，实现了物流和技术服务的深度融合。

（2）传统物流与电子商务的跨界融合。流通领域的新型物流模式在向制造业渗透过程中，在过去几十年的发展中，汽车产业一直处于引领地位。在新一轮信息技术对流通业颠覆发展中也不会例外，在已经形成稳定局面的零部件和整车物流领域，除电商技术逐步引入外，在面向大众消费的汽车整车和售后服务备件物流方面，电商发展存在无限商机。各大主机企业都在探讨电商在流通领域的变革，顺丰、京东、淘宝等知名电商和快递公司在过去一年中在探索汽车产业发展新机遇中表现活跃。

（八）行业技术创新活跃

2014 年，各汽车物流企业在行业创新方面又取得了一定的进步，在汽车整车物流、零部件入厂物流、售后服务备件物流三个方面涌现出 21 个创新项目。

1. 汽车整车物流创新项目

天津劳尔工业有限公司的“车辆运输中置轴挂车及列车”项目，天津港环球滚装码头有限公司的“滚装船舶作业危险源可视化管理”项目，精英（天津）物流有限公司的“OMS 操作管理系统、进程管理系统、客户查询平台”项目，安徽江汽物流有限公司的“商用车发运中心流程优化”项目，中国重汽集团进出口有限公司的“出口车辆海运物流报价管理平台”项目，重庆长安民生物流股份有限公司的“整车库房次通道标准研究”项目，重庆中集汽车物流有限责任公司的“VLM 汽车物流管理系统”项目，东风商用车有限公司市场销售总部物流管理部的“构建商品车运输线路危险源图谱，降低商品车事故率”项目。

2. 汽车零部件入厂物流创新项目

上海安吉通汇汽车物流有限公司的“汽车零部件循环取料管理系统移动客户端软件”项目，东风汽车有限公司东风日产乘用车公司的“一次物流 AGV 零件上线无人化改善”项目，广州风神物流有限公司的“东风雷诺汽车物流规划咨询”项目与“乘用车轮胎搬运与储存技术研究与应用”项目，南京长安民生住久物流有限公司的“汽车零配件物流周转箱管理系统”项目，奇瑞捷豹路虎汽车有限公司的“收发货道口自动分配系统”项目，武汉东本储运有限公司的“入厂车辆排队优化”项目，长春一汽国际物流有限公司的“关于汽车零部件入厂物流网格化模型的应用研究”项目，一汽物流（长春陆顺）储运有限公司的“汽车零部件产前物流水陆联运”项目，北京长久物流股份有限公司的“跨欧亚国际铁路多式联运”项目。

3. 售后服务备件创新项目

广州风神物流有限公司的“汽车售后备件配送物流信息化平台”项目，济南佳明汽车物流有限公司“基于 eTMS 信息系统汽车售后零部件物流 KPI”项目，一汽物流有限公司的“轿车备品中心基于模块化管理的包装中心”项目。

（九）行业交流活动丰富多彩

中物联汽车物流分会作为行业组织，2014 年围绕产业链发展组织举办了丰富多彩的交流活动。

（1）2014 年 3 月初，分会组织“2014 汽车零部件物流高端巡访（重庆站）”，此活动得到重庆长安民生物流，长安福特及长安汽车的大力支持。参加代表汇集国内汽车零部件物流和物流装备领域精英，走访了五处生产车间与重点项目，并与被参观企业代表就零部件物流领域的问题进行了座谈交流，在座谈中分会公布了汽车零部件物流 KPI 指标的调查结果。

（2）在零部件巡访同期，召开了“中国汽车零部件物流标准化推进会第一次会议”。分会广泛收集了汽车主机厂、零部件生产企业及物流企业零部件物流中较为关心的标准化问题，并根据企业实际情况，代表们就标准推进工作开展方式进行了深入讨论。

（3）4 月中旬，分会继续与英国汽车物流杂志在北京共同成功组织了第十一届中国国际汽车物流会议，会议依旧是中外汽车物流行业交流的最大平台，来自海内外的参会代表超过 400 人，是全球最具影响力的汽车物流国际会议之一，会议的很多观点在国际汽车物流发展中具有领航标作用。

（4）在国际汽车物流会议同期，分会组织举办了“第七届中国汽车出口物流国际研讨会”，本次活动为中国汽车进出口相关物流企业提供了有效的交流平台，通过推动物流与汽车出口的联动发展，进而推动我国汽车制造企业进出口业务成长，提高了我国汽车企业国际竞争能力。

（5）2014 年 6 月下旬，在西安召开了“第五届全国汽车售后服务备件物流研讨会”，会后安排代表们参观了比亚迪汽车在西安的售后备件物流库。备件物流作为汽车物流产业链中后市场中第一个环节逐渐受到企业的重视，此项活动推动了汽车物流产业链向后市场延伸。

（6）2014 年 8 月中旬，分会主办的“第五届全国商用车物流发展研讨会”在银川召开，本次活动由福田智科物流公司、长久物流公司共同协办。会议主要研究探讨了商用车市场变化对物流带来的影响、商用车物流发展的行业问题、全国商用车物流资源一体化建设问题，以及行业标准的制订问题，有力地推动了行业健康发展。

（7）2014 年 8 月下旬，在中铁特货、长久物流的支持下，分会在青岛组织召开了第三届全国汽车铁路和滚装物流研讨会。会议是行业内唯一的铁水领域汽车物流研讨会，活动得到了业内主机企业及汽车物流企业的高度关注，参会代表就商品车的铁路运输、车辆运输车新标准的实施情况、铁路线边的仓库选址及进场、铁路运输的经济批量等行业较为关心的问题进行了深度讨论。

（8）2014 年 10 月上旬，分会以通讯方式召开了三届三次理事会，审议了行业表彰和增补会员事宜。

（9）2014 年 11 月中旬，在武汉召开了“2014 全国汽车物流行业年会暨中物联汽车物流分会十周年庆典活动”。来自全国汽车物流领域 200 多家单位，以及来自英国、法国、美国、德国等国家的 550 余位代表参加了此次会议。同期，分会组织了隆重简朴的大型庆典活动，征询理事会意见对全国汽车物流行业十年来做出贡献的企业和个人进行了表彰。

二、2015 年汽车物流行业发展展望

如果用一个词来判断2015 年汽车物流行业发展的话，那就是“趋势”。从市场趋势看，院墙是汽车产业市场多年来形成的无形文化，但在趋势面前都将会开始逐渐发生改变。在移动互联大趋势下，电商和跨界将快速影响整个行业。从宏观环境看，新一届中央政府全面建成小康社会、全面深化改革、全面推进依法治国、全面从严治党的大背景下，交通运输领域存在的物流顽症将会提到日程上来，行业多年来形成的瓶颈问题有望得以逐步解决，作为服务业的汽车物流行业将会转向依靠管理、技术和服务等实力展开新一轮竞争和合作的新局面。

（1）受经济大环境影响，汽车市场规模增速有放缓趋势，汽车企业间的竞争将会加剧，物流企业将面临服务收入、质量和渠道下沉等多方压力，行业将面临多重挑战。

（2）汽车零部件企业和售后服务备件领域物流市场将会是行业最大的新增市场，汽车物流格局将会有更多“外来户”进入。

（3）随着公路治超趋紧趋严，车辆运输车新标准即将出台，整车物流公路运输格局处在巨变前夕，公铁水综合运输体系的完善和发展将对目前物流格局产生重大影响。

（4）移动互联时代的汽车流通模式，在 O2O（线下体验，线上购买）、F2C（工厂到消费）、会员制以及各种新型模式推动下汽车物流必将发生深层次变革，在商流变化下汽车物流将随之变化，并将深度融合。

（5）市场、技术、资金、人才对行业领军企业来讲，国际化发展已经具备条件。“一带一路”的国家战略，更为企业带来政策层面的积极保障。未来一段时间，我国汽车物流企业走出国门，走向世界的步伐将会加快。

（6）企业的发展和竞争维度增多，资金、市场、人才等传统企业竞争与合作的考量因素，将会扩展到如移动互联的理念、跨界融合多方合作的市场观、先进适用的现代物流技术、尊重法规标准的良好习惯、全面系统的管理、激发员工爱岗敬业的文化等多维度。

（7）规范化、标准化建设在行业发展中将发挥越来越重要的作用，行业协会牵头组织企业对现有汽车物流体系的重新构建，梳理出现有标准在国家标准、行业标准和团体标准等不同角度的重新定位，并推动标准切实解决行业和企业面临的不对称和不一致甚至是市场混乱问题，引导行业走上健康有序发展道路。

（8）小微型承运商作为汽车物流大市场中公路运输的主体，在移动互联、市场结构、法制建设、安全环保等大环境和背景下，面临更严峻的挑战，因此在广泛的行业活动中，领悟方向，抱团合作，广泛交流，在今后一段时期内尤为关键。

2015 年是“十二五”的收官之年，是我国经济领域实现转型发展的关键一年，新一届政府的很多经济新政在这一年都将启动。深刻领悟，付诸实施，将影响行业企业未来一段时间的发展。我们期待汽车物流行业作为专业物流领域的典范，在新的一年中继续迎接时代的挑战和机遇，引领我国物流行业继续快速发展和进步。

（中物联汽车物流分会　马增荣）

2014 年医药物流业发展回顾与 2015 年展望

2014 年，医药流通行业销售额仍然保持持续增长态势，增幅略有下降；大中型企业加快兼并重组步伐，行业集中化更加明显；医药企业更加注重软实力的提升；互联网技术的快速发展推动医药市场的转型升级，开启了医药电商元年；网络处方药开放在即，各巨头纷纷加大在医药电商方面的布局。伴随着传统医药市场高度同质化竞争的加剧，医药行业创新经营模式将迎来百花齐放。

一、2014 年医药物流市场发展回顾

2014 年医药物流依然保持了较快发展的态势，虽然医药行业增长速度有所放缓，但医药物流的质量有所提升，医药电商的启动成为 2014 年最大的亮点。

（一）医药市场规模持续较快增长，但增幅放缓

2014 年医药流通行业销售总额仍然保持了较快速度增长，但增幅同比略有下降，预计将达到 14700 亿元左右，医药电商成为医药流通行业销售的亮点。目前医药行业受到中国人口老龄化、政府对医药卫生投入加大、实行全民医保、单独二胎放开、慢性病需求增大、人均用药水平提高以及大健康领域消费升级等多方利好因素影响，医药行业依然保持较快发展。但是 2014 年由于受国家宏观经济增速下降和药价调整的影响，医药流通市场增长趋势趋于平稳，医药行业微利化的特征依然存在，预计 2014 年医药流通行业销售额的增速在 13% 左右，比 2013 年增速下降约 3 个百分点。

（二）国家发布相关政策促进医药物流发展

国家为提高医药企业经营质量管理，增强流通环节医药质量风险控制能力，推动医药物流发展，出台了一系列政策支持行业发展。继 2013 年 6 月国家出台新版的《医药经营质量管理规范》（GSP）后，国务院又颁发了《医疗器械监督管理条例》等一系列医疗器械法律法规和发布《中华人民共和国中医药法（征求意见稿）》公开征求意见，有力地促进医疗器械和中药的发展。

（三）医药物流项目投资依然强劲

随着新版 GSP 的实施，2014 年各医药流通企业继续加大在物流建设上的

投入，加快发展现代医药物流中心建设和布局，以提高自身的竞争力。

2014 年 10 月，以九州通医药集团投资 3.8 亿元在武汉东西湖建成全球最大的单体医药物流中心为标志，中国医药物流建设达到了新高潮。该物流中心总建筑面积 7.5 万平方米，应用了基于穿梭技术的密集式存储货架系统，目的是节约发货月台空间，实现自动排车，解决目前诸多物流中心在集货、发货环节的效率和空间问题。此外，2014 年新的医药物流项目建设还有：国药控股上海二期项目将建设近 5 万平方米现代医药物流中心，该物流中心引进了新型货到人自动化拆零拣选设备，开启了国内医药物流中心应用自动化拆零拣选系统的先河；广东深华药业有限公司投资 2.3 亿元建设 18000 平方米现代医药物流中心；四川泸州投资 2 亿元建设 8 万平方米医药物流中心；贵阳康心药业智慧医药建设 7.3 万平方米的物流中心二期工程；九州通在绵阳投资 8000 万元建设面积为 2.5 万平方米的现代医药物流中心；山东同科天地科技企业孵化器有限公司在济南建设 5 万平方米第三方医药物流中心；修正药业集团在钦州投资建设现代大型医药物流中心区域总部；湖北格奥欣打造华中医药物流中心，拟投资 3 亿元建设 3.6 万多平方米现代医药物流中心；国药控股新疆哈密药业有限公司在哈密投资 3000 多万元，建成 5040 平方米医药物流配送中心。

（四）医药电商市场政策突破在即，增势迅猛

1. 互联网医药企业呈爆发式增长

目前医药电商主要有三种运营模式：自营式 B2C 网上药店、第三方平台模式和 B2B 采购平台。截至 2014 年年底，持有互联网医药交易服务牌照的网站已达到 371 家，比 2013 年的 202 家增长了 169 家。其中，B2C 网站由 2013 年的 138 家增长到 2014 年的 272 家，B2B 网站由 2013 年的 53 家增长到 2014 年的 83 家，第三方经营服务平台由 2013 年的 11 家增长到 2014 年的 16 家。虽然第三方平台型医药电商数量较少，且起步较晚，但已占据半壁江山。

2010 年整个医药电子商务市场规模约为 2 亿元，2011 年规模翻一倍至 4 亿元，2012 年则增长到 16.6 亿元，2013 年线上医药市场规模达到 42.6 亿元。每年增长率超过 200%，预计 2014 年医药电商市场规模约在 70 亿元，医药电商正在以迅猛态势发展。

2. 互联网巨头纷纷布局医药市场

2014 年年初，阿里巴巴收购了中信 21 世纪有限公司，随后将其改名为阿里健康。成为国家药监部门“医药电子监管码的唯一服务提供商”，并获得了国内首个可开展互联网医药销售（B2C）的第三方平台试点牌照。其他互联网巨头如腾讯收购挂号网，推出微信挂号。京东和 1 号店也均已取得网上药品销售第三方平台资质，将对医药电商的发展起到巨大的推动作用。目前，阿里系

的天猫医药馆已成为国内规模最大的第三方医药电商平台。

3. 处方药市场开放临近，医药电商将会有大发展

数据显示，目前国内药品终端销售收入中，处方药约占80%、非处方药约占20%，目前处方药的市场规模在1万亿元左右。

目前医药电商仍然沿用2005年发布的《互联网药品信息服务管理办法》和2005年发布的《互联网药品交易服务审批暂行规定》两部管理办法。网上药店暂时只能销售非处方药和自行建立配送网络，这在很大程度上限制了医药电子商务的发展。2014年5月，国家食品药品监督管理总局公布了医药行业近年来最具影响力的政策——《互联网食品药品经营监督管理办法（征求意见稿)》，面向社会各界征求意见，规定取得相应资格证书的互联网平台不仅可以卖处方药，还可以由第三方物流配送平台进行药品或医疗器械的配送，若这一政策能够落地实施将大大推动医药电商的发展。预计处方药网上销售将以正面清单方式公布，第一批公布约300～500个品规，预计在2015年上半年启动实施。一旦公布慢性病、常见病用药将受益，医药电商大战才真正开启。

（五）移动医疗对传统医药物流提出了新课题

2014年医药行业最大的特点是移动医疗的兴起。中国互联网信息中心（CNNIC）发布的第35次《中国互联网络发展状况统计报告》显示，截至2014年12月，我国手机网民规模达5.57亿人，较2013年年底增加5672万人。随着移动设备终端的普及化和移动互联网的快速发展，移动医疗开始在国内兴起。

当前国内大多数的移动医疗项目都处于开始阶段，已经出现了如阿里健康、药急送、挂号网、春雨医生等移动医疗应用，虽然仍处于用户积累的初级阶段，且至今尚未形成较为成熟的盈利模式，但是随着移动医疗应用的功能越发完善和线上线下的资源整合，将会为移动医疗提供更为丰富的支持，为用户提供更为丰富的服务，从而使移动医疗产生质的飞跃。无论采取线上还是线下，最后牵涉的药品配送都离不开物流，但这和传统的医药物流有区别。如何应对快速、小批量的物流需求，如何对接线上，这都给传统的医药物流企业带来新的课题。

（六）医疗器械物流快速发展

2014年，中国医疗器械行业保持了较快发展速度，预计全年医疗器械市场规模为2556亿元，成为仅次于美国的全球第二大医疗器械市场。医疗器械电子商务成为医疗器械市场发展的亮点，传统零售门店的销售额在2014年几乎没有增长，而医疗器械电子商务快速发展，整个家用医疗器械零售市场的增量

几乎全部被电商占据。

但我们也应该清醒地认识到，虽然我国医疗器械行业已经成为仅次于美国的第二大市场，但医疗器械行业仍然集中度偏低，呈小而散的状态，还没有形成规模发展。绝大多数企业还停留在零散分布、低水平恶性竞争的粗放式增长阶段。2014 年，国家为促进中国医疗器械行业发展，不仅实施了新版的《医疗器械监督管理条例》，而且还完成了 5 个部门规章的编制，以及几十个规范性文件。市场的规范化虽然可能会给医疗器械企业的发展带来阵痛，但长期来看，对促进中国医疗器械市场的健康发展具有极大作用。

（七）我国医药物流和发达国家相比差距较大

虽然我国医药物流集中度有所提高、流通环节有所减少。但总体来看，由于受医院终端不允许跨区域配送、医药流通订货习惯、医药流通企业传统管理观念等因素的影响，流通环节较多，渠道库存透明度不够，供应商压库存现象严重，渠道库存一直居高不下，企业物流社会化程度低、网络化一体化运营程度不高、规模小、效率低、成本高。与美国相比，我国医药物流用了其 7 倍的费用，完成了其 30% 的流通额，整体效率仅为美国的 4%，物流效率和成本还有待进一步改善与提高。2014 年各大医药流通企业加快推进供应链整合，力图提升集中度，通过集采、请货、多仓运作等方式减少供应链环节，降低供应链库存，提高供应链效率。

伴随供应链整合的同时，中国医药物流业正朝着精益化管理方向发展。传统医药物流管理较为粗放，是由于医药流通业以前利润较高且供求不平衡。随着医药流通环节毛利逐步降低，行业竞争加剧，传统的低价竞争和粗放式管理已经不能满足货主、客户对物流服务与成本的需求，医药物流精益化管理的时代正在来临。目前国药物流、华润医药、上海医药均已开展物流精益化管理，并将精益化管理作为公司战略之一，以期达到降本增效，提高自身竞争力的目的。

新版 GSP 对医药物流信息提出了更高的要求，医药物流信息化水平进一步提高。目前医药物流行业加大了对仓库管理 WMS，运输管理 TMS 的投入，越来越多的医药物流企业使用无线射频（RFID）、全球卫星定位（GPS）、无线通信、温度传感等物联网先进技术，提高仓库分拣和冷链物流全程监控，优化业务流程，提高管理水平。

（八）冷链管理水平有一定程度的提高

新版 GSP 对冷链管理、技术、人才等方面的要求较以前有明显提高，随着新版 GSP 的实施落地，各医药流通企业加大对冷链管理、技术、人才的投入，取得了一定成果，冷链管理水平有一定程度的提高。主要体现在以下几个方面：

（1）冷链质量与风险管控意识加强，各企业出台了相应的风险管控措施和应急预案，并加强了内审力度，药监局也对此加大了检查力度；

（2）冷藏箱、冰排、无线温湿度采集监控系统等冷链相关技术的研发与应用取得了一定进展，为冷链安全提供了一定保障；

（3）冷链作业与管理相关信息系统的研发与应用也取得了长足进步，国药、上药、华润等企业开发应用相应的系统，实现了包装方案的自动确认、包装方案验证、冷链作业环节监控与管理、质量放行等功能，为下一步实现冷链全流程的可视化管理奠定了基础。

二、2015 年医药物流市场发展展望

预计 2015 年我国医药物流虽然增速会有所下降，但医药流通行业销售总额将会创出新高。医药电商特别是网络处方药、移动医疗和医疗器械将会是 2015 年的主要亮点。

（一）医药市场依然保持快速增长

虽然医药市场的增速有所放缓，但是未来一段时间内，国民经济仍然会保持快速增长趋势，医药行业受宏观经济影响也会保持较快速度发展。我国人口老龄化呈加速趋势、政府对医药卫生投入不断加大、积极推动实行全民医保、人们对慢病需求增大和对健康意识的提高仍然是未来医药市场的动力，医药市场整体规模将会持续扩大。

（二）企业的兼并重组仍将持续

新版 GSP 实施以来，虽然医药行业的“散、小、乱”的格局有所改观，但与国外发达国家相比，我国医药行业的集中度仍然较低。2015 年医药行业仍然会在《全国药品流通行业发展规划纲要（2011—2015）》的指引下，通过收购、合并、托管、参股和控股等多种方式做强做大，实现规模化、集约化和国际化经营，形成以全国性、区域性骨干企业为主体的遍及城乡的药品流通体系。

同时，《互联网食品药品经营监督管理办法》出台在即，第三方物流企业可以介入数千亿元的医药电商，传统医药物流和医药电商物流的整合也将会是 2015 年的一个亮点。

（三）网上处方药市场将迎来爆发式增长

虽然网上处方药市场开放还存在处方药和医保对接等问题，但从目前情况来看，网售处方药的开放只是一个时间问题，已经是大势所趋。相关数据显示，2013 年，中国非处方药市场规模为 1783 亿元，处方药市场总规模高达 9521 亿元，非处方药医药电商的规模为 42 亿元，仅占医药非处方药流通市场的 2.4% 左右，以非处方药的电商渗透率来计，网络处方药至少有 200 亿元的市场规模。而且随着医药电商渗透率的不断提高，网上处方药市场将呈扩大趋势。

（四）现代医药物流网络将进一步健全

2015 年医药行业仍然会保持较快速度发展，由于新版 GSP 的实施，医药流通企业在软硬件投入和升级改造方面仍将会有较大提升，全国性的医药物流网络将会进一步完善。

同时，随着医药电商的快速发展，医药物流最后一千米的建设成为一个新的瓶颈亟待解决。在现有政策下，网上药店只能销售非处方药，需要自行建立配送网络，但是网售处方药政策松绑在即，自建物流或与可靠的第三方平台合作成了医药电商平台可选择的两个物流配送模式。面对即将开放数千亿元医药市场，目前市面上能够达到标准的物流配送企业少之又少，医药电商的最后一千米建设将会在 2015 年有重大发展。

慢性病、常见病将会是医药电商第一波，是采取社区医院配送还是就近药店配送还是其他一些模式？2015 年都会有探索。不管哪种模式，最后一千米的配送都是重中之重，这个环节做的好坏直接关系客户体验，同时也反映到成本，这是医药电商成败的关键点之一。

（五）医药电商对零拣选技术要求不断提高

医药商业的业态决定其物流特性，同样决定物流拆零特性，传统的医药物流以分销和纯销为主，快批和零售连锁业务为辅，前者主要是整托和整箱出货，后者是需要拆零拣选。随着医药行业的发展和电商的崛起，越来越多的医药配送需要拆零拣选，这大大增加了物流中心的作业数量和难度。

医药物流和其他行业相比，受到 GSP 的严格限制，无论是存储、品类管理、批号管理等的要求更高，且由于受医药供应链协同差及医院强势的影响，医药物流订单相对不均衡，都给物流中心拆零拣选作业提出了更高的要求，2015 年将会产生几个医药电商拆零拣选模式，其他进军医药电商的物流企业可以学习和借鉴。

（六）医疗器械物流将快速增长

根据医疗器械目前发展现状，我们预计2015年中国医疗器械物流会呈现如下发展趋势：

1．行业发展仍将保持较高的增长幅度

相关数据显示：全球医药和医疗器械的消费比例约为1∶0.7，而欧美日等发达国家已达到1∶1.02，全球医疗器械市场规模已占据国际医药市场总规模的42%，并有扩大之势。我国医疗器械市场总规模2014年约为2556亿元，医药市场总规模预计为13326亿元，医药和医疗器械消费比为1∶0.19，比2013年的1∶0.2还略低一点。预计医疗器械仍然有广阔的成长空间，医疗器械市场比例将会有所提高。得益于医疗器械的快速发展，医疗器械物流也将保持较快发展趋势。

2．市场集中度不断提高

目前国内的医疗器械市场不管在生产还是在销售领域，集中度相对都比较低，中国目前虽然已成为世界第二大医疗器械市场，但世界排名前10位的医疗器械企业中没有一家中国大陆企业，更没有一家行业集中程度高的医疗器械物流企业。医疗器械物流与医药物流相比，其复杂性更高，要求更为严格，一般企业很难达到要求，随着行业法规日趋完善，国内外市场竞争加剧，最终将淘汰一批竞争力弱的医疗器械企业，扶持一批具有国际竞争力的企业，医疗器械行业集中度将不断提高。

3．互联网将成为医疗器械重要销售渠道

移动互联网时代的来临，将让更多的家用医疗器械通过互联网进行销售，电商渠道销售的比例将不断增加。电子商务与线下销售相比具有诸多优势，不仅突破了空间和时间的限制，而且效率更高费用更低，用户的权益也可以得到保障。因此，医药电商销售将成为医疗器械销售增长重要的渠道。

（七）医药物流信息化建设呈现互联网+趋势

伴随着移动互联网时代的来临，以用户为中心，去中心化，扁平化，平台化，建立新的医药物流生态圈已成必然，医药物流信息化建设将呈现“互联网+”的趋势：

（1）医药物流信息系统应用模式向模块化、平台化、行业化方向发展：通过平台集成模块化的子系统，实现企业内部信息互联，打破信息孤岛；通过功能上的进一步完善（如：电子监管码互联、药检报告电子网络化、人力劳动管理、耗材管理、资产管理、绩效管理、计费管理、客户服务管理等），逐步构建医药行业特色的物流信息系统；

（2）应用方式向移动化互联网方向发展，移动互联网技术在医药物流技术中应用将更加宽广，如：APP 终端实时自主下单、库存查询、物流信息查询跟踪、终端奖励支付、配送签单实施采集上传等；

（3）应用需求层次向智能化方向发展：储位优化、配送线路优化、装载优化、库存分布决策、分布式订单等优化模块逐步在 WMS、TMS 及供应链物流信息平台上应用；

（4）应用范围向终端客户及上游供应商信息化延伸，融合企业内部 ERP、WMS、TMS、冷链系统等系统，逐步推进医药供应链信息平台建设，以实现供应链上物流全程状态跟踪，库存信息、订单、储存资源、质量监管信息可视化等，为上下游企业、政府监管部门、企业内部用户提供云端服务。

（国药集团医药物流有限公司　覃拥　张少凯）

2014 年粮食物流发展回顾与 2015 年展望

2014 年中国粮食物流取得积极进展，政府扶持下的粮安工程、科技与人才兴粮工程等进一步实施，粮食物流数字化和智能化稳步推进，粮食电子商务物流成效初显。未来，立足于粮食安全的粮食物流，特别是粮食物流信息化仍是各级政府扶持的重点，粮食国际物流面临新的机遇，节粮减损等将得到进一步重视。

一、2014 年粮食物流发展回顾

2014 年我国粮食生产实现了“十一连增”，总产量达到 12142 亿斤，比上年增加 103.2 亿斤，连续 2 年跨上 1.2 万亿斤台阶；农民增收实现“十一连快”，农民收入增幅连续 5 年超过国内生产总值和城镇居民收入增幅。2014 年粮食行业的关键词是国家粮食安全。为了保障粮食安全，我国粮食物流工作在推进实施粮安工程，科技与人才兴粮工程，深入贯彻国家粮食安全战略与“五项改革”（粮食流通体制改革、粮食储备管理机制改革、国有粮食企业改革、粮食行政管理机制改革、粮食流通统计制度改革）等方面有了进一步发展。

（一）粮食物流受到各级政府的高度重视

2014 年是我国粮食行业全面实施深化改革的一年。不容乐观的是在国际粮食价格总体平稳的背景下，国内粮价因受托市收购价格等因素影响而长期维持高位，国内外粮价倒挂日益严重，粮食生产与流通成本不断抬高。在双重挤压下，我国粮食收储政策体制和粮食安全面临前所未有的挑战，粮食政策性储备高达 3 亿多吨，保障粮食安全的粮食物流也受到政府的高度重视。

2014 年中央一号文件提出，着力加强促进农产品公平交易和提高流通效率的制度建设，加快制定全国农产品市场发展规划，落实部门协调机制，加强以大型农产品批发市场为骨干、覆盖全国的市场流通网络建设，开展公益性农产品批发市场试点建设；健全大宗农产品期货交易品种体系；加快发展主产区大宗农产品现代化仓储物流设施，完善鲜活农产品冷链物流体系；支持产地小型农产品收集市场、集配中心建设；完善农村物流服务体系，推进农产品现代流通综合示范区创建，加快邮政系统服务“三农”综合平台建设；实施粮食收储、供应安全保障工程；启动农村流通设施和农产品批发市场信息化提升工程，加强农产品电子商务平台建设。得益于国家政策的扶持，各地积极打造功能齐全、服务现代化的农产品物流园区。国内影响较大的有山东省临邑县投资10亿元建设国家级农产品综合物流园，是鲁西北最先进的具有完整冷链物流的园区。该项目稳定运营后，线上线下将实现无缝对接，实现农产品“买全国、卖全国”，年交易量200万吨以上，交易额100亿元以上。湖北省上市公司中百控股联手17家粮油龙头企业共同打造粮食物流航母，集合省内行业资源优势，通过对产品、渠道等资源的整合，建立放心粮油专营渠道，让消费者购买到安全放心的粮油产品，带动湖北省粮油企业进一步做大做强。

此外，粮食安全上升到新的高度，粮食物流紧密关系到粮食安全，中央及各地方政府增加了对粮食物流建设及研发的资金扶持。2014年中央安排10亿元补助投资，继续支持主要跨省粮食物流通道的节点建设，以提升散粮装卸和中转能力；为农户建设标准化储量装具139.4万套，并在吉林和黑龙江省开展大农户试点；支持89个国家粮食质量监测中心和粮食质量监测站的建设。国家发改委会同国家粮食局下达投资计划，安排中央补助投资20亿元，重点在收储矛盾较为突出的东北地区和南方稻谷产区建设仓容130亿斤。政府加快推进“危仓老库”维修改造，中央财政补助资金从2013年的10亿元提高到20亿元，其中重点支持省从2013年的四个增加到十二个。截至2014年8月底，已完成翻建仓容126亿斤，大修仓容406亿斤，并在东北地区下达了350亿斤储粮罩棚，在部分南方稻谷产区下达了18亿斤储粮罩棚建设计划，缓解东北地区和南方部分稻谷产区粮食仓储设施严重不足等突出矛盾。

（二）粮食物流流通领域改革明显

2014年粮食市场形势错综复杂、收储压力前所未有、改革发展任务艰巨。在党中央、国务院的领导下，各级粮食部门深入学习贯彻习近平总书记关于保障国家粮食安全的一系列重要讲话精神，认真贯彻落实国务院第52次常务会议的决策部署，切实抓好粮食收储保供，扎实推进“五项改革”，大力实施“两项工程”，较好地完成了各项工作任务。

首先，为加快构建国家粮食安全保障体系，进一步明确地方政府维护国家粮食安全的责任，建立健全粮食安全省长责任制 。粮食安全省长责任制是贯彻国家粮食安全战略、保障国家粮食安全的一项基本制度。省长责任制要求地方政府稳定发展粮食生产，巩固和提高粮食生产能力；落实和完善粮食扶持政策，抓好粮食收购，保护农民种粮积极性；管好地方粮食储备，确保储备粮数量充足、结构合理、质量良好、调用高效；实施粮食收储供应安全保障工程，加强粮食流通能力建设；深化国有粮食企业改革，促进粮食产业健康发展；完善区域粮食市场调控机制，维护粮食市场稳定；健全粮食质量安全保障体系，落实监管责任；大力推进节粮减损，引导城乡居民健康消费等方面承担责任。

其次，为了提升服务宏观调控和保障粮食安全的能力，国家粮食局加强了粮食储备管理机制改革。强调地方储备粮主要用于保应急、控粮价、稳市场，是区域内应急保供的第一道防线；中央储备粮主要用于应大灾、守底线、稳预期，是保障国家粮食安全的“撒手锏”。最后，深化国有粮食企业改革，构建国有企业和其他市场主体共同发展的新格局。

（三）粮食物流技术更加数字化和智能化

2014 年，粮食物流技术在粮食收储等环节取得了积极进展。浙江省粮食局直属粮油储备库于 2008 年开始，着手进行包装仓散装化升级改造工程（包改散工程）的试点工程建设。截至 2014 年年末，已完成 9 幢仓库的改造，并通过封闭式太阳能光伏建筑屋顶，利用隔热效应和光伏电站对温控机进行供电和智能控制，使储备库走上了一条从传统储粮向现代化、科学化储粮的创新之路。长江以南直属库储存的中央储备稻谷已经全部采用降温通风、谷物冷却机、压盖隔热等控温技术措施，有效减缓了储粮品质变化问题。中储粮还集成创新并推广应用了富氮低氧储粮技术，这是一项纯绿色的储粮害虫防治技术。目前中储粮气调储粮规模超过 1000 万吨，在害虫防治、保质减损等方面取得了明显成效。

2014 年，在粮食物流信息技术方面的建设中，数字化和智能化是重点。国家粮食局大力推进“智慧粮食”工作，“智慧粮食”是运用物联网、云计算、空间地理和遥感信息集成等新一代信息技术，推进粮情监测、预测预警和服务管理的精细化、智慧化。其中库存粮食识别代码及电子标识追溯技术和标准，已经在 13 个省（区）和 3 大央企的 1000 多家企业试点。在国家发改委的支持下，由中储粮总公司、黑龙江省粮食局、江苏省粮食局、深圳粮食集团等部门和单位承担的“粮食储运监管物联网应用示范工程”，已经建成了 47 个物联网技术应用库点，开始发挥粮食信息互联互通的重要作用。与此同时，出于建立食品原产地可追溯制度和质量标识制度，健全农产品质量安全可追溯体系的要求，国家粮食局提出了以库存粮食识别代码为技术载体，建立贯穿收购、储存、运输、加工和销售，即“从田间到餐桌”的全过程质量追溯系统。按照国家粮食局部署，山东与江苏在全国率先启动库存识别代码的试点工作。山东省共有 163 家企业加入了识别代码试点工作，其中国有企业 151 家，约占已备案的国有企业的1/3，另有民营企业12家。山东省粮食局库存粮食识别代码系统平台已接收到各试点企业上传的3474个货位的库存粮食识别代码以及关联信息，涉及粮食367.7万吨。

中储粮也已在2014年完成114家直属库的智能化建设，搭建了集粮情远程监测、智能出入库监管、库存数量监测等多功能于一体的全新智能化粮库管理体系，计划今年扩大推广范围，实现系统内346家直属库智能化全覆盖。作为全国三个“农业物联网区域试验工程”实验区的天津市农业物联网已投入近1亿元，建成了国内首家省级农业物联网综合应用平台，涵盖市场价格、遥感等领域的17个数据库。共建设核心试验基地10个，开展了节能温室、工厂化养殖车间、养殖水面、大型企业牧场及养殖场的示范应用。

（四）粮食电子商务物流发展良好

2014年中央一号文件首次提出“加强农产品电子商务平台建设”，进一步推进了涉农电子商务的高速发展。据不完全统计，目前全国农产品电商平台已逾3000家，农产品网上交易量增长快速，以阿里巴巴平台为例，农产品销售额从2010年的13亿元迅速发展到2012年的198亿元，再到2013年前五个月的150亿元，年均增长超过200%。包括1号店、阿里巴巴和京东在内的主流电商，近两年纷纷争相布局地方特产项目，开设特色地方馆，用土特产撬动用户对于农产品的需求，拓宽农产品销路，解决县域经济尤其是县域农业的渠道问题。山西太行山农产品物流园区于2014年全面建成“太行山农产品物流网”电子商务平台，目前园区已入驻商户217家，交易品种1230种，日访客户5600人次，年交易额达到240万元，太行山农产品物流园将依托平台面向全国发布农产品价格信息，通过网络互通，编制一张供需大网，实现买全国的农产品、卖全国的农产品，力争打造“山西最大、华北一流、全国知名”的现代化农产品综合物流基地。2015年1月9日，中华粮网网络融资首笔贷款顺利投放，实现粮食行业网络融资零的突破，标志着粮食行业在电子化、信息化道路上迈出了一大步。2014年4月，在苏州粮食局的支持下，由全资子公司苏州国家粮食储备库、苏州市金仓粮食物流中心有限公司、苏州市军粮供应站有限公司以及控股子公司苏州市粮食批发交易市场服务有限公司组成的苏州市粮食集团有限责任公司成立，粮食集团投入巨资打造全国一流的垂直型粮食电子商务，借助信息技术平台实现线上做专做强，打造平台品牌，线下完善体验发挥电子商务供应链功能。顺丰嘿客凭借强大的物流能力，推出“产地直采”概念，推出“像水果一样新鲜”的大米。由吉林省延边朝鲜族自治州农委、州供销社联合搭建的中国长白山特产品物流网电子商务平台在2014年年底正式开通运营。该平台主推延边朝鲜族民俗美味、长白山人参、延边大米、食用菌、山珍 5 大类 500 余款产品，开辟了延边农特产品销售新渠道。

另外，围绕国家粮食安全工程、新增千亿斤粮食生产与粮食产业园区发展等一些规划获得了通过。

二、2015 年粮食物流展望

2015 年，世界经济仍处在国际金融危机后的深度调整期，是中国全面深化改革的关键之年，也是中国经济新常态下的“第二年”。应该充分认识物流业发展“三期叠加”的阶段性特征，结合粮食物流特性，准确把握新趋势。

（一）粮食物流仍是各级政府的扶持重点

“农是国之本，农伤则国贫”，2015 年中央一号文件继续关注三农问题，并着重强调了国家粮食安全战略。2015 年，我国将加快农产品市场体系转型升级，加强农产品市场设施建设和配套服务，健全交易制度。政府将持续完善全国农产品流通骨干网络，加大重要农产品仓储物流设施建设力度，特别将加快千亿斤粮食新建仓容建设进度，尽快形成中央和地方职责分工明确的粮食收储机制，提高粮食收储保障能力。粮食物流将更加关注农户科学储粮工程，加强农产品产地市场建设，加快构建跨区域冷链物流体系。各级政府将继续开展公益性农产品批发市场建设试点，强调农业生产全程社会化服务机制创新试点，为农户提供代耕代收、统防统治、烘干储藏等服务。完善国家粮食储备吞吐调节机制，加强储备粮监管。落实新增地方粮食储备规模计划，建立重要商品商贸企业代储制度 。支持电商、物流、商贸、金融等企业参与涉农电子商务平台建设。

2015 年全国粮食流通工作会议在京召开，强调要以全面落实粮食安全省长责任制为核心，进一步增强粮食安全保障能力。强化对粮食主产省和主产县的政策倾斜，保障产粮大县重农抓粮得实惠、有发展。粮食主销区要切实承担起自身的粮食生产责任。

（二）粮食物流信息化将是工作重点

过去一年，我国对于粮食物流信息化建设的投入取得积极成效，但是随着市场的迅速发展和客户的需求变化，对粮食物流信息化的要求越来越高。国务院印发的《物流业发展中长期规划（2014—2020 年）》提出，加强北斗导航、物联网、云计算、大数据、移动互联等先进信息技术在物流领域的应用。加快企业物流信息系统建设，发挥核心物流企业整合能力，打通物流信息链，实现物流信息全程可追踪。2015 年中央一号文件提出建立全程可追溯、互联共享的农产品质量和食品安全信息平台。国务院印发的《关于促进云计算创新发展培育信息产业新业态的意见》中提出要加快发展云计算，打造信息产业新业态，推动传统产业升级和新兴产业成长，培育形成新的增长点，促进国民经济提质增效升级。以进一步加强农业信息中心体系建设为主题的全国农业信息中心主任会议强调，部省信息中心要协同作战，加强顶层设计，努力研发全国信息中心体系都想用、都能用、都好用的信息系统，要充分利用 12316 信息服务已有的良好软硬件系统基础，建设一片协作、共赢、五彩缤纷的农业云；要用先进的信息理念丰富信息人的头脑，用现代信息技术提升信息人的技能，编织一张覆盖到村户的信息人网。一系列政策的发布进一步证明在未来粮食物流推进中信息化将是工作重点。

（三）粮食国际物流将面临新的机遇

据海关统计，我国 2014 年 12 月份进口谷物及谷物粉 237 万吨，全年累计进口 1951 万吨，上年同期累计为 1458 万吨，同比增长 33.8%；2014 年 12 月份出口大米 73703 吨，全年累计出口 419071 吨，上年同期累计为 478404 吨，同比下降 12.4%。2014 年中国全年进口大豆 7140 万吨，同比增加 12.7%，创下历史新高，农产品贸易逆差对我国粮食国际物流提出挑战，也提供了新的机遇。国家积极支持优势农产品出口，支持农产品贸易做强，加快培育具有国际竞争力的农业企业集团。创新农业对外合作模式，重点加强农产品加工、储运、贸易等环节合作，支持开展境外农业合作开发，推进科技示范园区建设，开展技术培训、科研成果示范、品牌推广等服务。完善农业对外合作的投资、财税、金融、保险、贸易、通关、检验检疫等政策，落实在境外从事农业生产所需的农用设备和农业投入品出境的扶持政策。充分发挥各类商会组织的信息服务、法律咨询、纠纷仲裁等作用。

2015 年 2 月 1 日，推进“一带一路”建设工作会议在北京召开，会议安排部署了 2015 年及今后一段时期推进“一带一路”建设的重大事项和重点工作。“一带一路”是“丝绸之路经济带”和“21 世纪海上丝绸之路”的简称。丝绸之路经济带战略涵盖东南亚经济整合、东北亚经济整合，并最终融合在一起通向欧洲，形成欧亚大陆经济整合的大趋势。21 世纪海上丝绸之路经济带战略从海上联通欧亚非三个大陆，和丝绸之路经济带战略形成一个海上、陆地的闭环。在“一带一路”战略下，为今后我国在粮食进出口和粮食跨国交易等方面创造良好的环境。

（四）粮食物流发展更加注重大数据、云计算

云计算是推动信息技术能力，实现按需供给、促进信息技术和数据资源充分利用的全新业态，是信息化发展的重大变革和必然趋势。2015 年 1 月 6 日，国务院印发《关于促进云计算创新发展培育信息产业新业态的意见》，强调要加快发展云计算，打造信息产业新业态，推动传统产业升级和新兴产业成长，培育形成新的增长点，促进国民经济提质增效升级。到 2017 年，我国云计算服务能力大幅提升，创新能力明显增强，在降低创业门槛、服务民生、培育新业态、探索电子政务建设新模式等方面取得积极成效，云计算数据中心区域布局初步优化，发展环境更加安全可靠。到 2020 年，云计算成为我国信息化重要形态和建设网络强国的重要支撑。

未来，我国粮食行业将继续实施“智慧粮食”工程，运用物联网、大数据、云计算、空间地理和遥感信息集成等新一代信息技术，促进粮情监测预测预警和服务管理精细化、智慧化，为政府部门、市场主体等提供及时全面的信息服务。实现从数据采集、标识、交换及制度等方面建立技术标准体系，加快全国和省级平台的建设，为建立大数据资源池，强化数据挖掘、可视化、云计算等先进信息技术的应用，提升粮情信息智能化分析和服务能力，为“智慧粮食”的实现打下坚实基础。由此可见，在国家政策的大力支持下，今后粮食物流的发展将更加注重大数据云计算的投入，粮食物流行业的运行效率有望实现质的飞跃。

（五）粮食物流将是实现节粮减损的重要突破口

财政部于 2015 年 3 月 5 日表示，将会在 2015 年投入 1546 亿元，用于储备粮食、食用油以及其他物资，这要比 2014 年提高 33%；国家发改委也表示，中国将在 2015 年维持小麦和大米的最低收购价格，粮食产量预期将超过 5.5 亿吨。为此需要在继续、积极推动实施“粮安工程”的同时，致力于减少粮食产后损失浪费，确保政策性投入的社会经济效益。实施农户科学储粮工程，可使受益农户的储粮损失平均下降 6%，同时开展仓储设施建设和“危老仓库”改造，使危旧仓房和露天储粮的损失率平均下降 3%。预计到今年年底，可累计为全国 26 个省配置 817 万套新型储粮装具，每年减少储粮损失达 90 万吨。

由于仓储、物流、装卸、搬运等设施不匹配，原粮从收购环节到加工环节需要反复经过打包、拆包、再打包的过程，包粮运输流通成本较高，同时粮食损失浪费比较严重。由于粮食生产越来越向产区集中，粮食产销衔接、跨省流通、区域调剂任务越来越重，而目前我国粮食流通过程“四散”（即“散装、

散运、散储、散卸”）化程度较低，使得浪费更为突出。针对这些现象，各地政府积极探讨粮食流通环节的节粮减损措施。例如政府积极推广节能减排技术改造传统粮食产业，应用高效保温、余热回收利用和烘干新热源等技术降低粮食的破损和二次污染；开发基于新材料的集装单元化技术，提高“四散”储运效率；加大基于库存粮食识别代码技术和电子射频标识（RFID）的物联网技术、全球定位系统、地理信息系统等技术科研投入，优化配置粮食流通资源、提高粮食物流效率、降低粮食流通成本、实现节粮减损的目标，保障国家粮食安全。

（南京财经大学营销与物流管理学院　吴志华　吴慧芬）

参考文献

[1] 何黎明.2014 年我国物流业发展回顾与 2015 年展望［EB/OL］. http://www.chinawuliu.com.cn/lhhkx/201501/16/297616.shtml.

[2] 中华粮网. 粮食行业网络融资零的突破［EB/OL］. http://www.cngrain.com/Publish/news/201501/580282.shtml.

[3] 经济观察网. 顺丰嘿客欲借“直采”大米吸引客流.［EB/OL］. http://www.hbgrain.com/InfoContent.aspx?id=9005&mid=359.

[4] 21 世纪经济报道. 中储粮动刀 20 多家收储公司：剥离政策性业务［EB/OL］. http://www.hbgrain.com/InfoContent.aspx?id=8747&mid=360.

[5] 国家粮食局. 国务院关于建立健全粮食安全省长责任制的若干意见［EB/OL］. http://www.chinagrain.gov.cn/n316630/n316665/n742585/c759086/content.html.

[6] 国家粮食局.2015 年全国粮食流通工作会议.［EB/OL］. http://www.chinagrain.gov.cn/n16/n3615/n3676/n5161751/n5161951/5163992.html.

[7] 国务院.2014 年中央一号文件公布.

[8] 国家粮食局. 湖北出台 19 条深化粮食流通改革意见［EB/OL］. http://www.chinagrain.gov.cn/n316630/n316665/n742585/c406356/content.html.

[9] 国家粮食局. 光明日报：节粮爱粮，从何入手？［EB/OL］. http://www.chinagrain.gov.cn/n317135/c473662/content.html.

[10] 吴子丹. 大力实施科技兴粮工程全面提高科技对粮食行业发展的支撑能力［EB/OL］. http://www.chinagrain.gov.cn/n16/n3615/n3676/

n5148814/n5150452/5161124. html.
[11] 国家粮食局. 深化“五项改革”[EB/OL]. http://www.chinagrain.gov.cn/n316630/n316665/n742585/c761517/content.html.
[12] 长治日报. 长治县“太行山农产品物流网”电子商务平台建成达效[EB/OL]. http://www.chinawuliu.com.cn/zixun/201501/28/298043.shtml.
[13] 德州新闻网. 中国供销临邑农产品综合物流园建设进展顺利[EB/OL]. http://www.chinawuliu.com.cn/information/201501/12/297425.sht ml.
[14] 中国农业网. 农业物联网技术让天津进入农业信息化时代[EB/OL]. http://www.moa.gov.cn/fwllm/xxhjs/dtyw/201411/t20141128_4256743.htm.
[15] 中国农业新闻网-农民日报. 中国长白山特产品物流网正式开通运营[EB/OL]. http://www.moa.gov.cn/fwllm/xxhjs/dtyw/201411/t20141118_4212057.htm.
[16] 中国商务网. 电子商务的兴起，让中国农产品流通的模式更为多样化[EB/OL]. http://www.moa.gov.cn/fwllm/xxhjs/dtyw/201501/t20150108_4327592.htm.
[17] 海关总署. 2014年我国粮油进口数据[EB/OL]. http://www.grainstorage.net/news/show-3238.html.
[18] 国务院. 关于促进云计算创新发展培育信息产业新业态的意见[EB/OL]. http://www.gov.cn/zhengce/content/2015-01/30/content_9440.htm.
[19] 国务院. 关于建立健全粮食安全省长责任制的若干意见[EB/OL]. http://www.gov.cn/zhengce/content/2015-01/22/content_9422.htm.

2014 年冷链物流发展回顾与 2015 年展望

一、2014 年冷链物流发展回顾

相较于 2012 年的“热闹非凡”、2013 年的“稳中有进”，2014 年是我国冷链物流真正快速发展的一年（包括冷链物流外部环境和基础设施）。生鲜电商的崛起赋予了冷链产业新的商机，而上海福喜事件等则再次敲响了冷冻冷藏食品安全的警钟，倒逼整个冷链行业自省深思。冷链基础设施的不断完善也使和路雪、麦当劳等为代表的外资企业纷纷提高冷链物流标准。同时，越来越多的冷链物流行业领军企业尝试向综合性一站式冷链物流服务供应商的方向发展。客观形势的动荡，机遇和挑战的博弈，将冷链行业推到了的“求变谋发展”的风口浪尖。总之，历经几年的市场培育和理念传播，我国冷链物流市场逐步进入由初级的基础物流服务向物流增值服务迈进的阶段。整体回顾如下：

（一）政策环境不断放宽、财政支持进一步加强

2014 年的中央一号文件明确提出“完善鲜活农产品冷链物流体系”继续发力冷链产业。此外《物流业中长期发展规划》《关于进一步促进冷链运输物流企业健康发展的指导意见》的提出也为冷链产业打了一针强心剂，一扫冷链资本市场的阴霾（具体政策摘要见下表）。

2014 年国家冷链物流政策摘要

发布月份	文件名称	发布单位	相关政策
1 月	《关于全面深化农村改革加快推进农业现代化的若干意见》	国务院	完善鲜活农产品冷链物流体系。支持产地小型农产品收集市场、集配中心建设

续　表

发布月份	文件名称	发布单位	相关政策
4月	《国家新型城镇化规划（2014—2020年）》	发改委 公安部 财政部	完善农产品流通体系，健全覆盖农产品各环节的冷链物流体系。加快培育现代流通方式和新型流通业态，大力发展快捷高效配送。积极推进“农批对接”“农超对接”等多种形式的产销衔接，加快发展农产品电子商务降低流通费用
8月	《全国电子商务物流中长期发展规划（2014—2020年）》	商务部	生鲜、医药电商
8月	《关于加快发展生产性服务业促进产业结构升级的指导意见》	国务院	发展第三方物流，加强仓储、冷链物流服务
9月	《国务院办公厅关于深化医药卫生体制改革2014年重点工作任务》	国务院	提升药品流通服务水平和效率，鼓励大中型骨干药品流通企业向农村和偏远地区延伸销售和配送网络
9月	《商务部关于促进商贸物流发展的实施意见》	商务部	提高专业化水平，加强冷链物流建设
10月	《物流业发展中长期规划（2014—2020年）》	国务院	加快食品冷链、医药、危险化学品等专业物流装备的研发，提升物流装备的专业化水平
11月	《国务院办公厅关于促进内贸流通健康发展的若干意见》	国务院	大力发展冷链物流，支持农产品预冷、加工、储存、运输、配送等设施建设，形成若干重要农产品冷链物流集散中心。推动城市配送车辆统一标识管理，保障运送生鲜食品、主食制品、药品等车辆便利通行

续　表

发布月份	文件名称	发布单位	相关政策
12 月	关于进一步促进冷链运输物流企业健康发展的指导意见	发改委	大力提升冷链运输规模化、集约化水平；加强冷链物流基础设施建设；完善冷链运输物流标准化体系；积极推进冷链运输物流信息化建设；大力发展共同配送等先进的配送组织模式

一系列的政策出台，对我国冷链产业而言，无论在当下还是中长期均是利好。除了宏观政策上的引导，中央和各级地方政府 2014 年在冷链产业上的财政支持力度进一步加大。2014 年银川市获得中央财政 3200 万元补贴，用于大型农批企业、流通企业的冷链仓储、配送中心建设；吉林农产品冷库获中央财政补助 3638.6 万元；6 月，福建省建宁县农产品产地初加工冷库项目获补助 280 万元；7 月杭州萧山 5 个冷链项目获补助 1250 万元；8 月国家投资 650 万元支持海南冷链物流项目。

（二）冷链市场规模稳步增长，基础设施不断完善

2014 年冷链需求市场规模进一步增加，达到 11200 万吨左右，较 2013 年增长了近 22%，地域范围上依然集中在中东部经济发达地区，如北京、天津、大连、山东、广东等。2014 年全国冷库总量达到 3320 万吨，折合 8300 万立方米，与去年 2411 万吨相比增长 36.9%。需要关注的是西南地区冷链投资情况，由于“21 世纪海上丝绸之路”等政策效应的推动，成都、云南等地的冷链设备需求市场明显增加，在 2014 年吸引了近 60 亿元的投入。

此外，2014 年年初《政府工作报告》提出全年淘汰黄标车及老旧车 600 万辆的任务，对此环保部、发展改革委、公安部、财政部、交通运输部、商务部六部门联合印发了《2014 年黄标车及老旧车淘汰工作实施方案》，这些举措使得我国商用车 2014 年大幅升级换代，冷藏车 2014 年产销量达到 2 万辆，与去年相比翻了一番。

2014 年的冷链基础设施投入继续加大，在物流地产普遍被看好的背景下，冷链物流园区的建设成为 2014 年冷链产业的亮点。据中物联冷链委不完全统计，2014 年全国运作（包含建成、开建、签约不包括建设中的）的重点冷链项目超过 40 个，投资额超过 550 亿元，相较于 2013 年的近 700 亿元，虽然新投资降幅较大，但考虑到大型冷链项目的工期一般在 2～3 年，所以 2014 年的

冷链基础设施建设依然火热。其中，2014 年完工的冷链项目超过 80 亿元，奠基开工、新签约的冷链项目达到 370 多亿元，涉及冷库 180 多万吨。2014 年运作的重点冷链项目地区分布依然不均衡，重点分布在华北地区（北京、天津、山东等），投资额超过 200 亿元，占比超过全国的 1/3；东北地区约 50 亿元；华南与华东地区（广东、上海、浙江等）约 60 亿元；西南地区（重庆、四川等）50 亿元；中部地区（安徽、湖北等）50 亿元。

2014 年建成的重点园区有：大连冷链物流基地一期、晨农集团崇明冷链物流中心、重庆凯尔冷链物流园区、包头市农产品冷链物流中心和中国食品谷中凯冷链物流园区。正式投建的包括泸州海吉星农产品商贸物流园项目、安必达冷链物流有限公司的黄冈农产品冷链物流配送中心、马鞍山御香苑冷链保护物流加工园、淮北市凤凰山农贸城冷链工程等。

（三）标准制定工作有序开展，标准化进程不断加快

2014 年由中物联冷链委负责起草的《物流企业冷链服务要求与能力评估指标》《水产品冷链物流服务规范》两项国家标准正式发布。此外，冷链委相继在食品和药品领域开展《食品冷链物流追溯管理要求》《药品冷链物流运作管理要求》《药品物流服务规范》等国家标准试点工作，累计有近 100 家企业获得标准试点资质。

同时，《餐饮冷链物流服务规范》行标进入报批阶段，《冷链运输车辆应用选型技术规范》和《冷链物流从业人员职业资质》两项行标进入调研阶段，《鲜活甲壳类海产品冷链运输规范》《肉禽类冷链温控运作规范》《药品阴凉箱》三项行标正式立项。

GB29753《道路运输易腐食品与生物制品冷藏车安全要求及试验方法》强标发布，2014 年 7 月 1 日开始执行，之前申请的公告一年缓冲期到 2015 年 6 月 30 日。本标准规定了冷藏车的分类、要求、降温和保温性能、机械制冷机组和试验方法。本标准适用于采用已定型汽车整车或二类底盘基础上改装，装备机械制冷机组，道路运输易腐食品与生物制品的冷藏车，冷藏半挂车参照此标准执行。

2014 年年底，冷标委对现有冷链标准情况进行梳理，要整合成一批对提高冷链流通率、保障品质有重大促进作用的标准。科学划分推荐性和强制性标准，针对冷冻、冷藏食品等重点品种，在零售交接规范、冷藏库能耗等级要求等关键领域推动出台 2 ~ 3 项强制性国家标准。此外，国家发展改革委等 7 部委联合出台了《关于我国物流业信用体系建设的指导意见》，要求完善物流信用法律法规和标准，并将冷链物流作为试点之一，这对于加快冷链标准化进程有很强推动作用。

（四）冷链市场分散，第三方物流规模有待提升

2014 年第三方冷链物流企业特点依然是规模小、压力大。冷链行业依然“看着热干着冷”，从中物联冷链委发布的“2013 冷链物流企业百强排名”来看，在规模方面，2013 冷链百强企业总收入为 109.02 亿元，只占全国冷链总收入的 10% 左右。其次，缺乏龙头企业，前 50 强占据绝大份额，后 50 强基数太小。在百强排名中，年收入在 5 亿元以上的有 7 家，年收入过亿元的有 25 家，8000 万元以上的有 33 家，6000 万元以上的有 51 家。可见，百强企业中有过半收入超过 6000 万元。将百强企业按照每 10 个企业一组，分析每组的企业收入，前十强企业占据 49% 的收入，接近一半。后面 5 组即 50% 的企业占据百强收入的 15%。可见，我国冷链物流发展不平衡的现象仍然很明显，冷链物流市场化水平和集中度仍较低。

（五）连锁零售餐饮稳步发展，冷链需求和服务双升级

中央八项规定如疾风劲雨，使得高端餐饮复兴之日不会再现。在经历了一年的艰难转型过渡期之后，餐饮行业逐渐恢复了元气，定位于大众消费的连锁餐饮品牌逐渐成为餐饮行业的中坚力量，上升势头明显，高端餐饮和街边饭馆愈加难以生存。而连锁餐饮标准化菜品和网点化扩张给冷链物流企业带了更多的发展机遇。

2014 年 7 月的“福喜”事件，无论对当事企业还是其他连锁餐饮企业都是一种打击，食品安全问题再一次刺痛了民众神经。促使餐饮企业加大食品安全监管力度，加强食材供应链管理，升级更新食材的温控设施。规范连锁餐饮市场竞争行为，已成为政府部门和行业必须去面对的问题。在食品安全的倒逼下，餐饮业的冷链配置将会由部分企业的营销点逐渐成为行业标配。为了更好地参与竞争，餐饮企业需加大冷链设施投入成为业界共识。

2014 年 10 月，商务部、国家发展改革委联合发布《餐饮业经营管理办法（试行）》指出，餐饮外卖企业须有营业资质和冷链，冷藏保温温控需有保障。政府出手管理规范餐饮行业发展的第一步已经迈出。

受电商冲击，以及店面租金成本、员工薪资上涨等压力，2014 年全国各地出现大面积商超关店潮，从《2014 年主要零售企业关店统计》发布的数据来看，2014 年全国主要零售企业（百货、超市）共计关闭 201 家门店，关店数同比增长超 4 倍，创历年之最。反之我们也发现连锁零售发力生鲜板块，建立生鲜网站、自建和外包生鲜加工配送中心，完善冷链配送系统，为第三方冷链物流企业带来新的机遇。截至 2014 年年底，沃尔玛在中国拥有 11 个生鲜配送中心。

（六）生鲜电商是亮点，发展前景仍需观望

2014 年生鲜电商虽然“雷声大雨点小”，但依旧是冷链行业亮点。首先资本疯狂进入生鲜电商领域，亚马逊 2000 万美元入股上海本地垂直生鲜电商美味七七，中粮我买网获得 IDG 资本和赛富基金 1 亿美元 B 轮融资……总之，有强劲资本输血的生鲜电商市场活力十足。

生鲜 O2O 也是当下很多电商大佬争先布局的版图。2014 年京东联手万家便利店和獐子岛，一号店则携手沃尔玛，顺丰嘿客布局 2500 家门店“入侵”冷链最后一公里。而在跨境生鲜电商领域，阿里巴巴、京东、亚马逊等电商巨头也是未雨绸缪。同时，一批有实力的生鲜跨境电商平台也先后崛起，像优鲜码头、百联电商等。

然而不得不面对的现实是，贴着“蓝海”标签的生鲜电商市场，初期的圈地成本依然很高，冷链设施的购置、全程冷链的设计与配送、消费者理念的培育等，都需要大量的时间和资金成本，甚至有统计称 99% 的生鲜电商都在亏损。

（七）进出口食品需求旺盛，临港冷链前景看好

2014 年中国与冰岛正式签订自由贸易协定，青岛港与冰岛最大的企业怡之航集团签署合资项目——青岛港怡之航冷链物流，筹划合力打造亚洲最大的冷链物流中转港。此外，中澳贸易协定意向书的签订，也在推动澳洲牛羊肉、红酒、奶制品的大量进口，例如，中物联冷链委去澳洲考察了解到，原来从澳洲每天运往上海的乳制品，运送方式已从客机改为专门货机。

而在临港冷链建设方面，大连獐子岛中央冷藏项目一期、宁波港冷链物流中心一期已经投入使用，天津东疆保税港区东疆大洋冻品物流配送中心、大连大窑湾保税港区毅都集发、深圳机场红酒物流中心、宁波港金枪鱼保税冷库、烟台港保税水产物流园、以及宇培投资 50 亿元的大连冷链物流和食品加工园等项目也在建设中。

（八）冷链人才缺口大

冷链物流是复合型产业，所需的种类涉及整个冷藏冷冻类食品、药品的生产、贮藏运输、销售，以及相关的冷链技术装备，到消费前的各个环节的管理、技术、组织、操作等多方面的人员。冷链物流人才大体可分为两种：技术和作业型人才、管理和规划型人才。

前者必须具备一定的物理化学知识，熟悉冷库常涉及一些化学物品，如制冷剂用到的氨、氟利昂和四氟乙烷等，还要懂得冷库里保温系统和制冷设备结

构和原理。除此之外，冷冻技术与食品特点等也是技术和作业型人才必须要掌握的。而管理和规划型人才不仅要了解前者所需掌握的知识，还得具备一定的管理才能，这就要求相关人才有一定的学历和学习能力，才可以管理好冷链物流的流程运作，并能为企业提出一些有利于冷链物流发展的解决方案和意见。

二、2015 年冷链物流展望

《物流业中长期规划》明确了物流业在国民经济发展中的基础性、战略性地位，极大地提升了产业地位，也对冷链物流业发展提出了新的要求。

（一）冷链大环境、大趋势继续向好

新一届政府对食品安全的重视进一步升级，中产阶级人口数量不断增加，对冷链产品的需求越来越大，政府和消费者对冷链物流理念的认识越来越深，冷链市场规模继续扩大。因此，2015 年冷链物流行业无论从宏观环境还是客观形势，都将持续向好。

2014 年无论是国务院、发改委、商务部，或是地方等各级等政府部门，都出台了冷链相关政策规划，从这一点上释放出明显的信号：国家自上而下重视冷链发展，公平的冷链物流竞争环境会越来越好。2015 年将是《农产品冷链物流发展规划》落地实施的最后一年，下一个五年规划将在冷链基础设施建设、冷链标准化、公平的冷链环境、冷链税费减免等方面进一步加强。

（二）冷链零担和宅配服务是亮点

生鲜电商 2014 年市场规模达 260 亿元，2015 年预计达到 520 亿元，增长势头十分迅猛。生鲜电商的发展关键在于产品的冷链物流能力，最先一公里和最后一公里配送的综合性差异化服务体验将是生鲜电商务模块的竞争核心，而目前的冷链物流企业服务还未形成产品化，因此可以预见，2015 年冷链零担和宅配服务市场规模会进一步扩大，传统冷链物流企业要想触碰这块蛋糕，必须在资源整合和服务品质上下功夫，目前刚刚成立的九曳供应链正在关注这个领域。

（三）关注冷链“最先一公里”

2014 年进口果蔬、海鲜走红国内，为何出现如此现象？国外进口果蔬反倒比国内价格低、品质高、物流快，这又是为何？究其原因就是农产品冷链“最先一公里”问题没有重视和解决。

国内往往放弃农产品产地加工，把粗加工和精加工一股脑地压在综合成本

居高的北上广沿海地区，反而使得农产品果蔬的整个冷链物流变成高成本的“长物流”，积重难返，销地又有多少物流商能够做得起或愿意做这样的“长物流”，更何况又岂是一家企业能够为之。

反观境外果蔬入境中国，因为“最先一公里”做得好，看似漫长的跨境物流却变得非常惬意，所以它就成了“短物流”。由此可见，“最先一公里”在整个供销链条中的地位是极其重要的，在全面质量管理的理念下，事前控制无论在控制效果还是控制成本上都是最优的，重视“最先一公里”才能根本解决产品品质差、损耗高的难题。

（四）传统企业跨界做冷链，做好服务是关键

2014 年，随着我国冷链政策环境和市场前景的利好，以及互联网崛起和金融创新，将会有更多搅局者和传统物流进入冷链领域，一方面将会为冷链行业注入新的血液和基因，另一方面对于传统冷链格局将带来巨大的冲击和挑战。

目前，除了阿里巴巴、京东、一号店这些互联网大鳄已经将触角延伸到冷链行业之外，在传统物流领域，像顺丰已经依托“顺丰冷运 + 顺丰优选 + 顺丰嘿客”完成冷链一体化的初步设想；在航空领域，像海航、东航已经通过不同方式打造航空冷链物流体系；在金融、融资租赁领域，像平安、民生、狮桥也都凭借各自优势提供不同的冷链金融解决方案；而在物流地产领域，像普洛斯、复星、宇培、平安不动产等也各自开始冷链物流网络的布局。

冷链物流的发展离不开金融和人才的支撑，但是只有这两个是不行的，物流毕竟是服务行业，快速扩张的同时一定要关注一线的基础服务。

（五）自贸协议、自贸区和“海上丝绸之路”溢出效应显现

中国—东盟大经济平台的形成离不开大物流的积极支持。习近平总书记提出的“海上丝绸之路”无疑使中国—东盟大经济体更加火热。对冷链产业而言，中澳自由贸易协议签订、国家对跨境电子商务的支持，航空、海运冷链及临港、临空冷链都将受益。如果说 2014 年是政策观望、市场考察的一年，2015 年则是积极介入抢占冷链物流市场的关键时间点，天津、广东、福建、广西、云南、成都冷链市场将会更热。

随着自由贸易区的拓展，进出口的食品和药品量越来越大，冷链物流业将会获得越来越多的机会。上海自贸区对物流业的影响不仅仅体现在业务上，自贸区对冷链物流的重视才是最重要的。

（六）探索冷链物流强制标准，尝试团体标准制定

国务院总理李克强 2015 年 2 月 11 日在国务院常务会议上所确定的“推进

我国标准化工作改革总的方向和具体措施”，提出今后标准将严格界定标准的层级，控制国标和行标的数量，对涉及健康、安全、环保制定强制性国家标准，由协会等依据市场需求制定团体标准，让标准真正解决现实问题。

从实施过程来看，要先对已有多项冷链国标和行标进行梳理和清理，向国家标准委提出已有标准的清理建议。制定团体冷链标准的相关制度与开展方案，在各环节和领域做好标准化改革的宣传，提高大家对标准化改革的认识，真正从标准有用的角度开展标准工作。

（七）冷链物流企业依然是百家争鸣

2015 年第三方冷链物流企业特点依然是规模小、压力大。冷链物流市场越做越热，随之衍生的企业模式也越来越多，在这个充满想象力的蓝海市场，各路企业可谓八仙过海，各有各的生存和盈利之道。但是，细细梳理常温物流的发展会发现，物流企业有了网络才真正有价值。冷链物流有一张天网和四张地网，天网是指强大的信息平台，地网是冷库网、干线（整车、零担）网、城配（区域）网、宅配网。能把其中任何一张网做好，企业就真正有价值了，但是由于企业的商业模式、资金和人才等的限制，现在的冷链物流企业短期内很难迅速建立其中一个网络。

（八）冷链人才缺口导致人力资源成本继续上涨

2015 年我国冷链产业继续快速发展，带动与之相关的食品和药品行业、冷链物流行业、餐饮和零售行业、制冷和保温行业一起发展，还有快速崛起的生鲜电商行业，但与之相对应的冷链人才却出现脱节，院校没有这个专业，刚毕业的相关专业学生又不能马上进入角色，冷链前进动力不足。从北京、上海等地的冷链物流企业调查中发现，企业“无人可用”是他们共同的心声，不仅管理人员面临断层，货车司机和冷库作业员工也越来越稀缺，越来越难找。物以稀为贵，人才的短缺导致企业用人成本快速上涨。

（中物联冷链物流专业委员会　秦玉鸣）

2014 年大宗商品电子交易市场发展回顾与 2015 年展望

大宗商品电子交易市场是一种利用网络平台对石油、钢材、粮食、煤炭等大宗商品进行批量交易的 B2B 电子商务模式。大宗商品电子交易市场是一种介于现货市场与期货市场之间的新型市场形态，是中国现代商品市场体系的重要组成部分。这类市场的出现对推动传统现货批发市场改造提升、促进商品流通、规避价格风险以及实现商品价格发现等功能具有重要意义。

一、2014 年大宗商品电子交易市场发展回顾

（一）大宗商品电子交易市场数量持续增加，中西部保持较高增长态势

2014 年是大宗商品电子交易市场快速发展的一年。截至 2014 年年底，据中国物流与采购联合会大宗商品交易市场流通分会不完全统计，目前我国大宗商品电子类交易市场共 739 家（如表 1 所示）[①]。其中，处于运营状态的市场为 661 家，处于暂停交易或停业状态的市场为 78 家。2014 年，我国大宗商品现代流通行业总体呈现向规范化、专业化和规模化发展的良好态势，行业整体综合实力与市场主体质量有明显提升。大宗商品电子类交易市场与实体经济的联系更加紧密，行业分布更加广泛，市场数量同比增长 37.4%，实物交易规模超过 20 万亿元。

表 1　大宗商品电子类交易市场地域分布表（截至 2014 年年底）

省份	数量	省份	数量
山东	80	云南	15
广东	73	陕西	14

① 数据来源：中国物流与采购联合会大宗商品流通分会 http：//www. cbca. org. cn/news/notice/2015 - 01 - 04/37f8b128159cc9a99bdd45eef2cf6316. html。

续　表

省份	数量	省份	数量
江苏	61	湖北	12
浙江	59	内蒙古	12
上海	50	黑龙江	10
北京	46	江西	10
天津	41	贵州	9
辽宁	31	山西	9
河南	31	吉林	8
湖南	25	宁夏	6
河北	24	海南	5
广西	20	甘肃	4
重庆	17	青海	2
新疆	17	西藏	2
四川	16	香港	1
安徽	15	总计	739
福建	14		

从地域分布看，我国大宗商品电子类交易市场已覆盖32个省（区、市）和特别行政区，但是地区差异明显，东部沿海地区分布最多，中部次之，西部最少。但是随着国家“一带一路”战略的提出，处于丝绸之路经济带上的省市加快对传统批发市场的转型升级，积极拥抱互联网和电子商务，推动传统产业与互联网进一步结合。大宗商品电子交易市场的数量逐年增加，从数量上在逐渐缩小与东部沿海地区的差距。中西部市场数量在2010年只占到全国大宗商品电子交易市场的27.4%，到了2014年，已经达到35%。同时，连续两年中西部市场数量的增长率高于全国增长率。但是我们看到，无论是全国大市场还是中西部市场的增长率都比2013年大幅回落，这是因为在2014年年初，贵金属交易市场集中爆发了一系列风险事件，各部门、省市在清理整顿工作之后，又加大了对交易市场的审查，将一部分违规的交易市场关闭或责令其整改（如表2所示）。

表2　　东西部大宗商品电子交易市场数量对比

年份	2009	2010	2011	2012	2013	2014
东部①	94	114	170	254	355	480

① 在这里将“北京、天津、上海、广东、江苏、山东、浙江、辽宁、河北、福建、香港”十一个省市、特别行政区计算为东部。

续 表

年份	2009	2010	2011	2012	2013	2014
中西部	34	43	73	103	183	259
总数	128	157	243	357	538	739
中西部百分比①（%）	26.6	27.4	30	28.9	34	35
总增长率（%）②	19.6	22.7	54.8	46.9	50.7	37.4
中西部增长率③（%）	13.3	26.5	69.77	41.1	77.7	41.5

从行业分布看，我国大宗商品电子交易市场涉及的行业已包括能源、化工、纺织、金属、酒类、矿产品、农产品、林产品、牧渔产品、医药等二十多个行业。其中，由于金属与农产品现货电子交易起步较早，所以比其他行业发展更快。其中，农产品大宗商品电子交易市场依然保持龙头地位，比2013年的161家增长36%（如表3所示）。

表3　大宗商品电子类交易市场行业分布表（截至2013年年底）

行业	数量	行业	数量
农产品	219	林木	18
金属	162	渔产品	14
化工	71	矿产品	14
能源	41	综合类	104
畜禽	27	其他	47
酒类	22	总计	739

其中，一些具有代表性的大宗商品电子交易市场经过多年的规范运营与管理，交易量稳步增长，并通过服务创新，带动现货市场、相关产业和商品流通的发展，成为我国大宗商品电子交易市场的典型代表。

宁波大宗商品交易所大胆尝试新的交易品种，推出国内首只皮革交易品种——牛蓝湿革。我国是全球皮革重要产地，2012年我国轻革（猪牛羊革）产量就达到7.47亿平方米，总产值达到1705亿元。但是，却没有相应的电子市场进行交易，严重阻碍了皮革类原材料行业在互联网时代的发展。而牛蓝湿

① 中西部百分比：中西部大宗商品电子交易市场数量占全国大宗商品电子交易市场数量的百分比。

② 2008年全国大宗商品电子交易市场总数为107家。

③ 2008年中西部大宗商品电子交易市场总数为30家。

革现货电子交易的上线正是填补国内该品种交易的空白。同时，牛蓝湿革现货电子交易也有利于形成我国皮革类产品的统一价格，为争夺全球定价的话语权做好准备[1]。

一些信息主导型大宗商品现货电子交易市场在2014年也获得了很大的发展。中国电子商务研究中心（100EC.CN）监测数据显示，2014年上半年，B2B电子商务服务商营收份额中，阿里巴巴继续排名首位，我的钢铁网紧随其后，市场份额达到8.0%①。找钢网实现交易额688亿元，同比增长超300%，完成钢材自营交易量304万吨，交易金额95亿元②。东方钢铁在线实现交易额1757亿元，同比增长超10%③。

（二）大宗商品电子交易与物流服务创新

作为现代物流的重要组成部分，大宗商品物流直接关系到生产资料流通的顺利运行。然而，由于大宗商品品种丰富、数量庞大、专业性强（化学产品、生鲜产品等）的特点，任何一家物流公司都无法全部承担，这就要发挥大宗商品电子交易市场的平台效应，汇聚不同特点的物流仓储企业，共同为大宗商品的流通提供优质服务，在为大宗商品交易提供服务的同时，也促进物流服务的创新。

在“滴滴”“快滴”等掀起颠覆客运服务模式浪潮之后，2014年货运O2O领域也取得了快速发展。一大批货运信息网站和货运APP如雨后春笋般出现。很多大宗商品电子交易市场也积极开展这项服务或是和已经拥有一定规模的货运信息网站进行对接，实现信息互联。通过大宗商品电子交易市场为货运企业或个人提供货源，通过货运信息网站为大宗商品电子交易聚集灵活的物流服务提供商。随着货运信息网站或货运APP的增加，这一行业的竞争会愈发激烈，必将迎来洗牌，行业集中度会进一步加强。

当大宗商品电子交易物流服务创新在行业实践中开展的如火如荼之时，政府部门也十分关注大宗商品物流服务的创新工作。商务部印发的《2014年流通业发展工作要点》和《商务部关于促进商贸物流发展的实施意见》指出，发展大宗商品物流服务创新要鼓励生产资料物流企业充分利用新技术和新的商业模式整合内外资源，延长产业链，跨行业、跨领域融合发展，增强信息、交易、加工、配送、融资、担保等一体化综合服务能力，由单纯的贸易商、物流商，向供应链集成服务商转型。

---

① 数据来源：《2014年（上）中国电子商务市场数据监测报告》。

② 数据来源：http：//www.100ec.cn/detail－－6225525.html，http：//www.100ec.cn/detail－－6229658.html。

③ 数据来源：http：//www.100ec.cn/detail－－6229680.html。

（三）贵金属交易再现风险，清理整顿工作继续发力

为规范各类交易场所健康有序发展，防范金融风险，2011年11月，国务院发布《国务院关于清理整顿各类交易场所切实防范金融风险的决定》（国发〔2011〕38号），要求各省级人民政府对本地区各类交易场所进行集中清理整顿。经过了两年的清理整顿工作，取得了一定的成果，但是还有不尽如人意的地方。2014年的“3·15”晚会曝光的“白银骗局”案件，又一次将人们的目光聚焦到混乱无序的交易场所。这次集中爆发问题的是贵金属交易所。从电视报道来看，这些交易场所存在夸大宣传、诱导投资者交易，层层设计陷阱，人为操纵交易数据等现象，导致一些投资者被欺骗，造成很大的经济损失。

贵金属交易所风险事件曝光后，清理整顿各类交易所部际联席会议在2014年4月11日成立打击非法证券期货活动局（清理整顿各类交易场所办公室），主要职责就是承担清理整顿各类交易场所的有关工作[3]。6月，公安部统一部署对国内多个大宗商品交易场所进行突击检查，范围涉及多个省市。与以往不同，此次检查不是由公安部经侦部门联合相关监管部门展开，而是由刑侦部门牵头，进行突击检查，打击力度大，主要目标就是有金融诈骗嫌疑的贵金属交易市场。随后，清理整顿各类交易场所部际联席会议办公室发出《关于开展各类交易场所现场检查的通知》（清整联办〔2014〕28号），要求对各类交易场所集中开展一次现场检查，此次检查的对象不仅仅是爆发危机的贵金属市场，还有已通过验收地区纳入清理整顿范围的各类交易场所，包括验收通过后新设的交易场所；重点检查对象是贵金属类、文化产权及艺术品类和股权类交易场所，以及验收通过后投诉举报和媒体负面报道较多的其他交易场所。

（四）规范在线供应链金融，降低大宗商品交易风险

大宗商品数量多、价值高、金额大的特点决定了大宗商品的生产与贸易需要大量的流动资金作为支撑。而“融资难”问题是一个困扰我国大多数企业非常棘手的问题，对于中小企业而言尤为突出。而供应链金融业务的出现使得这一现象大为改观。供应链金融是指以核心企业为出发点，基于供应链链条的交易关系和担保品，在供应链运作过程中向客户提供的融资、结算和保险等相关业务在内的综合金融服务。供应链金融帮助大宗商品企业盘活了手中的存货以及权益资产，拓宽了融资渠道，改善了经营状况，大大促进了大宗商品的生产和交易。随着电子商务的快速发展，大宗商品电子交易市场纷纷将传统的供应链金融业务移植于线上，并针对电子商务的特点加以改造升级，积极开展在线供应链金融服务。然而在供应链金融迅速发展的同时，也出现了一系列的问题，如信用风险、操作风险等风险不断加大，业务发展不规范、行业标准不完

善、政府监督不系统等。这些问题导致大宗商品供应链金融发生了一系列风险事件。

2012 年上海钢贸事件给供应链金融和大宗商品交易领域带来的负面影响还未消除，2014 年 6 月发生的青岛港骗贷案，7 月发生的淮矿物流风险事件又将大宗商品供应链金融推上了风口浪尖。青岛骗贷案的起因与上海钢贸事件类似，都是由于重复质押导致的。由于大宗商品具有很高的价值，贸易商可以通过质押或大宗商品进行融资。通过传统的动产质押业务，贸易商用大宗商品进行质押以获得银行的贷款。这样的物流金融业务需要第三方仓储物流企业对质物进行详尽和严格的检查，帮助银行妥善保存质物，并按银行指令与贸易商进行交接。但是由于利益的诱惑，贸易商和第三方仓储物流企业联手进行违规操作甚至是违法操作。对于同一批货物，仓库出具虚假仓单，由贸易商重复质押给多个银行以获取多次贷款。或者，贸易商以次充好，用品质较差的质物代替原有的质物。或者，当贸易商将钢材质押获得贷款后，在仓库的协助之下擅自将钢材变现，银行却浑然不知。更有甚者，钢贸商和仓库联手捏造虚假仓单向银行申请贷款。青岛骗贷案就是德正资源的全资子公司德诚矿业将一批矿石货品存于一家仓库，却勾结不同的仓储公司，出具了不同的仓单证明，并利用这些仓单去不同银行重复质押融得巨资。而后企业负责人被执法部门带走，从而激起业内狂澜。根据青岛银监局公开信息，盘子巨大的“德正系”在当地的金融授信额度就高达 148 亿元，外埠风险敞口仍在排查之中[4]。

而淮矿物流的风险事件更是让人唏嘘不已。淮矿物流提出并推行基于“平台＋基地”的全流程监管下供应链管理模式，获得了政府及业内的高度认可。由淮矿物流收购并控股的“斯迪尔”电商平台更是被誉为“生产资料领域的阿里巴巴”，然而就是这样一个在业内享有盛誉的大宗商品电子交易市场，却因为债务逾期，而作为第一被告被民生银行上海分行起诉，并在 2014 年 10 月 1 日申请破产重整。淮矿物流的钢贸债务危机从而浮出水面。经调查淮矿物流存在巨大的债权债务黑洞，以 2014 年 9 月 12 日为基准日，淮矿物流债权总额高达 161.57 亿元，债务总额高达 167.49 亿元，波及民生银行上海分行、光大银行武汉分行等 19 家银行。淮矿物流风险事件的爆发原因是多方面的，钢铁行业的全面亏损是造成此次事件的直接原因，产能过剩、需求萎缩、成本上涨导致钢铁市场供大于求，钢材价格倒挂，钢铁行业出现全面亏损，钢铁链上的企业风险急剧加大。盲目追求扩张、缺乏内部监管、滥用授信额度、业务流程不规范是导致此次事件的根本原因。淮矿物流和斯迪尔都一味地追求做大，要做最大的大宗商品电子交易市场，要做生产资料界的阿里巴巴。为了扩大规模，滥用授信额度，吸引更多的钢铁厂商进入平台。当风险初步显露的时候，缺乏内部监管，上下串通隐瞒风险，却没有好的办法解决，导致风险最终全面爆发[5,6]。

淮矿物流的破产并不意味着“平台＋基地”全流程供应链管理模式的失败，我们要区别对待，不能因为淮矿物流的风险事件就将“平台＋基地”模式的有益经验抛弃，而是要分析问题，总结经验，控制供应链金融的各类风险。例如，要构建市场诚信体系，引导企业规范发展；要完善标准体系，规范业务发展；要充分发挥行业协会作用，实行行业自律；更要加强理论和政策研究，促进物流金融创新持续发展。

在供应链金融爆发危机的时候，行业的正能量也在不断传递。2014 年 6 月 12 日，首届在线供应链金融推进大会在北京国际会议中心召开，大会由中国电子商务创新创业联盟主办，围绕在线供应链、在线互联、风险可控、产能结合、创新共赢等主题进行了深入研讨。2014 年 11 月 22 日，中国物流与采购联合会物流金融专业委员会在北京正式成立。2014 年 12 月 5 日，“第二届中国供应链金融服务联盟年会暨 2014 供应链金融合作与创新发展论坛”在西安隆重举行，中国供应链金融服务联盟专家委员会宣布正式成立。相信在新形势下，中物联物流金融专业委员会以及中国供应链金融服务联盟等行业组织会在相关金融主管部门的指导下，充分发挥行业组织的作用，在金融机构和物流企业、货主企业之间搭建起多层次、全方位、高效率的交流和服务平台。

二、2015 年大宗商品电子交易市场发展展望

（一）大宗商品延续良好发展势头，通关改革助推跨境贸易

2015 年第一个月，国内大宗商品现货交易市场密集成立，共有 30 家左右的交易市场开业或试营业。新成立的交易市场分布在多个省份，包括江苏、内蒙古、陕西、江西、广东等；业务覆盖多个行业，包括煤炭、珠宝玉石、纺织服装、橡胶轮胎等。除了现货类商品交易市场外，还有三家权益类交易市场，1 月 4 日南京市公共资源交易中心成立，1 月 15 日中新天津生态城版权交易中心正式运营，1 月 20 日江苏省公共资源交易中心省政务服务中心揭牌。日均近一家的成立速度，彰显了大宗商品现货及权益类商品现货交易发展的强劲势头，现货交易平台建设为大势所趋；与此同时，以宝钢、安钢、华通铂银交易市场为代表的具有雄厚产业背景、商贸实体交易市场背景的股东越来越多。大宗商品电子交易市场转型升级、服务经济探索发展的趋势越来越明显，行业逐步规范，发展势头良好[7]。大宗商品交易市场密集成立意味着大宗商品交易在国内受关注程度持续升温，虽然钢铁、煤炭等行业处于低谷，但国家的“一带一路”战略及相关政策刺激让市场普遍看好大宗商品交易的未来发展。

经中国人民银行批准，上海清算所自 2014 年 8 月 4 日起开展人民币铁矿

石掉期和人民币动力煤掉期中央对手清算业务。随着国际干散货航运市场中海运量最大的大宗商品铁矿石、动力煤掉期业务上线，上海清算所已构建了中国的场外航运及大宗商品金融衍生品清算平台。这将有效汇聚产业整体资源，提高市场流动性，深度带动航运、大宗商品和金融市场的联动发展，为我国大宗商品的跨境贸易迈出了坚实的一步[8]。

为促进我国跨境贸易电子商务的健康发展，同时统一各直属海关对跨境贸易电子商务出口商品的监管模式，完善海关统计，海关总署研发了跨境贸易电子商务通关服务平台，对接电商企业、支付企业和物流企业，实现海关与企业数据的互联互通。通过“清单核放、汇总申报”，实现了海关对跨境电子商务出口商品的有效监管。海关总署跨境贸易电子商务通关服务平台上线为全国其他口岸开展跨境电子商务业务奠定了坚实的基础[9]。与此同时，京津冀三地海关目前共有43个通关业务现场，通关一体化改革实施后，这些作业现场通过信息网络互联互通，形成一个虚拟的“区域通关中心”进行实际运作，实现“三地通关如同一关”。长江经济带海关区域通关一体化第二阶段改革实施，实现了长江流域的全覆盖，沿江的所有口岸和特殊监管区域都实现了一体化通关，企业可以直接在属地海关办理报关手续，实现“12关如同一关”的效果。广东地区各陆路口岸正式启用区域通关一体化模式。实现区域一体化通关后，省内企业无论在省内海关任何空运、海运港口、陆路口岸进出境，均可自由选择申报、纳税、放行地点。通过一体化改革可以降低物流成本、提高流通效率，进一步促进大宗商品进出口贸易。

（二）加快完善物流体系，突破大宗商品电子商务发展瓶颈

电子商务有一个核心两个支撑，一个核心是产品，电子商务的最终目的还是产品的流通，两个支撑分别是物流和支付。淘宝网的巨大成功就是利用支付宝很好地解决了支付的问题，而京东的崛起则很大程度上依赖于庞大的物流体系。在大宗商品电子商务领域，物流仍是限制大宗商品电子商务发展的瓶颈。目前大宗商品物流仍停留在对传统物流运输、仓储等单一环节进行改进的阶段，缺乏整体的物流体系建设方案，而且物流信息化程度不高，无法将国内分散的物流资源汇聚起来形成规模优势，也无法对货物进行实时监控实现全流程追踪。因此，在未来的一年，大力完善物流体系成为大宗商品电子交易市场的重要任务。

2014年被誉为中国产业互联网元年，并且出台了《物流业发展中长期规划（2014—2020年）》等重要物流业政策规划，因此，在2015年我国大宗商品物流体系的完善将会在行业自身建设和政府政策支持两个方面有所体现。

第一，大宗商品物流的信息化、智能化建设将得到加强。阿里巴巴、京东

先后赴美上市，阿里巴巴更是创下美国史上最大IPO。以百度、腾讯、阿里巴巴为代表的消费互联网像月亮的正面一样被大家所熟知；与之对应，以大宗商品电子商务为代表的产业互联网拥有几十万亿元的巨大产业，却如隐藏在月亮背面的巨大宝藏。钢铁、煤炭、石油、化工、农产品、白酒、红酒等传统大宗商品产业，像是惊醒的睡狮，开始全面拥抱互联网。用互联网思维和技术来改造升级传统物流业将成为大宗商品交易领域内的共识。无论是直接提供物流服务的物流仓储企业，还是集成整合物流服务的大宗商品电子交易平台都会重点关注物流的信息化、智能化建设。更多的物流企业将会采用RFID[①]等实时追踪技术以及货物实时监测技术，以GPS[②]为信息采集手段、以GSM[③]、3G、4G（LTE）为通信手段、以GIS[④]为信息表达手段，应用大数据技术对资源配置进行优化，对货物运输过程进行全程跟踪，以提高货物运输的安全性，提高运输效率和服务水平。更多的物流信息平台将会建成，并与相关的大宗商品电子交易市场平台进行整合对接，提供更全面、更快速、更准确的物流信息服务，数据交换、信息发布等传统功能将得到加强，同时，运力交易、货运人社区、云物流等服务将会得到快速发展。

第二，在《物流业发展中长期规划（2014—2020年）》等一系列重要物流业政策规划出台之后，各省市将会根据自身的情况，结合“中长期规划”的精神出台自己的相关政策，推出发展本省本地区物流业的具体办法和措施。例如，近期以雾霾为主的环境问题成为举国上下关注的焦点，煤炭行业更是得到了高度的关注。“中长期规划”也将“节能减排、绿色环保”列为发展的主要原则之一。在这样的背景下，2015年各省市将会重点关注大宗商品物流和供应链的低碳环保问题，出台一些政策法规促进大宗商品物流和供应链向绿色低碳的方向发展：一是煤炭加工、存储、配送等环节将逐步实现全密闭化；二是在煤炭储存、装卸、运输过程中有效防尘措施逐步得到应用，以控制扬尘污染；三是运煤列车、货车及其装卸设施将逐步进行全封闭改造，以减少运输过程中的原煤损耗和煤尘污染；四是大量燃油重卡公路运输工具将逐步减少，以LNG、CNG为燃料的新能源汽车应用范围将扩大；五是动态煤炭管理信息系统

---

① Radio Frequency Identification 技术，又称无线射频识别，是一种通信技术，可通过无线电信号识别特定目标并读写相关数据，而无须识别系统与特定目标之间建立机械或光学接触。

② Global Positioning System（全球定位系统）的简称。

③ Global System For Mobile Communications 的简称，由欧洲电信标准组织ETSI制订的一个数字移动通信标准。

④ Geographic Information System 的简称，是在计算机硬、软件系统支持下，对整个或部分地球表层（包括大气层）空间中的有关地理分布数据进行采集、储存、管理、运算、分析、显示和描述的技术系统。

将逐步建立，以实现对煤炭供应、储存、配送、使用等环节的动态监管[10]。

（三）自贸区建设提速，促进大宗商品交易蓬勃发展

2013 年 8 月 22 日国务院正式批准设立中国（上海）自由贸易试验区，上海自贸区的建立在我国经济和政治的发展进程上，都具有里程碑式的意义。

2014 年 12 月 26 日，十二届全国人大常委会第十二次会议举行第三次全体会议，会议通过关于推广上海自贸区试点经验，设立广东、天津、福建三个自贸试验区，并扩展上海自贸区的范围；在全部试点区内，对于国家规定实施准入特别管理措施之外的外商投资，暂时停止实施企业设立、变更等行政审批，改为备案管理的议案。

新批准建立的三个自贸区并不是对上海自贸区的简单复制，而是在上海自贸区经验基础上具有更明显的区域化特征、目标指向性更强，从区位角度看，福建对接台湾、广东侧重港澳，天津重点面向东北亚并统筹京津冀协同发展。各个自贸区都在积极规划，制定本区域内大宗商品交易发展的蓝图。作为福建自贸试验区最大的片区，厦门自贸试验区将建设跨境贸易电子商务基地；建设大宗商品交易中心；建设航运物流中心列入 2015 年重点培育的十大功能性产业。天津作为北方首个设立自由贸易区的城市，将充分发挥自由贸易港的功能，把大宗商品的资金流、物流安全高效地在自贸区内运转视为未来自贸区发展的重要方向。天津自贸区统筹京津冀协同发展辐射我国最重要的钢铁制造基地——河北省，有利于促进河北钢铁行业的贸易流通和转型升级。

自贸区的建立对于大宗商品交易来说具有重大的意义。2014 年 4 月 15 日，中国（上海）自由贸易试验区管委会出台《中国（上海）自由贸易试验区大宗商品现货市场交易管理暂行规定》（以下简称《规定》）[12]直指大宗商品交易市场。《规定》指出：①市场经营者应当建立健全交易、资金托管、清算、仓储、信息发布、风险控制、市场管理等业务规则与各项规章制度，做到“交易、托管、清算、仓储”分开，严格防范和妥善处置各类风险；②市场经营者应当确保交易各方的交易资金存储在第三方的资金存管机构开设的专用资金账户，不得侵占、挪用账户资金，由主办银行或独立第三方清算机构对交易资金进行清算，确保交易资金安全；③市场经营者应当建立完善的仓单管理及交收机制，由独立第三方仓单公示系统对仓单进行登记公示，确保仓单真实性和交收安全。指定交收仓库应为自贸试验区内的保税仓库或其他符合海关监管要求的保税仓库；④市场经营者及其工作人员不得以任何方式参与市场交易。这预示着不仅自贸区外的大宗商品交易市场经受严厉的清理整顿工作，自贸区内的大宗商品交易市场也要规范自己的行为、防范各类风险。

2014 年 12 月 2 日发布的“中国人民银行关于金融支持中国（上海）自由

贸易试验区建设的意见”更是给大宗商品交易的发展带来了新的机遇。例如，着力推进人民币跨境使用、人民币资本项目可兑换、利率市场化和外汇管理等领域改革试点；居民自由贸易账户及非居民自由贸易账户可办理跨境融资、担保等业务，条件成熟时，账户内本外币资金可自由兑换；完善结售汇管理，支持银行开展面向境内客户的大宗商品衍生品的柜台交易等意见都为开展大宗商品跨境交易带来了政策支撑。

2015 年伊始，上海自贸区大宗商品市场建设提速，八家市场建设方案通过评审。这八家大宗商品现货交易平台基础不同，业务也各有侧重，例如，“上海自贸区液化品国际交易中心”致力于打造亚洲最具影响力的液化品现货离岸交易中心和定价中心，首批上市交易品种为苯乙烯、乙二醇和甲醇。“上海华通白银国际交易中心”首批将上线的主要品种为国标一号白银，后续将推出铂、钯等更多品种；所有品种将采用人民币定价，随着未来交易量的增长和仓储规模的扩大有利于中国取得白银等贵金属的国际定价权。“上海钢联大宗商品国际交易中心”将为金属材料、矿产品、化工原料及产品、农产品、煤炭、石油、水泥、建筑材料等行业提供交易服务。这些平台全部是国际交易平台。即外国机构可以直接入场交易，这与上海自贸区作为深化改革开放、深入国际化的定位吻合，也为平台做大做强、最先对接国际市场提供了很好的基础[13]。

（四）推进“一带一路”建设，开辟大宗商品电子交易新市场

2013 年习近平总书记提出建设“丝绸之路经济带”和“21 世纪海上丝绸之路”的构想。随后，李克强总理在 2014 年 3 月 5 日所作的政府工作报告中提出，抓紧规划建设“丝绸之路经济带”和“21 世纪海上丝绸之路”。“一带一路”战略正式提上国家日程。11 月 4 日习近平总书记主持召开中央财经领导小组第八次会议，研究丝绸之路经济带和 21 世纪海上丝绸之路规划、发起建立亚洲基础设施投资银行和设立丝路基金。

“一带一路”战略在短期内并不能为我国的大宗商品行业带来明显的利好，但是从长远来看，“一带一路”战略对于我国大宗商品交易拓展市场、缓解产能过剩、争夺国际定价话语权具有重要意义。我国大宗商品尤其是煤炭、钢铁等产量已经严重过剩，国内市场供大于求、产品价格大幅跳水、企业利润不断走低的矛盾愈发严重，积极开拓海外市场是解决这一矛盾的重要途径。“丝绸之路经济带”和“海上丝绸之路”沿线涉及 53 个国家、94 个城市，涵盖中亚、南亚、西亚、东南亚和中东欧等国家和地区，主要是新兴经济体和发展中国家[14]。

“东盟”是海上丝绸之路的重要组成部分，仍处于工业化进程当中，当地钢铁工业不能满足其钢铁需求，目前是世界最大的钢铁产品进口地区[15]。以东盟中人口最多、钢材年消费量第二大的印度尼西亚为例，印尼本地钢厂产量

及品种与质量远不能满足印尼市场需求，因此印尼每年需要从国外大量进口各种钢材及半成品，并且进口幅度呈逐年递增之势。2013 年中国超越日本成为印尼最大的钢材进口国，但中国出口货品仍然以长材为主，钢材附加值较低。据印尼钢铁协会的预计，印尼钢材消费量未来有望以 8% 的速度保持增长，到 2020 年钢材消费量将可能达到 2000 万吨的水平[16]。这对中国钢铁企业来说是一次非常好的开拓海外市场、消化过剩产能的机会，同时印尼市场热镀锌、彩涂等冷轧品种的需求持续上升，也有助于倒逼国内钢企提升产品工艺、丰富产品种类。从中长期看，“一带一路”将会缓解国内的钢铁、水泥、电解铝等过剩产能压力，盘活外汇储备，推进人民币国际化，扩大地区的政治经济影响力。同时，“一带一路”战略的实施给中国建立了参与国际大宗商品交易和资源配置的平台，为开展能源产品、基本工业原料和大宗农产品的国际贸易提供了非常好的市场和机遇，可以大大增加中国在大宗商品市场的竞争力，为争夺大宗商品国际定价权积蓄力量。[17]

2015 年，“一带一路”工作将有实质性的推进，相关省份将会发挥自身优势对大宗商品电子交易做出具体规划。2 月 1 日，推进“一带一路”建设工作会议在北京召开，安排部署 2015 年及今后一段时期推进“一带一路”建设的重大事项和重点工作。虽然目前国家层面的“一带一路”规划尚未出台，但许多省份主动融入这一大战略。每个省份都结合自身特点积极融入“一带一路”的战略当中去。例如，新疆 2015 年的重点工作任务是以“政策沟通、道路连通、贸易畅通、货币流通”为目标，全方位推进与丝绸之路经济带沿线国家务实合作，在金融服务方面计划建设股权交易中心、跨境人民币结算中心、外汇交易中心和大宗特色资源产品期货市场，这将有助于大宗商品电子交易跨境贸易在新疆的有序推进。云南决定发挥北上连接丝绸之路经济带，南下连接海上丝绸之路的地理位置优势，坚持技术与经济结合、工程与管理结合，建设云南大物流产业群，从完善物流体系的角度推进大宗商品电子交易的发展[18]“一带一路”战略给大宗商品电子交易市场发展提供了新的机遇，大宗商品电子交易市场要发挥自身的优势，紧跟政策发展，创新交易模式、完善物流基础设施，积极融入“一带一路”战略。

（五）经济发展进入“新常态”，倒逼大宗商品交易改革创新

2014 年 5 月，习近平总书记在河南考察时强调，“我国发展仍处于重要战略机遇期，我们要增强信心，从当前我国经济发展的阶段性特征出发，适应新常态，保持战略上的平常心态”。我国经济发展进入“新常态”，从大的环境和趋势上倒逼大宗商品交易进行改革创新。改革体现在大宗商品产业结构方面，创新体现在大宗商品电子交易服务方面。

在改革产业结构方面，首先，产业集中度会得到进一步提升。以煤炭钢铁行业为例，一些污染高、产能低、质量差的钢厂煤矿会被叫停整改或被兼并，由实力雄厚、技术先进的大中型企业构成的产业集群将会得到进一步加强。其次，制造工艺得到提升、产品质量进一步提高。我国大宗商品电子类交易市场涉及的行业已包括能源、化工、纺织、金属、矿产品、农产品等二十多个行业，涉及的交易品种不胜枚举。其中存在不少工艺落后、质量不过关的产品，这不仅降低生产销售企业的利润，更会阻碍大宗商品生产的制造研发和技术创新。以煤炭行业为例，2014 年 8 月，国家发改委出台了《煤炭经营监管办法》。办法明确，煤炭经营主体应依法经营，公平竞争，禁止销售或进口高灰分、高硫分劣质煤炭，因此提升选煤、洗煤工艺，降低灰分、硫分，提升产品质量是煤炭生产企业下一阶段的工作重点。最后，大宗商品目标市场进一步细分，产品种类更加丰富。例如，国家把完善高速铁路、城际铁路网络作为发展的重点之一，专用铁轨的需求将维持在较高水平，在粗钢等低附加值钢材产量严重过剩的情况下，钢厂细分目标市场，丰富产品种类，挖掘新的需求增长点成为必然趋势。

在创新服务方面，大宗商品电子交易市场的平台作用会进一步显现。商流、物流、资金流、信息流在大宗商品电子交易市场的聚集程度会进一步提高，配套的物流服务、金融服务将会得到完善。物流信息化、集成化建设将会显著提升大宗商品物流服务质量，例如物流公共信息平台、综合型物流园区的建设。流通加工、物流配送、代理采购、贸易结算、物流金融等物流增值服务会得到进一步加强。虽然物流金融业务近几年暴露出较大的风险，但是随着监管体系的完善和管理制度的规范，物流金融业务的创新对整个产业的带动作用还将进一步增强。大宗商品电子交易市场正在经历快速的发展，从 2008 年的 107 家上升到 2014 年的 739 家。对于这样快速发展的行业，商业模式具有非凡的意义。尤其是在经历了数轮清理整顿之后，很多商业模式被禁止，很多被淘汰。商业模式的好坏成为大宗商品电子交易市场能否生存下去的前提。在国家进一步加强商品交易市场清理整顿力度后，倒逼大宗商品电子交易市场不断进行商业模式创新，降低交易风险，更好地服务于现货，促进我国商品流通体系的建立。

致谢：本项研究获国家自然科学基金项目（71390331 和 71390333）的支持。

（西安交通大学管理学院　卢继周　冯耕中　王能民
中国物流与采购联合会大宗商品交易市场流通分会　周旭
酒泉有种网交易中心有限公司　赵绍辉
西安市商用信息系统分析与应用工程实验室　刘缨缨）

参考文献

[1] 宁波大宗商品交易所将上线国内首个皮革原料现货［OL］，中国宁波网，2014 年 3 月 27 日，http：//news. cnnb. com. cn/system/2014/03/27/008021986. shtml.

[2] 孙丽朝. 公路货运 O2O 平台，上演抢滩大战［OL］. 中国经营报，2015 年 2 月 8 日，http：//www. siilu. com/20150208/123903. shtml.

[3] 打击非法证券期货活动局（清理整顿各类交易场所办公室）职能［OL］. 中国证券监督管理委员会网站，2014 年 11 月 11 日，http：//www. csrc. gov. cn/pub/zjhpublic/G00306215/201404/t20140411_ 246992. htm.

[4] 劳佳迪. 青岛港骗贷案始末［OL］，中国经济周刊，2014 年 7 月 7 日，http：//focus. news. 163. com/14/0707/14/A0IB9NS500011SM9. html.

[5] 王晶，易显强，洪涛. 淮矿物流资金坏账事件敲响的警钟［OL］. 现代物流报，2014 年 10 月 12 日，http：//www. cn156. com/article – 36347 – 2. html.

[6] 阮晓琴. 钢铁业第二波风险传导到国企：淮矿物流倒在托盘上［OL］. 上海证券报，2014 年 11 月 21 日，http：//business. sohu. com/20141121/n406235381. shtml.

[7] 2015 伊始现货交易场所密集成立［OL］. 大宗商品交易市场流通分会网站，2015 年 2 月 3 日，http：//www. cbca. org. cn/news/hynews/2015 – 02 – 03/dc389b36b8817040ac53ccba37b5f2a5. html.

[8] 大宗商品终于有了“中国价格”［OL］. 新华每日电讯，2014 年 8 月 6 日，http：//news. xinhuanet. com/mrdx/2014 – 08/06/c_ 133534874. htm.

[9] 海关总署跨境贸易电子商务通关服务平台试点在广东东莞启动［OL］. 中华人民共和国海关总署网站，2014 年 7 月 8 日，http：//www. customs. gov. cn/publish/portal0/tab65602/info712379. htm.

[10] 崔忠付. 我国煤炭物流与供应链发展现状和趋势［OL］. 中国物流与采购联合会网站，2014 年 8 月 11 日，http：//www. cbca. org. cn/news/hynews/2014 – 08 – 11/42912b8320ef78b68a1ff04c03779fca. html.

[11] 国务院拟扩大上海自贸区范围增设广东天津福建三区试点［OL］. 人民网，2014 年 12 月 26 日，http：//npc. people. com. cn/n/2014/1226/c14576 – 26281793. html.

[12] 关于印发《中国（上海）自由贸易试验区大宗商品现货市场交易管理暂行规定》的通知［OL］. 上海市商务委员会网站，2014 年 4 月 18 日，http：//www. scofcom. gov. cn/zxxgk/235937. htm.

［13］钟帮武．上海自贸区八家大宗商品交易市场背景大起底［OL］．大宗商品交易市场流通分会网站，2015 年 2 月 9 日，http：//www.cbca.org.cn/news/hynews/2015-02-09/0178ebe6720b2e51eebc39aa504090de.html.

［14］“一路一带”未来投资过万亿大宗商品市场长期利好［OL］．证券日报，2015 年 2 月 28 日，http：//news.xinhuanet.com/house/cs/2015-02-28/c_ 1114461465.htm.

［15］袁宇峰．东盟钢铁市场简析［J］．冶金管理，2012（7）：24-28.

［16］朱晓辰．印尼钢铁市场现况及未来展望［J］．世界钢铁，2014，14（6）.

［17］杨溧．“一带一路”战略实施将给中国大宗商品市场逐鹿全球带来契机［OL］．和讯网，2015 年 2 月 3 日，http：//gold.hexun.com/2015-02-03/173018636.html? from=rss.

［18］徐寿波．云南大物流建设：发挥区位优势融入“一带一路”［OL］．中国物流与采购网，2014 年 5 月 29 日，http：//www.cbca.org.cn/news/hynews/2014-05-29/bf092e984791f9319c8f42c3e5ff7d27.html.

2014 年电子商务（网络购物）物流发展回顾与 2015 年展望

2014 年是我国电子商务发展的重要一年。在电子商务市场继续保持快速增长的同时，中国网络购物市场开启上市热潮，聚美优品、京东集团、阿里巴巴先后赴美上市成功。电子商务市场的高速发展成为推动电子商务物流市场的重要驱动力，电商物流也成为物流市场发展最快的细分领域。

一、2014 年电子商务发展回顾

2014 年，我国电子商务市场继续保持快速增长。据艾瑞咨询统计数据显示，2014 年中国电子商务市场交易规模 12.3 万亿元，增长 21.3%，其中中国网络购物市场交易规模达到 2.8 万亿元，增长 48.7%，仍然维持在较高的增长水平。根据国家统计局 2014 年全年社会消费品零售总额数据，2014 年，网络购物交易额大致相当于社会消费品零售总额的 10.7%，年度线上渗透率首次突破 10%，成为推动电子商务市场发展的重要力量。如图 1、图 2 所示。

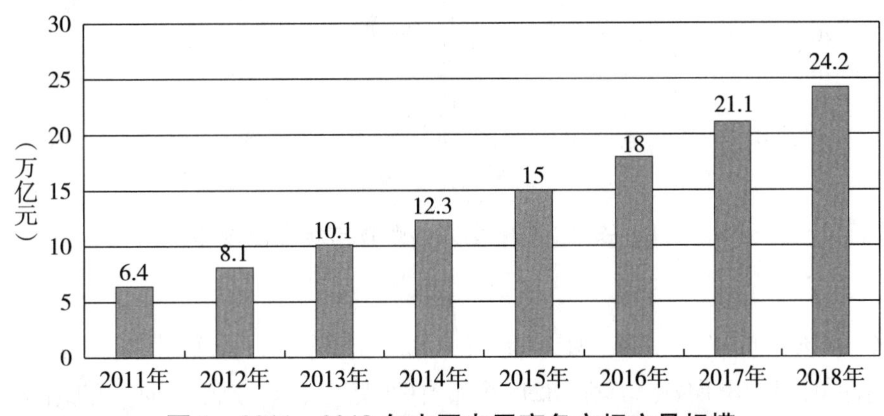

图 1　2011—2018 年中国电子商务市场交易规模

注：根据艾瑞咨询公开资料整理。

B2C 市场增长迅猛。艾瑞咨询数据显示，2014 年中国网络购物市场中 B2C 交易规模达 12882 亿元，在整体网络购物市场交易规模的比重达到 45.8%，较

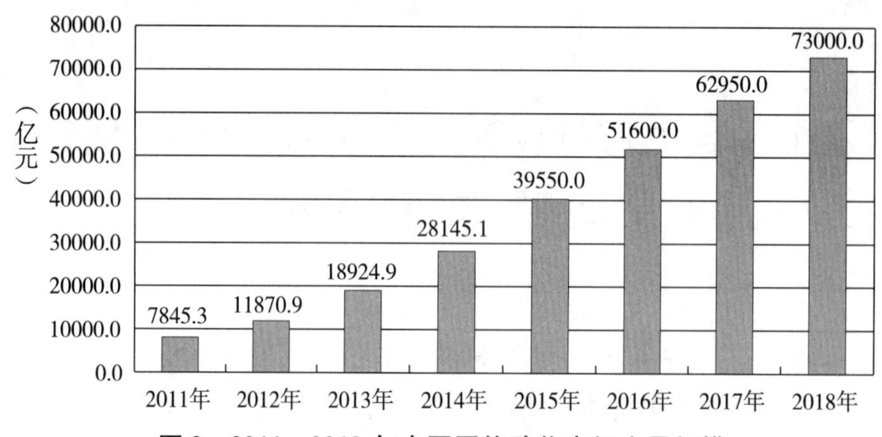

图 2　2011—2018 年中国网络购物市场交易规模

注：根据艾瑞咨询公开资料整理。

2013 年的40.4%增长了5.4 个百分点。从增速来看，B2C 市场增长迅猛，2014 年中国网络购物 B2C 市场增长 68.7%，远高于 C2C 市场 35.2%的增速，B2C 市场将继续成为网络购物行业的主要推动力，如图 3 所示。

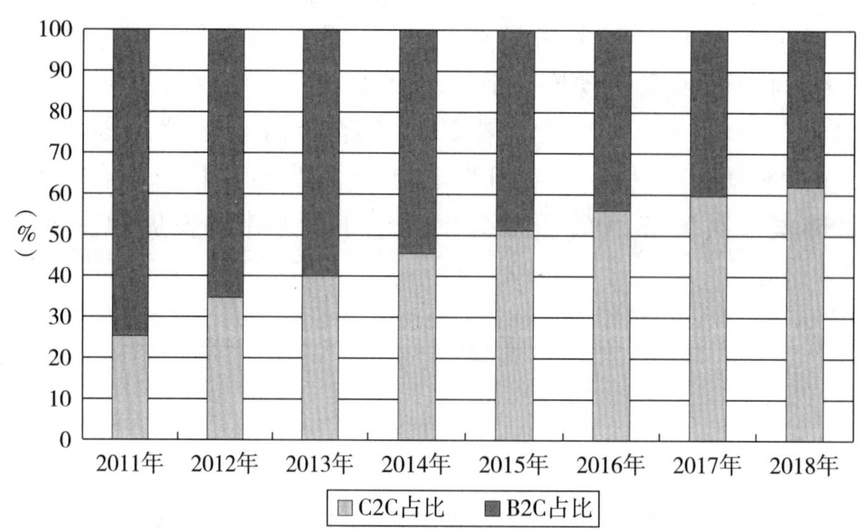

图 3　2011—2018 年中国网络购物市场交易规模结构

注：根据艾瑞咨询公开资料整理。

B2C 市场格局稳定。从 2014 年看，B2C 市场中，天猫市场份额占比超六成，京东占比为 18.6%，其余 B2C 企业中唯品会、1 号店、国美的增速均高于 B2C 市场整体增速。从自主销售为主 B2C 市场来看，京东占比近 50%，苏宁易购占比达到 8.5%，唯品会占比达到 7.7%，其他项中小米手机官网发展迅速，整个市场集中度依然较高。如图 4 所示。

移动购物市场异军突起。2014 年中国移动购物市场交易规模为 9297.1 亿

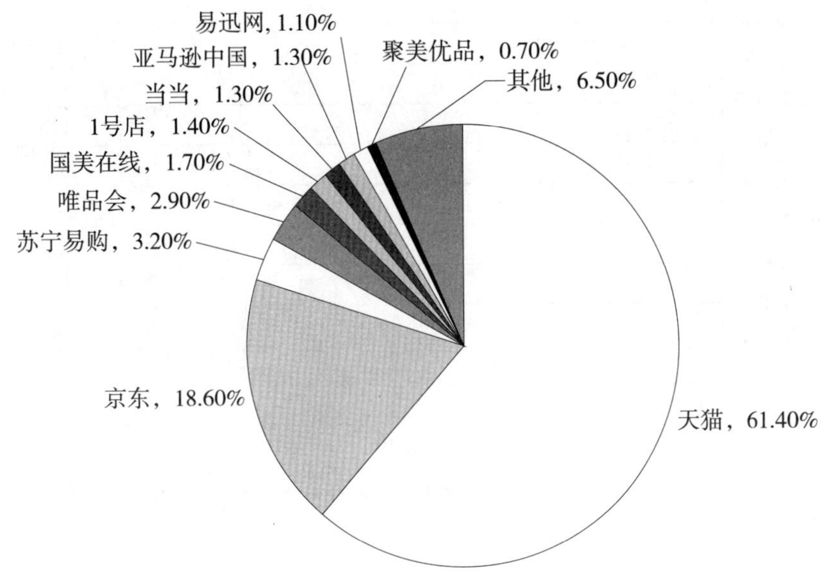

图4 2014年中国B2C购物网站交易规模市场份额

注：根据艾瑞咨询公开资料整理。

元，年增长率达239.3%，远高于中国网络购物整体增速。据艾瑞咨询预测，未来几年中国移动购物市场仍将继续保持较快增长，2016年将超过PC端网购交易占比，成为中国网民网购的重要选择；2018年移动购物市场交易规模将超过4万亿元。在2014年移动购物市场的企业份额中，阿里无线一家独大，占比86.2%，其无线端通过"淘宝+天猫"提供平台服务，在由交易入口向无边界生活圈转型。京东方面则联手腾讯，以手机客户端、微信购物、手机QQ购物、微店等全面布局移动端。唯品会、苏宁易购、聚美优品、1号店、国美在线、亚马逊、当当、买卖宝等也纷纷发力移动端，市场竞争较激烈。如图5所示。

二、2014年电子商务物流发展回顾

（一）京东自建物流模式得到资本市场认可

2014年5月，京东商城成功登录美国纳斯达克市场，其拥有的庞大自建物流网络基础成为上市成功的重要亮点。过去几年，京东投入巨资，建立了一套完整的覆盖全国的物流仓储配送体系。截至2014年9月30日，京东建立了118个仓库，总面积约为230万平方米。同时，还在全国1855个行政区县拥有2045个配送站和1045个自提点、自提柜。强大的物流基础网络优势支撑着京东独树一帜的"仓配一体"的电商物流运作模式，其核心理念是减少物品流动，使货物离消费者更近，降低搬运次数，提升整个产业链效率。根据京东公

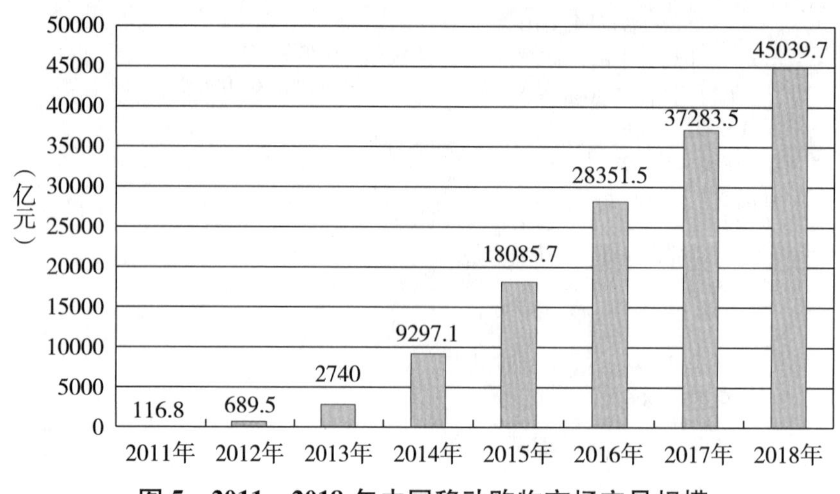

图5　2011—2018年中国移动购物市场交易规模

注：根据艾瑞咨询公开资料整理。

开的IPO数据显示，2013年，京东年度成交总额GMV为1255亿元人民币，总体运营费用占营业收入的10.3%，其中，物流占比为5.8%；库存周转天数为32天，远低于其他电商库存周转70～90天的水平。

其他电商企业的自建物流脚步也进一步加快。苏宁易购累计建成并投入使用的物流基地达到24个。当当网已在全国11个城市开设了20间仓库，总面积超过42万平方米。亚马逊目前在全国有15个运营中心，总运营面积超过70万平方米。唯品会宣布将在全国建立至少4个面积在1000亩以上的物流园，建立密集的仓储基地，整合调配资源，打通电商上下游，提升用户体验。此外，1号店、易迅等电商企业纷纷加快在全国布局物流基础网络。

（二）菜鸟网络对电商物流领域产生重要影响

2014年，菜鸟网络的"中国智能骨干网"——以"地网"为载体，以仓聚货、聚人、聚产业，用"数据"驱动的云供应链服务的协同平台的战略格局日益清晰。

2014年"双十一"期间，"天网"预警雷达数据驱动的云供应链平台发挥社会化物流的数据协同，对617个一级分拨中心、10000条国内干线、50000个末端网点进行事前预测、事中监控、事后统计，体现了大数据应用对智慧物流行业的决策支持。作为"天网"产品的电子面单于2014年5月上线试运营。该电子面单建立了行业统一的标准格式，推动了快递物流行业的信息化，赋能快递合作伙伴，最终提升商家的仓内运作效率。另外，菜鸟网络增强了对快递企业的控制力。在其信息系统与菜鸟网络全面对接后，快递企业的用户信息以及快递总部与网点间结算的关键信息亦将被菜鸟网络所掌控，这样一来难免会出现快递企业过度依赖菜鸟网络的局面，同时冲击加盟制企业建立在传统面单基础上的管控体制，削弱总部对网点的影响力。

“地网”的建设也在紧锣密鼓进行之中。根据菜鸟的战略布局，希望通过5～8年的时间，建立一张支撑日均300亿元网络零售额的智能骨干网络，加速在全国铺设自建仓库网络，形成一套开放共享的社会化仓储设施网络。“地网”已在全国14个核心骨干节点城市完成布局，预计于2016年年底交付150万平方米。

“人网”以菜鸟驿站的形式实现末千米基础设施的覆盖，目前已在全国26个省、101个市、494个县共签约18000个实体站点，日均单量在20万单。

毫无疑问，菜鸟网络整合了海内外大量物流服务资源，成为电商生态圈的重要组成部分，尤其是“天网+地网+人网”的结合给电商物流的运作和服务模式带来了更多的想象空间，被互联网深深影响的电商物流行业正在遭遇一场巨大的“变革”。

（三）O2O升温，物流迎来新挑战

O2O模式正在成为线下企业电商化的发展趋势。自从2013年开启实体门店互联网化进程后，苏宁推动线上线下融合的O2O模式在2014年上半年初显成效，遍布全国1600家苏宁实体门店都成为其物流配送网点，为线上销售平台提供落地化的本地服务，成为最新推出“急速达”服务强有力的支撑基础。2014年7月初，1号店在上海300个“全家便利店”开通订单包裹自提服务。天猫、京东等电商在社区的布局则更早，O2O脚步加快。

此外，非电商企业也在切入电商领域。2014年5月，顺丰快递在社区开“嘿客”，试水O2O，抢占社区资源。第三方支付平台“拉卡拉”也进军社区电商O2O，以社区为核心，“开店宝”为终端载体，连接供货源与社区，消费者通过“开店宝”完成选购、支付和收货流程。未来，拉卡拉将自建区域仓、中心店，以“前店后仓”的形式运营，形成“前端交易+后端仓储+落地配送”的全渠道构架。邮乐网作为中国邮政旗下的电商平台，其策略是通过O2O模式让网点成为电商落地点。一方面，这会形成“活动推动+村邮站代购+目录营销+投递配送”的工业品下乡模式；另一方面，此举亦在尝试“农产品加工企业+邮政网点+邮乐网”“农户+村邮站+邮乐网”的农产品进城模式。

物流是与客户直接接触的环节，是电商体验的直接渠道，也是O2O模式实现的重要因素。电商企业正在从线上竞争的“红海”转向线下“蓝海”竞争，而线上线下渠道全面打通所形成的物流网络覆盖和服务将成为竞争胜出的关键。随着O2O的真正发力，电商物流企业为适应客户新的服务要求，其模

式将出现创新性变革，具有较大的发展空间。

（四）跨境电商成行业热点，物流服务有待升级

跨境电商成为市场热点之一。据商务部统计数据显示，2013 年中国跨境电子商务交易额突破 3.1 万亿元，到 2016 年将增至 6.5 万亿元，年均增速接近 30%。蓬勃增长的市场为跨境电商提供了无限的发展空间，跨境电商物流迎来发展契机，物流服务转型升级势在必行。

政策红利刺激不断。在进出口稳中有升的大环境下，随着国家对跨境电商政策支持力度的加大，跨境电商成为我国对外贸易的新增长点。近年以来，广州、杭州、郑州、深圳、哈尔滨、长春等地先后获批“国家跨境电子商务试点城市”，试点城市将通过“规范贸易制度、制定贸易标准、强化在线支付、完善跨境物流、电商出口退税”五个方面给予政策支持。流程监管创新，通关便利化加速跨境电商的发展。全国首个统一版海关总署跨境电商通关服务平台于 2014 年 7 月 1 日在广东东莞正式上线运营。7 月 29 日，海关总署“56 号文”“57 号文”相继出台，通过电子商务交易平台实现跨境交易的企业和个人接受海关监管，推广“清单核放、汇总申报”的便利模式，解决了跨境电商货品以个人物品通过行邮的方式出境所存在的难以快速通关、结汇、退税难等问题。

海外仓成趋势。海外仓的广泛使用将改变跨境电商零售出口产业的物流生态，能够实现本地发货，加快商品配送速度，提升商品的销售速度。国内企业加快海外仓储布点和国际业务的布局。万邑通在英国和德国先后开通“海外仓”；出口易、递四方等物流服务商也大力建设海外仓储系统，不断上线新产品。跨境电商的迅速崛起也对跨国快递和物流企业提出了新的要求，国内快递企业也纷纷“出海”发展国际业务。依托邮政渠道，EMS 可以直达全球 60 多个国家；顺丰速运针对境外电商推出“全球顺”服务；申通快递先后进军俄罗斯、荷兰市场。

跨境电商物流出现多种模式共同发展的多元化业态。由于跨境电商单笔订单的商品数量较少、体积较小，所以在线外贸卖家向海外买家发货一般通过国际快递或国际外贸小包两种方式。由于邮政包裹配送时间长、包裹无法全程追踪、清关障碍等弊端明显，这不仅极大地考验海外用户耐心，也严重制约了跨境电商的进一步发展。随着“备货”模式兴起，通过仓储前置，传统集装箱海运的方式将得到青睐。天猫国际和六大跨境电商试点合作，依托港口，批量海运空运到保税区的模式，降低物流成本。同时，传统的快递和物流企业也开始做一些延伸布局，加大对保税仓、第三方转运等业务。跨境物流正在从单一的邮政包裹演变为“邮政包裹为主，其他模式并存”的多元化业态。

（五）电商物流差异化服务成竞争焦点

"送装一体化"服务成电商服务新的标杆。日日顺物流充分发挥"四网融合"（虚网、营销网、物流网和服务网）的优势，提出为用户提供24小时限时达、送装同步等差异化物流服务方案，实现送货、安装同步上门服务，解决了家电等大件商品电子商务"最后一公里"的难题，大大提升了客户的购物体验，专业化服务能力成为企业重要竞争优势。

随着电商渠道下沉，物流服务网络向三线、四线城市扩张。随着一线、二线城市市场日趋饱和，三线、四线城市和中西部地区成为电商发展新市场。京东2014年大力将渠道向三到六级的小县城渗透，目前已覆盖全国90%以上的县城区域。菜鸟网络联合日日顺物流，在中国2800多个县建立了物流配送站，布局了17000多家服务商，解决了三线、四级市场的配送难题。随着互联网和移动互联网的发展，二线、三线城市、县级城市的经济产业群也开始陆续拥抱电子商务，产业群基地互联网化成必然趋势，三到六线城市的物流需求激增，这对电商物流服务从深度、广度和速度等方面提出了更高的要求。

此外，电商物流竞争也日趋白热化，并购重组事件不断。错失了B2C模式快速发展时期，已掉出快递业第一梯队的宅急送引入复星投资，借此做出重大战略调整，提出"BBC模式"，即仓配一体化，定位企业客户，瞄准代收货款、跨境电商业务。在与凡客完成资产剥离后，国内较早开展电子商务配送业务的快递公司如风达在2014年6月30日宣布被中信产业基金全资控股的天地华宇集团收购，将作为天地华宇旗下的快递品牌独立运营。多起并购事件说明，电商竞争加剧了快递企业间的竞争激烈程度，中小快递如果没有充足的资本和网络支撑，很难在竞争中胜出。

三、2015年电商物流发展展望

2015年的全国人大三次会议上，国务院总理在政府工作报告中首次提出"互联网+"行动计划，指出"制定'互联网+'行动计划，推动移动互联网、云计算、大数据、物联网等与现代制造业结合，促进电子商务、工业互联网和互联网金融健康发展，引导互联网企业拓展国际业务"，这是首次将互联网建设上升到国家层面。几天后，李克强总理在"两会"闭幕后的中外记者见面会上，更是说道："我很愿意为网购、快递和带动的电子商务等新业态做广告。因为它极大地带动了就业，创造了就业的岗位，而且刺激了消费，人们在网上消费往往热情比较高。"高层领导对电子商务、网络购物、快递等新业态的重视为电商物流的发展营造了良好的政治环境。

2015年，我国电子商务市场仍将保持较高的增长速度，电商物流在此“风口”上也将呈现以下趋势。

大数据应用使电商企业与物流行业之间形成联动机制，“互联网+”与物流发生化学反应，互联网使物流更“聪明”，大幅提高物流效率，降低物流成本。同时，物流智能化趋势在电商领域越来越明显，亚马逊在美国已经推出出租车顺路送货平台；在运输环节，UPS、Google、DHL和国内的顺丰都自行开发了载货无人机，德国政府已经批准进入市场应用；在仓储环节，亚马逊的KIVA拣货机器人标志着电商仓储管理已经进入新时代；各国配送机器人项目也在研发中。

电商企业“向下走”的农村战略给三四线城市、农村消费带来巨大变化，扩大了物流覆盖半径和纵深。电子商务缩小了城乡差距，这使得生产、消费、物流的改变构筑了新的商业流通体系。

电商物流市场旺盛的需求成为吸引新加入者的重要动力。在此背景下，电商物流领域将进一步优胜劣汰，个性化、专业化发展将成趋势，差异化物流服务如预约定时服务、自提服务、退换货服务、售后服务等将成为行业新热点。

（中物联电商物流与快递分会　万莹）

2014 年跨境电子商务物流发展回顾与 2015 年展望

一、2014 年电子商务物流发展回顾

（一）国家支持电子商务物流发展

近年来，国家关于跨境电子商务的利好政策持续发酵。2013 年 7 月，国务院常务会议制定促外贸“国六条”，明确积极扩大商品进口，增加进口贴息资金规模。这为国内电子商务平台发展进口业务提供了契机；2013 年 8 月初，国务院发布《促进信息消费扩大内需的若干意见》，提出挖掘消费潜力、增强供给能力、激发市场活力、改善消费环境等要求；2013 年 8 月底，国务院办公厅转发商务部等部门《关于实施支持跨境电子商务零售出口有关政策意见的通知》，即国家支持跨境电商产业发展的“国六条”正式出台。该通知在上海、重庆、杭州、宁波、郑州 5 个城市试点跨境贸易电子商务服务，并从 2013 年 10 月 1 日起向全国有条件的地区推开实施；2013 年 9 月底，第二批国家电子商务示范城市创建工作启动；2013 年 11 月底，商务部发布《关于促进电子商务应用的实施意见》；2014 年 1 月，财政部、国税总局联合发布《关于跨境电子商务零售出口税收政策的通知》，明确跨境电子商务零售出口有关的税收优惠政策；2014 年 5 月，国务院发布《关于支持外贸稳定增长的若干意见》，提出进一步加强进口，出台跨境电子商务贸易便利化措施等。

政策春风下，地方政府主导的跨境电商细则也在逐步落地。2014 年 9 月 9 日，深圳跨境贸易电子商务进口试点正式在前海启动，标志着前海在跨境电商领域进出口双向通道的全流程开通。之前，上海“跨境通”依托于上海自贸区，吸引了诸多品牌入驻；杭州的节奏是“出口先行”；“保税进口”则成为宁波“跨境购”的主要运作模式；河南本土首家新型跨境贸易电商平台“E 贸易”主要依托中部物流枢纽。此外，各地还纷纷申报跨境电商试点城市，建起跨境电商产业园。

2014 年 12 月全国首个省级跨境电商政策出台：“浙江省跨境电子商务实施方案”。支持对象如下：一是自建跨境电子商务销售平台的电子商务出口企业（以下简称“自建平台企业”）；二是利用第三方跨境电子商务平台开展电子商

务出口的企业（含个体商户，以下简称“电商应用企业”）；三是为电商应用企业提供交易服务、物流仓储、报关、检验检疫、退税等专项服务或综合服务的跨境电子商务第三方平台或服务企业（以下简称“电商服务企业”）。

（二）跨境电商物流发展迅猛

近年来，跨境电子商务（Cross – border Electronic Commerce）在我国发展非常迅速，也进入了人们的生活。所谓跨境电子商务，是电子商务应用过程中一种比较高级的形式，是指在不同的国别或地区间交易双方通过互联网形式及其相关信息平台实现双方交易。跨境电子商务同样有 B2C、B2B、C2C 等电子商务形式，其中主要是 B2C 和 B2B。国际贸易进出口环节中一般要涉及国际结算、进出口通关、国际运输、物流保险等，同时还需要考虑其安全性及风险控制等方面，这使得跨境电子商务和境内电子商务有所区别。对于国内的中小企业来说，跨境电子商务更是备受推崇，因为其一方面可以增加更多的海外市场机会，另一方面会使国内市场变得更加丰富。互联网技术的广泛应用以及外贸业态的不断发展，让跨境电子商务成为我国企业寻求海外以及国内贸易新一轮的商机。

企业方面，除了亚马逊、天猫国际、1 号店，对“跨境电子商务”感兴趣的，还有跨行业的竞争者。如顺丰旗下的海淘网站“海购丰运”正式上线，为“海淘”用户提供转运服务，并通过“什么值得买”海淘专区向消费者提供“海淘”导购服务。新生的“跨境电商”市场就像一个能量巨大的旋涡，吸引着各方市场力量的参与。

从表 1 中可以看出，我国的跨境电子商务规模是十分庞大的，并且交易数额在不断攀升，这意味着跨境电子商务物流的需求也在攀升。因此，电子商务全球化与跨境网购的流行加速了全球经济一体化，使物流产业的发展进入全球集约化，也给电子商务企业带来了全新的物流配送问题。

跨境电子商务的快速发展给物流带来了潜在的巨大市场，但是，在跨境电子商务物流方面，我国的第三方物流企业还不能提供专业化、个性化的物流服务。另外，跨境电子商务企业本身对物流的运作也还没有进入专业轨道，并没有探索出一种适合跨境电子商务的物流运作模式。

表 1　我国跨境电子商务交易规模情况

年份	交易规模（万亿元）	交易规模增长率（%）	交易规模占进出口比例（%）
2008	0.8	—	4.6

续　表

年份	交易规模（万亿元）	交易规模增长率（%）	交易规模占进出口比例（%）
2009	0.9	9.2	6.0
2010	1.3	41.0	6.3
2011	1.8	40.1	7.5
2012	2.3	32	9.6
2013	3.1	31.3	12.1
2014	4.0	30.6	14.5

数据来源：《2008—2014 年中国进出口贸易及跨境电商市场交易规模》（艾瑞咨询集团发布）。

跨境电子商务物流作为物流产业中的新兴势力，正以其高速增长的发展趋势引领当下物流潮流，但是跨境电子商务物流在物流学界还是一个比较新的话题，也是一个值得深入思考的话题。国内学者近几年对此研究颇为火热，主要观点如表 2 所示。

表 2　　国内关于跨境电子商务物流的主要观点

作者	发表时间	主要观点
孟祥铭、汤倩慧	2014 年	跨境贸易电子商务健康发展的对策主要是提高通关效率、解决退税问题、完善跨境电子支付监管与外汇管理体系、建立新型跨境第三方物流企业模式
曹淑艳、李振欣	2013 年	发展跨境电子商务第三方物流
王永兴	2013 年	改善跨境电子商务物流服务能力
沐潮	2013 年	优化海关对跨境电子商务物流的监管
侯喆	2012 年	创建基于供应链思想的 B2C 电子商务物流体系
刘娟	2012 年	跨境电子商务物流服务创新

然而，目前相关研究多着重于从消费者角度探讨电子商务服务品质的重要性与电子商务从业者在单一国家内的递送方式，虽然最近几年有一些学者从宏观角度去研究跨境电子商务物流，但是鲜有从电子商务企业角度进行订单履行或者运作模式的研究。因此本研究以电子商务企业的跨境物流配送系统为切入点，配合国际物流企业以及国际快递企业提供的配送模式，来探讨可为电子商务企业在跨境网络购物趋势下提供服务品质较佳的物流运作模式。

（三）目前我国跨境电子商务下物流发展现状存在的不足

1. 我国跨境电子商务物流政策支持不足

跨境电子商务在中国的起步较晚，但是发展速度惊人，如最具代表性的阿里巴巴。尽管我国还没有出台扶持相关企业的政策，但由于跨境电子商务是我国内外贸新的增长点，越来越受到各方关注。2013 年，商务部出台了《关于实施支持跨境电子商务零售出口有关政策意见的通知》，对零售出口企业在海关、检验检疫、税收等方面遇到的问题提出了具有针对性的措施。这一政策无疑打破了出口的寒冰，对所有零售出口企业来说都是可遇而不可求的机会。

另外，国家积极建立基础信息标准和接口的规范准则，目前有一小部分地区实现了海关、国检、国税、外管等部门与电子商务企业、物流配套企业之间进行标准化信息流通。与发达国家相比，我国的政策支持尤为不足，这在某种程度上阻碍了跨境电子商务企业以及物流企业的快速发展。

2. 当前国际物流发展速度与跨境电子商务需求不匹配

我国跨境电子商务发展速度是十分惊人的，2011 年交易额为 1.6 万亿元左右，2012 年为 2 万亿元，2013 年为 3.1 万亿元左右。2014 年为 4 万亿元左右。其贸易规模增长速度较快。仅浙江省义乌市，2014 年上半年跨境快递日均出货量达到了 20 万票。与之相对应的物流企业，从事跨境电子商务的比较少，大多数是由国际快递公司完成物流配送服务。如此大的物流量，仅仅靠国际快递企业是远远不够的，尤其是在购物旺季，经常会出现快件积压、爆仓等现象，这给跨境电商的发展带来了巨大障碍。

3. 我国物流基础设施不完善

物流在我国出现的时间比较晚，整个的物流环境相对比较差，各种配套设施也有待完善。对于不同运输方式连接的交通枢纽也是比较少的。由于跨境电子商务涉及跨国境的仓储、配送、运输、报关、核税等一系列问题，为了使运输过程损耗尽可能减少，速度更快、成本更低，需要建立合理高效的物流体系，并且需要更先进和完备的物流设施。然而，目前国际快递的运输时间长、手续多、成本高违背了跨境物流电子商务快捷和便利的特点，严重制约了跨境电子商务的进一步发展。

4. 缺乏第三方物流提供专业化服务

我国第三方物流企业数量较多，但是大型的、专业化程度较高的第三方物流企业比较少，例如宝供物流、德邦物流等。大多数物流企业提供的是国内物流服务，即使是为电子商务服务都是为国内电子商务服务的。对于国际快递服务，也主要是以普通快递的形式，而没有专门为跨境电子商务企业提供全方位的专业物流服务。目前在我国，为跨境电子商务提供国际快递服务的也只有联合包裹服务公司（United Parcel Service，Inc.，UPS）、联邦快递公司（FedEx，Inc.，FDX）、敦豪速递公司（DHL）、中国邮政速递物流公司（EMS）、顺丰速运公司等。专业化的第三方物流服务是十分必要的，这有利于推动我国跨境电子商务更好地发展，并在国际市场竞争中处于有利地位。

二、2015 年跨境电子商务物流发展展望

（一）我国跨境电商物流市场潜力巨大

艾瑞统计数据显示，2014 年中国跨境电商物流进出口交易额为 4 万亿元，同比增长 30.6%，但相较于中国整体进出口贸易市场规模，占比仍处于较低水平，仅占 14.5%。艾瑞预测，中国跨境电商交易规模将持续高速发展，在中国进出口贸易中的比重将会越来越大，到 2015 年将会达到 16.9%，跨境电商交易规模达 5.2 万亿元。

从国际市场来看，一是经济全球化仍将深入发展，贸易自由化和区域经济一体化继续推进，双边和区域自由贸易协定数量不断增加，国际产业转移从加工制造环节向产业链两端延伸，为中国延伸产业链条、优化要素配置带来机遇；二是新兴经济体和发展中国家工业化、城镇化进程加快，经济有望保持较快发展，为中国开拓市场提供新的支撑；三是科技创新孕育新兴产业，加快产业升级，促进国际分工深化，推动产业内贸易发展，扩大国际贸易空间。

从国内市场来看，一是中国产业体系日益完备，基础设施明显改善，劳动力素质不断提高，科技创新日益深化，出口产业综合优势进一步增强；二是产业结构升级、城镇化和人民生活水平提高，带动各类生产资料和生活资料进口增长；三是战略性新兴产业快速发展带动相关产品和技术的进出口，专业市场开展对外贸易，将为外贸增长提供新的增长点；四是国家加快中西部开发，提升沿边开放水平，中西部地区和沿边地区贸易投资环境进一步改善，吸引投资和产业转移能力增强，进出口具备了更快发展的基础和条件。

（二）我国未来发展跨境电子商务物流的对策

1. 健全我国跨境电子商务物流的法律机制及政策

跨境电子商务作为一个新兴行业，相关法律法规还比较欠缺。良好的法制环境有利于促进跨境电子商务及其物流的发展，也有利于提高跨境电子商务物流的运作效率。目前，我国还没有对跨境电子商务物流的操作规范、通关程序、税收、仓储管理、相关企业管理办法等进行法制化。随着跨境电子商务的快速发展，法律法规是不可缺少的一部分，无论是对跨境电子商务企业及其相关物流企业还是对于消费者，都会有一定的保障作用，从而使这一新兴市场、新兴行业能够快速健康发展。

在我国，对于跨境电子商务还没有太多的政策支持。政府相关部门应该尽快推出新的政策来支持其发展，如在资金支持、程序简化、税收优惠等方面对

跨境电子商务物流进行扶持。例如，2013 年 9 月，由商务部会同国家发展和改革委员会、中国人民银行、海关总署等 9 个部门共同研究制定的《关于实施支持跨境电子商务零售出口有关政策意见》，其中将跨境电子商务零售出口纳入海关的出口贸易统计，提出了对跨境电子商务零售出口的支持政策以及出口检验、收结汇等具体措施。尽管如此，跨境电子商务物流的政策支持力度与发达国家相比还远远不够。

2. 电商企业的物流战略联盟

从电子商务企业的角度出发，单独自营物流会增加企业的物流成本，这对于电商企业来说是难以抉择的物流运作模式。但是，从规模经济效益来讲，跨境电子商务企业之间可以进行物流合作，建立物流战略联盟。由多个跨境电商企业分别在国内外成立物流仓储中心，联盟的会员可以将货物运输至国内物流中心储存，海外买家下单后，物流中心根据发货指令发货至海外配送中心，海外配送中心根据送货指令将货物配送至海外买家（如下图所示），反之亦然。

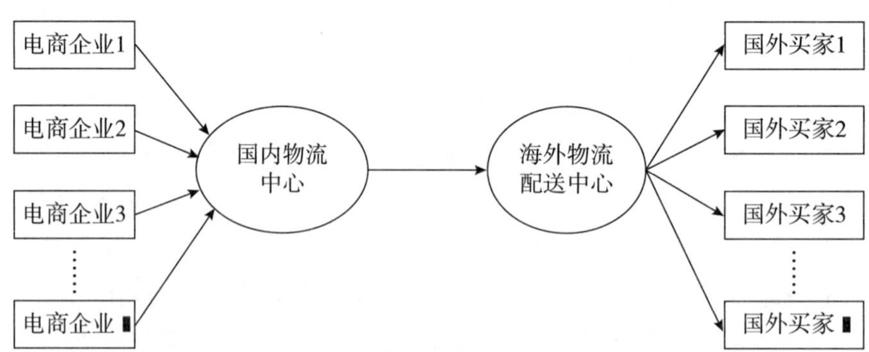

物流战略联盟正向运作示意图

3. 第三方物流企业提供专业化的物流服务

第三方物流企业作为专业的物流服务方，为其客户提供的是全方位、高品质的物流服务。在我国，第三方物流普遍存在，但是为跨境电子商务提供专业化物流服务的第三方物流企业几乎没有。跨境电子商务不同于国内的电子商务，是跨国界的交易，其交易流程、物流运作是比较复杂的。在整个过程中，涉及了国际运输、报关、报检等程序，这位跨境电子商务的运作带来了不便，如果有专业化的物流服务方，为其解决运输、仓储、海外配送、报关、报检等工作，不但提高了物流运作效率，也为跨境电子商务降低成本，提高了客户购物满意度。

4. 选择海外仓储

海外仓储是基于电商企业的实际需求出发的，主要有自营和外包仓储两种形式。外包仓储是目前跨境电子商务企业应用的物流运作方式，通过海外仓储专业供应商为其提供海外仓储服务，并为其配送商品服务完成交易。从成本方面考虑，对于跨境电商企业来说是较为符合其需求的一种物流运作方式。

对于企业规模相对较大的跨境电商来说，不仅需要从成本方面考虑，还需要从客户体验、客户满意度、市场机会、商品管理、库存控制等方面考虑，可以选择自营海外仓储的方式进行运作。其优势在于提高客户满意度、提高市场的相应速度、有效的降低库存等。所以对于 B2C 和 B2B 跨境电子商务企业来说，选择自营仓储是一种有效的物流运作方式。

（三）结语

跨境电子商务在我国出现的时间虽短，但其发展速度及其交易规模十分惊人。电子商务的发展离不开物流，物流发展也需要电子商务的推动，二者是相辅相成的。在我国，现代物流业仍处于发展阶段，各种基础设施、设备尚未完善，对于跨境电子商务物流更是缺乏专业化的操作，仅在物流领域进行，导致跨境电子商务的物流成本高、物流效率低。

面对快速发展的跨境电子商务，宏观领域要靠政府层面政策进行引导，微观层面上只有从专业化物流运作入手，才能从根本上解决跨境电子商务物流的基本问题，不断探索跨境电子商务物流运作的新模式，高效率、高质量、低成本地运作跨境电子商务物流，为跨境电子商务快速发展提供良好的支持和保障。

（吉林大学珠海学院　张滨）

第三章

物流技术与装备

2014 年物流装备行业发展回顾与 2015 年展望

一、2014 年物流装备行业发展回顾

1. 物流装备行业发展环境

2014 年中国面对复杂多变的国际环境和艰巨繁重的国内发展任务，国民经济在新常态下平稳运行，结构调整出现积极变化，发展质量不断提高，民生事业持续改善。2014 年全年国内生产总值 636463 亿元，比上年增长 7.4%。工业生产平稳增长。全年全部工业增加值 227991 亿元，比上年增长 7.0%。规模以上工业增加值增长 8.3%。其中制造业增长 9.4%。全年社会消费品零售总额 262394 亿元，比上年增长 12.0%，扣除价格因素，实际增长 10.9%。与物流装备行业相关的制造业、商贸业增长速度都高于全年 GDP 增速。

从固定资产投资看，2014 年全年全社会固定资产投资 512761 亿元，比上年增长 15.3%。从交通运输角度看，2014 年全年货物运输总量 439 亿吨，比上年增长 7.1%。货物运输周转量 184619 亿吨千米，增长 9.9%。全年规模以上港口完成货物吞吐量 111.6 亿吨，比上年增长 4.8%，其中外贸货物吞吐量 35.2 亿吨，增长 5.9%。规模以上港口集装箱吞吐量 20093 万标准箱，增长 6.1%。与物流行业密切相关的固定资产投资、货物运输量、货物周转量增长趋缓，进入中高速增长阶段。

2014 年宏观经济运行对物流装备行业的影响体现在：经济增长速度下滑对一般的物流装备产品，如叉车、托盘等的市场需求带来较大影响，这类普通物

流装备产品开始进入总需求波动、产能过剩的低速增长阶段。具体表现在：叉车、托盘等装备产品市场增长乏力，增长速度由原来30%左右的高速增长下降到仅仅一位数的增长，增速下滑幅度较大。如叉车在经历了多年高速增长后，自2011年以来，已经连续三年产量在30万台左右徘徊，托盘预计2014年也仅仅增长9%左右，增长速度大幅下降。

2014年对物流装备行业影响较大的还有行业政策环境。国务院正式通过《物流业发展中长期规划（2014—2020年）》（以下简称《中长期规划》），把物流业定位于支撑国民经济发展的基础性、战略性产业。规划要求，到2020年，基本建立布局合理、技术先进、便捷高效、绿色环保、安全有序的现代物流服务体系，明确了中长期发展的战略目标。规划提出三大发展重点、七项主要任务、十二项重点工程和九项保障措施，抓住了制约物流业发展的关键问题，明确了我国物流业“新常态”下健康发展的顶层设计。国家对物流行业的支持和重视将带动物流装备行业的快速发展。

当前，对物流装备行业影响较大的还是经济结构的调整。随着制造业产业结构调整和劳动力成本上升，企业纷纷改造物流系统，用机械化取代人力，用自动化提升效率成为趋势，极大带动了机械化、自动化和智能化物流装备的高速增长。2014年物流系统的自动化与机械化设备需求大幅增长，冷链物流技术装备、自动化立体库系统等进入快速发展阶段。尤其是适合电子商务物流的快速分拣系统，智能终端自提货柜系统，智慧物流信息系统等发展较快。现代信息技术革命不仅对电子商务领域产生了巨大影响，也将对现代物流装备行业带来巨大变革，目前不仅货运车联网系统和快递业的智慧物流系统发展日新月异，大数据对现代物流体系的优化与变革已经引起亚马逊、谷歌等信息产业巨头的关注，纷纷进入物流领域。最先进的无人机配送技术已经成为UPS、顺丰速运的关注焦点，开始进行技术测试和尝试性的推广应用。现代物流业已经由人搬肩扛快速进入自动化与信息化阶段。

2. 物流业对物流装备行业的影响

2014年全年社会物流总额将超过210万亿元，可比增长8%左右；物流业增加值超过3.4万亿元，可比增长9%左右，两项指标增速与上年相比均小幅放缓，但仍高于同期GDP增速，处于中高速增长区间。社会物流总费用将超过9.7万亿元，同比增长8%左右，增速延续小幅回落态势。社会物流总费用与GDP的比率为17%左右，物流业发展的质量和效率有所提升。中国物流景气指数全年处于55%上下区间波动，物流运行总体趋稳。中国物流业总量发展平稳，需求结构与发展环境变化巨大，对物流行业的技术改造和装备升级带来了巨大影响。主要体现在：电商物流仓储建设加快；资本市场推动带来了物流信息化模式创新，促进了物流企业对新技术与新装备需求；物流细分市场的快速增长带动了医药、商贸、食品、家电、电子等行业对物流装备的需求。

2014 年，第三方物流企业也纷纷加大技术改造和装备升级力度。城市配送企业更加关注配送效率提升和配送中心建设，关注物流标准化、信息化的发展，对新型叉车、货架、分拣输送设备、自动化立体仓库等现代化物流装备的需求快速提升；托盘租赁共用循环使用系统得到国家及政府部门关注，在快速消费品领域获得较快发展。

3. 物流装备行业发展情况

根据全世界先进国家的经济发展规律，很多国家在经济进入经济转型升级阶段的时候，往往是物流装备大发展的时期。国际经验表明，人工、土地等成本不断上升，经济增速开始放缓，靠降低成本或扩大销售难以获得利润，物流业“第三利润源”的战略地位将凸显。产业升级将直接带动物流机械化、自动化大发展，带动物流装备市场需求快速增加。可以说，经济增长进入“新常态”，物流装备行业将进入“非常态”。主要有以下三大原因：

一是大变革：物流装备行业已经进入大变革时代。这首先是由电子商务快速发展引起的，电子商务的发展改变了现代物流的系统结构，物流服务向消费者转变，带动了物流技术与装备的变革。其次，随着物联网、大数据、云计算和移动互联网的发展，推动了以“产业互联网”为特征的工业 4.0 革命，也必然带来物流互联网的大变革。

二是大发展：经济转型带来了劳动力成本、土地成本、仓储租金成本的大幅上升，带来了企业对物流机械化、自动化的需求，促进了高架立体库、全自动立体库、自动分拣系统的设施建设，直接带动了物流装备行业的大发展。目前中国物流装备市场已经超越日本、美国及欧洲各国，成为世界上最大、最具活力的市场。

三是大创新：信息技术的发展推动了以“产业互联网”为特征的新工业革命，其主要体现是“智慧制造、智慧工厂的信息物理系统”，也被德国概括为工业 4.0。工业 4.0 带来的物流技术创新主要体现在以物联网、云计算、大数据、移动互联网应用的物流信息系统创新和以自动化、智能化、绿色环保为方向的装备创新。

十年前，物流装备行业高速发展的主要驱动力是以叉车、托盘、货架等为主体的普通物流装备。自 2013 年以来，市场驱动主体已经升级换档为：自动化物流设备、智能穿梭车、智能机器人、输送分拣系统、感知与识别系统等技术与装备。2014 年这一趋势更为明显。初步分析，2014 年中国物流装备行业整体发展好于预期，整体增长速度接近 20%，是经济增速的 2.5 倍以上。

（1）叉车行业

据中国工程机械工业协会工业车辆分会数据统计显示，2014 年全年销售机动工业车辆359622台，比上年增长9%，全年出口机动工业车辆96947台，比上年增长7%，其中仓储类叉车有20%以上的增长。2014年叉车销售增长得益于国内物流大环境对叉车销售的带动作用，得益于物流企业实施机械化搬运代替人工，得益于电子商务物流的快速发展。各地区包括城乡、县镇和农村的生活资料配送需求量日益增加，带动了叉车的快速增长。

从叉车行业总体成长态势分析，叉车行业连续十多年来总体一直处于上升通道，并且实现了连续十多年接近30%的高速增长，叉车市场年销售量也从过去的不足2万台，增长到30万台左右，成为世界最大的叉车生产制造基地。2011年以来，中国叉车行业开始进入循环型上升的增长阶段，呈现出增长速度上下波动，整体产量缓慢增长的态势。2011年以来一直在30万台左右徘徊，今年产量接近36万台，创出历史新高。在世界总销量中，中国市场占有四分之一的份额，继续位列世界第一大销售市场。如图1所示。

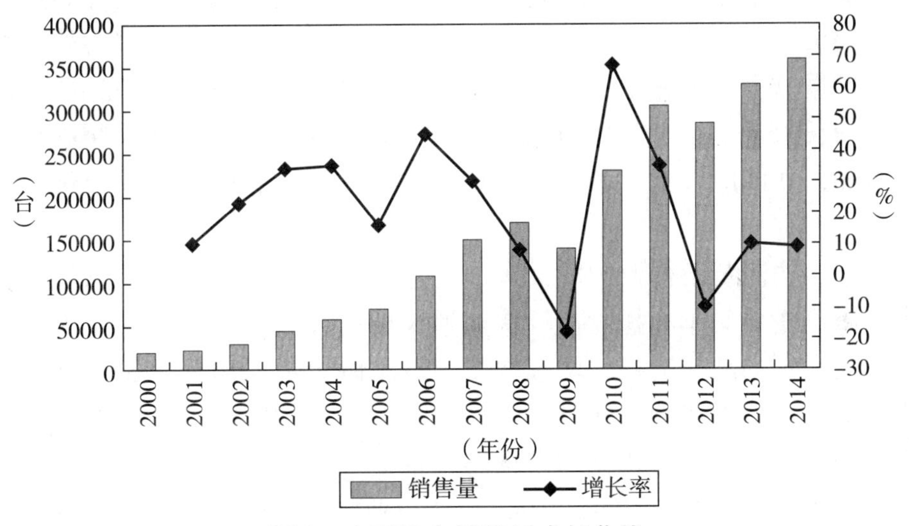

图1　中国叉车销售量成长曲线

在市场占有率方面，大企业继续保持了自己的优势与市场地位，内资企业在产量上继续保持优势，仓储叉车高速增长，增长率达到20%，仓储叉车占比与上年相比有一定的提升。

（2）托盘行业

2014年以来，托盘行业产销增长速度平稳。受石油价格大幅下调影响，塑料托盘企业市场销售开始好转。整体来看，2013年托盘产量呈现中速增长态势，年产量达到24837万片，同比增长9%左右，托盘保有量突破9亿片。木托盘行业受中国经济和环保压力影响，市场销售一般。

根据对托盘生产量增长趋势分析，托盘产量由2003年的年产3500万片增长到2013年的年产2.28亿片，增长了6.5倍左右。同期叉车产量从每年

45482 台增长到每年 30 万台左右，也增长了 6.5 倍左右，叉车和托盘保持了同步增长，目前，叉车生产增长已经趋缓，托盘年产量增长速度也将下降。根据目前趋势预测，中国托盘保有量还将保持一段时间增长，但随着每年托盘更新量的增加，托盘总产量将逐步趋稳。

在托盘标准化方面，根据调查，目前，澳大利亚标准规格托盘使用占比最高，托盘保有量中标准规格托盘占 95%；欧洲次之，标准规格托盘占总保有量 70%；美国第三，标准规格托盘占总保有量 55%；亚洲的日本和韩国标准规格托盘占托盘总保有量比例不高，日本为 35%，韩国为 26.7%。根据中国物流与采购联合会托盘专业委员会调查，中国标准规格托盘占托盘总保有量 23% 左右。

（3）货架市场

2014 年以来，随着物流自动化的快速发展，制造业对自动化立体库需求快速增长。在商贸物流领域，随着仓储业转型升级步伐加快，企业仓储投资大幅增加。货架市场需求整体上仍处于中速增长阶段，高端立体库货架处于高速增长状态。根据监测及不完全调查统计，2014 年全年预计货架出货量超过 63 亿元，同比增长 15%，其中，仓库改造及立体库建设的大型货架系统项目所占比重大幅增加，立体库（含一般立体仓库和自动化立体仓库）的货架预计占比超过 80%。

近几年，物流装备行业中的叉车、托盘、货架出现联动发展态势，普通的工业货架市场随着叉车和托盘市场快速增长而增长。但是，2011 年以来，叉车行业经过几十年的高速增长，增长幅度出现下降，进入循环增长阶段，普通工业货架的增长也趋于缓和。同时，受产业转型升级的影响，立体库货架系统的增长速度开始高于叉车与托盘的市场增长幅度。

2014 年在传统的货架需求领域，烟草行业物流配送工程建设项目进入十二五收尾阶段，市场需求增长稳定，是中高端货架市场的主力军；医药行业受新医改政策影响，医药配送中心建设步伐加快，医药企业与医药流通企业自动化立体库建设步伐加快，是货架需求的主要行业；电子商务物流领域、服装行业与快速消费品行业对货架需求也越来越多，此外机械、汽车、电子等行业增长平稳，也是货架市场主要应用行业。

（4）物流系统设备集成

2014 年仍是中国物流系统设备大发展的一年。新年伊始，很多物流系统工程项目纷纷开工，自动化立体库项目建设市场一片繁荣，据不完全统计，截至 2014 年 12 月，全国自动化立体库保有量超过 2600 多座。预计 2014 年物流系统设备集成的市场需求增速超过了 35%，年立体库建设超过 400 座以上。2000—2013 年中国物流系统市场需求增长情况如图 2 所示。

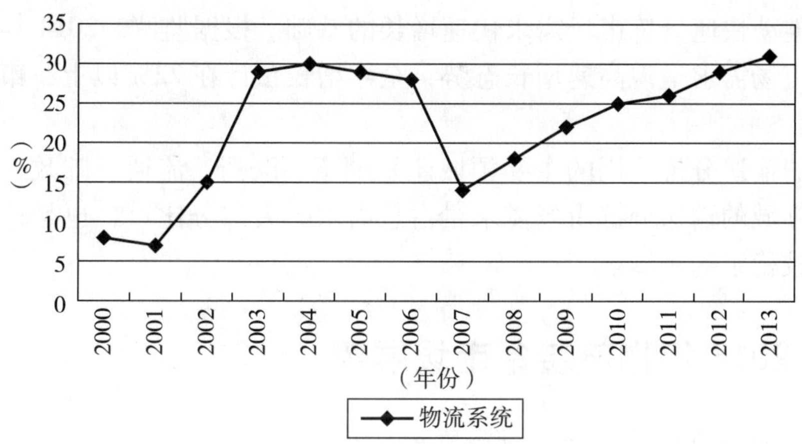

图 2　2000—2013 年中国物流系统市场需求增长分析

数据来源：中国物流技术协会信息中心。

从自动化立体库建设规模来看，目前自动化立体库建设规模越来越大，很多自动化立体库平均货位超过 1 万个，高度超过 20 米，系统越来越复杂，应用范围越来越广。

2014 年海外物流系统供应商继续加快本土化制造与生产，除核心部件外基本采用国产设备，同时物流系统供应商的设备出口也开始增加。据不完全统计，目前全国物流系统集成商约 40 家，其中核心企业 10 多家，内资企业占一半左右，核心企业能够承包物流系统工程项目，掌握自动化立体库总体规划、机械电气控制、软件系统等全面技术，拥有专属的安装制造实体。

随着中国物流系统设备市场的繁荣，很多企业不断进入这一领域，使得该领域企业越来越多，竞争越来越激烈。根据观察与分析，新进入这一领域的物流系统集成供应商主要有如下几类：一是原来的物流系统规划与咨询企业，借助于自身多年的咨询经验，随着业务发展，开始承接物流集成项目。比较有代表性的企业有伍强、兰剑等企业；二是过去建设自动化物流系统较多的企业，具有本行业经验，也开始组建队伍进入该领域。代表性的企业有在医药领域建设物流自动化较早的九州通等企业；三是过去从事货架系统生产与销售的部分企业等。

（5）输送分拣设备

2014 年是电子商务大发展的一年，电子商务配送的包裹总数量突破 140 亿件。随着电子商务物流的发展，对物流输送分拣设备的市场需求日益增长，输送分拣设备在物流系统中所占比例近年来有较大提升，市场需求增长较快。

用机械化和自动化的快速分拣技术，可以取代大量的人工分拣，同时还可以提高分拣的准确率，降低劳动成本。因此随着劳动力成本的大幅上升，极大促进了输送分拣设备行业快速发展。电子商务配送的多品种、小批量、高频次特征，是推动快速分拣市场需求快速增长的基础。根据监测，2014 年输送分拣设备行业市场需求呈现高速增长态势，全年增长预计在 22% 以上，市场规模超过 35 亿元。

传统的输送分拣应用的主要领域还是烟草、医药、流通、邮政、图书等领域，这些领域的输送分拣市场需求量占总需求的大部分比重，也是输送分拣需求增长比较稳定的领域。

二、2015 年物流装备市场展望

1. 物流装备业面临的宏观环境分析

目前，中国经济下行压力继续加大，国家经济调控力度也不断加强。春节刚过，国务院就出台了降低中小企业税费的政策，减税额度达到 600 多亿元，人民银行也不断放松银根，定向降低了部分银行的资金准备金率。2015 年是“十二五”收官之年，为了保持国民经济稳定健康发展，预计国家还将出台一系列的宏观调控政策，预计中国经济将继续围绕 7.5% 左右波动，保持在 7% 以上增长速度，不会大起大落。尤其值得关注的是中国推出的“一带一路”国家战略，这一战略实施对拉动中国西北和西南地区物流业大发展将起到极为重要的作用。

本届政府对物流业发展极为重视，习近平、李克强多次到物流企业和物流基地视察，汪洋副总理非常关注城市物流和商贸物流发展，国家领导人对现代物流业发展做出了一系列指示，极大推动了物流业发展。2015 年是全面完成“十二五”规划的收官之年，也是《中长期规划》和三年行动计划的启动之年，物流业发展面临新的机遇和挑战。

根据上述分析，2015 年中国物流技术装备行业面临的宏观经济环境是稳定的，行业政策环境是良好的，相关行业的发展环境是稳定向好的。同时，中国经济结构调整，人力成本上升，将给物流机械化和自动化带来巨大的市场机遇，电子商务物流快速发展将继续推动物流装备行业超常发展。因此，预计 2015 年，中国物流信息化与标准化将处于快速发展阶段，促进物流机械化与自动化发展；商贸物流发展和城市物流配送中心建设将带动物流仓储技术装备市场需求；总之，2015 年中国物流装备行业将面临良好的发展环境。

2. 产业物流变革促进物流装备发展

预计 2015 年中国社会物流总额将保持中速增长，干线运输将向集约化方向发展，城市配送将成为物流业关注的焦点和难点。在城市物流配送领域，随着电子商务发展，城市污染加剧和道路拥堵，城市物流将面临变革压力，一方面城市物流要面对高速增长的物流配送需求，另一方面也要控制和减少物流配送车辆进城频次。如何解决这个两难问题摆在物流行业面前。因此，预计2015年城市物流共同配送将获得快速发展，城市物流公共基础设施建设将提到规划层面，城市宅配、智能自提终端等新模式与新技术得到发展，智慧物流系统得到应用。

从产业物流角度看，随着工业革命的推进，工业4.0的快速发展，制造业将不断向智能化和自动化产业升级，因此将带动产业物流进一步发展。据预测，医药、烟草、机械、汽车、家电、服装等行业物流继续稳定增长；冷链物流、物资管理物流、快递物流、电力物流等领域物流发展迅速。这些产业的现代物流业的快速发展将推动物流装备行业的市场需求快速增长。

3. 中高端物流装备市场进入历史机遇期

进入21世纪以来，是中国物流装备行业大发展的时期。特别是2002年以后，物流装备行业整体发展速度大大超过同期GDP的增速，多年保持在30%以上。2002—2014年，叉车市场销售量由2万台左右增长到36万台左右，托盘保有量由1亿片左右增长到9亿片，工业货架年出货量由不足10亿元发展到超过63亿元的市场规模，自动化立体仓库保有量由不足1000座发展到2400座左右。

目前，中国物流装备市场上，叉车、托盘等产品总量需求即将进入饱和期，进入以更新换代为主的循环增长阶段。而自动化立体库、智能物流设备、高端物流产品、物流机器人系统、智能分拣系统、识别与感知系统等中高端物流装备将进入高速成长期，成为行业领跑者。开拓国际市场，成为中国物流装备企业的发展目标。预计中国物流装备行业发展速度将继续保持世界第一，并逐步成为世界第一大市场，预计行业发展战略机遇期还有8~10年。

4. 物流装备市场热点分析

根据产业发展规律，我们认为2015年物流装备市场热点：①物流自动化与机械化设备市场需求继续高速增长；②智能物流装备将迎来发展机遇。智能穿梭车、智能搬运机器人、智能分拣系统等市场空间广阔；物流自动化与机械化设备将通过物联网技术接入互联网，推动物流互联网发展；③标准化、模块化的物流技术是关键。商品包装、载具容器、存储设备、拣选设备、输送设备、搬运设备、分拣设备、装运设备都将走向标准化与模块化，电商包裹可循环包装技术具有发展机遇；④物流全程信息化技术大发展，信息技术成为物流装备翅膀。其中识别、跟踪、交互、定位、大数据分析、智能控制市场广阔；⑤输送分拣技术与设备市场空间巨大。自动分拣、货到人拣选、输送设备等进入快速发展阶段；⑥物流装备后市场即将进入爆发期。叉车租赁、托盘租赁、货架租赁、立体库后期改造、维护与升级等专业的后市场服务空间广阔；⑦绿色物流技术装备获得市场青睐；⑧终端配送的技术与装备高速发展。例如，智能终端货柜、可穿戴识别技术、无人机配送、车辆装卸技术、单元化包装技术等。

5. 物流装备主要产品市场预测

（1）叉车市场将在调整中前行

由于行业特性，叉车销售情况对经济发展有一定的滞后性，由于叉车市场基数比较大，国内年销售机动工业车辆已经有26万多台。预计2015年，在整个经济放缓的新常态下，国内叉车销售会经历一个小的调整期，叉车市场增长速度将有所下降，但会保持正增长。

随着经济转型和绿色物流发展，电动叉车、新能源环保型叉车将成为市场热点。2014年电动叉车市场份额明显加大，提高了三个百分点，是近年来增长最快的一年。随着市场的发展，对环保的重视以及绿色仓储与配送的开展，开发和研制电动叉车、环保型叉车日渐成为一种新产品开发趋势。

目前很多叉车企业加大了电动仓储叉车和新能源叉车产品的研究，如合力等企业研制的LNG、LPG内燃叉车，比亚迪的锂电池叉车、中力、诺力、如意等研制的电动仓储车等。在叉车的配套件方面，LNG、LPG天然气发动机、国产电动叉车电控系统、锂电池等也有国内企业开发和研制生产，并且已经给整机进行配套。随着经济发展、自动化水平提高，客户的使用需求从单纯完成搬运向智能、高效和良好使用体验转变。同时，国家对非道路移动机械排放要求更加严格，在未来低端市场为主的市场分布情况将会有所改变。预计2015年，中国叉车企业也将转型升级，中端叉车市场的竞争将会展开，中端叉车市场需求将上升。

在叉车出口方面，外资品牌叉车继续担当主力军角色。一方面，由于近年来外资企业在中国的生产能力进一步加强，产品品种类型更加丰富，一些品牌中国工厂承担了亚洲、欧洲的生产销售任务，其中，以三菱、丰田为代表的中国新工厂产能进一步释放；另一方面，国内叉车技术水平与世界知名品牌还有明显差距，需要改变国内企业对叉车仅仅只是搬运设备的传统理念，在质量、寿命、智能水平、使用体验、销售渠道及售后服务方面有所突破，如果国内企业没有实质性改善，2015年内资企业出口将面临更加严峻的考验。

此外，具有特殊用途的专用叉车将会被不断开发，例如称重叉车、专用的冷链叉车、适用于立体仓库的10米以上的高起升叉车、适用于更加严格爆炸环境的C级防爆叉车、自动导向叉车等特殊叉车将不断涌现。

（2）托盘行业产销量稳定增长

2015年全球石油市场将缓慢回升，但石油价格难以回到高位，因此塑料托盘市场仍将处于平稳回升态势。近年来，国产大型注塑加工设备开发成功，使塑料托盘生产加工设备的投入大幅下降，推动塑料托盘生产能力扩大。截至

2014 年年底，预计塑料托盘生产能力已经突破 65 万吨 3000 万片左右，预计 2015 年塑料托盘将稳步发展。

近年来，钢质托盘的使用开始普及，尤其是新结构、新工艺的平托盘抢占塑料托盘市场。国外部分专业的钢质托盘制造企业进入中国市场，带来了众多新工艺、新设计。预计 2015 年钢材价格仍将低迷，对钢托盘生产是个利好，但由于金属托盘自重大，其适用范围仍有局限，未来市场空间也不会很大。

根据有关统计，近年来纸托盘产量快速增长，在托盘年产量中所占比重快速上升。根据中国物流与采购联合会托盘专业委员会第三次托盘普查显示，托盘保有量中纸托盘比例上升较快，已经占到总量的 5%，按照这一数据和纸托盘占比上升趋势推断，2015 年纸托盘年产量将继续快速增长。目前，中国有多家机械生产企业推出了蜂窝纸芯生产线，如湖北京山等。蜂窝纸板制作的托盘主要用于日用品和家电包装上。一些大型家电生产企业如科龙、海尔和长虹等都陆续采用了蜂窝纸板托盘。预计随着纸托盘技术的改进，环保、自重轻的纸托盘市场空间较大。

根据最新调研，目前五大类托盘中，木托盘仍占绝对数量，为 80%，塑料托盘由前几年的 11% 增至 2012 年的 12%，其他各类材料托盘占比合计为 8%。

综合分析，预计 2015 年托盘市场将继续保持一定速度增长，但增长趋缓，增速在 7% 左右。托盘产量超过 2.57 亿片，托盘保有量继续增加，标准规格托盘所占比例将有较大幅度提升。

（3）物流系统设备将继续保持快速增长

2015 年预计中国自动化立体库将继续保持快速增长，增长速度保持在 30% 左右；新建的具有一定规模的自动化立体库将超过 400 ~ 500 座，如果包括小型立体库则新建立体库更多。如果把自动输送分拣物流系统包括在内，2015 年物流系统集成领域市场规模将超过 500 亿元以上，其中自动化仓储市场规模将超过 100 亿元；自动分拣系统市场规模将超过 58 亿元。

（4）货架系统市场需求保持中速增长

2015 年工业货架系统随着物流系统装备行业快速成长而快速发展，立体库货架市场需求将保持高速增长，普通的工业货架随着物流业进入中速增长阶段，市场需求增长将趋缓。综合来看，预计 2015 年货架系统市场将保持中速增长，增速在 13% 左右，市场规模将达到 70 亿元。

（物流技术与应用　王继祥）

2014 年包装行业发展回顾与 2015 年展望

一、2014 年包装行业发展回顾

1. 包装行业布局良好，产业规模发展迅速

2014 年，随着中国经济规模扩大，包装产业有了新的发展。中包联第八次全国代表大会召开，进一步完善了我国包装行业组织体系建设，提升了我国世界包装大国的地位。中国包装产业规模已经形成，成为全球第二大包装产业。据统计，国内约有 25 万多家包装企业，以民营企业和外商投资企业为主体，吸收了一批世界级的跨国公司，与我国全球经济第二大国的地位较为匹配。企业结构发生了新的变化，涌现出了一批年销售额超亿元，甚至超十亿元的龙头企业。我国包装工业总产值突破 1.4 万亿元，形成了集中度较高的产业链特征。从地域分布看，主要集中在经济发达的珠三角、长三角等地区。同时，企业经营增长速度放缓；产品从关注数量转向关注质量；从依靠劳动、资源和技术要素转向资本市场的运作，有数十家包装企业在沪、深、香港和美国上市。产业结构进一步调整，在高端制造业上有了新进展，与中国经济新常态相吻合。

2. 中包联八大顺利召开，五个平台创新发展

2014 年 12 月 25 日，中国包装联合会第八次全国代表大会在北京召开。世界包装组织副主席、中国包装联合会第七届理事会会长石万鹏，中国包装联合会第八届理事会会长候选人徐斌，国务院国有资产监督管理委员会秘书长阎晓峰出席大会。国资委秘书长阎晓峰在致辞中阐述了包装行业对国民经济和社会发展的重要作用以及改革开放以来的重大成就，肯定了中国包装联合会在服务企业发展、促进行业进步中发挥的重要作用。他指出，行业协会要积极适应社会组织管理制度改革要求，加强自身建设、加快自我提升，真正走上自治管理、自律发展的健康道路。石万鹏代表第七届理事会作题为《高举改革创新的旗帜　为建设现代包装强国而奋斗》的工作报告。报告对第七届理事会工作做了简要回顾，并对十年来的工作做了总结。大会选举产生了新一届理事会。同期召开了八届一次理事会，会议选举产生了中国包装联合会第八届理事会会长徐斌；王利等 45 人当选副会长；秘书长由副会长王跃中兼任。常务理事 271

人。理事522名。

3. 电商物流飞速发展，快递包装顺势井喷

据统计，2014年中国网购包裹达到90亿件，2015年预计可达到110亿件。高达百亿的快递包装市场使用了约25亿个纸箱、上百万吨的透明胶带、气泡袋等塑料包材。在外贸出口包装和奢侈品包装萎缩的情况下，快递包装撑起了中国包装工业的一片天。

快递大量使用透明胶带，使得中国透明胶带的市场需求呈现井喷现象。据统计，2014年，快递使用的透明胶带可绕地球120圈。此外，快递包装大量使用的气泡袋、泡沫塑料、EPE等缓冲包装材料也大幅增加。

快递包装不仅给包装的产品结构带来重大变化，而且对中国包装的市场格局也造成全局性的影响。前些年，由于中国世界工厂的地位，中国包装工业集中分布在长三角、珠三角、环渤海等东部沿海地区。随着外贸产业萎缩，内地日用快消品市场蓬勃发展，中国包装工业的重心将趋于分散并呈现向内地转移的趋势。

快递包装纸箱因为生产工艺简单，利润不高而一直不受大型纸箱厂家的重视。但是，一些纸业龙头企业开始越来越重视快递纸箱这个欣欣向荣的市场，同时也诞生了若干提供电商快递解决方案服务的包装印刷企业。

4. 企业关停重组洗牌　行业增速总体趋缓

2014年，以劲嘉、合兴、美盈森、裕同、胜达为代表的包装企业凭借独特的经营模式、富有成效的营销战略，加上原纸价格低位徘徊的有利条件，取得了良好业绩。面对行业洗牌期的有利时机，企业进一步加快了并购的步伐。深圳劲嘉先后收购了江苏顺泰包装、贵州瑞源包装，上海绿新包装材料科技股份有限公司受让云南省玉溪印刷有限责任公司60%的股权等。

但是，受大形势影响，包装行业的利润日趋微薄，人工成本高涨，再加上制造业转移和内需疲弱导致订单锐减，使部分包装企业无法支撑下去。一些纸包装行业频频出现问题，如江苏宿迁富士达包装有限公司在自有资金不足情况下盲目扩张，借民间高利贷无力偿还，老板跑路。浙江杭州荣海包装制品有限公司由于投资房地产造成资金链断裂，老板失联，企业已被当地政府接管。永春宏泰和永春联盛则是无力偿还银行贷款，在银行停贷的情况下老板跑路。

香港旺达纸品集团旗下的通达纸品，深圳旺达彩印，江苏旺达纸品，江苏旺达纸业及东莞市弘安纸品在两年内悉数关闭。香港长盛集团接连关闭旗下位于东莞的恒泰、群胜、信胜三家大型瓦楞包装厂。香港洛琪及子公司镇泰包装也悄然关停。香港上市公司合丰集团在公司一直盈利的情况下，将公司大本营，位于凤岗的工厂出售。不久，另一家大型港资包装企业华通集团悄悄地关停了位于深圳宝安石岩的华通纸品厂。

关停的上述十几家工厂均是规模较大、设备先进、享有很高知名度的港资企业。这一方面是基于中国世界工厂大退潮的大背景下收缩投资的考量；另一方面也反映出中国包装企业经营越来越困难的事实。仅以软包装行业为例，2014 年，软包装企业呈现出“旺季不旺，淡季真淡”的特点。约 80% 的企业年产值下滑约 20%。行业增速普遍趋缓，市场需求减少，行业经营困难。

5. 食品包装制定新规　食品标准整合规范

2014 年 7 月 1 日起，包括肉制品在内的 11 类预包装食品有了新国标——GB 29921《食品中致病菌限量》。该标准对肉制品、水产制品、即食蛋制品、粮食制品、即食豆类制品、巧克力类及可可制品、即食果蔬制品、饮料、冷冻饮品、即食调味品、坚果籽食制品 11 类食品分别规定了致病菌指标、限量要求和检测方法。在实施日期前已生产的食品可在保质期内继续销售。进口食品的标准执行时间应按照此标准实施。其他相关标准不一致的应按照此标准执行。致病菌检验应按照 GB 29921 引用的检验方法执行。

此标准制定的目的在于解决我国之前涉及食品致病菌限量的超过 500 项标准中，指标设置存在重复、交叉、矛盾或缺失等问题。此标准的实施，对于整合分散在不同食品标准中的致病菌限量规定，具有重要意义。

6. 包装机械差距缩小　行业创新仍需努力

我国包装机械行业已整体进入产品结构调整和创新能力提升时期，有些包装机械填补了国内空白，已能基本满足国内市场的需求，部分产品还有出口，但从整体上看还是大而不强，素质不高，自主创新能力薄弱，国际竞争力不强。我国包装机械以中小企业为主，随着包装产业向小型化、数字化方向发展，企业提升技术、更换设备都需要大量资金支持，同时操控高端设备的高级技工人才缺乏，也令不少企业举步维艰。用工成本提升和人民币升值倒逼企业转型，需庞大资金投入。为解决该难题，往往采取数家企业合资的合作模式，由 OEM 代工成功转型高科技企业。

目前，我国包装机械企业的技术水平与世界发达国家相比竞争力明显不足，主要表现为：首先，我国包装机械专业技术人才少，缺乏专业研发团队。产品技术落后，一味模仿并不能解决行业根本问题。其次，自动化程度低，这也是国内设备不能与发达国家包装设备相媲美的重要关键点。最后，企业及机械都缺乏国际认证检测。如果不能尽快做强做大，提升技术水平和档次，则与发达国家的差距将进一步被拉大。

7. 利乐包装地位削弱，国内厂商抢占份额

利乐包由瑞典利乐公司（TetraPak）开发，是一种典型、成熟的复合包装，广泛应用于牛奶等软饮料的包装。它具有广阔的市场空间和较好的盈利能力，目前利乐包在国内的市场规模超过 250 亿元。利乐自 20 世纪 70 年代进入中国

市场后，通过专利保护、捆绑销售和控制产业链等方式，长期占据国内无菌包装市场垄断地位。然而随着国内外厂商的进入与市场需求、政策环境的变化，与利乐包功能相似的无菌包装形式出现，利乐包装行业垄断格局不断被削弱，国内企业不断壮大，进一步抢占了原由利乐包装占有的无菌包装市场份额。

8. 传统包装亟待变革，冷链包装方兴未艾

随着电商物流行业的兴起以及人们对农产品、加工食品的配送要求不断提高，冷链物流成为了新的行业发展点。电商巨头纷纷抢滩冷链物流，冷链物流的发展要求传统的物流包装必须转型为具有保鲜、保温、环保等功能的新型包装，目前已投入使用的新型包装有复合保温纸箱、复合瓦楞纸箱、EPP 环保保温箱等，无论从功能角度还是环境保护角度都能较好地满足冷链物流包装的需求。在冷链物流下游方面，农产品是冷链包装的主要品类。其中，水果蔬菜市场年产基数大，增长迅速，冷链技术成熟度持续提高，是冷链物流发展的重要动力。

二、2015 年包装行业展望

2015 年是不平凡的一年，就国家层面来说，既是“十二五”规划的收官之年，又是全面深化改革的关键之年。2015 年中国经济将保持平稳发展，但是相对于前几年，其增速明显放缓。出口产品形势严峻，内需消费难以显著提升，加之国家环保治理力度加大，企业人工成本持续上升。包装企业日子过得将会日益艰难，这一切要求包装企业做好充分的准备。

但是，困难重重，不意味着没有发展的机会。日子还是要过，刚性的需求还是有的，技术还是要进步的。目前，国际上包装机械向高端化转变已经出现强劲的发展势头。随着科技的不断发展与进步，微电子、电脑、工业机器人、图像传感技术和新材料等在包装机械中将会得到越来越广泛应用，我国相关企业应学习和引进新技术，向生产效率高、自动化程度高、可靠性好、灵活性强、技术含量高的包装设备进军。打造出新型包装机械，引领包装机械向集成化、高效化、智能化等方向发展。新型包装机要求具有简洁化、高生产率、配套完善，更具自动化等特点。未来的包装机械将配合产业自动化趋势，促进包装设备总体水平提高。如高智能数控系统、编码器及数字控制组件、动力负载控制等新型智能设备已经普遍应用到包装机械设备中，使设备使用者在操作过程中更具有独立性、灵活度、操作正确性、高效率和兼容性。面对如此之大的市场需求和发展机遇，我国包装机械行业应该尽快改变中低端产品过剩、高端产品不足的局面，加快制定行业标准规范；生产企业需要加大自动化设备改造，提升产品技术含量，开发出产销对路的大型成套生产线，从而在国内外市

场中立于不败之地。

包装材料在当前低碳环保的趋势下应当有较大的创新和发展，环保化、功能化消费理念催生新型包装材料。2015 年，“新型包装”要在传统包装的基础上，融入先进的科学技术，让传统包装在功能、设计和环境保护上都具有较大的创新。材料创新是指采用新型材料，使得包装在获得不亚于原有产品性能的前提下更加环保、更加满足消费者需求，行业中关注度较高的几种新型包装主要集中于材料创新和功能创新。用途的扩大，合理的价格，低碳环保的特点，使得这类包装材料成为包装行业中发展最快的制品，这主要包括纳米包装、可食性包装和绿色包装。功能创新是指运用新技术使得包装物实现其原来不具备的功能，主要包括复合包装、活性包装和自加热与自冷却包装等。随着整个包装行业对环保要求的不断提高、对包装功能需求的拓展，新型包装将迎来更大的发展空间。

从总体上看，包装行业高端人才还不够多，创新能力还不够强，主要装备研发水平还不够先进，研发投入还不能满足需求，内生动力亟待增强。2015 年要下定决心，不懈努力，改变这一状况。着力建设一支以企业为主体的研发力量，形成比较完整的专业化技术研发体系；大力开展产学研合作创新，充分利用国家创新资源和高新区的创新能力，攻克发展难题；积极开拓国际高端合作，加速追赶步伐；加强高级专业人才的培养和吸纳，积蓄发展后劲。在转型升级和科技创新两个关键环节上，下真功夫、苦功夫、硬功夫，推动行业平稳健康发展。

（天津科技大学　韩永生　刘立琮）

2014 年工业车辆行业发展回顾与 2015 年展望

2014 年世界工业车辆总销量首次突破 100 万台，达到历史最好水平。而中国工业车辆行业在国内经济增速放缓、国际局势复杂多变的大背景下，继续保持稳定的增长，国民经济结构的优化和人民生活水平的提高，企业工作效率提升、机器代替人工、物流规模水平的发展等原因，使工业车辆的市场需求量不断增加。

一、2014 年世界工业车辆市场发展回顾

来自世界工业车辆统计协会（WITS）的数据显示，2014 年世界工业车辆总销量为 1063029 台，首次突破 100 万台，增幅达 7.51%。从车型方面看，电动平衡重叉车的销量为 176567 台，电动乘驾式仓储叉车 100379 台，电动步行式仓储叉车 310852 台，内燃平衡重叉车为 475231 台。

从各大洲的工业车辆销售情况看，金融危机后到 2014 年，除欧洲外，各大洲销量均已恢复或超过危机之前的水平。其中，亚洲的销量达到 432098 台，增幅达 9.65%，其中电动平衡重叉车的销量为 66807 台，电动乘驾式仓储叉车为 33874 台，电动步行式仓储叉车为 49818 台，内燃平衡重叉车为 281599 台。

2014 年世界工业车辆销售量前十位的国家分别为：中国、美国、日本、德国、法国、英国、意大利、俄罗斯、巴西、韩国。

二、2014 年中国工业车辆市场发展回顾

2014 年中国工业车辆的总销量为 359622 台，增幅达 9.39%，其中，电动平衡重叉车的销量为 42002 台，电动乘驾式仓储叉车 6177 台，电动步行式仓储叉车 249403 台，内燃平衡重叉车 196272 台。

中国工程机械工业协会工业车辆分会（CITA）通过对会员单位 2000—2014 年的销售情况进行统计分析后发现，会员企业总销量增长迅速，2014 年总销量是 2000 年的 16 倍。进入 21 世纪，中国市场一直保持着较好的增长，即使是金融危机时期世界主要经济体工业车辆销量均有 50% 左右跌幅的情况下，中国市场依然持平，之后不断迈上新的台阶，自 2009 年以来，中国连续五年

位列世界第一大市场。

2014 年国内工业车辆的销量为 268910 台，增幅达 10%，其中电动平衡重叉车的销量为 34313 台，电动乘驾式仓储叉车 5571 台，电动步行式仓储叉车 32754 台，内燃平衡重叉车 196272 台。

影响 2014 年国内工业车辆销售的主要因素：一是国内物流大环境对叉车销售有很好的带动作用；二是随着国内企业生产效率的提升、人工成本的不断增加，机器代替人工的趋势越来越显著，进而促进工业车辆需求增长；三是得益于电子商务的发展，各地区包括城乡、县镇和农村的生活资料的配送需求量日益增加，带动了叉车的增长，其中仓储类叉车有 20% 以上的增长。

在产品类型方面，过去内燃叉车占 80% 左右的比例，但是 2014 年内燃叉车占比下降到 72.99%，电动叉车的市场份额明显加大，占 27.01%，提高了 3 个百分点，是近年来增长最快的一年。各大企业都加大了电动仓储叉车和新能源叉车产品的研究，如合力等企业研制的 LNG、LPG 内燃叉车，比亚迪的锂电池叉车，中力、诺力、如意等研制的电动仓储车等。在叉车的配套件方面，LNG、LPG 天然气发动机、国产电动叉车电控系统、锂电池等近年来也有国内企业开发和生产，并且已经给整机进行配套。

从各地区销售情况来看，华东地区销售量最高，为 119060 台，市场份额占 44.40%；其次为华南地区，销售量为 39266 台，市场份额占 14.64%；再次是华北地区，销售量为 33494 台，市场份额占 12.49%；华中地区销售量为 27591 台，市场份额占 10.29%；西南、西北、东北的市场份额分别为 6.69%、5.96%、5.56%。具体到各省市情况，广东省以 32587 台占据销售量第一的位置，占 2014 年国内市场份额的 12.15%，与 2013 年相比下降 0.01%；江苏与之相差不多，销售量为 31408 台；其后分别为山东、浙江、上海、河北、河南、福建、安徽、湖北。

从分行业销售情况看，交通运输、仓储物流行业占比达到 17.07%，与 2013 年相比上涨了 7.86%；电气、机械行业占比达到 13.63%，比 2013 年上涨了 19.18%。此外，食品饮料、批发零售、石油化工等行业占比也相对较高。另外，从 2013 年和 2014 年外资企业分行业销售情况来看，上涨形势比较好的行业是租赁、农林牧副渔和批发零售业；而下跌比较大的是医药医疗器材、造纸业及纸制品、冶金金属制造行业。

在内外资销售占比方面，总销售量中，内资占 82.18%，外资占 17.82%；国内市场销售量中，内资占 85.94%，外资占 14.06%。总的来看，由于外资企业在中国的产能进一步扩大，车型更加丰富，加上兼并收购等因素，总销售量中外资占比有所扩大，而国内市场上外资占比近年变化不大，主要表现在外资品牌在中国生产的产品出口量明显扩大。

在市场占有率方面，2014 年销售量前三家企业的总销售量占比为 49.89%，国内销售量占比为 57.05%；销售量前五家的企业的总销售量占比为 58.48%，国内销售量占比为 64.01%；销售量前十家企业的总销售量占比为 73.07%，国内销售量占比为 73.86%。由此可见，市场集中度进一步提高。

在工业车辆进出口方面，根据海关总署的相关数据，2014 年的出口量为 92694 台，增长率为 7.10%，内资占总出口比重为 71.83%；2014 年的进口量为 12572 台，同比增长 4.22%。进口金额达 291695891 美元，同比下降 3.23%。总体上看，2014 年的出口增长幅度相比前几年有所下降，市场竞争更加激烈，内资品牌占总出口比重有明显下降；2007—2014 年工业车辆进口呈现下降的趋势，主要原因是世界各大品牌在中国的生产能力进一步加强，车型种类越来越丰富，可以满足国内市场的大部分需求。

三、2015 年工业车辆发展展望

展望 2015 年的中国工业车辆市场，由于工业车辆市场的涨跌滞后于经济发展的变化，预计 2015 年将出现继 2012 年调整之后的新一轮调整。中国市场占世界总销量接近 4/1，随着中国市场进入调整期全球销量会受到影响，预计 2015 年比 2014 年会持平或略有增长。

从发展趋势看，国内工业车辆市场竞争将会加剧，并开始由低端向中端和高端市场蔓延；受多方因素影响，内资企业出口面临挑战；兼并重组方面，虽然各方意向强烈，但难度也在增大；叉车后市场方面，服务和盈利模式需要提升和创新。

车型方面的变化也应引起注意，电动叉车的比例将继续增大。目前国内依然以内燃叉车为主，但客观环境的变化使开发和研制电动叉车、环保型叉车日渐成为一种新产品开发趋势。例如，排放标准提高，非道路移动机械国三排放标准实施、北京等地制定更高的地方排放标准；仓储车需求加大，物流配送范围由城市向乡村发展、仓储智能化管理、电子商务等因素加大了仓储车的市场需求量。可以说，随着各大叉车企业对绿色仓储与配送行动的推行，电动叉车将会成为中国工业车辆市场竞争的焦点。

（中国工程机械工业协会工业车辆分会　张洁）

2014 年载货车行业发展回顾与 2015 年展望

一、2014 年载货车行业发展回顾

2014 年，我国经济整体上延续了 2011 年以来的下行趋势，房地产投资增速较 2013 年进一步下降，产能过剩和内需不足也进一步导致固定资产投资增速下降，在这些因素影响下，载货车市场需求重返低迷。

（一）载货车行业情况

2014 年我国实现载货车生产 3195901 辆，销售 3184406 辆，销售同比下降 8.9%。其中，重型载货车、中型载货车和轻型载货车的生产和销售均比 2013 年下降，微型载货车的产量和销售量同比略有增长（见表 1）。

表 1　2014 年载货汽车细分市场情况　（辆）

	2014 年生产	2013 年生产	2014 年销售	2013 年销售	销售同比增长（%）
重型载货车	747451	760581	743991	774104	-3.9
中型载货车	247899	285461	247839	286839	-13.6
轻型载货车	1661643	1894993	1662634	1908328	-12.9
微型载货车	538908	527466	529942	527019	0.6
载货车合计	3195901	3468501	3184406	3496290	-8.9

1. 重型货车行业

2014 年，固定资产投资增速超预期下行，使重型载货车销售没有延续 2013 年增长态势，在上半年同比增长 7% 的形势下，下半年需求急转急下，导致全年销售下降 3.9%。

在细分市场上，2013 年非完整车辆销售 266057 辆，占重型载货车市场份额 35.8%，市场份额连续 5 年下滑；半挂牵引车销售 278990 辆，占重型载货车市场 37.5% 份额，市场份额进一步提升；整车销售 198944 辆，占重型载货车市场 26.7% 份额（见表 2）。

表 2 重型载货车细分市场情况 （辆）

年份	2007	2008	2009	2010	2011	2012	2013	2014
重型货车整车	93087	106746	134281	247698	269907	202121	219967	198944
半挂牵引车总计	177776	194155	211106	354623	257574	190645	263383	278990
重型货车非完整车	216618	239547	290784	415112	353160	243235	290754	266057
合计	487481	540448	636171	1017433	880641	636001	774104	743991

从 2014 年分季度销售趋势看，重型载货车销售形势与 2013 年相反，全年高开低走，销售形势逐步恶化。第一季度销售 202937 辆，同比增长 20%；但后三季度却逐步陷入低迷，销售同比下降分别达到 3%、7% 和 22%。

2. 中型货车行业

受经济持续低迷影响，2014 年中型载货车新增需求不足，而近年支撑中型载货车市场发展的更新需求也受物流业增速放缓的影响，出现车辆更新需求下降趋势。在此影响下，中型载货车市场需求出现近年来的首次大幅下降，降幅同比达到 13.6%。

在细分市场上，2014 年整车销售 150278 万辆，市场份额连续 5 年下滑，降至 60.6%；非完整车辆销售 97561 辆，市场份额 39.4%（见表 3）。

表 3 中型载货车细分市场情况 （辆）

年份	2007	2008	2009	2010	2011	2012	2013	2014
中型货车整车	131256	124563	181577	179424	191843	184050	175897	150278
中型货车非完整车	105466	82546	76389	92342	100116	106219	110942	97561
合计	236722	207109	257966	271766	291959	290269	286839	247839

从分季度销售情况看，2014 年首季中型载货车市场需求就出现快速下滑，当季实现销售 66702 辆，同比下降 9%；第二季度则销售 63078 辆，较去年同期下降 27%；在中型载货车传统淡季的第三季度，销售 51078 辆，为近年来单季销售最低值，同比下降 18%；第四季度销售有所好转，单季销售 66981 辆，同比增长 3%。

3. 轻型载货车行业

2014 年轻型货车销售总量大幅下降，全年销售 1662634 辆，同比下降

12.9%。2014年轻型载货车市场需求下降主要来自低端市场，低端市场运力过剩，轻型车对农用车替代日渐减弱，都是导致低端轻型车需求下降的主要因素。

细分市场上，轻型载货车非完整车辆销售103114辆，同比略有下降，但市场份额增至6.2%；整车销售1559520辆，同比下降13.5%（见表4）。

表4　　轻型载货车细分市场情况　　（辆）

年份	2007	2008	2009	2010	2011	2012	2013	2014
轻型货车整车	1016787	1103597	1461371	1883634	1756188	1733974	1803504	1559520
轻型货车非完整车	99613	96306	98227	141987	123872	108736	104824	103114
合计	1116400	1199903	1559598	2025621	1880060	1842710	1908328	1662634

2014年第一季度，轻型载货车当季销售同比增长4%；第二季度销售43万辆，同比出现16%降幅；第三季度市场需求进一步恶化，销售量31.6万辆，创近6年单季销量新低，同比大幅下降28%；第四季度，当季轻型载货车销售降幅趋缓，实现销售40.3万辆，同比下降14%。

4. 微型货车行业

2014年微型载货车是唯一没有出现下降的载货车类型，全年实现销售529942辆，销量同比增长2900余辆，比上年略增0.6%。不过，2014年微型非完整车市场需求依然没有实质增长，全年销售2191辆，只占微型载货车市场总量0.4%（见表5）。

表5　　微型载货车细分市场情况　　（辆）

年份	2007	2008	2009	2010	2011	2012	2013	2014
微型货车整车	275245	261466	472914	520539	484020	533247	526527	527751
微型货车非完整车	28662	31186	32776	25732	8156	1565	492	2191
合计	303907	292652	505690	546271	492176	534812	527019	529942

2014年微型车产品与低端轻卡之间的产品分界进一步模糊。微型载货车产品在城乡结合地区的小批量零担货物运输中发挥着越来越重要的作用，同时在舒适性和功能性方面进一步加强，与低端皮卡形成客户群重叠和竞争。

2014年分季度销售情况看，第一至第四季度微型载货车销售呈现低开高走态势，销售同比分别增长-7%、-4%、2%和13%。

（二）载货车进口情况

2014年国内进口载货类汽车11977辆，较2013年同期累计增长3.4%。其中重型载货车进口3825辆，占进口载货车总量的31.96%，进口重型载货车与国产重型载货车的比值为0.51%，两者比值创近年来新低（见表6）。

表6　2008—2014年进口重型载货车占国内重型载货车市场比例

年份	2008	2009	2010	2011	2012	2013	2014
比例（%）	1.71	1.28	1.33	1.86	2.43	0.89	0.51

（三）载货车企业

1. 重型载货车企业

2014年前5家重型载货车企业销售606894辆，占重型载货车市场份额81.6%，较2013年的81.9%下降0.3个百分点。前10家企业实现销售718329辆，占市场份额96.6%，同比下降0.2%。

2014年市场份额占比10%以上的5家主流重型载货车企业销售情况有涨有跌。其中，东风汽车实现销售155142辆，同比下降6.4%，但依然保持市场份额第一的位置；中国重汽销售121306辆，同比增长0.4%，市场份额升至16.3%，排名从第三位升至第二位；一汽集团销量116634万辆，同比下降10.8%，市场排名从第二位降至第三位；北汽福田和陕西汽车分列第四和第五位，其中陕汽凭借在替代能源汽车领域的优势，取得3%的销售增长，市场份额增至14.1%。

2. 中型载货车企业

2014年，前5家中型载货车企业共实现销售191156辆，占中型货车市场总销量的77.1%，较2013年前5家市场份额上升6.1个百分点；前10家企业总计销售中型载货车235376辆，市场份额95%，同比增长4.3个百分点。

前5家企业中，各企业排名与2013年相同。东风汽车实现销售63661辆，较2013年销量下降21.3%，市场份额降至25.7%，但依然领先居第二位的一汽5.6个百分点；一汽实现销售49718辆，销量略降1.7%，市场份额20.1%，同比增长2.5个百分点；中国重汽实现销售32651辆，同比增长5.1%，占中型载货车市场13.2%的份额，排在第三位；重庆力帆2014年销售同比增长15%，市场份额达到10.7%；庆铃汽车销售略有增长至18597辆，市场份额升至7.5%。

3. 轻型载货车企业

2014年主要轻型载货生产企业中，前5家企业实现销售972159辆，市场份额合计为58.5%，较2013年市场集中度略有下降；前10家企业实现销售1320741辆，市场份额79.4%，同比增长0.7个百分点。

2014年轻型车企业竞争格局有所变化。在产品竞争方面，延续了2013年以来的趋势，中高端产品市场稳步发展，低端产品市场空间快速缩小。2014 年轻型载货车技术进一步提升，在替代能源和新能源汽车领域新产品推出加速，城市物流车辆围绕环保、节能与专用化三个方面的需求加快升级。

在主要企业中，北汽福田在轻型载货车领域依然保持领先地位，但其市场份额进一步下降至 18.0%，竞争优势下降；江铃汽车凭借在中档产品领域的优势地位，通过产品多样化和发展专用汽车，实现销售 179880 辆，同比增长 20.5%，市场份额升至 10.8%，排在第二位；江淮汽车 2014 年实现销售 175763 辆，销售同比下降20.5%，市场份额降至10.6%，居行业第三位；东风汽车和金杯汽车市场份额与 2013 年变化不大，分别排在行业第四和第五位。

4. 微型载货车企业

2014 年排名前 5 家的微型载货车企业合计销售微型货车 483093 辆，市场份额 81.2%，较 2013 年增加 4.2 个百分点，微型载货车行业前 4 家企业已经形成一家独大、三家跟随的竞争格局。

2014 年上汽通用五菱在微型载货车领域继续保持大幅增长，全年实现销售 219466 辆，同比增长 25.4%，市场份额从 2013 年的 33.2% 增至 41.4%；北汽福田实现销售 91210 辆，同比下降 14.7%，市场份额跌至 17.2%，排在第二位；重庆长安实现销售 82293 辆，同比增长 4.1%，市场份额升至 15.5%，超越东风汽车排在第三位；东风汽车销售 72848 辆，同比下降 11.8%，市场份额连续两年大幅下降至 13.7%；奇瑞汽车实现销售 1.7 万辆，排在第五位，但市场份额只有 3.3%。

二、2015 年载货车行业市场展望

2014 年，我国经济在下半年经历了近年来最困难的时期，随着下半年以来各项针对性宽松政策的出台和大型工程建设计划的颁布，预计 2015 年我国固定资产投资增速将有所回升。但房地产领域受货币贬值预期和高房价影响，预计还难以摆脱目前低迷态势。同时产业转型与新兴产业的发展，还有待进一步落实。我们认为，整体上，2015 年我国经济还将处于调整与恢复期，经济增长速度将与 2014 年持平。

我们预计，2015 年载货车市场需求在 2014 年基础上小幅回暖。重中型载货车方面，预计全年销售总量将在 105 万辆左右；轻型和微型载货车市场需求总量将在 230 万辆左右。

（中国汽车技术研究中心　潘增友）

2014年货架行业发展回顾与2015年展望

2014年的中国货架行业如年初预计的那样，随着物流业的蓬勃发展，市场规模持续扩大，行业发展进入了一个快速增长期。

一、2014年货架行业市场回顾

（一）货架市场总体情况分析

2014年国内货架行业市场整体保持了较快的增长，增幅超过20%。钢材价格在2013年走低的情况下，2014年再度走低，货架按产量计算的增长率仍要高于按订单额计算的增长率，因此市场实际增长应超过25%，总体市场规模在50亿~60亿元。自动化立体仓库货架、以电商需求为代表的组合货架和穿梭小车货架成为市场的三大主力军，占据绝对的市场份额。

1. 货架市场的地域分布情况

华东、华北和华南地区依然是市场销售的主战场，在市场规模扩大的情况下，其所占的比例仍有上升的态势，体现“强者恒强”。华中、西南地区得益于“中部崛起”“一带一路”等国家战略的实施，需求有较大幅度增长，是市场的板块新亮点。而东北、西北市场仍无明显增长迹象。在海外市场方面，单纯的货架出口没有亮点；相反地，在包括安装的工程项目出口中，中国货架企业已成功完成或正在施工数个项目，这将为中国货架企业开辟新的广阔市场空间。

2. 货架市场的行业分布状况

2014年货架需求与上一年基本保持一致，商业物流、医药化工、食品饮料三个行业牢牢占据货架需求前三名，表明货架在关于民生的领域中需求最高。其中商业领域排名不断上升，市场份额不断扩大，这主要得益于电商的迅猛发展。

3. 货架行业竞争状况

受项目大型化、复杂化趋势影响，对货架厂商的资金实力、设备工艺、工期保证等提出了更高的要求，这些直接导致在货架厂商的竞争中，第一梯队相较于第二梯队明显处于有利地位，但第一梯队之间的竞争仍旧非常激烈。

2014年年初我们提到，一些货架厂商出于种种考虑，开始逐步向系统集成方向发展。但有趣的现象是，也有原来的货架厂商在向集成商走了一段时间后，又重新把货架作为经营主攻方向。市场上还有集成商在酝酿建厂，大规模制造货架的传闻。在转型升级的时代，一切皆有可能，但均需面临市场考验。做专做强，一门深入，是多数货架企业的选择。

（二）货架市场发展特点分析

1．货架新技术新产品应用提速

应用主要集中在两个方面，一是自动化立体仓库货架向更高、更重型方向发展中的应用，二是货架在密集式高效率存储系统发展中的应用。

2．电商行业货架需求依然保持爆发式增长

电商行业的货架需求在近两年保持爆发式增长，电商货架并不是单一类型的货架，而是以电商需求定制的一揽子货架总称，通常包括但不限于阁楼式货架、搁板式货架和横梁式货架。其目的都是为了实现电商的高效率存储、高速度拣选，突出货物快速流动的特点。电商行业订单下单量大，工期严苛，加工复杂，对货架公司综合能力考验巨大。

3．项目大型化趋势再上台阶

单个货架项目金额从超 1000 万元开始，短短两三年迅速达到超 3000 万元。2014 年市场出现了单个货架项目超 5000 万元、超亿元的大单，使项目大型化趋势再上台阶。如笔者所在公司 2014 年就有两个亿元大单。

4．东南亚货架工程项目获得起步

以往的海外出口，以纯货架买卖居多。以印尼、泰国、越南、马来西亚为代表的东南亚市场，由于地少人多，再加上近几年来全球劳动密集型制造业的迁入，货架需求保持增长。中国货架企业在东南亚市场已成功起步，目前，实施了多个项目。最具代表性的是上海精星公司在印尼某烟草公司获得超亿元人民币的“库架合一”大单，目前该项目第一个库已经主体吊装完毕。

二、2015 年货架行业发展展望

（一）货架企业面临的挑战

目前，中国经济面临转型之际，经济下行压力不小，中国制造行业面对诸多挑战，货架企业身处制造行业自然不能幸免。概括来说，有四个方面的挑战需要面对。

1．总体产能过剩

虽然相较许多不景气的行业而言，货架市场需求旺盛，但是从总体上来说，产能也是过剩的，开工不足的货架企业不在少数。许多原来从事出口或其他机械、金属加工的企业很容易进入中低端的货架制造领域。

2. 成本上升压力巨大

这里的“成本”主要是指以劳动力、土地为主体的生产经营成本。近几年来，尽管货架行业每年增长率不低，但和平均工资的上涨幅度相比仍是“差着一大截”。长此以往，企业所承受的压力可想而知。钢材价格目前处于近20年的低位，2015年上涨可能性增大，届时对签有年度协议的订单和延期实施的订单极为不利。

3. 资金流动性风险

一方面，流入实体经济部门的资金持续降低，造成项目付款条件差、付款周期长、垫资多（货架企业钢材采购要全额付现）、垫资时间长、现金少、承兑汇票多，货架企业应收账款压力不小；另一方面，是全社会的融资难、融资贵。两面夹击下，货架企业资金的流动性风险凸显，要管控好、平衡好绝非易事。

4. 创新能力不足

大家都已形成这样的共识：自主创新，提高企业核心竞争力。可现在问题的关键是两个，一个是投入，一个是思路。在激烈竞争的市场环境中，利润是微薄的，企业没有足够的积累，没“钱”创新。企业首先是生存，没有足够的时间让企业静下心来研发创新。同时，创新的方向在哪里，创新的机制体制保证，知识产权的保护，这些现实问题也困扰着企业。

（二）货架企业的发展机遇

展望2015年，机遇和挑战并存。货架企业纷纷采取措施，迎接挑战，把握行业发展机遇，简单梳理如下：

（1）以客户需求为导向，紧跟国际物流装备行业发展趋势，引进国际国内先进制造设备，加速货架新技术新产品的应用。

（2）聚焦优势产品和领域，有所为，有所不为，实行错位竞争。

（3）自觉维护行业市场秩序。大到具有国际水准的高含金量的国家标准的制定，小到坚持维护正常的付款条件，每一个行业内成员的努力，都将为营造良好的行业发展生态“添砖加瓦”。

（4）利用资本市场多渠道融资功能，解决资金问题。有企业引进风险投资，有企业准备上市。

（5）异地建厂，以期降低土地、劳动力和运输等成本，扩大产能，抢占当地市场并辐射周边，最终完成全国布局。

总之，我们认为货架行业正处于国内物流行业发展的快速上升期，在未来较长一段时间内会保持高速增长。前文所分析到的2014年货架市场的特点和趋势将持续深入发展，2015年的货架市场充满期待。

（上海精星仓储设备工程有限公司　崔雄）

2014 年自动化立体库发展回顾与 2015 年展望

一、2014 年自动化立体库发展回顾

1. 市场状况

当前，世界经济仍处在金融危机后的深度调整期，我国经济发展步入“新常态”。中国物流业正处于产业地位的提升期、现代物流服务体系的形成期和物流强国的建设期。物流业在“新常态”下转型升级，健康发展面临严峻挑战，快递、电商、医药、粮食、大健康、冷链等细分物流市场品牌集中、企业集聚、市场集约的趋势进一步显现。

2014 年，随着《物流业发展中长期规划（2014—2020 年）》把物流业定位于支撑国民经济发展的基础性、战略性产业，物流产业地位进一步得到提升。自动化立体库顺应了经济发展“新常态”，成为物流市场中的核心系统，保持了较强的需求态势，市场规模和应用领域进一步扩大。在快速兴起的电商、医药综合物流、大健康产业、冷链等领域，对自动化物流设备、自动化立体库的需求呈现较快增长趋势，成为继烟草、医药生产、服装、制造业之后的新兴应用领域。同时，我国自动化立体库的设计能力、集成能力和创新能力不断增强。

据不完全统计，2014 年国内建成的自动化立体库接近 300 座，共生产了 2000 多台不同规格型号的有轨巷道堆垛机，自动化立体库的总产值超过 40 亿元人民币。截至 2014 年年底，全国累计建成的自动化立体库接近 2500 座，在役的自动化立体库接近 2000 座。

2. 供应商发展状况

自动化立体库供应商主要分为两类，一类是系统集成商，另一类是设备制造商。2014 年，一些系统集成商向设备制造商拓展，而一些设备制造商向系统集成商迈进，使自动化立体库国内市场竞争日趋激烈。国外知名厂商通过独资、合资、并购等多种形式进入中国市场，成立了本土公司；国内其他行业的一些企业也看中未来自动化立体仓库的市场潜力，加入到此行业；国内一些厂商正在积极运作上市，拓展融资渠道。目前，参与国内自动化立体库市场竞争的国内外厂商稳定在 50 家左右，本土品牌和外资品牌（含港资、台资）各占

一半，成为泾渭分明的两大阵营，各自占据市场的两端。初步估计，按年度项目数量划分，本土企业约占70%，外资企业约占30%；按年度合同总额划分，本土企业约占60%，外资企业约占40%。

3. 产品技术发展状况

近几年来，网络技术和电子商务飞速发展，以及各行业规模化企业实力增强，对自动化仓储系统的需求总量越来越大，类型越来越多，推动了自动化立体库的技术发展和创新，自动化立体库呈现出存储单元微型化、SKU多样化、功能组合增多和作业速度高速化等趋势。为适应这些发展趋势、满足客户需求，国内多种新技术应运而生，有的已经有实际案例，主要体现在以下几方面：

（1）件箱堆垛机

件箱堆垛机（MINILOAD）在近两年市场需求旺盛，特别是高速度性能要求的件箱堆垛机。国内外众多厂商瞄准这一商机，纷纷推出高速件箱堆垛机产品。从技术水平看，欧洲产品技术性能独领风骚，早已形成系列产品，市场应用成熟，成为国内厂商追赶的目标。国内主流厂商已经在进行高速件箱堆垛机的试制，运行速度达到400 m/min，起升速度达到100 m/min，采用全新的控制和驱动技术，定位精度在±3mm以内，存取货装置作业效率极高，可以做到最快3.5秒完成一个存取循环作业。

（2）多层穿梭车技术

多层穿梭车是在货格中搬运件箱物料的紧凑型穿梭车技术产品，该穿梭车与固定于立库端部的垂直提升机、连续提升机或提篮式货架自由组合、配合使用，替代堆垛机，完成件箱物料的快速存取作业。多次穿梭车走行速度可达140m/min，加速度$1.5m/s^2$，货叉取放周期4秒。由于作业有效载荷与设备自重比值比较小，意味着大大降低了每个仓储单元存取作业的能耗，具有绿色节能概念，符合目前世界发展的潮流。2014年又有多个厂商推出了该类系统和产品。

（3）穿梭板技术

为解决在托盘高层立体库密集存储的要求，一般采用立体驶入式货架的密集存储方式，穿梭板是其中一种新型的存取货设备，它能在货架中各层穿梭运行，深入到托盘载荷下方，采用顶升机构将托盘顶起离开货架支承面，满足出入库流量要求不高但存储量要求很大的立库系统需要，配置简单，可节约设备投资。

在自动化程度较高的系统中，通过穿梭板与堆垛机或AGV联合作业，可以实现高密度立库货架内货物的存取以及端头的货物存、取作业，对于空间利用率要求高的冷库以及旧仓库升级改造更加适用。

（4）货到人拣选技术

利用前述多层穿梭车拥有超高的处理能力，可以实现件箱物料在立库内的缓存和出入库的排序，再配置人工拣选站，存货和发货料箱自动进出拣选站，把存货送到拣选员面前，不需要拣选员为了拣取每项物品而在货架区或拣选区内走来走去，再通过人机工程设计，拣选员无须将手臂举过肩，也无须过多伸展手臂而造成不适，提高了操作舒适度，将疲劳度降到最低，消除了拣选员反复抬举或推动纸箱和料箱的动作，确保高生产力的持续性，大幅度提高拣选人员的作业效率。每组拣选站的拣选率可以达到约500～800个订单/小时。

以上四种有代表性的新技术，国内厂商已经掌握相关技术并开发成功产品，有的已得到实际应用。未来随着客户的认可和采用，它们必将成为自动化立体仓库的标志性技术产品，促进自动化立体仓库技术的升级换代，推动物流行业发展。

二、2015年自动化立体库发展展望

随着国内经济和产业结构调整，各行业均出现产能过剩现象。但由于我国自动化物流技术和装备发展水平还处于朝阳阶段，市场需求空间巨大，自动化立体库依然处于快速发展期。

2015年是全面完成“十二五”规划的收官之年，也是《物流业发展中长期规划（2014—2020年）》和三年行动计划的启动之年，物流业发展面临新的机遇和挑战，企业要有新思路、新模式、新对策。据初步推算，我国自动化立体库市场还在稳步扩大，未来几年该领域市场规模年复合增长率仍将保持在20%以上，2015年自动化立体库市场总额在60亿元人民币左右。

（昆明昆船物流信息产业有限公司　姜荣奇）

2014 年托盘业发展回顾与 2015 年展望

一、2014 年托盘业发展回顾

2014 年，我国托盘业尽管在经济下行压力下遇到诸多困难，但整体状况依然处于上升区间，成绩显著，主要表现在以下几个方面。

（一）商务部、国标委等部门推进托盘业发展

2014 年，商务部为贯彻落实汪洋副总理在部分城市物流工作座谈会上关于“推进物流标准化建设”的指示精神，根据国务院《物流业发展中长期规划（2014—2020 年）》（国发〔2014〕42 号）和《国家标准委、商务部关于加快推进商贸物流标准化工作的意见》（国标委服务联〔2014〕33 号），决定与国家标准委在全国范围内开展商贸物流标准化专项行动。该《专项行动》从托盘标准化入手，以降低物流成本，提高物流效率为目标，在快速消费品、农副产品、药品流通领域，率先开展标准化托盘应用推广及循环共用。其主要工作任务包括：提高标准托盘普及率；推进相关领域托盘标准化进程；提升托盘循环共用水平；制定相关服务规范等。

为了加快《专项行动》的实施，商务部和国标委选择了第一批重点企业。其中有招商路凯、集保等托盘租赁企业 4 家；华润、国药、物美等大型商贸连锁企业 9 家；中粮集团、北京顺鑫等快消品生产企业 6 家；山东力扬、新创（天津）等托盘生产企业 3 家以及中国储运、五矿集团等第三方物流企业 8 家，共 30 个相关企业。第二批重点企业将在 2015 年年底选定。

近 2 ~ 3 年来，商务部高度重视物流标准化建设，尤其是托盘标准化。多次展开调查研究、座谈讨论、征求意见。还专门组团赴国外考察调研，在郑州召开专题会议落实工作任务。

（二）国家烟草专卖局推进烟草托盘联运

2014 年 3 月，国家烟草专卖局向全国烟草管理部门，企事业单位发出通知（国烟办综〔2014〕134 号），要求全行业充分认识开展卷烟托盘联运的重要性、大力推进行业托盘标准化，全面开展同城卷烟托盘联运工作；系统规划工商卷烟托盘联运；协同制定同城卷烟托盘联运实施方案；联合成立同城卷烟托

盘联运专项工作领导小组，共同研究确定操作办法。

国家烟草专卖局在《通知》中提出：托盘联运是现代物流的重要标志和必然趋势。在行业工商企业间开展卷烟托盘联运，有利于建立以托盘为载体的卷烟物流流转单元，通过实现整托盘出入库和整托盘运输，可大幅度降低重复装卸和卷烟损耗，大量减少劳动用工和作业强度，显著提升工商物流对接效率和作业质量。在行业工商企业间开展卷烟托盘联运，有利于建立以电子标签为媒介的卷烟物流信息单元，通过实现整托盘件烟信息存储和读取，可有效提升行业卷烟生产经营决策管理系统（以下简称决策管理系统）运行效率，促进工商企业物流信息资源共享，提高企业内部数字仓储管理水平。在行业工商企业间开展卷烟托盘联运，有利于增强烟草供应链上下游企业战略伙伴合作意识，提高客户服务水平和市场响应能力，推进工商物流一体化进程，实现企业物流向行业物流、行业物流向供应链物流的转变和提升，构建工商物流共同面向消费者的敏捷卷烟供应链流通体系。

近年来，随着工商物流一体化工作不断推进，工商企业间托盘联运工作快速展开。目前共有 9 家省级工业公司 21 个生产厂与同城地市级局（公司）开展了卷烟托盘联运，4 家省级工业公司与同省级局（公司）协同实现了全省范围内工商卷烟托盘联运，1 家省级工业公司与行业 165 家地市级局（公司）实施了卷烟托盘联运，工商卷烟托盘联运总量达到 650 万箱；同时，随着行业联运通用平托盘、卷烟联运平托盘电子标签等行业标准的推广实施，工、商企业卷烟托盘标准化率明显提高，分别达到 72%、87.7%，为全国开展同城卷烟托盘联运工作奠定了基础和条件。

（三）中国物流与采购联合会向全国人大、国务院报送托盘政策建议

2014 年 6 月，中国物流与采购联合会（以下简称“中物联”）向全国人大、政协、国务院以及相关部委报送“关于推行标准化托盘利用的政策建议”。该《政策建议》除了全面介绍我国托盘市场的基本情况、阐述标准化托盘利用的重大意义等内容外，还明确建议从超市、连锁零售企业、电子商务及快递等区域入手，推行标准托盘的利用；采取灵活多样的政策支持此项工作广泛深入地展开；尤其要加强托盘质量认证，确保标准化托盘符合国家标准和质量要求。

（四）大型托盘共用系统公司——中国智能物流包装公司问世

2014 年 11 月，中国智能物流包装公司问世。该公司是在我国大型央企中国诚通集团的支持下，由中国包装总公司负责组建的大型托盘共用系统企业，

中国铁路总公司、中国物资储运总公司、中国物流有限公司、北京市首都公路发展集团有限公司、浙江中烟工业有限公司、联想集团、苏宁电器、华润等大型企业积极参与，吴清一教授给予指导。公司新闻发布会借第九届托盘国际会议之机举行，2015 年 1 月在上海主办了“加快推进智能物流包装循环共用系统建设研讨会暨物流标准化行动系统联盟启动仪式”。

（五）“第九届中国托盘国际会议暨 2014 全球托盘企业家年会”成功举办

由中物联托盘专业委员协同亚洲托盘系统联盟举办的“标题”会议和托盘展览，于 2014 年 11 月 27 日在安徽芜湖落幕。作为专业性很强的国际会议达到约 500 人的规模，比前几届人数增加了近 50% 之多。中物联崔忠付副会长、商务部王选庆副司长、国务院发展研究中心任兴洲所长以及韩国、日本、欧洲托盘行业协会负责人作精彩致辞和演讲，会议内容丰富、切合现实，多角度、全方位、精辟透彻地分析阐述了会议主题，对企业老总们转变经营理念、提高改革创新意识、解决企业面临的困惑大有帮助。大家普遍反映，会议的质量高，参会收获大。

（六）中国成为亚洲托盘系统联盟主席国

2014 年 9 月 25 日，亚洲托盘系统联盟在泰国曼谷举行年度会议，中国、日本、韩国等 11 个成员国代表出席，会上投票一致决定由中国担任轮值主席国，吴清一出任主席。同时，经吴清一推荐提议，全体代表通过，苏州安华总经理孙延安任副主席。亚洲托盘系统联盟章程规定，轮值主席在中、日、韩三国之间轮流担任，每两年轮换一次。轮值主席主持该联盟各项工作，组织会议讨论，决定重大事项。

（七）“中国托盘质量保障体系”工作取得明显进展

为了促进托盘标准化，扩大符合质量要求的托盘利用范畴，托盘委从 2012 年起开展了构建“托盘质量保障体系”的工作，草拟了一整套“托盘质量保障体系”文件资料，通过全国托盘工作会议、座谈会、论证会等形式，广泛征求行业意见，反复修改完善，形成了实施方案，2013 年开始尝试在木质托盘企业展开企业认定，2014 年开始对塑料及金属托盘企业展开认定，取得了良好的社会反响，也得到了军队等相关部门的认可。部分招标文件中已明确规定，凡参与招标项目必须是托盘委认定的企业，否则不允许参加竞标。托盘质量认定具有现实意义和长远利益，也是与欧洲托盘认定相应的具有国际主权意义的大事。

二、2015 年托盘业发展展望

2015 年，我国全面进入中高速增长的新的历史阶段，全球经济缓慢复苏，国内经济面临下行压力。我们也应该看到，新常态下的中国已成为世界经济增长的引擎，对外投资规模已大于吸引外资规模，经历改革历练的中国企业，在组织创新、管理创新、技术创新和模式创新等方面已积累了大量经验，其在国际经济舞台上竞争力不可小觑。从托盘发展规律看，托盘的发展并不一定与经济社会发展趋同。从国外一些国家情况来看，往往越是在经济不景气的时候，托盘的发展状况越好。理由之一是企业越是在经济不振情况下，越重视增收节支，压缩人工费首当其冲，这种情况下托盘的用量会徒然增大，我国近几年的状况也证明了这一点；理由之二是随着物流瓶颈问题凸显，人们愈发认识到，解决物流效率和成本问题的有效途径之一是利用托盘。近几年我国托盘的总产量和总用量双双明显上升，也足以验证这一说法；理由之三是我国托盘行业已逐渐发展并趋于成熟。托盘行业组织的认可度、影响力显著扩大，托盘行业队伍建设和凝聚程度显著加强；理由之四是托盘企业的经营管理水平、技术创新程度、抗险解困能力等发生了可喜变化；理由之五是我国政府对托盘业的重视和支持力度明显加大。商务部采取的一连串政策举措就是有力的见证。所以，我们认为，2015 年托盘业充满期待。

（中国物流与采购联合会托盘专业委员会　靳伟）

2014 年自动导引车发展回顾与 2015 年展望

一、机器人热解读

近年来，关于机器人技术发展，国际大环境下出现两个代表性事件：美国总统奥巴马提出的“再工业化”和欧洲提出的“新工业革命”战略。这两个战略在全球范围内掀起了一股自动化、数字化、智能化的浪潮，其核心设备就是机器人。

2014 年 6 月，习近平总书记在两院院士大会讲话中提到，“机器人革命”有望成为“第三次工业革命”的一个切入点和重要增长点，将影响全球制造业格局，而且我国将成为全球最大的机器人市场。总书记明确提出要求：“我们不仅要把我国机器人水平提高上去，而且要尽可能多地占领市场。”“以空间换面积，以机器换人力”的装备发展战略受到重视，各行业对传统装备的升级换代充满了期待。

2013 年 12 月 30 日，工信部发布《工业和信息化部关于推进工业机器人产业发展的指导意见》，已经明确把 AGV 产品纳入工业机器人范畴，要求到 2020 年形成较为完善的产业体系。工业机器人主要分关节式机器人和移动式机器人，目前科技界把移动机器人称为自动导引车（Automated Guided Vehicle, AGV），是实现柔性制造和自动化物流输送的重要设备。

从国内因素来看，随着中国人口红利消失，劳动力成本的上升，对工业产品质量要求的提高以及产业升级转型需求的更加迫切，企业对高效、节能、环保的自动化生产和自动化搬运的需求越来越高，对 AGV 的需求也将呈不断增长态势，AGV 市场规模将不断扩大，直接推动了相关企业的快速发展。

从微观上看，很多地方为促进本区域产业升级都在积极发展机器人产业，如重庆、上海、青岛、沈阳、杭州等地制定了很多优惠政策吸引机器人项目落地。在上述因素影响下，正是因为看到了 AGV 的市场潜力，除了原有的 AGV 企业在加大投入、扩充产能外，国内大大小小 AGV 厂家不断涌现，由过去三四家迅速扩展到几十家，很多企业从零部件、集成商、用户等角色进入该领域。而且 AGV 行业还引起资本市场的浓厚兴趣，其他行业的一些企业纷纷成立 AGV 研发部门，甚至通过并购进入这一新兴领域，对 AGV 行业发展起到良好推动作用。中国坐拥全球最有活力的消费市场和最大的制造体系，正面临一场机器人产业带来的盛宴，吸引了政府、媒体、企业、资本的关注和期待。预计在 2015 年，这股机器人行业的投资热潮还难以退烧。

二、2014 年国内自动导引车（AGV）行业发展回顾

1. 市场销售情况

AGV 在中国的应用领域由传统生产制造物流领域扩大到电商分拣、户外运输巡检以及医疗服务领域，且随着“数字化车间”和“智能物流”趋势加快发展，AGV 市场需求增长势头愈发迅猛。按笔者通过 2014 年招投标信息及对 AGV 企业调研的保守估计，2014 年国内 AGV 的市场销售总额约为 7 亿元人民币，AGV/AGC（Automated Guided Cart）产品的销售数量大约为 2500 台。

2. 需求行业

汽车制造业对 AGV 的需求仍然保持了旺盛态势，主要需求体现在两大领域：一是新建和改造的汽车总装车间底盘合装 AGV，该领域应用的 AGV 需要与汽车装配工艺相结合，因此对 AGV 的行走控制、举升控制、同步跟踪技术要求非常高，且对 AGV 稳定性及可靠性要求非常严格，这一市场基本上被富有经验的国内外 AGV 生产厂家垄断。二是汽车生产中物料车输送，也就是简易 AGC，其特点是控制简单，固定路线，不需要复杂的调度管理，稳定性对车间生产没有实质性影响。此类 AGC 产品的入门门槛较低，价值偏低，但市场需求量大。

烟草行业作为传统 AGV 需求大户，因“十二五”技改计划基本完成，2014 年市场需求与往年相比呈下降趋势，未来几年基本围绕 AGV 更新换代及少量新厂投资购买。

2014 年 AGV 新兴市场需求集中在国家电网机器人户外巡检领域，这一领域因行业特殊性，市场需求取决于户外导航技术可靠性及产品实用性有待行业认可与运行时间检验。

其他 AGV 传统需求行业如家电、造纸、医疗、印刷、食品、化工、军事等，对 AGV 的需求也呈旺盛态势。特别是家用电器行业，2014 年 AGV 需求量比往年应当成倍增长，但受生产企业利润影响，此类企业基本局限于使用简易 AGC 产品。

3. 技术创新

2014 年中高端 AGV 的技术创新主要体现在导航技术先进性、负载大功率突破、户外应用技术提升以及供电方式多样化等方面。

从导航技术来说，越来越多的 AGV 生产商着眼于未来，研发更多先进的

导航技术，也就是由原来固定路径导航逐渐向自由路径导航发展。如自主激光导航、惯性导航、二维码导航、差分 GPS 导航及自然轮廓导航等等，有的已经有了成熟实际应用案例，有的已经具备市场应用条件。

从 AGV 负载能力来说，国内企业通过对 AGV 液压浮动轮系技术开发，已经成功生产出负载 40 ~ 80 吨的 AGV，且可以通过双车协调来满足更大体积物体在狭窄空间的输送需求。

此外，为满足 AGV 连续运转及环保要求，非接触供电模式 AGV 在 2014 年也取得更大技术进步。

4. 竞争态势

2014 年国产自主品牌 AGV 无论是市场份额还是产品国产化率都达到 80%。同时国内又新增了有能力出口海外市场的 AGV 厂家，使海外市场对中国 AGV 产品质量及稳定性的认识得到整体提升，间接促进行业快速发展。

国内传统 AGV 企业基本有自己固定领域客户，中高端需求市场因为对 AGV 稳定性和可靠性要求比较严格，基本由几家国内企业及国外供应商占领。而新进入这一行业的 AGV 企业通过低端 AGC 市场迅速扩大业务范围，逐渐向中高端领域靠拢，整体形成公平的市场竞争态势。新兴领域对 AGV 市场需求，打破了过去行业内出现第一个成功案例后其他需求企业才效仿采购的应用模式，2014 年出现了同一新兴行业内几家企业在同一时间段对 AGV 提出采购需求。这种市场需求的集中出现，规避了因一家企业对 AGV 应用失败而导致整个行业失去应用 AGV 的信心，从而使市场竞争更趋公平化。发生这一变化的主要原因是市场对 AGV 需求迫切，这对 AGV 研发企业迅速开拓新兴市场应用起到至关重要的作用。

三、2015 年 AGV 行业发展展望

通过对国内外影响因素分析，AGV 作为机器人领域最柔性的自动化装配及搬运设备，越来越受到各行各业的青睐。2015 年随着机器人热潮继续发酵，笔者认为 AGV 市场需求将会在历史上首次出现井喷的势头。

首先，2015 年传统生产制造企业升级改造压力大于往年，改造步伐慢或犹豫不决的企业将逐渐被行业所淘汰，机器人换人趋势已经不可避免，加速了 AGV 的应用。

其次，新兴行业对高端 AGV 需求态势明显，如：国家电网巡检 AGV 将扩大采购规模，码头集装箱应用、电商分拣系统等也将扩大对 AGV 的需求规模。

最后，传统应用 AGV 较多的行业领域如汽车、家电、造纸、医疗、印刷、食品、化工、军事，通过这几年的市场培育，已经到了全产业链推广应用阶

段，预计60%以上AGV市场需求将应用到传统行业。

2015年AGV技术发展趋势，一是开放式结构、通用性器件与平台发展，从单片机到PC机到工业控制计算机到PLC，AGV控制将多元化，单机控制技术更加人性化，使AGV更为智能，更加易用，更便于维护。二是稳定可靠的分布式总线结构（CANopen）成为AGV主流控制技术。三是AGV混合供电技术提高，以适应不同客户需求。四是与互联网技术相结合。互联网技术为移动机器人未来发展打开了一扇窗口，互联网大数据与智能移动机器人相互交融的时代已经来临。

2015年市场需求发展趋势，一是AGV与周边设备将紧密结合。AGV性能必须与应用行业领域的“工艺要求”相结合。二是AGV需求将多样化。侧出叉式、货架式、双车协调式以及高位取货式与传统AGV模式相结合。三是AGV导航方式多样化，混合导航、户外导航、无自由路径导航将成为需求热点。四是中低端AGC应用会迅速普及，市场销售额在未来几年会接近高端AGV市场。五是适合户内、户外应用的重载AGV需求呈几何倍数增长。个人乐观估计，2015年中国AGV市场需求将突破3500台左右，市场销售额将达到历史峰值10亿元人民币左右。

长期来看，AGV市场的蓬勃发展源于各行业开始普及应用AGV。在这一过程中，拥有自主技术、雄厚资金、稳定研发技术人员、本土化服务以及对国内行业工艺熟悉等优势的国内AGV企业将是最终受益者。AGV产品集中了传感器技术、机械工程、电子工程、计算机工程、自动化控制工程以及人工智能等多学科的研究成果，代表机电一体化的最高成就，是目前科学技术发展最活跃的领域之一，拥有自主知识产权是未来国内AGV行业发展的必然趋势。国内企业应当继续加强AGV领域的人才培养，通过建立并优化创新人才成长环境，着力培养一批高水平的科研带头人以承担技术创新重任，同时加快完善AGV行业技术标准，提供AGV专业人员相互交流的平台等，是所有从事AGV领域的业内人士的共识。

（新松机器人自动化股份有限公司　王玉鹏）

2014 年物流业物联网发展回顾与 2015 年展望

一、2014 年物流业物联网发展回顾

（一）物联网技术应用推动物流业进入 4.0 时代

现代物流是具有流动特征的复合型产业，一边连接着制造业，一边连接着消费者。我们认为，传统的物流系统是物流 1.0 时代；随着信息技术的发展，科学技术的进步，使得原材料、在制品、制成品从供应地到消费地的运动和储存等相关活动的信息可以通过各种手段更方便地沟通，现代物流各环节可以统一考虑，系统运筹。这使得企业在研究客户需求信息的基础上，能够对物流作业各功能环节的活动进行高效而经济的计划、执行和控制，从而引发了现代物流理念的变革，现代物流进入了一体化物流（logistics）时代，这就是物流 2.0 时代。当现代物流与制造业信息深度融合与共享，制造业在采购获得、制造支持和产品销售等各环节均能以客户需求为导向，不仅实现企业信息系统的快速反应及生产线的柔性制造，还可以实现企业信息流、物流与资金流信息的全面融合，物流进入供应链管理时代，这是物流 3.0 的时代。

2014 年，随着物联网技术的发展，物联网技术在物流业应用也不断深入，物联网与云计算、大数据、移动互联网等现代信息技术不断融合，逐步形成了综合的互联网与实体物流网的融合，“互联网 + 现代物流”的模式发展越来越清晰，现代物流进入了 4.0 时代。基于这一背景，在 2014 年我们首次提出了物流互联网概念。

什么是物流互联网？简单地说，物流互联网是实体物理世界的物流系统与线上互联网世界的物流信息系统实现一体化融合的互联网。在这一系统中，互联网成为物流实体运作的主导与控制核心，成为物流系统的“大脑”和神经系统，并通过物流信息互联网向网下物流系统延伸和无缝对接，实现物理世界物流系统全方位的互联互通。

（二）2014 年物流业物联网技术发展回顾

物联网技术是地网（实体物流）与天网（互联网）互相融合的基础，现代物流的自动识别领域是物联网技术的发源地，基于 RFID/EPC 和条码自动识别等技术、各类传感器的感知技术、GPS/GIS 的定位追踪技术，实现了物流系

统的信息实时采集与上网，实现了“物与物自动通信（M2M）”，从而使得物理世界的实体物流网络“地网”与虚拟世界的互联网“天网”对接与融合，进入互联网的物流信息在互联网集合、运算、分析、优化、运筹，再通过互联网分布到整个物流系统，实现对现实物流系统的管理、计划与控制。

随着物联网的发展，2014 年大数据、云计算逐步成为物流信息系统的重要计算与分析手段，其计算与分析模式是分布式和网格式的云计算模式，适应了现代物流实体网络体系的运作，2014 年大数据与云计算与物联网技术融合，在物流领域得到了较大应用。

物联网技术是天网与地网互联互通的核心，物联网技术的落地应用需要各类智能设备来完成。2014 年随着物联网技术的发展，嵌入了物联网技术的物流机械化和自动化智能设备发展很快。如嵌入了智能控制与通信模块的物流机器人、物流自动化设备；嵌入了 RFID 的托盘与周转箱；安装了视频及 RFID 系统的货架系统等都得到了巨大发展。

在制造业物流领域，2014 年随着工业 4.0 技术发展，工业智能化和自动化水平越来越高，对制造业物流中心的智能化发展提出了很高要求。根据调研，2014 年中国制造业新建全自动化立体库突破 300 座，大部分自动化立体库均应用了物联网技术，尤其是传感器感知技术和智能控制技术应用最多。其中，10% 的自动化立体库具备了较高智能化，与生产线的信息系统联网互通，物流中心的现代物流系统与制造系统无缝对接，实现了智能化和自动化，物联网逐渐覆盖企业供应链和物流全系统。

在货物运输领域，2014 年车联网技术飞速发展，货运物联网新的商业模式和技术模式层出不穷，物联网对运输系统的覆盖也由过去的车辆追踪与定位开始向车队管理、车辆维修、金融服务、车辆智能调度等领域全方位延伸，极大促进了货运领域的发展，使小、散、乱、差的货运领域出现了巨大变革。如：G7 货运人将物联网技术融入大车队管理；深圳易流推出了“好多车”全面整合货运资源，把货运透明管理理念融入车队管理；中交兴路推出了车旺云平台……目前基于车货匹配和信息服务的 O2O 货运信息平台就有数百个，各类物流公共物流信息平台超过 1000 个，卡行、安能等企业通过信息平台整合货运市场已经得到了资本投资，实现了快速发展。

在电子商务领域，2014 年阿里巴巴的智能物流骨干网建设逐步落地实施，阿里在智慧物流领域最主要的优势是对货源的大数据分析和优化，通过物流大数据的分析与优化，借助物联网和互联网技术，与快递企业和物流公司实现平台对接，促进了智慧物流发展。京东自建的现代物流系统越来越完善，初步实现了物流作业智能化和透明化管理，配送包裹实现了全面追踪和追溯。2014 年，国际上亚马逊最新的电商物流中心智能机器人联网运作，让货架动起来，实现货到人拣选，引起业界广泛关注。

（三）2014年智慧物流技术与设备发展回顾

智慧物流系统技术与装备主要集中在三个方面：一是传统物流设施设备的智能化与网络化，这是实现物流设备互联网的基础；二是物流设备的自动化和标准化，这是实现物流作业互联网的基础；三是智能追溯系统应用，这是物流系统信息互联互通的基础。

传统的物流设施设备智能化与网络化，主要体现在仓储设施互联网和仓储设备互联网领域，仓储设施互联网一般通过视频监控的物联网技术、各类传感器技术和仓储信息化技术来实现。视频监控联网是实时了解仓库情况；传感器的感知技术是实时感知仓储的温度、湿度和感知监控危险品，主要用在危险品仓库、冷库等特殊仓库领域；仓库信息化技术是对仓储互联网的管理与控制，涉及WMS等多种信息技术；在仓储设备联网方面，目前主要体现在叉车互联网，物流周转箱和托盘加装RFID实现联网追踪。

2014年，仓储设施互联网方面，视频联网监控技术发展较快，增长速度在15%左右；各类感知技术主要用于特定领域，发展一般，增长速度在10%左右；仓储设备互联网的增长速度最快，应该在20%左右；仓储信息化技术应用最广泛。

2014年物流系统自动与智能作业方面，物流自动化技术发展最快，主要体现在自动化立体库集成技术、自动输送分拣技术设备、智能穿梭车与货架系统、物流机器人搬运、无人机配送等方面。首先，在全自动立体库建设领域，近年来进入快速增长阶段，据预测，2014年市场需求增长在35%以上；在自动输送分拣系统领域，随着电子商务物流高速增长，市场需求预计呈现30%左右的增长；智能穿梭车与货架系统由于能够有效地提升仓库的利用面积，提高物流作业效率，技术门槛不高，近两年出现高速发展，增长速度超过50%；物流机器人是世界机器人的七大应用领域之一，机器人搬运，机器人堆码跺等技术装备近两年进入快速发展阶段，市场增长速度预计在30%以上；物流配送无人机也属于物流机器人系统，2014年国内几大快递与电商企业都在测试配送无人机，制定了无人机配送计划，随着中国低空领域放开和电子商务物流发展，未来预计将进入快速增长阶段。

在智能追溯领域，应用最普遍的物联网感知技术是RFID技术，其次是GPS/GIS移动追踪定位技术和智能手持终端产品。根据最近调研，2014年中国快递行业手持终端扫描设备增长超过20%，很多快递企业的快递员都配备了手持终端扫描设备，通过这个设备，可以实现配送终端接货信息的实施上网，实现对配送货物的透明化管理和信息追踪。在手持终端扫描设备领域，中国企业勇于创新，紧跟互联网可穿戴智能技术发展大潮，研发出了可穿戴的扫描戒指，解放了配送人的双手，创造了世界先进的技术。

物流智能追踪与追溯的互联网应用在物流领域开展的最早，技术最成熟，发展也最快。2014 年物品追溯系统继续获得较快发展，预计发展速度在 32% 以上。在产品追溯领域，食品和医药仍是主要的产品，此外，危险品追溯、疫苗追溯、贵重物品追溯、古董产品追溯、奢侈品追溯等领域也发展很快。随着人们对食品安全和药品安全的重视，这两个领域的智能双向追溯将获得巨大发展。随着社会发展，危险品追溯、贵重物品追溯也会得到巨大发展。

综合来看，在 2014 年，在物流技术与装备领域，借助物联网技术，实现设备的自动化与智能化作业得到了很快发展，综合发展速度超过了 30%，这是目前智慧物流系统物流互联网最实用，应用最落地的智能技术领域。

二、2015 年物流业物联网技术应用发展展望

进入 2015 年，国内外三大国家级战略将对物流业物联网技术应用产生极大影响。

一是德国推出工业 4.0 战略得到全球响应，智能制造和智慧工厂发展得到各国重视，与之配套的物流 4.0 系统也将得到推动与发展。为应对工业 4.0 发展，中国也提出了中国工业 4.0 战略——“中国制造 2025”战略，因此可以预计，2015 年中国制造业物流物联网技术应用将保持快速发展。

二是在今年两会上，国务院总理李克强作的政府工作报告将互联网 + 战略纳入国家战略，“互联网 + 物流”就是物流行业物联网应用的核心，是物流 4.0 的体现——物流互联网。可以预见，2015 年中国物流互联网将获得巨大发展，物联网将更加全面的与大数据、云计算、移动互联网、互联网、实体物流网络和设备全面融合，一个崭新的物流互联网时代将开启，物流行业物联网应用将进入物流互联网时代。

三是 2015 年 1 月 23 日，日本政府正式发布了《日本机器人发展国家战略》，推出了推动机器人发展的一系列政策措施。2014 年物流行业机器人发展成为行业焦点和热点，中国物流机器人发展进入高速增长时代，中国即将成为全球最大的机器人市场，中国机器人行业技术创新也不断加快。

因此，2015 年中国物流物联网技术应用将是大发展的一年。这一年，智能物流技术与装备将获得更快发展，物流实体网络和物流信息网络将借助于物联网技术进一步融合，创造巨大市场空间，获得巨大的发展，更会创新出更多商业模式，在智能追溯领域仍将保持快速发展。

在物流领域物联网技术与产品应用会更加广泛，RFID、GPS、传感技术、

视频技术、条码技术等各项技术都会获得广泛应用，预计增长速度会达到30%以上。

在智能技术与装备领域，预计智能穿梭车与货架系统将继续获得高速发展，增长速度有所回落，预计在50%左右；智能叉车将会获得较快发展，增长速度将达到20%；智能周转箱系统几年来发展很快，预计2015年出货量增长将达到20%；在智能搬运与堆码垛等物流机器人领域，预计2015年也将获得较快发展，发展速度在30%左右；在输送分拣领域的智能分拣技术与装备的应用，随着电子商务物流的快速发展，预计增长幅度将超过40%。

未来物流技术装备将全面向智能化、可视化方向发展，这一领域的发展空间极为广阔，发展也方兴未艾，发展速度预计也将保持在30%左右。

2015年配送终端的自动化与智能化将会取得突破。一方面，无人机送货将取得局部应用，智能货柜终端自提系统增长速度达到40%。另一方面，手持终端设备向可穿戴和小型化发展；智能追溯也会快速发展，中国智能追溯领域的发展速度将在26%以上。

在物流业物联网技术方面，发展的大趋势是物联网技术与互联网技术、移动互联网技术、大数据技术、云计算技术融合，未来物联网技术应用将不再突出，物流互联网概念和模式将取代物流物联网技术模式。在信息系统对货运运力整合方面，将进入万众创新和激烈竞争阶段，大部分货运APP将被市场淘汰，新的货运APP将不断涌现，具有核心竞争力的货运物联网将逐步确立龙头地位。

总之，2015年必将是物联网技术在物流业应用飞速发展的一年，是物联网技术实现落地应用的一年，是中国物流4.0：物流互联网元年。

（《物流技术与应用》杂志　王继祥）

第四章

物流行业基础工作

2014 年物流标准化工作回顾与 2015 年展望

在 2014 年 3 月召开的全国标准化工作会议上，国家质检总局局长支树平在讲话中要求必须以改革创新的精神，全面深化标准化改革。国家标准委主任田世宏在会议上强调，企业标准备案制度改革的目的，就是减少政府过多干预企业行为，减轻企业负担，切实落实企业主体责任，要逐步改为企业产品、服务标准自我声明和公开制度。这也标示着我国物流标准化改革正式拉开了序幕。

回顾 2014 年，物流标准化工作得到了国家领导、各级政府部门、社会团体的重视，越来越多的企业将标准和品牌相结合，物流标准化工作在经济转型升级的背景下，在标准化改革的大方向下，逐步走向市场，经受市场的检验。

一、2014 年物流标准化工作回顾

（一）物流标准化政策环境回顾

1. 多部门和地方发布政策文件要求加强物流标准化工作

（1）国务院《物流业发展中长期规划（2014—2020 年）》

2014 年 9 月 12 日，国务院印发了《物流业发展中长期规划（2014—2020 年）》（国发〔2014〕42 号），《规划》多处提到物流标准化工作，在《规划》的主要发展原则中提出要“积极发挥政府在战略、规划、政策、标准等方面的引导作用”，要“完善标准，提高效率”；在七个主要任务中提出要“加强物流标准化建设”，要求“加紧编制并组织实施物流标准中长期规划，完善物流

标准体系。按照重点突出、结构合理、层次分明、科学适用、基本满足发展需要的要求，完善国家物流标准体系框架，加强通用基础类、公共类、服务类及专业类物流标准的制定工作，形成一批对全国物流业发展和服务水平提升有重大促进作用的物流标准。注重物流标准与其他产业标准以及国际物流标准的衔接，科学划分推荐性和强制性物流标准，加大物流标准的实施力度，努力提升物流服务、物流枢纽、物流设施设备的标准化运作水平。调动企业在标准制修订工作中的积极性，推进重点物流企业参与专业领域物流技术标准和管理标准的制定和标准化试点工作。加强物流标准的培训宣传和推广应用”。将物流标准化工作纳入了未来几年开展的 12 个重点工程中，要“重点推进物流技术、信息、服务、运输、货代、仓储、粮食等农产品及加工食品、医药、汽车、家电、电子商务、邮政（含快递）、冷链、应急等物流标准的制修订工作，积极着手开展钢铁、机械、煤炭、铁矿石、石油石化、建材、棉花等大宗产品物流标准的研究制订工作。支持仓储和转运设施、运输工具、停靠和卸货站点的标准化建设和改造，制定公路货运标准化电子货单，推广托盘、集装箱、集装袋等标准化设施设备，建立全国托盘共用体系，推进管理软件接口标准化，全面推广甩挂运输试点经验。开展物流服务认证试点工作，推进物流领域检验检测体系建设，支持物流企业开展质量、环境和职业健康安全管理体系认证。”《规划》为未来五年物流标准化工作提出了总的纲领。

（2）国务院《关于加快发展生产性服务业促进产业结构调整升级的指导意见》

2014 年 7 月 28 日，国务院印发《关于加快发展生产性服务业促进产业结构调整升级的指导意见》（国发〔2014〕26 号），提出要“完善物流建设和服务标准，引导物流设施资源集聚集约发展”，要“提高物流行业标准化设施、设备和器具应用水平以及托盘标准化水平”“推进货运汽车（挂车）、列车标准国际化”“推动城市配送车辆标准化、标识化”“在关系民生的农产品、药品、快速消费品等重点领域开展标准化托盘循环共用示范试点”，在物流设施、标准化设备的应用，以及与国际标准的衔接方面提出了指导意见。《意见》还提出要健全节能环保的标准体系增强节能环保指标的刚性约束，严格落实奖惩措施。在保障措施中也提出应重点支持标准体系等的建设，探索完善财政资金投入方式，推动建立统一开放、规范竞争的服务业市场体系。

（3）国务院《关于依托黄金水道推动长江经济带发展的指导意见》

2014 年 9 月 12 日，国务院印发《关于依托黄金水道推动长江经济带发展的指导意见》（国发〔2014〕39 号），提出了“依托长江黄金水道，高起点高水平建设综合交通运输体系，推动上中下游地区协调发展、沿海沿江沿边全面开放，构建横贯东西、辐射南北、通江达海、经济高效、生态良好的长江经济带”的总体任务，将加快发展多式联运作为重要任务之一，要求“加快推进铁水、空铁、公水等联运发展，扩大辐射范围，提高联运比重。抓紧制定多式联运标准规范，完善运输装备技术标准体系，推广标准合同范本，统一多式联运单证。培育多式联运经营人”。

（4）交通运输部、公安部、商务部《关于加强城市配送运输与车辆通行管理工作的通知》

2014 年 1 月 20 日，由交通运输部、公安部、商务部联合发文加强城市配送运输与车辆管理的通知，“鼓励企业加快标准化托盘、装卸辅助设备等先进技术和装备的应用”，要求“城市配送车辆应当符合《道路货物运输及站场管理规定》的相关要求和《城市物流配送汽车选型技术要求》（GB/T 29912）的具体规定”，要共同“推动城市配送车辆的标准化、专业化发展”，以解决提高城市配送效率，解决城市配送车辆“进城难、停靠难、装卸难”等突出问题，规范城市配送服务。

（5）国家发展改革委《关于我国物流业信用体系建设的指导意见》

2014 年 11 月 18 日，国家发展改革委会同交通运输部、商务部、国家铁路局、中国民用航空局、国家邮政局、国家标准委联合印发《关于我国物流业信用体系建设的指导意见》（发改运行〔2014〕2613 号），提出“利用信用记录建立企业分类监管制度。针对运输、仓储、代理等不同行业和不同运输方式分别制订信用考核标准，逐步建立行业管理部门和社会信用评价机构相结合，具有监督、申诉和复核机制的综合考核评价体系”，要求“建立完善物流信用法律法规和标准”，“根据物流行业特点和政府监管需要，研究制订物流行业信用信息采集分类共享、物流业信用评价指标体系、物流企业诚信管理体系等标准，形成物流业信用建设的标准体系”，同时“鼓励物流行业协会积极参与物流业信用体系建设，在信用信息采集、评估、标准制订等方面发挥更大作用”。《指导意见》将物流业信用体系建设作为社会信用体系建设的重要组成部分，希望通过信用标准体系的建立，加强政府信用监管，发挥行业协会在诚信体系建设中的引导作用，积极带动物流企业诚信经营，进而提高我国物流业的诚信意识和信用水平，规范市场竞争秩序，实现健康可持续发展。

（6）商务部《关于促进商贸物流发展的实施意见》

2014 年 9 月 22 日，商务部印发了《关于促进商贸物流发展的实施意见》，提出多措并举加快推进商贸物流业发展。《意见》提出，要“创新商贸物流标准宣传贯彻和实施促进的工作机制，提高标准的通用性和统一性。根据社会需求与工作重点，利用各种形式，加强商贸物流标准化理念推广与知识普及。支持各类企业、社会团体积极参与商贸物流标准的制修订。加快商贸物流管理、技术和服务标准的推广，鼓励有关企业采用标准化的物流计量、货物分类、物品标识、物流装备设施、工具器具、信息系统和作业流程等。以标准化托盘循环共用试点工作为切入点，逐步提高全社会标准托盘普及率，促进相关配套设施设备的标准化改造。”并将“选择基础较好、积极性高的地区、园区和企业开展商贸物流标准化应用推广工作，鼓励和指导上述单位加大基础设施、装备技术、服务流程、内部管理等领域的标准化实施力度，培育商贸物流标准化服务和管理品牌；加强行业与行业、企业与企业之间的标准衔接和统一，引导全行业提高标准应用水平、经营管理水平、产品质量水平和从业人员资质水平。”

（7）财政部、商务部、国家邮政局《关于开展电子商务与物流快递协同发展试点有关问题的通知》

2014 年 11 月，财政部、商务部、国家邮政局联合下发了《关于开展电子商务与物流快递协同发展试点有关问题的通知》，决定在天津、石家庄、杭州、福州、贵阳 5 个城市开展电子商务与物流快递协同发展试点。试点工作的发展目标包括：在试点城市建立适合电子商务快速发展的物流快递管理制度和服务体系；将电商物流快递基础设施建设纳入城市总体规划，完善骨干节点和末端投递服务站点建设；建立完善配送车辆标准体系，实现配送车辆规范运营；建立从业人员服务和考核标准，完成对从业人员的培训和考核，全面实现持证上岗。

（8）交通运输部印发贯彻落实《国务院关于促进海运业健康发展的若干意见》的实施方案

为了落实国务院《关于促进海运业健康发展的若干意见》（国发〔2014〕32 号），交通运输部2014 年 10 月 8 日印发了《〈国务院关于促进海运业健康发展的若干意见〉的实施方案》，《方案》提出由交通运输部水运局、运输司牵头制定完善联运单证、标准和集装箱铁水联运规则，大力发展铁水联运、江海联运、滚装甩挂运输，推广应用江海直达船型和联运设施，由交通运输部海事局和安全质量司牵头推进国内海运标准规范的国际化工作，以上工作要在 2015 年取得阶段性成果；由交通运输部科技司、水运局、海事局共同牵头，加强绿色海运标准体系建设，制定完善船舶能效规范、清洁能源动力船舶检验规范等标准规范，并要求在 2016 年取得阶段性成果。

2.《物流标准化中长期发展规划》编制工作启动

为落实国务院发布的《物流业发展中长期规划（2014—2020 年）》，国家标准化管理委员会组织中国物流与采购联合会、北京交通大学交通运输学院、中国标准化研究院等单位于 2014 年 4 月份启动了《物流标准化中长期发展规划（2015—2020 年）》的编制工作，本次编制主要完成三项工作，一是修订和完善物流标准体系，二是提出未来五年的物流标准化工作重点，三是还将在《规划》的基础上提出未来三年的标准项目计划。

2014 年，《规划》经过前期的广泛调研，已组织召开了 15 次研讨和论证，并向社会公开征集意见，目前《规划》完成了送审稿，预计将于 2015 年由国家标准化管理委员会会同十个部门共同发布。本次《规划》分析总结了物流标准化现状、存在的问题，提出了未来五年的指导思想、发展目标、主要任务，标准制修订重点领域，还将针对目前行业内的瓶颈问题提出多项物流标准化工程。《规划》结合了我国标准化整体改革思想，将创新物流标准化工作方法、建立物流标准化的协调机制，开展团体标准试点、发挥行业组织在团体标准工作中的主导地位，标准科学划分层级、加强重点标准研制，强化标准推广实施、加强标准效用评估等内容列入了指导思想、主要任务和标准化工程中，旨在解决目前物流标准“用”的不到位等问题，从而提升物流标准化水平，增强物流标准竞争力，为促进国民经济转型升级和物流业可持续发展提供有力的支撑。

（二）物流标准制修订情况

2014 年新发布物流国家标准 30 项，其中由全国物流标准化技术委员会提出并归口的标准 16 项；新发布物流行业标准 23 项，其中由交通运输部发布的行业标准 16 项，由商务部发布的行业标准 7 项；上海、山东、江苏、四川、黑龙江、海南等 11 个省发布了物流地方标准，2014 年在国家标准委备案的物流地方标准 24 项。内容涉及钢铁物流、危险品物流、石油化工物流、药品物流、汽车物流、烟草物流、粮食物流、水产品物流、家电物流、物流金融、农副产品物流、冷链物流、应急物流、国际货贷等专业类物流标准，以及术语、物流设备、物流单证、甩挂运输、物流信息、节能减排、品牌价值评价等基础类、通用类物流标准。（见表 1 ~ 表 3）。（由全国物流标准化技术委员会归口管理的标准制修订情况及标准内容介绍见附件）

表 1　　　　2014 年发布的物流国家标准目录

序号	标准编号	标准名称	实施日期
1	GB/T 30672—2014	模压平托盘 植物纤维类	2015 - 07 - 01
2	GB/T 30673—2014	自动化立体仓库的安装与维护规范	2015 - 07 - 01
3	GB/T 30674—2014	企业应急物流能力评估规范	2015 - 07 - 01
4	GB/T 30675—2014	阁楼式货架	2015 - 07 - 01
5	GB/T 30676—2014	应急物资投送包装及标识	2015 - 07 - 01
6	GB/T 31078—2014	低温仓储作业规范	2015 - 07 - 01
7	GB/T 31080—2014	水产品冷链物流服务规范	2015 - 07 - 01
8	GB/T 31081—2014	塑料箱式托盘	2015 - 07 - 01

续　表

序号	标准编号	标准名称	实施日期
9	GB/T 31083—2014	乘用车公路运输栓紧带式固定技术要求	2015－07－01
10	GB/T 31084—2014	国际货运代理运输单证交接规范	2015－07－01
11	GB/T 31085—2014	国际货运代理单证签发规范	2015－07－01
12	GB/T 31086—2014	物流企业冷链服务要求与能力评估指标	2015－07－01
13	GB/T 31046—2014	品牌价值评价 交通运输业	2014－12－31
14	GB/T 31005—2014	托盘编码及条码表示	2015－02－01
15	GB/T 31006—2014	自动分拣过程包装物品条码规范	2015－02－01
16	GB/T 31148—2014	联运通用平托盘 木质平托盘	2014－12－01
17	GB/T 31149—2014	汽车物流服务评价指标	2014－12－01
18	GB/T 31150—2014	汽车零部件物流 塑料周转箱尺寸系列及技术要求	2014－12－01
19	GB/T 31151—2014	汽车整车物流质损风险监控要求	2014－12－01
20	GB/T 31152—2014	汽车物流术语	2014－12－01
21	GB/T 31003—2014	化纤物品物流单元编码与条码表示	2015－02－01
22	GB/T 31300—2014	担保存货第三方管理规范	2015－03－01
23	GB/T 30838—2014	契约承运人服务质量要求	2014－08－01
24	GB/T 15634—2014	行政、商业和运输业电子数据交换 段目录（修订，替代标准 GB/T 15634—2008）	2015－08－01
25	GB/T 15635—2014	行政、商业和运输业电子数据交换 复合数据元目录（修订，替代标准 GB/T 15635—2008）	2015－08－01
26	GB/T 17699—2014	行政、商业和运输业电子数据交换 数据元目录（修订，替代标准 GB/T 17699—2008）	2015－08－01
27	GB/T 20799—2014	鲜、冻肉运输条件（修订，替代标准 GB/T 20799—2006）	2015－01－10
28	GB/T 4996—2014	联运通用平托盘 试验方法（修订，替代标准 GB/T 4996—1996）	2015－06－01
29	GB/T 4995—2014	联运通用平托盘 性能要求和试验选择（修订，替代标准 GB/T 4995—1996）	2014－12－01
30	GB/T 20154—2014	低温保存箱（修订，替代标准 GB/T 20154—2006）	2015－12－01

表 2　　　　2014 年发布的物流行业标准目录

序号	标准编号	标准名称	实施日期	标准主管部门
1	JT/T 911—2014	危险货物道路运输企业运输事故应急预案编制要求	2014－11－01	交通运输部
2	JT/T 912—2014	危险货物道路运输企业安全生产管理制度编写要求	2014－11－01	交通运输部
3	JT/T 913—2014	危险货物道路运输企业安全生产责任制编写要求	2014－11－01	交通运输部
4	JT/T 914—2014	危险货物道路运输企业安全生产档案管理技术要求	2014－11－01	交通运输部
5	JT/T 915—2014	机动车驾驶员安全驾驶技能培训要求	2014－11－01	交通运输部
6	JT/T 916—2014	道路运输驾驶员 特殊环境与情境下安全驾驶技能培训与评价方法	2014－11－01	交通运输部
7	JT/T 917. 1—2014	道路运输驾驶员技能和素质要求 第 1 部分：旅客运输驾驶员	2014－11－01	交通运输部
8	JT/T 917. 2—2014	道路运输驾驶员技能和素质要求 第 2 部分：货物运输驾驶员	2014－11－01	交通运输部
9	JT/T 917. 3—2014	道路运输驾驶员技能和素质要求 第 3 部分：出租汽车驾驶员	2014－11－01	交通运输部
10	JT/T 919. 1—2014	交通运输物流信息交换 第 1 部分：数据元	2014－11－01	交通运输部
11	JT/T 919. 2—2014	交通运输物流信息交换 第 2 部分：道路运输电子单证	2014－11－01	交通运输部
12	JT/T 919. 3—2014	交通运输物流信息交换 第 3 部分：物流站场（园区）电子单证	2014－11－01	交通运输部
13	JT/T 697. 6—2014	交通信息基础数据元 第6 部分：船员信息基础数据元（JT/T 697. 6—2008）	2014－11－01	交通运输部
14	JT/T 856—2013	道路运输行业节能评价方法	2014－01－01	交通运输部
15	JT/T 857—2013	道路运输企业节能评价方法	2014－01－01	交通运输部
16	JT/T 869—2013	汽车货运站（场）节能评价方法	2014－01－01	交通运输部
17	SB/T 1036—2013	药品物流设施与设备技术要求	2014－06－01	商务部
18	SB/T 1038—2013	中药材流通追溯体系专用术语规范	2014－06－01	商务部

续　表

序号	标准编号	标准名称	实施日期	标准主管部门
19	SB/T 1039—2013	中药材追溯通用标识规范	2014－06－01	商务部
20	SB/T 11068—2013	网络零售仓储作业规范与评价	2014－12－01	商务部
21	SB/T 11069—2013	城市配送统计指标体系及绩效评估方法	2014－12－01	商务部
22	SB/T 10408—2013	中央储备肉冻肉储存冷库资质条件	2014－12－01	商务部
23	SB/T 10384—2013	中央储备肉活畜储备基地场资质条件	2014－12－01	商务部

表3　　2014年在国家标准委备案的物流地方标准目录

序号	标准编号	标准名称	实施日期	标准主管部门
1	DB31/T 843—2014	钢材质押融资仓储企业管理规范	2015－01－01	上海市质监局
2	DB31/T 826—2014	中药饮片包装编码与条码表示	2014－11－01	上海市质监局
3	DB46/ 284—2014	石油化工可燃液体储存场所消防安全规范	2014－09－01	海南省质监局
4	DB53/T 607.30—2014	烤烟生产 第30部分：仓储、运输、标识管理	2014－10－01	云南省质监局
5	DB36/ 788—2014	道路运输液体危险货物罐式车辆常压罐体定期检验规则	2014－09－01	江西省质监局
6	DB23/T 1533—2013	粮食储存场所消防安全管理技术规范	2013－12－21	黑龙江省质监局
7	DB23/T 1552.2—2014	甩挂运输站场建设要求 第2部分：零担货物 甩挂运输站场	2014－02－23	黑龙江省质监局
8	DB23/T 1553—2014	甩挂运输站场信息化建设要求	2014－02－23	黑龙江省质监局
9	DB23/T 1554—2014	甩挂运输车辆装卸货站台技术要求	2014－02－23	黑龙江省质监局

续 表

序号	标准编号	标准名称	实施日期	标准主管部门
10	DB51/T 1726—2014	危险化学品钢制包装容器安全性能检验规则	2014－05－01	四川省质监局
11	DB32/T 2666—2014	水产品冷链物流服务规范	2014－04－30	江苏省质监局
12	DB52/T 847.5—2013	施秉太子参 初加工与储藏运输	2013－12－01	贵州省质监局
13	DB21/T 2215—2013	动物及动物产品运输防疫技术规范	2014－01－12	辽宁省质监局
14	DB37/T 2342—2013	第三方物流家电配送服务规范	2013－07－10	山东省质监局
15	DB37/T 2343—2013	物流金融风险控制指南	2013－07－10	山东省质监局
16	DB37/T 2344—2013	物流金融服务规范	2013－07－10	山东省质监局
17	DB37/T 2439.1—2013	鲜活农产品生产流通管理规范 第1部分 蔬菜	2014－02－01	山东省质监局
18	DB37/T 2439.2—2013	鲜活农产品生产流通管理规范 第2部分 猪肉	2014－02－01	山东省质监局
19	DB37/T 2454—2013	普通货物运输物流单证数据元规范	2014－02－01	山东省质监局
20	DB37/T 2455—2013	商贸流通产品数据元规范	2014－02－01	山东省质监局
21	DB46/T 269—2013	农产品流通信息追溯系统建设与管理规范	2014－02－01	海南省质监局
22	DB22/T 1960—2013	药品运输管理要求	2013－12－31	吉林省质监局
23	DB22/T 1938—2013	物流快递质量服务规范	2013－12－31	吉林省质监局
24	DB22/T 1939—2013	物流仓储服务质量规范	2013－12－31	吉林省质监局

（三）标准的实施、宣传、推广情况

1. 服务业标准化试点

为了加快服务业发展，由国家标准化管理委员会和国家发展和改革委员会牵头并会同国务院有关部门和地方质量技术监督局、地方有关部门共同组织的“服务业标准化试点”工作。从2009年开始到2014年已有43家物流企业申请试点，标准化试点是一项以建立和实施服务业标准体系为主要内容，以实现管理规范、服务质量良好、顾客满意度高为目标探索性活动，参加试点的企业要求三年内未发生重大产品（服务）质量、安全健康、环境保护等事故，能够体现行业特色，服务提供的各个环节应有标准可依，标准齐全。标准覆盖率达到

80%以上，与本行业、本单位有关的国家标准、行业标准、地方标准和企业标准应得到有效实施，实施率达到90%等。2013年经审查新确定了10项物流“国家级服务业标准化试点”项目，10家物流企业申请并确定为标准化试点单位，标准的试点项目从2014年开始到2015年结束，企业通过标准的实施与企业自身的持续改进相结合，与企业的服务品牌创建相结合，以不断提高服务标准化效果，引导服务企业向标准化、品牌化的方向发展。

2．商贸物流标准化服务试点

2014年国家标准委、商务部联合印发《关于加快推进商贸物流标准化工作的意见》，在全国部署实施商贸物流标准化工作。12月12日，商务部流通发展司、国标委服务业部在京召开商贸物流标准化专项行动工作部署会议，进一步落实专项工作。此次专项行动以降低物流成本、提高物流效率为目标，坚持市场主导，从托盘标准化入手，在快速消费品等领域，率先开展标准托盘应用推广及循环共用，带动上下游关联领域物流标准化水平的提高；从物流综合信息服务平台建设规范和服务规范入手，增强平台服务功能，促进资源共享和信息互联互通。此次专项行动计划实施时间约为5年，其中，第一阶段为2015—2016年，通过重点推进企业充分利用专项行动的契机，使得自身标准化建设迈上新台阶，第一批确定了40家“全国商贸物流标准化重点推进企业”，包括30家重点企业，如托盘租赁服务企业招商路凯、集保（CHEP）、上海百联等；商贸连锁企业华润集团、国药集团、1号店等；快速消费品生产企业中粮集团、珠江啤酒、顺鑫农业等；托盘生产企业山东力扬、上海新通联等；第三方物流企业青岛日日顺、顺丰速运、宝供物流等。

3．冷链物流标准试点

2014年，由中国物流与采购联合会冷链物流专业委员会牵头组织，相继在食品物流企业和药品物流企业开展了《食品冷链物流追溯管理要求》和《药品冷链物流运作规范》两项国家标准试点活动。《食品冷链物流追溯管理要求》和《药品冷链物流运作规范》是2012年发布的两项国家标准，标准规定了食品和药品冷链物流全过程的管理要求，以及物流过程中的温控要求等。目前，加工食品和冷藏药品的规范管理已经成为各级政府、药品生产企业、经营企业、使用单位十分关注的问题，中物联冷链委依据标准的主要内容，从企业从业人员、制度、设施设备、流程控制等多个方面进一步细化了指标，并从申报的企业中分别选取了有代表性的30家食品物流企业和32家医药物流企业开展标准的试点。中物联冷链委将通过标准试点，通过一到两年考察企业的KPI达标情况，从试点企业中推出冷链服务的示范企业。关键标准的试点对行业和企业发展均是一个良好的开端，通过标准的试点活动一是提升企业对食品药品安全保障的社会职责感，同时通过标准的达标，也是对服务方、对药品使用者和社会服务承诺的展示。二是通过试点帮助企业建立品牌服务意识，标准化管理意识，把标准作为提升企业服务质量的重要手段之一，在共同的标准下谈服务、谈能力，为行业创造健康的、规范的市场环境。

4. 一些重点物流国家标准和行业标准贯彻实施

《物流企业分类与评估指标》从2005年发布已有十个年头，中国物流与采购联合会依据标准开展的物流企业评估工作也取得了很好的成效。2014年7月1日新修订的标准正式实施，中物联物流企业评估办公室针对新标准于4月和9月召开了标准的宣贯培训研讨会议，进行了《物流企业分类与评估指标》国家新旧标准修改部分的对照解读，先后有600余人参加了培训和宣贯会议。

金融物流创新业务中质押融资已经成为广大企业尤其是众多中小企业获取业务发展资金，改善融资渠道的一个重要手段，动产的质押监管开展十余年间没有具体标准进行规范，造成这项对金融机构、商贸制造业、物流企业多方有利、互惠共赢的业务在实际操作环节中出现了许多不该发生的事件。2014年，为加强物流行业自律，促进物流市场的健康、规范发展，中国物流与采购联合会依据《质押监管企业评估指标》（SB/T 10979—2013）行业标准启动并开展了物流企业质押监管评估工作，全年评估质押监管企业52家，通过标准的贯彻实施对规范物流市场，完善服务体系，提升物流服务质量，扩充融资渠道，提高企业服务能力起到了重要作用。

2014年还开展了多样的标准化活动，如在汽车物流企业中开展“汽车零部件物流标准化倡议活动”，在物流园区企业中开展的《物流园区服务规范与评估指标》国家标准的宣贯研讨活动；与厦门市标准化院成立两岸食品冷链物流标准工作组，共同推动的开展两岸食品冷链物流标准的对标活动；珠海市港口管理局开展的“物流市场新发展、政策及标准系列培训”，陆续举办了物流仓储系列标准、物流园区系列标准、物流合同及单证系列标准、口岸物流标准、物流企业服务和质押监管评估系列标准、物流统计及企业物流成本构成系列标准等几大系列15项国家标准的培训等标准的宣传贯彻工作，提升了行业和企业整体的标准化认知。

（四）2014年物流标准化工作的特点

1. 标准的制定与实施相结合

一是政府监管与标准相结合，如交通运输部发布的道路运输车辆动态监督管理，在管理办法中明确要求道路运输车辆卫星定位系统平台和定位装置应符合现行的7项国家和行业标准，将标准与政府管理相结合；二是行业主管部门积极采取多项措施，在行业内推动标准的实施，如国家标准化管理委员会和商务部共同开展的标准化托盘推广，从托盘标准化入手，依据现有的两项联运平托盘国家标准开展标准托盘应用推广及循环共用，带动上下游关联领域物流标准化水平的提高；如交通运输部联合物流龙头企业进行电商平台、快递、运输仓储、物流园区等企业开展的交通运输物流信息互联共享平台标准的发布与实施，将标准与平台运行相结合，使用标准具体可更强的操作性。

2．与民生相关的物流标准受到关注

我国发布的农副产品和食品冷链物流标准已达到了150余项，但冷链物流仍存在着标准实施有待加强，涉及安全的标准无监管等问题。随着居民消费水平的提高和食品安全意识的增强，我国冷链运输物流需求将快速增长，2014年国务院转发了国家发改委《关于上半年经济形势和做好下半年经济工作的建议的通知》，要求进一步促进我国冷链运输物流企业健康发展，提升冷链运输物流服务水平。发改委为了落实通知要求，发布了《关于进一步促进冷链运输物流企业健康发展的指导意见》，提出要“制修订食品冷链配送操作规范、食品冷链温度控制等冷链基础、冷链管理、冷链设施、冷链技术等层面的标准”，加强冷链物流标准的培训宣传和推广应用，要“研究制定冷藏保温车辆分类及技术要求”，推动冷链运输车辆标准化、专业化”，要“研究探索对关系到居民食品安全的肉类、水产品等农产品运输执行强制性标准”。国家标准委也正在研究冷链物流标准化实施方案，下一步将在农副产品和食品冷链物流标准的清理、涉及安全标准的实施上加大力度。

随着互联网与电子商务的高速发展，快递服务不仅在企业数量、市场规模等方面迅速发展，与民生直接相关，还与信息技术紧密结合，快递收派作业专用的电动三轮车安全要求、邮政快递业的信息安全及信息交换问题也日益变得重要和突出，2014年国家邮政局审查通过的《快递专用电动三轮车技术要求》行业标准规定了快递专用电动三轮车的设计要求、时速要求、使用管理要求等，不仅可以为使用部门提供可靠的技术依据，还可引导快递专用电动三轮车有序发展、规范运行，提升快递服务形象，提高快递服务质量。即将开展的快递服务与银行、民航、电子商务、制造服务等信息交换标准也将进一步保证各类信息安全，保障用户合法权益等方面提供技术支撑。

3．公益类物流标准成为标准制定重点

物流业是新兴行业，绿色物流还刚刚起步，2014年，国务院发布的《物流业中长期发展规划》将大力发展绿色物流作为主要任务之一，在优化运输方式、节能减排、发展先时的物流组织模式、设施设备的有效利用、物流包装的循环使用等方面提出了要求，要求加快建立绿色物流评估标准和认证体系。交通运输部2014年行业节能减排工作要点也提出“组织完善交通运输节能减排规划标准，提出交通运输行业节能减排标准体系规划”。国家邮政局提出的《快递服务温室气体排放测量方法》行业标准通过审查，政府已开始从宏观管理上将绿色物流的推进与物流标准化工作提上日程。

物流诚信是物流企业对社会的一种信义的践行承诺，据北京交通大学交通运输学院做的物流诚信企业调查，物流企业诚信存在着虚假承诺高质服务、违规泄露客户信息、不按合同执行、企业信息造假等失信或不诚信现象，社会对物流业诚信的认可度总体偏低。2014 年，一些公共服务平台、企业联盟相继制定诚信联盟标准，通过标准的实施在平台和联盟的范围内发布失信企业名单、司机和快递员黑名单等，实现信息共享。

2014 年，由中国物流与采购联合会主持向国家质监局申报拟开展的质检公益课题研究，也将《绿色物流指标构成》《绿色仓储与配送要求及评估》《绿色仓储与配送技术装备要求及评估》《物流设施设备的选用参数要求》《托盘单元化物流系统规范》等绿色物流关键标准，以及《物流企业诚信要素构成》《商贸物流企业信用评价实施规范》等国标作为制定的重点。

二、2015 年物流标准化工作展望

（一）物流标准化面临的形势

1. 国家标准化改革

党的十八大以来，党中央、国务院提出实施创新驱动战略，在促进经济提质增效升级等方面提出了许多新要求，标准化法的修订、标准化改革是 2014 年标准化工作的一项重点。国务院总理李克强 2 月 11 日主持召开国务院常务会议，确定推进标准化工作改革措施、促进经济提质增效升级。会议提出，必须深化改革，优化标准体系，完善标准管理，着力改变目前一些方面存在的标准管理“软”、标准体系“乱”和标准水平“低”的状况，拟全面清理和修订现行国家、行业、地方标准，整合现行各级强制性标准，在涉及公众利益的健康、安全、环保等领域建立统一的强制性国家标准，逐步缩减推荐性标准，推动向公益类标准过渡。

会议指出，推动中国经济迈向中高端水平，提高产品和服务标准是关键。必须深化改革，优化标准体系，完善标准管理，着力改变目前一些方面存在的标准管理“软”、标准体系“乱”和标准水平“低”的状况，促进提升产品和服务竞争力，激发市场活力，推进经济提质增效升级。会议确定，一是完善标准化法规制度，开展标准实施效果评价，强化监督检查和行政执法，严肃查处违法违规行为，让标准成为对质量的“硬约束”。二是全面清理和修订现行国家、行业、地方标准，整合现行各级强制性标准，在涉及公众利益的健康、安全、环保等领域建立统一的强制性国家标准，逐步缩减推荐性标准，推动向公益类标准过渡。三是鼓励学会、协会、商会和产业技术联盟等制定发布满足市

场和创新需要的团体标准，选择部分领域开展试点。允许企业自主制定实施产品和服务标准，建立企业标准自我声明公开制度。四是提高标准国际化水平。进一步放宽外资企业参与中国标准制定工作，以有效的市场竞争促进标准上水平。努力使我国标准在国际上立得住、有权威、有信誉，为中国制造走出去提供“通行证”。

2. 物流标准化面临的新形势

当前，伴随着经济全球化深入发展，改革全面深化、经济转型持续升级、产业结构不断调整、物流市场快速发展、企业对物流标准需求日益增加等变化，我国物流标准化工作面临新的形势。一是随着标准化工作改革，物流标准化的创新，物流标准层级科学化分，开展多样化、实用性强的物流团体标准是物流标准化的新趋势；二是随着科技进步促进生产工艺不断变革、产品更新速度持续加快，催生了一系列物流新技术、新服务与新模式，亟须在相关领域制修订一批物流标准，提高采购、生产、销售、回收等供应链各环节标准的协调一致性，以保障优质、高效、稳定、便捷的物流服务，推动产业融合发展。三是经济社会的快速发展和人民生活水平的不断提高，促使公共利益维护意识不断增强，对资源节约、环境保护、市场秩序稳定、诚信建设、消费者利益维护等方面提出更高要求，亟须在相关领域开展物流标准制修订工作，并加强标准的执行力与监管力，保证公共利益不受侵害。四是物流市场的统一开放、深入发展，要求打破地区间、行业间的技术封锁和交流障碍，这就需要物流标准化规范市场秩序、构建公平竞争环境，为物流市场运行提质增效提供规范化支撑。五是随着国际产业转移发展和我国“走出去”战略的实施，与采购、生产、销售、回收全球化相适应的物流模式正在形成，我国物流企业参与国际竞争的程度不断加深，迫切需要从服务品质、设施设备、术语标识等方面与国际标准对接。

（二）2015 年物流标准化工作重点

2015 年国家质检总局将会同有关部门负责加强技术标准体系建设工作，总的思路是管放结合，把该管的管住管好，把该放的放开放到位。2015 年基本建成强制性与推荐性标准协调配套、符合经济社会和科技发展需要的技术标准体系。2015 年物流标准化工作将在以下几个方面重点开展。

1. 建立物流标准化的协调机制

将由国家标准化管理委员会牵头，建立物流标准化的协调工作组，一是建立与物流相关的政府管理部门的标准化管理部门协调工作组，二是建立与物流相关的标准化技术组织协调工作组，三是组建物流标准化专家委员会，力争在物流标准化的顶层设计及重大问题方面，在标准的立项、征求意见及审查等方面实现沟通与协调。

2．团体标准工作体系建设及制定

开展物流团体标准的试点活动，组织搭建团体标准工作体系，研究制定工作流程及管理办法，开展团体标准制定。

3．物流诚信要素构成和信息化平台建设

了解物流行业目前的诚信信息平台建设、企业联盟诚信、企业诚信建设情况，从政府监管、行业管理、企业自律等维度制定《物流企业诚信要素构成》标准，统一要素的概念，为诚信信息平台的数据共享提供依据。

4．信息接口与信息安全标准制定

重点研究制定物流信息基础数据元标准、信息公共服务平台接口标准，快递物流信息交换安全规范等信息标准的制定。

5．设施设备和集装单元化标准制定

在物流设施设备方面，重点研究制定物流设施、物流仓储设备、运输设备等的设计尺寸参数标准，制定集装单元化的托盘标准，以提高设施的有效利用和设备间相互转换的有效衔接。

附件：

全国物流标准化技术委员会归口的标准情况介绍

1. 新发布国家标准

2014 年，国家标准委批准发布、由全国物流标准化技术委员会提出并归口管理的国家标准 16 项，这些标准中有 6 项于 2014 年 12 月 1 日开始实施，其余 10 项分别于 2015 年 6 月和 7 月 1 日实施（见附表 1）。

附表 1　　2014 年新发布的物流国家标准

序号	标准名称	标准号	发布日期	实施日期
1	联运通用平托盘 性能要求和试验选择	GB/T 4995—2014 替代 GB/T 4995—1996	2014－09－03	2014－12－01
2	联运通用平托盘 木质平托盘	GB/T 31148—2014	2014－09－03	2014－12－01
3	汽车物流服务评价指标	GB/T 31149—2014	2014－09－03	2014－12－01
4	汽车零部件物流 塑料周转箱尺寸系列及技术要求	GB/T 31150—2014	2014－09－03	2014－12－01

续　表

序号	标准名称	标准号	发布日期	实施日期
5	汽车整车物流质损风险监控要求	GB/T 31151—2014	2014-09-03	2014-12-01
6	汽车物流术语	GB/T 31152—2014	2014-09-03	2014-12-01
7	联运通用平托盘试验方法	GB/T 4996—2014 替代 GB/T 4996—1996	2014-10-10	2014-06-01
8	塑料箱式托盘	GB/T 31081—2014	2014-12-22	2014-07-01
9	水产品冷链物流服务规范	GB/T 31080—2014	2014-12-22	2014-07-01
10	低温仓储作业规范	GB/T 31078—2014	2014-12-22	2014-07-01
11	物流企业冷链服务要求与能力评估指标	GB/T 31086—2014	2014-12-22	2014-07-01
12	模压平托盘 植物纤维类	GB/T 30672—2014	2014-12-31	2014-07-01
13	自动化立体仓库的安装与维护规范	GB/T 30673—2014	2014-12-31	2014-07-01
14	企业应急物流能力评估规范	GB/T 30674—2014	2014-12-31	2014-07-01
15	阁楼式货架	GB/T 30675—2014	2014-12-31	2014-07-01
16	应急物资投送包装及标识	GB/T 30676—2014	2014-12-31	2014-07-01

★ 联动通用平托盘系列标准

托盘作为物流基础的作业单元，在运输、仓储、装卸搬运、配送等物流各环节中起着有效衔接、顺畅贯通的关键作用，对提高物流作业效率、降低物流成本也至关重要。我国托盘的循环利用正在引起社会、政府和企业的高度重视。联运通用平托盘的系列标准对标准化托盘的尺寸和质量进行了明确规定，相关系列标准的制定和实施是提高托盘利用水平、实现托盘共用的基础和有力保障。

我国已发布的、现行的“联运通用平托盘”系列国家标准主要有四个：《联运通用平托盘主要尺寸及公差》《联运通用平托盘 性能要求和试验选择》《联运通用平托盘 试验方法》和《联运通用平托盘 木质平托盘》。其中《联运通用平托盘主要尺寸及公差》于1982年首次发布，1996年、2007年分别两次进行了修订，《联运通用平托盘 性能要求和试验选择》《联运通用平托盘 试验方法》于1985年首次发布，1996年进行了第一次修订，本次为第二次修订，《联运通用平托盘 木质平托盘》为新发布标准。

（1）《联运通用平托盘 性能要求和试验选择》（GB/T 4995—2014，替代GB/T 4995—1996）

新发布的《联运通用平托盘 性能要求和试验选择》是一项修订标准，标准替代《联运通用平托盘 性能要求》（GB/T 4995—1996）国家标准。本次标准的修订主要依据国内托盘行业现阶段发展的新要求，对应新修订发布的国际相关标准，修改采用了ISO 8611－2－2011《物料搬运托盘　平托盘　第2部分：性能要求和试验选择》，标准规定了联运通用平托盘的性能要求和试验选择原则，适用于公路、铁路和水路的联运通用平托盘的设计、生产、检验及使用。

本次修订的主要内容包括：一是增加了有关选择预处理环境条件的内容；二是修改了托盘性能要求；三是增加了试验选择原则，即增加了根据托盘用途选择所需进行的试验项目的内容；四是增加了确定试验载荷方法的内容。

（2）《联运通用平托盘试验方法》（GB/T 4996—2014，替代GB/T 4996—1996）

新发布的《联运通用平托盘试验方法》是一项修订标准，标准替代《联运通用平托盘试验方法》（GB/T 4996—1996）国家标准。标准规定了联运通用平托盘性能的试验方法，适用于公路、铁路和水路的联运通用平托盘的设计、生产、检验及使用。为了确保与国际标准的相互衔接，本次修订的标准为修改采用ISO 8611－1：2011《物料搬运托盘　平托盘　第1部分：试验方法》。标准共分九章，给出托盘主要试验方法14项，包括：抗弯试验、叉举试验、垫块或纵梁抗压试验、堆码试验、底铺板抗弯试验、翼托盘抗弯试验、气囊抗弯试验、静态剪切试验、角跌落试验、剪切冲击试验、顶铺板边缘冲击试验、垫块冲击试验、静摩擦系数试验和滑动角试验。以考量托盘及其构件在堆码、叉举、货架存取、吊索提升等不同工作环境的承载能力、抗变形抗冲击能力以及防滑性能等，确保在整个物流过程中托盘及所承载的货物不受损坏。

本次修订的标准为修改采用ISO 8611－1：2011《物料搬运托盘　平托盘　第1部分：试验方法》，为了确保与国际标准的相互衔接，修改内容包括：

修改了试验方法的分组方法，修改了“堆码试验”的内容，修改了试验方法在试验载荷、试验时间、加载设备结构尺寸及其安放位置、挠度或变形量的测量与评定、试验次数等方面的内容；新增加了“叉举试验”“垫块或纵梁抗压试验”“气囊抗弯试验”“静态剪切试验”“静摩擦系数试验”和“滑动角试验”等试验项目。

（3）《联运通用平托盘　木质平托盘》（GB/T 31148—2014）

本标准主要规定了适用于联运通用以及公用系统用的木质平托盘样式、要求、试验方法、检验规则以及标志、包装、运输与贮存，一次性托盘也可参照使用。

标准的发布对于推行托盘的循环使用，实现托盘共用，更好引导企业设计与生产符合共用要求的优质托盘，降低用户的采购成本，减少资源消耗具有积极的意义。

★其他托盘、货架及仓库标准

（1）塑料箱式托盘（GB/T 31081—2014）

《塑料箱式托盘》国家标准规定了塑料箱式托盘的分类、技术要求、试验方法、检验规则、标志、运输和储存。适用于以高密度聚乙烯、共聚聚丙烯等塑料为主要原料，满足一定额定载荷、堆码载荷等性能要求的可重复使用的塑料箱式托盘。该标准的实施，将可以更好指导企业设计与生产符合共用要求的优质托盘，减少资源消耗。

（2）模压平托盘 植物纤维类（GB/T 30672—2014）

《模压平托盘 植物纤维类》国家标准规定了模压平托盘的产品分类、技术要求、试验方法、检验规则、标志、运输、储存，适用于以竹木加工剩余物或农作物秸秆为主要原料、添加少量胶黏剂，并通过模压成型工艺制成的能四向进叉载荷的单面使用的模压平托盘。该标准的发布与实施，将在促进技术进步、改进产品质量、提高市场竞争力，提高社会经济效益等方面具有积极意义。

（3）自动化立体仓库的安装与维护规范（GB/T 30673—2014）

《自动化立体仓库的安装与维护规范》国家标准规定了自动化立体仓库的安装与维护要求，适用于采用巷道堆垛机，对货物单元进行自动存储作业的立体仓库的安装与维护。本标准对规范行业内自动化立体仓库的安装与维护保养，提高我国自动化立体仓库的应用水平起着积极的作用。

（4）阁楼式货架（GB/T 30675—2014）

《阁楼式货架》国家标准规定了阁楼式货架的术语和定义、分类与标记、材料、要求、试验方法、检验规则和标志、包装、运输、储存，适用于用型钢制成的、由立柱、支撑梁、楼面板、楼梯、护栏、货架等组成的、楼层不低于二层（含二层）的阁楼式货架。本标准的制定，对阁楼式货架产品的质量提升，进一步规范仓储设备的健康发展具有积极意义。

★汽车物流系列标准

汽车物流是伴随着汽车工作的迅速发展而发展起来的专业物流服务领域，是将汽车零部件、商品车整车及服务备件从生产运送到经销商的一系列物流过程。目前我国专业从事汽车物流的骨干大中型企业近 100 家，具体从事汽车运输、仓储的企业上千家，已形成了一体化全方位的综合物流服务格局。

近几年，在中国物流与采购联合会汽车物流分会及大型汽车生产企业、物流企业共同努力下，已经研制了一批汽车物流标准，新的四项国家标准发布对解决汽车物流领域基础概念不统一、服务流程及指标缺失、汽车物流服务技术标准空白，规范汽车物流服务，提高服务质量，完善汽车物流标准化建设，推动我国物流业整体水平的发展具有重要的作用。

本次发布的汽车物流系列标准包括了基础类标准、汽车整车物流管理标准、汽车零部件物流管理标准和汽车服务备件物流管理标准。

（1）《汽车物流服务评价指标》（GB/T 31149—2014）

《汽车物流服务评价指标》（GB/T 31149—2014）规定了汽车整车物流服务评价指标、零部件物流服务评价指标和售后服务备件物流服务评价指标。适用于对从事经营性汽车物流服务企业的仓储、运输、装卸作业、流通加工等物流服务能力进行评价。标准综合了现阶段汽车物流仓储、运输、装卸作业、流通加工等物流环节服务能力要求，以及汽车生产企业对服务品质以及商品车质量保证的需求，依据汽车生产企业对汽车物流服务商（包括汽车零部件入厂物流企业、汽车整车物流企业和汽车服务备件物流企业）的考核指标，以及汽车物流服务商自身的 KPI 指标，选取了物流服务品质、物流服务成本、物流服务交付、物流服务管理、物流安全及改善等方面的重点关键性评价指标，清晰地界定了指标的构成。

（2）《汽车零部件物流 塑料周转箱尺寸系列及技术要求》（GB/T 31150—2014）

汽车零部件入厂物流由于物流过程直接到了汽车生产线边，是与汽车整车生产企业联系最为紧密的物流环节，是各个环节衔接十分紧密的高技术行业，是国际物流业公认的最复杂、最具专业性的物流领域。在我国汽车零部件入厂物流有两种物流模式，一种是直接送货模式，一种是 milk - RU 循环取货方式，目前已有大约 60% 的企业不同程度的采用国际上比较先进的循环取货物流模式。在取货环节中，物流商用使用的料箱是重要物流器具之一，也是 milk - RU 物流模式的基础与先决条件，随着零部件入厂物流模式的不断进步，采用可循环使用的塑料周转箱已成为汽车生产企业和物流服务商的首选。

《汽车零部件物流 塑料周转箱尺寸系列及技术要求》（GB/T 31150—2014）规定了汽车零部件物流用塑料周转箱的尺寸系列和技术参数要求，标准适用于以注射成型法生产的塑料周转箱。标准规定的塑料周转箱的尺寸适用于《 联运通用平托盘——主要尺寸及公差》（GB/T 2934—2007）国家标准中推荐的联运通用平托盘。并以减少消耗、资源有效利用为原则，尽量做到提出标准的先进性、合理性。

(3)《汽车整车物流质损风险监控要求》(GB/T 31151—2014)

《汽车整车物流质损风险监控要求》(GB/T 31151—2014)规定了汽车整车物流运作过程中对有可能产生质损的环节进行监控的要求，适用于汽车整车物流运作的过程管理。标准充分借鉴了在汽车业广泛应用的失效模式和后果分析系统，以及在汽车领域广泛使用的FMEA方法，通过识别物流过程每个步骤的失效情况和质量风险，对风险的严重度、发生度、难检度的分析，提出了汽车整车物流环节中的质损关键控制点，以及监控方法及要求，对保障汽车整车的物流质量具有重要的意义。

(4)《汽车物流术语》(GB/T 31152—2014)

《汽车物流术语》(GB/T 31152—2014)是基于汽车物流的基础类标准，标准确定了汽车物流的基础术语、作业服务术语、设施设备术语、信息术语、管理术语及其定义，适用于汽车物流及相关领域的信息处理和信息交换。

★冷链物流系列标准

(1) 水产品冷链物流服务规范(GB/T 31080—2014)

《水产品冷链物流服务规范》规定了水产品冷链物流服务的基本要求、接收地作业、运输、仓储作业、加工与配送、货物交接、包装与标志要求和服务质量的主要评价指标，标准适用于鲜、活、冷冻和超低温动物性水产品流通过程中的冷链物流服务，水产品生产过程中涉及的水产品冷链物流服务亦可参照执行，标准规范了水产品冷链物流服务行为，对提高水产品冷链物流服务质量具有重要的指导与促进作用。

(2) 低温仓储作业规范(GB/T 31078—2014)

《低温仓储作业规范》规定了低温仓储的入库作业、储存作业、出库作业、环境控制、安全控制及信息处理的要求，适用于公共低温仓库的仓储作业活动。标准规范了低温仓储作业活动，对提升我国低温仓储企业的作业水平，促进现代服务业发展具有十分重要的意义。

(3) 物流企业冷链服务要求与能力评估指标(GB/T 31086—2014)

《物流企业冷链服务要求与能力评估指标》规定了物流企业从事农产品、食品冷链服务所应满足的基本要求，以及物流企业冷链服务类型、能力级别划分及评估指标，适用于物流企业的农产品、食品冷链服务及管理，对规范物流企业冷链服务行为、提高物流企业冷链服务水平具有重要的指导作用。

★应急物流系列标准

应急物流是政府应急管理体系的有机组成部分，在加强政府应急管理能力、有效应对突发事件、维护社会安全与稳定等方面发挥着不可替代的作用。应急物流具有突发性、不确定性、弱经济性、非常规性等特点，2008年发生5.12汶川特大地震后，国家发展改革委针对救灾过程中所暴露出的物资包装标识不规范、所使用的应急物流力量能力参差不齐等问题，着手组织相关力量开展应急物流体系建设研究、制订应急物流专项规划，物流标准化技术委员会也开始着手组织开展相关应急物流标准的研究和制订，已制定的应急物流系列标准有三项，分别为：《企业应急物流能力评估规范》《应急物资投送包装及标识》和《应急物流仓储设施设备配置规范》，本次发布了前两项国家标准，另一项《应急物流仓储设施设备配置规范》国家标准已报批国家标准化管理委员，目前正在审批的过程中。

（1）企业应急物流能力评估规范（GB/T 30674—2014）

《企业应急物流能力评估规范》国家标准规定了企业应急物流能力分类与分级方法和企业应急物流能力评估指标，适用于为应对自然灾害、事故灾难、公共卫生事件及社会安全事件等突发事件应急物资保障时，企业应急物流能力的建设与管理。

（2）应急物资投送包装及标识（GB/T 30676—2014）

《应急物资投送包装及标识》国家标准规定了应急物资投送包装及包装标识的要求。适用于储存到应急物资储备仓库中的或由各级应急物资保障机构筹措的应急物资投送前的包装及标识。应急采购物资或社会捐赠物资投送前的包装及标识可参照执行。两项应急物流国家标准可用于各级政府应急物流管理部门对参与应急物流的企业应急保障能力的认定，还可为企业开展应急物流建设提供参考，标准的发布与实施对建立国家应急物流体系，进一步提升我国应对突发事件水平，做好救灾减灾工作具有重大的现实意义。

2. 2014 年已报批和通过审查的标准

（1）国家标准

2014 年，由全国物流标准化技术委员会提出并归口，已向国家标准委报批的国家标准项目 7 项，经全国物流标准化技术委员会组织专家审查通过的国家标准项目 6 项（见附表 2）。

附表 2　　2014 年已报批和通过审查的国家标准项目

序号	标准计划编号	标准名称	完成情况
1	20075403 - T - 469	物流设施与设备图示符号	已报批
2	20080042 - T - 469	人造纤维车载物固定装置	已报批
3	20091368 - T - 469	媒介购物的物流服务质量要求	已报批
4	20091373 - T - 469	医药生物冷藏箱通用规范	已报批
5	20100341 - T - 469	木质及木制品箱式托盘	已报批
6	20100359 - T - 469	应急物资仓储设施设备	已报批
7	20120507 - T - 469	塑料吹塑平托盘	已报批

续　表

序号	标准计划编号	标准名称	完成情况
8	20100344 – T – 469	汽车及零部（配）件物流信息系统功能及基本要求	已通过技术审查
9	20120493 – T – 469	钢铁物流包装标识规范	已通过技术审查
10	20120494 – T – 469	钢铁物流统计指标体系	已通过技术审查
11	20120495 – T – 469	钢铁物流验货操作规范	已通过技术审查
12	20120496 – T – 469	钢铁物流作业规范	已通过技术审查
13	20120506 – T – 469	汽车物流统计指标体系	已通过技术审查

（2）行业标准

2014 年，由中国物流与采购联合会提出、全国物流标准化技术委员会技术归口，已通过技术审查的标准 4 项（见附表 3）。

附表 3　　2014 年已通过技术审查的行业标准项目

序号	标准名称	完成情况
1	物流企业岗位设置及能力要求	已通过技术审查
2	汽车零部件物流器具分类及编码	已通过技术审查
3	餐饮冷链物流服务规范	已通过技术审查
4	商用车背车装载技术要求	已通过技术审查

3. 在制标准

2014 年，还重点开展了物流单证、托盘共用、城市共同配送、冷链物流、化工物流、粮食物流，棉花物流、煤炭物流等标准研制，截至年底，在制国家标准 39 项，行业标准 19 项。

（中国物流与采购联合会标准化工作部　李红梅）

2014 年物流信息化发展回顾与 2015 年展望

回望刚刚走过的 2014 年，我国经济步入新常态，物流业也面临结构调整、转型升级的新局面。国务院印发《物流业发展中长期规划》是对中国物流业的重大利好，同时将极大地促进我国物流信息化的快速发展。本报告首先回顾了 2014 年中国物流信息化的发展现状，探讨了中国物流信息化现阶段的特点和存在的问题，然后对 2015 年中国物流信息化的发展趋势进行了预测和分析。

一、2014 年物流信息化回顾

（一）国家对物流信息化工作高度重视

2014 年 6 月 11 日，李克强总理主持召开国务院常务会议，讨论通过《物流业发展中长期规划（2014—2020 年）》（以下简称《中长期规划》），9 月 12 日以国发〔2014〕42 号文正式发布。这是继 2009 年国务院《物流业调整和振兴规划》出台以来，又一个指导物流业发展的纲领性文件。《中长期规划》在主要任务中，要求进一步加强物流信息化建设。加强北斗导航、物联网、云计算、大数据、移动互联等先进信息技术在物流领域的应用。加快企业物流信息系统建设，发挥核心物流企业整合能力，打通物流信息链，实现物流信息全程可追踪。加快物流公共信息平台建设，积极推进全社会物流信息资源的开发利用，支持运输配载、跟踪追溯、库存监控等有实际需求、具备可持续发展前景的物流信息平台发展，鼓励各类平台创新运营服务模式。进一步推进交通运输物流公共信息平台发展，整合铁路、公路、水路、民航、邮政、海关、检验检疫等信息资源，促进物流信息与公共服务信息有效对接，鼓励区域间和行业内的物流平台信息共享，实现互联互通。《中长期规划》特别是提出了“标准化、信息化、智能化、集约化”的“四化”要求。这进一步明确了物流业的发展方向和目标，将极大地促进物流信息化的快速发展。

2014 年 7 月 28 日，国务院发布的《关于加快发展生产性服务业　促进产业结构调整升级的指导意见》明确要求，优化第三方物流企业供应链管理服务，提高物流企业配送的信息化、智能化、精准化水平，推广企业零库存管理等现代企业管理模式。加强核心技术开发，发展连锁配送等现代经营方式，重点推进云计算、物联网、北斗导航及地理信息等技术在物流智能化管理方面的应用。加强综合性、专业性物流公共信息平台和货物配载中心建设，衔接货物信息，匹配运载工具，提高物流企业运输工具利用效率，降低运输车辆空驶率。提高物流行业标准化设施、设备和器具应用水平以及托盘标准化水平。这为我国第三方物流企业的转型升级指明了方向。

2014 年 3 月 4 日，交通运输部、公安部和国家安监总局联合发布《道路运输车辆动态监督管理办法》，明确要求道路危险货物运输企业和拥有 50 辆及以上重型载货汽车或者牵引车的道路货物运输企业应当按照标准建设道路运输车辆动态监控平台，或者使用符合条件的社会化卫星定位系统监控平台，对所属道路运输车辆和驾驶员运行过程进行实时监控和管理。道路旅客运输企业和道路危险货物运输企业监控平台应当接入全国重点营运车辆联网联控系统。道路货运企业监控平台应当与道路货运车辆公共平台对接，按照要求将企业、驾驶人员、车辆的相关信息上传至道路货运车辆公共平台，并接收道路货运车辆公共平台转发的货运车辆行驶的动态信息。这将有助于建立全国统一的车辆监控平台，同时可引导全国物流公共信息平台的健康发展。

2014 年 7 月 17 日，交通运输部正式对外发布《交通运输物流信息互联共享标准（2014）》（简称新《标准》），其中数据元、道路运输电子单证、物流站场（园区）电子单证三项行业标准同步发布。新《标准》由基础标准、平台互联与交换标准、应用与服务规范、标准升级维护管理规范和标准符合性测试规范组成。企业可免费获取标准代码，进行简单的接口改造即可实现对接。新《标准》的应用，将有助于解决物流链上下游企业间信息“孤岛”问题。

2014 年 9 月 22 日，商务部发布的《关于促进商贸物流发展的实施意见》，明确要求商贸物流企业提高信息化水平：支持商贸物流企业与生产企业、批发零售等企业通过共用信息系统，实现数据共用、资源共享、信息互通。通过中央和地方两级示范，支持以企业为主体的物流综合信息服务平台发展，发挥平台整合调配物流资源，解决物流信息不对称、接口标准不统一等矛盾，实现精准化、可视化管理等功能，并搭载企业诚信、托盘循环共用、物流金融、跨境电子商务、商品溯源、通关便利化、多式联运等各种增值服务，为广大商贸物流企业特别是中小企业提升组织化和信息化水平，降低交易成本提供有利条件。有条件的地区还可协调相关部门，开展政府物流信息共享平台建设，将现有交通、工商、税务、海关等部门可公开的电子政务信息进行整合后，向社会公开，实现便民利企的物流政务资源共享。这将极大地促进我国商贸物流信息化的发展。

2014 年 11 月 18 日，国家发展改革委、交通运输部、商务部、国家铁路局、中国民用航空局、国家邮政局、国家标准委联合发布了《关于我国物流业信用体系建设的指导意见》，《意见》明确要求推动物流信用信息的整合共享。各地区要对本地区各相关部门的物流信用信息进行整合，建立信用信息交换共享机制，按照共享目录和统一标准，及时交换共享，形成统一的信用信息共享平台。依托国家统一的信用信息共享交换平台，逐步实现全国物流信用信息的互通和共享，消除“信息孤岛”，确保信用信息及时、全面、准确、翔实、安全，使物流企业的信用状况透明、可核查，让守信行为得到褒扬，让失信行为无处藏身。信用记录依法应当向社会公开的，要及时公开，并为社会查询提供便利。这将极大地促进我国物流信息平台及物流电子商务的健康发展。

（二）物流企业信息化投资有所下降，物流信息技术的应用更加普及

2014 年 6 月，工业和信息化部信息化推进司发布了《2013 年物流信息化监测报告》，从物流信息化基本建设、物流信息技术应用情况和物流信息化应用效果三个方面对物流企业进行了调研，调查结果如下：

1. 物流信息化基本建设

（1）物流信息化投资率有所回落

2013 年，受到经济大环境的影响，物流企业在信息化相关领域的投资率较前两年有所下降，参与调研的企业中只 38. 14% 进行了当年的信息化投资。其中，7. 69% 的企业信息化投资率不足 1%，23. 08% 的企业信息化投资率介于 1% ~5%，38. 46% 的企业信息化投资率在 5% ~10%，7. 69% 的企业信息化投资率在 10% ~15%，同时，约有 20. 08% 的样本企业投资率超过 15%，如图 1 所示。

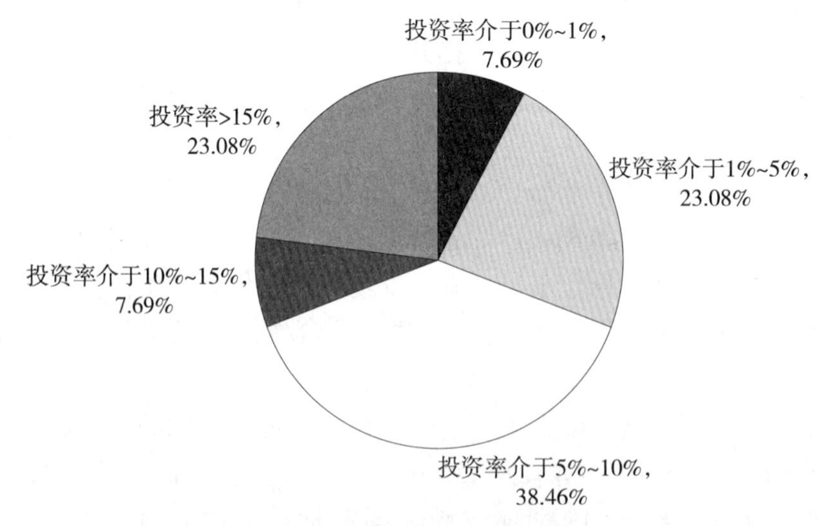

图 1　样本企业信息化投资率

在物流信息化建设形式的选择上，信息化建设外包能获得更为专业的系统

建设和系统集成方案，成熟度较高；而采用自主研发的信息化系统则对自身业务流程的需求更为熟悉，针对性更强。在本次调查的企业样本中，选择外包服务和自建信息系统的企业差别不大，分别占样本企业的42.86%和40%，如图2所示。

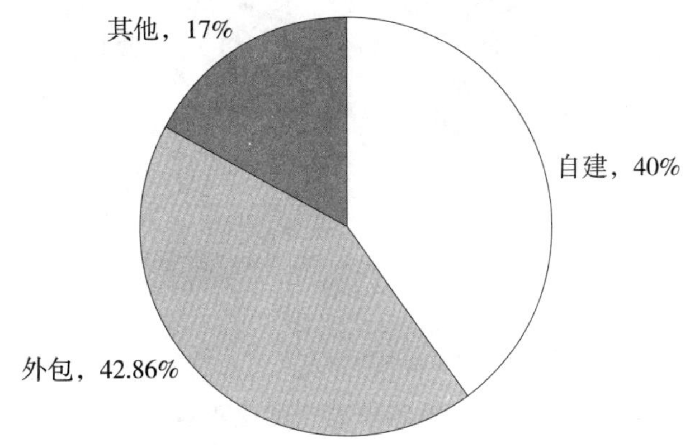

图2　物流信息化建设形式

（2）信息平台/门户网站大多用于信息发布

样本企业中，超过85.71%的企业建有自己的门户网站/信息平台；其中，大多门户网站/信息平台的用途仍是单纯定位在信息发布上，占比达76.67%；只有23.33%的企业将电子交易纳入其中并逐步推行应用，这一数据较之去年略有上升，信息平台的作用由单纯的信息发布逐渐向电子交易等多种形式拓展，如图3所示。

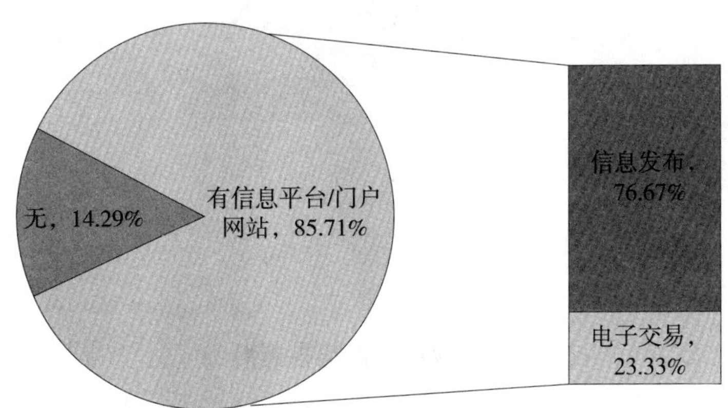

图3　门户网站/信息平台用途

（3）物流信息集成日渐成为建设重点

物流信息集成受到大多数企业的关注，70.97%的样本企业将构建信息平台（内部信息处理、OA、增值业务）作为信息化建设的重点；此外，部分企业将软件开发、RFID/RF/GIS/GPS/条码等信息技术的应用、数据分析、数据挖掘等作为物流信息化建设的重点，如图 4 所示。

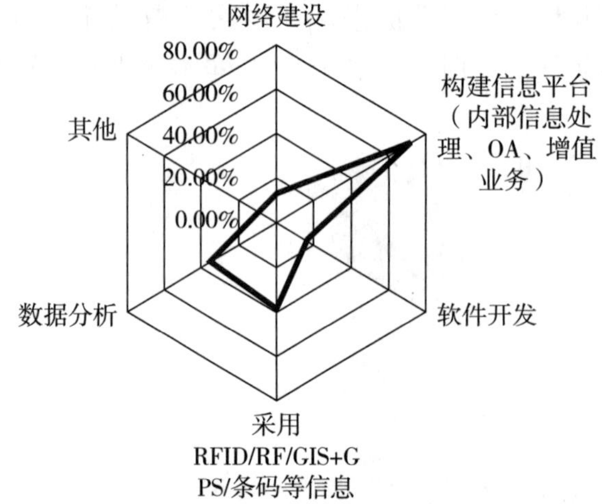

图 4　物流信息化建设重点

（4）资金和人才问题持续制约企业物流信息水平提升

监测结果显示，较之去年更多的样本企业任务信息化人才短缺是制约企业物流信息化发展的主要原因，占比 44. 45%；其次，缺少资金和行业标准缺失也是企业物流信息化建设中的主要问题，分别各占 24. 44%，如图 5 所示。

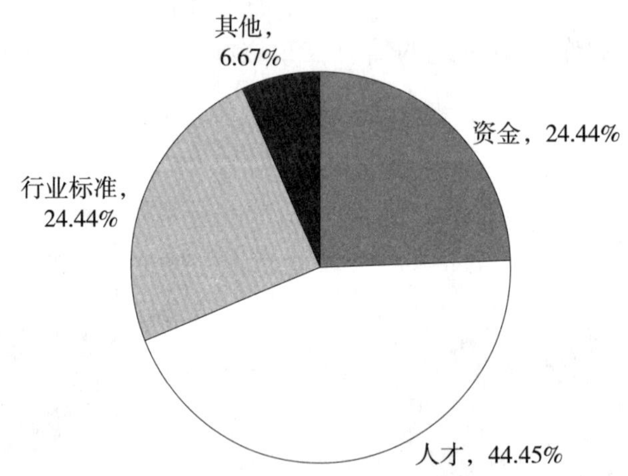

图 5　物流信息化建设瓶颈

2. 物流信息技术应用

（1）条码、电子单证等技术得到基本应用

2013 年，条码和电子标签等技术在物流业务中的应用程度继续提升。其中，条码应用率达到 58. 21%，较 2012 年增长 4. 9%；电子标签应用率达到 38%，较 2012 年增长 10. 44%；而电子单证使用率 48. 85% 与 2012 年相比则略有下降。但物流信息技术总体上的发展趋势是毋庸置疑的，这些技术的应用在很大程度上提升了企业的信息化水平，物流信息技术的创新应用是推进物流信息化发展的重要手段，如图 6 所示。

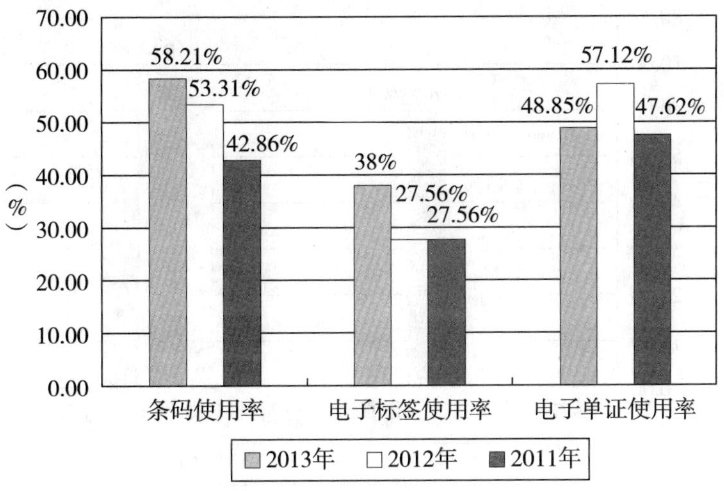

图 6　2011—2013 年条码、标签、单证使用率

（2）物流软件得到普及应用

本次调查选取了常见的七种物流业务管理软件，通过对比其应用率可以看到近年来物流软件的应用率逐步提升，应用种类更加丰富，不同软件之间的均衡性更加明显，更加注重软件与业务的切合度以及与企业未来发展的相关性，如图 7 所示。

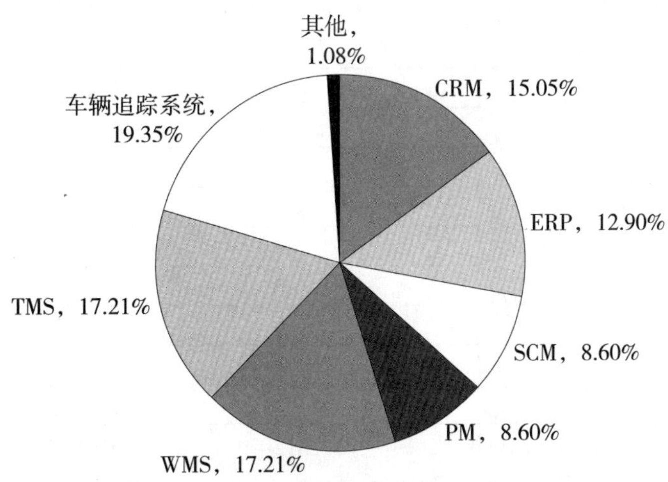

图 7　物流软件应用占比

（3）信息交换方式逐渐以信息化交换为主导

监测结果表明，物流企业与外部主体业务信息交换中，以 EDI（电子数据交换）和互联网等为代表的信息化交换方式逐渐成为市场主导。信息交换方式的变革直接影响着物流业务进行中信息交换速率和准确度的提升，如图8所示。

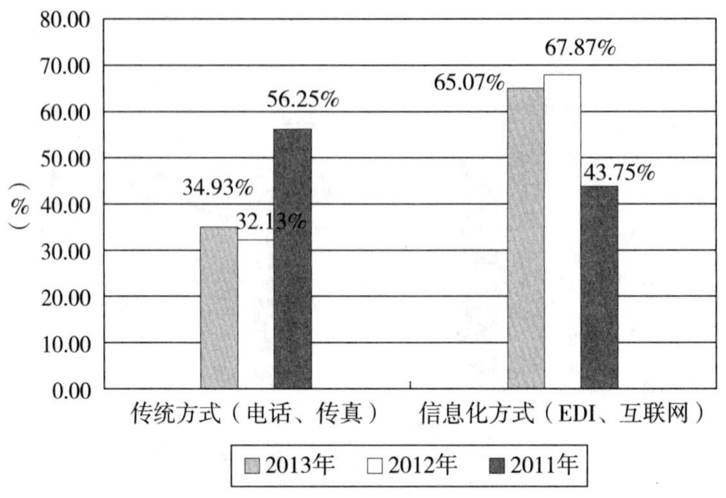

图8　样本企业信息交换方式

3. 物流信息化应用效果

（1）订单（运单）准时率

样本企业调查数据显示，有超过86.67%的物流企业订单（运单）准时率超过70%，其中企业订单（运单）准时率超过90%的企业占比达到70%左右。随着市场竞争日益激烈，企业仍需继续加大信息化建设力度，提升信息技术的应用水平，提高订单（运单）准时率，满足客户需求，如图9所示。

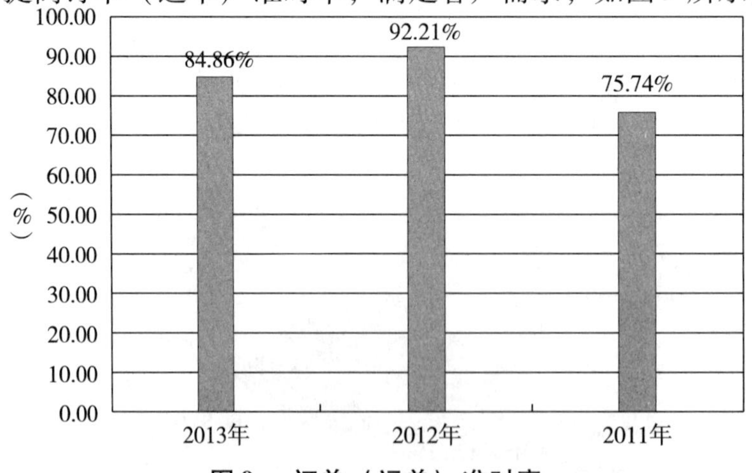

图9　订单（运单）准时率

（2）车辆追踪水平

监测结果显示，87.38%的企业实现了对自有车辆的追踪，其中，有61.11%的企业自有车辆追踪率达到100%。有68.46%的企业实现了对委外车辆的追踪，其中，有 66.67% 的企业对外部车辆的追踪率超过 50%；26.67% 的企业达到了外部车辆的追踪率 100% 的水平，如图 10 所示。

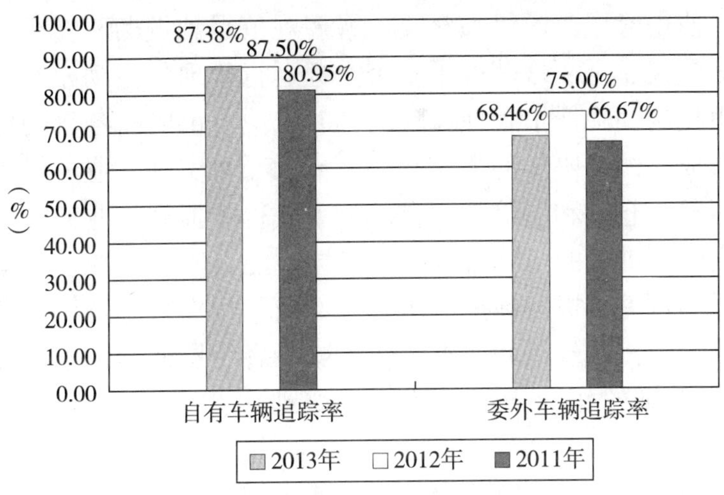

图 10　样本企业车辆追踪率

(3) 全程透明可视化率

本次监测的样本企业中，有 63.64% 的企业全程透明可视化程度超过 50%；36.36% 的企业的全程透明可视化能力达到 100%。

(三) 产业物流以流程透明化为基础，通过数据共享和协同作业提高效率

1. 产业物流信息化以统一数据接口为基础，通过信息共享和协同作业来提高物流效率

唯智信息技术有限公司为深圳欧唯特公司打造的物流管理系统建立了 EDI－SERVER 数据总线，集中处理各系统接口，一方面处理平台内部系统（OMS，TMS，WMS 等）之间的数据交互，另一方面处理外部系统（NC，SAP，TES，POD，B2B 平台等）与物流平台的数据交互；集成的 EDI 接口平台极大地减轻了 IT 部门接口维护的复杂度，同时提供标准接口及接口预留，保证平台的扩展性；基于统一的订单管控平台，驱动协同仓储 WMS 与运输 TMS 系统间的作业，使运输调度部门与仓储备货部门并行作业；OMS 进行订单下发后，通过 EDI 实现实时信息传递，实时传递到各作业系统，运输调度部门承运商指派及调度交接信息会实时反馈到仓储部门，仓储部门依据信息进行集货交接，同时仓储部门的作业情况也将实时反馈到运输部门，运输部门根据指示进行装车发运，改变了之前串行的作业模式，各部门之间信息孤岛的情况，极大地提高了作业协同性及效率。

安徽江汽物流有限公司应用的整车仓储调度系统实现了协同运作。将主机

厂，营销公司，仓库与承运商纳入一个平台。保障了物流信息链的完整与及时，使企业整合上下游资源的能力大幅提升。通过实施出厂物流公司整车物流信息化项目，使得管理要求得到落实，管理规范得到贯彻，整车从仓储到运输整个过程全面受控，全面地获得了整个业务运行管理的主动权利。项目中引入了良性的竞争机制，降低了管理风险的同时也使得供应商各自的优势得到了充分的发挥，形成了团结协作的工作态势。借助项目实施，业务管理流程得到全面贯彻，使得整车仓储和运输效率在总体上获得了提升。业务管理部门借助信息系统，方便快捷准确的下达各种指令，同时能及时地获取业务运行的状态并对整体运作做出调整，极大地提升了管理部门的运作效率。供应商在业务流程和系统的帮助下，按照规范和要求运作，减少各个层面上的模糊和反复，不仅极大地提高了现场的作业效率，还能很好地完成之前无法达到的各项考核要求。

2. 电子商务加供应链的服务体系是产业物流发展的新模式

河南众品食业股份有限公司助互联网、物联网技术，围绕公司肉类产业链的上、中、下游建立农产品、食品集采平台，通过众品的温控供应链集成服务体系，实线网上平台调动网下资源，通过网下资源整合网上平台。通过互联网为更多中小农产品、食品企业提供“线上＋线下”的一站式服务。公司通过线下强大的温控物流供应链服务体系，在150个重点消费城市，构建贸易分销平台，帮助企业或客户搭建高效的产品分销平台，实现产品快速销售。通过信息平台＋供应链联盟，帮助企业建立一个农产品（食品）中小企业的服务平台，如采购平台，销售平台，资金支持，物流支持等。这里面涵盖B2B、B2C等多种服务模式。形成了以“电子商务＋温控供应链服务体系”为核心新的商业模式。

创捷供应链专注于“垂直电商加供应链金融”的新模式，搭建了以“创捷供应链E－SCM平台”为基础的大型跨国商贸综合服务平台供应链管理与电子商务相互结合，产生供应链管理领域的重大创新——电子商务供应链管理（E－Commerce Supply Chain Management，E－SCM）。即利用互联网完全的自助交易方式与网络业务伙伴实时进行合作和重要计划信息的交流，实现供应链服务业务间的协同。电子商务供应链管理有利于供应链中的企业通过运用电子商务手段掌握跨越整个供应链的各种有用信息，实现有组织、有计划的统一管理，减少流通环节、降低流转、结算、库存等成本、缩短需求响应和市场变化时间，提高运营绩效，为客户提供全面服务，实现最大增值。

3. 智慧物流是产业物流发展的方向

一汽大众应用的入厂车辆智能调度系统（VCS）通过RFID物联网技术VCS系统的推进与实施，一汽大众致力于打造“优质、高效”为核心的仓储物流管理一体化平台，此系统对内满足一汽大众零部件运输车辆入厂卸货提供了信息支持，全员绩效考核提供了数据支撑，运输车卸货率提高40%，停靠指定卸车位效率提高70%。通过实施系统信息化管理，企业改造优化主业务流程，并打造了全国最先使用RFID射频技术的车辆智能调度系统管理。以满足整车仓储要求，以达到车辆运输过程透明化、提高车辆和货物可调配性、卸货过程可控性、提高要货的平衡性、提高车辆的利用率、减少车辆在公司内滞留时间，全过程的跟踪式的信息化物流服务体系。作为新兴的物联网技术，LVCS系统开创中国整车仓储使用物联网RFID射频技术的先河，达到了世界先进水平。

浙江中烟工业有限责任公司应用了支持烟草全供应链的全物料单件批次追踪与溯源关键技术，本项目为了克服传统卷烟仓储管理系统的缺点，充分利用了超高频RFID技术，结合金属介质对超高频RFID电子标签的影响因素，提出了一种超高频RFID电子标签用于金属表面的解决方案，设计了安装于托盘上和一种地埋式货位标签，标签总体性能达到国内领先水平。在应用中，生产仓储中的每个托盘上安装一个RFID电子标签，对托盘电子标签的信息进行数据采集和实时处理，攻克了基于多层楼库的托盘货位化仓储全程信息自动感知技术难题，自主研发出一套基于RFID的货位化管理方案，实现了在楼房型仓库中实行托盘货位化管理。并结合WMS应用到仓储物流的各个环节，研发了基于RFID的数字化仓储管理系统，为烟草工业企业实现对各种物流资源的实时跟踪和及时履行采购、销售订单，提高物流资源的跟踪、定位和管理水平，提升烟草制造企业物流自动化水平和整体运作效率提供了新思路和新手段。

（四）云平台、大数据、移动互联、O2O并融合供应链管理模式是物流信息平台的发展方向，融合物流金融等增值服务使平台增强盈利能力

1. 供应链+O2O模式的物流信息平台发展迅速

车杰盟云服务平台让互联网成为线下交易的前台。这样线下服务就可以用线上来揽客，消费者可以用线上来筛选服务，成交可以在线结算，很快达到规模。O2O电子商务模式的运用对连锁服务行业来讲是一条能令企业迅速发展的“高速公路”，较之传统渠道而言，有着无法比拟的优势。O2O之下的互联网化，意味着以“互联网思维”理解传统的商业形态，改造供应链，并以数据为基础，提高线下运营效率。在新的体系中，从商品采购、仓储管理、物流配送到销售渠道建立，都要运用数据进行资源配置。不仅渠道变了，客户挖掘方式变了，营销手法变了，而且商家提供产品和服务的方式也变了，以用户为中心的模式成为主导。

2. 与上下游信息共享与协同作业是物流信息平台的发展方向

民生货代营运管理信息系统努力打造同政府公共物流信息平台、上游客户企业信息系统、下游物流服务商信息系统实现信息共享与协同的能力，进而打通产业链上下游，探索制造业、流通业、金融业等多种产业的融合渗透，促进生产方式转变和流通方式转型，提升货代物流业对整个供应链的掌控能力，为整个供应链创造差异化竞争优势提供重要支撑，最终成为地区性甚至全国性的综合货代服务公共信息平台。

泰德煤网供应链信息化管理平台是支撑泰德煤炭流通网络运行的数字化平台，由企业 ERP 系统、供应链管理平台、先进计划系统、决策支持系统、其他支持系统和协同平台与电子商务系统等部分构成。通过使用协同的供应链信息管理平台，健立完备的硬件基础设施平台，将企业内外部资源同一化管理。同时实现客户、供应商、运输提供商、合作伙伴及企业内部管理部门和员工之间协同的敏捷作业。实现采购、物流、配煤、销售、资金、信息等煤炭流通服务能力的建设和整合。使用现代管理技术和工具，实施创新和集约的煤炭供应链管理服务。以达到整合价值链资源，建立煤炭流通标准，提升协同运行能力。

中兴供应链的供应链信息平台，通过对商流、物流、资金流和信息流重新梳理优化，并通过信息系统加以固化执行，使得各个流程有机集成。并借助信息化的手段，与供应链上下游企业进行信息的有效共享和快速传递；同时系统具备良好的可扩展性，能够快速适应业务向上下游延伸而发展出的不同业态的业务模式，始终保持与整个供应链更加紧密的合作。供应链的透明可视，能推动供应链上下游更好地协同，商贸流通企业更高效地业务运营，为客户提供更优质的服务。中兴供应链依托供应链信息平台，实现了供应链的 360 度透明可视。

3. 移动互联技术在物流信息平台的应用越来越广泛

在移动互联时代，泰德煤网及时推出泰德易通手机客户端，通过东北亚煤炭交易会以及分散在各地的销售网络向客户进行推广，泰德易通可以实现煤炭咨询信息、行业信息、泰德可供产品的信息推送，同时支持在线评价、交流、预约下单、订单跟踪等功能，同时还能记录客户关心的咨询和产品信息，泰德易通将公司的优质客户资源复制到了线上，并通过互联网改善了客户服务体验，提高了客户对泰德品牌的认可。

泉州天地汇公路港 I 配货项目对司机来说以移动互联为基础的配货方式使得选择面大大增加，可以实现全国范围内配货，行驶途中就可回程，司机最头痛的，问题迎刃而解；等待时间大压缩（平均配货时间可由 24 小时下降到6 ~ 8 小时），使得运价单价即使降低，因为更多的运输次数，月收入反倒大幅增加，形成良性循环，I 配货对物流企业的信用控制，使得司机更加有保障；线上配货大幅缩短提货路程，既便捷也省钱。

路歌物流电子商务平台提供了海量的运力资源、快捷的调度功能及有力的整合手段，并开发了路歌好运宝 APP，可在线交易，征对司机及物流经纪人的特点，开发了各自不同功能的 APP，可以完成运力的采购和调度。

（五）物流金融等增值服务使平台增强盈利能力

中铁物资集团进军大宗商品电子商务领域，为推动业务发展，加快商业模式创新，实现“产融深度结合”，中国大宗物资网作为供应链核心企业，与中信、华夏、华润、建行、中金支付等金融机构大力推进银企合作和在线支付平台建设，通过平台共建、渠道共享、金融创新、资源整合等手段，实现对平台交易上下游客户的在线支付结算、订单融资、仓单质押、线上融资等“在线供应链金融”服务。通过构建“在线供应链金融”服务可以将物化的资金流转化为在线数据，无缝嵌入核心企业的电子商务平台，从而在线连接供应链核心企业、贸易商、供应商、物流公司和银行，把供应链交易所引发的资金流、物流、信息流实时传输与展现在共同的数据平台上并可授权共享。

中信信通国际物流公司开发的三方质押监管平台开展的质押监管业务涉及包括汽车在内的十余个品类，实时监管物资金额达几十亿元，遍布全国的 1600 多个网点，相同数量的监管人员，还涉及银行、质押方等。质押监管交互系统，系在银行、经销商、监管公司、主机厂四方的框架下研发而成，主要模块包含“风险信息提醒功能”“业务操作功能”“数据统计功能”“信息查询功能”等，全面涵盖了三方质押监管的各个业务环节。其核心突出创新和科技含量是融合四方不同的 ERP 系统的嵌入式物流系统，在中国复杂的 IT 环境下具有标杆意义。目前公司这个系统获得各合作银行普遍认可，在行业内处于绝对领先地位。

（六）物流园区信息化主要向信息共享及智慧物流园区方向发展

盖世集团在数字化物流园区信息化建设中，本着统筹规划的原则，打造盖世物流数字化园区平台。数字化园区由一体化整合平台、公共信息服务平台、物流作业管理平台、企业内部管理平台及智能化配套支持平台等部分组成。运用 3G、3S、云计算、物联网等新技术，站在产业的前沿，搭建符合园区业务战略的一体化平台，推动实现园区公共服务一体化、经营管理标准化、物流作业自动化、配套支持智能化。抓住园区物流管理的各个环节，建立科学、简便、高效的应用系统，面向园区、企业、公众、政府等各层人员，打造支撑业务演化的、统一标准规范的数字物流园区，充分整合园区内外信息资源，重组流程，打通业务环节，提升管理服务，提高物流园区的市场竞争力和品牌影响力。一个有效集成的数字物流园区平台，应该能够为用户提供一个统一高效的沟通界面，为客户提供完整、综合、全面的且符合客户个性需求的解决方案。

湖南天骄物流信息科技有限公司开发的车海通物流园区公共平台用层次化和整体的观点来规划、实施物流的信息化建设，借鉴企业信息门户思想构建一个全面、稳定、开放、安全、可扩展的中国物流信息平台；使得所有应用系统在统一的物流信息平台上集成和协同，并完成各个系统之间的数据传输、安全认证、用户统一管理和共享等功能，以保证物流信息系统安全、高效、可靠运行。

物流园区的信息化建设要考虑到本地产业发展与供应链的整合作用。物流园区的信息化建设决不是建个网站这样简单，更不是购买一部分软件发给企业应用就算信息化，或者说物流园区的信息化建设不是为了信息化而信息化。建一个网站，用几套管理软件，虽然也是信息化的一部分，但对当地产业升级发展起不到推动和促进作用。虽然一个地方经济发展有一个地方的特点，但在现代社会中离不开与其他地区经济的配合，离不开上下游产业的配合。如何通过信息化摆脱当地的地理、交通、资源的不足，与其他相关地区进行上下游资源的整合，这才是物流园区信息化的关键。

二、2015 年物流信息化展望

（一）“互联网 + 物流”将会颠覆传统物流模式，极大地推动物流信息化的发展

“互联网 + ”不是指传统意义上的信息技术，它既包含云计算、大数据、物联网、移动互联等信息技术，又包含制造业、商贸业、物流业等传统产业，是一种信息技术与传统产业的相互融合，是一种新业态，是互联网思维下实体产业的发展，不是实体产业简单的互联网化。“互联网 + ”模式有以下特点：

（1）组织机构扁平化，指令能尽快地传递下去，有利于效率的提高。

（2）表现形式是互联互通，信息共享，开放平等。

（3）输出形式是个性化的服务，差异化的服务，而不是成形的产品。

（4）商业模式是分工协作，互利共赢的合作关系。

（5）价值形式是关注用户的数量，流量的大小，而不是产品的价格。

“互联网 + 物流”模式将会在推动物流行业结构调整、转型升级方面探索出一条新的道路。

（二）《物流标准化中长期发展规划（2015—2020 年）》（以下简称《规划》）即将颁布，制约物流信息化发展的物流标准问题将不复存在

《规划》将于 2015 年上半年，由国家标准委会同十个部委共同发布。该

《规划》力求通过编制和实施，分析我国物流标准化工作的发展现状和面临的形势，明确“十三五”期间我国物流标准化工作的指导思想和发展目标，定位未来五年物流标准化工作的主要任务、重点领域和重点工程，进一步做强优势环节，补齐薄弱环节，确定配套的保障措施和实施方案，并为定制物流标准专项规划、年度计划和加强物流标准化管理工作提供依据。《规划》的编制原则是按照国务院关于深化标准化工作的改革精神，以“用”为核心来规划今后的标准化工作，解决问题，达到效果。强制性国家标准严格限定在保障人身健康和生命财产安全、国家安全、生态环境安全和满足社会经济管理基本要求的范围之内，鼓励具备相应能力的学会、协会、商会、联合会等社会组织和产业技术联盟协调相关市场主体共同制定满足市场和创新需要的标准，供市场自愿选用，增加标准的有效供给。团体标准和企业标准将发挥重要作用，长期制约物流信息化发展的物流标准问题将不复存在。

（三）以移动互联为代表的新信息技术在物流行业将应用越来越普遍

有人预计，移动互联网的规模是互联网的10倍，移动互联在物流行业的应用表现形式无疑是货运APP的热潮。2015年可能就是货运APP的大发展年，有三方面原因：

（1）庞大车货市场的诱惑，我国公路货运市场规模大约3万亿元，其中零担占30%多，约为9000多亿元。

（2）人们希望复制滴滴和快的成功模式，把运人变成运货，以至于风投、IT精英、物流人都一拥而上，希望自己能成功。

（3）较低的技术壁垒，APP是一个开放的外接端口软件，如果切入点准确，会在很短的时间积累起流量，这也是资本倚重之处。

（4）最关键的是成本很低，现在的司机每人都有智能手机，只要下载一个免费的APP软件就可以找到货，还有许多增值服务，这很有诱惑力。

在货运APP热潮后面，我们也要清醒地看到，这其中存在着巨大的泡沫，也许2~3年之后，一大批货运APP会死掉，但正如比尔·盖茨预测的那样，泡沫也是有价值的：泡沫会推动市场在短时间内前行；泡沫会促使资本迅速集合和离去；泡沫使得投资过重与其商业价值不匹配。但有一点不容置疑，那就是将会极大地推动物流行业信息化的发展。

（中国物流与采购联合会网络事业部　晏庆华）

2014 年物流教育培训发展回顾与 2015 年展望

2014 年，在相关政府部门的指导和支持下，物流行业教育培训各项工作扎实稳步推进。重点在联系部委，服务企业和院校等方面做了大量工作，并在物流人才培养模式创新、完善物流行业人才培养体系、物流行业职业标准体系和现代物流职业教育体系建设等方面进行了积极探索和大胆实践。

一、2014 年物流教育培训发展回顾

（一）物流人才培养体系得到完善

加快构建中国物流行业人才标准体系。“中国物流行业人才标准体系”建设项目于 2012 年启动，构建了由“职业标准、职业资格、能力单元”三层结构组成的标准体系，该框架得到了行业教育主管部门、企业和院校的认可。2014 年，《物流行业从业人员职业能力要求》的第 1 部分、第 2 部分已经通过标准审查，另外 3 个部分已经完成征求意见稿，全部工作计划 2015 年完成。此外，针对专业领域的职业能力标准《冷链物流从业人员职业资质》也即将进入公开征求意见的阶段。行业职业标准编制为提升企业人力资源管理水平和院校人才培养质量打下了坚实的基础。

推进国家开放大学物流学院学分银行建设。2013 年，中物联与国家开放大学合作成立了国家开放大学物流学院，依托双方优势和资源，积极探索行业学院的办学模式，引入职业资格、学习单元和学分，并通过学分银行实现非学历继续教育和学历继续教育有效衔接。目前此项工作正在与国家开放大学学分中心共同推进。

开发系列物流职业教育现代学徒制标准规范。针对物流行业需求和专业特点，中物联牵头开发了系列标准规范，包括《物流现代学徒制框架》《物流学徒制课程设计与开发规范》《物流学徒制导师培训标准》《物流学徒制评估师培训标准》《物流学徒制评估员工作规范》等，为试点项目实施打下了坚实基础。

密切关注国际物流、采购供应链方面的有关认证开展情况。重点将行业培训项目与当前市场上热门的国际主流培训认证项目进行比对分析，为下一步开发和强化物流行业培训认证工作提供了依据。

（二）培训认证工作面临新的机遇和挑战

2014 年是国家职业资格认证工作的改革之年，对所有认证工作来说也是个调整年。本次国家对职业资格改革，从长远看对行业今后取得职业资格认定、组织职业资格认证的主体地位十分有利。同时，2014 年职业资格培训认证工作也是重新梳理定位、夯实基础、深化内涵、创新产品和服务发展的一年，在标准体系建设、开发培训项目、升级产品和服务等方面做了一系列积极有效的工作。

（三）行业职业资格认证各项工作稳步推进和完善

建立物流师的后市场服务机制，完善年审服务平台。为提升对物流师认证的后期服务，2014 年结合当前新型在线教学形式，对物流师年审平台进行改版升级，以物流师需求为导向，开发微课堂、多类型教学课程，丰富了学习内容，为广大学员后期继续学习、提高自身专业素质和技能搭建了平台。2014 年年审人员比去年同期增长 50%。

建立行业培训机构联席会议机制，以提升培训质量，掌握市场动态，及时了解培训机构诉求。联席会议成员由各省优秀培训机构组成，定期召开成员会议，围绕培训及行业发展，研究新问题、交流新理念、探讨新方法，共同制定下一步工作计划。同时，联席会的代表成员在当地起到了示范、引领及带动作用。

签署新一轮 ITC 合作协议，为注册采购师、ITC 资格认证的推进奠定了坚实的基础。联合国推出的模块 17 运营管理与模块 18 供应链财务管理在 2014 年起纳入培训与考试体系中，完善了注册级别和国际文凭级别的架构和内涵。

（四）开展企业高端人才培训和师资培训工作

全力打造“中国物流企业家高级研修班”高端品牌项目。经过两年的筹备，首期“中国物流企业家高级研修班”于 2014 年 3 月正式启动。研修班聘请国内知名学者与企业家授课，理论和企业调研实践结合，满足物流企业家及高级管理人员对更新理念、知识、扩大视野、提升领导力的需求。首期研修班由来自全国各 A 级物流企业及大型物流企业总裁、总经理、物流总监共计 42 名组成，为学员、企业家和学者提供一个集学术、商务、联谊于一体的交流平台。

实施物流人才知识更新工程。“现代物流与供应链管理高级研修班”项目为人社部《专业技术人才知识更新工程 2014 年高级研修项目计划》之一，培训具体由行业承办。2014 年 11 月来自全国行业协会、A 级物流企业、大中型制造企业共计 70 名学员齐聚武汉参加培训。培训邀请到国内权威专家授课，既有行业发展政策解读，也有企业发展前沿理念、业务模式创新，新技术、新方法的介绍，对提高参培人员职业素养及专业技术技能具有很大的帮助。

开展物流院校骨干教师培训工作。2011 年开始，行业每年组织 2 ~ 3 次物流专业骨干教师国内外培训，组织教师深入企业实习、培训的同时积极推荐企业专家走进学校走上课堂，积极创新教师培养的机制，强化师资队伍建设。2014 年 1 月和 7 月分别在东莞、台湾组织了 4 次师资培训。截至目前共有 600 多名来自全国各地职业院校的教师参与培训。

（五）物流教育得到国家的支持和肯定

近年来，中物联在物流行业人才培养方面做了大量具体细致的工作，尤其在推动物流职业教育发展方面的努力得到了政府部门的肯定。2014 年 6 月 23 日，国务院召开全国职业教育工作会议，习总书记作了重要批示。中物联任豪祥副会长作为行业代表出席了会议，并提报经验交流材料。12 月 12 日教育部在唐山召开全国职业教育现代学徒制推进大会，会议安排中物联作为唯一一家行业代表发言介绍联合会在中英合作开展现代学徒制试点项目的成功经验。同年教育部以购买服务的方式委托行业承担三个研究和建设项目，并划拨了相应的项目经费。

（六）物流专业设置趋向精细化、标准化

完成《物流专业教学质量国家标准》编制工作。按照教育部《教学质量国家标准》编制的要求，在评价环节中行业参与要与行业标准和需求接轨。中物联和教指委牵头在全国范围内组织了行业和专业调查，专家组根据分工于 2014 年 3 月份提交了标准（草案），通过对国内高校物流教师和企业专家多次征求意见，使标准内容更加完善。最后由专家组修改定稿，于 10 月份按时提交至教育部，标准的编制组织工作得到教育部的肯定。

制定高等职业学校专业目录工作。物流行指委参与了教育部《高等职业学校专业目录》的修订工作。按照本次专业目录修订指导思想主动适应、科学发展的原则，物流行指委提交了高等职业学校专业目录下增设“物流大类”的专业设置方案。根据目前的专家意见物流类有望在财经大类下作为一个二级类，《目录》正在进行最后一轮的征求意见。

（七）教育教学改革研究不断深化

2014 年年初，中物联共收到 106 个课题立项申请，经评审共确定 98 个课题列入“2014 年物流教改教研课题计划”。2014 年上半年，秘书处组织专家对

列入“2013 年物流教改教研课题计划”的 158 个课题进行结题验收，经过网评和会评，最终共确定 112 个课题完成结题。该项工作对推动物流教育教学改革，提高教学质量，促进物流教学研究活动的开展具有积极的推动作用。

2014 年下半年为调动职业院校教师投身物流教学改革研究与实践的积极性，提高人才培养质量，推广先进教学成果，物流行指委组织开展了 2014 年度物流职业教育优秀教学成果奖评选工作。根据 2014 年度物流职业教育优秀教学成果奖评选工作程序和办法，共收到推荐成果 151 个，评出一等奖 14 项、二等奖 28 项、三等奖 41 项，其中 1 项获得国家级教学成果二等奖。

（八）物流教育在国际交流与合作方面进一步深化

开展高校物流专业国际交流与合作情况调查。拓展高校物流专业的国际合作与交流是教指委 2014 年重点工作任务之一，中物联根据工作安排，设计《高校物流专业国际交流与合作情况调查表》，于 2014 年 3 月启动调查工作。调查内容涵盖合作办学、科研合作、教师交流、学生交流、总体评价等内容。秘书处根据调查结果，梳理撰写了《高校物流专业国际交流与合作情况调查报告》，为下一步推进院校国际交流与合作工作提供依据。

成立中国物流高等院校国际合作联盟。为推动我国物流高等教育国际交流与合作，中物联与教指委共同发起成立中国物流高等院校国际合作联盟，目前共有 50 多所院校加入联盟。联盟将统筹高校对外合作的资源、项目与活动，建立物流高等教育国际交流与合作的工作平台和信息平台，推进联盟单位与国外知名高校在学术交流、科研合作、师生交流与培训、合作办学等方面的合作。

中英双方物流职业教育项目合作有了实质性进展。中物联于 2012 年开始积极与英国文化协会、英国物流技能协会合作，推动国内中职院校开展现代学徒制物流专业的试点工作。2014 年 8 月上海试点项目进入实质性运行阶段，首批学员进入试点企业，严格按照英国学徒制模式进行培训，10 余名来自企业的专家和院校的老师完成了导师和评估员的培训，并在英国专家的指导下开展学徒指导和评估的实践。2014 年 10 月 27 日，英国商业、创新和技能部官员访问试点项目后，评价为英国现代学徒制在中国迄今“最成功的一次”。

（九）物流交流平台形式多样化

举办“第十三届全国高校物流专业教学研讨会”。今年 8 月，中物联和教指委共同在天津召开了第十三届全国高校物流专业教学研讨会。来自全球 13 个国家和地区的物流专家学者和教师共计 400 多人参加了会议，会议开设了 4 个分论坛，共有 30 多位来自国内外的专家登台演讲，会议同期还召开了亚太物流联盟年会。

举办第六届全国职业院校物流专业教学研讨会。会议由中物联和行指委共同举办，搭建了广泛的交流合作平台，会议共有来自全国各地300多名专家学者及物流企业高管参加，内容涉及院校人才培养模式创新、校企合作、信息化、“学徒制”试点等多方面，引入企业与院校对话和体验式教学环节收到非常好的效果。为发挥物流职业教育先进单位的带头、示范和辐射作用，会议期间还举办了第三批“全国物流职业教育人才培养基地”授牌仪式，本次共有16家单位被评为“全国物流职业教育人才培养基地”。

完成2015年中、高职物流技能大赛筹备工作。由行业牵头申报的中职组物流运输作业团体赛和高职组现代物流作业方案设计与实施两个赛项顺利进入最后一轮答辩评审。经过近几年发展，物流技能大赛参与的院校越来越多，对物流教学的引领作用越来越强，对方案的设计要求也越来越高，物流行指委争取把2015年的赛事办成一场高水平、高质量的比赛。

二、2015年物流教育培训发展展望

新时期物流产业的发展对物流人才的培养工作提出了新的要求，2015年将继续围绕根据党的十八届三中全会精神和《国家中长期教育发展和改革规划纲要（2010—2020年）》确定的战略目标，不断整合物流企业、行业协会资源，借鉴国外的先进经验，努力提高我国物流人才教育培训质量。

加快建立完善的行业人才标准体系。借鉴发达国家先进经验，逐步探索并建立我国物流行业人才标准体系，构建职业标准、能力单元、职业资格、培训课程多层次的物流职业标准体系，物流行业从业人员培训和评估标准由通用标准向各特定领域专业标准延伸，形成完善的与国际接轨的人才标准体系。

完善职业资格认证体系。根据行业人才标准，调整培训大纲、修订培训教材、完善培训内容；规范资格考试认证流程，在完善题库建设的同时，实现试卷考试和网络考试的有机结合；充分发挥亚太物流联盟主席国作用，推动亚太地区物流人才培养水平提高，实现资格证书互认。

引领院校物流人才培养工作向国际化水平迈进。发挥教指委和行指委的作用，切实提升教师队伍水平和教材质量，推动教学改革，大力推行产教合作，实现教学和实践的有机结合。配合教育主管部门，积极推动中职、高职和本科教育教学立体衔接，向国际化物流人才培养目标迈进。以国家开放大学物流学院为平台开展中专、专科、本科学历继续教育和非学历继续教育，并通过国家继续教育学分银行实现非学历继续教育和学历继续教育有效衔接。

深化国际交流与合作。充分发挥行业组织在教育和人才培养工作中的引领

作用，继续与各国行业组织和教育机构加强合作，学习发达国家在教育和人才培养工作中的先进经验，加强在标准制定、课程引进、项目合作、师资培训和合作办学等领域合作。

提高行业人才服务水平。建立物流行业人力资源需求预测和就业状况定期发布制度；为从业人员提供终身学习的全程服务；与其他行业、各省市、各专业领域合作，提供专业化、体系化的中高层人员培训和企业人才培养管理咨询等服务；围绕A级企业，以中国物流企业家商学院为服务平台，开发针对不同企业的人才培养合作服务。

（中物联教育培训部　郭肇明）

第三篇

资料汇编

2014 年全国物流运行情况通报

2014 年我国物流需求规模增速减缓，物流业转型升级加快，社会物流总费用与 GDP 的比率有所下降。

一、社会物流总额增速减缓

2014 年全国社会物流总额 213.5 万亿元，按可比价格计算，同比增长 7.9%，增幅比上年回落 1.6 个百分点。分季度看，一季度 47.8 万亿元，增长 8.6%，回落 0.8 个百分点；上半年 101.5 万亿元，增长 8.7%，回落 0.4 个百分点；前三季度 158.1 万亿元，增长 8.4%，回落 1.1 个百分点；全年呈现稳中趋缓的发展态势。

从构成情况看，工业品物流总额 196.9 万亿元，同比增长 8.3%，增幅比上年回落 1.4 个百分点；进口货物物流总额 12.0 万亿元，同比增长 2.1%，增幅比上年回落 4.3 个百分点；再生资源物流总额 8455 亿元，同比增长 14.1%，增幅比上年回落 6.2 个百分点；农产品物流总额 3.3 万亿元，同比增长 4.1%，增幅比上年提高 0.1 个百分点；单位与居民物品物流总额 3696 亿元，同比增长 32.9%，增幅比上年提高 2.5 个百分点。

二、社会物流总费用与 GDP 的比率有所下降

2014 年社会物流总费用 10.6 万亿元，同比增长 6.9%。社会物流总费用与 GDP 的比率为 16.6%，比上年下降 0.3 个百分点。其中，运输费用 5.6 万亿元，同比增长 6.6%，占社会物流总费用的比重为 52.9%；保管费用 3.7 万亿元，同比增长 7.0%，占社会物流总费用的比重为 34.9%；管理费用 1.3 万亿元，同比增长 7.9%，占社会物流总费用的比重为 12.2%。

三、物流业总收入平稳增长

2014 年物流业总收入 7.1 万亿元，同比增长 6.9%。

说明：由于货运量、货运周转量及 GDP 的调整，社会物流总费用及与

GDP 的比率、物流业总收入也进行了相应调整。

国家发展和改革委员会
国家统计局
中国物流与采购联合会

2014年中国物流行业十件大事

中国物流与采购联合会

（二〇一四年十二月三十一日发布）

1. 国务院发布《物流业发展中长期规划》（2014—2020年），明确物流业为基础性、战略性产业。

2. “一带一路”（“丝绸之路经济带”和“21世纪海上丝绸之路”）、长江经济带、京津冀协同发展上升为国家战略，区域物流互联互通成为突破口。

3. 商务部印发《关于促进商贸物流发展的实施意见》等系列文件，城市物流配送试点进一步扩围。

4. 京津冀、长江经济带、广东地区三大区域通关一体化改革全面实施，通关模式创新助推贸易便利化。

5. 铁路货运改革深入推进，零散货物班列、电商班列、高铁行包等新兴业务推向市场。

6. 电商物流持续快速增长，物流网络全面向农村延伸，跨境电商加紧海外物流布局。

7. 广东、天津、福建特定区域再设三个自由贸易园区，推动更高水平对外开放。

8. “中国物流金融服务平台”上线运行，金融物流风险管控引起广泛关注。

9. 阿里巴巴和京东相继上市，兼并重组案例频频出现，货运平台等新模式受到资本市场追捧。

10. 货运APP集中上线，传统产业O2O借助物流渠道，物流业互联网化加速推进。